Visual Basic Develo[...] to ASP and IIS

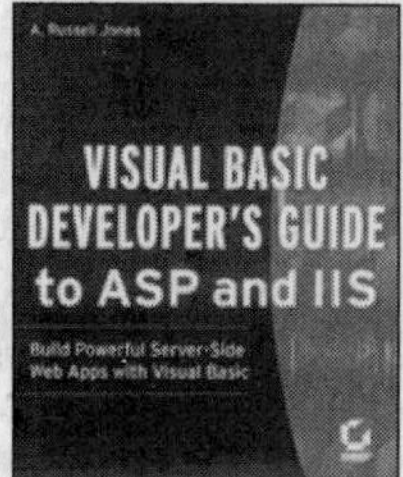

by A. Russell Jones
ISBN: 0-7821-2557-3
416 pages; 7.5" x 9"
$39.99 U.S.

The core components of Web application development for programmers using Microsoft technologies are ASP (Active Server Pages) and IIS (Internet Information Server). This book gives experienced Visual Basic developers everything they need in order to develop sophisticated Web applications. The book features in-depth information on writing IIS server-side applications and coverage of the new VB WebClasses.

Mastering Active Server Pages 3

by A. Russell Jones
ISBN: 0-7821-2619-7
928 pages; 7.5" x 9"
$49.99 U.S.

Active Server Pages is Microsoft's technology for delivering dynamic, interactive Web applications. Mastering Active Server Pages 3 gives comprehensive coverage of the latest version for Visual Basic, VBScript, and Visual InterDev programmers. The book also covers the newest Linux/Unix version of ASP (ChiliASP) and discusses both VBScript and JScript implementations.

ASP, ADO, and XML Complete

SAN FRANCISCO ▸ PARIS ▸ DÜSSELDORF ▸ SOEST ▸ LONDON

Associate Publisher: Richard Mills

Contracts and Licensing Manager: Kristine O'Callaghan

Acquisitions and Developmental Editor: Denise Santoro Lincoln

Compilation Editor: Justin Whitney

Editors: Donna Crossman, Pete Gaughan, Carol Henry, Susan Berge, Anamary Ehlen, Jeff Gammon, Suzanne Goraj, Susan Hobbs, Patrick J. Peterson, Linda Stephenson, Colleen Strand, Sharon Wilkey, Emily Wolman

Production Editor: Shannon Murphy

Technical Editors: Greg Guntle, Piroz Mohseni, Dominic Selly, Dianne Siebold, Tim Sneath

Book Designer: Maureen Forys, Happenstance Type-O-Rama

Graphic Illustrator: Tony Jonick

Electronic Publishing Specialist: Adrian Woolhouse

Proofreaders: Laurie O'Connell, Yariv Rabinovitch, Nancy Riddiough, Monique van den Berg

Indexer: Nancy Guenther

Cover Designer: Design Site

Cover Photographer: David Rickerd/Photonica

Library of Congress Card Number: 2001090456

ISBN: 0-7821-2971-4

Manufactured in the United States of America

10 9 8 7 6 5 4

Trademarks

SYBEX has attempted throughout this book to distinguish proprietary trademarks from descriptive terms by following the capitalization style used by the manufacturer.

The author and publisher have made their best efforts to prepare this book, and the content is based upon final release software whenever possible. Portions of the manuscript may be based upon pre-release versions supplied by software manufacturer(s). The author and the publisher make no representation or warranties of any kind with regard to the completeness or accuracy of the contents herein and accept no liability of any kind including but not limited to performance, merchantability, fitness for any particular purpose, or any losses or damages of any kind caused or alleged to be caused directly or indirectly from this book.

Screen reproductions produced with Collage Complete.
Collage Complete is a trademark of Inner Media Inc.

Internet screen shot(s) using Microsoft Internet Explorer reprinted by permission from Microsoft Corporation.

Acknowledgments

This book incorporates the work of many people, inside and outside Sybex.

Richard Mills and Denise Santoro Lincoln defined the book's overall structure and contents. Justin Whitney offered his technical expertise in adapting the material for publication in this book.

A large team of editors, developmental editors, production editors, and technical editors helped to put together the various books from which *ASP, ADO, and XML Complete* was compiled: Denise Santoro Lincoln handled developmental tasks; Raquel Baker, Susan Berge, Elizabeth Campbell, Jennifer Campbell, Jennifer Durning, Anamary Ehlen, Jeff Gammon, Pete Gaughan, Suzanne Goraj, Susan Hobbs, Leslie H. Light, Chad Mack, Shannon Murphy, Patrick J. Peterson, Linda Stephenson, Colleen Strand, Sharon Wilkey, and Emily Wolman all contributed to editing or production editing; and Greg Guntle, Piroz Mohseni, Dominic Selly, Dianne Siebold, and Tim Sneath provided technical edits.

Justin Whitney deserves particular thanks for making sure all of the material in this book was up-to-date, organized, and flowed in a seamless manner. Similarly, thanks to Donna Crossman, Pete Gaughan, and Carol Henry for their hard work in editing the book.

The *ASP, ADO, and XML Complete* production team of electronic publishing specialist Adrian Woolhouse, production editor Shannon Murphy, and proofreaders Laurie O'Connell, Yariv Rabinovitch, Nancy Riddiough, and Monique van den Berg worked with speed and accuracy to turn the manuscript files and illustrations into the handsome book you're now reading. Rachel Boyce, Liz Paulus, Dan Schiff, Keith McNeil, and Erica Yee also helped in various ways to keep the project moving.

Finally, our most important thanks go to the contributors who agreed to have their work excerpted into *ASP, ADO, and XML Complete*: Kurt Cagle, Mike Gunderloy, Noel Jerke, A. Russell Jones, and Evangelos Petroutsos. Without their efforts, this book would not exist.

Contents at a Glance

Contents

INTRODUCTION

ASP, ADO, and XML Complete is a one-of-a-kind computer book—valuable both for the breadth of its content and for its low price. This thousand-page compilation of information from some of the very best Sybex books provides comprehensive coverage of three essential programming technologies used for Web programming. This book, unique in the computer book world, was created with several goals in mind:

- To offer a thorough guide covering all the important features of ASP, ADO, and XML at an affordable price
- To acquaint you with some of our best authors—their writing styles and teaching skills, and the level of expertise they bring to their books—so you can easily find a match for your interests as you delve deeper into Web programming

ASP, ADO, and XML Complete will take you from programming essentials, to beginning ASP programming, to database development, to advanced ASP programming, to using XML with your Web applications. It will then cover real-world programming. This book provides the essential information you'll need to get the most from these three technologies while also inviting you to explore the even greater depths and wider coverage of material in the original books.

If you've read other computer "how-to" books, you've seen that there are many possible approaches to the task of showing how to use software effectively. The books from which *ASP, ADO, and XML Complete* was compiled represent a range of the approaches to teaching that Sybex and its authors have developed—from the concise and specific *Developer's Guide* style to the wide-ranging, thoroughly detailed *Mastering* style. These books also address readers at different levels of computer experience. As you read through various chapters of this book, you'll see which approach works best for you. You'll also see what these books have in common: a commitment to clarity, accuracy, and practicality.

You'll find in these pages ample evidence of the expertise of Sybex's authors. Unlike publishers who produce "books by committee," Sybex authors are encouraged to write in individual voices that reflect their own experience with the software at hand and with the evolution of today's personal computers. Nearly every book represented here is the work of a single writer or a pair of close collaborators, and you are getting the benefit of each author's direct experience.

In adapting the various source materials for inclusion in *ASP, ADO, and XML Complete*, the compiler preserved these individual voices and perspectives. Chapters were edited only to minimize duplication and update or add cross-references so that you can easily follow a topic across chapters. A few sections were also edited for length so that other important Web programming information could be included.

Who Can Benefit from This Book?

ASP, ADO, and XML Complete is designed to meet the needs of any Microsoft Web programmer who wants a complete reference to the most popular technologies for building Web applications. The Contents and the Index will guide you to the subjects you're looking for.

How This Book Is Organized

ASP, ADO, and XML Complete has six parts, consisting of 26 chapters.

Part i: Programming Essentials The first five chapters cover necessary programming tools, including Visual Basic, and introduce VBScript and JScript.

Part ii: Beginning ASP The next five chapters explore IIS and ASP applications.

Part iii: Database Development The following five chapters go into developing databases. SQL and ADO 2.5 are introduced.

Part iv: Advanced ASP and WebClasses The next three chapters cover advanced ASP programming, including client-side scripting.

Part v: XML The four chapters in Part v explore using XML. They also discuss using BizTalk in business-to-business communication.

Part vi: Building Real-World Web Applications The final four chapters cover real-world programming and implementing specific features on a Web site, such as sale items and a shopping basket.

NOTE

See the Sybex Web site at `www.sybex.com` and search for this book to find the code that is used within this book.

A Few Typographical Conventions

When a Windows operation requires a series of choices from menus or dialog boxes, the ➢ symbol is used to guide you through the instructions, like this: "Select Programs ➢ Accessories ➢ System Tools ➢ System Information." The items the ➢ symbol separates may be menu names, toolbar icons, check boxes, or other elements of the Windows interface–anyplace you can make a selection.

`This typeface` is used to identify Internet URLs and code, and **boldface type** is used whenever you need to type something into a text box.

You'll find these types of special notes throughout the book:

TIP

You'll see a lot of these—quicker and smarter ways to accomplish a task, which the authors have based on many, many months spent testing and using ASP, ADO, and XML.

NOTE

You'll see these Notes, too. They usually represent alternate ways to accomplish a task or some additional information that needs to be highlighted.

WARNING

In a few places you'll see a Warning like this one. When you see a warning, do pay attention to it.

YOU'LL ALSO SEE "SIDEBAR" BOXES LIKE THIS

These boxed sections provide added explanation of special topics that are noted briefly in the surrounding discussion but that you may want to explore separately. Each sidebar has a heading that announces the topic, so you can quickly decide whether it's something you need to know about.

For More Information...

See the Sybex Web site, `www.sybex.com`, to learn more about all of the books that went into *ASP, ADO, and XML Complete*. On the site's Catalog page, you'll find links to any book you're interested in. Also be sure to check the Sybex site for late-breaking developments about the applications themselves.

We hope you enjoy this book and find it useful. Happy programming!

PART I

Programming Essentials

Chapter 1

The Microsoft Toolset

Choosing the right tools to build your Web site is, of course, a critical step. There are turnkey outsource solutions, such as Delphi.com, that you can utilize to add functionality to your Web site. There are also third-party development packages you can utilize as well for adding features to your site.

You most likely wouldn't be reading this book unless you were interested in doing a little programming of your own! The Visual Basic language is a key tool in the community developer's arsenal. There are, however, many tools in the supporting cast that make up a successful Web site deployment. This chapter explores these tools and, of course, takes an in-depth look at the Visual Basic language and how it will be utilized.

Adapted from *E-Commerce Developer's Guide to Building Community and Using Promotional Tools*, by Noel Jerke

ISBN 0-7821-2865-3 544 pages $49.99

The Toolset

The tools range from server software to programming languages to encryption technology. Each is critical in building the complete solution. An overview of each tool is given in this chapter along with a list of features that are critical for building a Web application. Don't worry if some of the terminology doesn't make sense yet. The rest of the book will cover programming basics in more detail.

Presently, Microsoft has taken on a new and significant initiative called .NET that seeks to fundamentally change the way Web development is done. The following sections focus on the core NT/2000 tools that are currently available and examine where Microsoft is headed down the road.

Microsoft Windows NT/2000

The Windows NT/2000 platform is the foundation for building a Visual Basic programmed solution. It provides the core Web server, security, TCP/IP functionality, and other fundamental requirements for a Web server operating system. Table 1.1 discusses the key features for building a Web application.

TABLE 1.1: Web Features

Feature	Description
Security	As with any Web server, it is critical to provide solid security to protect the network and operating system from hackers and mischief-makers.
TCP/IP networking	TCP/IP is, of course, the standard networking protocol used across the Internet that allows computers to communicate with each other.
Component Object Model (COM) support	When using Visual Basic to build the necessary business objects for an e-commerce Web site, COM is a key tool.
Web server	Internet Information Server (IIS) is the server that supports the core Web server functionality. (See the next section.)

It is important that Windows is set up properly to ensure security integrity, scalability, and other key issues. Certainly there are differences between the Windows NT and Windows 2000 platforms. Some of the core tools, such as SQL Server, IIS, Active Server Pages (ASP), and so on, are significantly enhanced on the Windows 2000 platform. Windows 2000 also offers more server-side software options for managing your Web site. From a coding development standpoint, however, the work is pretty much the same. The code developed in this book for both SQL Server and ASP will work on either platform.

Internet Information Server

IIS is the Web server that is provided with Windows NT/2000. The latest version on NT is IIS 4.0 and is provided with the Windows NT Option Pack. Windows 2000 comes with IIS 5.0. Table 1.2 gives an overview of the key features of IIS.

TABLE 1.2: IIS Web Server Features

Feature	Description
Index Server	Site content indexing, including HTML pages and Word documents, is supported with Index Server and enables your Web site to have site search functionality.
FTP service	IIS provides the basic functionality to support the File Transfer Protocol (FTP).
HTTP service	IIS provides the basic HTTP service.
SMTP service	IIS provides the support for SMTP mail protocol for sending e-mail from the Web server.
NNTP service	Internet newsgroups can be set up and supported in IIS.
Certificate server	Certificate server allows you to manage your own set of certificates to enable authentication between the server and the client.
Message Queue Server	Microsoft Message Queue Server (MSMQ) is a fast store-and-forward service for Microsoft Windows NT/2000 Server.
Transaction server	The Option Pack also comes with Microsoft Transaction Server for developing high-performance, mission-critical applications. In Windows 2000 it is integrated into the operating system.
Management console	The management console is the interface for managing the Web server.
Active Server Pages (ASP)	Active Server Pages represent the foundation for Web server development. The ASP engine provides a hosting environment for a number of scripting languages with integrated support for VBScript and JScript (Microsoft's version of JavaScript). See Table 1.4 for information on what is new in ASP for IIS 5.0.

CONTINUED →

TABLE 1.2 continued: IIS Web Server Features

Feature	Description
FrontPage extensions	The FrontPage extensions are key tools for supporting site development in Microsoft FrontPage and Microsoft Visual InterDev. These extensions allow InterDev and FrontPage to manage the Web site over a standard TCP/IP connection.

IIS provides the basic Web server functionality required to serve Web pages. IIS 5.0 has its underpinnings significantly enhanced to be more scalable and stable, but provides the same basic services. The biggest changes for the developer are found in the implementation of ASP.

Active Server Pages/Visual InterDev

The heart of the toolset for building our applications is the ASP component of IIS. Combine that with the Visual InterDev development tool for creating Web pages, working with SQL Server, and building e-commerce applications. Table 1.3 reviews the key features of ASP.

TABLE 1.3: ASP Key Features

Feature	Description
VBScript language	ASP provides the capability to combine client-side HTML code with server-side VBScript, a slightly slimmed-down version of the popular Visual Basic programming language. This code will allow you to access your database, control the code being sent to the client browser, and much more.
Built in objects	IIS has several key objects built in that provide the core functionality for programming from ASP, such as the Response and Request objects. Through these objects you can manage cookies, maintain session state, access other server functions, and more.
COM components	There are a number of COM components that come with ASP, including ADO for accessing data from a range of remote sources, and browser objects for checking the user's browser capabilities, managing ad rotation, and much more.

Significant enhancements to the ASP environment in IIS 5.0 are outlined in Table 1.4.

TABLE 1.4: ASP Development Enhancements

FEATURE	DESCRIPTION
ASP Self Tuning	ASP is now much better at detecting resource bottlenecks, especially with regard to thread allocation. If there is CPU overhead available and requests are backed up, additional threads are allocated. Likewise, if the CPU is being overburdened, threads are deallocated.
Encoded ASP Scripts	This feature provides basic script encoding so that script logic cannot be easily read. The script code is de-coded during execution.
Application Protection	IIS, in general, provides better protection for Web applications by separating all applications into a segmented memory space from the core IIS processes.
XML Integration	The XML parser provided in Internet Explorer can be utilized to parse XML in your ASP applications.
Windows Script Components	Code written in VBScript can now be compiled into re-usable COM components for use in Web applications.
Flow Control Capabilities	There are now two methods for redirecting a user to another Web page. The traditional method used was the Response object, which sent a message to the browser, and required a trip back to the server. Now the Server object has a redirect option that happens at the server level.
Error Handling	The Server object has a new error handling capability that can help to track down script errors.
Scriptless ASP	Many sites are built with all ASP pages, even though there may be no script on certain pages. That means even an HTML-only page is run through the ASP parser in IIS 4.0. In IIS 5.0 a check is now done to see if a script is actually included on the page before invoking the ASP parser.
Performance-Enhanced Objects	All of the core objects built into IIS 4.0 are provided, but they have been significantly enhanced for performance.

In IIS 5.0, Microsoft has focused significantly on the performance of aspects of ASP to improve its scalability. In general, they have tuned IIS 5.0 for overall performance. There have been some enhancements for easier coding, with the major change being the capability to compile scripts into COM objects.

Visual InterDev is a key tool for designing Web applications and can be used for the code samples listed throughout this book. It is our primary development environment for building our Active Server Pages–based applications. Table 1.5 provides an overview of the key features of Visual InterDev.

TABLE 1.5: Visual InterDev Features

Feature	Description
SQL database tools	Visual InterDev provides an excellent interface when working with remote database environment. Queries can be built, tables managed, stored procedures worked with, and all of the critical functions for building data-driven e-commerce applications can be accomplished.
Remote server site management	Through the use of FrontPage server extensions, you can manage your server-based Web projects remotely with Visual InterDev.
Active Server Pages development	The key use of the tool is for is Active Server Pages, VBScript, or JScript programming.
Team project development/Visual Source Safe integration	In conjunction with Visual Source Safe and the FrontPage server extensions, team project development can be done easily on the same set of pages. Pages that are "checked out" can be locked from use by anyone else.
Client side HTML/ script editor	Not only can you work on server-side script development, but you can also work on client-side scripts, DHTML development, cascading style sheets, and so on.
Debugging tools	As is good practice with any development tool, debugging tools are provided for that occasional error a programmer might make.

NOTE

See the Microsoft.NET section later in this chapter to get a peek at what is coming in Visual Studio.NET 7.0.

Visual InterDev combined with ASP provides the Microsoft primary programming toolset for Web-based applications. The toolset has been a successful combination that many Web sites are built upon and provides the core tools for the functionality built in this book.

SQL Server

As critical to community building as programming is, even more critical is the database. Without a database to store messages, polls, profiles, and much more, there would be no community at all. Microsoft SQL Server provides a robust development platform for building multi-tier Web applications. You can place as much or as little logic in the database tier as needed. If you are running a multi-server Web farm, then partitioning the client, Web server, and database tier become crucial to ensuring solid performance and balancing server load.

SQL Server can be configured for different security levels, segmentation with replication, programming logic in stored procedures, and so on. With Microsoft's ActiveX Data Objects (ADO) and an OLE DB provider (or ODBC), you can connect from nearly any Microsoft development tool and interface with the underlying database.

NOTE

Microsoft Access can be used as the database for your site. For a Web site that is going to get any kind of extensive traffic, however, a robust scalable database such as SQL Server should be used.

There are three versions of SQL Server still in primary use by developers. SQL Server 6.5 was the first robust version to run on Windows NT 4.0. That was followed by SQL Server 7, which provided a significant revamp of the core infrastructure and greatly increased functionality and scalability. The newest version is SQL Server 2000, which requires Windows 2000. The SQL Script code developed in this book should work on any of these versions and, with a little work, can be ported to other popular enterprise SQL-based database servers.

In this book, Microsoft SQL Server will be used as the database behind the functionality.

NOTE

We assume that you are familiar with setting up and creating SQL Server databases. If you are unfamiliar with this technology, you might want to check out Sybex's *Mastering SQL Server 2000*, by Mike Gunderloy and Joseph L. Jorden.

Visual Basic 6

While ASP provides a powerful environment for server-based Web applications in itself through the scripting languages it exposes, it can be further enhanced by the use of compiled code written in a language such as

Visual Basic. There are multiple ways in which you can interface from Visual Basic to the Internet, as explored in Table 1.6.

TABLE 1.6: Visual Basic 6 Internet Features

FEATURE	DESCRIPTION
IIS applications	A new feature has been added to Visual Basic 6. IIS applications enable you to create Visual Basic programs with a standard HTML-based browser as their interface. These applications allow the programmer to utilize all of the familiar tools in VB, such as classes, database programming, and so on. The only difference is that the interface is a browser instead of a standard form. These applications are centrally run on a Web server and can be accessed on your intranet or Internet Web site.
COM objects	A key tool for Web application development is the creation of Component Object Model (COM) business objects. For example, in an e-commerce application, we might build objects for tax and shipping calculations encapsulating existing logic. These COM objects could then be called from our ASP script code.
WIN INET tools/ browser control	Of course, there is a traditional capability to create Web applications in a standard Visual Basic forms interface. Visual Basic contains an ActiveX control that can be placed on a form and provides a subset of Internet Explorer. This may be attractive for building management tools for an online store.
ActiveX controls	ActiveX controls can be created in Visual Basic for use in the Internet Explorer browser interface that will run on the client's computer. Again, this may be attractive for encapsulating functionality on the management side of a store.
DHTML applications	In conjunction with IIS applications, DHTML applications are introduced in version 6. DHTML applications allow the Visual Basic programmer to create DHTML interfaces in Internet Explorer, but the language is full-fledged Visual Basic instead of JScript or VBScript. Note that DHTML runs on the client side where IIS applications run on the server side.

This book primarily focuses on building applications in Visual InterDev with Active Server Pages. There might be times, though, when you will want to consider using Visual Basic as part of your Web development arsenal. Usually that is when you need to build complex logic that isn't possible in a scripting context. Often this logic is encapsulated in a COM object and can be used both on the Internet and in a client/server context. You can also use Visual Basic to create your own reusable ASP components. Part IV covers this process in more detail.

Table 1.7 outlines some of the different situations in which you might want to use Visual Basic.

TABLE 1.7: Visual Basic Utilization

Feature	Description
Legacy Code Migration	If you have existing code in Visual Basic, then using it in a Web application environment is possible with Visual Basic's Internet capabilities.
Performance	Generally speaking, compiled code will execute much more quickly than script code. You can develop extensive COM objects in Visual Basic for performance gains and then use them in ASP.
Logic Segmentation	Visual Basic provides a full-featured object-based development environment complete with many of the features of object-oriented development. The Visual Basic development environment provides a much more robust development interface and programming language.
Mixed Functionality	If you are building a LAN-based application that also needs to have a Web-based intranet-type interface, Visual Basic can provide the capability to do both right out of the box.

The good news is that the Visual Basic developer has options for what implementation of Visual Basic to use and can "right-size" the solution appropriately.

Microsoft Site Server 3.0

Microsoft's Site Server 3.0 is the big gun in Microsoft's arsenal for developing extended community and e-commerce applications. Site Server 3.0 provides a number of tools, including the core programming environment for directory level security, site personalization, membership tracking, site log file analysis, staging and development server support, and much more. With this toolset that is built on an ASP programming foundation and SQL Server, high-end, feature-rich Web sites can be built. Sample sites include those of Dell Computers (`www.dell.com`), Martha Stewart (`www.MarthaStewart.com`), and Ulla Popken (`www.ullapopken.com`).

In reality, it is important to point out that Site Server is primarily a framework of COM objects and applications that support the commerce and community processes. Table 1.8 gives an overview of the key feature set of Site Server, Commerce Edition. If your goal is to start out developing in Site Server, it is still important to understand all the concepts and programming techniques outlined in this book. If you are going to be building a significant e-commerce aspect to your site, then using Site Server 3.0, Commerce Edition (SSCE) will provide the commerce development foundation.

TABLE 1.8: Site Server 3.0 Key Features

Feature	Description
Membership Server	Membership Server provides a way to create a membership-based site with appropriate security and tracking. Security can be based on a database or on the Lightweight Directory Access Protocol (LDAP) used by the Windows 2000 Active Directory, among others.
Personalization Server	Personalization Server offers a way to provide targeted content to the user based on the user's membership profile.
Commerce Server (SSCE Only)	Commerce Server is the key toolset for building e-commerce applications. The Commerce Interchange Pipeline (CIP) provides a series of COM objects to manage the purchasing process and can support business-to-business integration as well.
Ad Server (SSCE Only)	Ad Server provides the ability to manage banner ad campaigns on a Web site. A complete Web-based management interface is provided for adding, updating, and deleting ad campaigns and, in particular, tracking the success (or failure) in terms of "click-throughs."
Site Analysis	Site traffic analysis is an important aspect of understanding your Web site. Site Server provides Web log analysis tools to analyze traffic patterns.

Commerce Server 2000

Microsoft's Commerce Server 2000 product for the Windows 2000 platform is the next generation of the Site Server product. Table 1.9 provides a breakdown of its main features.

TABLE 1.9: Commerce Server 2000

Feature	Description
Profile and Targeting	Site Server 3.0 provides a profile and targeting solution. The new twists in Commerce Server 2000 are much more e-commerce focused and built on the underpinnings of the Windows 2000 platform.

CONTINUED →

TABLE 1.9 continued: Commerce Server 2000

Feature	Description
Product Catalog	Based on SQL Server, the new Product Catalog System helps create catalogs, and import and export from existing data sources. Integrated and powerful search capabilities also make product information easy to find.
Analysis	Provides extended features including Web log file analysis as well as integrating in actual activity based on the Web site database.
Advertising	Banner advertising is provided as a type of business processing pipeline similar to the commerce pipelines for purchasing.

There is certainly much more available in the product; for additional information, check out `www.microsoft.com/CommerceServer/`. Commerce Server 2000 is a significant overhaul of the Site Server platform, but it does require Windows 2000. Making a careful selection between Commerce Server 2000 and Site Server will have a significant impact on your development requirements down the road. Either way, both have significant features, especially in an e-commerce context, with which to build an application.

Secure Sockets Layer (SSL)/Verisign Certificates

Security on a Web site is crucial for securing private data—especially credit card data. On the management side, passwords and other business-critical data should be encrypted between the browser and the server.

IIS 4 supports SSL 3. There is a simple process for requesting a certificate on the server and then submitting the certificate request to an authority, such as Verisign (`www.verisign.com`). Once the certificate request is made, the keys will be sent back installed on the server.

Miscellaneous Tools

There are many other tools available for Internet development. Certainly many non-Microsoft tools are available for development on Windows NT or on any other operating system.

WYSIWYG

WYSIWYG, or "What You See Is What You Get," is the drag-and-drop method of Web design. WYSIWYG tools simplify the creation of a Web page by allowing you to design visually, then automatically constructing the underlying HTML code for you. The drawback is that they sometimes add more code than you need or want. Whether or not to use a WYSIWYG editor is a matter of personal taste and coding style for developers.

Table 1.10 reviews other Microsoft tools.

TABLE 1.10: Microsoft's Web-Enabled Tools

Feature	Description
Microsoft Exchange Server	If you want to build extended e-mail capabilities, provide e-mail boxes for customer support, and other related functions, Exchange Server provides a robust e-mail platform.
Microsoft FrontPage 2000	While Visual InterDev does provide WYSIWYG editing, FrontPage 2000 is an excellent WYSIWYG HTML editing tool for creating static content on the Web site.
Microsoft Office	Microsoft Office provides extended tools for working with the Web. Microsoft Word can also be utilized for creating and editing Web page documents. Microsoft Access can be an excellent database tool to use in conjunction with Microsoft SQL Server.
Internet Explorer	Internet Explorer provides much more than a standard Web page display. There are a number of tools provided along with the browser itself. Remote Data Service (RDS) objects are provided for interfacing with data on the Web server via HTTP, ActiveX controls can run in the browser interface, and there is the capability to create client-side scripting in VBScript and JScript.
Visual Source Safe	Visual Source Safe provides a source code control toolset for storing source code and related files in a source database. It provides source code version management as well as an infrastructure for checking code in and out. This is particularly useful for avoiding version conflicts in team-based environments.

CONTINUED →

TABLE 1.10 continued: Microsoft's Web-Enabled Tools

Feature	Description
Remote Data Services (RDS)	RDS provides a toolset for querying databases across the Internet via HTTP. It provides a direct link between the browser and the database without having to make a trip to the server to work through ASP or some other server-side development tool.
Microsoft Visual Studio	Two tools included in Visual Studio have already been mentioned: Visual InterDev and Visual SourceSafe. Also included are Visual C++ and Visual J++ along with other development tools, such as Visual Modeler. All of these may be useful at various points in the development process. In Visual Studio.NET, the next generation of C++ programming environment, C# will be introduced.
BizTalk Server 2000	BizTalk makes it easy to integrate applications and businesses together with graphical tools for building Extensible Markup Language (XML) schema, performing schema transformation, establishing trading partner relationships over the Internet, as well as tracking and analyzing data and documents that are exchanged. BizTalk Server 2000 extends the features of traditional e-commerce and electronic data interchange (EDI). Chapter 23 explores the use of this tool in detail.
Application Center	Application Center 2000 is Microsoft's deployment and management tool that makes managing groups of servers as simple as managing a single computer. It provides a complete toolset for managing Web server farms. For large community Web sites with extensive server farms, this is an invaluable tool.

Microsoft continues to enhance and hone its overall product offering for the Internet. Which Microsoft or third-party solutions you use will greatly depend on the scope and scale of the Web application you are building. The next section takes a look at Microsoft's much-promoted .NET initiative.

Microsoft .NET

In mid-1999, Microsoft announced a significant shift in its Internet strategy, called .NET. Bill Gates and Steve Ballmer likened it to the decision to move from DOS to Windows, or when Microsoft made its infamous

Internet strategy shift in the 1990s. It is important to understand that this isn't a shift that happens overnight. It will be a progression over many years.

The expansiveness of the .NET strategy touches nearly every piece of software that Microsoft produces, which is a bit beyond the scope of this book to explain. For more information, check out `www.microsoft.com/net/`.

For developers, there are significant initiatives that need to be considered. Table 1.11 outlines some of the highlights.

TABLE 1.11: Microsoft's .NET Development Initiatives

Feature	Description
Web Services	Web Services are building blocks for constructing distributed Web-based applications in a platform, object model, and multi-language manner. Web Services are based on open Internet standards, such as HTTP and XML, and form the basis of Microsoft's vision of the programmable Web. In other words, it's a URL-addressable resource that programmatically returns information to clients who want to use it. One important feature of Web Services is that clients don't need to know how a service is implemented. They communicate through using standard Web protocols and data formats, such as HTTP and XML.
Visual Studio	Visual Studio.NET includes exciting features, some of which are enhancements to previous versions and some of which are brand-new. A few of the most significant additions include the new Microsoft programming language called C#; a new, smarter integrated development environment (IDE); new object-oriented features in Visual Basic.NET; and development lifecycle tools.
ASP.NET	ASP.NET is a new version of ASP that has been rebuilt from the ground up. ASP.NET provides for cleaner code that is easier to write, and simple to reuse and share. ASP.NET boosts performance and scalability by offering access to complied languages; development is more intuitive with Web Forms, and an object-oriented foundation facilitates reuse. Other important features include page events, Web controls, and caching. Server controls and improvements in data binding are also new with ASP.NET. Libraries for use with ASP.NET, and the Microsoft .NET Framework, which allows custom business functions to be exposed over the Web, provide more new development opportunities.

CONTINUED →

TABLE 1.11 continued: Microsoft's .NET Development Initiatives

Feature	Description
Web Forms	ASP.NET Web Forms are Web pages that enable you to write code just as you do for ASP today. More than that, though, ASP.NET Web Forms are designed on top of an object-oriented programming model, enabling code reuse and separation of the application code from page content. In Visual Basic you draw the controls on a form, then implement the event procedures underneath. In traditional ASP this isn't possible because there's no link between the controls and their server-side code. In ASP.NET, however, there is a link; instead of having to manually pull out values from the form variables, you can write code directly.
ADO+	ADO+ is the new set of data access services for the .NET Framework. ADO+ is a natural evolution of ADO, built around n-tier development and architected with XML at its core. Two key enhancements are extensive support for the disconnected programming model and rich XML integration.

Extensible Markup Language (XML)

Woven throughout the .NET platform is XML for data sharing. XML is a meta-markup language that provides a format for describing structured data. This facilitates more precise declarations of content and more meaningful search results across multiple platforms. XML enables Web-based data viewing and manipulation applications.

In XML you can define an unlimited set of tags. While HTML tags can be used to display a word in bold or italic, XML provides a framework for tagging structured data. An XML element can declare its associated data to be a retail price, a sales tax, a book title, the amount of precipitation, or any other desired data. With XML there is the capability to search for and manipulate data regardless of the applications within which it is found. Once data has been located, it can be presented in a browser, such as Internet Explorer, in any number of ways, or it can be handed off to other applications for further processing and viewing. More information can be found at `msdn.microsoft.com/xml/`.

The goal of this book is to explore the development techniques behind building robust Web applications. This will be primarily done through the use of VBScript code created in Visual InterDev and SQL code in Microsoft SQL Server.

Browsers

There are two primary browsers used on the Internet. The first is Netscape Navigator (or Communicator) 6.*x*, and the second is Internet Explorer 5.*x*; Figures 1.1 and 1.2 show the two browsers, respectively. Even though Internet Explorer has seen strong growth in use, Netscape is still a significant player in the marketplace.

Both browsers support standard HTML and some extended features, such as cascading style sheets, dynamic HTML, and JavaScript. The only thing you can be sure will work in both, however, is standard HTML. Even then, the visual rendering might be a little different in each.

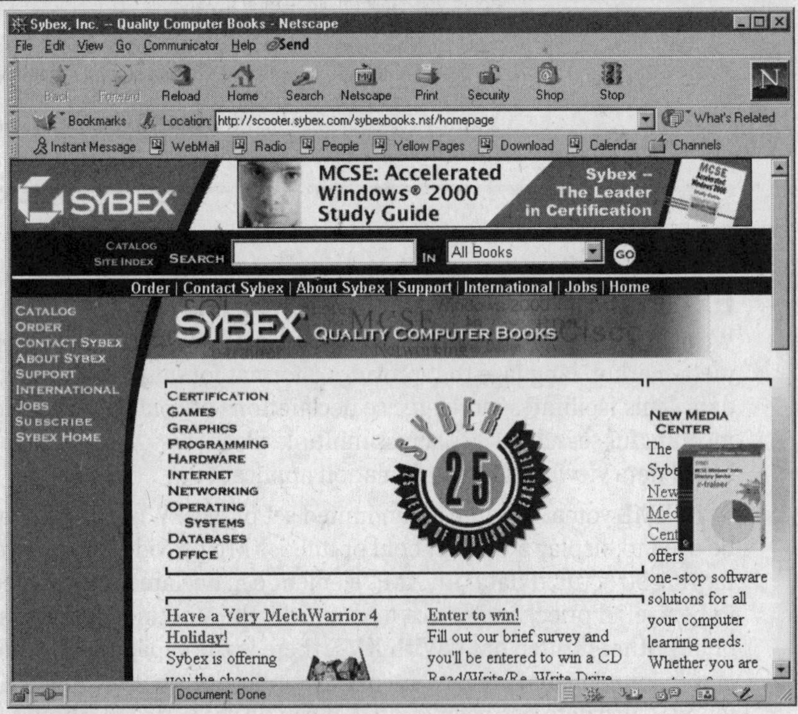

FIGURE 1.1: Netscape Navigator 4

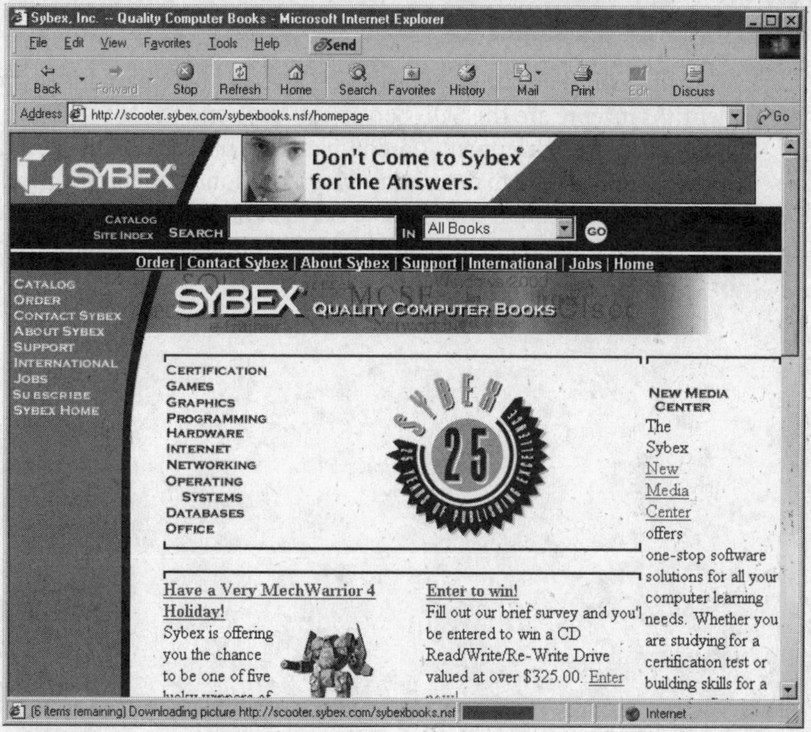

FIGURE 1.2: Internet Explorer 5

Trying to design a truly unique and advanced interface on the client side can be tricky when trying to ensure support in both browsers. Even if you decide to build two different interfaces for those two browsers, you still have issues of supporting smaller segment browsers, such as earlier versions, specialized browsers, and so on.

This book does not explore the difficult issues of cross-browser development of client-side JavaScript, etc. In certain cases, this book will offer some specific development with VBScript on the client side in Internet Explorer.

NOTE

For more information on building client-side browser-based applications, see the following books: *Mastering JavaScript and JScript* by James Jaworski (Sybex, 1999), *Visual Basic Developer's Guide to ASP and IIS* by A. Russell Jones (Sybex, 1999), and *Mastering Visual Basic 6* by Evangelos Petroutsos (Sybex, 1998).

What's Next?

The Microsoft platform provides a rich Internet development environment. At its core are the SQL Server database and the Visual Basic Script programming environment. Careful planning based on the size and scope of your site will help to determine what additional tools you'll need. In the next chapter, we'll cover Visual Basic in more detail, as well as define some of the fundamental concepts and terminology used in building a Web-based application.

Chapter 2

Visual Basic and the Web

Visual Basic was an instant hit in the Windows programming community but so far it hasn't been a major force in the Web programming world, except peripherally, through VBScript. (Microsoft selected Visual Basic's young "challenged" cousin, VBScript, as the default programming language for their Active Server Pages, or ASP, technology.) There are several reasons why VB hasn't been the language of choice for Web programming.

First, Visual Basic runs on only one platform, Windows. Until Microsoft's Web server, called Internet Information Server (IIS), became commonplace (about three years ago, with the introduction of version 3), VB couldn't talk directly to the Web server. This made it tough to use VB for the Web. You could do it, though, and some people did.

Adapted from *Visual Basic® Developer's Guide to ASP and IIS*, by A. Russell Jones
ISBN 0-7821-2557-3 416 pages $39.99

Second, VB has a large runtime dynamic-link library (DLL) that gets loaded whenever you run a VB application, even if the compiled application is only a few kilobytes of code. The large runtime made VB programs running on the Web painfully slow. Each time a client browser requested a Web page, the Web server had to dutifully load the runtime DLL, load the application, process the request, and then unload the application and the runtime DLL. Because the Web works on a get-in, get-the-data, get-out-quickly schedule, it's overkill to load a 1MB-plus application-support DLL simply to provide a little marked-up HTML text. Furthermore, because your application "died" after each request, storing data values between requests was difficult–which meant that the approach was primarily useful for formatting simple requests and database reports, not full applications.

In an attempt to alleviate these problems, Microsoft provided an application programming interface (API) called Internet Server API (ISAPI), through which programs could communicate with the Web server. However, the company neglected to provide VB with the means to access the API. Microsoft also "solved" the problem of large support DLLs (after all, Visual C++ has one, too) by letting you load DLLs directly into the Web server's address space. That way, they stay loaded all the time, which dramatically speeds up response time. ISAPI was an instant hit, but you couldn't take advantage of it until Visual Basic 5 provided the capability to create compiled DLLs. Unfortunately, this capability also dramatically decreased the stability of the Web server, because if one of the in-process DLLs crashed, the Web server often went down with it.

Meanwhile, several methods of connecting VB applications to the Web server appeared. A freeware DLL called Object Linking and Embedding Internet Server Application Programming Interface (OLEISAPI and later OLEISAPI2) provided connectivity between VB applications and the Web server. Other, relatively full-featured solutions not only provided connectivity, but also loaded a configurable number of instances of your application, provided load balancing between them, and enabled you to connect one instance to a single user so that programs could keep user-specific data between requests on the server. These solutions also kept program instances alive between client calls to the Web server, so you could store data easily in program variables.

In addition, you could (and still can) program directly to the underlying protocols. Carl Franklin (of Carl and Gary's Visual Basic Home Page) wrote an excellent book called *Visual Basic 4.0 Internet Programming*, in which he discusses Winsock programming, the use of various Internet protocols, and other low-level programming topics for the Internet. All that information is still valid, and if you want to get "under the hood," Carl's book (since updated for VB 6) can do more for you than this one.

Luckily, with VB 6, Microsoft has finally provided Visual Basic with a direct connection to the Web. The method they provide works via Component Object Model (COM) automation through one or more ASP pages. You build a DLL that exposes a WebClass object. The client calls an ASP page that loads a copy of your DLL. From then on, you use the WebClass methods, properties, and events to deliver content created from template files and/or created on the fly to the client browser.

If you don't understand all of this right now, don't worry. The important point to remember is that WebClasses aren't a brand-new technology and they aren't difficult to understand. They don't do anything you can't do with Visual Basic 5 and an ASP page or two—they just do it more easily.

What's a Web Application?

A Web application is different from a Web site. A Web site provides information that has been pre-built and can be stored (more or less) in static Hypertext Markup Language (HTML) files. Information in a Web site moves primarily from the server to the client. When the user must enter information, the server provides a generic, canned response. Between requests, the server doesn't care what the client does. The client can skip from one place to another with no effect on the Web site, because each page is a stand-alone unit; the Web is composed of discrete groups of hypertext documents. In contrast, a Web application provides information specifically retrieved and formatted for a single user or group of users. Information moves in both directions—the user's input or identity often determines the content that appears on the browser.

A Web application serves dynamic information, not static HTML files. The application extracts content as needed, often from a database server. A Web application not only provides information, but also accepts information from you and responds to your actions with a specific custom response.

A Web application does care what you do from one request to another. It needs to track you to serve your needs. You can't always skip around in a Web application the way you can in a Web site. Sometimes, you need to follow a process from start to finish (for example, filling out an online application), or the entire process is suspect and must be discarded.

WHY WRITE A WEB APPLICATION IN VB?

You can write Web applications in many languages: Perl, Python, Java, C, C++, even QuickBasic or Unix shell scripts. So why would you choose to write a Web application in Visual Basic? Whenever you need to make decisions, it's always good to look at the requirements first. Let's look at the requirements of a Web application and at how well VB meets those requirements. The five major requirements are:

Database connectivity A Web application often accumulates and manages critical information, storing it in a database for future reference. It also uses that information store to provide specific services. Therefore, a Web application language should be good at storing and retrieving information—preferably in databases. Since version 3, VB has had industry-leading database connectivity, and it still does.

Speed A Web application must often service many clients. Visual Basic, compiled into native code, is nearly as fast as C.

String handling A Web application must be able to handle string searches, concatenation, and token replacements. Visual Basic has excellent string-handling ability.

Security A Web application must be able to handle security demands. Any compiled language provides greater security than an interpreted language. Visual Basic meets this requirement equally as well as C, and better than Java or a scripting language such as VBScript or JavaScript.

Transactions A Web application often needs to perform several actions that must complete successfully for the data to remain valid. When working with a database, you usually wrap such actions in a transaction. A transaction is a contract that guarantees that the entire set of operations either will succeed or will fail in such a way that no changes will be made to data. The classic example of a transaction is that of a checking account. When you deposit a check, the bank debits the amount from one account and credits the same amount to another account. Both must succeed, or both must fail. The dual act of debiting one account and crediting another is a transaction. Through Microsoft Transaction Server, you can perform multiple actions in your Web pages, even use multiple objects to accomplish the transaction. Although you don't always need transactions, when you do need them, you need them badly.

In addition to the five major requirements, there are others that are somewhat less important:

Familiarity You'll write better code faster if you're familiar with the language. Because many of you are Visual Basic programmers, you're ahead of the game here.

Debugger You'll also write better code if you have a powerful debugger. Here Visual Basic and Visual Studio are leaders. The capability to view and change the contents of variables, rewrite code on-the-fly, move the execution pointer, step through code in DLL projects, step through code in ASP files, and step through code running in the browser—all from your Visual Basic project group—is awesome debugging power. Until Visual Studio 6 was released last year, ASP debugging was done through Response.Write statements in concert with Response.End statements, which is analogous to working in Visual Basic if the only debugging capabilities you could use were Debug.Print and Stop statements.

Code/object reuse Sure, you can do this in any language, but I'll bet no other language has as many third-party tools, libraries, and examples available as Visual Basic. I suspect that many of you reading this book also have a large set of routines and objects that you reuse when appropriate. Many of these routines will work just fine in a VB-based Web application, so once again, you're probably ahead of the game here.

As you can see, Visual Basic is as suited for Web application development as it is for any other type of program—it's a general-purpose language and meets these requirements easily.

What's the Difference between IIS and DHTML Applications?

Visual Basic has two built-in kinds of Web projects:

IIS applications These applications run on the Web server, under Microsoft's Internet Information Server. You can write Web applications for any kind of browser (or even non-browser) client using an IIS project.

DHTML applications These applications run on the client and use the built-in dynamic HTML (DHTML) capabilities of Microsoft's Internet Explorer (IE) browser to provide fast response to user input. These types of applications are well suited to games, simulations, and data-input applications.

Unfortunately, they're limited to Internet Explorer version 4 and higher at this time.

If you're going to write games or applications that need fast response time and don't have heavy database requirements, and all your clients are running the IE browser, DHTML applications can be a good choice.

More on IIS Applications

I choose IIS applications for several reasons:

- IIS applications run with multiple browsers and multiple versions of those browsers. You can write an IIS application that will run on anything from version 1*x* browsers all the way to the latest versions, and anything in between. They'll also run on multiple platforms, including the Mac and Unix machines. This makes IIS applications admirably suited for business applications used by clients who may not all be running Windows or have the latest browser.
- IIS applications have a single code base. Because the application resides in its entirety on the Web server, you can update the entire application with a single code change. The advantages of this are hard to beat when you realize how often business rules and database requirements change.
- There are no client-side installation issues. This alone makes IIS applications worth considering. I'm sure your Information Technology (IT) department won't be excited about supporting a new type of application on every computer in the enterprise. There are also no versioning issues, because you control the only public version of the application.
- The application is available from any location. After an IIS application is up and running, any client computer that can connect to the server can run your application. The application may run more slowly over a dial-up connection than over a 100Mbps network connection, but it will run.
- A client isn't bound to one computer. You can use sign-on and password or other security measures to identify clients no matter which computer they're running on. That means, for example, that if you build a training application, a person could sign on to your application and begin a lesson in Des Moines, get called overseas,

and finish the application from the Netherlands the next day—all without worrying about saving data or installing anything.

- All the data is centralized. Your clients won't ever lose data when they use your application (assuming you have backup procedures in place on the server). Additionally, you have the ability to prove (or disprove) how useful your application is to the business because you can (and should) track use of the application down to the page level. This kind of tracking capability is priceless when it comes to justifying the cost of an application.

DHTML applications, Visual Basic's other type of Web project, are a completely different sort of animal. They're inextricably bound to the IE browser, version 4 and higher. To try to do justice to both DHTML and IIS applications in the same book would do a disservice to both types. Believe me, you'll have enough to keep you busy with IIS applications alone.

WHAT'S NEXT?

In the next chapter, we'll take a closer look at these applications and how they evolved from the simple, static HTML pages of yesterday. We'll also begin exploring how IIS actually uses Visual Basic and Active Server Pages, or ASP, to create dynamic, interactive Web sites.

Chapter 3

Web Applications and ASP

In the early days of the Web, just being able to navigate through the pages of a site, or jump from one site to another with a mouse click, was a major breakthrough. This interaction model that was based on the single click of the mouse, not even the double click, was responsible for the tremendous success of the Web. Yet, in a few short years, this model of interaction was proven inadequate, because it didn't allow viewers to interact with the Web server in the way they interacted with a typical Windows application.

The Web was based on the premise that clients request documents from Web servers. This was a reasonable assumption for the early days of the Web, but the unexpected adoption of this technology led very quickly to the need for a more elaborate scheme of information flow between clients and servers. We are no longer interested in simply requesting documents from a

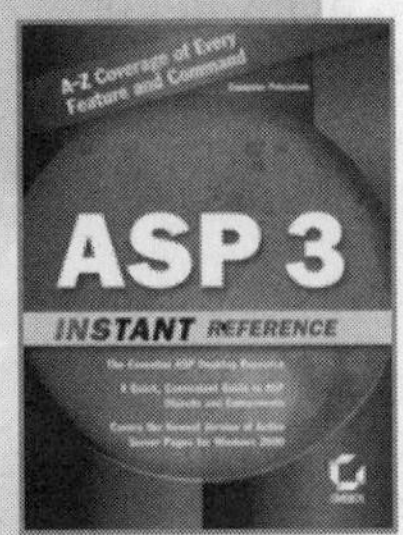

Adapted from *ASP 3 Instant Reference*, by Evangelos Petroutsos

ISBN 0-7821-2781-9 496 pages $24.99

server. People need up-to-date, live information. They need to search databases, look up stock prices, place orders, and in general send, as well as retrieve, information from the server.

To allow for a better two-way communication between clients and servers, the HTML standard was enhanced with Forms and controls. A Form is a section of a page where users can enter information (enter text in Text controls, select an option from a drop-down list, or check a radio button). The controls are the items that present or accept information on the Form. The values of the controls are sent to the server by the browser, where they're processed by an application, or a script, that runs on the server. HTML Forms and controls are quite rudimentary when compared to VB Forms and controls, but they are the only means of interaction between clients and servers (excluding the click of the mouse on a hyperlink).

Therefore, if you want to build a Web application, you must limit yourself to these controls. Your page may not look quite like a Windows application, but this is something you must live with and it doesn't seem like it's going to change any time soon. Yet, these controls coupled with hyperlinks are adequate for building applications that run over the Internet.

There was another limitation that had to be overcome. Browsers are designed to communicate with Web servers in a very simple manner. They request documents by submitting a string known as a URL (Uniform Resource Locator). URLs are the addresses of HTML documents on the Web. The URL of the desired document is embedded in the document itself. The browser knows how to extract the destination of the selected hyperlink and request the document. Alternatively, you can specify the URL of the desired document by entering its name in the browser's Address box. To interact with servers, clients should be able to request not only static HTML pages, but also programs (executable files or scripts) on the server. A script can create a new HTML page on the fly; moreover, this page can be different for different clients. If a client requests the details of an item, you could look up the item in a database the moment it's requested and retrieve the most up-to-date information. For instance, the units in stock is a piece of information that can't be stored in a static page; it must be looked up in a database the moment it's requested.

Requesting Server-Side Scripts

It is possible for the browser to request the name of a script on the server just as it would request an HTML page. The browser doesn't really have to know anything about the requested document. It simply sends a request for the document specified in each hyperlink and the server submits another HTML page. If the requested document is a script, the script is executed on the server and it generates an HTML page on the fly, which is returned to the client in response to the initial request.

For a richer interaction model, browsers should be able to pass more than a single URL to the server. Sometimes, they have to pass a lot of information back to the server, such as query criteria, registration information, and so on. To enable this two-way communication, the client attaches all the information to be passed to the server in the destination's URL. The URL of a page that contains a Form is the name of the script that will process the Form, followed by the parameter values entered by the viewer on the Form. Figure 3.1 shows what happens when you use the AltaVista search engine to locate articles on database programming. The search argument is "+ASP +programming" (this argument will return all the titles on ASP programming) and the browser passes the following URL to the server. The following line won't be broken in your browser's Address box and you may not see the entire string.

```
http://www.altavista.com/cgi-bin/query?pg=q&
sc=on&hl=on&q=%2BASP+%2Bprogramming&kl=XX& stype=stext
```

This is not a common URL. The first part is the URL of an application that runs on the server. It's the query application in the *cgi-bin* folder under the Web server's root folder. The question mark separates the name of the application from its arguments, while the ampersand symbol separates multiple arguments. The query application accepts six arguments: the *pg, sc, hl, q, kl,* and *stype* arguments. Most of the arguments are of no interest to us. The *q* argument is the search string. Notice that spaces are replaced by the plus (+) sign. The plus sign itself (which is a special symbol in URLs) was replaced by the string %2B (the hexadecimal representation of the plus character). The query application will read the information passed by the client, query the database with the specified keywords, and return another HTML document with the results of the query (you will probably see different documents at the top of the page if you perform the same query).

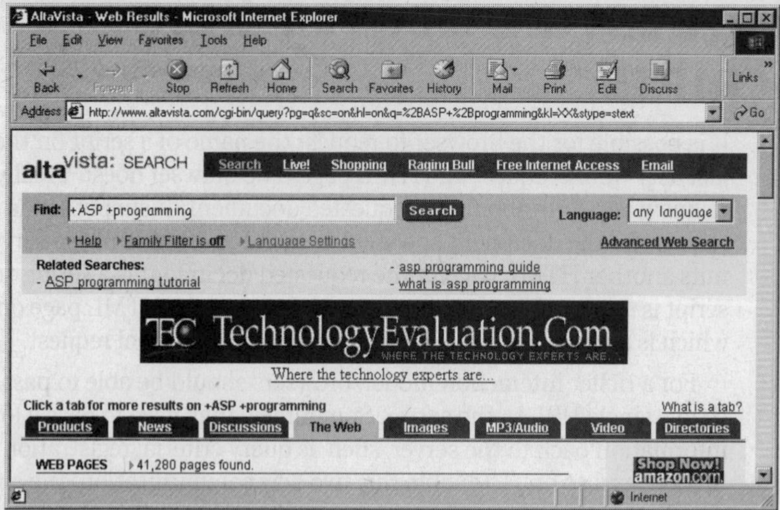

FIGURE 3.1: Invoking a server application and passing arguments to it from within the browser

In effect, we fool the browser into thinking that the destination document has a really long URL. The Web server will figure out what the URL means; it will invoke the query application and pass the specified parameters to it.

The application that runs on the server is not an EXE file. Different Web servers allow different types of applications to be invoked. IIS works with ASP (Active Server Pages) scripts. An ASP script is a program written in VBScript (or JScript) that uses several objects to communicate with the client. These objects are the ASP objects and they're explained in this guide. In the future, more objects may be added (you can actually write your own components for use with ASP pages). VBScript need not be changed in major ways. Additional functionality will be supported through new objects.

NOTE

***JScript* is Microsoft's unique flavor of JavaScript. See Chapter 5 for more details on syntax and how JScript differs from VBScript.**

VBScript is a simple scripting language, based on Visual Basic. Likewise, JavaScript is another scripting language, though it has no relation to Java. Both languages support the basic flow-control statements and can manipulate variables. They're core languages and don't provide any mechanisms for interacting with the client. If you're familiar with Visual Basic, you're ready to write ASP scripts in VBScript. The real power of VBScript is that it can access the ASP built-in objects, as well as any COM+ component installed on the server. For example, you can use the ADO objects to access databases, or the File Access component to access the server's file system. If you have developed middle-tier components for use with an application that runs on a local area network, you can use the same components to interface a Web application to a database.

Most ASP developers use VBScript, the default scripting language of IIS. The scripts run on the server and produce HTML code that can be viewed on any browser. In addition to server-side scripts, there are client-side scripts. These scripts are executed on the client and can be written either in VBScript or in JavaScript. Internet Explorer supports both VBScript and JavaScript, but Netscape's Communicator supports only JavaScript. Most examples of client-side script used in this book will be in JavaScript so that the code can be executed on all browsers. Chapter 16 will explore the use of both languages for client-side scripting, their advantages, and their differences. The bulk of this book, however, is about server-side scripts and unless stated otherwise, I'm going to use VBScript for all scripts that run on the server.

Server-Side Scripts

A server-side script is a script that's executed on the server. It is possible to write scripts that are downloaded to the client, along with the HTML page (client-side scripts), and are executed on the client, but this will be covered in later chapters. A server-side script is a mix of HTML statements and VBScript statements. The following script generates a simple page that displays the date and time on the server computer:

```
<HTML>
<H1>Active Server Pages</H1>
The date on the server is <% =Date() %>
and the time is <% =Time() %>
</HTML>
```

The tags <% and %> delimit the VBScript statements in the HTML document. When this script is executed, all HTML elements are sent to the client without any processing. The VBScript statements are executed and the output they produce is transmitted to the client in the place of the actual statements. The expression =`Date()` will be replaced by the output of the function `Date()`, which is the current date. Likewise, the expression =`Time()` will be replaced by the output of the function `Time()`.

If you store the previous lines in a text file with the extension ASP in your Web server's root folder, and then open the file from within the browser, the following HTML code will be transmitted to the client:

```
<HTML>
<H1>Active Server Pages</H1>
The date on the server is 4/5/00
and the time is 8:02:53 AM
</HTML>
```

This is straight HTML. All VBScript statements embedded in a pair of <% and %> tags were replaced by the output they produced.

NOTE

Unlike HTML pages, ASP pages can't be opened by double-clicking their names. You must start your browser and connect to the server where the file is stored. If you're using a single machine to test the samples in this book, you must start the Web server (the Personal Web Server or Internet Information Server) and connect to the URL of the desired file. To test the file `Test.asp`, use the URL `127.0.0.1/Test.asp`. 127.0.0.1 is the address of the local Web server and the file `Test.asp` is assumed to be in the server's root folder. If the Web server is running on another computer on the LAN, replace the address 127.0.0.1 with the name, or IP address, of the server. If the file is stored in a virtual folder under the root folder, replace the filename `Test.asp` with the appropriate relative path (`Samples/Test.asp`, for example).

You can also explicitly create output to be transmitted to the client by using the Response object (one of the ASP objects discussed in detail later in the book):

```
<%
Response.Write "<HTML>"
Response.Write "<H1> Active Server Pages</H1>"
Response.Write "The date on the server is" _
```

```
    & Date()
Response.Write "and the time is " & Time()
Response.Write "</HTML>"
%>
```

The tags <% and %> delimit an entire section of the script, consisting of multiple lines.

Finally, you mix and match HTML and VBScript code by embedding VBScript statements in a pair of <% and %> tags. Here's a slightly modified version of the same script. The difference is that all VBScript statements are on separate lines and they're a bit more complicated than before. This script formats the date and time values with the `FormatDateTime` function.

```
<HTML>
<H1>Active Server Pages</H1>
The date on the server is
<%
Response.Write FormatDateTime(Date, 1)
%>
and the time is
<%
Response.Write FormatDateTime(Time(), 3)
%>
</HTML>
```

You can also use VBScript to generate Forms that would normally be coded in straight HTML. For example, you can create a List control and populate it from within a script. See the section "The Select Control" later in this chapter for an example.

The Structure of Web Applications

The Web started as a global network that simplified the sharing of information. Some people post information in the form of Web pages, or HTML pages, or HTML documents, and many more people view this information. With the introduction of HTML Forms and specialized software that runs on the server, the Web has become an environment for running applications. The Web is no longer a simple click-and-view environment. It has become a client/server environment for running elaborate applications.

The browser is the client, which can display HTML documents and interact with the viewer through HTML controls and scripts that run on the server. The Web server processes the information and sends the results to the client in the form of HTML pages. Nowadays, we talk about Web applications. People using Microsoft's tools to build applications that run on the Web over the HTTP protocol call them ASP-based applications, because ASP plays such an important role in developing scripts on the server.

A Web application is a site with multiple HTML pages and server-side scripts. HTML pages call server-side scripts and pass parameters to the scripts. These scripts are executed on the server, just like applications would be. They process the values submitted by the client, format the results as HTML documents on the fly, and send the new documents to the client. One side of the script sees the client and interacts with the viewer by accepting information posted by the client and sending HTML pages to the client. The other side of the script sees the components on the server. Such components include databases, the server's file system, e-mail applications, and so on.

Web applications have a special requirement. Where typical desktop applications use Forms to interact with the user, Web applications are based on HTML pages. In a VB application, for example, there are many options for its Forms to communicate with one another. They can use public variables, they can read directly the values of the controls on any Form, and they can set each other's properties. The situation is different on the Web. Each page is a separate entity and it can't interact directly with another page of the same site. Not to mention that any user could bookmark any page and jump to this page directly.

A Web application is a site that works much like a Windows application, and specifically like a client/server application. Viewers enter information on a Form. This information is then transmitted to the server, and the result of the processing returns to the client as another HTML document. In most cases, the processing that takes place on the server is a database search. The results of the search are then furnished back to the client in the form of another HTML page.

Here's another major difference between a desktop application (like an application written in VB) and a Web application: the windows of a desktop application can remain open on the desktop and users can switch from one to the other with a mouse-click. This is not true with a Web application. A Web application can only display one Form (page) at a time. In order to switch to another page we must either select a link on the current page, or click the Back button to view a page we've already visited.

Creating a Web Site

A Web site is a collection of HTML documents that reside on the server. To access your site, a client must connect to a URL, which is the site's domain name. You could store all the documents making up the site in the folder `C:\Web\MySite`. Viewers need not know the actual name of the folder where the documents are stored. The `C:\Web\MySite` folder is the site's root folder and users can connect to it by specifying an address like `www.ComputersRus.com`. You can also specify the document that will be displayed by default when a viewer connects to your site. This document is usually a static HTML page named `default.htm` or `index.htm`.

Your documents can be organized in folders under the root virtual folder. As long as you use relative path names to call one document from within another, you can move a site to a different location on the hard disk and you won't have to change the references.

To create a new site with IIS under Windows 2000 Server, just start the Internet Information Services by selecting Start ➢ Programs ➢ Administrative Tools. If you're using Windows 2000 Professional, you will find the IIS in the Control Panel. When you see the IIS Console window, right-click the name of the server and select Properties to see the properties of the default site. Its root folder is in `C:\InetPub\WWWRoot`, but you can map the site's root folder to any folder on your system. You can also create virtual folders under the root folder and store the samples there. To test the samples, you must specify not only the Web server's domain name, but the name of the virtual folder as well. If you have a virtual subfolder named "Samples," use the following URL to open the `Test.asp` file in this folder: `http://www.domain.com/Samples/Test.asp`.

If you're using a server that doesn't have its own domain name, use the IP address of the local host, which is always `127.0.0.1`: `http://127.0.0.1/ Samples/Test.asp`.

The root folder is where all the pages making up the site must be placed. Of course, you can place them in subfolders of the root folder. For example, you can create an Images folder and place all images there, or a Scripts folder and place all scripts there. As long as these pages are referenced relative to the root folder, you'll be able to move your site to another root folder, or computer, as is.

Since you're reading this book, I'm assuming some of your pages are ASP scripts. You can use the extension ASP for all the documents of the site, even if they don't contain any VBScript statements. ASP 3.0 is very efficient in processing ASP pages that don't contain any scripts (just HTML code).

In addition to the ASP scripts (and static HTML pages, if you have any), a typical site contain a few more special files. These are the GLOBAL.ASA files, which contain declarations, and one or more INCLUDE files, which contain declarations and useful functions that can be included in any other script of the same site. These files are discussed in the last section of this chapter.

For readers who are familiar with VBScript, or even Visual Basic, I will discuss briefly the HTML statements for creating Forms with HTML controls. These pages are the application's user interface and your task as a Web developer is to design the application's user interface and the scripts that will accept and process the data entered on the various Forms. The Web designers will dress up your pages. A Web designer is responsible for the look and feel of the page. Your task is to fill the page with different data, which are usually the result of the execution of a script. The designer will create a good-looking page with dummy data (a table with fake data, for instance). The developer will populate the table with data retrieved from a database. To do so, you must write a script that reads the parameter values submitted by the client, builds the appropriate SQL statement, executes it against the database, and formats the rows returned by the database as an HTML table.

HTML Forms and Controls

To interact with the viewer, besides the ubiquitous hyperlinks, HTML recognizes a few special tags that insert controls on a Form. An HTML control is a stripped-down version of the ActiveX controls you use to build Forms with Visual Basic. You can use controls to collect information from the user for registration purposes, take orders over the Internet, or let the user specify selection criteria for record retrieval from databases. HTML provides the following controls:

Text control A box that accepts a single line of text, similar to Visual Basic's default TextBox control.

TextArea control A box that accepts multiple lines of text, similar to a TextBox control with its MultiLine property set to True.

RadioButton control A circular button that can be checked or cleared to indicate one of multiple options. This control is similar to Visual Basic's Option control.

CheckBox control A box that can be checked or cleared to indicate that an option is selected.

Password control A text control that doesn't display the characters as they are typed.

Select control A list of options from which the user can select one or more. This control is equivalent to Visual Basic's ListBox control.

Command Button control A button that can trigger various actions, similar to Visual Basic's Button control.

NOTE

The HTML keywords are not case sensitive, but I use uppercase to make it easy to distinguish them in the text. VBScript statements are also case insensitive, but we capitalize the first letter in each keyword (Statement, Keyword, and so on).

Before you place any controls on a page, you must create a Form, with the FORM tag. All controls must appear within a pair of FORM tags:

```
<FORM NAME = "myForm">
{your Controls go here}
</FORM>
```

The NAME attribute is optional, but it's a good practice to name Forms. Beyond the NAME attribute, the FORM tag also accepts the METHOD and ACTION attributes, which determine how the data will be submitted to the server and how they'll be processed there. The METHOD attribute can have one of two values: POST or GET. The ACTION attribute specifies the script that will process the data on the server. To specify that the contents of a Form must be submitted to the script `ReadValues.asp`, use the following <FORM> tag:

```
<FORM NAME = "myForm" ACTION =
    "ReadValues.asp" METHOD="POST">
```

The values entered by the viewer on the Form's controls are sent to the server with the Submit button. Every Form has a Submit button (even if it's named something different), which extracts the ACTION attribute from the <FORM> tag and the values of the controls, creates a new URL, and sends it to the server. Because the name of the requested document is `ReadValues.asp`, the Web server executes the `ReadValues.asp` script, which in turn uses the Request object to read the values of the controls.

WARNING

For security purposes, the Web server will not execute any executable file specified as a URL. By default, IIS will execute the ASP scripts in the site's root folder and its subfolders. It's also common to turn off the Write privileges of the root folder, so that no one can place scripts there except the administrator.

The values of the various controls can be retrieved through the Request.Form collection. There are other methods to retrieve the control values, which are discussed later. The simplest one is through the Form collection and I'll use this technique for the examples of this chapter. The Form collection has one member for each control on the Form and you can access the individual control's value by name. If the Form contains a control named "UserValue" you can access this control's value with the expression `Request.Form("UserValue")`.

SPECIFYING THE COLLECTION

You don't actually have to specify which collection of the Request object you are referring to. In other words, Request.Form("User-Value") and Request("UserValue") work the same. If you leave off the collection, ASP will automatically search all the collections in the following order for the key you've specified:

QueryString

Form

Cookies

ClientCertificate

ServerVariables

This is especially convenient if you're not sure how a particular variable will be sent to your page, whether by QueryString or by Form. However, for clarity I'll continue to specify the collection for now.

The CheckBox Control

The CheckBox control is a little square with an optional check mark. The check mark is a toggle, which turns on and off every time the user clicks the control. It is used to present a list of options, from which the user can select one or more. When the check mark is turned on, the check box is said to be checked, and when it's turned off, the control is said to be cleared.

The CheckBox control can be inserted in a document with the following tag: `<INPUT TYPE = CHECKBOX NAME = "Check1">` where *Check1* is the control's name. You'll use it later to find out whether the control is marked or not, for instance. By default, a check box is cleared. To make a check box checked initially, you use the CHECKED option in its INPUT tag:

```
<INPUT TYPE = CHECKBOX NAME = "Check1" CHECKED>
```

To read the value of the Check1 control from within your script, use the following expression:

```
If Request.Form("Check1") = "on" Then
    ' these statements are executed
    ' if Check1 was checked
Else
    ' these statements are executed
    ' if Check1 wasn't checked
End If
```

The RadioButton Control

The RadioButton control is similar to the CheckBox control, only it's round, and instead of a check mark, a solid round mark appears in the center of a checked RadioButton. RadioButton controls are used to present a list of options, similar to a group of CheckBox controls, but only one option can be selected in a group of RadioButtons. Not only that, the responsibility of clearing the previously checked button lies on the control itself; there's nothing you must do in your code to clear the checked button every time the user makes a new selection.

To insert a RadioButton in a document, use a line similar to the one for the CheckBox, only this time replace the control type with `RADIO`: `<INPUT TYPE = RADIO NAME = "Radio1">`. Whereas each CheckBox on a Form has its own name, you can have several RadioButtons with the same name. All RadioButtons with the same name form a group and only one member of the group can be checked at a time. Every time the user clicks a RadioButton to check it, the previously checked one is cleared automatically. To initially check a RadioButton, use the CHECKED attribute, which works similarly to the attribute with the same name of the CheckBox control. Notice that the options are mutually exclusive and only one of them can be checked.

Since a number of RadioButton controls may belong to the same group, and only one of them can be checked, they must also share the same name. The following statements will place a group of RadioButton controls on a Form:

```
<B>Income Range:</B>
<P>
<INPUT TYPE=RADIO NAME="IncomeBracket" VALUE=1>
Less than 10K
<BR>
<INPUT TYPE=RADIO NAME="IncomeBracket" VALUE=2>
More than 10K but less than 30K
<BR>
<INPUT TYPE=RADIO NAME="IncomeBracket" VALUE=3>
More than 30K but less than 100K
<BR>
<INPUT TYPE=RADIO NAME="IncomeBracket" VALUE=4>
More than 100K
<BR>
```

To read the value of the IncomeBracket control from within your script, use an expression like the following one:

```
Range = Request.Form("IncomeBracket")
```

The Text Control

The Text control is a box that can accept user input and is used for entering items such as names, addresses, and any form of free text.

To insert a Text control on a page, use the INPUT tag and set the TYPE attribute to TEXT. The line:

```
<INPUT TYPE = TEXT NAME = "Publisher"
       VALUE = "Sybex">
```

will display a Text control on the page, with the string "Sybex" in it. The viewer can enter any string, overwriting the existing one or appending more text at its end. The usual text editing and navigational keys (Home key, arrows, the DEL and INS keys) will work with the Text control. However, you can't format the text in a Text control by using different fonts or even font attributes like bold and italic.

Finally, you can specify the size of the control on the page with the SIZE attribute, and the maximum amount of text it can accept with the MAXLENGTH attribute. For example, the TextBox control defined as:

```
<INPUT TYPE = TEXT NAME = "Publisher"
    SIZE = 40MAXLENGTH = 100
    VALUE = "Sybex">
```

can accept user input up to 100 characters, while its length on the page corresponds to the average length of 40 characters in the current font.

To read the value of the Publisher Text control from within your script, use an expression like the following one:

```
PubName = Request.Form("Publisher")
```

The Password Control

The Password control is a variation on the Text control. Its behavior is identical to that of the Text control, but the characters entered are not displayed. In their places, the user sees asterisks instead. It's meant for input that should be kept private. To create a Password control you use an input tag similar to that for a Text control, but specify the PASSWORD type:

```
<INPUT TYPE = PASSWORD NAME = "Secret Box"
    SIZE = 20 MAXLENGTH = 20>
```

Other than a different TYPE attribute, Password controls are identical to Text controls.

The TextArea Control

You can also provide your users with a control that accepts multiple lines of text. It is the TextArea control, whose operation is quite similar to that of the TextBox control, but it handles the carriage return character, which causes it to change lines. All navigational and editing keys will work with the TextArea control as well. To place a TextArea control on a Form, use the </TEXTAREA> tag:

```
<TEXTAREA NAME = COMMENTS ROWS = 10
     COLS = 50></TEXTAREA>
```

This tag creates a box on the page, whose dimensions are 10 rows of text, with 50 characters per line. The ROWS and COLS tags specify the dimensions of the control on the page (in units of the current font).

Besides its attributes, another difference between the TextArea control and the other controls you've seen so far is that the TextArea control must end with the </TEXTAREA> tag. The reason for this is that the TextArea control may contain lengthy, multiple-line default text, which must be enclosed between the two tags and can't be assigned to an attribute:

```
<TEXTAREA NAME = COMMENTS ROWS = 10
     COLS = 50>
This is the greatest Web site I've
seen in years! Congratulations!!!
</TEXTAREA>
```

The text between the two </TEXTAREA> tags is displayed initially in the box. In the unlikely event that the user is less than excited about your pages, he can overwrite your initial comments. Notice that all line breaks in the text will be preserved. There's no need to use paragraph or line break tags to format the initial text of a TextArea control (and if you do include HTML tags in the text, they will be displayed in the Text box as you typed them). If the text can't fit in the space provided, the appropriate scroll bars will be added to the control automatically. Notice the lack of any HTML formatting tags in the text. The line breaks are preserved, but the control isn't going to process any HTML tags. Remember that the TextArea control doesn't insert line breaks on its own, so you must try not to exceed the maximum line length (as defined with the ROW attribute) if you want the contents of the control to be entirely visible along each line.

The Select Control

The Multiple Selection List control, as it's called, is a control that presents a list of options to the viewer, and lets him or her select none, one, or more of them. The tag for the List control is <SELECT> and it must be followed by a matching </SELECT> tag. The attributes that may appear in a <SELECT> tag are NAME (the control's name), SIZE (which specifies how many options will be visible), and MULTIPLE (which specifies whether the user may choose multiple items or not). To place a List control on your Form, use the following tag:

```
<SELECT NAME = "UserOptions" SIZE = 4
     MULTIPLE = MULTIPLE>
</SELECT>
```

Between the two SELECT tags you can place the options that make up the List, each one in a pair of OPTION tags:

```
<SELECT NAME = "UserOptions" SIZE = 3
     MULTIPLE = MULTIPLE>
<OPTION>Computer</OPTION>
<OPTION>Monitor</OPTION>
<OPTION>Printer</OPTION>
<OPTION>Modem</OPTION>
<OPTION>Speakers</OPTION>
<OPTION>Microphone</OPTION>
<OPTION>Mouse</OPTION>
</SELECT>
```

The control displayed on the Form with the statements shown above contains seven options, but only three of them are visible. The SIZE attribute will help you save space on your pages when you have a long list of options to present to the user. The user can also select multiple options (with the Shift and Control keys) even if some of them are not visible. To disable multiple selections, omit the MULTIPLE attribute.

To minimize the List control's size on the Form, omit the MULTIPLE attribute (if possible) and don't specify how many items will be visible. The result will be a list with just one visible element. If the user clicks the arrow, the list will expand and all its elements will become visible until the user makes a selection. Then, the list collapses back to a single item.

The OPTION tag has a VALUE attribute too. This attribute specifies the string(s) that will be sent back to the server when the user submits the Form with that option selected. In other words, it is possible to display one string in the list, but send another value to the server. Here's a modified version of the previous list:

```
<SELECT NAME = "UserOptions" SIZE = 6
```

```
    MULTIPLE = MULTIPLE>
<OPTION VALUE=1>Computer</OPTION>
<OPTION VALUE=2>Monitor</OPTION>
<OPTION VALUE=3>Printer</OPTION>
<OPTION VALUE=4>Modem</OPTION>
<OPTION VALUE=5>Speakers</OPTION>
<OPTION VALUE=6>Microphone</OPTION>
<OPTION VALUE=7>Mouse</OPTION>
</SELECT>
```

When the selection on this list is submitted to the server instead of the actual string, the server sees a number, which corresponds to the viewer's selection.

Quite often, we use VBScript to create and populate Select controls on a Form. If the control's options are read from a database, for example, you don't know the options that will appear on the control at design time. You must write a script that reads the appropriate values and then produces the HTML code that will display the control and its options on the page.

The following example shows you how to create a Select control with the month names. First, it places the <SELECT> tag to the output stream and then it goes through the names of the 12 months with a `For ... Next` loop. At each iteration it outputs the month's number (this is the control's VALUE attribute) and the month's name (this is what the viewer sees). The If statement outputs a slightly different <OPTION> tag when the month happens to be the current month. The SELECTED attribute preselects the current month on the control.

THE VBCRLF CONSTANT

vbCrLf is a predefined constant you can use to add line breaks to your output. It sends two "invisible" characters—a Carriage Return (Cr) and Line Feed (Lf)—to the output stream. These holdovers from the dot matrix days (and typewriters before that) simply add a hard return to the resulting line of code. Otherwise, the HTML output appears as one long line, like this:

```
<OPTION VALUE=1>January</OPTION><OPTION VALUE=2>...
```

CONTINUED ➞

Your site's visitors won't know the difference because browsers don't care one way or the other. But using vbCrLf makes for readable HTML, which makes for easier debugging should you need to view the output of your ASP code.

```
<%
Response.Write "<SELECT NAME = 'Months' _
    SIZE = 1>"
For iMonth = 1 To 12
    MName = MonthName(iMonth)
    If iMonth = Month(Date()) Then
        Response.Write "<OPTION VALUE=" _
                        & iMonth & " SELECTED>" & _
                        MName & "</OPTION>" & vbCrLf
    Else
        Response.Write "<OPTION VALUE=" _
                        & IMonth & ">" & MName & _
                        "</OPTION>" & vbCrLf
    End If
Next
Response.Write "</SELECT>"
%>
```

If you open this script from within your browser and examine the page's source code, you'll see the following HTML code:

```
<SELECT NAME = 'Months' SIZE = 1>
    <OPTION VALUE=1>January</OPTION>
    <OPTION VALUE=2>February</OPTION>
    <OPTION VALUE=3>March</OPTION>
    <OPTION VALUE=4 SELECTED>April</OPTION>
    <OPTION VALUE=5>May</OPTION>
    <OPTION VALUE=6>June</OPTION>
    <OPTION VALUE=7>July</OPTION>
```

```
        <OPTION VALUE=8>August</OPTION>
        <OPTION VALUE=9>September</OPTION>
        <OPTION VALUE=10>October</OPTION>
        <OPTION VALUE=11>November</OPTION>
        <OPTION VALUE=12>December</OPTION>
    </SELECT>
```

To read the selected value(s) on a Select control from within your script, use a statement like the following one:

```
Options = Request.Form("Month")
```

The value of the Select control is the same as the selected option's VALUE attribute. The *Options* variable, for example, will be assigned a numeric value, which is the selected month's number.

If the viewer has selected multiple options on the control, you can access them with the same name and an index value:

```
Option1 = Request.Form("Month")(1)
Option2 = Request.Form("Month")(2)
```

The Command Button

The Command Button is a control that can be clicked to trigger certain actions. Typically, Command Buttons are used to trigger two actions: Submit the data to the server, or reset all controls on the Form to their original values. Command Buttons can also be used to trigger any actions you can program in your pages with VBScript (or JavaScript) statements that are executed on the client, but we are not going to discuss client-side scripting yet. If you want to include client-side scripts in your pages, use JavaScript to make sure your pages can be viewed on all browsers.

There are two types of Buttons you can place on a Form. The most important one is the SUBMIT Button; it transmits the contents of all controls on the Form to the server. The RESET Button clears the controls on the Form (or resets them to their initial values) and doesn't submit anything.

These two types of Buttons can be placed on a Form with the following INPUT tags:

```
<INPUT TYPE = SUBMIT VALUE = "Send Data">
```

and

```
<INPUT TYPE = RESET VALUE = "Reset Values">
```

where VALUE is the caption that appears on the Button. Each Form should contain at least a SUBMIT Button to transmit the information entered by the user to the server. (If the page contains a client-side script, then you can submit the data to the server via the script and you don't have to include a SUBMIT Button.)

Figure 3.2 shows a Web page with a Form that contains all of the HTML controls we use in developing Web applications, with the exception of the TextArea and Password controls. The output of the AllControls.htm page is shown in Figure 3.2.

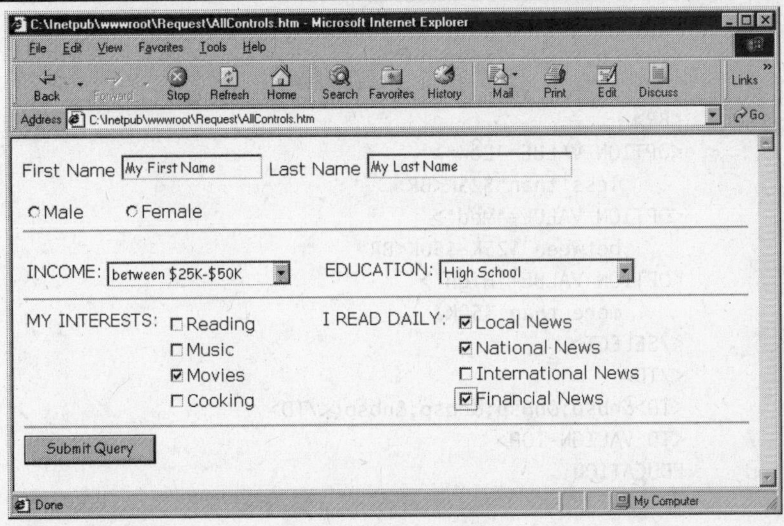

FIGURE 3.2: The output of the AllControls.htm page

Listing 3.1: The AllControls.htm Page

```
<HTML>
<FONT FACE="Verdana">
<FORM NAME=Personal ACTION=
     ReadParameters.asp METHOD=GET>
First Name
<INPUT TYPE=Text NAME=FirstName
     SIZE=20 VALUE='My First Name'>
Last Name
<INPUT TYPE=Text NAME=LastName SIZE=30
     VALUE='My Last Name'>
<BR><BR>
```

```
<INPUT TYPE=Radio NAME="Sex" VALUE="Male">
Male
    
<INPUT TYPE=Radio NAME="Sex"
    VALUE="Female">
Female
<BR>
<HR>
<BR>
<TABLE>
<TR><TD VALIGN=TOP>INCOME:</TD>
<TD><SELECT NAME="IncomeRange">
<OPTION VALUE="invalid">
    Select your income range
<BR>
<OPTION VALUE="Low">
    less than $25K<BR>
<OPTION VALUE="Med">
    between $25K-$50K<BR>
<OPTION VALUE="High">
    more than $50K
</SELECT>
</TD>
<TD>    </TD>
<TD VALIGN=TOP>
EDUCATION:
</TD>
<TD>
<SELECT NAME="Education">
<OPTION VALUE="invalid">
    Select your highest degree
<BR>
<OPTION VALUE="HSchool">
    High School
<BR>
<OPTION VALUE="College">
    College
<BR>
<OPTION VALUE="University">
    University
</SELECT>
</TD>
```

```
</TR>
</TABLE>
<HR>
<TABLE><TR>
<TD VALIGN=TOP>MY INTERESTS:
</TD>
<TD VALIGN=TOP>
<TABLE>
<TR><TD>
<INPUT TYPE=CheckBox NAME="Books">
     Reading</TD></TR>
<TR><TD>
<INPUT TYPE=CheckBox NAME="Music">
     Music</TD></TR>
<TR><TD>
<INPUT TYPE=CheckBox NAME="Movies">
     Movies</TD></TR>
<TR><TD>
<INPUT TYPE=CheckBox NAME="Cooking">
     Cooking</TD></TR>
</TABLE>
</TD>
<TD>     
       </TD>
<TD VALIGN=TOP>I READ DAILY:</TD>
<TD VALIGN=TOP>
<TABLE>
<TR><TD>
<INPUT TYPE=CheckBox NAME=Local>
     Local News</TD></TR>
<TR><TD>
<INPUT TYPE=CheckBox NAME=National>
     National News</TD></TR>
<TR><TD>
<INPUT TYPE=CheckBox NAME=International>
     International News</TD></TR>
<TR><TD>
<INPUT TYPE=CheckBox NAME=Financial>
     Financial News</TD></TR>
</TABLE>
</TABLE>
<HR>
```

```
<INPUT TYPE=SUBMIT>
</HTML>
```

Directives and Server-Side Includes

Besides VBScript (or JavaScript) statements and HTML encoded text, ASP files may contain two special items, *preprocessing directives* and *server-side includes.* A preprocessing directive is a command to the ASP interpreter; it tells the interpreter to execute some statements before it starts processing the script. If you're familiar with C programming, you'll recognize that the preprocessing directives are equivalent to compiler directives. A server-side include is a statement that tells the interpreter to load a file and replace the statements with the file's contents. If several of your scripts use the same code segment, you can place these statements in a text file and include it in any script by placing a server-side include at the beginning of the script.

The preprocessing directives have the following syntax:

```
<%@ directive=value%>
```

To specify multiple directives, separate them with a single space, as shown here:

```
<%@ directive1=value1 directive2=value2%>
```

Since the space delimits successive directives, there shouldn't be any spaces around the equals sign. Finally, the line with the directive must be the first one in the script. The only exception is the `<% =var %>` directive, which instructs the ASP interpreter to replace the entire directive with the value of the *var* variable.

ASP recognizes the following directives. Notice that most directives have an equivalent property in the Session object.

CODEPAGE This property determines which code page will be used to prepare the output and it must match the code page used by the client. Different languages and locales use different code pages. The value 932 corresponds to the code page of Japanese Kanji.

ENABLESESSIONSTATE This property determines whether ASP will maintain state across the pages of your application. The default value of this property is True and we rarely change it. ASP relies on client-side cookies to maintain state. If a client doesn't accept cookies, ASP won't be able to maintain state across pages, regardless of the setting of this directive. This directive doesn't have an equivalent property in the Session object.

LANGUAGE This directive specifies the scripting language. It's equivalent to setting the LANGUAGE attribute of the <SCRIPT> tag. The language you set with the LANGUAGE directive becomes the default language. You can overwrite this setting in a script with the LANGUAGE attribute.

LCID This directive sets the Locale ID for the current page. The Locale ID determines how numbers and dates will be formatted. The value 1036 corresponds to the French locale.

TRANSACTION The TRANSACTION directive tells the interpreter to treat the entire page as a transaction.

A server-side include (SSI) is similar to a directive: it tells the interpreter to replace the SSI with the contents of a file or another value. ASP recognizes the following server-side includes:

#include Tells the interpreter to replace the SSI line with the contents of a file. The #include SSI is described in detail in the last section of this chapter.

#config Sets the format for error messages, dates, and file sizes.

#echo Inserts the value of an environment variable (a member of the Request.ServerVariables collection) at the current location in the script.

#exec Inserts the result of a command or application. The command or application is executed before the script is processed, so that the result can be inserted at the current location in the script.

#flastmod Inserts the date/time when the file was last modified.

#fsize Inserts the current file's size in the script (this is the script's file size).

The #include SSI

The most important server-side include is #include, which inserts an entire file into the script. The syntax of this SSI is:

```
<!- #include fileType = filename ->
```

fileType specifies whether the file is referenced with a virtual or relative path and its value can be one of the literals "file" or "virtual." The following statement places the navigational buttons or hyperlinks at the top of the page:

```
<!- #include virtual="/Common/NavBar.inc" ->
```

The NavBar.inc file contains the code for the navigational buttons and it resides in the Common folder under the Web server's root folder.

What's Next?

Now that you can put together a form, the next step is deciding what to do with it. This is where the beauty of ASP comes into play. In the next chapter, you'll discover VBScript, one of the core languages of ASP. You'll learn VBScript syntax, including functions and logic structures, as well as how to bring it all together into a Web page. By the end of the chapter, you'll know how to use this versatile scripting language to respond to your visitor's input and to create a dynamic Web experience.

Chapter 4

Introduction to VBScript

Forms help make up the foundation of an interactive Web application. Now that you understand how Forms work, we can expand on the concept of interactivity by discussing the scripting languages used by ASP. The previous chapter gave you some examples of VBScript in action. In this chapter, you'll learn the different elements of VBScript as a language, as well as some basic programming concepts every developer can use.

Adapted from *Mastering™ Active Server Pages 3*, by A. Russell Jones

ISBN 0-7821-2619-7 928 pages $49.99

Scripting Languages vs. Other Computer Languages

Scripting languages are interpreted languages. The server must parse, compile, and execute the script on-demand. In contrast, languages like C++ are compiled languages. You use a program called a compiler to perform the first two steps—parsing and compiling the code—before executing the code. Compilers store a machine-language translation of the code. Interpreted languages are easier to use, while compiled languages are faster and more efficient.

ASP script languages have only one variable type—the `Variant` variable. A `Variant` is a relatively large (16-byte) variable that can hold any type of value—`Integer`, `Long`, `String`, `Array`, `Object`—any type. Variants are large because they need to be able to contain all other variables, as well as a value describing the type of value they contain.

While scripting languages are easier to use than compiled languages, they also have a large overhead. Because of the extra load on the server required to parse and compile scripting languages, code you write in ASP will not scale as well as code you write in compiled languages. Also, ASP scripts must run on the server. In contrast, compiled code can run on other servers and return the values to an ASP script.

In short, try to think of your ASP scripts as presentation code only. Use script to format responses and make calls to compiled code for efficiency. Use compiled components for database connectivity and to process business logic.

ASP Scripting Options

So far you've seen only VBScript examples in this book; but ASP isn't limited to VBScript. You can currently use any of several scripting languages. Any scripting language that conforms to the Microsoft Scripting Host requirements will work.

VBScript

VBScript is a subset of the Visual Basic for Applications (VBA) language used in the Microsoft Office suite and in many other commercially available applications, which in turn is a subset of Microsoft's Visual Basic language. All of these languages share an (almost) identical set of keywords, properties, and functions. The biggest difference between them, besides the lack of a few methods in VBScript, is that you can compile VB, but you can't compile VBScript.

VBScript is the default ASP scripting language. Most of the example code available in this book and in other resources is VBScript code.

JScript

JScript is Microsoft's ECMAScript-compatible version of JavaScript. Unlike the relationship between VBScript and VB, JavaScript is *not* a subset of Sun's Java language. The two languages share some common syntax, but Netscape developed JavaScript, not Sun. JScript is a powerful scripting language. Developers commonly use JScript to write client-side scripts because it's the common standard for browser scripting, and not all browsers can run VBScript.

You don't have to limit yourself to using JScript on the client; you can use it on the server as well. ASP ships with JScript. To use JScript on the server, you can change the default ASP language to JScript by using the Internet Service Manager application. You can also change the language on a page-by-page basis in your ASP scripts by changing the language tag at the top of each ASP page to the following:

```
<%@Language="JScript"%>
```

PerlScript

Perl is a powerful text-processing language used extensively in Common Gateway Interface (CGI) scripting, before ASP and other choices were available. PerlScript is a subset of Perl that retains most of Perl's functionality. Microsoft does not ship PerlScript with ASP, but you can download it from the Internet. There are both free and commercial versions of PerlScript available.

Others

Any scripting language that conforms to the Microsoft Scripting Host requirements will work. When ASP first appeared, there were many references to a Rexx scripting language. That seems to have disappeared, but it might be underground. I've also seen hints of a PythonScript scripting language. My recommendation is, stick to VBScript or possibly JScript on the server. Most of the comments in ASP newsgroups about scripting languages other than VBScript tend to center around poor support and buggy implementations. If you're more comfortable with Python or Perl than with VBScript or JScript, consider using CGI rather than ASP.

Getting Started with VBScript

The VBScript language provides built-in functions and methods for most common programming tasks. Version 5 added powerful search capabilities and support for creating your own classes and objects.

Keywords

Scripting is a combination of keywords, built-in functions, calls to custom routines, and object methods. Keywords are words that the parser recognizes—they're part of the language. You can't create variables with the same name as a keyword, so it's good to list them up-front, so you can avoid problems.

Table 4.1 lists the VBScript keywords in alphabetical order and a brief description of where/how you use them.

TABLE 4.1: VBScript Keywords

Keyword	Type	Description
Abs	Function	Returns the absolute value of a number.
Addition (+)	Operator	Used to add values.
And	Operator	Used to perform Boolean comparisons and operations.
`Array`	Function	Creates a `Variant` array.
`Asc`	Function	Returns the ASCII value of a character.
Assignment (=)	Operator	Assigns one value to another. In VBScript, you also use the = operator to test for equivalence.
`Atn`	Function	Returns the arctangent of a number.
`Call`	Statement	Calls a subroutine or function.
`CBool`	Function	Returns a `Variant` of subtype `Boolean` (either `True` or `False`).

CONTINUED ➞

TABLE 4.1 continued: VBScript Keywords

KEYWORD	TYPE	DESCRIPTION
CByte	Function	Returns a Variant of subtype Byte (single-byte integer).
CCur	Function	Returns a Variant of subtype Currency (8 bytes).
CDate	Function	Returns a Variant of subtype Date (8 bytes).
CDbl	Function	Returns a Variant of subtype Double (8 bytes).
Chr	Function	Returns the character representation of an ASCII integer value.
Cint	Function	Returns a Variant of subtype Integer (2 bytes).
Clear	Method	Clears the Err object.
CLng	Function	Returns a Variant of subtype Long (4 bytes).
Class	Object	The object returned when you create a class definition using the Class statement.
Class	Statement	Creates a class. You provide the class name, properties and methods.
Concatenation (&)	Operator	Concatenates strings. You can also use the Addition (+) operator to add strings, but it's not a good idea to do so.
Const	Statement	Creates a constant.
Cos	Function	Returns the cosine of an angle.
CreateObject	Function	Creates an object variable.
CSng	Function	Returns a Variant of subtype Single (8 bytes).
CStr	Function	Returns a Variant of subtype String.
Date	Function	Returns a Variant of subtype Date.
DateAdd	Function	Returns a date or time offset by month, week, day, year, minute, second, or hour.
DateDiff	Function	Returns the difference in months, weeks, days, years, minutes, seconds, or hours between two dates or times.
DatePart	Function	Returns the part of a date or time representing the day, weekday, month, quarter, year, minute, second, or hour.
DateSerial	Function	Returns a date offset by the specified number of days, months, and years.
DateValue	Function	Returns a Variant of subtype Date corresponding to a string date parameter—turns strings into dates. CDate does this as well.

CONTINUED →

TABLE 4.1 continued: VBScript Keywords

Keyword	Type	Description
`Day`	Function	Returns the day of the month.
`Description`	Property	Returns the description of an error stored in the Err object.
`Dictionary`	Object	A collection object that holds key-value pairs.
`Dim`	Statement	Declares a variable.
Division (/)	Operator	Divides one number by another.
`Do...Loop`	Statement	Surrounds code to be repeated in a loop.
`Empty`	Value	The value of an uninitialized `Variant`.
`Eqv`	Operator	Identical to Boolean And.
`Erase`	Statement	Clears an array.
`Err`	Object	Contains error information.
`Eval`	Function	Evaluates script passed to the function as an expression. You may evaluate only one expression at a time. Refer to the `Execute` statement for a way to execute multiple lines of code.
`Execute`	Method	Executes a regular expression search for the specified `string` argument.
`Execute`	Statement	Executes one or more lines of code passed to the statement as a string. You may separate statements with colons or with carriage return/linefeed characters. Script executed in this manner can access global variables, but may only be executed within the context of the currently executing procedure.
`ExecuteGlobal`	Statement	Executes one or more lines of code passed to the statement as a string. You may separate statements with colons or with carriage return/linefeed characters. Script executed in this manner runs in the global context, can access global variables, and may be called from anywhere else in the script.
`Exit`	Statement	Exits a subroutine, function, or repeated code block.
`Exp`	Function	Returns the natural base of logarithms (e) raised to an exponential power.
Exponentiation (^)	Operator	Raises a value to an exponential power.
`False`	Value	Boolean logical `False` value of 0.

CONTINUED ⟶

TABLE 4.1 continued: VBScript Keywords

KEYWORD	TYPE	DESCRIPTION
FileSystem-Object	Object	Object that performs disk file operations.
Filter	Function	Returns a subset of a string array based on conditions passed as a parameter.
FirstIndex	Property	Returns the character offset of the first character of a Match object returned from a regular expression search. Translated, that means that the search string was found in the target string, and it appears at the index position pointed to by the FirstIndex property. Unlike most other VB collections and the Instr function, the character offset of the first character in the searched string is 0, not 1.
Fix	Function	Returns a number truncated to an integer value.
For...Next	Statement	Surrounds code to be repeated in a loop a fixed number of times.
For Each...Next	Statement	Surrounds code to be repeated for the number of items in a collection object or array.
FormatCurrency	Function	Formats currency values according to specific criteria.
FormatDateTime	Function	Formats dates and times according to specific criteria.
FormatNumber	Function	Formats numbers according to a specific format string.
FormatPercent	Function	Formats numbers or numeric expressions as percentages.
Function	Statement	Defines the beginning of a function.
GetLocale	Function	Returns the LocaleID of the computer on which the script is running.
GetObject	Function	Returns an object reference for an object loaded from a file. You provide the filename, and optionally, a ProgID. A ProgID consists of a ProjectName.ClassName construction, like Excel.Worksheet, or Word .Application.
GetRef	Function	Returns a function pointer that you can bind to a DHTML event.
Global	Property	Determines whether a regular expression search should match all occurrences or only the first occurrence.
Hex	Function	Returns a numeric value as a hexadecimal string.

CONTINUED ➡

TABLE 4.1 continued: VBScript Keywords

KEYWORD	TYPE	DESCRIPTION
HelpContext	Property	Sets or returns a HelpContextID value representing the ID of a topic in a help file.
HelpFile	Property	Sets or returns the name of the help file associated with an object.
Hour	Function	Returns the hour from a specified time expression.
If... Then...Else	Statement	Surrounds code you want to execute only if a specified condition is True. If the condition is not True, you want to execute the code surrounded by the Else condition.
IgnoreCase	Property	Determines whether or not a regular expression search is case-sensitive.
Imp	Operator	Used to perform a logical implication on two numbers. I've never found a good reason to use this operator, although there may be one.
Initialize	Event	Occurs when a VBScript Class object is instantiated.
InputBox	Function	Asks a user for input. Doesn't work for server-side script.
InStr	Function	Returns the index of the first character of a matching sub-string within a string.
InStrRev	Function	Returns the index of the last character of a matching sub-string within a string.
Int	Function	Casts a variable value to an Integer value. Use this to change a string to an Integer or to truncate real values.
Integer Division (\)	Operator	Divides two numbers and casts the result to an Integer (no decimal points).
Is	Operator	Tests for object equivalence. Returns True if two object pointers both point to the same object.
IsArray	Function	Returns True if the argument is a Variant of subtype Array. Equivalent to the expression varType (someVar) And vbArray = vbArray).
IsDate	Function	Returns True if the argument is a Variant of subtype Date or can be converted to a Date subtype.
IsEmpty	Function	Returns True if the argument is a Variant with the value Empty.
IsNull	Function	Returns True if the argument is a Variant with the value Null.

CONTINUED ➞

TABLE 4.1 continued: VBScript Keywords

KEYWORD	TYPE	DESCRIPTION
`IsNumeric`	Function	Returns `True` if the argument is a number or can be converted to a number.
`IsObject`	Function	Returns `True` if the argument is a `Variant` of subtype `Object`.
`Join`	Function	Accepts an array of strings and returns a string separated by the specified delimiter. `Join` is the opposite of `Split`.
`LBound`	Function	Returns the lower-bound of the array argument.
`LCase`	Function	Returns a string with all of the characters changed to lowercase.
`Left`	Function	Returns a string consisting of the beginning of a string through the specified index.
`Len`	Function	Returns the length of the `string` argument.
`Length`	Property	Returns the length of a Match object found in a regular expression search.
`LoadPicture`	Function	Returns a picture object. The command loads an image file from disk. This function works on the server, but doesn't seem to recognize any known properties or methods.
`Log`	Function	Returns the natural logarithm of a number.
`LTrim`	Function	Returns a string with all white space (tabs, spaces, carriage returns) trimmed from the left side (front) of the string.
`Match`	Object	Object returned as the result of a match during a regular expression search.
`Matches`	Collection	Collection of Match objects resulting from a successful regular expression search.
`Mid`	Function	Returns a sub-string of a string starting with a specified index and a specified number of characters in length.
`Minute`	Function	Returns the minute of the hour as an integer from 0 to 59.
`Mod`	Operator	Performs modulo arithmetic.
`Month`	Function	Returns the month of the year as a number from 1 to 12.
`MonthName`	Function	Returns the name of the month number passed as an argument.

CONTINUED →

TABLE 4.1 continued: VBScript Keywords

Keyword	Type	Description
MsgBox	Function	Displays a Windows message box containing the specified message, title, and icon or buttons. Returns a constant designating the button the user clicked. This is useful for client-side script. On the server, VBScript writes MsgBox messages to the NT Application log.
Multiplication (*)	Operator	Multiplies two numbers.
Negation and Subtraction (-)	Operator	Returns a number multiplied by –1, or the difference of two numbers, depending on context. When used between two numeric values with a trailing space, VBScript interprets the minus symbol as a minus sign. When used in front of a numeric value with no trailing spaces, VBScript interprets the minus symbol as the negation operator.
`Not`	Operator	Used to negate an expression.
Now	Function	Returns the current date and time.
`Nothing`	Value	The value of an uninitialized `object` variable.
`Null`	Value	A value meaning no value, not zero, not a null string, not `Empty`, and not `Nothing`.
`Number`	Property	The error number property of an Err object.
`Oct`	Function	Returns a numeric value as an octal string.
`On Error`	Statement	Used to control what happens after an error occurs at runtime.
`Option Explicit`	Statement	Used to force variable declaration. When `Option Explicit` is in effect, VBScript raises a compile error when it encounters unrecognized symbols. Without `Option Explicit` in effect (the default), VBScript creates a new variable when it encounters an unrecognized symbol.
`Or`	Operator	Used to compare two expressions using Boolean `Or` logic.
`Pattern`	Property	Used to set or return the pattern string for a regular expression search.
`Private`	Statement	Used to create a private (script-level) variable, subroutine, or function.

CONTINUED ⟶

TABLE 4.1 continued: VBScript Keywords

KEYWORD	TYPE	DESCRIPTION
PropertyGet	Statement	The procedure code to return a property value for a Class object.
PropertyLet	Statement	The procedure code to set a property value for a Class object.
PropertySet	Statement	The procedure code to set an object property value for a Class object.
Public	Statement	Used to create a public variable, subroutine, or function.
Raise	Method	Used to raise an error. The result of raising an error depends on whether On Error Resume Next is in effect and on the current error-processing state.
Randomize	Statement	Used to seed the random number generator.
ReDim	Statement	Used to change the dimensions of an array. You can use this to change the last dimension of a multi-dimensional array only.
RegExp	Object	A regular expression object. Used to perform complex pattern-based searches in a target string.
Rem	Statement	Used to create a comment. Mostly obsolete. Use a single-quote instead.
Replace	Function	Replaces one or more occurrences of a specified sub-string within a string with a different sub-string. The replacement sub-string need not be the same length as the original sub-string.
Replace	Method	Replaces one or more occurrences of a specified sub-string within a string with a different sub-string in a regular expression search. The replacement sub-string need not be the same length as the original sub-string.
RGB	Function	Changes a set of three individual color values into a single Long color value in RGB format.
Right	Function	Returns the specified number of characters from the right-hand side (end) of a string.
Rnd	Function	Returns a random number between 0 and 1.
Round	Function	Rounds floating-point numbers to a specified number of decimal places.
RTrim	Function	Removes white space (tabs, spaces and carriage returns) from the right-hand side of a string.

CONTINUED →

TABLE 4.1 continued: VBScript Keywords

KEYWORD	TYPE	DESCRIPTION
ScriptEngine	Function	Returns a string containing the name of the currently executing script engine.
ScriptEngine-BuildVersion	Function	Returns the build version number of the currently executing script engine.
ScriptEngine-MajorVersion	Function	Returns the major version number of the currently executing script engine.
ScriptEngine-MinorVersion	Function	Returns the minor version number of the currently executing script engine.
Second	Function	Returns the second of the minute of the specified Time value.
Select Case	Statement	Block statement that executes code conditionally upon evaluating an expression against several possible cases.
Set	Statement	Sets an object variable reference.
SetLocale	Function	Sets the LocaleID for the script context. You use this to output dates, times, and currency values in the format for the assigned LocaleID.
Sgn	Function	Returns the sign of a number.
Sin	Function	Returns the sine of an angle.
Source	Property	Returns the source where an error occurred. In server-side VBScript, the source always contains the page name where the error occurred.
Space	Function	Returns a string filled with spaces a specified number of characters in length.
Split	Function	Splits a string into an array of sub-strings according to a defined delimiter. Split is the opposite of Join.
Sqr	Function	Returns the square root of a number.
StrComp	Function	Compares two strings. Returns –1 if the first string is less than the second string, 0 if the strings are equal, and 1 if the first string is greater than the second string. You select whether the comparison is case-sensitive.
String	Function	Returns a string filled with a character repeated a number of times.
StrReverse	Function	Returns a string in which the characters have been reversed.
Sub	Statement	Defines the beginning of a subroutine.

CONTINUED →

TABLE 4.1 continued: VBScript Keywords

Keyword	Type	Description
Subtraction (-) and Negation	Operator	Returns the difference of two numbers or a number multiplied by –1, depending on context. When used between two numeric values with a trailing space, VBScript interprets the minus symbol as a minus sign. When used in front of a numeric value with no trailing spaces, VBScript interprets the minus symbol as the negation operator.
`Tan`	Function	Returns the tangent of an angle.
`Terminate`	Event	Occurs just before a VBScript Class is destroyed. You use this to clean up by destroying object references and variables.
`Test`	Method	Executes a regular expression search.
`Time`	Function	Returns the current time, accurate to 1 second.
`Timer`	Function	Returns the number of seconds since 12:00 midnight.
`TimeSerial`	Function	Returns a time offset by the specified number of hours, minutes, and seconds.
`TimeValue`	Function	Returns the time from the argument. If the argument contains both date and time information, the `TimeValue` function returns the time only.
`Trim`	Function	Removes white space from both the left- and right-hand sides of a string, and returns the string.
`True`	Value	Boolean `True`. In VBScript, `True` is equal to –1.
`TypeName`	Function	Returns the VBScript internal type name of a `scalar` variable or object.
`UBound`	Function	Returns the upper-bound of an array.
`UCase`	Function	Returns a string with all the characters changed to uppercase.
`Value`	Property	Returns the text of a Match object resulting from a successful regular expression search.
`VarType`	Function	Returns a constant or (for arrays) combination of constants that represent the VBScript internal type of a variable.
`Weekday`	Function	Accepts a `Date` argument and returns a number from 1 to 7 representing the day of the week corresponding to the day portion of the argument.

CONTINUED ➞

TABLE 4.1 continued: VBScript Keywords

Keyword	Type	Description
WeekdayName	Function	Accepts a `Date` argument and returns the string for the day of the week corresponding to the day portion of the argument.
`While...Wend`	Statement	Conditional loop block. The loop executes until the condition following `While` evaluates to `True`.
`With...` `End With`	Statement	Holds a local reference to an object while you perform multiple operations on that object. Using `With...End With` speeds up your code and improves readability.
`Xor`	Operator	Performs a Boolean Exclusive `Or` operation.
`Year`	Function	Accepts a date and returns an integer corresponding to the year portion of the argument.

Variables

VBScript has only one type of variable—the `Variant` type—but it can hold any of three kinds of values: scalar variables, arrays, and object pointers. VBScript, by default, assumes that any symbol that is not a keyword is a variable. That can cause serious problems in your application if you accidentally mistype a variable name. VBScript accepts the mistyped variable without complaint, but interprets it as a new variable. For example, if you type `Email` when you meant to type `E_mail`, VBScript will create two completely different variables. To keep this from happening to you, include the `Option Explicit` command at the top of every ASP file, then use `Dim` statements to declare your variable names. When `Option Explicit` is in effect, VBScript raises a compile error when it encounters an unrecognized symbol. If you use `Option Explicit` faithfully, you will catch all of your mistyped variable names in testing during the design phase of your project rather than in production.

Scalar variables are simple variables like strings and numbers. The `variant` subtypes for scalar variables are `Boolean`, `Integer`, `Long`, `Single`, `Double`, `Date`, `Currency`, and `String`. To create a scalar variable, you define the variable using the `Dim` statement, then you can assign values to the variable. For example:

```
Dim x
x = 100
Response.Write x
```

Arrays are variants that hold lists of scalar or object pointer values. An `array` variable doesn't really hold a list of values–it holds a pointer to the first position of the collection in memory. If you think about it, you can see that the memory positions must be contiguous–when you create an array, the computer sets aside enough memory to hold the entire array. VBScript supports dynamic arrays, which means you can resize an array after it's created. Although when you do this, the computer creates another memory space that's large enough to hold the new array size, then copies the original array values into the new memory location. Therefore, resizing an array is extremely slow in comparison with creating an array of the maximum size to begin with.

You create an array in one of two ways: either dimension the array when you declare the variable, or dimension a variable, then create an array using the `Array()` function:

```
Dim iArr(25) ' create a 26 item array
```

Alternatively:

```
Dim iArr
iArr = Array()
Redim iArr(23)
```

You use an index to access the values in an array. For example:

```
iArr(0) = 0
iArr(1) = 2
iArr(2) = 4
```

By default, VBScript creates arrays in which the first index is `0`, so a statement like `Dim x(10)` creates an 11-item array. Zero-based indexing is often confusing for beginning programmers, who are used to counting items starting with 1. VBScript lets you dimension arrays starting with any integer value–even negative values. For example, you can create a 10-item array with the following statement:

```
Dim x(1 to 10)
```

Now you have a 10-item array in which the lowest index is `1` and the highest index is `10`.

The range of valid array index values is the array bounds. You can find the lower-bound with the `LBound(arrayVariable)` function and the upper-bound with the `UBound(arrayVariable)` function. For example:

```
Dim x(1 to 10)
Response.Write "Lower bound=" & _
```

```
        LBound(x) & "<br>"
    Response.Write "Upper bound=" & _
        UBound(x) & "<br>"
```

I can assure you that you'll have fewer problems with your code if you always use zero-based arrays. The reason doesn't have anything to do with the way the code works; it's for consistency. If you always use zero-based arrays, then the number of items in your array is always one more than the upper-bound of the array. In any case, even if you decide not to standardize on zero-based arrays, you can find out the number of items in the array with this formula:

```
    TotalItems = (ubound(anArray) - _
        lbound(anArray) + 1)
```

The third type of value you can hold in a `Variant` is an object pointer. When you create an object with the `Server.CreateObject` function, VBScript sets aside an area of memory to hold the object's data. The `Server.CreateObject` function returns a pointer to that position in memory. Your `object` variable holds that pointer in much the same way a `Variant` array holds a pointer to the first item in an array. So that VBScript can tell the difference between an object pointer and a value, you must use the `Set` keyword to create object variables. For example:

```
    Dim objDictionary
    Set objDictionary = _
      Server.CreateObject("Scripting.Dictionary")
```

THE DICTIONARY OBJECT

Though used here as only an example of a server object, the Dictionary object will be used at length in upcoming chapters. The Dictionary object is a simple object that holds key/item pairs, much like an array. One of the main differences is that you name the key, rather than trying to use an ordinal or additional variables. You'll understand this helpful object better over the next several chapters as you start using it in larger code samples.

You can determine whether a variable holds an object with the `isObject()` method. After you create an `object` variable, you call its methods and properties using dot notation. For example:

```
objDictionary.Add someKey, someValue
```

ASP destroys all locally defined variables when the page ends. Nonetheless, when you're done with an `object` variable, it's good programming practice to set it to the value `Nothing`:

```
Set objDictionary = Nothing
```

Setting the variable to `Nothing` frees up the memory used by the object, making it available for another process to use.

Subroutines and Functions

VBScript gives you the ability to place code into named code blocks, generically called routines or methods. Some languages have only one type of routine–the function. VBScript has two: subroutines and functions. Subroutines are routines that do not return values. They are equivalent to `void` functions in other languages. Functions do return values. In many cases, you could write a routine either as a function or as a subroutine. For example:

```
Sub addStrings(string1, string2, _
     stringTarget) ' concatenate strings
   stringTarget = string1 & string2
End Sub
```

The subroutine `addStrings` concatenates the argument `string1` with the argument `string2` and places the result in the argument variable `stringTarget`. It might be more useful to write the routine as a function. For example:

```
Function addStrings(string1, string2)
   addStrings = String1 & string2
End Function
```

The `addStrings()` function (note the use of parentheses to differentiate subroutines from functions) also adds the strings, but it returns the result. Most languages use an explicit `return` statement to return values. VBScript creates a variable that uses the name of the function itself, so you return the value by assigning the result of the function to the name of the function.

You call subroutines and functions differently. To call the `addStrings` subroutine, use either of these:

```
addStrings string1, string2, stringResult
Call addStrings(string1, string2, _
    stringResult)
```

To call a function, you should assign the function result to a variable. For example:

```
NewString = addStrings(s1, s2)
```

Note that in neither case do the names of the arguments in the call have to match the names of the arguments in the function or subroutine. The types don't have to match either, but you should make every effort to ensure they do, because VBScript will change the variable types as needed to try to make the call work. If the types don't match, you may not get the expected result. For example:

```
Function addStrings(string1, string2)
   addStrings = String1 + string2
End Function

' call the addStrings function
Dim s
s = addStrings(1,2) ' returns 3
s = addStrings("1", "2") ' returns "12"
```

The two examples are not the same—the first example isn't sending strings—it's sending numbers. The `addStrings` function will happily add the numbers, possibly leading to an error in your program.

A COMMENT ABOUT COMMENTS

Documenting your code as you go will save you a lot of headaches when you need to come back for changes. Any developers who may follow in your footsteps will also appreciate the courtesy. Here is a list of syntax you can use for the different languages presented in this book:

' (apostrophe) Used in Visual Basic and VBScript

CONTINUED →

REM Short for REMark; also used in Visual Basic by more nostalgic developers

-- (two hyphens) Used in SQL code

// (two slashes) Used in JScript and JavaScript

<!-- --> The Comment tag for HTML; comment must be opened with <!-- and closed with -->; can also be used to comment out multi-line sections of code

Variable typing problems are ubiquitous in VBScript because it has no typed variables. Therefore, as you write functions—especially if you write functions for others to use—you should check the input types. Use the casting operators (`CInt`, `CBool`, etc.) to change types where appropriate, and raise errors where casting might be inappropriate. For example:

```
Function addStrings(string1, string2)
   If varType(string1) <> vbString Then
      string1 = cStr(string1)
   End If
   If varType(string2) <> vbString Then
      string2 = cStr(string2)
   End If
   addStrings = String1 + string2
End Function

' call the addStrings function
Dim s
s = addStrings(1,2)
     ' returns 12 as expected
s = addStrings("1", "2")
     ' returns "12" - no change
```

The previous example checks the type of both input arguments and casts them to strings if they're not already strings. Sure, checking input argument types takes a small amount of time, but a small loss in speed is often better than errors.

VBScript lets you create recursive routines. A recursive routine is one that calls itself repeatedly until some condition becomes `True`. For example, Listing 4.1 changes all or part of a string array to uppercase. You supply the string array variable and the starting and ending index of the items to change to uppercase.

Listing 4.1: Recursive Routine Example

```
<%@ Language=VBScript %>
<% option explicit %>
<%
Sub ucaseArray(sArr, istart, iend)
   If istart <= iend Then
      sArr(istart) = ucase(sArr(istart))
      istart = istart + 1
      Call ucaseArray(sArr, istart, iend)
   End If
End Sub
Dim i
Dim istart
Dim iend
Dim sArr
sArr = Array("one", "two", "three")
Response.Write "The original array is:<br>"
For i = lbound(sArr) to ubound(sArr)
   Response.Write sArr(i) & "<br>"
Next
Response.Write "<p>"
Response.Write "Change all of the items _
     to upper case<br>"
Call ucaseArray(sArr, lbound(sArr), _
     ubound(sArr))
For i = lbound(sArr) to ubound(sArr)
   Response.Write sArr(i) & "<br>"
Next

Response.Write "<p>"
Response.Write "Change only the item at"& _
     " position 1 to upper case<br>"
sArr = Array("one", "two", "three")
Call ucaseArray(sArr, 1, 1)
For i = lbound(sArr) to ubound(sArr)
   Response.Write sArr(i) & "<br>"
```

```
Next
%>
```

Figure 4.1 shows the output of the previous example.

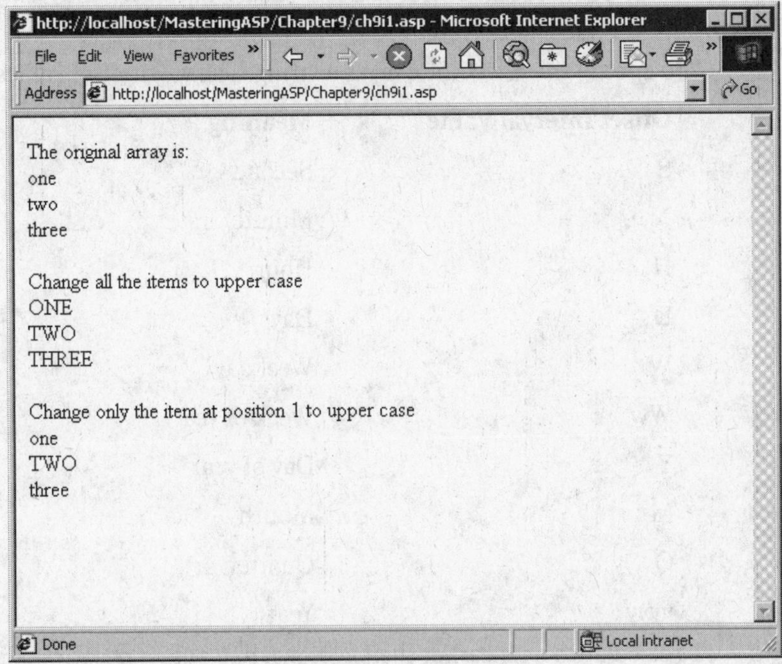

FIGURE 4.1: Recursive routine example

Built-In Functions and Methods

I've already listed all of the built-in functions, but you probably need to see some of them in action, particularly the date and time functions, and the error-handling methods.

The simplest of these is the `Now()` function. `Now` returns the current date and time in a `Date` variable. For example:

```
Response.Write Now()
        ' writes the current date and time
```

A closely related function, `Date()`, returns just the date without the time portion.

When you need to calculate a date offset from a known date, such as "two weeks from today," use the `DateAdd` function. You provide the starting date, the interval, and the size of the offset. For example:

```
Response.Write DateAdd("ww", 2, Now())
    ' Two weeks from today
```

You specify the offset interval as a string. The valid offset values are:

Offset Interval Value	Meaning
S	Second
N	Minute
H	Hour
D	Day
W	Weekday
Ww	Week of year
Y	Day of year
M	Month
Q	Quarter
yyyy	Year

To calculate a date earlier than a known date, use a negative offset size. For example, the following code fragment shows how to calculate a date exactly one year ago:

```
Response.Write DateAdd("yyyy", Now(), -1)
```

A related function, `DateDiff`, calculates the interval between two known dates. For example, to find the number of days since January 1, 1900, you would use:

```
Response.Write _
    DateDiff("d", #1/1/1900#, Now())
Response.Write _
    DateDiff("d", "1/1/1900", Now())
```

NOTE

You can specify a date literal (a constant) by surrounding it with number signs. You can freely intermix `Date` variables, date literals, and date strings in the date and time functions—VBScript performs any necessary conversion for you transparently.

The `DateDiff` function always subtracts the first date from the second date; therefore, if you reverse the order of the two dates, the function returns a negative number. For example:

```
Response.Write _
      DateDiff("d", Now(), #1/1/1900#)
```

VBScript did not inherit the ubiquitous `Format` function from Visual Basic. VB programmers use the `Format` function to format numbers and strings. Instead, VBScript has several separate built-in functions to format numbers and dates.

The `FormatDateTime` function formats dates in the most common formats. You provide the date and a formatting constant as arguments. For example:

```
Response.Write _
      FormatDateTime(Now, vbGeneralDate)
```

The built-in formats leave a little to be desired—there are only five of them. The table below shows the constants and a sample result for the date January 20, 1999.

Constant	Result
`vbGeneralDate`	01/20/1999 04:22:13 PM
`vbLongDate`	Wednesday, January 20, 1999
`vbShortDate`	01/20/99
`vbLongTime`	04:22:13 PM
`vbShortTime`	04:22

It helps at this point to know a little about how VBScript stores dates and times internally. A VBScript `DateTime` (subtype `Date`) variable is a `Double`—8-byte value. The integer portion represents the date and the fractional portion represents the time. Therefore, you can truncate a `DateTime` to get a date. In addition, if you add or subtract whole numbers from a `DateTime` value, you change days. For example, if you add 1 to the current date:

```
Response.Write Now() + 1
```

VBScript returns a date one day later at the same time. Similarly, you can write:

```
Response.Write _
    FormatDateTime(CLng(Now()), vbShortDate)
```

Note that you must format the result of the conversion to a `Long` by using the `FormatDateTime` function to force VBScript to interpret the value as a `Date`. Alternatively, you could convert the result of the `Long` conversion to a date by using the `CDate` function:

```
Response.Write CDate(CLng(Now()) + 1)
```

Formatting numbers is very similar to formatting dates and times in VBScript. The `FormatNumber`, `FormatPercent`, and `FormatCurrency` functions provide you with the most common formats. All of them work similarly. You must provide the value or expression to format. Optionally, you can provide the number of digits you want to display after the decimal point, whether to use parentheses around negative values, and whether to place commas (or another character, depending on your computer's regional settings) between groups of numbers (as in 1,000,000). The syntax is:

```
FormatCurrency(Expression, DecimalPlaces, _
    AddLeadingDigit, _
    NegativeNumbersInParentheses, _
    AddSeparators)
```

The last three optional arguments all take one of the values from a group of intrinsic constants called `TriState` constants.

Constant	**Value**	**Description**
`TristateTrue`	-1	True
`TristateFalse`	0	False
`TristateUseDefault`	-2	Use the setting from the computer's regional settings.

For example, to format the value 1009.7386 as currency, rounded to the nearest penny, you could write:

```
Dim s
```

```
s = FormatCurrency(1009.7386, 2, _
    True, True, True)
Response.Write s
' writes $1,009.74
```

The same call applied to the value `-.0246` yields `($0.02)`. The result is in parentheses because the result is a negative number and the function call set the argument `NegativeNumbersInParentheses` to `True`.

Logical Structures

Every modern language has several logical structures. Logical structures let you execute code conditionally. A completed structure forms a code block.

If...Then

There are actually several variations on the `If...Then` structure, but all of them have the same basic syntax—a conditional test, followed by `Then`, and the code to execute when the condition is true. The final statement in the code block must be `End If`. For example:

```
Dim i
i = 1
If i = 1 Then
    ' do something
End If
```

A slightly more complex variation adds one or more `ElseIf` tests:

```
Dim i
i = 2
If i = 1 Then
    ' do something
ElseIf i = 2 Then
    ' do something else
End If
```

In some cases, you want to execute some code when all of the `If` and `ElseIf` conditions fail. You use an `Else` condition to do that. For example:

```
Dim i
i = 2
```

```
If i = 1 Then
    ' do something
ElseIf i = 2 Then
    ' do something else
Else ' no condition is true
    ' code to execute when all conditions fail
End If
```

In general, it's a good idea to include an `Else` whenever you write an `If`. You'll soon see that, as a human being, you're highly unlikely to consider all of the possible conditions when you first write the routine. The `Else` condition handles those that you miss. For example, suppose you're writing an e-commerce application. The customer will submit a form containing a product type. You want to test the customer's choice against an internal list of product types, taking specific action for each type. If no type matches, you want to raise an error. For example:

```
If productType = "Clothing" Then
    ' do something
ElseIf productType = "Books" Then
    ' do something else
' place other productType conditions here
' after the last condition write the
' Else condition
Else
    ' no valid product type
   Err.Raise INVALID_PRODUCT, _
     "thisFile.asp", "Invalid Product Type."
End If
```

The `Else` condition catches product types that don't match any item in the list. In the example, the code raises an error, but you might just as easily decide to set the `productType` variable to a default value. For example, `UnknownProduct`, if no known products match.

Select Case

Structures like the product type example in the previous section work just fine as `If...ElseIf..Else...End If` blocks, but VBScript has another conditional block that takes less code. `The Select Case...`

Case...End Select statement selects a matching case from among many possible cases. For example, you could rewrite the product type example as a Case structure:

```
Select Case productType
Case "Clothing"
    ' do something
Case "Books"
    ' do something else
' place other case conditions here
' after the last condition write the
' Else condition
Case Else
    ' no valid product type
   Err.Raise INVALID_PRODUCT, _
      "thisFile.asp", "Invalid Product Type."
End If
```

When each condition has only one possible value, the Select Case statement doesn't improve your code much. The real power of Select Case occurs when you need any of several possible values to execute a single statement. For example, suppose that instead of the string Clothing, your application also had to recognize a list of alternate terms such as Clothes, Apparel, Millinery, Lingerie, etc. Written as an If statement, multiple conditions rapidly become awkward and hard to read. For example:

```
If productType = "Clothing" or _
     productType = "Clothes" or _
     productType = "Apparel" or _
     productType = "Millinery" or _
     productType = "Lingerie" or _
     productType = "Hosiery" or _
     productType = "Outer Wear" Then
    ' do something
End If
```

In contrast, as a Select Case statement, the statement is easy to read. For example:

```
Select Case productType
```

```
Case "Clothing", "Clothes", "Apparel", _
    "Millinery", "Lingerie", _
    "Hosiery", "Outer Wear"
  ' do something
Case Else
  ' perform default action
End If
```

Boolean Logic

You probably use Boolean logic every day. For example, when you make a decision to buy one item OR another item, but not both, you are using Boolean logic. All Boolean logic has a single output value—either True or False. There are four main Boolean operations. Three of these (AND, OR, and XOR) are binary operators—they require two *operands*—one on either side of the operator. Each operand may be a single value or expression. The NOT operator negates a value and is a unary operator—it requires only one operand. Boolean operations assume that each operand has the value True (non-zero) or False (zero). To the computer, that means you can use any type of numeric value or expression as an operand, because all numeric expressions evaluate to either zero or non-zero. Table 4.2 lists each operation along with a brief description of the results.

TABLE 4.2: Boolean Operands

Operation	Result
AND	True if both operands are True.
OR	True if either operand is True or if both operands are True.
XOR	True if either operand is True, but not if both operands are True.
NOT	True if the operand is False and False if the operand is True.

Strictly speaking, the logic is slightly more complicated than that, because one or both operands could be Null. Logical operations work with Null values. Because a Null value is not a numeric expression, it doesn't evaluate to either True or False; therefore, Null values generally cause Boolean expressions to evaluate to Null. There are only two exceptions:

- For an AND operation, the expression evaluates to False if the first operand is False. That's because the AND operation looks no further than the first value if it is False. There's no point in looking at the second value.
- For an OR operation, the expression evaluates to True if the first operand is True. That's because the OR operation doesn't look at the second value if the first one evaluates to True.

Your best bet is to avoid nulls altogether. You won't generally need to worry about Null values until you retrieve data from a database.

Looping

Very often, you need to perform an operation or series of operations many times. For Each...Next works especially well over the intrinsic ASP collection objects. The For Each...Next syntax iterates over each object in a collection. For Each...Next requires a collection object that supports iteration.

When you aren't dealing with objects or when your objective isn't to operate on a collection, you can use one of VBScript's other loop structures. Sometimes you need to loop a predetermined number of times. For these loop structures, use a For...Next structure. Sometimes, you need to loop while a condition is True, or until a condition is True. For these loops, use a While...Wend or a Do...While...Loop structure.

For...Next

When you need to loop a predetermined number of times, use a For...Next loop structure. The structure uses a loop control variable to control the number of loops through the code. You provide the loop control variable, the starting value, the ending value, and optionally, an increment or step. You place the code you want to repeat between the For and the Next statements. The syntax is:

```
For <control variable> = <start value> _
   to <end value> Step <increment>
   ' do something
Next <counter>
```

Traditionally, programmers use the variable `i` (meaning integer) for a control loop variable. For clarity, you can include the control loop variable after the `Next` statement. The default step value is 1; you do not have to provide a step for loop control variables that should increment by 1. For example, the following `For...Next` loop executes three times:

```
<%
Dim i
Dim counter
counter = 0
For i = 1 to 3
  counter = counter + 1
Next
Response.Write counter ' writes 3
%>
```

At the end of each loop through the code, VBScript increments the loop control variable and compares it to the ending value. The loop ends when the loop control variable equals the ending value. At the end of the loop in the previous example, the value of the variable `counter` is `3`. The value of the loop control variable itself is, according to the documentation, undefined; therefore, you should not rely on the value of the counter after the loop has completed.

You can change the increment by adding the optional `Step` value. You must provide a `Step` value if you want to step backward. For example, the following loop steps backward from `3` to `1`:

```
<%
Dim i
Dim counter
counter = 4
For i = 3 to 1 step -1
  counter = counter - 1
Next
Response.Write counter ' writes 1
%>
```

You can exit a For...Next loop early by using the Exit For command. For example, the following loop exits when the value of counter is 1 less than the value of the loop control variable:

```
<%
Dim i
Dim counter
counter = 0
For i = 4 to 1 step -1
  counter = counter + 1
  If counter = i - 1 Then
      Exit For
  End If
Next
Response.Write counter ' writes 2
%>
```

The Step value can be anything you want. For example, to print the even numbers from 0 to 100, you provide a Step value of 2:

```
<%
Dim i
For i = 0 to 100 step 2
   Response.Write i & "<br>"
Next
%>
```

For...Next loops help keep you from coding endless loops, but you must still be careful with them. For example, the following code runs until the Server.ScriptTimeout value stops the file from executing:

```
<%
Dim i
counter = 0
For i = 2 to 1 step -1
   i = i + 1
Next
%>
```

The previous example loops forever because the test comparing the loop control variable to the ending value always fails. Although the `Server.ScriptTimeout` provides a safety net, endless loops use nearly all of a server's processing power while executing. Avoid coding loops carelessly—endless loops potentially interfere not only with your own application, but also with other applications running on the server.

You can nest loops to any depth you desire, but you cannot cross-nest them. Again, by tradition, programmers use the variable names `j` and `k` for nested control loop variables. Of course, you're free to use any valid variable name. The following loop shows how you can nest `For...Next` structures:

```
<%
Dim i
Dim j
For i = 1 to 100
    For j = 1 to 100
        Response.Write i & ", " & j & "<br>"
    Next
Next
%>
```

In the previous example, the `Response.Write` statement in the inner (nested) loop executes 10,000 (100 * 100) times.

While...Wend Loop

A `While...Wend` loop executes until the conditional statement following the `While` becomes `True`. The syntax is:

```
While <condition>
    ' do something
Wend
```

You can see that a `For...Next` loop is actually a `While...Wend` loop in disguise, because the `For...Next` loop has an implicit condition—it tests the control loop variable for equality with the ending value. For example, the following two loops produce identical results:

```
<%
Dim i
For i = 1 to 3
```

```
    Response.Write i & "<br>"
Next
i = 0
While i <= 3
    i = i + 1
    Response.Write i & "<br>"
Wend
%>
```

Both loops execute until the variable `i` equals `3`. While all `For...Next` loops are `While` loops, the reverse is not true. For example, you cannot write the following loop as a `For...Next` loop:

```
<%
Dim s
s = "a"
While s <> "abcdefghijklmnop"
    s = s & Chr(Asc(Right(s,1)) + 1)
    Response.Write s & "<br>"
Wend
%>
```

`While...Wend` loops are essentially obsolete. They were included in VBScript primarily for compatibility with VB. A newer and more versatile version is the `Do...While` loop.

Do...While Loop

The `Do...While` loop, like `While...Wend` is a conditional loop, but you can place the condition test at either the start or end of the loop structure. This provides you with the ability to force a loop to execute at least once. The syntax is:

```
Do While <condition>
    ' do something
Loop
```

or

```
Do
    ' do something
Loop While <condition>
```

In addition, the `While` condition statement is optional. You can write an unconditional loop using the syntax:

```
Do
    ' do something
Loop
```

The last version is useful for programs where you want to loop forever, but isn't particularly useful on the server, where the `Server.ScriptTimeout` value limits the execution time of the script. However, it is useful when you don't need or want a conditional test at the beginning or end of the loop. For example, if you want to perform a conditional test in the middle of the loop code, the `Do...Loop` structure is completely appropriate.

The `Do...While (condition)` version may not execute even once because the conditional test at the start of the loop may not evaluate to `True`. In contrast, the `Do...Loop While (condition)` version places the conditional test at the end of the loop, so the loop must execute at least once.

String-Handling

Visual Basic has always had decent string-handling ability. VBScript not only inherited all of Visual Basic's functionality, but also added some extra features. You've already seen how to concatenate strings, but you haven't seen many of the other string operations. VBScript can extract and find sub-strings, compare strings, and split delimited strings into string arrays or create string arrays from delimited strings—all with built-in commands.

Just one mild warning: Strings, to a computer, are arrays of characters. Despite the apparent ease with which you can manipulate strings, you are actually copying contiguous blocks of memory from one place to another. Minimizing the number and size of these operations will make your programs run faster.

Left, Mid, Right, Instr, InstrRev, Split, Join

The three functions `Left`, `Right`, and `Mid` return the leftmost characters, the rightmost characters, or a section from the middle of the string, respectively. For the `Left` and `Right` functions, you specify the number of characters to return. For the `Mid` function, you specify the starting position and optionally, a length. If you don't specify a length, the `Mid` function returns the portion of the string from the specified starting position to the end of the string. Examples:

```
Left("Charlie", 3) ' returns "Cha"
Left("Bill", 22) ' returns "Bill"
Right("Charlie", 3) ' returns "lie"
Right("Bill", 22) ' returns "Bill"
Mid("Charlie", 3, 3) ' returns "arl"
Mid("Charlie", 3) ' returns "arlie"
Mid("Charlie", 3, 24) ' returns "arlie"
```

The examples show that you can easily extract a portion of a string. They should also show you what happens with each of these functions when you request more characters from a string than can be returned. In each case shown above, VBScript returns the number of characters possible, not the number of characters requested; and it does not raise an error when you request more than the number of possible characters.

The `Instr` and `InstrRev` functions locate the position of sub-strings within strings. Both functions return the index of the starting position of the sub-string within the main string. For example, the string `"intentions"` contains the sub-string `"ten"` starting at position `3`:

```
Response.Write instr("intentions", "ten")
    ' writes 3
Response.Write instrRev("intentions", "ten")
    ' writes 3
```

Both functions optionally accept a starting position and a `compare` flag that determines whether VBScript performs a case-sensitive or case-insensitive search for the sub-string. Unfortunately, the position of the arguments differs between the two functions. The `Instr` function expects the `start` argument *before* the main string, whereas the `InstrRev` function expects the start argument *after* the search string. Both functions expect the last argument to be one of the `CompareMode` constants.

There are two `CompareMode` constants, `VbBinaryCompare`, which has a value of `0` and `vbTextCompare`, which has a value of `1`. Use `VbBinaryCompare` to perform case-sensitive comparisons and `vbTextCompare` to perform case-insensitive comparisons.

Here's a full version of each of the functions:

```
Response.Write instr(1,"event", "vent", _
    vbBinaryCompare)
```

```
        ' writes 2
    Response.Write instr(1,"event", "Vent", _
        vbBinaryCompare)
        ' writes 0
    Response.Write instr(1,"event", "Vent", _
        vbTextCompare)
        ' writes 2
    Response.Write instrRev("event", _
        "vent",5,vbBinaryCompare)
        ' writes 2
    Response.Write instrRev("event", "Vent",5, _
        vbBinaryCompare)
        ' writes 0
    Response.Write instrRev("event", "Vent",5, _
        vbTextCompare)
        ' writes 2
```

Note that although the InstrRev function searches backward from the end of the main string, Response returns the index position of the substring, if found, calculated as an offset from the beginning of the main string. Also, note that the start argument for the InstrRev function is also an offset from the beginning of the string. In other words, if you want InstrRev to search the entire string, you must pass the length of the string in the start argument.

Boolean Operations

Most programmers eventually run into situations where they must use Boolean logic. Boolean operations and computers were made for each other because there are only two possible values for the result of a Boolean operation between two bits: 1 and 0.

The computer stores values as binary numbers. A binary number is a series of bits. Moving to the left, each bit can take only one of two values—0 or 1. When set (non-zero), each bit has a value of 2n, where n is the position starting with 0. The rightmost bit in an 8-bit number, when set, is 20, or 1. The next bit is 21, or 2. Each bit doubles the value of the bit to its right. Therefore, the value 12, to a computer, is 00001100 (no ones, no twos, one four, and one eight).

VBScript supports four Boolean operations: AND, OR, NOT, and XOR. You use the AND operator to see if the bit pattern in two values is the same. Whenever both values contain a 1 in the same position, the result also has a 1 in that position.

If you AND that value with the number 16 (00010000) you get 00000000, because neither pattern contains a 1 bit in the same column as the other. For example:

```
00001100
00010000
________
00000000
```

An OR operation compares two bit patterns and produces a 1 if either or both bits in a column are 1. For example, the expression 13 OR 17 produces the number 29:

```
00001101
00010001
________
00011101
```

An XOR operation is the opposite of an OR. It produces a 1 if only one, but not both, of the bits in a column is a 1. For example:

```
00001101
00010001
________
00011100
```

Finally, the NOT operator reverses the value of its operand. The expression: NOT 01010101 produces 10101010.

Regular Expressions

VBScript version 5 inherited powerful regular expression matching capabilities. I say inherited, because the code to perform regular expression searches was apparently ported more-or-less directly from JScript regular expression searches without regard to anything remotely VB-like. This port serves to keep the two scripting languages roughly in sync, but at the cost (for VBScript programmers) of dealing with zero-based string indexes, which is totally opposed to the general spirit and usual practice of VBScript and VB. In addition, the pattern matching characters (and the documentation) were created for Java/JavaScript/C programmers and not VBScript/VB programmers. Despite this gripe, regular expression searches are extremely powerful and can do much more than the simple `instr()` function.

A regular expression consists of text you want to search for combined with special characters or commands that describe how you want to search. To initialize a regular expression search, you create a RegExp object and set its `Pattern` property. For example:

```
// explicit RegExp creation
rgxp = new RegExp
rgxp.Pattern = "boy"
```

You can perform global (find all matches) searches using the `Global` property and case-insensitive searches with the `IgnoreCase` property. Both properties take Boolean `True/False` values. For example:

```
// case-insensitive search
rgxp.IgnoreCase = True

// global search
rgxp.Global = True
```

After creating a RegExp object and setting its properties, you perform the search with either the `Test` or the `Execute` method. The difference lies in whether you only need to test whether the pattern exists in the target string or whether you want to know where and how often the pattern appears. The result of the `Test` method is `True` if the pattern appears in the target string; otherwise, the method returns `False`.

For example, the following code searches for the word "boy" in the string "Every good boy does fine."

```
Dim s
Dim rgxp
s = "Every good boy does fine."
Set rgxp = New RegExp
rgxp.Pattern = "boy"
Response.Write rgxp.Test(s) & "<br>"
      ' writes True
```

In contrast, the `Execute` method returns a `Matches` collection. Each Match object in the `Matches` collection represents a single match and has properties for the matched string, the index of the start of the matched string in the target string, and the length of the match. For example:

```
Dim s
Dim rgxp
s = "Peter Piper picked a peck of" & _
  " pickled peppers."
Set rgxp = New RegExp
rgxp.Pattern = "p"
rgxp.IgnoreCase = False
rgxp.Global = True
Set matches = rgxp.Execute(s)
Response.Write "Testing for the pattern " _
    & Chr(34) & rgxp.Pattern & Chr(34) _
    & " in the string " & _
    Chr(34) & s & Chr(34) & "<br><br>"
For Each aMatch In matches
    Response.Write "Found a match at" & _
    " position " & aMatch.FirstIndex & _
    ". Matched string=" & Chr(34) & _
    aMatch.Value & Chr(34) & ". " & _
    aMatch.Length & " character(s) were" & _
    " matched. <br>"
Next
```

The preceding example finds each lowercase p and returns a collection of Match objects. The output looks like this:

```
Testing for the pattern "p" in the string "Peter Piper picked
a peck of pickled peppers."Found a match at position 8.
Matched string="p". 1 character(s) were matched.Found a match
at position 12. Matched string="p". 1 character(s) were
matched.Found a match at position 21. Matched string="p". 1
character(s) were matched.Found a match at position 29.
Matched string="p". 1 character(s) were matched.Found a match
at position 37. Matched string="p". 1 character(s) were
matched.Found a match at position 39. Matched string="p". 1
character(s) were matched.Found a match at position 40.
Matched string="p". 1 character(s) were matched.
```

The output shows the Match object's `FirstIndex`, `Value`, and `Length` properties.

The power of regular expression searching lies in its ability to match patterns using special characters and character sequences. Table 4.3 lists the special characters and sequences you may use in a regular expression.

TABLE 4.3: VBScript Regular Expression Pattern Special Characters and Sequences

CHARACTER	DESCRIPTION
\	Specifies that the next character is either a special character or a literal (an exact special character match). A literal character preceded by the backslash is called an *escaped* character. Some characters must be escaped because they have other meanings in regular expression syntax. The characters you must escape are: () - left and right parentheses [- left bracket] - right bracket \ - backslash * - asterisk . - period $ - dollar sign The special characters \b, \B, \d, \D, \f, \n, \r, \s, \S, \t, \v, \w, and \W appear individually in this table.
^	Limits matches to the beginning of a line or string.
$	Limits matches to the end of a line or string.
*	Matches the character preceding the asterisk zero or more times. For example, bo* matches both bed and book.
+	Matches the character preceding the plus sign one or more times. bo+ matches book, but not bed.
?	Matches the character preceding the question mark zero or one time. For example, be? matches `best` and `bit`, but not been.
.	Matches any single character except a newline (`vbCrLf`) character.
`(pattern)`	Enclose a pattern in parentheses to find matched patterns. You can retrieve the matched patterns from the `Matches` collection using the `Item` property and an `index` from `0...N`. Use `\(` and `\)` to match parentheses.

CONTINUED ➞

TABLE 4.3 continued: VBScript Regular Expression Pattern Special Characters and Sequences

CHARACTER	DESCRIPTION
a|b	Matches either a or b.
{n}	Matches exactly n times, where n is an integer greater than or equal to 1. For example, m{2} matches immediate but not magic.
{n,}	Matches at least n times, where n is an integer greater than or equal to 1. For example, e{2} matches seer but not her.
{nMin, nMax}	Matches between nMin and nMax times, inclusive, where both nMin and nMax are integers greater than or equal to 1.
[abc]	Matches any of the characters enclosed in the brackets. [mno] matches the n in bin or the m in Mom.
[^abc]	Matches any character *not* enclosed in the brackets. [^mno] matches the b and i in bin, and the M in Mom.
[a-z]	Matches any one of a range of characters. For example, [a-z] matches any lowercase alphabetic character in the range a through z.
[^d-g]	Matches any one of the characters *not* in the range. For example, [d-g] matches any character not in the range d through g.
\b	Matches a word boundary, such as a space, tab, or punctuation. For example, p\b matches the p in the word help in the phrase please help me and in the phrase please help. Place the /b before the pattern to find matches at the beginning of words or at the end of the pattern to find matches at the end of words.
\B	Matches text *not* on a word boundary. For example, \Bp matches the p in the word help in the phrase please help me, but not the p in the word please in that same phrase. That's because the p in please lies at the start of a word.
\d	Matches any digit character. Equivalent to [0-9].
\D	Matches any non-digit character. Equivalent to [^0-9].
\f	Matches a formfeed character.
\n	Matches a newline (vbCrLf) character.
\r	Matches a carriage return character.
\s	Matches any white space including space, tab, formfeed, etc. Equivalent to [\f\n\r\t\v].
\S	Matches any nonwhite space character. Equivalent to [^\f\n\r\t\v].

CONTINUED ➞

TABLE 4.3 continued: VBScript Regular Expression Pattern Special Characters and Sequences

Character	Description
\t	Matches a tab character.
\v	Matches a vertical tab character.
\w	Matches any alphanumeric character, including the underscore. Equivalent to [A-Za-z0-9_].
\W	Matches any non-alphanumeric character. Equivalent to [^A-Za-z0-9_].
\num	Matches num, where num is a positive integer. \1 matches the first Item in the Matches collection.
\o	Matches o, where o is an octal value. Octal values must be 1, 2, or 3 digits long. For example, \11 and \011 both match a tab character. Octal values that exceed 256 are treated as if they were two patterns. For example, the pattern \0011 is the equivalent of the patterns \001 & 1. This pattern type lets you use ASCII codes in regular expressions.
\xn	Matches n, where n is a hexadecimal (hex) value. Hex values must be exactly two digits long. For example, \x41 matches the character A. Hex values that exceed two characters are treated as if they were two patterns. For example, the pattern \x041 is the equivalent of the patterns \x04 & 1. This pattern type lets you use ASCII codes in regular expressions.

VBScript Classes

Classes are another feature new to VBScript version 5. Unlike the regular expression syntax, VBScript classes fit the pattern of the language well. A class consists of properties and code that work together as a unit. Most classes contain properties, which are values you can set and retrieve, and methods, which are callable functions or subroutines. Classes may contain both hidden (private) and visible (public) properties and methods.

Unlike most other objects in VBScript, you can't create a Class object directly. Instead, you provide the code for the class, and VBScript returns a reference to the Class object. You'll find that classes can be extremely useful in both client- and server-side code when you want to:

- Package functionality

- Hide method implementations
- Reuse code
- Simplify your code

You can create classes at both design and runtime. To create a class at design time, you write a `class` script. The `class` script defines the `class` properties and methods. To create a class at runtime, you concatenate the code that defines the class in a string, then issue either an `Execute` or `ExecuteGlobal` statement. Subsequently, you can create a new class instance—more commonly known as an object—and use the properties and methods of that object. Objects instantiated from `Class` code act the same whether you created the class at runtime or design time.

Here's an example. Suppose you want to create a `User` class that exposes first- and last-name properties and a list of telephone numbers. You would like to create an instance of the `User` class whenever a page starts and save the User information in a `Session` variable each time the page ends. You need to be able to add telephone numbers and display the User information.

To do that, you need to create a `User` class. For example, you might define a `User` class as follows:

WARNING

There are some VBScript code features in the following code that you haven't seen yet. This is not a simple example, but I included it because it illustrates the power of VBScript classes in an ASP page. If you don't understand all of the code right now, you may wish to return to this section later.

```
Class User
   Private mLastName
   Private mFirstName
   Private dTelephones
   Private Sub Class_Initialize()
      Set dTelephones = _
         Server.CreateObject("Scripting.Dictionary")
   End Sub

   Private Sub Class_terminate()
```

```
      Set dTelephones = Nothing
   End Sub

   Public Property Let LastName(s)
      mLastName = s
   End Property

   Public Property Get LastName()
      LastName = mLastName
   End Property

   Public Property Let FirstName(s)
      mFirstName = s
   End Property

   Public Property Get FirstName()
      FirstName = mFirstName
   End Property

   Public Sub addTelephone(atype, anumber)
      If dTelephones.Exists(atype) Then
         Response.Write "This person" & _
         " already has a phone of type " & _
         atype & "<br>"
         Response.end
      Else
         dTelephones.Add atype, anumber
         Response.Write "Added telephone " _
         & atype & ", "& anumber & "<br>"
      End If
   End Sub

   Public Property Get PhoneInfo()
      Dim V
```

```
      Dim s
      For Each V In dTelephones.keys
         s = s & V & "=" & _
              dTelephones(V) & "<br>"
      Next
      PhoneInfo = s
   End Property

   Public Property Get PhoneCount()
      PhoneCount = dTelephones.Count
   End Property
End Class
```

Starting at the top of the class definition, you first see three private variables: `mLastName`, `mFirstName` (the `m` in the variable names stands for `member` as in `member` variable), and `dTelephones`. The class uses the first two to hold the last and first names. The `dTelephones` variable will become a Dictionary object where the keys are telephone types like `home`, `work`, etc. and the values are the phone numbers.

Next, you see a `Private` subroutine called `Class_Initialize`. This subroutine and the corresponding `Class_Terminate` subroutine are event procedures, and are optional. They're called event procedures because VBScript raises a `Class_Initialize` event, which executes the code in the `Class_Initialize` method (if it exists) when you instantiate an object from a class. Similarly, just before VBScript destroys an object, it raises a `Class_Terminate` event, which executes the `Class_Terminate` method for the class (if it exists). You can use these event procedures to initialize and destroy (terminate) objects and property values. I've used them to create and destroy the Dictionary object to hold the telephone types and numbers.

The next four `Public` properties let you assign and retrieve the names. A `Property Let` method assigns a value to a property. A `Property Get` method retrieves the value. The names of `Public` properties and `Private` variables do not have to match.

The `Public` method `addTelephone` adds a telephone to the `dTelephones` Dictionary. I should warn you that the class has minimal error-checking. It won't let you add two Home phones, but there's no check for valid telephone numbers or types—feel free to add whatever you like.

The PhoneInfo property returns a string consisting of some number of telephoneType=telephoneNumber items, and the PhoneCount property returns the number of telephone type=number items defined for this User.

To create a new User object, use the VBScript New keyword. For example:

```
Dim aUser
Set aUser = new User
```

The variable aUser now holds a reference to an object—a new instance of the User class. You may now set the object's properties. For example:

```
aUser.LastName = "Jones"
aUser.FirstName = "Russell"
Response.Write aUser.LastName & "<br>"
    ' writes "Jones"
Response.Write aUser.FirstName & "<br>"
    ' writes "Russell"
aUser.AddTelephone "Home", "555-1212"
Response.Write aUser.PhoneCount & "<br>"
    ' writes 1
Response.Write aUser.PhoneInfo
    ' writes "Home=555-1212"
```

All this is interesting, but not particularly useful, because it takes more code than simply storing the values in Session variables and retrieving them for each page. But the next example should show you a sample of the power of objects.

You can take advantage of the Class_Initialize and Class_Terminate methods to automatically save and retrieve User objects to a Session variable. You need a name for the Session variable—I've opted to save the User object in a Session variable keyed to the Session.SessionID property, as follows:

```
dim aSessionID
aSessionID = cstr(Session.SessionID)
```

Here are the altered event procedures:

```
Private Sub Class_Initialize()
    Response.Write "User initialize<br>"
    Dim arr
    Dim i
```

```
    Dim aTelephone
    Set dTelephones = _
       Server.CreateObject("Scripting.Dictionary")
    If Not IsEmpty(Session(aSessionID)) Then
       arr = Session(aSessionID)
       mLastName = arr(0)
       mFirstName = arr(1)
       For i = 2 To UBound(arr) Step 2
          dTelephones.Add arr(i), arr(i + 1)
       Next
    Else
       ' first initialization
       mLastName = ""
       mFirstName = ""
       Set dTelephones = _
          Server.CreateObject("Scripting.Dictionary")
    End If
 End Sub

 Private Sub Class_terminate()
    Response.Write "User terminate<br>"
    ' write class info to a Session variable
    Dim arr
    Dim i
    Dim j
    Dim V
    arr = Array()
    ReDim arr(1)
    arr(0) = mLastName
    arr(1) = mFirstName
    i = UBound(arr)
    For Each V In dTelephones.Keys
       i = i + 1
       ReDim Preserve arr(i)
```

```
            arr(i) = V
            i = i + 1
            ReDim Preserve arr(i)
            arr(i) = dTelephones(V)
        Next
        Session(aSessionID) = arr
        Set dTelephones = Nothing
    End Sub
```

These two routines automatically store (persist) the `User` object to an array stored in a `Session` variable associated with the current SessionID. In the `Class_Terminate` event, the class stores the first and last names in the first two array positions, then sequentially fills the array with telephone types and numbers. Finally, it stores the completed array in the `Session` variable.

When the class re-instantiates on subsequent requests, it performs the operations in reverse. The class retrieves the array from the `Session` variable, sets the first and last name `Private` property variables, then loops through the array adding items (telephone type and telephone number) to the Dictionary.

I've added `Response.Write` statements so you can see when the `Class_Initialize` and `Class_Terminate` events occur relative to other code in the page.

You must initialize the object the first time the page runs. You can determine whether the page has been run for the current session by testing the value of the `Session(SessionID)` variable—if it's empty, it's the first request for the page. Listing 4.2 contains the complete page script.

Listing 4.2: VBScript Class Example

```
<%@ Language=VBScript %>
<% option explicit %>
<html>
<head>
</head>
<body>
<%
Dim aSessionID
aSessionID = CStr(Session.SessionID)
```

```
Class User
   Private m_ID
   Private mLastName
   Private mFirstName
   Private dTelephones
   Private Sub Class_Initialize()
      Response.Write "User initialize<br>"
      Dim arr
      Dim i
      Dim aTelephone
      Set dTelephones = _
Server.CreateObject("Scripting.Dictionary")
      m_ID = aSessionID
      If Not IsEmpty(Session(aSessionID)) Then
         arr = Session(aSessionID)
         mLastName = arr(0)
         mFirstName = arr(1)
         For i = 2 To UBound(arr) Step 2
            dTelephones.Add arr(i), arr(i + 1)
         Next
      Else
         ' first initialization
         mLastName = ""
         mFirstName = ""
         Set dTelephones = _
Server.CreateObject("Scripting.Dictionary")
      End If
   End Sub

   Private Sub Class_terminate()
      Response.Write "User terminate<br>"
      ' write class info to a Session variable
      Dim arr
      Dim i
      Dim j
      Dim V
      arr = Array()
      ReDim arr(1)
      arr(0) = mLastName
      arr(1) = mFirstName
      i = UBound(arr)
      For Each V In dTelephones.keys
```

```
      i = i + 1
      ReDim Preserve arr(i)
      arr(i) = V
      i = i + 1
      ReDim Preserve arr(i)
      arr(i) = dTelephones(V)
   Next
   Session(aSessionID) = arr
   Set dTelephones = Nothing
End Sub

Public Property Let LastName(s)
   mLastName = s
End Property

Public Property Get LastName()
   LastName = mLastName
End Property

Public Property Let FirstName(s)
   mFirstName = s
End Property

Public Property Get FirstName()
   FirstName = mFirstName
End Property

Public Sub addTelephone(atype, anumber)
   If dTelephones.Exists(atype) Then
      Response.Write "This person" & _
      " already has a phone of type " & _
      atype & "<br>"
      Response.end
   Else
      dTelephones.Add atype, anumber
      Response.Write "Added telephone" & _
      atype & ", "& anumber & "<br>"
   End If
End Sub
Public Property Get PhoneInfo()
   Dim V
   Dim s
```

```
        For Each V In dTelephones.keys
            s = s & V & "=" & _
                dTelephones(V) & "<br>"
        Next
        PhoneInfo = s
    End Property
    Public Property Get PhoneCount()
        PhoneCount = dTelephones.Count
    End Property
end class
Dim aUser
Dim i
If IsEmpty(Session(aSessionID)) Then
    Response.Write "Initializing new" & _
    " user<br>"
    Set aUser = New User
    aUser.LastName = "Russell"
    aUser.FirstName = "Jones"
    Call aUser.addTelephone("Home", _
        "111-111-1111")
Else
    Response.Write "Found User:<br>"
    Set aUser = New User
End If
'Response.Write "SessionID = " & _
   aSessionID & "<br>"
If Request.Form("Add") = "Add" Then
    aUser.addTelephone _
    CStr(Request.Form.Item("PhoneType")), _
    CStr(Request.Form.Item("PhoneNumber"))
End If
With aUser
    Response.Write "<b>User Info:</b><br>"
    Response.Write "LastName=" & _
        .LastName & "<br>"
    Response.Write "FirstName=" &_
        .FirstName & "<br>"
    Response.Write "PhoneCount=" & _
        .PhoneCount & "<br>"
    Response.Write "<b>Phones:</b><br>" & _
        .PhoneInfo
End With
```

```
%>
<form name="frmTel" method="post" action="">
<table width="60%" align="center" border="1">
   <tr>
      <td colspan="2">
         Add a phone number:
      </td>
   </tr>
   <tr>
      <td>
         <b>Type:</b>
      </td>
      <td>
         <input type="text" name="PhoneType">
      </td>
   </tr>
   <tr>
      <td>
         <b>Number:</b>
      </td>
      <td>
         <input type="text" name="PhoneNumber">
      </td>
   </tr>
   <tr>
      <td colspan="2" align="center">
         <input name="Add"
            type="submit" value="Add">
      </td>
   </tr>
</table>
<br>
</form>
</body>
</html>
```

Try adding several telephone numbers. You should see them appear in the printed list at the top of the screen.

I could give the `User` class to another programmer as an `include` file. That's the package functionality aspect of object-oriented programming. That programmer could be trained to create and use User objects very quickly—that's the code reuse aspect.

It's important to understand that I implemented the list of telephone numbers as a Dictionary. If I later change my mind and simply keep them in an array for performance reasons, from the other programmer's viewpoint, the code wouldn't have changed; the `PhoneCount` and `AddTelephone` methods would act exactly the same and the store-and-retrieve scheme would still work properly. In other words, I've hidden the method implementation.

Finally, it's much easier for a programmer to use well-named objects with methods and properties than to use function calls.

Because VBScript can run on both the client and the server, you can create objects in client-side script as well. Classes are obviously not necessary—there are thousands of sites that work perfectly well without classes and objects. Nevertheless, you'll find that creating classes and using objects soon becomes an integral part of your programming toolkit.

WHAT'S NEXT?

As powerful as VBScript is, you have alternatives as an ASP developer. ASP also includes an interpreter for JScript, Microsoft's version of Javascript. Developers who are accustomed to C and related languages often prefer the syntax and structure of JScript. But what language is right for you? The next chapter will help you decide by introducing you to the primary features of JScript and how to use it in your Web applications.

Chapter 5

Introduction to JScript

I'll start this chapter with both a confession and a warning. I don't use JScript on the server—I use VBScript. My recommendation to you is that you not use JScript on the server either, unless you already know it from client-side scripting and you just need to get started quickly. The reason has nothing to do with JScript's intrinsic worth as a language; it's because Microsoft provides far more support and examples for VBScript than for JScript as a server-side language.

With that said, JScript works for most of ASP's functionality extremely well. If you plan to use JScript all the time, you should change the default language setting for your site to JScript. Be aware that this does not mean you should write pages that omit the language declaration—they will work on your server, but probably will not work on other servers where the server administrator has not changed the default language setting.

Adapted from *Mastering™ Active Server Pages 3*, by A. Russell Jones

ISBN 0-7821-2619-7 928 pages $49.99

JScript vs. VBScript

JScript is, in some ways, more powerful than VBScript, although VBScript version 5 has almost closed the gap. JScript is case-sensitive, where VBScript is not. JScript is considerably more object-oriented than VBScript. JScript is a standard because it conforms to the ECMAScript requirements, but Microsoft has added many proprietary extensions so that JScript can interact with COM objects easily.

JScript is a larger and more complex language than VBScript. It has a more stringent syntax, but less stringent code formatting requirements. For example, white space is irrelevant in JScript. You don't need a line-continuation character; you simply finish the command on the next line. That's because JScript requires a line-termination character (the semicolon). Until version 5, JScript had no error-handling capability, which means you had to perform more data and parameter checking to avoid errors. In contrast, VBScript has had an `On Error Resume Next` command since its inception. You can use the JScript `eval` function to execute code dynamically—in other words, you can execute code by writing more code. VBScript has no such capability.

JScript is much more aware of HTML than VBScript (which is essentially oblivious to HTML) and has numerous formatting and parsing methods for creating and analyzing HTML tags. This reflects its heritage as a client-side language, but it makes it easier to use than VBScript for writing HTML with script.

JScript is case-sensitive—which is a major shift for VB programmers, but natural and familiar to C and Java programmers. The convention for creating function names, method names, and properties is that they should start with a lowercase letter. Object names begin with a capital letter. You should concatenate multi-word names and capitalize the first letter of all words except the first; for example, `getObject`, or `toString`. Unfortunately, the language doesn't always follow these conventions. The result is that you must memorize the capitalization requirements for the built-in names to be productive. I'm not a fan of case sensitivity in programming languages for exactly that reason. The problem gets worse when two different programmers write similar methods—but with differing case in the names. For example, one programmer's object may expose an `isString` property, while an equivalent function in a different programmer's object may expose an `isstring` property.

Even in JScript's keywords there are numerous examples of inconsistent case. For example, the multi-word keyword `fontsize` is all lowercase, whereas the function `getDay` follows the normal convention, and the function `GetObject` begins with a capital letter. The JScript keywords are listed in Table 5.1.

TABLE 5.1: JScript Keywords

KEYWORD	TYPE	DESCRIPTION
$1 through $9	Keyword	Contains values from the result of the RegExp function.
`abs`	Method	Returns the absolute value of a numeric expression.
`acos`	Method	Returns the arc cosine of a numeric expression.
`ActiveXObject`	Object	Creates and returns references to ActiveX (COM) objects. You provide the class identifier of the object you want to create. For example, `var myOjb = new ActiveXObject ("Scripting.Dictionary")`.
Addition (+)	Operator	Adds values. In JScript, use the addition operator for addition and for string concatenation.
`anchor`	Method	Surrounds the text of a String object with an <a> anchor tag.
`arguments`	Property	Contains an array of the arguments passed to the currently executing function.
`Array`	Object	Contains arrays of any data type. JScript can also handle COM (VBScript-type) arrays via special language extensions.
`asin`	Function	Returns the arcsine of a numeric expression.
Assignment (=)	Operator	Assigns a value to the variable on the left side of the equals sign.
`atan`	Function	Returns the arctangent of a numeric expression.
`atan2`	Function	Returns the angle (in radians) from the x-axis to a specified point (x, y).
`atEnd`	Method	Returns `True` if an Iterator object has reached the end of its associated collection.
`big`	Method	Surrounds the text of a String object with `<big>` tags.
Bitwise AND (&)	Operator	Performs a Boolean AND operation on two values.

CONTINUED ➡

TABLE 5.1 continued: JScript Keywords

Keyword	Type	Description
Bitwise Left Shift (<<)	Operator	Shifts the bits of a value one position to the left.
Bitwise NOT (~)	Operator	Negates a value by flipping all the bits from 1 to 0 or from 0 to 1.
Bitwise OR (|)	Operator	Compares two bit patterns and produces a 1 if either or both bits in a column are 1.
Bitwise Right Shift (>>)	Operator	Shifts the bits of a value one position to the right.
Bitwise XOR (^)	Operator	Compares two bit patterns and produces a 1 if only one of the bits, but not both, in a column is a 1.
`blink`	Method	Surrounds the text of a String object with <blink> tags.
`bold`	Method	Surrounds the text of a String object with <b> tags.
`Boolean`	Object	Creates a Boolean value.
`break`	Statement	Used to end processing in a loop or code block. Processing starts at the code line following the code block.
`caller`	Property	Provides a reference to the function that called the current function. In other words, the caller property gives you access to the item immediately preceding the current item on the call stack.
`ceil`	Method	Returns the smallest integer value greater than the value of the argument passed to the method.
`charAt`	Method	Returns the character at a specified offset within a string.
`charCodeAt`	Method	Returns the character code for the character at a specified offset within a string.
Comma (,)	Operator	Causes multiple expressions to be evaluated in sequence, as if they were a single expression. It returns the value of the rightmost expression in the list.
Comment (//) Single-line version	Statement	Used to place a comment on a single line. You may place the slashes anywhere in the line. The compiler ignores any text on that line following the slashes. For multi-line comments use the /*...*/ syntax.
Comment (/*...*/) Multi-line version	Statement	Used to surround comment lines. The compiler ignores all text between the starting /* characters and the ending */ characters.

CONTINUED ➞

TABLE 5.1 continued: JScript Keywords

KEYWORD	TYPE	DESCRIPTION
Comparison	Operators	Less than (<), Greater than (>), Less than or equal to (<=), Greater than or equal to (>=), Equal (==), Not equal (!=), Identity equality—same object (===), Identity inequality (!==).
compile	Method	Compiles a regular expression. Used to improve the speed of loops and repeated code.
Compound Assignment	Operators	Addition (+=), Bitwise AND (&=), Bitwise OR (|=), Bit-wise XOR (^=), Division (/=), Left Shift (<<=), Modulus (%=), Multiplication (*=), Right Shift (>>=), Subtraction (-=), Unsigned Right Shift (>>>=).
concat (Array)	Method	Concatenates two arrays.
concat (String)	Method	Concatenates two strings.
Conditional Compilation	Language Extension	Use in situations where non-Microsoft browsers or servers may not be able to compile the code. You begin conditional compilation using the @cc_on statement, or the @if or @set statements.
Conditional Compilation	Language Variables	These are built-in variables that are either True or Language Extensionevaluate to NaN. @_win32—true if running on a Win32 system. @_win16—true if running on a Win16 system. @_mac—true if running on an Apple Macintosh system. @_alpha—true if running on a DEC Alpha processor. @_x86—true if running on an Intel processor. @_mc680x0—true if running on a Motorola 680x0 processor. @_PowerPC—true if running on a Motorola PowerPC processor. @_jscript—Always true. @_jscript_build—Contains the build number of the JScript scripting engine. @_jscript_version—Contains the JScript version number in major.minor format.

CONTINUED ➡

TABLE 5.1 continued: JScript Keywords

KEYWORD	TYPE	DESCRIPTION
Conditional (trinary) (?:)	Operator	Used to execute one of two statements based on an expression. If the expression evaluates to True, JScript executes the first statement. If the expression evaluates to False, JScript executes the second statement. The syntax is `expression ? statement1 : statement2.`
constructor	Property	The name for a function that constructs an object.
continue	Statement	JScript does not process code following a continue statement in a loop. Instead, it begins processing again at the top of the loop.
cos	Method	Returns the cosine of a numeric expression.
Date	Object	JScript object for manipulating date and time values.
Decrement (--)	Operator	Decrements a value by 1.
delete	Operator	Deletes a property or an array element.
description	Property	Holds a description of a runtime error.
Dictionary	Object	Object that holds key-value pairs. You can look up a value if you know the key name. The Dictionary object also supports iteration over either the keys or the values.
dimensions	Method	Returns the number of dimensions in a VBArray array.
Division (/)	Operator	Divides two numbers.
do...while	Statement	Loop structure that always executes at least once.
E	Property	Returns Euler's constant, the base of natural logarithms, approximately 2.718.
Enumerator	Object	Object for enumerating or iterating over collections.
Equality (==)	Operator	Tests for equality between two values or expressions.
Error	Object	Object to hold runtime error information. This object is essentially the equivalent of the VBScript Error object, but has only number and description properties.
escape	Method	HTTP-encodes strings.
eval	Method	Evaluates JScript code. Use this to execute code strings you build at runtime.

CONTINUED →

TABLE 5.1 continued: JScript Keywords

Keyword	Type	Description
exec	Method	Searches a string for a regular expression.
exp	Method	Returns e to the power you supply as an argument to the method.
FileSystemObject	Object	Object used to manipulate the file system.
fixed	Method	Surrounds the text of a String object with <tt> teletype tags. The browser renders this text in a fixed-width font such as Courier.
floor	Method	Returns the largest integer value less than the value of the argument passed to the method.
fontcolor	Method	Surrounds the text of a String object with <font> tags where the starting tag includes a color attribute.
fontsize	Method	Surrounds the text of a String object with <font> tags where the starting tag includes a size attribute.
for	Statement	Used at the start of a `for` loop structure. The syntax is: `for (value; test; increment) statement or block` Equivalent to VBScript's `For...Next` statement block.
for...in	Statement	Executes a statement or block for each item in a collection or array. Equivalent to VBScript's `For Each...Next` statement block.
fromCharCode	Method	Creates a string from a list of Unicode values.
Function	Object	Creates a new function.
function	Statement	Declares a new function.
getDate	Method	Returns the integer (1-31) value for the current day of the month stored in a Date object.
getDay	Method	Returns the integer (0-6) value for the current day of the week stored in a Date object.
getFullYear	Method	Returns the year as a four-character integer (for example, 2001), for the date stored in a Date object.
getHours	Method	Returns the hour of the date stored in a Date object.
getItem	Method	Returns the item at a specified position in a VBArray.

CONTINUED ➞

TABLE 5.1 continued: JScript Keywords

Keyword	Type	Description
getMilliseconds	Method	Returns the milliseconds past the current second for the time stored in a Date object.
getMinutes	Method	Returns the number of minutes past the hour for the time stored in a Date object.
getMonth	Method	Returns the month as an integer (1–12) for the current month stored in a Date object.
GetObject	Function	Returns a reference to a COM or OLE object stored in a file.
getSeconds	Method	Returns the number of seconds past the minute for the time stored in a Date object.
getTime	Method	Returns the time stored in a Date object.
getTimezoneOffset	Method	Returns the difference (in minutes) between the local time on the computer and Universal Coordinated Time (UTC).
getUTCDate, getUTCDay, getUTCFullYear, getUTCHours, getUTCMilliseconds, getUTCMinutes, getUTCMonth, getUTCSeconds	Method	These methods are identical to the getDate, getDay, etc., methods except that they perform all calculations using Universal Coordinated Time (UTC) rather than the date and time on the local computer. Note that because the computer must calculate UTC dates and times as an offset of the local computer's date/time, your date/time operations are still only as accurate as the local computer's time.
getVarDate	Method	Returns a JScript date from the date stored in a Date object in COM VT_DATE format. You only need to use this method if you're working with date or time arguments received from a VBScript or ActiveX control function or object.
getYear	Method	Returns the two-digit year from the date stored in a Date object.
Global	Object	A JScript object that holds functions that are globally available.
Greater than (>)	Operator	Compares the relative size of two numeric values or expressions. Returns True if the value of the expression on the left side of the operator is larger than the value of the expression on the right side.

CONTINUED ➞

TABLE 5.1 continued: JScript Keywords

Keyword	Type	Description
Greater than or equal to (>=)	Operator	Compares the relative size of two values or expressions. Returns True if the value of the expression on the left side of the operator is larger than or equal to the value of the expression on the right side.
Identity (===)	Operator	Compares two object variable references and returns True if both variables refer to the same object.
`@if`	Statement	Conditional `if` structure. Used to conditionally compile code where the host-scripting environment may not be able to interpret the code correctly.
`if...else`	Statement	Code block. Performs a Boolean test on an expression and executes the code within the block if the expression evaluates to True.
Increment (++)	Operator	Increments a value by 1.
`index`	Property	For a RegExp object, returns the index of the first successful search for a regular expression.
`indexOf`	Method	Returns the starting position of the first matching sub-string within a String object.
Inequality (!=)	Operator	Compares two values or expressions. The operation evaluates to True if the value on the left side of the operator is not equal to the value on the right side.
`Infinity`	Property	Number object property that contains an initial value of POSITIVE_INFINITY.
`input`	Property	For a RegExp object, the `input` property returns the string that was searched.
`instanceOf`	Method	Returns True if the object is an instance of the specified `class` argument.
`isFinite`	Method	Returns True if the argument supplied is a finite number.
`isNaN`	Method	Returns True if the argument supplied is NaN (Not a Number).
`italics`	Method	Surrounds the text of a String object with <i> italics tags.
`item`	Method	Property of an Enumerator object. Returns the current item in an enumerated collection.

CONTINUED ➡

TABLE 5.1 continued: JScript Keywords

KEYWORD	TYPE	DESCRIPTION
`join`	Method	Returns a string consisting of all the elements in a string array joined into a single string with an optional separator character between the values.
`Labeled`	Statement	A unique identifier that marks a position or label in code. To create a label, append a colon (`:`) to the end of the label text. For example, `myLabel:`. The code line following the label is called a `labeled` statement. If you include a label after a `continue` statement in a loop, execution continues at the code line following the label.
`lastIndex`	Property	Property of a RegExp object that returns the index of the last matching sub-string within a string.
`lastIndexOf`	Method	Returns the starting position of the last matching substring within a String object.
`lbound`	Method	Returns the lower-bound of a VBArray.
`length` (Array)	Property	Returns the size of an array or collection.
`length` (Function)	Property	Contains the number of arguments defined for a function.
`length` (String)	Property	Returns the length of the text for the String object.
Less than (<)	Operator	Compares the relative size of two numeric values or expressions. Returns `True` if the value of the expression on the left side of the operator is smaller than the value of the expression on the right side.
Less than or equal to (<=)	Operator	Compares the relative size of two values or expressions. Returns `True` if the value of the expression on the left side of the operator is less than or equal to the value of the expression on the right side.
`link`	Method	Surrounds the text of a String object with an <a> anchor tag containing an HREF attribute.
`LN2`	Property	Returns the natural logarithm of 2.
`LN10`	Property	Returns the natural logarithm of 10.
`log`	Method	Returns the natural logarithm of a numeric value or expression.
`LOG2E`	Property	Returns the base 2 logarithm of E (Euler's constant).
`LOG10E`	Property	Returns the base 10 logarithm of E (Euler's constant).

CONTINUED ➞

TABLE 5.1 continued: JScript Keywords

Keyword	Type	Description
Logical AND (&&)	Operator	Performs a Boolean AND operation.
Logical NOT (!)	Operator	Performs a Boolean NOT operation.
Logical OR (||)	Operator	Performs a Boolean OR operation.
match	Method	Performs a search for a sub-string using a RegExp object.
Math	Object	A JScript intrinsic object used to perform math operations and retrieve constants.
max	Method	Returns the larger of two arguments.
MAX_VALUE	Property	The largest number you can use in JScript, approximately 1.79E+308.
min	Method	Returns the smaller of two arguments.
MIN_VALUE	Property	The smallest number you can use in JScript, approximately 2.22E-308.
Modulus (%)	Operator	Performs modulo arithmetic.
moveFirst	Method	Resets the current item of an Enumerator object to the first item of its associated collection.
moveNext	Method	Moves the current item of an Enumerator object to the next item of its associated collection.
Multiplication (*)	Operator	Multiplies numeric values.
NaN (Global)	Property	Contains the global initial constant for NaN (Not a Number).
NaN (Number)	Property	NaN is a special value meaning Not a Number.
NEGATIVE_INFINITY	Property	A value that represents negative infinity.
new	Operator	Creates a new object variable.
Nonidentity (!==)	Operator	Returns True if the operand on the left side of the operator does not refer to the same object as the operand on the right side.
Number	Object	Used to hold numeric values and constants.
number	Property	Contains a numeric value for a runtime error.
Object	Object	Parent object for all object variables.

CONTINUED ➡

TABLE 5.1 continued: JScript Keywords

KEYWORD	TYPE	DESCRIPTION
`parse`	Method	Parses the text of a String object. Returns the elapsed number of milliseconds between a string or Date and the constant date `January 1, 1970`.
`parseFloat`	Method	Parses the text of a String object and returns a floating-point value if the String contains a text representation of a number.
`parseInt`	Method	Parses the text of a String object and returns an integer value if the String contains a text representation of a number.
`PI`	Property	Returns the value of `pi` (approximately `3.14159`).
`POSITIVE_INFINITY`	Property	Returns a value representing positive infinity.
`pow`	Method	Returns the value of a numeric expression to the power of an argument you supply to the function.
`prototype`	Property	Returns a reference to a `prototype` object. New instances of that object type inherit the behavior of the prototype.
`random`	Method	Returns a pseudo-random number between 0 and 1.
`RegExp`	Object	Contains the results of a regular expression search.
`Regular Expression`	Object	Contains the patterns for a regular expression search.
`replace`	Method	Replaces sub-strings found by a regular expression search with other sub-strings.
`return`	Statement	Exits a function and (optionally) returns a value.
`reverse`	Method	Reverses the order of elements in an array.
`round`	Method	Returns a number rounded to the nearest integer value.
`ScriptEngine`	Function	Returns a string containing the name of the scripting language in use.
`ScriptEngine-BuildVersion`	Function	Returns a string containing the build version of the scripting language in use.
`ScriptEngine-MajorVersion`	Function	Returns a string containing the major version number of the scripting language in use.
`ScriptEngine-MinorVersion`	Function	Returns a string containing the minor version number of the scripting language in use.
`search`	Method	Searches a string for matches to a regular expression.

CONTINUED ⟶

TABLE 5.1 continued: JScript Keywords

KEYWORD	TYPE	DESCRIPTION
`@set`	Statement	Conditional variable creation statement.
`setDate`	Method	Sets the date value of a Date object.
`setFullYear`	Method	Sets the year of the date value of a Date object.
`setHours`	Method	Sets the current hour of a time value contained in a Date object.
`setMilliseconds`	Method	Sets the number of milliseconds past the second for the time value contained in a Date object.
`setMinutes`	Method	Sets the minutes past the hour for the time value contained in a Date object.
`setMonth`	Method	Sets the current month of the date value contained in a Date object.
`setSeconds`	Method	Sets the number of seconds past the minute for the time value contained in a Date object.
`setTime`	Method	Sets the time value of a Date object.
`setUTCDate`, `setUTCFullYear`, `setUTCHours`, `setUTCMilliseconds`, `setUTCMinutes`, `setUTCMonth`, `setUTCSeconds`	Methods	These methods are identical to the `setDate`, `setFullYear`, etc., methods except that they perform all calculations using Universal Coordinated Time (UTC) rather than the date and time on the local computer. Note that because the computer must calculate UTC dates and times as an offset of the local computer's date/time, your date/time operations are still only as accurate as the local computer's time.
`setYear` Method	Method	Sets the year of the date value contained in a Date object.
`sin`	Method	Returns the sin value of a numeric value supplied as an argument.
`slice` (Array)	Method	Returns a portion of an array. You supply the starting and ending indexes.
`slice` (String)	Method	Returns a portion of a string. You supply the starting and ending indexes.
`small`	Method	Surrounds the text of a String object with `<small>` tags.
`sort`	Method	Returns a sorted array.
`source`	Property	Returns the text of a regular expression pattern.

CONTINUED ➞

TABLE 5.1 continued: JScript Keywords

KEYWORD	TYPE	DESCRIPTION
`split`	Method	Splits the text of a String object into an array of strings separated at the delimiter value you supply.
`sqrt`	Method	Returns the square root of a numeric argument.
SQRT1_2	Property	Returns the square root of 0.5, or one divided by the square root of 2.
SQRT2	Property	Returns the square root of 2.
`strike`	Method	Surrounds the text of a String object with `<strike>` strikethrough tags.
`String`	Object	Object that contains text and exposes methods and properties to manipulate that text.
`sub`	Method	Surrounds the text of a String object with <sub> subscript tags.
`substr`	Method	Returns a sub-string from the text of a String object beginning from a specified offset with a specified length.
`substring`	Method	Returns a sub-string from the text of a String object beginning from a specified `start` offset and extending to a specified end offset.
Subtraction (-)	Operator	Subtracts numeric values.
`sup`	Method	Surrounds the text of a String object with <sup> superscript tags.
`switch`	Statement	A code block that conditionally executes one of a group of statements depending on the value of the condition.
`tan`	Method	Returns the tangent of a numeric value or expression.
`test`	Method	Returns `True` if a specified pattern exists in a string, otherwise returns `False`.
`this`	Statement	Contains a reference to the current object.
`throw`	Statement	Raises an error.
`toArray`	Method	Converts a VBArray to a JScript array.
`toGMTString`	Method	Obsolete. Use the `toUTCString` method instead.
`toLocaleString`	Method	Returns a string representation of a date. Uses the local computer's locale settings.

CONTINUED ➟

TABLE 5.1 continued: JScript Keywords

KEYWORD	TYPE	DESCRIPTION
`toLowerCase`	Method	Returns a string with all the characters converted to lower case.
`toString`	Method	Returns a string representation of an object.
`toUpperCase`	Method	Returns a string with all the characters converted to upper case.
`toUTCString`	Method	Returns a string representation of a date in Universal Coordinated Time (UTC).
`try...catch`	Statement	Sets up error-handling. Requires two code blocks: a `try` block and a `catch` block. If an error occurs in the `try` block, execution resumes at the start of the `catch` block. You can handle the error locally or raise it to the next level using the `throw` statement.
`typeof`	Operator	Returns the type of an object or expression as a string. The return value is `number`, `string`, `boolean`, `object`, `function`, or `undefined`.
`ubound`	Method	Returns the upper-bound of a VBArray.
Unary Negation (-)	Operator	Negates a value or expression.
`unescape`	Method	Accepts an escaped (HTTP-encoded) string. Returns the string converted to normal text.
Unsigned Right Shift (>>>)	Operator	Shifts bit patterns to the right. Zero-fills the bits on the left.
UTC	Method	Returns the number of milliseconds between the constant `January 1, 1970` and the supplied date. Uses UTC time to make the calculation.
`valueOf`	Method	Returns the primitive value of the object argument. The method returns Arrays as comma-separated strings; Boolean values as strings; dates and times as milliseconds (see UTC method); Functions as the text of the function; Numbers as a numeric value; Objects as themselves; and Strings as text.
`var`	Statement	Used to declare a variable.
`VBArray`	Object	Used to contain and manipulate COM safe-array arrays, known as `VBArrays`.
`void`	Operator	Used to evaluate an expression. The `void` operator returns the value `undefined`.

CONTINUED →

TABLE 5.1 continued: JScript Keywords

KEYWORD	TYPE	DESCRIPTION
`while`	Statement	Begins a conditional code block. The block executes if the condition following the `while` statements evaluates to `True`.
`With`	Statement	Sets the default object for the following statement or group of statements. Equivalent to the `With` statement in VBScript.

VARIABLES AND SYNTAX

JScript, like VBScript, does not use typed variables, everything is a Variant; however, like VBScript, you can declare variables using the `var` statement. Unlike VBScript, you can declare a variable and initialize its value in the same statement. For example:

```
var myVar = 3;
var myString = new String("This is a string");
```

Note that each line in the script requires a semicolon. Also, remember that JScript is case-sensitive. The following code will not work correctly:

```
var myVar = 3
Response.Write(MyVar);
```

You can assign expressions in JScript during variable declaration:

```
var myVar = (3 * 6);
```

You can also declare several variables on one line. Separate the individual variable declarations with commas. For example:

```
var myVar = 3, myString =
new String("Test"), i, j;
```

The keyword `var` is optional. JScript, like VBScript, tries to interpret unrecognized keywords as variables. Unlike VBScript, there's no equivalent to the `Option Explicit` statement, which forces variable declaration. When you mix automatic variable creation with case sensitivity, you have a recipe for trouble. In longer scripts, such problems may be very difficult to find and debug.

In JScript, you can create both single and compound statements. A compound statement is a group of statements surrounded by braces. For example, an `if` conditional structure is a single statement if it has only one executable code line. For example:

```
if (true)
    x = 1;
```

If the preceding statement had two lines, you would write it as a compound statement, because you want to execute both of the code lines following the `if` condition when the condition evaluates to `true`. For example:

```
if (true) {
    x = 1;
    y = 1;
}
```

NOTE

In VBScript, the constant for a Boolean True value is `True`, with a capital T. In JScript, the constant is `true` with a lowercase t. In both languages, the value of `True` is –1, and the value of `False` is 0.

The equals sign is an overloaded operator in VB and many other languages because you use it for both assignment and equality tests. In JScript, however, like C, you use a single equals sign for assignment and a double equals sign (==) for an equality test. This is hard to remember, mostly because using the single equals sign doesn't normally cause an error. JScript happily assigns the value you think you're testing to the variable on the left side of the equals sign.

To test object variables for equality in JScript, use a triple equals sign (===), and an exclamation point (often called a bang) with a double equals sign (!==) to test objects for inequality.

Using the ASP Objects with JScript

The ASP objects have exactly the same properties and methods using JScript as they do with VBScript, but the syntax is slightly different. For example, you must remember to add the semicolons at the end of each line, and you must remember to enclose the arguments to the built-in methods in parentheses. For example, in VBScript, you could write:

```
Dim myVar
myVar = 2
Response.Write myVar & "<br>"
```

In JScript, you could code the same functionality as:

```
var myVar = 2;
Response.write(myVar + "<br>");
```

Use the same syntax alterations for Request object methods. For example, to enumerate the keys and values in the `Request.ServerVariables` collection, use a `for` loop and an `Enumerator` object:

```
var en = new
    Enumerator(Request.ServerVariables);
for (;!en.atEnd(); en.moveNext())
   Response.Write(en.item() + "="
      + Request.ServerVariables(en.item())
      + "<br>");
```

The `for` loop shown above is equivalent to the following VBScript code:

```
For Each V in Request.ServerVariables
   Response.Write V & "=" & _
   Request.ServerVariables(V) & "<BR>"
Next
```

Interestingly, although JScript itself is a case-sensitive language (for example, you can't write `For` when you mean `for`), JScript ignores case for the ASP-intrinsic object methods and properties, but not for the objects themselves. In other words, this code works:

```
Response.Write("Hello");
```

and this code works, too:

```
Response.write("Hello");
```

but this code does not:

```
response.write("Hello");
```

Apparently, after you create the variable reference, non-case-sensitive code running internally in the ASP engine itself must interpret all method and property references; otherwise, JScript would force you to write the references with proper case.

The lesson in this section is that you must constantly remain aware that case and syntax are more important in JScript than in VBScript.

USING JSCRIPT ARRAYS

Although most variable types are roughly equivalent in JScript and VBScript, arrays are not. In JScript, arrays are objects; in VBScript, arrays are not objects. In JScript, the lowest array index is always 0; in VBScript, you can create arrays where the lowest index is any integer value. But they do have similarities. Both VBScript and JScript arrays are dynamic—you can extend or truncate them at runtime. Both VBScript and JScript arrays can hold any kind of value—in other words, the elements of the array do not have to have the same data type; you can freely mix objects and scalar values.

You can create a JScript array both explicitly, by declaring the array, and implicitly, using the `split` function. For example:

```
// create an array with 4 elements
var arrWords1 = new Array(3);

// implicit array creation
var sWords = "one,two,three,four";
var arrWords2 = sWords.split(",");
```

You can also create an array using a list of constants:

```
var arrWords3 = new Array("one", "two",
     "three", "four");
```

After creating an array, you access individual elements using an index:

```
var arrWords3 = new Array("one", "two",
     "three", "four");
Response.Write(arrWords3[0]);
// writes "one"
```

The `length` property of a JScript array returns the number of elements in the array:

```
var days = new Array("Sun", "Mon", "Tue",
     "Wed", "Thu", "Fri", "Sat");
Response.Write(days.length);
// writes 7
```

You can also extend or truncate the number of elements in a JScript array using the `length` property:

```
var arr = new Array();
arr.length=10;
Response.write(arr.length);
```

Note that the number of elements of an array is not necessarily the same as the number of assigned values in the array. `Array` elements with unassigned values have the initial value `undefined`.

BUILT-IN METHODS

You've seen all these methods in the JScript keywords table in this chapter (Table 5.1), but some of them require a little more explanation. JScript uses both primitives and objects to manipulate values. For example, an integer constant is perfectly viable—so is a `Number` object containing an integer value:

```
var myInt = 2;
var myIntObject = new Number(2);
Response.Write(myInt + "<br>");
Response.Write(myIntObject.toString() +
    "<br>");
```

JScript contains a large number of built-in date and time methods. You access these through a `Date` object. For example:

```
var myDate = new Date('2/1/99 4:54:23 pm');
Response.write(myDate.toString() + "<br>");
// writes " Mon Feb 1 16:54:23 CST 1999"
Response.write(myDate.getMonth() + "<br>");
// writes 1 (month numbers are 0-based)
Response.write(myDate.getSeconds() + "<br>");
// writes 23
Response.write(myDate.getUTCSeconds() +
    "<br>");
// writes 23
```

LOGICAL STRUCTURES

JScript has two main logical structures: the `if...else` structure and the `switch` statement. In JScript terminology these are logical statements. You've already seen both of these in action in the previous section. In this section, you'll take a closer look at the syntax and requirements.

The *if...else* Statement

In JScript, a single statement may cover several lines, but each statement must end with a semicolon (`;`), the statement terminator. JScript `if...else` statements are no exception, but they look like an exception because most people write the statement on two lines, as follows:

```
if (condition)
    do something;
```

Note that the `else` portion of the statement is optional. Most people break the statement into two lines for clarity, but it's perfectly legal to write:

```
if (condition) do something;
```

Even most of the spaces are optional. For example:

```
var s="1234";
// the space between var and s is required
// The following line works even without spaces
if(s=="1234")Response.Write("1234");
// writes 1234
```

Note that JScript requires spaces only where no other separator divides the text into recognizable parts. In the variable declaration line of the previous fragment, if you omit the space between `var` and `s`, JScript creates a variable called `vars`. No error occurs until the following line, where JScript attempts to compare the value `1234` to the now undefined variable `s` as shown in the following example:

```
//This code causes an error
vars="1234" // no error
Response.Write(s + "<br>"); // error
```

The previous line causes the error because `s` is undefined. At any rate, one of the most common syntax errors in JScript with the `if...else` structure is that beginners often forget to create a compound statement for multi-line conditional code. In other words, if you need to execute more than one conditional statement for an `if` or `else`, add braces around the statements. For example:

```
//This code does not work properly
var i = 3;
if (i < 3)
   Response.write("Hello ");
   Response.write("World<br>");
else
   Response.write("i is not less than" +
   " three<br>");


//This code works properly
var i = 3;
if (i < 3) {
   Response.write("Hello ");
   Response.write("World<br>");
}
else
   Response.write("i is not less than" +
   " three<br>");
```

The first version causes a hard-to-understand error—a syntax error on the line containing the first `else`. The cause of the problem though isn't the `else`, it's that the `if` statement is a compound statement, and thus requires braces. The second version works properly.

JScript, unlike VBScript, has no `elseif` and there is no equivalent construction. Instead, you must chain `if` statements. For example:

```
' VBScript version
Dim i
i = 3
If i = 1 Then
   Response.Write "1<br>"
Elseif i = 2 then
   Response.Write "2<br>"
```

```
Elseif i = 3 then
   Response.Write "3<br>"
Else
   Response.Write "i is not 1, 2, or 3.<br>"
End If


//JScript version
var i = 3;
if (i == 1)
  Response.Write("1<br>");
if (i == 2)
  Response.Write("2<br>");
if (i == 3)
  Response.Write("3<br>");
else
  Response.Write("i is not 1, 2, or 3.<br>");
```

The *switch* Statement

When you want to test a single condition that may have multiple values, it's much easier to use the `switch` statement than the `if` statement. The `switch` statement conditionally executes code based on the value of a condition. The syntax is:

```
switch (condition) {
   case 1:
      code when condition is 1;
      break;
   case 2:
      code when condition is 2;
      break;
   default:
      code when condition is neither 1 or 2;
}
```

The `switch` statement acts in several ways. First, Microsoft's JScript documentation states that the `switch` statement causes execution to jump to a label based on the value of condition. The documentation defines a label as a text string followed by a colon. In the `switch` statement, the labels follow the keyword `case`. That's confusing because the label, in this case, can be a numeric value. Listing 5.1 shows an example of a `switch` statement that executes code based on a numeric value. If you run the code, you may get a surprise!

Listing 5.1: `switch` **Statement Example**

```
<%@ Language=JScript %>
<%
var i = 1;
var iValue
if (Request("Submit") == "Go") {
   iValue = new Number(Request("iValue"));
   if (iValue != NaN)
      i = iValue.valueOf();
}


Response.Write("The variable i has a value of "
   + i + "<br><br>");
switch (i) {
   case 1:
      Response.Write("This statement" +
         " prints when i=1<br>");
      break;
   case 2:
      Response.Write("This statement" +
         " prints when i=2<br>");
      break;
   case 3:
      Response.Write("This statement" +
         " prints when i=3<br>");
      break;
   default:
      Response.Write("This statement" +
         " prints when i does not equal" +
         " 1, 2, or 3<br>");
}
%>
<html><head><title>ch10i1.asp</title></head>
```

```
<body>
<form name="frmSwitch" method="post">
Enter a value for the variable i
<input type="text" maxlength="5" name="iValue">
 
<input type="Submit" name="Submit" value="Go">
</form>
</body>
</html>
```

I've added a form to the file in `ch10i1.asp` that lets you change the value of `i` interactively. If you view the file in your browser, it looks like Figure 5.1. (Note that the figure represents the file on this source book's CD, not the previous listing.) The default value for the variable `i` is `1`.

When you view the file in the browser, you'll see that initially, when `i` is `1`, all the statements print. That doesn't make sense because only one of the statements should print. The example points out the most important difference between the `switch` statement and VBScript's `Select Case` structure–the `switch` statement requires a `break` command after each `case`. In JScript, if you neglect to insert the `break` statements, JScript executes all the statements following the first `case` statement that meet the condition. In contrast, the `Select Case` structure doesn't fall through to the next statement.

If you're still confused, try changing the value of the variable `i` to `3`. When `i=3` only the statement at `case 3` and the default statement will print. Listing 5.2 contains a fixed version of the `switch` statement. After adding the `break` statements to each condition, the statement works properly–only one message prints for any value of `i`.

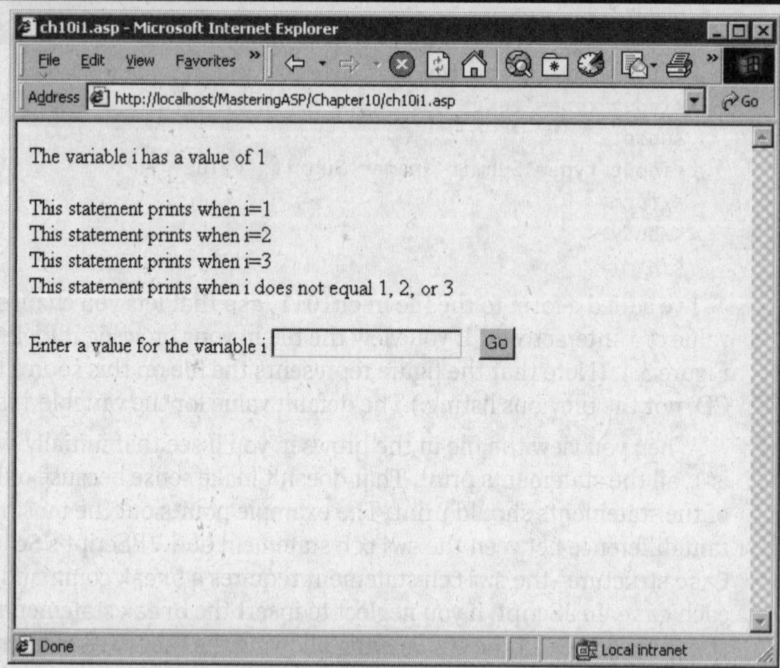

FIGURE 5.1: Switch statement example

Listing 5.2: Fixed `switch` Example

```
switch (i) {
   case 1:
      Response.Write("This statement prints" +
         " when i=1<br>");
      break;
   case 2:
      Response.Write("This statement prints" +
         " when i=2<br>");
      break;
   case 3:
      Response.Write("This statement prints" +
         " when i=3<br>");
      break;
   default:
      Response.Write("This statement prints" +
         " when i does not equal 1, 2," +
```

```
        " or 3<br>");
}
```

The Trinary (?:) Operator

JScript has one special operator that behaves like an `if...else` statement. The syntax is:

```
condition ? execute if true : execute if false
```

It's called the trinary operator because it has three parts—the condition, the statement to execute when the condition is `true`, and the statement to execute when the condition is `false`. For example:

```
var i = 1; y = 0;
(i==0) ? y = 1: y = 2;
Response.Write(y);
// writes 2
```

The operator evaluates the condition, then executes the statement following the question mark when the condition evaluates to `true` or the statement following the colon if the condition evaluates to `false`. VBScript has a similar (but less efficient) function—the `Iif` function. The logic for the trinary operator is exactly the same as the following `if` statement:

```
if (condition)
   execute if true;
else
   execute if false;
```

The code statements for the trinary operator may be compound statements.

Looping

JScript has fewer looping constructs than VBScript, but the ones it has are more flexible. Use a `for` loop when you know how many times you want the loop to execute. The syntax of the `for` statement is:

```
for(start counter; end condition; statements) {
   loop code
}
```

For example, the following code builds an array, then displays the value of each item in the array:

```
var i;
var arr = new Array(10);
for (i = 0; i < 10; i++) {
   arr[i] = "Item " + i.toString();
}
for (i = 0; i < 10; i++) {
   Response.write(arr[i] + "<br>");
}
```

A more generic example tests the `length` property of the array as the loop end condition:

```
for (i = 0; i < arr.length; i++) {
   Response.write(arr[i] + "<br>");
}
```

You can iterate through an array using the `for...in` syntax. Interestingly, the item retrieved for each element in an array is the index, not the value. For example:

```
var aList = new Array("1","2","3","4","5");
for (i in aList)
   Response.write(i + ", ");
Response.Write("<br>");
// writes the index numbers: 0, 1, 2, 3, 4,
```

More typically, you want to retrieve the values. To do that, use code like this:

```
var aList = new Array("1","2","3","4","5");
for (i in aList)
Response.write(aList[i] + ", ");
Response.Write("<br>");
// writes the list of values:
1
2
3
4
5
```

JScript treats objects and arrays essentially the same. For example, JScript indexes property values. You can retrieve a value with either the name or the index. Therefore, JScript's `for...in` structure can also iterate through the properties of an object. The following example shows a function to create an object and a `for...in` loop to iterate through its properties:

```
// function to create an object
function myObj() {
    var name;
    var type;
    return this;
}
var obj = new myObj();
obj.name="A. Russell Jones"
obj.type="Person"
for (i in obj) {
    Response.write(obj[i] + "<br>");
}
// writes:
// A. Russell Jones
// Person
```

NOTE

You cannot use JScript's `for...in` syntax to loop through the properties of a VBScript array. To use `for...in` on a VBScript array, you must first convert it to a JScript array using the `toArray` method. Similarly, you cannot use `for...in` to loop through the items in any of the ASP object collections.

String-Handling

JScript treats strings as objects. You can declare a variable as a String object explicitly, or you can let JScript create a String object implicitly by assigning a string value to a variable. For example:

```
var s = new String();
var s1 = new String("This is a string");
```

```
var s2;
s2 = "This is another string";
Response.Write(typeof[s] + "<br>");
    // writes "object"
Response.Write(typeof[s1] + "<br>");
    // writes "object"
Response.Write(typeof[s2] + "<br>");
    // writes "object"
```

Note that you can use either the single-quote (') or the double-quote (") character as the string delimiter:

```
var s = new String("This is a string");
var s = new String('This is a string');
```

You can't use some characters directly in JScript because it treats them as special characters. To print or use the special characters in code, you use a combination of the backslash character (called the escape character) plus another character. These two-character combinations substitute for the special characters shown in Table 5.2.

TABLE 5.2: JScript Special Characters

Escape Sequence	ASCII Character Value	Description
\r	13	Carriage return
\n	10	New line (line feed)
\f	12	Formfeed
\t	9	Tab
\'	39	Single-quote
\"	34	Double-quote
\b	8	Backspace

For example, to embed a tab in a string, use the \t special character:

```
var s="Fruit\tPrice\n\rApple\t" +
    "$0.20\n\rBanana\t$0.22";
Response.Write("<pre>" + s + "</pre>");
```

Note that the Response.Write method uses the <pre> tag to display the contents of the variable s; otherwise the browser will ignore the tabs and carriage return/linefeed characters. Here's a complete example:

```
<%@ Language=JScript %>
<html>
<head>
<title>
JScript Special Characters Example
</title>
</head>
<body>
<h2 align="center">
JScript Special Characters Example
</h2>
<%
var s="Fruit\tPrice\n\rApple\t" +
     "$0.20\n\rBanana\t$0.22";
Response.write("<b>With &lt;pre&gt; tag in" +
     " effect</b>:<p>");
Response.Write("<pre>" + s + "</pre>");
Response.write("<hr><p>");
Response.write("<p><b>Without &lt;pre&gt;" +
     " tag in effect</b>:<p>");
Response.Write(s);
%>
</body>
</html>
```

Figure 5.2 shows how the previous listing displays in a browser, both with and without the <pre> tag.

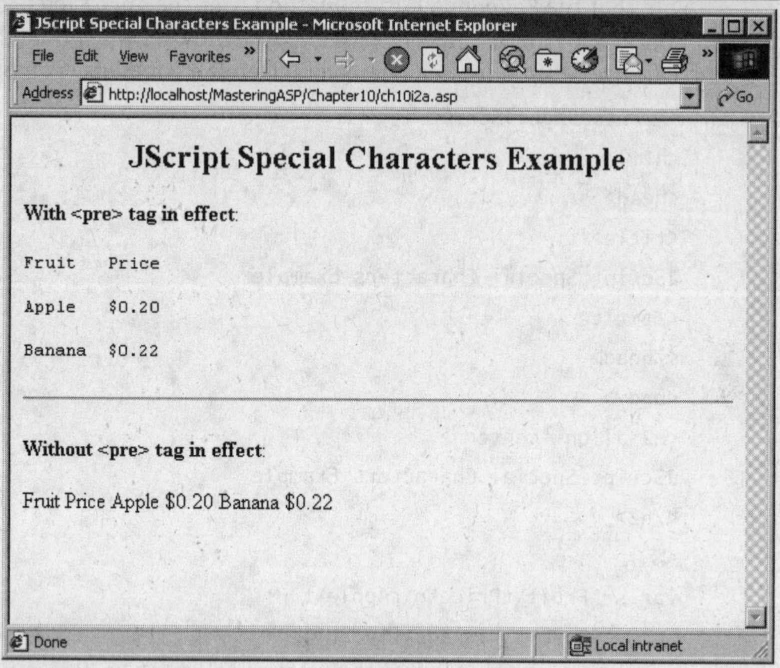

FIGURE 5.2: JScript special characters example

NOTE

To embed the escape character (\) itself in a string, use two consecutive escape characters. For example, to display the string `c:\somePath\someFile .txt`, use the syntax `Response.Write("c:\\somepath\\someFile .txt");`

To concatenate two strings in JScript, you can use either the concat method or the concatenation (+) operator. For example:

```
var s1 = new String("Happy ");
var s2 = new String("Birthday");
Response.Write(s1 + s2 + "<br>");
// writes "Happy Birthday"

s1 = s1.concat(s2);
Response.Write(s1 + "<br>");
// writes "Happy Birthday"
```

```
Response.write("Happy ".concat(s2));
// writes "Happy Birthday"
```

JScript contains several functions to wrap HTML tags around text. For example:

```
s = new String("This is bookmarked text.<br>");
Response.Write((s.anchor("bookmark1")) +
     "<br>");
// creates the HTML string
//<A NAME="bookmark1">This is bookmarked
//   text.<br></A><br>s = new
//   String("Link to ch10i1.asp<br>");
Response.Write((s.link("ch5i1.asp")) +
     "<br>");
// creates the HTML string
// <A HREF="ch5i1.asp">Link to
//   ch5i1.asp<br></A>
```

Of course, after the browser renders the response, you can't see the HTML unless you right-click and select View Source. Listing 5.3 shows the other JScript functions that create HTML.

Listing 5.3: JScript String Object HTML-Producing Methods

```
s = new String("This is bold text.");
Response.Write(s.bold());
Response.Write ("<br>");

s = new String("This is big text.");
Response.Write(s.big());
Response.Write ("<br>");

s = new String("This is blinking text" +
     " (Netscape Browsers Only).");
Response.Write(s.blink());
Response.Write ("<br>");

s = new String("This is blue text.");
Response.Write(s.fontcolor("0000FF"));
Response.Write ("<br>");
```

```
s = new String("This is size 5 text.");
Response.Write(s.fontsize(5));
Response.Write ("<br>");

s = new String("This is italicized text.");
Response.Write(s.italics());
Response.Write ("<br>");

s = new String("This is small text.");
Response.Write(s.small());
Response.Write ("<br>");

Response.Write("Normal Text");
s = new String("Superscript");
Response.Write(s.sup());
Response.Write ("<br>");

Response.Write("Normal Text");
s = new String("Subscript");
Response.Write(s.sub());
Response.Write ("<br>");
```

Figure 5.3 shows how the previous listing displays in a browser.

Many of the String object methods become even more useful when you wrap them in function code as shown in the next section.

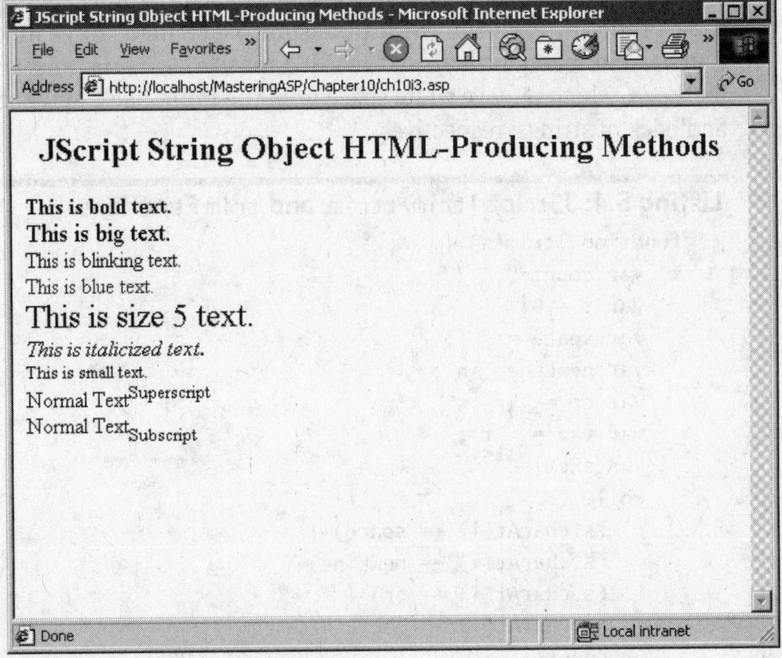

FIGURE 5.3: JScript string object HTML-producing methods

FUNCTIONS

The body of a function is a compound statement. Therefore, you must surround the function body with braces. The syntax for a function in JScript is:

```
function name(argument1, argument2,
    ... argument n) {
   function body code here
}
```

Arguments are optional. It's perfectly acceptable to create a function that accepts no arguments. The position of the braces surrounding the function body (or any compound statement, for that matter) is unimportant other than for style or clarity. Because JScript ignores white space, you can place all of your code on a single line if you wish.

As a simple but useful function example, you can duplicate some of the methods available in VBScript. Listing 5.4 contains three functions that are JScript equivalents to the VBScript `LTrim`, `Rtrim`, and `Trim` methods, which remove white space from the front, back, and both front and back of strings, respectively.

Listing 5.4: JScript `ltrim`, `rtrim`, and `trim` Functions

```
function ltrim(s) {
   var count=0;
   var i = 0;
   var space = " ";
   var newLine="\n";
   var cr = "\r";
   var tab = "\t";
   var sRet;
   while (
      (s.charAt(i) == space) |
      (s.charAt(i) == newLine) |
      (s.charAt(i) == cr) |
      (s.charAt(i) == tab)){
      count++;
      i++
   }
   if (count > 0)
      sRet = s.substring(count, s.length);

   return(sRet);
}
function rtrim(s) {
   var count=0;
   var i = s.length - 1;
   var space = " ";
   var newLine="\n";
   var cr = "\r";
   var tab = "\t";
   var sRet;
   while (
      (s.charAt(i) == space) |
      (s.charAt(i) == newLine) |
      (s.charAt(i) == cr) |
      (s.charAt(i) == tab)) {
```

```
        count++;
        i-
    }
    if (count > 0)
        sRet = s.substring(0, s.length - count);

    return(sRet);
}

function trim(s) {
    return(ltrim(rtrim(s)));
}
```

The `ltrim` and `rtrim` functions do the real work—the `trim` function simply calls both of the other functions. Each function accepts a string argument. Because string concatenation is a relatively expensive operation, the function counts the number of white-space characters, then performs a single string copy in both the `ltrim` and `rtrim` functions. Note that the return value from each function is a String object—the functions don't alter the original string. In addition, because the return value is a String object, you can treat the function exactly as you would treat any other String object.

Having defined the functions, you may subsequently use them just like any other function call. For example:

```
var s = "   This is a string containing "
  + "leading and trailing spaces.    ";
Response.Write("<pre>'" + s + "'</pre>");
Response.Write("<hr>");
Response.Write("<b>ltrim(s)</b>:<pre>'" +
   ltrim(s) + "'</pre><br>");
Response.Write("<hr>");
Response.Write("<b>rtrim(s)</b>:<pre>'" +
   rtrim(s) + "'</pre><br>");
Response.Write("<hr>");
Response.Write("<b>trim(s)</b>:<pre>'" +
   trim(s) + "'</pre><br>");
```

Figure 5.4 shows the results of the previous code in a browser.

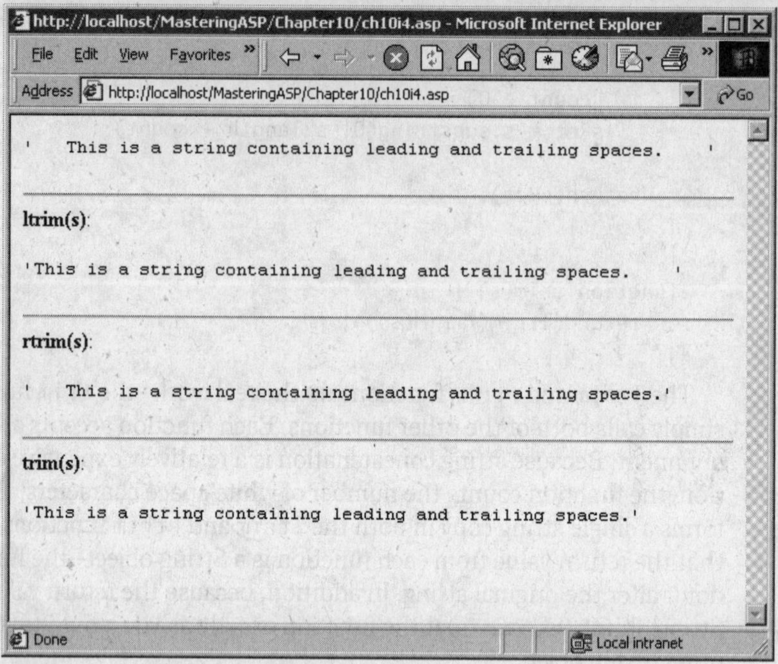

FIGURE 5.4: `ltrim`, `rtrim`, and `trim` function examples

Listing 5.5 shows a slightly more complex function to count the number of words in a string argument passed to the function.

Listing 5.5: `CountWords` **Function Example 1**

```
function countWords(s) {
   var count = 0;
   var i;
   var lastCharWhiteSpace = 0;
   // loop through the string
   for (i = 0; i < s.length; i++) {
      // get the character at position i
      if (s.charAt(i) == " ") {
         // if it's a space
         lastCharWhiteSpace = true;
      }
      else {

         // it's not a space
```

```
         if (lastCharWhiteSpace == true |
            i == 0 )
            count++;
         lastCharWhiteSpace = false;
      }
   }
   return count;
}

var s = "  This is a string  ";
Response.Write("The number of words" +
   " in the string '" + s + "' is: ");
Response.Write(countWords(s) + "<br>");
// The Response.Write statements above write:
// The number of words in the string 'This is
// a string' is 4
```

The function iterates through each character in the string and tests to see if the current character is a space. If so, it sets a flag called `lastCharWhiteSpace` to `true`. If the character is not a space, and the last character was a space *or* the current character is the first character in the string, the function increments the `count` variable. At the end of the function, `count` contains the number of words in the string argument. You use the `return` statement to return the value of any variable or expression.

A function can return only one value. To exit a function without returning a value, use the `return` statement by itself with no associated variable or expression.

There are two problems with the function in Listing 5.5. The first is that the function will fail if you pass it anything except a string. The second is that the function only looks for spaces, but spaces aren't the only word separators. Carriage returns, tabs, and, in some cases, punctuation can separate words as well. For example, in JScript, you can embed a carriage return using the syntax `\n`, called a newline character. As written, the `countWords()` function would not count the words separated by the newline character as separate words. The following code shows the JScript version:

```
var s = "  This is\n\na string  ";
Response.Write("The number of words in" +
   " the string '" + s + "' is: ");
Response.Write(countWords(s) + "<br>");
// writes 3
```

Listing 5.6 contains an improved version of the function. The `countWords2()` function iterates through the characters in the string using the `switch` statement to determine the character code of each character. If the character is a space, a tab, or a newline character, the function treats it as white space.

Listing 5.6: Improved `CountWords` Function Example 1

```
function countWords2(s) {
   var count = 0, i, charCode,
      lastCharWhiteSpace = false;
   if (!(typeof(s) == "string")) {
      Response.Write("The countWords2" +
        " function expects a String" +
        " argument.");
      return;
   }
   for (i = 0; i < s.length; i++) {
      switch (s.charCodeAt(i)) {
      case 32:
         lastCharWhiteSpace = true;
         break;
      case 10:
         lastCharWhiteSpace = true;
         break;
      case 13:
         lastCharWhiteSpace = true;
         break;
      case 9:
         lastCharWhiteSpace = true;
         break;
      default :
         if (lastCharWhiteSpace == true |
            i == 0 ) {
            count++;
            lastCharWhiteSpace = false;
         }
      }
   }
   return count;
}
```

The `countWords2` function improves on the original in three ways: First, the function checks the argument type using the `typeof` function.

If the argument is not a string, the function writes a message and exits. Second, the function tests for white space consisting of characters other than spaces by checking the character code for each character in the string argument. It obtains the character code using the `charCodeAt()` function, which returns the character code for a character at a specific offset in a string. Finally, the function trims the string by calling the `trim()` function shown earlier in this chapter before counting the words in the string.

Creating Objects in JScript

As I stated at the beginning of this chapter, JScript is more object-oriented than VBScript, although VBScript version 5 has narrowed the gap. You've already seen how to use the built-in objects. Since version 3, JScript has had the ability to create objects. To create an object in JScript, you create a constructor function. The constructor function creates and initializes the object's properties, then returns the object. For example, to create an audio CD object, you might want a `title` property, an `artist` property, a `trackCount` property, a variable to hold an array of track titles, and the name of the record company:

```
function CD() {
   var title;
   var artist;
   var trackCount;
   var trackTitles;
   var recordCompany;
   return(this);
}
```

To create the new CD object, you call the constructor function preceded by the new keyword:

```
var myCD = new CD();
```

After creating the object variable, you can now set its properties as shown in the following fragment:

```
myCD.title="Fraser and DeBolt Together Again";
myCD.artist = "Alan Fraser and Daisy DeBolt";
myCD.trackCount = 12;
myCD.trackTitles =
```

```
        new Array(myCD.trackCount - 1);
    for (i=0; i < myCD.trackCount; i++)
        myCD.trackTitles[i] = "Track " +
        i.toString();
    myCD.recordCompany="Columbia Records";
```

There are some quirks to JScript object creation. Note that you must set the `trackTitles` property to an Array object from outside the constructor function. If you create the Array object inside the constructor function, but try to change its size from outside the constructor function as shown below, the code causes a runtime error. However, you can call an initialization function to make the constructor function assign default values to the properties. You can even pass default values to the constructor function. For example:

```
function CD() {
    var title;
    var artist;
    var trackCount;
    var trackTitles = new Array();
    var recordCompany;
    return(this);
}
myCD.title="Fraser and DeBolt Together Again";
myCD.artist = "Alan Fraser and Daisy DeBolt";
myCD.trackCount = 12;
myCD.trackTitles.length = myCD.trackCount - 1
//the previous line causes an error.
```

Regular Expressions

JScript has powerful regular expression–matching abilities. A regular expression consists of text you want to search for combined with special characters or commands that describe how you want to search.

Microsoft's MSDN documentation is somewhat confused on this topic. It documents two separate objects, stating that the Regular Expression object holds search criteria, and the RegExp object holds the results of a search or match operation, but you can create only one object—the RegExp object.

You can create a RegExp object either implicitly, by surrounding the search criteria with forward slashes, or explicitly, by creating a new Regular Expression object and providing the search criteria as a String argument:

```
// implicit RegExp creation
rgxp = /boy/;

// explicit RegExp creation
rgxp = new RegExp("boy");
```

You can perform global (find all matches) and case-insensitive searches using an optional argument in both the implicit and explicit forms. The possible flag values are:

i Perform a case-insensitive search.

g Perform a global search.

You can combine the flags in any order. For example:

```
// case-insensitive search
rgxp = /boy/i

// global search
rgxp = /x/g

// case-insensitive global search
rgxp = new RegExp("boy", "ig");
```

You can approach using a RegExp object from two directions: by passing a RegExp object as an argument to the String object's `search` and `match` methods, or by passing a String argument to the RegExp object's `exec` method. The String object's `search` method returns the zero-based character offset of the first matching character in the string, or `-1` if no match is found.

For example, the following code uses the `String search` method to search for the word boy in the string `Every good boy does fine.`

```
var s1 =
    new String("Every good boy does fine.")
var s2 = /boy/i
```

```
Response.write(s1.search(s2));
// writes 11
```

The difference between searches and matches is that a search returns the index of the first match for the regular expression in a string, whereas the return value of a match is an array.

The String object `match` method and the RegExp object's `exec` method are functionally identical. It doesn't matter whether you perform the `match` method on a RegExp object or `exec` a String, both methods return an array. You can use the `compile` method of the RegExp object to improve the speed of matches run multiple times, for example, in a loop.

The power of regular expression–searching lies in its ability to match patterns using special characters and character sequences. Table 5.3 lists the special characters and sequences you may use in a regular expression.

TABLE 5.3: JScript Regular Expression Special Characters and Sequences

CHARACTER/ SEQUENCE	DESCRIPTION
\	Escape character. Use this to embed newline, tab, or other special characters into the regular expression string.
^	Limits matches to the beginning of a line or string.
$	Limits matches to the end of a line or string.
*	Matches the character preceding the asterisk zero or more times. For example, /bo*/ matches both bed and book.
+	Matches the character preceding the plus sign one or more times. /bo+/ matches book, but not bed.
?	Matches the character preceding the question mark zero or one time. /be?/I matches `best` and `bit`, but not been.
.	The period is a wildcard character. It matches any single character other than a newline.
`(pattern)`	Enclose a pattern in parentheses to find matched patterns. You can retrieve the matched patterns using the RegExp object's `$1...$9` properties. Use \(and \) to match parentheses.
a|b	Matches either a or b.

CONTINUED →

TABLE 5.3 continued: JScript Regular Expression Special Characters and Sequences

CHARACTER/ SEQUENCE	DESCRIPTION
`{n}`	Matches exactly n times, where n is an integer greater than or equal to 1. For example, `/m{2}/` matches `immediate`, but not `magic`.
`{n,}`	Matches at least n times, where n is an integer greater than or equal to 1. Non-negative integer. For example, `/e{2}/` matches `seer`, but not `her`.
`{nMin, nMax}`	Matches between nMin and nMax times, inclusive, where both nMin and nMax are integers greater than or equal to 1.
`[abc]`	Matches any of the characters enclosed in the brackets. `/[mno]/` matches the n in `bin` or the m in Mom.
`[^abc]`	Matches any character not enclosed in the brackets. `/[^mno]/` matches the b in `bin` and the M in Mom.
`\b`	Matches a word boundary, such as a space, tab, or punctuation. For example, `/p\b/` matches the p in the word `help`, in the phrase `please help me`, and in the phrase `please help`. Place the /b before the pattern to find matches at the beginning of words or at the end of the pattern to find matches at the end of words.
`\B`	Matches text not on a word boundary. For example, `/\Bp/` matches the p in the word `help` in the phrase `please help me`, but not the p in the word `please` in that same phrase. That's because the p in `please` lies at the start of a word.
`\d`	Matches any digit character. Equivalent to [0-9].
`\D`	Matches any non-digit character. Equivalent to [^0-9].
`\f`	Matches a formfeed character.
`\n`	Matches a linefeed character.
`\r`	Matches a carriage return character.
`\s`	Matches any white space including space, tab, formfeed, and so on. Equivalent to `[ \f\n\r\t\v]`.
`\S`	Matches any non-white space character. Equivalent to `[^\f\n\r\t\v]`.
`\t`	Matches a tab character.
`\v`	Matches a vertical tab character.
`\w`	Matches any word character including underscore. Equivalent to `[A-Za-z0-9_]`.

CONTINUED ➡

TABLE 5.3 continued: JScript Regular Expression Special Characters and Sequences

CHARACTER/ SEQUENCE	DESCRIPTION
\W	Matches any non-word character. Equivalent to [^A-Za-z0-9_].
\num	Matches num, where num is a positive integer. \1 matches what is stored in RegExp.$1.
/n/	Matches n, where n is an octal, hexadecimal, or decimal escape value. Allows embedding of ASCII codes into regular expressions.

The array returned by the `match` or `exec` functions contains items at several positions.

Position 0 The string that was searched.

Position 1 The index of the first match, if any.

Position 2 The index of the first character after the last match. In other words, this holds the match index in position 1 to the length of the matched portion of the string. Start at this position to search for the next match.

Position 3 The portion of the searched string that was matched.

Position 4 to n Holds matched items (duplicate of `$1...$9` properties).

The number of items in the array increases as the match list grows longer. For example, Listing 5.7 searches the word `immediate` for the regular expression `/(med)\S/`. The expression will match any occurrence of the string med followed by any character.

Listing 5.7: Match Example

```
function matchExample(re, str)
{
  var s = "";
  var arr = re.exec(str);
  for (i in arr)
   s += "\'" + arr[i] + "\'<br>";
return(s);
}
Response.Write (matchExample(/(med\S)/ig,
```

```
    "immediately") + "<br>");
// OUTPUT
// 'immediately' (string searched)
// '2' (first match index)
// '6' (index of first character
//   after first match)
// 'medi' (matched string)
// 'medi' ($1 property)
```

In addition to the information in the array shown above, when you use the pattern syntax shown in Table 5.3, the built-in properties $1 through $9 hold the results of a match operation. Listing 5.8 shows the same search as Listing 5.7, but the code displays the RegExp properties $1 through $4.

Listing 5.8: Extended Match Example

```
function matchExample(re, str)
{
  var s = "";
  var arr = re.exec(str);
  for (i in arr)
     s += "\'" + arr[i] + "\'<br>";
  s += "$1 contains: " + RegExp.$1 + "<BR>";
  s += "$2 contains: " + RegExp.$2 + "<BR>";
  s += "$3 contains: " + RegExp.$3 + "<BR>";
  s += "$4 contains: " + RegExp.$4 + "<BR>";
  s += "$5 contains: " + RegExp.$5 + "<BR>";
  s += "$6 contains: " + RegExp.$6 + "<BR>";
  return(s);
}
Response.Write
    (matchExample(/i(m{2})(e.)(i\S)(tel)(y)/ig,
    "immediately") + "<br>");
```

Figure 5.5 shows the output from Listing 5.8.

Part i

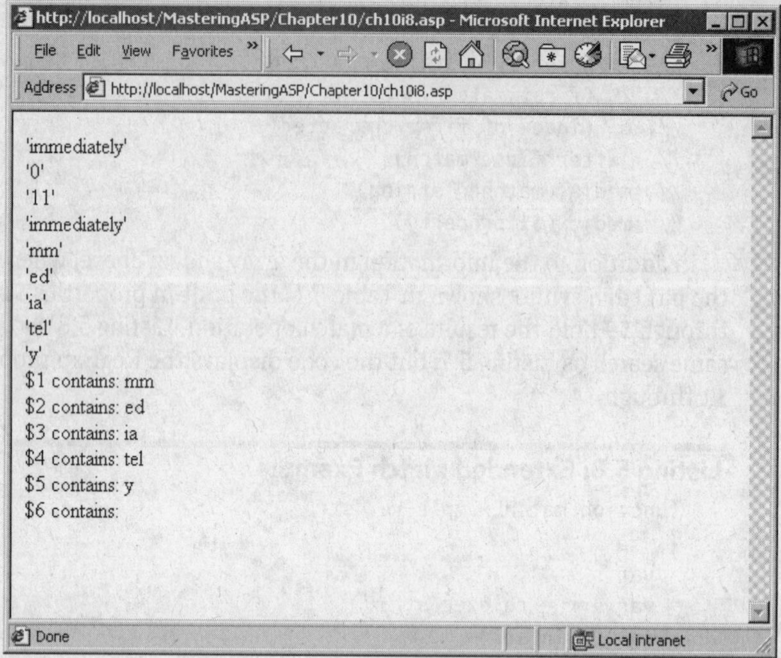

FIGURE 5.5: Extended match example

WHAT'S NEXT?

Now that you're familiar with using both VBScript and JScript as your ASP scripting language, it would help to take a step back and look at ASP as a whole. In the next chapter, you'll see how an ASP page actually works: how a browser requests your page, what IIS does to answer that request, and what the ASP object model actually looks like. Knowing this kind of behind-the-scenes structure will help you in making the right coding decisions as you begin designing your ASP applications.

PART ii
BEGINNING ASP

Chapter 6

IIS Applications

In spite of their graphical power, browsers act more like mainframe terminals than Windows clients in a client-server program. Unless you add client-side script, browsers simply display the information sent by the server. In other words, browsers show a great deal of intelligence about how to display information but little intelligence about content. To write an effective Web application, you need to understand how a browser requests information and how the server responds to each request.

Adapted from *Visual Basic® Developer's Guide to ASP and IIS*, by A. Russell Jones

ISBN 0-7821-2557-3 416 pages $39.99

How Browsers Request Files

When you type a Uniform Resource Locator (URL) into your browser's address field, many things happen. The browser parses the URL and sends a message to a Name server to translate the text name (for example, `microsoft.com`) into an Internet Protocol (IP) address (for example, `207.84.25.32`). The browser then connects to the server with that IP address and requests the file. The server reads the file and sends the contents back to the browser. The browser parses the HTML, using the embedded commands to figure out how to format the file. Most HTML files contain references to graphics. These references are in the form of URLs as well, so the entire process repeats for each graphic reference, sometimes many times for files that contain many graphics or other file references.

So, the process of displaying an HTML file consists of a series of small transactions between the client (the browser) and the server (the Web server).

IIS applications work like the Web–in small transactions. First, a client browser makes a page request to the Web server. The request is always for a specific file. The server's response depends on the type of file requested. If the file is an HTML file (having an .htm or .html extension), the server simply reads the file contents, URL-encodes the content string, and then sends the encoded string back to the requesting browser. The entire process, from request to response, is a *transaction* between a client and a server. The client always initiates the transaction, then waits until the server returns a response, at which time the transaction is complete.

The file request to the Web server is similar to what happens when you double-click a network file in Windows Explorer, with two differences:

- The Web server never lets your local application (the browser) open or write to the requested file; instead, the Web server opens the file and returns the file contents.
- The connection is *transient*. You don't need to assign a drive letter to contact the Web server. After the Web server finishes processing your request, it disconnects.

As soon as the transaction is complete, the Web server forgets all about you. If you immediately click the Refresh button, the Web server simply repeats the transaction–it doesn't remember that you requested the file five seconds ago.

With a standard Hypertext Transfer Protocol (HTTP) connection, most Web files require several such transactions–one for the base HTML file, then one for each referenced graphic in that file. So to display a file with five embedded graphics, the browser makes *six* separate requests to the Web server (see Figure 6.1).

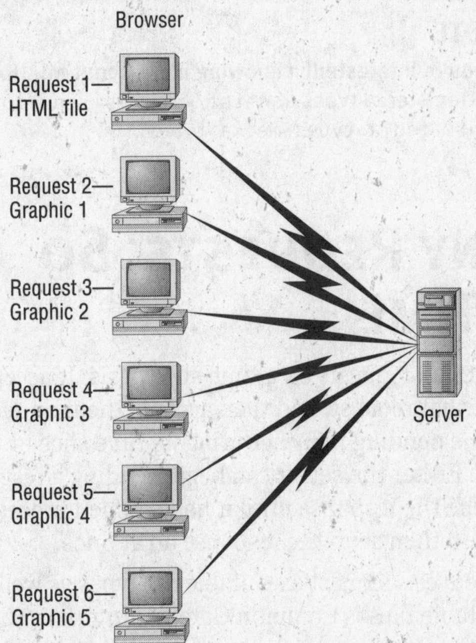

FIGURE 6.1: Browser-server request cycle

Note that in Figure 6.1 the first request is for an HTML file. The next five requests, for the graphics, are for a different file type (often referred to as the MIME type) that contains binary data. For each file type, both the server and the browser can treat the request and response differently. I won't explain all the MIME types right now; it's enough that you realize that browsers and Web servers respond differently to different kinds of files.

File extension associations control how IIS responds to file requests. These associations are stored in the Registry. This is the same method used by Windows Explorer to open the appropriate application when you double-click a file. With browsers, the MIME-type header returned by the server controls how the browser responds to different file types. MIME stands for Multipurpose Internet Mail Extensions. The server returns the file's MIME type with each request. Browsers use the MIME-type header to determine how to display the file. In most cases (text/.html files, .gif files, and .jpg files), the browser can display the files directly. For other types, such as .doc and .avi, the browser will find the MIME type in a custom list, then launch the appropriate application to display the file.

NOTE

If you're interested in knowing more about MIME, you can find a list of all the registered types at `http://www.isi.edu/in-notes/iana/assignments/media-types/media-types`.

So Many Requests, So Little Time

IIS handles all requests on a time-slice basis. It accepts a request, begins to service that request, and then accepts the next request. It continues to process the pending request during its time slice until that request is complete. Either the server can begin sending a response immediately, or it can cache the response until it has finished processing the entire request and then send the response all at once.

Browsers can request executable file types as well. The generic term for executable files is Common Gateway Interface (CGI) files or programs. As I explained in Chapter 2, you can use Visual Basic to create a CGI program. Here's a pseudocode model:

```
Read any data sent by the browser from StdIn
Process the data
Write the response to StdOut
```

When the requested file is an ASP file, the server handles the request slightly differently. It retrieves the file, either from disk or from the cache, then sends the file contents to the ASP engine.

The ASP engine parses the file to determine which parts are script code (code in ASP files is enclosed in percent signs and brackets, for example, `<% this is code %>`).

At this point, I should warn those who are thinking, "This isn't VB! I don't need to read this part!" that you really *do* need to read this part. VB's connection to the Web server is through the ASP engine. You have to work with the Web server through the objects exposed by ASP. Luckily, a Visual Basic WebClass exposes these ASP objects globally, so you don't have to declare them or receive them from an event call.

Because these objects are so important to Web applications built with Visual Basic, I'm going to explain each object briefly, then go through their properties, methods, and events in some detail, showing you how to use each one.

ASP Object Model

The ASP object model has changed very little since version 1. The version described here and that you'll work with in this book is ASP 3, but almost everything in the book will work with version 2. For those of you already familiar with ASP 1, the only significant object model changes are that the Application and Session objects expose a `Contents` property and that ASP now exposes a ScriptingContext object. The `Contents` property can be helpful when you need a list of the items stored in the Application or Session objects. Until now, you had to maintain that list yourself.

There are six objects in the ASP type library:

- Server
- Application
- Session
- Request
- Response
- ScriptingContext

Each is described in the following sections.

Server Object

There's only one Server object for a Web server. All the applications share a single Application object. In an ASP page, you use the Server object to create other object instances—this is equivalent to the Visual Basic command `Set myObject = new someObject`. The Server object also contains methods and properties to map virtual Web paths to physical paths. In other words, if your Web application is located in the `myWeb` virtual directory, you can find out where the files for `myWeb` are physically located. The Server object can also encode and decode string information for transmission to or from the HTTP protocol.

Table 6.1 lists the Server object's properties and methods.

TABLE 6.1: The Server Object

NAME	DESCRIPTION

`CreateObject` method	Returns an object instance. The following example creates a Dictionary object:
	`Dim d`
	`Set d = Server.CreateObject ("Scripting.Dictionary")`
	The `Server.CreateObject` method is equivalent to the following Visual Basic code:
	`Dim d as Dictionary`
	`Set d = new Dictionary`
	You would normally use the `CreateObject` method only from an ASP page. From VB, use the standard syntax to create a new instance of an object.

MapPath method	Returns the physical path corresponding to the virtual path parameter. Example: `MyPhysicalPath = Server.MapPath(myVirtual-Path)` You use this function to find physical file locations when you know only the virtual path (the URL) for the file. You need physical paths to read and write files.
HTMLEncode method	Encodes the string parameter in a manner suitable for transmission over HTTP.
URLEncode method	Encodes a string so that the server can transmit it via Transmission Control Protocol/Internet Protocol (TCP/IP) as a valid URL. URL encoding involves replacing non-text and numeric characters with a percent sign and the hex ASCII value of the character. For example, a space (ASCII 32) is equivalent to %20 (hex 32). You need to use this method to build valid URL strings.
`ScriptTimeout` property	Sets or returns an integer value that specifies the number of seconds the server should wait for a specific request to finish executing before it returns a timed out message to the requesting browser.

Application Object

There's one Application object for each Web application. An application, to the ASP engine, is the set of all files and subdirectories within a directory that contains a file called `global.asa`. The .asa extension stands for Active Server Application. The Application object is a container object that can hold other values. In fact, although it's not a Dictionary object, it's easiest to think of the Application object as a Dictionary. Dictionaries, like Visual Basic collections, are lists of key-value pairs.

The name for such pairs is *associations*. The association key is a string value, but the value associated with each key is a variant; therefore, each key can be associated with a value of any variant subtype, including Object and Nothing. You can use the Application object in the same way that you normally use global variables in your application. Tempting as it is, don't use the Application object to store anything except simple data types and arrays. You can't store apartment-threaded objects in the Application object, and there are good reasons not to store anything there if you don't have to. Table 6.2 lists the Application object's properties, collections, methods, and events.

TABLE 6.2: The Application Object

NAME	DESCRIPTION
Contents collection	Returns a collection of key-value associations. Because this is a collection, it also supports the `For Each`...`Next` syntax, the `Count` and `Item` properties, and the Remove method.
Lock method	Locks the Application object, restricting access to it so that only the current session can use the object. Obviously, you want to minimize the time that any given session locks the Application object. To release the lock, use the `Application.Unlock` method. If you don't release the lock, the ASP engine releases it when the current page ends.
`Unlock` method	Unlocks the Application object, freeing it for use by another session.
OnEnd event	Occurs when the last session for a Web application either times out or is abandoned (see `Session.Timeout` and/or `Session`.Abandon in the following section). You can write code to perform application cleanup in the `Application`_OnEnd event procedure in the `global.asa` file.

CONTINUED ➡

TABLE 6.2 continued: The Application Object

Name	Description
`OnStart` event	Occurs the first time that any user requests any page in your application. You can write code to perform Application-level variable initializations in the `Application_OnStart` event procedure in the `global.asa` file.
StaticObjects collection	Returns a collection of all the objects created with `<object>` tags that have been stored in the Application object. Like other collections, it has a `Count` property and an `Item` property. You can also use `For Each` to iterate through the collection. This is a read-only property.

Session Object

Each application may have many sessions, one for each user accessing the application. The Session object is a container object like the Application object. It's also similar to a Dictionary object, with keys and values. The biggest difference is that each user gets a unique Session object, whereas all users of the application share the Application object. Table 6.3 lists the Session object's properties, collections, methods, and events.

TABLE 6.3: The Session Object

Name	Description
Contents collection	Returns a collection of key-value associations. Because this is a collection, it also supports the `For Each...Next` syntax, the `Count` and `Item` properties, and the Remove method.
`SessionID` property	Returns the ID for the current session. The `SessionID` is a pseudo-random identifier that is generated automatically by the ASP engine the first time a user requests any page in the application. This is a read-only property.
`Timeout` property	Sets or returns an integer value that specifies the number of minutes before a session will expire if no activity occurs.
Abandon method	Forces the current session to expire when the current page finishes executing.

CONTINUED ➞

TABLE 6.3 continued: The Session Object

NAME	DESCRIPTION
OnEnd event	Occurs when a session times out or is abandoned. You can write code to perform end-of-session cleanup in the `Session_OnEnd` event procedure in the `global.asa` file. If the current session is the only active session, this event fires immediately before the `Application_OnEnd` event.
`OnStart` event	This event occurs the first time that any user requests any page in your application. You can write code to perform Application-level variable initializations in the `Session_OnStart` event procedure in the `global.asa` file. If the current session is the first active session in the application, this event fires immediately after the `Application_OnStart` event.
StaticObjects collection	A collection of all the objects created with `<object>` tags that have been stored in the Session object. Like other collections, it has a `Count` property and an `Item` property. You can also use `For Each` to iterate through the collection.
CodePage property	Sets or returns the CodePage used for representing characters.
LCID property	Sets or returns the `LocaleID` setting for the client machine.

WHAT'S A SESSION?

At this point, it may be useful to explain what a *session* is. Unfortunately, this is more complicated than it should be. A session begins when a user requests any file in your Web application *and* that user's browser does *not* send a valid ASP-generated SessionID cookie for that site. That's confusing, I know, but bear with me; I'll explain it shortly.

As soon as the ASP engine sees a request from a browser without a valid SessionID cookie, it creates a new Session object, generates a pseudo-random SessionID value, and sets the cookie. On all subsequent requests from that browser, the ASP engine reads the SessionID cookie and uses the value to match the Session object it

CONTINUED ➡

generated on the first request to this request. That's how ASP manages to store information about a specific user between page requests.

If the user's browser refuses the cookie (either the browser doesn't support cookies, or the user has opted to refuse them), the ASP SessionID cannot be stored in the browser, and the user will not have a valid Session object.

Note that the request created a Session object although the server can't use that Session object to save data between requests.

Because of the missing cookie value, the ASP engine won't be able to connect subsequent requests to the Session object. When the user's browser refuses the cookie, the ASP engine will create a brand new Session object for each request. Therefore, you can still use the Session object to store values when the user refuses cookies, but you will lose the values after the page is complete. Although you can code around the cookie problem, most ASP sites don't work as intended if the user's browser refuses the cookie.

NOTE

Cookies are key-value pairs stored on the client computer, either in memory (transient cookies) or on disk (permanent cookies).

Request Object

Browsers send a good deal of information to the server for each page request. You don't normally see any of this "header" information when you're browsing a site, but it is available at the server for applications to use. The ASP engine packages this information nicely in an object called the Request object. The Request object contains all this header information as well as information about the specific page request and any form information submitted by a user. You can retrieve the information through the properties and collections of the Request object. Table 6.4 lists the Request object's properties, collections, and methods.

TABLE 6.4: The Request Object

Name	Description
BinaryRead method	Reads binary information from submitted form data.
ClientCertificate collection	Returns a collection of client security certificates. You can use this to provide secure services.
Cookies collection	Returns a collection of cookies sent by the client. The Request.Cookies collection is read-only. To set, alter, or remove a cookie from the collection, use the Response.Cookies collection instead.
Form collection	Returns a collection of form key-value associations sent by the client browser. The collection contains information from the input controls enclosed in a <form> tag. The keys are the names or IDs of the controls; the values are the contents. You'll see more about this in Chapter 8.

QueryString collection	Returns a collection of key-value associations from the URL sent by the client browser. For example, if the client browser navigates to the URL `myFile.asp?Action=1 &Total=2`, there would be two values in the QueryString collection:
	`Action=1`
	`Total=2`

ServerVariables collection	Returns a collection of header key-value associations sent by the client browser. These variables are sent regardless of the method (`Post` or `Get`) used to request the page. This is a read-only property.
`TotalBytes` property	Contains the size of the client form data, in bytes, when the client sends information to the Web server via the `Post` method. This value is empty when the request method is `Get`. This is a read-only property.

Response Object

You use the methods of the Response object to send a response to the client browser. The Response object is your primary way to communicate with the client. Table 6.5 lists the object's properties, collections, and methods.

TABLE 6.5: The Response Object

NAME	DESCRIPTION
AddHeader method	Adds an HTTP header value to the page.
AppendToLog method	Logs a message to the Internet server log file.
BinaryWrite method	Writes binary information (information that should not be HTTP encoded) to the client browser.
Buffer property	As you process a request, you can either begin returning information immediately, or you can buffer the information and begin returning it only after you have completed processing the request. In practice, you will usually buffer the information; otherwise, you cannot add headers or redirect after processing begins. The Buffer property sets or returns whether the Response object will buffer information. You can set it to True or False.
CacheControl property	Controls how a client proxy server caches the page. The default value is False. Setting the value to True enables proxy servers to cache the page, which can improve the response time for ASP pages on which the information rarely changes.
Charset property	Controls which character set the browser will use to display information on the client browser.
Clear method	Clears all the information from the response buffer.
ContentType property	Lets you control the contents of the MIME-type header sent to the client browser.
End method	Ends processing immediately. The server will send any buffered information to the client browser.
Expires property	Controls how long the information you send to the client remains valid before the client must return to the server to refresh the page. You specify the interval in minutes. A value of 0 tells the browser that the page expires immediately.
Cookies collection	Provides access to the browser's cookie collection for this site. You can add and delete cookies from the collection by using the Append and Remove methods.
ExpiresAbsolute property	The Expires property lets you set the number of minutes until the content in a page is no longer valid. In contrast, the ExpiresAbsolute property lets you set a specific date and time when the information will become invalid.
Flush method	Sends the contents of the response buffer immediately.

CONTINUED →

TABLE 6.5 continued: The Response Object

Name	Description
`IsClientConnected` property	Lets you find out whether a specific SessionID is currently connected. Note that this is not a way to determine whether the client browser is still using your program, only whether it is currently requesting a page.
PICS property	Adds an HTTP header value containing a Platform for Internet Content Selection (PICS) label. The PICS label contains a rating for the page. Using this system, parents can determine the levels of content that their children can see. For more information, see the PICS specification on the W3C Web site: `http://www.w3.org`.
`Redirect` method	Sends a redirect header to the client browser specifying a page to which the browser should navigate. When the browser receives a redirect header, it immediately requests the specified page from the server.
`Status` property	Sets the value of the status line returned by the server. You've probably seen this one before: `404 Not Found`. You set the `Status` property to return a specific number and explanation to the browser.
`Write` method	You'll use this method most often. The `Response.Write` method sends string information to the browser. If buffering is on, the method appends new string information to the string that the server will return.

ScriptingContext Object

This is a wrapper object that enables an external ActiveX object to obtain references to the other ASP objects. VB 6 WebClasses provide these references automatically, so the ScriptingContext object is not important. The preferred method for gaining references to the ASP objects from external ActiveX objects is to get a reference to the ObjectContext object by calling the `getObjectContext` method.

The ScriptingContext object provides a "wrapper" that encloses all the other ASP objects in a single object that can be passed as a parameter. When a page containing ActiveX object references starts, the ASP engine calls the `OnStartPage` method for each ActiveX object on the page with a ScriptingContext object as a parameter. The ActiveX objects use the ScriptingContext parameter to gain reference pointers to the Server, Application,

Session, Request, and Response objects. Following is a list of the ScriptingContext object properties:

```
Server
Application
Session
Request
Response
```

These five properties return reference pointers to the ASP objects.

WARNING

Microsoft recommends that you use the `getObjectContext` method rather than the ScriptingContext object. Although the ScriptingContext object still exists for backward compatibility reasons, it is obsolete, and you should no longer use it.

ObjectContext Object

The ObjectContext object is the communications channel to Microsoft Transaction Server (MTS). Through MTS, you can let ActiveX objects participate in transactions initiated by an ASP page. You can also gain references to the other ASP objects through the ObjectContext object. The ObjectContext object has no properties. Table 6.6 lists its methods and events.

TABLE 6.6: The ObjectContext Object

NAME	DESCRIPTION
`SetComplete` method	Calling the `SetComplete` method tells MTS that, as far as the calling component is concerned, the transaction was a success. MTS declares the transaction successful only when all the participating components call `SetComplete`.
`SetAbort` method	Calling the `SetAbort` method tells MTS that the transaction was unsuccessful. MTS declares the transaction unsuccessful if any participating component calls `SetAbort`.

CONTINUED ➞

TABLE 6.6 continued: The ObjectContext Object

NAME	DESCRIPTION
`OnTransactionCommit` event	MTS raises the `OnTransactionCommit` event only if the transaction was successful. You can write code in an `OnTransactionCommit` subroutine to perform specific actions if the transaction is successful.
`OnTransactionAbort` event	MTS raises the `OnTransactionAbort` method only if the transaction was unsuccessful. You can write code in an `OnTransactionAbort` subroutine to perform specific actions if the transaction fails.

WEB APPLICATIONS VS. CLIENT-SERVER APPLICATIONS

Now that you've seen the ASP objects, let's explore a typical Web request. Figure 6.2 shows the entire ASP request cycle from client to server and back.

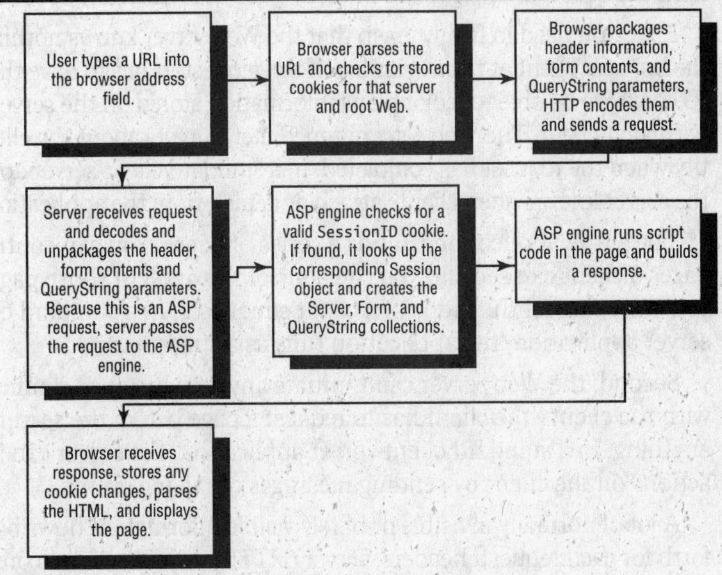

FIGURE 6.2: The ASP request cycle

I've left out some facts and processes showing how the browser finds the server's IP address and how the Web server and the ASP engine communicate, because these processes don't have any immediate bearing on Web application development.

The actions shown in Figure 6.2 occur *every time* the browser sends a request, so there's a lot of work going on behind the scenes. You need to keep the request cycle in mind because it has a direct effect on how well your applications will work and how much of a load you will place on the network and the server. For example, suppose you store 2KB of information in a cookie and update some part of that cookie for each request. Those 2,048 bytes must travel to the server and back for each subsequent request. If you have 10 clients connected, you are responsible for 40KB of network traffic above and beyond the page content, form content, or `QueryString` variables for *each page* those clients request. If you have 100 clients, you've increased network traffic by 4MB for each page.

I'm not advocating that you never use cookies—the problem is just as acute if you use `QueryString` or `Form` variables to maintain state. The point is that you want to minimize your application's footprint on the network and the server so that your application will respond quickly, scale easily, and be a good Net citizen.

Although the ASP request cycle in Figure 6.2 looks similar to a standard client-server application request cycle, it is different in several ways.

First, you need to firmly grasp that the Web server knows nothing about the browser client at the beginning of the request. It has to have the SessionID cookie to be able to look up any information stored on the server for that particular client. The Web server immediately forgets about the client's identity when the request has completed. In a standard client-server application, the server knows when clients attach or detach from the application.

The entire application runs as a series of pages. You can control which pages a client can see and you can control the order of those pages, but you can't control the scope of a client's requests. In a standard client-server application, the application runs as a single entity.

Second, the Web server can't initiate any activity on or communication with the client—the client has to request a page before the server can do anything. In a standard client-server application, the server can initiate actions on the client by sending messages or raising events.

A lot of normally invisible or barely visible information flows back and forth for each request: headers, server (HTTP) variables, form contents, URL or `QueryString` parameters and values, and cookie values. You can take advantage of these values if you're aware of them. There's no need for all this invisible information in a standard client-server application because the connection doesn't disappear; therefore, after either the client or the server transfers information, it's there for the duration of the session.

Third, after completing a request, you never know if or when the client will return. If the client does return, you can't control which page it will request next. You can't guarantee that any IDs you send to the client will be valid the next time the client requests a page, because you have no control over the time between requests. In a standard client-server application, you have some control over what happens next. In any case, you will know if the client disconnects. Because the server portion of the application has only a few entrance and exit points, you don't have problems with the client suddenly requesting unexpected pages.

The point of all this is that you have to plan Web applications differently than you plan standard applications, because you have such little control over the client portion of the application.

As an example, suppose you have built a series of three form pages that a user must fill out to complete a job application. The user completes the first page and posts it to the server. You store the page and return the next page. The second page has a Cancel button, but the user clicks the browser's Back button instead. What should you do? Redisplay the first form empty? Redisplay the first form filled in? Are you going to allow changes on the first page? Suppose the client had completed the form, then clicked back? Would you then allow the client to make changes? Suppose the client bookmarks page 2 of your form, and then uses the bookmark a week later. You don't want to display page 2 first. For your application to work correctly, you'll need to plan for and solve all these potential problems.

In contrast, in a standard client-server application, such problems rarely arise because clients don't have a Back button or a bookmarking capability unless you give it to them.

What's Next?

Handling the myriad possibilities is what creating a successful Web application is all about. In the next chapter, you'll learn how to view your application as a whole and begin planning for the different paths your visitor can take. You'll start by taking a look at the one file that ties it all together: the `global.asa` file.

Chapter 7

Introduction to ASP Applications

What is an ASP application? You can argue that any Web site that uses ASP to provide dynamic content is an ASP application. But for the purposes of this book, I'm going to define an ASP application as a set of pages that uses HTML forms and user input to store or alter persisted data on the server. In that sense, you've already seen a number of applications (albeit short ones) in this book. You should recognize that my definition doesn't cover all possible ASP applications, but it probably covers the ones you're most likely to write.

Adapted from *Mastering™ Active Server Pages 3*, by A. Russell Jones

ISBN 0-7821-2619-7 928 pages $49.99

Applications vs. Web Sites

A Web site provides information. An ASP application not only provides information. It lets users interact with that information, often adding to or altering the information, thus changing the future display of that information, either for themselves (user-specific changes) or for everyone using the application. For example, an online contact information program is user-specific; when a user enters or changes information, the display of that information changes for only that user. In contrast, when a user adds an item to a discussion group application, the display changes for everyone using the application.

In both cases, the critical factor is that the information isn't static. Users feel more involved in a Web application than in a Web site because they have to interact with (and therefore think about) the content. Because the content changes significantly over time, there are some fundamental differences between creating a Web site and creating a Web application that you should recognize. Ask these questions when you begin planning the application:

- How does the application obtain information—where's the data?
- Where should the application store information? Do you need global (application-level) information? Do you need to store data in `Session` variables?
- Must the application be moveable? Will it run on one server or on many servers? In one location or many locations?
- How many simultaneous users must the application support?
- How responsive must the application be?
- Is the application critical; will a failure cause critical business functions to be lost?
- Must the application be secure? Is the information sensitive or private? Do you require a secured site?

The answers to questions like these play a large role in determining how you should set up the application. For example, an e-commerce application may use a database to store product and order information, but use cookies to store user information during the shopping and ordering process. Only when the order is complete does the application need to update the database. On the other hand, a note-taking application needs to store user-entered information immediately, and has little need for cookies.

As the starting point for your application and for each session, you need to pay particular attention to the `global.asa` file.

THE *GLOBAL.ASA* FILE

In the previous chapter, you read about the `global.asa` file and the events that fire during Application and Session initialization and termination. Now I want to discuss the `global.asa` file in relation to an application.

To create an ASP application, you need to create a virtual directory in IIS 4 and higher, and mark it as an application using the IIS administration program. You place your `global.asa` file in the root application directory. If you don't mark the virtual directory as an application, IIS will not process the `global.asa` file at all. This is different from IIS version 3. In that version, the presence of a `global.asa` file in a virtual directory automatically made that virtual directory an application, which led to confusion when multiple directories within an application contained `global.asa` files. The new version is simpler. The rule is: IIS processes only `global.asa` files contained in a virtual directory marked as an application, and then only when the request references the virtual root directory as the root of the request. I know; that's not as simple as I had hoped, but here are some examples that may help.

First, create two physical directories. The top-level directory is `AppRoot`. The `AppRoot` directory has one subdirectory, called `App1`. Each directory contains two files, a `global.asa` file and a `default.asp` file (see Listing 7.1).

Part ii

Listing 7.1: Sample `global.asa` and `default.asp` Files

```
' ***********************************************
' Global.asa file in AppRoot
' ***********************************************
<SCRIPT LANGUAGE=VBScript RUNAT=Server>
Sub Application_OnStart
  Application("AppName") = "AppRoot"
End Sub
</SCRIPT>

' ***********************************************
```

```
' Default.asp file in AppRoot
' ************************************************
<html><head><title>
AppRoot Default File
</title></head>
<body>
<%
Response.write "Application Appname" & _
    " variable=" & Application("AppName") & _
    "<br>"
Response.write "Got to AppRoot Default File"
%>
</body>
</html>

' ************************************************
' Global.asa file in App1
' ************************************************
<SCRIPT LANGUAGE=VBScript RUNAT=Server>
Sub Application_OnStart
  Application("AppName") = "App1"
End Sub
</SCRIPT>

' ************************************************
' Default.asp file in App1
' ************************************************
<html><head><title>
App1 Default File
</title></head>
<body>
<%
Response.write "Application Appname" & _
    " variable=" & Application("AppName") & _
    "<br>"
Response.write "Got to App1 Default File"
%>
</body>
</html>
```

Each `global.asa` file creates an `Application` variable containing the name of the corresponding directory. The `default.asp` files display the value of that `Application` variable, as well as the location and name of the file. Create an AppRoot virtual directory with the physical directory pointed to the physical AppRoot directory. Create an App1 virtual directory with the physical directory pointed to the physical App1 directory. Now try running the default files. Table 7.1 shows the URL and result for each of three requests.

TABLE 7.1: Result of URL in Browser

URL	Result in Browser
`http://localhost/AppRoot/default.asp`	Application Appname variable=AppRoot Got to AppRoot Default File
`http://localhost/AppRoot/App1/default.asp`	Application Appname variable=AppRoot Got to App1 Default File
`http://localhost/App1/default.asp`	Application Appname variable=App1 Got to App1 Default File

The first and third URLs act just as you would expect; they display the value.

The `global.asa` file is different from other ASP files. When ASP receives a request, it checks to see if an Application object has been instantiated for that virtual directory. If not, it searches upward through the directory hierarchy for a `global.asa` file. ASP uses the highest-level `global.asa` file it finds in a directory marked as a virtual Web site in the IIS administration program and processes the contents.

As the starting point for your application, the location of the `global.asa` file is critical; it must reside in the root directory of the application. IIS assumes that the `global.asa` file is always at the highest directory level for your application.

Part ii

How Do *GLOBAL.ASA* Files Interact in Subdirectories?

You can mark any directory as a virtual directory. From another point of view, every virtual directory is a pointer to a physical directory. If the directory is marked as an application and contains a `global.asa` file, IIS assumes any files you run in that directory are part of that application. Therefore, if you mark a subdirectory of an existing application as another application, and you place a `global.asa` file in that subdirectory, IIS will treat it as the start of a new application. A user requesting files first in one, and then the other of those two directories, will switch applications as well as `Session` and `Application` variables each time they move between applications.

Here's a scenario. Suppose you have a directory structure for your company's intranet such that people normally enter at the top-level application. Beneath that top-level directory, you have another application directory. Each application directory contains a `global.asa` file. For example:

```
MyCompany
    App1
```

When a user requests a file in the `MyCompany` application, IIS processes the `global.asa` file in that directory (if there is one). If a user subsequently requests a file in the `App1` application, IIS will execute the `global.asa` file in the `App1` directory. Thus, from your point of view as the programmer, the user has changed applications.

Most people prefer to have a single, top-level application directory and place only subordinate content in the subdirectories because managing resources is much easier that way, but IIS lets you arrange applications in hierarchies as well.

What to Put in *GLOBAL.ASA* Files

The `global.asa` file should contain resource information, global application and session-scope `<object>` tags, and initialization and shutdown code. For example, you should create Application-level variables for connection information, file resources needed throughout the application like error log or user-specific file references, and any other values used globally for the entire application, or session-wide for a specific session.

You should try to limit declarations and assignments in `global.asa` to string resources for application startup, but you often must include database operations during the `Session_OnEnd` and `Application_OnEnd` events, because that's the only sure way to perform clean-up. Unfortunately, it's also difficult to debug Session and Application shutdown code in `global.asa` because the browser is no longer available during those events. So you can't use `global.asa` to write debug information and you won't receive any error messages from ASP because, again, the browser isn't available.

There are a few things you can do to ease this problem. First, you can develop the shutdown code in another page. Developing `global.asa` code in another page lets you use the Response object to track errors. If you develop in Visual InterDev, you can use the debugger to step through the code. You can also develop VBScript code in Visual Basic, which gives you better debugging capabilities, as long as you're careful to stick to the capabilities of VBScript and avoid features that are specific to VB. After you have the code thoroughly debugged, you can place it into the `global.asa` file. Second, you can log shutdown operations (and shutdown errors) to a file, or if you have access to the server, to the event log. I recommend you always log `global.asa` shutdown code, as there is no other way that you can track errors during production.

WHAT NOT TO PUT IN *GLOBAL.ASA* FILES

Always remember: *Do not create any apartment-threaded objects at Application or Session scope*. For example, it's tempting to create one Connection object for each Session and store it in a `Session` variable rather than creating a new Connection on each page. Avoid that temptation. Don't store Dictionary objects at Application or Session scope either.

Other than that, the only restrictions to keep in mind are that you don't have access to the Session object during the `Application_OnStart` or `Application_OnEnd` events, and you don't have access to the `Session` values during the `Session_OnEnd` event.

Useful Directory Structures

Because of the way IIS treats virtual directories, you can have applications that share data as long as you place them in a subordinate position to a virtual directory marked as an application. For example, if you own a chain of hotels, you might want an individual site for each hotel, but you would want to gather data about individuals who visit any of the sites in one location. To do that, you could set up a virtual directory as the application `root`, but place each of the hotel sites below that directory, without a `global.asa` file. When people visit one of the subordinate sites, IIS will run the `global.asa` file at the root level. Now people can move between the hotel sites and their `Session` variables will remain constant.

You can use this capability to gather statistical information about all hotel guests in one place. For example, by giving each browser a cookie, you would be able to count the number of repeat visits even if the guest chose a different hotel during the next visit to the site. You wouldn't need to have any content in the `root` directory other than a list of links to the lower-level sites.

What's Next?

For many developers, the `global.asa` file is not only one of the trickiest aspects of a Web application, but also the foundation of it as well. Now that you understand this crucial element, you're ready to begin building your project. The next chapter will walk you through the structure of an ASP application, as well as several more of its key elements. You'll also explore some extensive sample code so you can see how it all comes together.

Chapter 8

Building ASP Applications

With the `global.asa` file in place, you have essentially defined your application. Now you can begin populating that application with some ASP programming. In this chapter, you'll see how to set up an ASP Web site and how IIS maintains user data for an application. You'll also build two projects that illustrate the flexibility and power of ASP development.

Adapted from *Visual Basic® Developer's Guide to ASP and IIS*, by A. Russell Jones

ISBN 0-7821-2557-3 416 pages $39.99

Understanding the Structure of an ASP Application

An application, to the ASP engine, is the set of all files and subdirectories within a directory that contains a `global.asa` file. Most ASP applications consist of ASP files and include files, both of which can be any mixture of HTML, code, and graphics files; however, you can freely intermix ASP files with HTML files or any other file type that the server understands.

NOTE

Include files can have one of several different extensions, such as `.asp`, `.htm`, or even `.txt`. As a matter of convention, many developers use the `.inc` extension to distinguish which files are used as includes.

Figure 8.1 shows the directory structure for a typical ASP application.

Name	Size	Type
images		File Folder
include		File Folder
default.htm	2KB	HTML Document
global.asa	2KB	Active Server Application
mainMenu.asp	4KB	Active Server Document
register.asp	4KB	Active Server Document
signon.asp	4KB	Active Server Document

FIGURE 8.1: A typical ASP application directory structure

As you know, the `global.asa` file always runs first, regardless of which file was requested. At this point, you can gain control of the request by redirecting the browser to the page of your choice in the `global.asa` file. As people use your application, they're likely to save bookmarks or favorites. These bookmarks may or may not point to the starting file in your application. If your application depends on users starting at a particular point, or if you have security requirements, you should route users to the appropriate page by redirecting them in `global.asa`.

The application shown in Figure 8.1 contains several ASP files, as well as two subdirectories: `images` and `include`. No single directory structure fits all applications; you can put all the files in a single directory if you wish. In practice, though, it's much easier to build and maintain the application if you arrange files according to their function.

NOTE

The virtual Web root and the ASP application root do *not* have to be the same.

For example, you might have a single `global.asa` file that applies to several ASP applications. You could place that `global.asa` file in a directory and then define each subdirectory in that directory as a virtual root, named according to the application. The directory structure in Figure 8.2, for example, contains four applications: 401k, Paycheck, Retirement, and Timesheet.

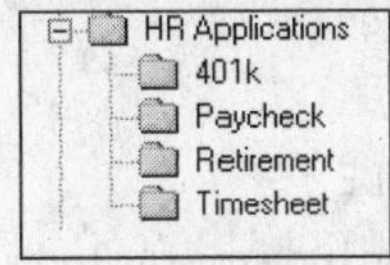

FIGURE 8.2: Directory structure with a shared `global.asa` file

The highest-level directory, called `HR Applications`, contains the `global.asa` file. Whenever a user attaches to any of the four applications, the ASP engine climbs the directory tree until it reaches the `HR Applications` level, where it finds the `global.asa` file. One reason to set up an application in this manner might be that all four sites share security arrangements. Another reason might be that all four applications share a common database connection or other data, and you want to initialize that information in the `global.asa` file.

Using Include Files

To reduce the amount of repetitive code or HTML in your ASP pages, you can *include* external files inside your ASP page. An include file is code from an external file that the server places in the ASP page at runtime. You control where the server places the content of an include file with an include *directive*. An include directive is formatted as an HTML comment, so servers that don't understand the directive will ignore it, as will browsers. The entire process is exactly the same as if you were to cut and paste the contents of the file into your ASP page. Here's an example of an include directive:

```
<!-- #INCLUDE
     FILE="c:\include\myInclude.inc" -->
```

The include directive tells the server to replace the include directive with the contents of the file—in this case, `myInclude.inc`. There are two forms of include directives: `#INCLUDE FILE` and `#INCLUDE VIRTUAL`. The `FILE` form requires a physical path for the file, whereas the `VIRTUAL` type references a file in a virtual directory.

Regardless of which form you use, the ASP engine performs all include replacements *before* it processes any code. Therefore, you cannot use code to determine *which* file to include or *whether* to include a file. The following code will not work as intended—the ASP engine will include both files.

```
<%
if myVar=True then
    %>
    <!-- #INCLUDE
    FILE="c:\include\myInclude.inc" -->
    <%
else
    %>
    <!-- #INCLUDE
    FILE="c:\include\yourInclude.inc" -->
    <%
end if
%>
```

When the ASP engine parses this file, it will replace the two include directives with the contents of `myInclude.inc` and `yourInclude.inc`—and it will make the replacement *before* it runs the code for the `if...end if` structure. This is a common misconception, so I'll repeat. Once again, with emphasis: *You cannot use code to determine which file to include and you cannot use code to determine whether a file will be included.*

Despite this, with a little planning, you can still take advantage of include files. Using the preceding example, suppose `myInclude.inc` contains the HTML to display the graphic `HappyBirthday.gif` and that `yourInclude.inc` contains HTML to display the graphic `HappyAnniversary.gif`. In this case, the code would work even though the ASP engine replaces both include directives. This time, although the ASP engine inserts the HTML code for both files, the `If...Then` structure ignores one of them, depending on the value of the `myVar` variable. Therefore, only one of the files displays on the browser, which is the intent.

Include files are useful for inserting often-used functions or subroutines into an ASP page. By placing the code in an include file, you can update all pages that reference the code by making changes in only one place. Using include files in this way is like placing your favorite routines in a module in VB.

Include files are not limited to code. I've seen many sites that use them for toolbars, common graphics, common sections of text, etc. You can create include files that are all code, all HTML, or a mixture of both–just like any other ASP page. You can and should use include files to enforce consistency and reuse code in your application.

Understanding Language Independence

ASP pages can be written in several scripting languages because the ASP engine is a *scripting host*, not a language. Currently, VBScript and JScript (Microsoft's implementation of ECMAscript) are included with the ASP engine installation, but you can also use Practical Extraction and Report Language (Perl), Restructured Extended Executor (REXX), or any language that conforms to the Microsoft debugging protocol. Almost all the code examples in this book use VBScript. However, you will see some JavaScript as well because you're going to write browser-independent applications, and you can't use VBScript for client-side script unless you're running Internet Explorer.

The ASP engine even supports pages written in more than one language. Each ASP page has a primary language, designated by the `<%@ LANGUAGE= %>` directive at the top of each page.

Within a page, however, you can use other languages by wrapping the code in `<script></script>` tags, for example:

```
<script language=someLanguage runat=server>
</script>
```

Each page in an ASP application can set the default language for that page.

If you use multiple languages on a single page, or for any server-side script contained in `<script></script>` tags, remember to include the `runat=server` parameter and value. Otherwise, the parsing engine will think you're writing client-side code. You must always keep in mind whether you're writing code that will execute on the browser or on the server. On the server, you have access to the ASP objects—the Server, Application, Session, Request, and Response objects. On the client, you have access to the document and all its properties and methods.

This can be a tough concept to master, because you probably haven't written code in an environment where you're mixing and matching server-side code, client-side code, and HTML all in a single file.

Always remember:

- Code inside code-delimiter brackets (`<% and %>`) runs on the server.
- Code outside the brackets that is wrapped in `<script>` `</script>` tags will run on the client unless the `<script>` tag includes the `runat=server` parameter.
- The ASP engine sends all other text in the page to the browser as part of the response. Usually, this other text consists of HTML tags and content.

Using the Scripting.Dictionary Object

A Scripting.Dictionary object is similar to a Visual Basic collection object, but faster and much more flexible. The documentation describes it as similar to a Perl associative array, if that helps you. Both the VB collection object and the Dictionary object have keys, values, and `Add`, `Remove`, and `Item` methods; however, for the Dictionary `Add` method you must supply the key first, then the value. The `Add` method for a VB collection requires the value first, then the key. I find the Dictionary object syntax more natural. In addition, the Dictionary object has methods to get the list of keys or values, and has an `Exists` method, which lets you find out whether a specified key exists.

In VB, to find out whether a Dictionary key exists, you would use code like this:

```
Dim d as new Dictionary
d.Add "Name", "Bill"
Debug.Print d.Exists("Name") ' prints True
```

In contrast, to find out whether a key exists in a VB collection object, you have to use `On Error Resume Next`, attempt to retrieve the value, and check for errors.

```
Sub keyExists(c as Collection, _
    aKey as string) as Boolean
    Dim V as variant
    On Error Resume Next
    V = c(aKey)
    KeyExists = (Err.Number <> 5)
End Sub
```

NOTE

The preceding code explicitly checks for `Err.Number=5` rather than just checking if any error occurred. This is because if the key exists, but the associated value is an object variable rather than a scalar variable, you will get Error 450 instead of Error 5.

The keys are strings. The values are variants, which means that they can be any data type, including objects. You can imagine that a Dictionary object looks like a table with two columns, as shown in Table 8.1.

TABLE 8.1: Dictionary Object Keys and Values Example

KEY	VALUE
"FirstName"	"John"
"LastName"	"Davis"
"City"	"Albuquerque"
"State"	"New Mexico"
"Address"	"1723 Candelaria"
"Age"	42
"Telephones"	(Array) "555-555-5555", "555-555-5556"

The keys must be unique. Having unique keys enables the Dictionary object to keep a sorted key list so that it can find any specific value with a fast binary lookup. This makes the Dictionary object larger than an array of the same size but much more efficient at finding values quickly.

Part ii

Several other features of the Scripting.Dictionary object are worth noting. Unlike a VB collection object, you don't have to use the Add method to add new items; if you assign a value to a key that doesn't exist, the Dictionary creates a new key for you.

You can change the values of associations in the Dictionary through simple assignment—you don't have to remove the key and then add it again with a new value. Here's a VBScript example:

```
Dim d
Set d = _
      Server.CreateObject("Scripting.Dictionary")
d("newKey") = "This is a new key"
Response.Write d("newKey")
      ' displays "This is a new key"
d("newKey") = "This is a changed value"
Response.Write d("newKey")
      ' displays "This is a changed value"
Response.Write d("NewKey")
      ' fails to display
```

When this code runs, it creates a new Dictionary object with one key, newKey, and one value, the string "This is a new key", which displays in the browser. The code then assigns a new value to the association with the key newKey, and displays that. Finally, to show that keys in the Dictionary object are case sensitive by default, the program tries to display the key NewKey. That statement fails to display because the Dictionary object can't find the key, but unlike referencing missing keys in a VB Collection object, it doesn't cause a runtime error.

You can control how a Dictionary object treats case sensitivity in keys by using the CompareMode property. There are three CompareMode constants defined in the Microsoft Scripting Runtime Library: BinaryCompare, TextCompare, and DatabaseCompare, which are equivalent (and equal in value) to the VBScript CompareMode constants vbBinaryCompare, vbTextCompare, and vbDatabaseCompare. One restriction: You must set the CompareMode property before adding any items to the Dictionary; otherwise, a runtime error occurs. To avoid having to define the Scripting CompareMode constants, use the built-in VBScript CompareMode constants. Alter the code so it looks like this:

```
Dim d
```

```
Set d = _
    Server.CreateObject("Scripting.Dictionary")
d.CompareMode = vbTextCompare
d("newKey") = "This is a new key"
Response.Write d("newKey")
    ' displays "This is a new key"
d("newKey") = "This is a changed value"
Response.Write d("newKey")
    ' displays "This is a changed value"
Response.Write d("NewKey")
    ' displays "This is a changed value"
```

Now, when you browse to the page, the browser displays all three lines.

Although the Object Browser lists the `DatabaseCompare` constant as one of the available `CompareMode` constants, the documentation for the Dictionary object doesn't include it as a valid value. Using it doesn't raise an error, though. As an experiment, set the `CompareMode` property of the Dictionary object to `vbDatabaseCompare` and run the file. Running it the first time appears to cause the Dictionary to treat keys as case insensitive; however, if you refresh the file, the third line disappears. Add a line to display the `CompareMode` property. The first time, the file properly displays 2, the value of the `vbDatabaseCompare` constant. If you run the file again, though, it will display the `CompareMode` property as 0, which corresponds to the `vbBinaryCompare` constant. I don't have a good explanation for this behavior (yet). Don't set the `CompareMode` property to `vbDatabaseCompare`.

Remember that, by default, Dictionary keys are case sensitive. This case sensitivity, coupled with the lack of a runtime error when you reference missing keys, goes against the case-insensitive theme of VB and VBScript and caused me several hours of frustrated debugging before I realized the reason. I don't like using the Dictionary in case-sensitive mode. If you don't either, you can avoid this problem altogether by wrapping the code that creates the Dictionary object in a function:

```
Function newDictionary()
    Set newDictionary = Server.CreateObject _
        ("Scripting.Dictionary")
    newDictionary.CompareMode = vbTextCompare
End Function
```

The function returns a case-insensitive Dictionary object.

NOTE

Like VB, VBScript uses the name of the function to return values; it creates a local variable with the same name as the function. You can often use this feature to make your code more readable, save yourself typing, and avoid the overhead of creating an extra local variable.

Table 8.2 shows the complete list of methods and properties for the Scripting .Dictionary object.

TABLE 8.2: Scripting.Dictionary Object Methods and Properties

NAME	TYPE	DESCRIPTION
Add *key, value*	Method	Adds a new string key to the Dictionary associated with the specified value. If the key already exists, an error occurs.
`CompareMode` (`CompareMethod`)	Property Get, Let	Controls the way the Dictionary object compares keys. Sets or returns one of the CompareMethod enumeration constants. `vbBinaryCompare (0)` (case-sensitive) `vbTextCompare (1)` (case-insensitive) `vbDatabaseCompare (2)` (N/A)
`Count`	Property Get (read-only)	Returns the count of the number of associations in the Dictionary object.
`Exists` *key*	Property Get (read-only)	Returns a Boolean value that shows whether the specified key exists.
`Item` *key* or *index*	Property, Get, Let, Set	Returns or sets a value associated with the specified string key or integer index.
`Items`	Method	Returns a variant array of all of the values currently stored in the Dictionary.
Key *key*	Property Let (write-only)	Changes a string key from one string to another.
Keys	Method	Returns a variant array of all of the keys currently stored in the Dictionary.
Remove *key*	Method	Removes the specified key, if it exists.
`RemoveAll`	Method	Removes all keys.

NOTE

The Microsoft VBScript documentation doesn't list the `vbDatabaseCompare` as a valid `CompareMode` value for a Dictionary object. Although it doesn't raise an error if you use it, it exhibits some strange behavior, so don't use it.

A (Very) Brief Introduction to HTML and Forms

In Chapter 3 you learned about the different controls of a form. Before you move on to the other projects in this chapter, I want to review how to actually put a form together and interact with it.

Developers originally used HTML files for read-only display of information. Very quickly though, they realized that they needed a way for people to interact with the pages—specifically, to enter form data, such as names and e-mail addresses, in a way that they could be collected on the central server. It's important to realize that the *display* portion of a form requires nothing beyond standard HTML; however, to save the information generated by a form requires a program running on the server.

All HTML files begin with an `<html>` tag and end with an `</html>` tag. This tag is a containing or block tag—a tag that contains other tags. Following, or "inside" the HTML tag, you always have `<head></head>` tags. Any tags appearing between the `<head>` and `</head>` tags are in the *head* section. The head section contains browser directives, but most importantly, it contains the document title. The title of the document goes inside `<title>` and `</title>` tags. You should be seeing a pattern here. The `</tag>` form ends a tag begun with the `<tag>` form. Tags are not case sensitive in HTML, but they are in XML, SGML, and other markup languages, so you should work on making yourself write case-sensitive HTML right from the beginning. I'm afraid I'm guilty of mixing case in tags, so don't do as I do, do as I say.

After the head section comes the *body* section, which (you guessed it) is delimited by `<body>` and `</body>` tags. All the information displayed by the browser belongs in the body section except for the title, which is in the head section.

Believe it or not, you now have enough information to write a simple HTML file. Here's an example:

```
<html>
<head>
<title>
    Extremely Simple HTML
</title>
</head>
<body>
   Enter your name,
   then click the Submit button.
</body>
</html>
```

Figure 8.3 shows how this file looks in a browser. To run it, enter the preceding code listing into Notepad or an HTML editor. Save the file, then navigate to it in the browser. I recommend you create a virtual Web site rather than simply saving the file to disk and browsing to it, because you're going to write server-side code next, which requires the Web server.

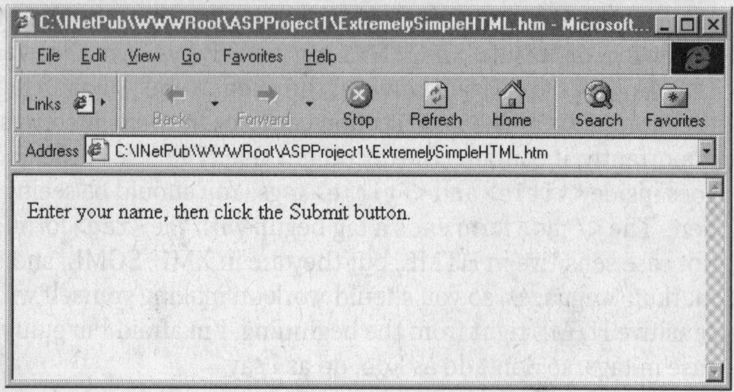

FIGURE 8.3: Extremely simple HTML file

Wait—there's no Submit button! To display a button using standard HTML, you need to create a form. (Sounds like VB, doesn't it?) An HTML form begins with a `<form>` tag and ends (like most containing HTML tags) with a </form> tag. The form tag can take several parameters; these are the most common:

Name The name of the form. Although this parameter isn't required, it's good practice to name your forms so you can refer to them easily in client-side scripts.

Action The URL to which the form will submit data. You may include additional URL-encoded variables in the value portion of the `Action` parameter (the part after the equals sign), but only if the `Method` parameter is `Post`. If you don't specify an action, the form will post itself to the originating filename (in other words, it posts to itself).

Method You can use either the `Post` or the `Get` method. If you use the `Get` method, the browser will create a URL string that consists of the action URL (minus any explicit parameters) with URL-encoded form data appended. You'll see an example of this in a minute.

Here's a very simple form:

```
<form name="frmTest" METHOD="POST"
    action="testform.asp?submitted=true">
    <input type="text" name="Text1" value="">
    <input type="submit" name="Submit"
        value="Submit">
</form>
```

Copy the form code and insert it after the line that ends with `click the Submit button`. Save the file as `TestForm.asp`. Now navigate to the file in your browser. The page should now look similar to Figure 8.4.

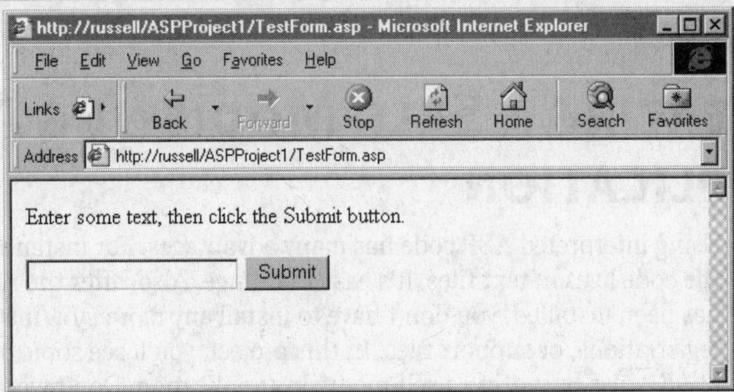

FIGURE 8.4: The `TestForm.asp` file

Enter some text in the text field and click the Submit button. Nothing happens. That's because you need to write a program to make something happen. Let's do that. Go back into the TestForm.asp file you just saved and add the following code above the <html> tag. Be sure to enter the <% and %> code delimiters.

```
<%@ Language=VBScript %>
<%
if Request("Submitted") = "true" then
     Response.Write "Request(Text1) = " & _
          Request("Text1") & "<BR>"
     Response.End
end if
%>
```

Refresh the file, enter some text into the text box, and submit the form again. This time, the server should display the text you typed.

You've just written your first ASP program. If you're not familiar with ASP and forms, I encourage you to experiment with this form a little before moving on to the next project. Specifically, you should try these tasks:

- Change the form method from Post to Get. What happens? (Hint: Look at the address line of your browser.)
- The Action parameter is optional. What happens if you delete the Action parameter from the <form> tag? What if you enter just action=?submitted=true as the parameter?
- What values besides the Text value does the form submit to the server?

Creating a Self-Modifying ASP Application

Using interpreted ASP code has many advantages. For instance, because the code lives in text files, it's easy to change. Also, after the ASP engine has been installed, you don't have to install any more DLL installations, registrations, or support files. In this project, you'll see some of the power of ASP files by writing a self-modifying application. Don't worry if you don't completely understand everything in the project at this time—you will by the time you finish this book.

Using Visual InterDev or your favorite HTML editor, start a new text file. This file will consist of a form with a drop-down selection list. When you select a color from the list and submit the form, the file will rewrite itself to reflect your choice, then redisplay itself.

Listing 8.1 shows the entire code. Note that system constants are used in several places. In order for these values to be recognized, you can set a reference to the Microsoft Scripting Runtime, or you can define the constants in an include file or in your code. I recommend that you set a reference. You can do this using the References item on the Project menu or by adding a META tag to your `global.asa` file. For example, the following line adds a reference to the Microsoft ActiveX Data Objects 2.5 library:

```
<!--METADATA TYPE="TypeLib" NAME="Microsoft ActiveX Data
Objects 2.5 Library" UUID="{00000205-0000-0010-8000-
00AA006D2EA4}" VERSION="2.5"-->
```

NOTE

The preceding line is a single unbroken comment line in the VI code editor.

Here are the constants defined for the Scripting Runtime:

```
BinaryCompare = 0
DatabaseCompare = 2
TextCompare = 1
ForReading = 1
ForWriting = 2
ForAppending = 8
TristateFalse = 1
TristateMixed = 2
TristateTrue = -1
TristateUseDefault = -2
SystemFolder = 1
TemporaryFolder = 2
WindowsFolder = 0
StdErr = 2
StdIn = 0
StdOut = 1
```

Listing 8.1: Self-Modifying ASP File (`selfMod.asp`)

```
<%@ Language=VBScript %>
<% option explicit %>
<%Response.Buffer=True%>
<%
dim submitted
dim backcolor
dim fs
dim ts
dim s
dim afilename
dim colors
dim curColor
dim V
dim aPos
dim i
set colors = server.CreateObject _
    ("Scripting.Dictionary")
colors.Add "Black", "000000"
colors.Add "Red", "FF0000"
colors.Add "Green", "00FF00"
colors.Add "Blue", "0000FF"
colors.Add "White", "FFFFFF"

submitted=(Request("Submitted") ="True")
if submitted then
    Session("CurColor")=Request("newColor")
    curColor = Session("CurColor")
    afilename=server.MapPath("selfMod.asp")
    Response.Write afilename & "<BR>"
    Response.Write Session("CurColor") & _
      "<BR>"
    set fs = server.CreateObject _
        ("Scripting.FileSystemObject")
    set ts = fs.OpenTextFile _
        (afilename,ForReading,false)
    s = ts.readall
    ts.close
    set ts = nothing
    aPos = 0
    do
```

```
        aPos = instr(aPos + 1, s, _
            "bgcolor", vbBinaryCompare)
    loop while (mid(s, aPos + 7, 1) <> "=")
    aPos = aPos + 9
    if aPos > 0 then
        s = left(s, aPos) & _
            Session("CurColor") & _
            mid(s, aPos + 7)
        set ts = fs.OpenTextFile _
            (afilename,ForWriting,false)
        ts.write s
        ts.close
        set fs = nothing
        Response.Redirect "selfMod.asp"
    else
        set fs = nothing
        Response.Write _
            "Unable to find the position" & _
            " in the file to write the" & _
            " new color value."
        Response.End
    end if
else
    if isEmpty(Session("Curcolor")) then
        Session("CurColor") = "FF0000"
    end if
    curColor = Session("CurColor")
end if
%>
<html>
<head>
</head>
<body>
<form name="frmColor" method="post"
    action="selfmod.asp?Submitted=True">
<input type="hidden" value="<%=curcolor%>">
<input type="hidden"
    value="<%=Session("curcolor")%>"
    id=hidden1 name=hidden1>
<table align="center" border="1"
    width="80%" cols="2">
    <tr>
```

```
            <td align="center" colspan="2"
               bgcolor="#FF0000">
                <% if curColor = "000000" then %>
                    <font color="#FFFFFF">
                <% else %>
                    <font color="#000000">
                <% end if %>
                Select A Color
                    </font>
            </td>
        </tr>
        <tr>
            <td align="left" colspan="2"
               bgcolor="#FFFFFF">
                Select a color from the list,
                then click the "Save Color Choice"
                button.
            </td>
        </tr>
        <tr>
            <td align="right" valign="top"
               width="20%">
                <b>Color</b>:
            </td>
            <td align="left" valign="top"
               width="80%">
                <select name="newColor">
                    <%
                    for each V in colors
                      Response.Write "<option "
                      if colors(V)=curColor then
                         Response.Write _
                           "selected "
                         end if
                         Response.Write _
                           "value='" & _
                           colors(V) & "'>" & V
                         for i = 1 to 12
                           Response.Write " "
                         next
                         Response.Write _
                           "</option>"
```

```
                        next
                        %>
                    </select>
                </td>
            </tr>
            <tr>
                <td align="center" valign="bottom"
                   colspan="2">
                <input type="submit"
                   value="Save Color Choice"
                    id=submit1 name=submit1>
                </td>
            </tr>
        </table>
        </form>
        </body>
        </html>
        <%set colors = nothing%>
```

Web development environments such as Visual Basic and Visual InterDev create Web applications for you automatically, but if you're not using one of these tools, you'll need to create one manually.

If you're still using IIS 3, ignore this procedure. If you're using IIS 4, though, you must create a Web application before IIS will run the `global.asa` file. If you ever notice that an application isn't running any of the code in `global.asa`, you should check to make sure that the virtual directory containing your `global.asa` file is marked as a Web application. To mark the virtual directory for your project as an application, open the Internet Service Manager, select or create your application's virtual directory, then right-click the virtual directory name in the left-hand pane.

Look at the button to the right of the Name field in the Application Settings portion of the Virtual Directory properties dialog. If the button's caption is Create, click the button to create a new Web application, then enter the name for the application in the Name field. If the button is called Remove, then the directory is already marked as a Web application, and you don't need to do anything (see Figure 8.5).

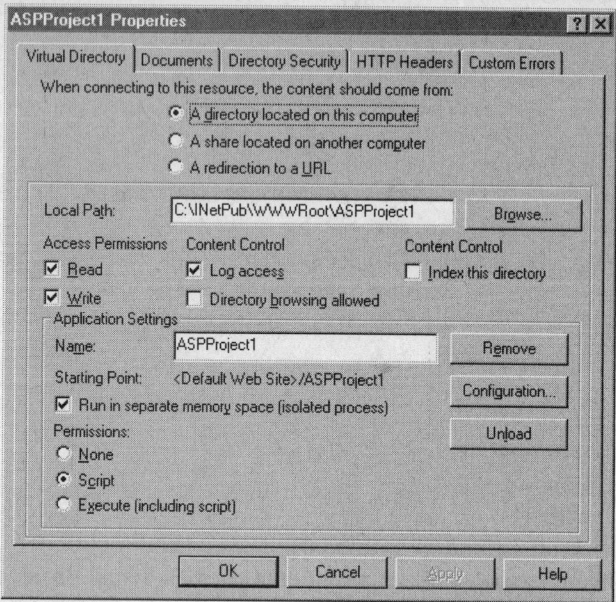

FIGURE 8.5: Internet Service Manager Virtual Directory properties

SETTING UP THE PROJECT IN VISUAL INTERDEV

To set up the project outlined in this section in Visual InterDev, you should reference the Microsoft Scripting Runtime Library. You'll also need to allow write access to the virtual directory through the Internet Service Manager program before the project will work. To specify write access, open the Internet Service Manager program, find your virtual directory in the Default Web Site, and right-click it. Select Properties. In the dialog box, make sure the Write check box is checked. For IIS 4, the dialog box looks like Figure 8.5.

In the rest of this chapter, I'll explain the code in the `selfMod.asp` file.

```
<%@ Language=VBScript %>
```

This line is required in every ASP file (but of course, the language doesn't have to be VBScript—remember, ASP files can host multiple languages).

```
<% Option Explicit %>
```

Just as in VB, the `Option Explicit` command forces you to declare variables before you use them. Although the command is not required, you should always use this in both ASP and VB.

```
<%Response.Buffer=True%>
```

The server normally writes the HTTP headers immediately, then begins sending output as the ASP engine generates it. If you want to redirect within your code (which requires a change to the HTTP headers), you have to include this line. When you set the `Response.Buffer` property to `True`, the server buffers the entire response until page processing is complete. For long requests, this can slow down the perceived response time, because the user has to wait until the entire request has finished processing before the browser can begin to display the result. You should usually use this command in a page only if you plan to redirect, write cookies, or alter the HTTP headers.

```
set colors = _
     Server.CreateObject("Scripting.Dictionary")
```

There are several things to explain in this line. First, the `Server.CreateObject` method is equivalent to the following VB code:

```
Dim colors as Dictionary
Set Colors = New Dictionary
```

In an ASP file, you need to enter both the project name (`Scripting`) and the class name (`Dictionary`) to obtain a reference to an object.

At any rate, the next five lines simply add the colors to the Dictionary object with the color name as the key and the HTML color string (which is a text representation of a long, or RGB, value) as the value. Each of the six-character strings represents three hexadecimal byte values. Colors are a combination of red, green, and blue. Each color may take a value from 0 to 255 (00 to FF in hex) and requires two characters. You read the value in pairs. The pairs of characters represent the red, green, or blue values, respectively.

```
colors.Add "Black", "000000"
colors.Add "Red", "FF0000"
colors.Add "Green", "00FF00"
colors.Add "Blue", "0000FF"
colors.Add "White", "FFFFFF"
```

This form submits to itself by posting the values entered by the user back to the same page that the form came from—unheard of for straight

Part ii

HTML forms, but common as dirt with ASP files. Submitting a form to itself puts all the code that deals with the form in one file, where you can test it easily, and makes one less file to maintain. If the user has submitted the form, you want to process the submitted request; otherwise, you just want to display the form. The following line determines whether the form is being shown for the first time or whether the user has submitted the form. The Request object will contain a string value of `"Submitted=True"` if the form has been submitted. The following code assigns a local variable called `submitted` a Boolean value of `True` if the form was submitted by the user:

```
submitted=(Request("Submitted") ="True")
if submitted then
    Session("CurColor")=Request("newColor")
    curColor = Session("CurColor")
```

NOTE

In the preceding code, note that you do not have to dimension Session variables before using them—even if `Option Explicit` is in effect.

Another way to test whether a user has posted a form is to check the value of `Request.ServerVariables("REQUEST_METHOD")`. The value will be `POST` when the user has posted content, and `GET` when you should display the form. I've used both and prefer using the local variable method. I find that using a local variable is more intuitive and works regardless of whether you use the `Post` or `Get` method.

You can think of the Session object as a Dictionary object (although it's not) because it exhibits almost identical behavior:

```
afilename=Server.MapPath("selfMod.asp")
```

The `Server.MapPath` method translates a virtual directory or filename into a physical directory or filename. In this case, when you pass it the name of the current file, it will return the full physical `drive:\pathname\filename` for the file. On my system, it returns

```
"c:\inetpub\wwwroot\ASPProject1\selfMod.asp"
```

The next few lines create two of the other objects in the Microsoft Scripting Runtime Library—a FileSystemObject and a TextStream object. The FileSystemObject provides methods and properties to work with the native file system. One of those methods is the `OpenTextFile` method, which returns a TextStream object. The TextStream object lets you read from and write to text files. In this case, open the file in read-only mode, then read the entire file at one time by using the ReadAll method. Finally, close the TextStream.

```
set fs = server.CreateObject _
     ("Scripting.FileSystemObject")
set ts = fs.OpenTextFile _
     (afilename,ForReading,false)
s = ts.readall
ts.close
set ts = nothing
```

At this point, the content of the string "s" is the same as the file that's running! You can do this because the ASP engine doesn't lock the file while it's executing—it reads the whole file into memory. You're going to search the string for the first occurrence of the word bgcolor that's followed by an equals sign.

```
aPos = 0
do
     aPos = instr(aPos + 1, s, "bgcolor", _
       vbBinaryCompare)
loop while (mid(s, aPos + 7, 1) <> "=")
aPos = aPos + 9
```

The code loops to find the last occurrence of the word bgcolor because the first occurrence is inside the loop itself! The final line sets the value of the aPos variable to point to the color string value in the first row of the table—the position after the first pound (#) sign in the file, right before the color value you're going to update.

After it finds the position of the color string for the first row of the table, the code simply substitutes the selected color value and saves the file. It then redirects so that the browser will request the just-altered file.

```
if aPos > 0 then
     s = left(s, aPos) & _
          Session("CurColor") & _
          mid(s, aPos + 7)
     set ts = fs.OpenTextFile _
          (afilename, ForWriting, _
          false)
```

```
        ts.write s
        ts.close
        set fs = nothing
        Response.Redirect "selfMod.asp"
    else
        set fs = nothing
        Response.Write _
            "Unable to find the position" & _
            " in the file to write the" & _
            " new color value."
        Response.End
    end if
```

If the form was not submitted, the file provides a default color value of red—FF0000—and assigns it to both a Session variable and a local variable called `curColor`. In general, you should assign Session variable values to local variables if you're going to use them more than once in a file, because looking up the Session variable value based on the key you provide takes several times longer than simply retrieving the value of a local variable. This follows the same principle you use in VB; always assign objects to local variables if you're going to use them more than once in a routine. Similarly, it's the principle behind the introduction of the `With...End With` block in VB. Local references are much faster than COM references.

```
if isEmpty(Session("Curcolor")) then
    Session("CurColor") = "FF0000"
end if
curColor = Session("CurColor")
```

That's almost all the VBScript code in the file. The remainder of the file displays the table, the drop-down list, and the button inside a `<form>` tag.

```
<form name="frmColor" method="post"
    action="selfmod.asp?Submitted=True">
```

There are several types of input controls. The available input types correspond roughly to text fields, buttons, combo boxes, and list boxes, although they act slightly differently than the equivalent Windows common controls.

You saw the text field and submit button types in the previous project. The drop-down list is slightly different. It's not an `<input>` tag at all, it's a `<select></select>` tag. The `<select>` tag contains a list of `<option>` tags that contain the list data. Each option tag can take a `value` parameter that specifies the value returned to the server. By default, the browser returns the option value for the item that's visible in the drop-down list. This is similar to a VB list box, which contains both visible items and `itemdata`. The ItemData array contains a list of long values, one for each item in the list. In contrast, the `<option>` tag can take any type of value, although it returns them all as text. You can also preselect a specific option by adding a `selected` parameter to that option tag. The `selected` parameter does not require a value.

One special type of input control is hidden. A hidden input doesn't display, so you can use it to pass values from one file to another. In this case, I'm using hidden inputs just so you can view the value by selecting View Source from the browser.

```
<input type="hidden" value="<%=curcolor%>">
<input type="hidden"
     value="<%=Session("curcolor")%>">
```

This is a trivial example that you would never use in practice because you would have problems if more than one person accessed the file. However, it does illustrate two important points about ASP files:

- *Because ASP files are text files, you can change them easily.* To update an ASP-based application, you simply update the text files that contain the application code. No registration entries to worry about, no need to stop the server, no DLLs or large executables, and no installation programs to write. That's powerful stuff.
- *ASP files can rewrite themselves.* You can't do that in VB (although you can write VB code that writes ASP pages). You can do this because the code contained in the ASP file is loaded into memory for compilation from the ASP file. After the file is loaded, the ASP engine releases the file lock. Depending on your server settings, the ASP engine can cache the file—but it does check to see if the file has changed for each request. Therefore, when you change the file, the ASP engine will display the contents of the changed file for the next request.

In the next section, you'll learn how to cache data in HTML or simple ASP files, rewriting them as needed when the data changes.

TYING IT ALL TOGETHER—CACHING TABLE DATA

Imagine that, instead of changing a color value, you wanted to display the contents of a table. Sure, you can query a database for each request, but if the table data didn't change often, wouldn't it be nice if you could "cache" the table in an HTML file? And whenever the table data changed, you could re-create the HTML file.

I'm going to present the project here despite the data access requirements. Those of you who are not familiar with ActiveX Data Objects (ADO) may want to return to this example after reading Chapter 16. You can also read up on ADO by taking a look at the *VB Developer's Guide to ADO* by Mike Gunderloy (Sybex, 1999).

NOTE

The `pubs` database comes with SQL Server. If you don't have SQL Server, you can download a Microsoft Access database containing the tables of the `pubs` database from the Sybex Web site.

This project consists of one ASP file. Each time you run the file, it lets you select a table from the `pubs` database. When you submit your selection, the program checks to see whether it already has the table data cached in an HTML file. If the table cache file exists, the ASP file simply returns the contents of the HTML file. If the table cache file does not exist, the program reads the table from the database, writes a cache file, then displays the contents of the file. The program also refreshes cached data if you pass a `Refresh=True` parameter in the URL. Administrators could use this feature to force the cached data to refresh.

NOTE

To download code (including the Access database), go to `http://www.sybex.com`. Click Catalog and search for this book's title. Click the Downloads button and accept the licensing agreement. Accepting the agreement grants you access to the downloads page for the book.

The complete code for the program is in Listing 8.2 at the end of this chapter. Just like the code in the previous project in this chapter, the `selectTable.asp` file is a form that submits to itself. The first part of this file contains the logic needed to differentiate between a request containing form data (Submitted=True) and an unsubmitted request, before the user has selected a table to display. Unlike the previous project, though, this one gets all its information from a database by using ADO. To read database information, you need to open a connection to the database:

```
Set conn = _
    Server.CreateObject("ADODB.Connection")
conn.ConnectionString="pubs"
conn.CursorLocation= adUseClient
conn.Mode= adModeRead
conn.Open
```

In this case, you create the Connection object and set its ConnectionString property to a valid Data Source Name (DSN), pubs. Next, you set the Connection object's CursorLocation property to adUseClient, which tells the Connection object that you're going to use open database connectivity (ODBC) client cursors rather than SQL Server server-side cursors for any recordsets you retrieve using the connection. Because you're only going to be reading data, not updating, you set the Mode property to adModeRead. Finally, you open the connection using the Open method of the Connection object.

Next, you want to retrieve information about the tables in the database so you can populate the drop-down list. To do that, you need to get a recordset from the connection.

```
set R = Server.CreateObject("ADODB.Recordset")
R.CursorLocation=aduseclient
call R.Open("SELECT Name FROM SysObjects" & _
    " WHERE Type='U' ORDER BY Name ASC", _
    conn, adOpenForwardOnly, adLockReadOnly, _
    adCmdText)
end if
```

This code creates a Recordset object, tells it to use a client-side cursor, and to get a list of all tables in the pubs database. The rest of the code in the file displays the data from the recordset. It's fairly straightforward and similar to the code in the previous project, so I won't spend any time on it.

When the user selects a table from the drop-down list, the code redirects to the relative URL showTable.asp. You'll use redirection extensively in Web applications to provide messages and feedback, and to process requests based on user selections or input. The `Response.Redirect` method sends a header to the client browser. The header essentially means that the browser can find the information requested at a new address. The browser immediately makes a new request to the server for the specified page. So, (right now) redirection requires a round-trip to the client.

NOTE

Microsoft will soon provide server-side redirection, which won't require the round-trip to the client and will therefore be much more efficient.

The `showTable.asp` file contains almost no static HTML—just the bare minimum markup and two placeholders for the table data.

```
<html>
<head>
</head>
<body>
<!--Start--><!--End-->
</body>
</html>
```

The first thing the `showTable.asp` file does is check the `TableName` parameter. If the parameter is empty, the program redirects the user "back" to the `selectTable.asp` file:

```
if Request.QueryString("TableName") = "" then
    Response.Redirect "selectTable.asp"
end if
```

This code exists because, as I stated earlier, you don't know and can't control the order in which a user might request files from your application. If users simply type the URL to `showTable.asp` into their browsers, the program wouldn't know which file to display. Simply displaying whichever table the file may currently contain might be confusing; therefore, the code forces the user to make a choice before displaying any table.

Next, it caches the `TableName` parameter in a local variable:

```
requestedTablename= _
    Request.QueryString("TableName")
```

If the requested table name is the same as the previous request, the file simply shows the data already cached in the file; otherwise, it reads and formats the table data. It also refreshes the table data if you pass a "Refresh=True" parameter in the URL. You'll need some way to refresh the file if the table data changes. An "optional" parameter such as this gives you the opportunity to refresh the file if, for example, an administrator changes the data. Another way of doing this is to keep track of the data by looking at the highest Identity value (AutoNumber in Access), the date/time at which the table was last changed, or via a trigger that updates a row in a separate table whenever data in the main table is changed.

In this project, you "change" the table data by selecting a different table or by passing a "Refresh=True" parameter to the ASP page:

```
if requestedTablename <> tablename or _
  Request.QueryString("Refresh") = "True" then
  ' open the file, change the contents to that
  ' of the new table, then save the file.
End if
```

The process of opening a file is similar each time. You query the Server object by using the MapPath function to obtain the physical path for the file.

```
set fs = server.CreateObject _
    ("Scripting.FileSystemObject")
aFilename = server.MapPath("showTable.asp")
set ts = fs.OpenTextFile _
    (afilename,ForReading,false)
s = ts.readall
ts.close
set ts = nothing
```

TIP

Microsoft's documentation states that one way to speed up sites is to limit or eliminate the use of the MapPath function. For greatest efficiency, you should cache path information in Application or Session variables when appropriate. Don't ever hard-code file paths in a Web application unless you're absolutely sure that the path will never change.

Next, you'll want to replace the old table name with the selected table name. Find the old table name parameter and value in the file string. Use VB's new replace function to perform string replacements.

```
s = replace(s, "tablename=" & _
        chr(34) & tablename & _
        chr(34), "tablename=" & _
        chr(34) & requestedTablename & _
        chr(34), 1, 1, vbBinaryCompare)
```

Now replace the table data. Because browsers ignore comments, you can conveniently use them as markers inside HTML files. I've used the two comment tags `<!-Start-->` and `<!-End-->` to mark the beginning and end positions for the table data. To make the replacement, you need to find the markers.

```
do
        startPos = instr(startPos+1, s, _
            "<!--Start",vbBinaryCompare)
loop while mid(s, startPos + 9 ,1) <> "-"
startPos=startPos + len("<!--Start") + 3
do
        endPos = instr(endPos + 1, s, _
        "<!--End", vbBinaryCompare)
loop while mid(s, endPos + 7, 1) <> "-"
```

To get the data, you create a database connection and read the data from the selected table.

```
set conn = server.CreateObject _
        ("ADODB.Connection")
conn.ConnectionString="pubs"
conn.CursorLocation=aduseclient
conn.Mode= adModeRead
conn.Open
set R = Server.CreateObject("ADODB.Recordset")
R.CursorLocation=aduseclient
set R = conn.Execute("SELECT * FROM " & _
        requestedtablename,,adCmdText)
```

Whenever you retrieve data, you should check to make sure that the data you think is there is actually there. The `Execute` method returns a recordset regardless of whether it retrieves any data. Always check the recordset's `End-of-File` (`EOF`) property. The property will return `True` if the recordset is empty—that is, if no rows were retrieved. If the recordset contains data, then you can format the column headers by using the `Field.Name` property to get the name of each column.

```
if not R.EOF then
    tableData="<table align='center'" & _
       " border='1' width='95%' COLS='" & _
       R.Fields.Count & "'>"
    sTmp="<TR>"
    for each F in R.Fields
        sTmp = sTmp & "<TD><B>" & _
               F.Name & "</B></TD>"
    next
    sTmp = sTmp & "</TR>"
    tableData = tableData & sTmp
end if
```

At the end of this loop, the recordset is still on the first row. You loop until the EOF property becomes true, placing each field value in a table cell. Note that this is a nested loop; the outer loop creates the rows while the inner loop fills the columns with data.

```
while not R.EOF
    sTmp = "<TR>"
    for each F in R.Fields
        if (F.Attributes and adFldLong) = _
          adFldLong then
            if F.Type=adLongVarBinary then
                sTmp = sTmp & _
                "<TD valign='top'>" & _
                "(binary)</TD>"
            elseif F.ActualSize=0 then
                sTmp = sTmp & _
                "<TD valign='top'> </TD>"
            else
                sTmp = sTmp & _
                "<TD valign='top'>" & _
                F.GetChunk(F.ActualSize) & _
                "</TD>"
```

```
                end if
            else
                if isNull(F.Value) then
                    sTmp = sTmp & _
                    "<TD valign='top'> </TD>"
                else
                    sTmp = sTmp & _
                    "<TD valign='top'>" & _
                    F.Value & " </TD>"
                end if
            end if
        next
        sTmp = sTmp & "</TR>"
        tableData = tableData & sTmp
        R.MoveNext
    Wend
```

You need to decide what to do if the recordset does not contain any rows. In this case, the program returns a message in the first table row.

```
tableData= "There is no data in the" & _
    " table: " & requestedTablename & ".<BR>"
```

Finally, don't forget to close the recordset and the connection and set them to `Nothing`. Setting them to `Nothing` frees up the memory. Strictly speaking, you don't have to do this at the end of a page because the ASP engine destroys the objects and frees the memory for variables created during page processing when the page ends. However, it's good practice for you to clean up explicitly. It also frees the memory somewhat sooner than the ASP engine can.

```
R.Close
set R = nothing
conn.Close
set conn= nothing
```

Finally, concatenate the table data into the file string between the start and end position markers in the file, then write the file string to disk.

```
s = left(s, startPos) & tableData & _
    mid(s, endPos)
```

```
set ts = fs.OpenTextFile _
     (afilename,ForWriting,false)
ts.write s
ts.close
set ts = nothing
set fs = nothing
```

Now the file is ready to display, so you can redirect to the file you just wrote.

```
Response.Redirect "showTable.asp?" & _
     "TableName=" & requestedTablename
```

Listing 8.2: Code for Providing Fast Access to Table Data ASP Project (`selectTable.asp` and `showTable.asp`)

```
'****************************************
' The selectTable.asp file
'****************************************
<%@ Language=VBScript %>
<% option explicit %>
<%Response.Buffer=True%>
<%
dim submitted
dim tablename
dim R
dim conn
submitted=(Request("Submitted") ="True")
if submitted then
     Response.Redirect _
       "showTable.asp?TableName=" & _
       Request("TableName")
Else
     set conn = server.CreateObject _
       ("ADODB.Connection")
     conn.ConnectionString= _
       "DSN=pubs;UID=sa;PWD="
     conn.CursorLocation=aduseclient
     conn.Mode= adModeRead
     conn.Open
     set R = Server.CreateObject _
       ("ADODB.Recordset")
     R.CursorLocation=aduseclient
```

Part ii

```
        call R.Open("SELECT Name FROM " & _
          "SysObjects WHERE Type='U' " & _
          "ORDER BY Name ASC", _
          conn, adOpenForwardOnly, _
          adLockReadOnly,adCmdText)
    end if
    %>
    <html>
    <head>
    <meta name="generator"
       Content="Microsoft Visual Studio 6.0">
    </head>
    <body>
    <form name="frmTable" method="post"
       action="selectTable.asp?Submitted=True">
    <table align="center" border="1"
       width="80%" cols="2">
         <tr>
           <td align="center" colspan="2"
            bgcolor="#FF0000">
              Select Table</font>
           </td>
         </tr>
         <tr>
           <td align="left" colspan="2"
            bgcolor="#FFFFFF">
              Select a table name from
              the list, then click the
              "Display Table" button.
           </td>
         </tr>
         <tr>
           <td align="right" valign="top"
            width="20%">
              <b>Table</b>:
           </td>
           <td align="left" valign="top"
            width="80%">
              <select name="TableName">
                <%
                do while not R.EOF
                  Response.Write "<option "
                  if R("Name").value = _
```

```
                tableName then
                Response.Write "selected "
              end if
              Response.Write "value='" & _
                R("Name") & "'>" & _
                R("Name") & "</option>"
              R.movenext
            loop
            R.close
            set R = nothing
            conn.Close
            set conn=nothing
            %>
          </select>
        </td>
      </tr>
      <tr>
        <td align="center" valign="bottom"
        colspan="2">
          <input type="submit" value="Display
           Table">
        </td>
      </tr>
</table>
</form>
</body>
</html>

****************************************
 ' The showTable.asp file
****************************************
<%@ Language=VBScript %>
<% option explicit %>
<%Response.Buffer=true%>
<%
dim submitted
dim tablename
dim tabledata
dim sTmp
dim requestedTablename
dim afilename
dim fs
dim ts
```

Part ii

```
dim s
dim startPos
dim endPos
dim conn
dim R
dim F
tablename="authors"
if Request.QueryString("TableName") = "" then
  Response.Redirect "selectTable.asp"
end if
requestedTablename= Request.QueryString _
  ("TableName")
if requestedTablename <> tablename or _
  Request.QueryString("Refresh") = "True" _
  then _
   set fs = server.CreateObject _
     ("Scripting.FileSystemObject")
   aFilename = server.MapPath("showTable.asp")
   set ts = fs.OpenTextFile _
     (afilename,ForReading,false)
   s = ts.readall
   ts.close
   set ts = nothing
   s = replace(s, "tablename=" & chr(34) & _
     tablename & chr(34), "tablename=" & _
     chr(34) & requestedTablename & _
     chr(34),1,1,vbBinaryCompare)
   do
     startPos = instr(startPos+1, s, _
     "<!--Start",vbBinaryCompare)
   loop while mid(s, startPos + 9 ,1) <> "-"
   startPos=startPos + len("<!--Start") + 3
   do
     endPos = instr(endPos + 1, s, _
       "<!--End", vbBinaryCompare)
   loop while mid(s, endPos + 7, 1) <> "-"
   set conn = server.CreateObject _
     ("ADODB.Connection")
   conn.ConnectionString="pubs"
   conn.CursorLocation=aduseclient
   conn.Mode= adModeRead
   conn.Open
   set R = Server.CreateObject _
```

```
  ("ADODB.Recordset")
R.CursorLocation=aduseclient
set R = conn.Execute("SELECT * FROM " & _
  requestedtablename,,adCmdText)
if not R.EOF then
   tableData="<table align='center'" & _
     " border='1' width='95%' COLS='" & _
     R.Fields.Count & "'>"
   sTmp="<TR>"
   for each F in R.Fields
     sTmp = sTmp & "<TD><B>" & _
       F.Name & "</B></TD>"
   next
   sTmp = sTmp & "</TR>"
   tableData = tableData & sTmp
   while not R.EOF
     sTmp = "<TR>"
     for each F in R.Fields
       if (F.Attributes and adFldLong) = _
       adFldLong then
         if F.Type=adLongVarBinary then
           sTmp = sTmp & _
             "<TD valign='top'>" & _
             "(binary)</TD>"
         elseif F.ActualSize=0 then
           sTmp = sTmp & _
             "<TD valign='top'>" & _
             " </TD>"
         else
           sTmp = sTmp & _
             "<TD valign='top'>" & _
             F.GetChunk(F.ActualSize) & _
             "</TD>"
         end if
       else
         if isNull(F.Value) then
           sTmp = sTmp & _
           "<TD valign='top'>" & _
           " </TD>"
         else
           sTmp = sTmp & _
           "<TD valign='top'>" & _
           F.Value & " </TD>"
```

Part ii

```
            end if
          end if
        next
        sTmp = sTmp & "</TR>"
        tableData = tableData & sTmp
        R.MoveNext
      wend
    else
      tableData= "There is no data" & _
        " in the table: " & _
        requestedTablename & ".<BR>"
    end if
    R.Close
    set R = nothing
    conn.Close
    set conn= nothing
    s = left(s, startPos) & tableData & _
      mid(s, endPos)
    set ts = fs.OpenTextFile _
      (afilename,ForWriting,false)
    ts.write s
    ts.close
    set ts = nothing
    set fs = nothing
    Response.Redirect _
      "showTable.asp?TableName=" & _
      requestedTablename
end if
%>
<html>
<head>
</head>
<body>
<!--Start-->
<!--End-->
</body>
</html>
```

What's Next?

You've set the table, seated the guests, and given them a menu. How do you remember what they ordered? How do you help them navigate through each course of the meal? Somehow your application must remember each visitor's current *state*. It must accept, remember, and respond to the visitor's feedback. The next chapter explains how to do just that. In fact, you'll find several different methods for maintaining state in your application, as well as the drawbacks and benefits of each. Soon you'll have your visitors eating out of your hand.

Chapter 9

State Maintenance in ASP Applications

State maintenance is the process of keeping track of the state of your application as it applies to a specific individual or to the application as a whole. One example is a shopping cart at an e-commerce site. As a potential customer moves from page to page placing items into the cart, you need to maintain the list of items selected. If the customer purchases one or more items from the cart, you must remove those, but maintain the remaining items. You may also need to know other information about that person: whether they've ever visited the site before, what they bought or selected during previous visits, what promotions or discounts apply to that person, etc.

You definitely need to keep track of this information during any specific visit, but you probably have longer-term storage needs as well. What if the customer leaves, but returns in half an hour? Do you make the customer re-select each item? If not,

Adapted from *Mastering™ Active Server Pages 3*, by A. Russell Jones

ISBN 0-7821-2619-7 928 pages $49.99

how long should you maintain the information? For one day? For one month?

In this chapter, you'll see the various options for state maintenance and the advantages and disadvantages of each.

Don't Cache Data

"The best Web application doesn't need to cache data; it's a stateless application." I've seen this statement over and over in the press and have come to believe that stateless applications aren't really applications, they're Web sites. If you don't need to maintain the state of your application, then your application doesn't do anything other than allow the user to click links. If your application involves security or user input, you must maintain state. What the term *stateless* application really means is that you persist information between pages either on the client or the server in such a way that you can retrieve the applicable state during each request. In other words, the application doesn't use `Session` variables, `Application` variables, or (in some cases) cookies.

These applications are called stateless because you don't maintain the state in memory; you retrieve state as needed. You then use that state information to service the request, alter the information if necessary, and store it again at the end of the request. Each time you see *stateless application* in this book, think of it as meaning applications that retrieve persisted-state information for each request.

You maintain state in a typical client-server application with variables. You know when the session started and you know before it ends, so you can persist the information stored in variables to disk. You have control over when and how individuals move from screen to screen. You know which screen the individuals are on now, and which page they're requesting. In short, you have a large body of knowledge about any specific individual, their history, and what they can do next. You don't have to do anything special to maintain the data—put information in a variable and it's available until the person closes the application (barring machine crashes).

In a Web application, much of this information is difficult to obtain and even more difficult to store. You have a thin client—the browser—where your data-storage options are limited, in most cases, to cookies (approximately 4 KB or 4096 bytes). You have a limited amount of resources on the server—you often can't simply move the data you would normally store on the client to the server because it's too large. Even if you have sufficient memory on the server to hold the information, the length of time to service requests rises as the volume of information required for that request rises. Therefore, storing all the data in server memory soon begins to limit scalability—the number of simultaneous users that can access your application.

So if you can't cache much data on the client and you can't cache much data on the server, where should you cache the data? The answer is: Don't cache data. Design your application so you minimize the data necessary for any particular request. This takes planning; you can't simply have an idea and begin coding like you can with many stand-alone applications.

The idea of building stateless applications is probably the single most difficult skill to master for programmers moving from stand-alone and client-server applications. The task gets much easier if you immediately begin thinking of each page as a tiny program. For each request, you're going to accept input from the browser, process the request, provide the requested information, and end the program. That means that tasks you would normally think of as a single operation may in fact be several linked operations.

The key to this kind of processing is to force the browser to provide sufficient information so you don't have to maintain the entire application state on the server. You do this by sending pointers to information from the browser rather than the information itself. For example, when a person selects an item from the shopping cart, you store an `ItemID` cookie on the browser rather than the item title or description. Using the `ItemID` cookie value, you can display the associated information on the browser screen, and you can use the `ItemID` to look up related information on the server for each request. You haven't reduced the need to display the associated information, but you have reduced the volume of that information. Of course, you've also complicated your programming because now you must look up the information for each request.

You should spend a considerable fraction of your application-planning time deciding how and where to store information, and how much information you must maintain from one request to the next. Web application design is a process of compromise between ease of development and scalability. It's easiest to store all the information once, then retrieve it from memory. The most scalable applications look up everything from a minimum number of cached information pointers, but they take longer to develop. As you develop more applications, you'll begin to plan these lookups more carefully. The interface between the browser and the page is similar to the interface between a function and the calling code, and you can think of them in the same way. The items of information the browser sends are the input arguments. The HTML returned by the page is the return value.

Advantages and Disadvantages of Sessionless Applications

A stateless application either must be designed as a series of small, independent transactions, or at minimum, must be able to identify a browser from one request to another. You'll see two kinds of stateless applications—those that use cookies and those that don't.

IIS uses cookies to associate a browser with a specific SessionID, and subsequently, to associate information stored for that SessionID with a request. There are two problems with this scheme. First, not every browser accepts cookies. For example, with IE 5, you can refuse cookies by clicking the Tools menu and selecting Internet Options, then the Security tab and clicking the Custom Level button. You'll see the Security Settings dialog (see Figure 9.1).

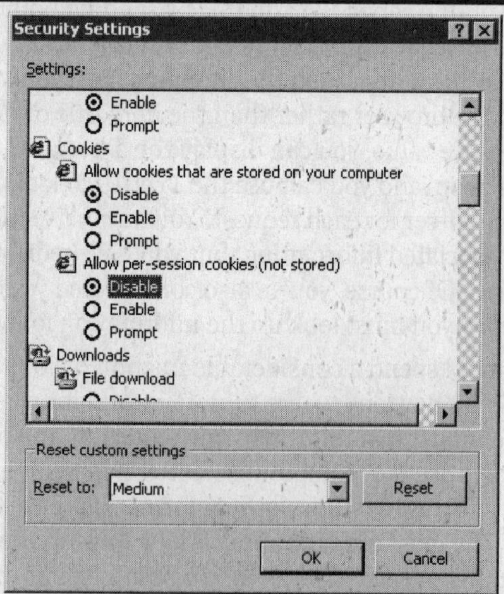

FIGURE 9.1: Internet Explorer 5 Security Settings dialog

The Security Settings dialog lists two types of cookies: per-session cookies and cookies stored on your computer. The difference is that when you write a cookie, if you give it a valid future expiration date, the browser writes the cookie to the user's browser cache folder (the cookie is stored on the computer). If you omit the expiration date, the browser maintains the cookie in memory only as long as the browser is open. When the user closes the browser, the cookie disappears (the per-session cookie). Note that the term *per-session* as used by Microsoft has nothing to do with ASP sessions. A person using a browser may move through many ASP sites during the course of a browser session.

You cannot only enable and disable cookies, you can also set the browser to warn you with a message box whenever a server tries to write a cookie value. Many people use the warning setting—don't ignore it!

ASP tries to write the `SessionID` cookie to the browser during the response to the first request by a browser to that server, regardless of the application. For subsequent applications the browser accesses on the same server during the same browser session, IIS uses the `SessionID` cookie already written to the browser. For requests after the browser has accepted the `SessionID` cookie, ASP doesn't fire the `Session_OnStart` event. In other words, for each application, ASP uses the presence of the `SessionID` cookie value to determine whether to fire the `Session_OnStart` event or not.

This logic leads to a problem when a browser doesn't accept cookies. Because the `SessionID` cookie never exists, ASP runs the `Session_OnStart` event code for each request. In IIS 3 that meant that people who had the cookie warning setting enabled avoided ASP sites altogether because they received two cookie warnings for each request (unless they accepted the cookie). This was an unfortunate, but also unavoidable, consequence of using ASP. With IIS 4, Microsoft added a setting that lets you disable all use of Sessions for an ASP application. When you turn Sessions off, IIS doesn't check for a `SessionID` value, doesn't try to write a `SessionID` cookie, and you have no access to Sessions (no Session object, `Session` variables, and `Session_OnStart` or `Session_OnEnd` events).

At first, this may seem like a foolhardy act—after all, isn't one of the major advantages of ASP the ability to associate data with a specific request? That's true, but like most advantages, there are tradeoffs. When you use `Session` variables, you're tied to a specific server. This problem won't affect most ASP sites, but if your application must scale beyond the number of users a single server can support, it becomes a major problem.

In return for disabling Session use, you gain the ability to process requests on any server. Because you no longer depend on the `SessionID` cookie to associate the browser with a specific set of data, you can process the request on any server that has access to the user's information. For example, a Web farm is a set of Web servers that can handle requests. You also gain speed if you disable Sessions. It's often (but not always) faster to make an association between data sent by the browser and server-side data yourself than it is to rely on ASP Sessions to do it for you.

If you don't use Sessions, you must store the information required to connect a browser with a specific set of data yourself. You can use cookies just like ASP does, if the browser has cookies enabled. If the browser doesn't have cookies enabled, you'll need to use embedded `form` variables or `QueryString` variables to maintain state pointers on the browser.

Why would this be faster? As I stated, it isn't always faster. If you can store all the information required in cookies, embedded `form` variables, or `QueryString` variables, you eliminate the time required to create a Session object and look up any associated data between the `SessionID` cookie and the data stored for that Session. You can eliminate some processing overhead by limiting your dependence on `Variant` variables and out-of-process object instantiations.

I started this section with the cookie discussion because Sessions and cookies are two separate considerations, but they influence each other. The primary decision of whether to use Sessions depends on two factors:

- Whether you need multiple servers to service the application
- How much planning and programming you're willing to do to improve the response time of your application

The primary decision of whether to support browsers that don't accept cookies depends on how friendly you want to be to the clients. In an intranet situation, the company might decide that all browsers must accept cookies. In a commercial Internet application, you probably have to plan for browsers that don't accept cookies or risk losing business.

State Maintenance Options

In an ASP application you can maintain user state with the following:

- `Session` variables
- Cookies

- `QueryString` variables
- `Hidden form` variables
- Database tables or files

I'll discuss all these options and show you when each might be appropriate. For each method I'll use this example. You have a database table containing demographic information about registered users; UserIDs, sign-ons, names, etc. When a user signs on, you use the `signon` value the user entered to look up the user's information in the database.

Now assume your application needs access to the user's demographic data for each page in the application. To be able to retrieve the user's information, you need to somehow make, and keep, an association between the user's browser and the information related to that browser. Remember that you may decide to disable Sessions, in which case you cannot rely on ASP to make the association for you.

For purposes of this discussion, I'm going to assume you have decided to support only browsers with cookies enabled, and that you have access to `Session` variables. At the end of the discussion, I'll show you what you need to do if you disable Sessions, and how to write applications that support browsers with cookies disabled.

Basically, there are only two places to store state information–on the client or on the server. I don't necessarily mean on the Web server itself, but on the server side of the browser-server relationship.

Maintaining State with Cookies

Cookies are highly efficient from the server point of view because they push the burden of maintaining data onto the browser. You can write persistent or temporary (per-session) cookies, depending on your needs. However, if you rely on cookies you have six considerations:

1. **Cookies increase network traffic.** Each time you store a cookie on a browser, the browser subsequently sends the cookie name and value(s) back to the server for each request. Assume you store the maximum amount of information (approximately 4 KB) of information in your cookies set. If you have 20 users on your site, it won't make a significant impact on network traffic; but if you have 2000 users, each making requests 4 times per minute, you've increased network traffic

to 32 MB per minute. While that may not bring your network and server to its knees, you should consider that your application may not be the only one on the server, and is most certainly not the only traffic on the network.

2. **Cookies increase the time required to service a request.** The server must parse the cookie string and create the `Request.Cookie` collection for each request. Therefore, the more values you store in the cookie string, the longer it takes the server to parse the string, thus increasing your response time and reducing scalability. Again, this is a minor consideration for a small user base, but all those milliseconds add up.

3. **Cookies are machine-dependent.** When you write a persistent cookie to a computer, the browser will return that cookie value the next time a user visits your application. But if the person uses a different computer to access your application, the cookie value won't be there. You may not think this is a serious problem, but it is. Consider an individual who accesses a travel reservations site from work, makes a reservation, then accesses the same site from home. That person has every right to expect that the application will remember the prior access. If the site relies on cookies to maintain state, the user's reservation information will be on the work computer, but not on the home computer.

4. **Cookies are browser-dependent.** The problem is actually worse than described in the previous paragraph. Cookies belong to a specific browser. Suppose a user has two browsers. After accessing the travel application with IE, the user later (that same day) returns to the site with Netscape. The two browsers maintain cookies independently. That means that any cookie you write with IE isn't sent with Netscape, and vice versa. Therefore, the application won't have access to the information stored in cookies for visits by other browsers, even if the machine and user are the same.

5. **Cookies may disappear.** Perhaps worst of all, because browsers store persistent cookies in directories accessible to the users, those users can delete the files, or the machine can crash, or the user can rebuild the machine. In other words, you can't store critical data in cookies because you can't rely on the information to be present in the future.

6. **Users control cookies.** Even with per-session cookies, there's a small chance that a person may start your application with cookies enabled, but turn cookies off during the session. That means your application may lose cookie values in the middle of the application—not an attractive scenario for critical applications. Therefore, to be absolutely safe, you must check constantly to ensure that the expected cookie values exist, and plan for application flow if the cookies suddenly disappear—or at least trap any errors that result.

The point of this discussion isn't to tell you not to use cookies; it's that cookies aren't necessarily the best place to store data. They're limited in size, aren't guaranteed to be present between sessions (or even during a session), and not all browsers accept them. Nevertheless, cookies are the method that Microsoft chose to associate a browser with server-side data, because they work most of the time. I agree with that decision—it's the best of a bad bargain.

Cookies do have some advantages. You can create and read cookies easily with both client- and server-side code, they work in all modern browsers, and you can create secure (encrypted) cookies so people watching the network can't read the values.

In your hypothetical application, you could use cookies to store all the demographic user information, or you could store just the UserID in a cookie, then look up the user information on the server each time you need it. In other words, you can use cookies the same way the ASP engine uses them to identify users. The browser associates the cookie with a given site and sends the cookie information along with each request.

From the ASP server-side scripting point of view, a cookie is a collection of keyed values, much like a Dictionary object. You use the Request object to retrieve cookie values and the Response object to create or alter them. Therefore, in the example, you would store the UserID in a cookie after you have authenticated the user during sign-on:

```
Response.Cookies("UserID") = rs("UserID").Value
```

To retrieve the value in subsequent requests, use:

```
aUserID = Request.Cookies("UserID")
```

Even better, a cookie can have multiple keyed values, called sub-keys. You can group the user information in a single cookie. For example:

```
Response.Cookies("User")("UserID") = _
   rs("UserID").Value
```

```
Response.Cookies("User")("Signon") = _
   rs("UserSignon").Value
Response.Cookies("User")("LastName") = _
   rs("UserLastName").Value
Response.Cookies("User")("FirstName") = _
   rs("UserFirstName").Value
Response.Cookies("User")("UserEMail") = _
   rs("UserEmail").Value
' etc.
```

To retrieve a sub-key value from a cookie, use this syntax:

```
aUserID = Request.Cookies("User")("UserID")
```

If you're not sure whether a cookie has sub-keys, you can check by using the `HasKeys` property. The `HasKeys` property returns `True` when the cookie contains sub-keys. For example:

```
If Request.Cookies("myCookie").HasKeys then
   ' do something
End If
```

When the server receives a request, it parses the cookies into a Collection object, which understands the `For...Next` syntax. To process all the cookies in a request, you can use a loop like this:

```
With Request
   For Each aKey In .Cookies
      If .cookies(aKey).HasKeys Then
         For Each subKey In .Cookies(aKey)
            response.write subKey & "=" _
            & .cookies(aKey)(subkey) & "<BR>"
         Next
      End If
   Next
End With
```

If you don't need to store much information between requests and you aren't much concerned about losing the information, cookies are an excellent way to maintain state because they don't take up any memory on the server. You can even write permanent cookies that store data on the client's hard drive. Permanent cookies make it possible to store state between sessions.

To make a cookie permanent, use the `Expires` property. When you set the `Expires` property to a date later than the current date, the browser will store the cookie on the user's hard drive. For example, use the following to create a cookie that expires in one week:

```
Dim nextWeek As Date
NextWeek = dateAdd("d", 7, now())
Response.Cookies("User").Expires = NextWeek
```

By default, the browser sends all cookies set by an application back to that application. If your application has more than one directory, you can specify which cookies the browser should send to each directory in your application by adding a path to the cookie. The browser compares the path of the request to each cookie and sends the cookie only if it matches the path. To add the path, use the `Path` property:

```
Response.Cookies("myCookie").Path = "/myPath"
Response.Cookies("myCookie") = "someCookie"
```

In the example above, the browser would send the `"myCookie"` cookie only to requests for pages in the `/myPath` virtual directory.

For cookies that have an expiration date, you can set the domain as well as the path, which lets you create a cookie in one application that the browser will send to a different application in another domain.

In the background, transparent to developers, the Response object writes an HTTP header to tell the browser to save the cookie. You can use the Response object `AddHeader` method to bypass the automatic cookie-management and storage functions. To add a cookie, use this syntax:

```
Response.AddHeader "Set-Cookie", _
   "<name>=<value> " & _
   "[; <name>=<value>]...[; expires=<date>]" & _
   "[; domain=<domain_name>]" & _
   "[; path=<some_path>][; secure]"
```

Here's an example:

```
Response.AddHeader "Set-Cookie", _
   "myCookie=someCookie"
```

The result is the same as if you had used the `Response.Cookies` collection—the browser stores the cookie.

Part ii

The browser stores cookies in a `Cookies` subdirectory of your `Profile` directory. On Windows NT, your profile is in the `Profiles` subdirectory of the `$systemRoot$` path—usually called `WinNT`. On Windows 95/98, your profile in is a subdirectory of the `$systemRoot$` path—usually called `Windows`. On Windows 2000, your profile is under the Documents and Settings directory under your username. When you add a cookie using the `Response.Cookies` collection, you can set the `Expires` parameter using any valid date format. When you use the HTTP method, you need to specify the date in the format `ddd, dd-mmm-yyy hh:mm:ss GMT`.

You can look in the appropriate `Cookies` directory to check that your application sent the cookie in the correct format—if it did, the browser will create a file like `username@domain.txt` that stores the cookie information.

The browser stores and transmits cookies as text files, so you need to encrypt the cookie if the information is sensitive, such as sign-on and password information. You can manually encrypt the information or tell the browser to encrypt the data automatically. Cookies have a `Secure` attribute that tells the browser to store cookies in encrypted form, and send them only to sites that support Secure Sockets Layer (SSL) encryption.

Maintaining State with *QueryString* Variables

There's been a great deal of press coverage (mostly negative) about how unscrupulous Web sites are stealing your privacy by storing unwanted information on your computer in cookies. Therefore, some of the more paranoid individuals have improved their privacy by turning cookies off. For clients that won't accept cookies, you can't store anything in the Session object because the ASP engine won't find the `SessionID` cookie, and (if Sessions are enabled for the application) will try to create a new `Session` cookie for each request. Of course, you can't use cookies to maintain state either. Instead, you can pass information through the `QueryString` collection.

Remember that `QueryString` data is text appended to the URL. On the server, you receive the data in the Request object as the `Request.QueryString` collection. As is typical with Web communications, the raw data is in `key=value` form like cookies, `form` variables, etc. Ampersands separate the key-value pairs. A question mark separates the entire query string from the URL. The following URL example contains two QueryString values—LastName (1) and FirstName (2):

```
http://myServer/mySite.com?LastName=Doe&FirstName=John
```

Most browsers support up to about 1024 characters in QueryString data. The server parses the QueryString data into a collection, so you can retrieve it using keys or indexes (1-based, not 0-based). The QueryString collection supports standard For Each...Next syntax. Using the QueryString values from the previous example:

```
Response.Write Request.QueryString("LastName")
        ' prints Doe
Response.Write Request.QueryString.Count
        ' prints 2
Response.Write Request.QueryString(2)
        ' Prints John
```

That makes it extremely easy to retrieve the data sent by the browser. You can add QueryString parameters to HTML you send to the browser by concatenating strings together to produce a valid URL.

Concatenating strings together is a straightforward process, you just need to remember to separate the first key-value pair with a question mark and all subsequent pairs with ampersands. For example, suppose you had a record set of usernames. You want to display the names as a list of links. When an administrator clicks on one of the names, you want to display a form to edit the user's information. For each link, you'll want to return the user's ID, as follows:

```
While Not R.EOF
   With Response
      .Write "<a href=somepage.asp?ID=" & _
        R("UserID").Value & ">" & _
        R("Name").Value & "</a><br>"
   End With
   R.MoveNext
Wend
```

Now, when the administrator clicks on the link, you'll be able to pull the UserID from the QueryString collection to display the form to edit the user's information. For example:

```
Dim anID
```

Part ii

```
anID = Request.QueryString("ID")
' display form based on anID
```

When you show the form, you'll need to keep track of the ID in the form page too, and possibly in several subsequent pages—that's the application user's state—editing the user with the ID anID. All that concatenation can become painful when you're trying to keep track of multiple variables. Imagine trying to append enough information to keep track of 20 or 30 critical variables in an application!

There are some undesirable characteristics of using QueryString data to maintain state. First, the user (and other observers) can see the data because it appears in the address bar. Therefore, you should never use this method to send any private information unless you also apply your own encryption scheme to the data. Second, if you use QueryString data and your data contains spaces or other non-alphanumeric characters, you must apply the Server.URLEncode method to the query string before appending it to a URL.

NOTE

The Server.URLEncode method replaces characters with a percent sign followed by the hex value of the character. For example, a space (ASCII 32) is "%20".

Finally, because the information in the QueryString on the browser appears in the address field, users can change the QueryString data, which can lead to errors in your application. Therefore, you can't always depend on the validity of the information in the QueryString variables.

Maintaining State with *Hidden Form* Variables

Yet another way of maintaining state on the client is to use hidden form variables. If you do this, you need to create a <form> tag and insert the hidden form variable for each page for which you need to pass state back to the server. You also need to ensure that the client submits the form using the POST method so the browser returns the values to the server. That means either you will have to have a Submit button for each page, or you need to write client-side script to submit the form when a navigation event—such as a click on a link or button—occurs.

For example, to pass a variable called "ID" with a value of 2817 from one page to another, the first page could contain:

```
<form name="frmHidden" method="post">
   <input type="hidden" name="ID" value="2817">
   <input type="submit" value="Submit">
</form>
```

When the user clicks the Submit button, the form will send the value ID=2817 to the server. You can retrieve the value using the Request.Form collection, then use the value in a form on the next page.

To submit the form from a link, use client-side script such as this:

```
<script language="javascript">
   function doSubmit() {
      document.frmHidden.submit();
   }
</script>
<form action="mypage.asp"
   name="frmHidden" method="post">
   <input type="hidden" name="ID" value="2817">
   <input type="submit" value="Submit">
</form>
```

Somewhere on the page you would put a link to the ASP page to which you want the user to navigate. For example:

```
<a href='mypage.asp' onClick='doSubmit();">
   Click Here</a>
```

If you wanted to continue the sequence, you would retrieve the ID value in mypage.asp script, using Request.Form("ID") and send the ID forward to the next page. The process of setting and retrieving the ID variable would continue as long as you needed the variable value on the server to maintain state.

Hidden form variables are in some ways better than cookies or QueryString variables. There's no size restriction on hidden form variables, they're not visible in the browser's address field, and users can't change them; but they are visible to users savvy enough to use the View Source feature of the browser. You should not use them for values you don't want the user to see (e.g., answers to test questions) unless you encrypt them.

Maintaining State with *Session* Variables

`Session` variables are the easiest way to maintain state. You can store any data type in a `Session` variable. You'll recall that the Session object is an associative array much like a Scripting Dictionary object. A Session can hold practically an unlimited number of name-value pairs. Each `Session` variable name must be unique. The value associated with that name is a `Variant`; therefore, you can store both primitive data types, such as strings or numeric values, and COM objects, like Dictionary or custom ActiveX objects.

So you could store the UserID in a `Session` variable. Now, whenever the user makes a request, you can use the value of the `Session("UserID")` variable to look up the user's information in the database, as seen in the example.

```
Set R = conn.execute("SELECT * FROM Users " & _
    "WHERE UserID=" & Session("UserID"), , _
    adCmdText)
```

But wait! Retrieving database data is an expensive operation in terms of both time and server resources. You may not want to perform a database lookup for each user request. You retrieved the data once during the `signon` request—you could store the entire row in `Session` variables during the `signon` operation. That way, you wouldn't need to go back to the database for each subsequent request. Instead, you can create a `Session` variable for each field in the table row for that user. For example:

```
Session("UserID") = _
    rs("UserID").Value
Session("UserSignon") = _
    rs("UserSignon").Value
Session("UserLastName") = _
    rs("UserLastName").Value
Session("UserFirstName") = _
    rs("UserFirstName").Value
Session("UserEMail") = _
    rs("UserEmail").Value
' etc...
```

Now you have access to the user data from anywhere in the application without returning to the database. In essence, you've cached the demographic data for this user in the Session object.

This is absolutely the easiest way to cache data for an individual user of your application, and probably the one you'll use most often. There's only a couple of problems with it (you knew this was coming, didn't you?). First, think about what the ASP engine must be doing while it retrieves the variable values for each user. Imagine that the Session object is a Dictionary where each key is a SessionID and each value is itself a Dictionary. The keys of this sub-dictionary are the names you give your `Session` variables, and the values are your `Session` variable values. I don't know exactly how the Session object stores data, but it must be with a method similar to what you see in Figure 9.2.

The point is that using `Session` variables at all forces the server to access a single object for each request. Therefore, the use of `Session` variables must force the server to serialize requests, at least during retrieval of the sub-dictionary containing the `Session` variables associated with that user's SessionID.

So why use sessions at all? You can disable them, either for your entire server or for a specific site, using the IIS administration program. Sessions can be enabled or disabled at either the Web level or at the virtual directory level, so you'll need to decide how you want to set up your server. To disable Sessions for the entire server, start the IIS administration program. The checkbox to enable/disable sessions is in the Application Configuration dialog. Right-click on the Default Web Site entry in the left-hand pane, select Properties, then click the Home Directory tab. Click the Configuration button, then the App Options tab (see Figure 9.3).

Uncheck the Enable Session State checkbox. When you do that, IIS will ask if you want all the other child applications to inherit that setting (assuming there are other applications on that server). You can select the specific applications for which you want to disable sessions. You can disable sessions for a specific application by first right-clicking on that application, then following the same process you just saw with the Default Web Site.

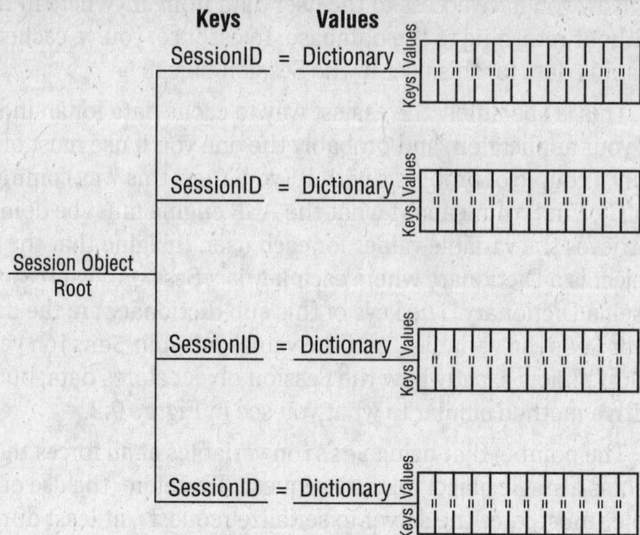

FIGURE 9.2: Hypothetical Session object structure

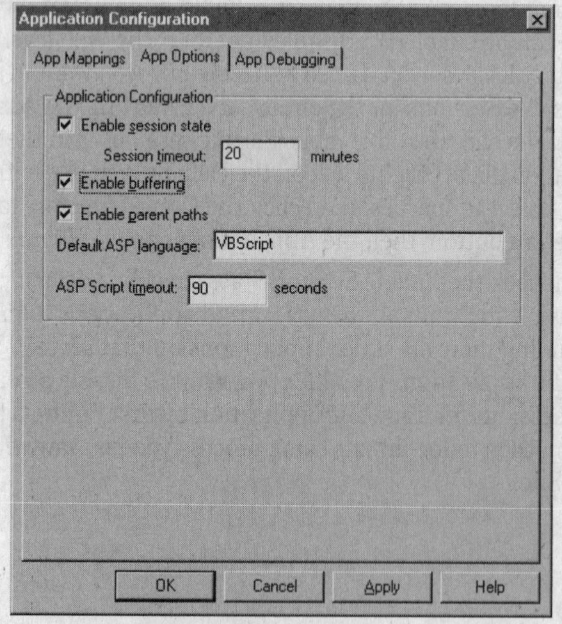

FIGURE 9.3: IIS Application Configuration dialog

Sessions are a mixed blessing. They make development extremely easy, but Microsoft itself recommends that you should use another method besides Sessions to maintain state if you want to build Web sites that will scale to large numbers of users.

Consider a Web farm where you use more than one server to service requests. If you use `Session` variables, you need some method to route requests from one browser to the same server for each request. If you don't have such a method (and the ASP engine doesn't currently provide one), the Session information either won't be available or will be different on each server.

Commercial routers are available that let you use Sessions on sites with multiple servers; you can consider one of these as an alternative to disabling Sessions if you build a site with heavy use. For smaller sites, it's relatively easy to write your own multi-server router. Suppose you have a single, publicly available address for your site; e.g., `http://www.mySite.com`. You have four servers, only one of which has a public IP address corresponding to the `mySite.com` IP address. The other three servers' IP addresses are not mapped to the `mySite.com` address. Together, all four servers constitute a Web farm. The public server receives all initial requests for your site.

The first time a new request arrives, the public server uses a script to route the request to one of the three Web farm servers. That server then provides a SessionID. Subsequent requests by the same browser bypass the public server and go directly to the Web farm server. The script on the public server uses a round-robin method to ensure that each of the servers in the Web farm receives an equal number of requests. You need to use relative paths to ensure that graphics and other resources are available on all the servers. Because you need to balance the load, you may want to ensure that people can't bookmark pages on a specific server by redirecting any users without SessionIDs (new Sessions) back to the public server for routing.

Note that this scheme doesn't truly balance the load between servers—it only balances the number of browsers assigned to each server. Load balancing itself is beyond the scope of this book, but you can easily write a simple round-robin scheme. Depending on your setup and application requirements, that may be sufficient, but typically you'll want to at least poll the servers to find out if they're running, which one currently has the smallest load, etc. You will probably need fail-over protection and may even want to bring additional servers online, as needed.

Finally, although it may not always be an issue, you need to be aware of the memory requirements when you use Session variables. Storing a few small strings and numbers for each user won't use much memory, but storing entire record sets, even as arrays, will use up large amounts of memory in a hurry. If the server runs out of RAM, it will begin spooling the data out to virtual memory, and that will definitely adversely affect your application's response time and scalability.

MAINTAINING STATE WITH FILES

Although reading a file for each request may sound like a totally inefficient method for maintaining state, it's not as bad as it sounds. IIS caches files–in fact, you can set the number of files it caches to suit the resources available on your server. Because requests tend to come in clusters–a single user will use your application, then quit–you can rely on IIS's file caching services to improve the speed of file reads and writes.

You still need to rely on one of the previous forms of data-caching to make the association between the browser and the file, but you may use any of them. For example, you may save a UserID as a cookie, place it in the QueryString, save it as a Session variable, or submit it as a hidden form variable; the method you select doesn't matter. The result is that you obtain the UserID value and use that value to open a file. For example, Listing 9.1 shows a file to obtain a user's first and last name. When the user requests the file it does the following:

1. Checks to see if the browser sent a cookie called Filename; if so, it redirects to the ch9i2.asp file.
2. Checks to see if the user submitted the form; if so, it checks and processes the form contents, then writes a file containing the user's first and last name, writes a cookie to the browser, and redirects to ch9i2.asp.
3. If neither condition 1 nor condition 2 are true, the file displays a form into which users enter their names.

Listing 9.1: User Name Form (ch9i1.asp)

```
<%@ Language=VBScript %>
<% option explicit %>
<%
If Request.Cookies("FileName") <> "" Then
```

```
      Response.Redirect "ch9i2.asp"
   End If
   If Request("Submit") = "Submit" Then
      Dim fs
      Dim ts
      Dim aFilename
      Dim LastName
      Dim FirstName
      Dim ForWriting
      Dim TriStateUseDefault
      Dim aPath
      Dim pathLen
      aPath = Request.ServerVariables _
        ("PATH_TRANSLATED")
      pathLen = Len(aPath)
      Do While (pathLen > 0) And _
        (Mid(aPath, pathLen, 1) <> "\")
        pathLen = pathLen - 1
      Loop
      aPath = Left(aPath, pathLen)
      ForWriting = 2
      TriStateUseDefault = -2
      FirstName = Request("FirstName")
      LastName = Request("LastName")
      If LastName <> "" And FirstName <> "" Then
         ' write the user's name into a file
         ' create a file name
         aFilename = LastName & FirstName & _
           "_" & year(now) & _
           "_" & month(now) & "_" & day(now)
         Set fs = server.CreateObject _
           ("Scripting.FileSystemObject")
         Set ts = fs.OpenTextFile _
           (aPath & aFilename & ".txt", _
           ForWriting, True, TriStateUseDefault)
         ts.write "LastName=" & LastName & vbCrLf
         ts.write "FirstName=" & FirstName
         ts.Close
         Set ts = Nothing
         Set fs = Nothing
         ' write a cookie to the browser
         ' so you'll know that the file
         ' was created in future pages
```

Part ii

```
        Response.Cookies("FileName") = aFilename
        Response.Cookies("FileName").Expires = _
          DateAdd("d", 2, Now())
        Response.Redirect "ch9i2.asp"
      End If
End If
%>
<html>
<head>
<title>Maintaining State With Files</title>
</head>
<body>

<form name="frmUserName"
   method="post" cols="2">
<table align="center" border="1">
<tr>
  <td colspan=2>
    Enter your first and last names.
  </td>
</tr>
<tr>
  <td width="40%">
    <b>First Name</b>:
  </td>
  <td width="*">
    <input type="text" name="FirstName"
      value="<%=FirstName%>">
  </td>
</tr>
<tr>
  <td width="40%">
    <b>Last Name</b>:
  </td>
  <td width="*">
    <input type="text" name="LastName"
      value="<%=LastName%>">
  </td>
</tr>
<tr>
  <td colspan=2 align="center">
    <input type="submit" name="Submit"
      value="Submit">
```

```
  </td>
 </tr>
 </table>
 </form>
 </body>
 </html>
```

The `Filename` cookie has an expiration date of two days from today, making it a persistent cookie. Therefore, when users return to the application within two days, they won't have to re-enter their names. Instead, the browser will redirect to the `ch9i2.asp` file, which displays the name (see Listing 9.2), as follows:

1. Reads the cookie to construct the filename.
2. Reads the file and extracts the first and last names.
3. Displays Hello <name>.

Listing 9.2: Using a Persistent Cookie as a File Pointer

```
<%@ Language=VBScript %>
<% option explicit %>
<html>
<head>
</head>
<body>
<%
' read the file
Dim fs
Dim ts
Dim aFilename
Dim s
Dim FirstName
Dim LastName
Dim aPos
Dim ForReading
Dim TriStateUseDefault
Dim aPath
Dim pathLen
aPath = Request.ServerVariables _
  ("PATH_TRANSLATED")
pathLen = Len(aPath)
Do While (pathLen > 0) And _
  (Mid(aPath, pathLen, 1) <> "\")
```

```
    pathLen = pathLen - 1
  Loop
  aPath = Left(aPath, pathLen)
  ForReading = 1
  TriStateUseDefault = -2
  aFilename = Request.Cookies("Filename")
  If aFilename = "" Then
    Response.Redirect "ch9i1.asp"
  End If
  Set fs = server.CreateObject _
    ("Scripting.FileSystemObject")
  Set ts = fs.OpenTextFile _
    (aPath & aFilename & ".txt", _
    ForReading, False, TriStateUseDefault)
  Do While Not ts.AtEndOfStream
    s = ts.readLine()
    aPos = InStr(1, s, "=", vbBinaryCompare)
    If aPos > 0 Then
      Select Case LCase(Left(s, aPos - 1))
        Case "firstname"
           FirstName = Mid(s, aPos + 1)
        Case "lastname"
           LastName = Mid(s, aPos + 1)
        End Select
     End If
  Loop
  ts.Close
  Set ts = Nothing
  Set fs = Nothing
  Response.write "Hello " & FirstName & _
    " " & LastName & "."
  %>
  </body>
  </html>
```

NOTE

The IUSR_MACHINENAME account must have read/write-access to the Chapter9 directory for the code to run properly.

You should be able to extrapolate from this example to see how you could associate a reasonably large amount of data with a single pointer item stored on the client—in this case, the filename. This method works well, but is not without problems. For example, the files become hard to manage when you have 10,000 or 1,000,000 users. You also have the problem of managing obsolete files and duplicates. If a user visits the site once, how long should you maintain the data? For some sites, you'll need to maintain the data forever. For others, you can delete it when the session ends. But how would you associate the file with a SessionID so you can find it to delete it at the end of the Session? You can't rely on the browser to find the filename during the `Session_OnEnd` event because, by definition, the browser isn't visiting the application at that point—otherwise, the Session wouldn't have timed out.

In this particular example, you could delete any user files older than two days—the expiration date for the cookie; however, if users re-visit the site within the two-day period, you would need to update the file date by writing data to the file so it didn't get deleted. As you can see, it would be nice to have a more robust way to associate data with a pointer stored on the client. And you do have access to that method—with a database.

Maintaining State in a Database

Databases are probably the most scalable way to maintain state. Storing state in a database is definitely slower when your application has only a few users, but as the number of users and the size of the data increases, using a database to store state quickly outstrips using `Session` variables. It's also easier to script than using `QueryString` or `Form` variables, especially when you have a large application where you must store many more state variables.

Another major advantage of storing state in a database is that you can maintain state not only during a session, but also between sessions. The only other way to maintain state between sessions is to use persistent cookies or files. Cookies maintain state on the client, whereas state stored in a database resides on the server. Maintaining cross-session state on the server is better. People frequently change computers, delete cookie files, or sign on to their computers using other sign-ons, so client-side state is less certain.

To store state in a database table, you must set up the table properly. By that, I don't mean you must have a column for every variable, but you must be able to identify the data row or rows that belong to an individual or session. You do this by setting a single identifying cookie that acts as a primary key to the table, then retrieving the data using that cookie value when each request starts. You can create and set your own cookie value—for secured sites, you will probably want to use the user's unique ID or sign-on. For cross-session state maintenance, you'll need to have each user sign on with a login and password. For single-session state maintenance, you can use the `SessionID` cookie as long as you don't care about storing state for an individual user, just an individual session.

Here's how to store state in a database on a single-session basis:

1. In the `Session_OnStart` event in the `global.asa` file, create a new row(s) for the new SessionID or sign-on.
2. At the start of each page in your application, read the cookie, then retrieve the appropriate row(s) from the database.
3. During page processing, add or remove state information as appropriate.
4. At the end of each page, update the database with any changed state information.
5. In the `Session_OnEnd` event in `global.asa`, delete the row(s) from the database.

To store state between sessions, you defer Step 1 until after the user has signed on, and create a new row only if the user doesn't already have data. You would eliminate Step 5 unless an administrator deletes the sign-on.

You'll need a scheme to delete or archive obsolete state data (data you've stored for individuals that never return to your site). For many public sites, this is the bulk of the data collected; for internal sites, it may occur only when an employee leaves the company. If you use persistent cookies to connect people to their data, you will probably also want a way for a user whose cookie has been lost to reconnect to his or her data. That's why many sites ask you to provide special personal information so they can ask you about it if you lose or delete the site cookie.

Summing Up State Maintenance Options

If you only need to store small amounts of data (less than 4 KB), and especially if you don't need cross-session data, use cookies. Cookies work well and you'll be able to develop the application quickly.

If you don't expect to ever have to scale the site beyond a single server, use `Session` variables. If you need to keep data across sessions, or if the data you need to maintain is large, you can use a file or database to persist the data.

If your client doesn't have cookies enabled, use `hidden form` or `QueryString` variables to store a pointer value on the client. Use the pointer value to retrieve associated information from files or database tables on the server. You can also use these methods if your server doesn't have sessions enabled.

If you need high scalability, use database tables in combination with any other method that can store a pointer to the data. Remember that the less data you must retrieve for any request, the faster and more scalable your application becomes.

Finally, you can use more than one method at the same time—database tables, files, and cookies to store information between sessions, as well as `Session` variables, QueryString variables, `hidden form` variables and cookies to store information during a session. I usually work to get the best of both worlds—the persistence of databases and the in-memory access to `Session` variables except in sites that can't use Sessions.

What's Next?

In the next chapter, you'll bring together all of the skills you've learned so far by building a simple e-commerce application that handles purchase and subscription information for a publication. You'll start with the database behind the application, then build an HTML form and the ASP code to process it. Finally, you'll look at a simple report generator to help you administer your new project.

Chapter 10

Sample Application

Before we go full bore into database design in Part III, we are going to build a very simple e-commerce application based on Active Server Pages and SQL Server. This will help to get our feet wet with the ASP development environment.

Our sample application will be a simple form to purchase a subscription to a publication. This form will take in name and address information and credit card data.

Adapted from *Visual Basic® Developer's Guide to E-Commerce with ASP and SQL Server™*, by Noel Jerke

ISBN 0-7821-2621-9 752 pages $49.99

Building the Data Table

The first thing we will need is a simple database table that we can insert our subscriptions into. The obvious fields are in the table for the subscriber's name, address, credit card information, etc., as shown in Listing 10.1.

CREATING A TABLE IN SQL SERVER

Database management will be covered in more depth in the next few chapters. But if you want to create the following table now, you have a couple of options. In SQL Server Enterprise Manager, you can open the database you want to use, right-click Tables, and choose New Table. Then manually create the fields with the names and vartypes shown in Listing 10.1. Another option is to open Query Analyzer and connect to your database. Then simply type the code exactly as you see it and execute the code by either pressing F5 or choosing Query and then Execute.

Listing 10.1: Subscription Database Table

```
CREATE TABLE dbo.Subscriptions (
  idSubscription int IDENTITY (1, 1) NOT NULL ,
  chrFirstName varchar (100) NULL ,
  chrLastName varchar (100) NULL ,
  chrAddress varchar (150) NULL ,
  chrCity varchar (100) NULL ,
  chrState varchar (10) NULL ,
  chrZipCode varchar (15) NULL ,
  chrPhone varchar (25) NULL ,
  chrEmail varchar (100) NULL ,
  chrCardName varchar (150) NULL ,
  chrCardType varchar (50) NULL ,
  chrCardNumber varchar (25) NULL ,
  chrExpDate varchar (50) NULL ,
  intProcessed tinyint NULL DEFAULT 0,
    /* Default to 0 */
  dtEntered datetime NULL
    DEFAULT GETDATE(),
    /* Default to current date */
```

```
intLength tinyint NULL
)
```

A couple of status fields are included in the table. The `intProcessed` field would be used to flag the order as processed so an indication of what subscriptions have been retrieved can be easily tracked. This field should be defaulted to 0, to indicate "unprocessed." The next status field is the `dtEntered` field. This defines the date the subscription was entered into the database. It should be defaulted to the current date.

Building the HTML Form

To build the HTML page, we will need to create an HTML form and HTML elements on the page. Then we will build a script page to process the data entered by the user.

The first part of the page is straightforward, as shown in Listing 10.2. The standard HTML headers for the page are created. We also start out the form by setting it to post results to the `ProcessSub.asp` page, which will process the subscription.

Listing 10.2: `Subscription.asp` **Page**

```
<%@ Language=VBScript %>
<HTML>
<HEAD>
<META NAME="GENERATOR" Content="Microsoft
    Visual Studio 6.0">
</HEAD>
<BODY>

<BR><BR>

<center>

<!--  Setup the Header --!>
<font size="4" color="blue"><b>
XYZ Publication
</b></font>

<!--  Start the form that will post to the
      ProcessSub.asp page. --!>
<form method="post" action="ProcessSub.asp">
```

The next section of the page is the table that contains the form for displaying the input fields of the subscription page (see Listing 10.3). There are several key actions on the page. First, if the user enters invalid data, we want to be able to send him back to this form and have the data he entered repopulated into the form.

The repopulation is done by reading session variables set in the `ProcessSub.asp` page when the data is in error. Our first challenge is the length of the subscription (set in `intLength`). If the user selected two-year or three-year subscriptions, then we will want to set the proper radio button. If not, then the one-year option will be set.

Listing 10.3: `Subscription.asp` **Continued**

```
<!-- Next the table starts that will
     layout the data entry form -->
<table border=1>

<!-- Subscription Length -->
<tr>
  <td align="right">Subscription Length:</td>
  <td>
<%
    '  Check to see if a length was set. If so
    '  then default the radio button selected.
   if session("intLength") = "1" then
     CheckOne = "Checked"
     Flag = 1
   end if

   if session("intLength") = "2" then
     CheckTwo = "Checked"
     Flag = 1
   end if

   if session("intLength") = "3" then
     CheckThree = "Checked"
     Flag = 1
   end if

    '  If this is the first time the form is
    '  displayed in the session then default to
    '  a length of one year.
```

```
    if Flag <> 1 then CheckOne = "Checked"

%>
  <!--  Radio buttons for selecting
        the length -->
  <input type="radio" value="1"
     name="intLength" <%=CheckOne%>>
     One Year
  <input type="radio" value="2"
     name="intLength" <%=CheckTwo%>>
     Two Year
  <input type="radio" value="3"
     name="intLength" <%=CheckThree%>>
     Three Year
  </td>
</tr>

<!--  First Name -->
<tr>
  <td align="right">First Name:</td>
  <!--  Input field for the first name -->
  <td><input type="text"
    value="<%=session("chrFirstName")%>"
    name="chrFirstName"></td>
</tr>

<!--  Last Name -->
<tr>
  <td align="right">Last Name:</td>
  <!--  Input field for the last name -->
  <td><input type="text"
    value="<%=session("chrLastName")%>"
    name="chrLastName"></td>
</tr>

<!--  Address -->
<tr>
  <td align="right">Address:</td>
  <!--  Input field for the address -->
  <td><input type="text"
    value="<%=session("chrAddress")%>"
    name="chrAddress"></td>
</tr>
```

```
<!--  City -->
<tr>
  <td align="right">City:</td>
  <!--  Input field for the city -->
  <td><input type="text"
    value="<%=session("chrCity")%>"
    name="chrCity"></td>
</tr>

<tr>
  <td align="right">State:</td>
  <td><input type="text"
    value="<%=session("chrState")%>"
    name="chrState" size=2></td>
</tr>

<!--  Zip Code -->
<tr>
  <td align="right">Zip Code:</td>
  <!--  Input field for the zip code -->
  <td><input type="text"
    value="<%=session("chrZipCode")%>"
    name="chrZipCode"></td>
</tr>

<!--  Phone Number -->
<tr>
  <td align="right">Phone:</td>
  <!--  Input field for the phone number -->
  <td><input type="text"
    value="<%=session("chrPhone")%>"
    name="chrPhone"></td>
</tr>

<!--  Email Address -->
<tr>
  <td align="right">Email Address:</td>
  <!--  Input field for the email address -->
  <td><input type="text"
    value="<%=session("chrEmail")%>"
    name="chrEmail"></td>
</tr>
```

```
<!--  Name on Card -->
<tr>
  <td align="right">Name on Card:</td>
  <!--  Input field for the email address -->
  <td><input type="text"
    value="<%=session("chrCardName")%>"
    name="chrCardName"></td>
</tr>
```

A process similar to the length of subscription logic needs to take place for the card type. If the user selected MasterCard or American Express, then we want to reselect those options when the user is returned to the form (see Listing 10.4).

Listing 10.4: `Subscription.asp` **Continued**

```
<!--  Input field for the credit card type -->
<tr>
  <td align="right">Card Type:</td>
  <td>

<%
    ' Check to see which card was selected
    ' previously if there was an error.
    if session("chrCardType") = "Visa" then
      SelVisa = "Selected"
    end if

    if session("chrCardType") = _
      "MasterCard" then
      SelMC = "Selected"
    end if

    if session("chrCardType") = "AmEx" then
      SelAmEx = "Selected"
    end if
%>

    <!--  Select box for the type of cards -->
    <select name="chrCardType">
      <option value="Visa"
        <%=SelVisa%> >Visa
      <option value="MasterCard"
        <%=SelMC%>>MasterCard
```

```
            <option value="AmEx"
              <%=SelAmEx%>>American Express
          </select>

        </td>
      </tr>

      <!--  Credit Card Number -->
      <tr>
        <td align="right">Card Number:</td>
        <!--  Input field for the credit
           card number -->
        <td><input type="text"
           value="<%=session("chrCardNumber")%>"
           name="chrCardNumber"></td>
      </tr>

      <!--  Credit card expiration date -->
      <tr>
        <td align="right">Expiration Date:</td>
        <!--  Input field for the expiration date -->
        <td><input type="text"
           value="<%=session("chrExpDate")%>"
           name="chrExpDate"></td>
      </tr>
```

The last section of our page is the HTML Submit button for sending the form data to the server (see Listing 10.5). Then the form and the page are closed out.

Listing 10.5: The End of `Subscription.asp`

```
      <!--  Submit button -->
      <tr>
        <td colspan="2" align="center">
          <input type="submit" value="Subscribe!"
             name="submit">
        </td>
      </tr>

      </table>

      </center>
```

```
<!--  Closing tag for the end of the form -->
</form>

</BODY>
</HTML>
```

The input page is fairly straightforward. If you are new to ASP coding, then mixing script code and HTML tags in the same page might take some getting used to. But it is precisely this powerful integration that makes ASP such a rich development environment for building Web applications.

Programming the Script Code

Now the real programming fun begins on the processing of the subscription request. Our goal in this page is several-fold. First, we want to retrieve the data from the user and validate it. We want to ensure that she has entered in values for all required fields, and when possible we want to validate that the data is correct.

Second, we want to then give feedback to the user if there is an error. A message will be displayed telling the user certain fields are incorrect. We will provide a link back to the subscription page for the user. That is where the session variables and repopulating the subscription form come into play.

Third, if the data is valid, we want to thank the user. In this case, we are going to re-display the input data for good customer service feedback. And of course, we need to be sure to insert the subscription data into the database for later retrieval.

As with the `subscription.asp` page, the `processsub.asp` page opens up with basic HTML tagging. Listing 10.6 shows the page code.

Listing 10.6: `ProcessSub.asp` **Page**

```
<%@ Language=VBScript %>

<HTML>

<BODY BGCOLOR="WHITE">
```

Our first task is to retrieve the data from the form. We utilize the Request object to retrieve the data and reference the field names on the form (see Listing 10.6). The data is stored in variables for later use.

NOTE

Variables do not have to be used to store the form data. The Request object could be used throughout the page. But the variable use makes for easier manipulation of the data later.

Listing 10.7: `ProcessSub.asp` **Continued**

```
<%

'  Retrieve all of the data that the
'  user entered by using the request object.
intLength = Request("intLength")
chrFirstName = Request("chrFirstName")
chrLastName = Request("chrLastName")
chrAddress = Request("chrAddress")
chrCity = Request("chrCity")
chrState = Request("chrState")
chrZipCode = Request("chrZipCode")
chrPhone = Request("chrPhone")
chrEmail = Request("chrEmail")
chrCardName = Request("chrCardName")
chrCardType = Request("chrCardType")
chrCardNumber = Request("chrCardNumber")
chrExpDate = Request("chrExpDate")
```

The next step is to check each field and validate it (see Listing 10.8). For most of the fields, we are simply going to ensure that the field is not blank. For the state field, we do a little more validation to ensure that the length is not more than two characters. On the credit card expiration date, we can use the `IsDate` function to validate that it is a valid date.

Listing 10.8: `ProcessSub.asp` **Continued**

```
'  Check to see if the first name was entered.
if chrFirstName = "" then

  '  Give an error if not.
  strError = "You did not enter in your" & _
    " first name.<BR>"

end if
```

```
' Check to see if a last name was entered.
if chrLastName = "" then

  strError = strError & "You did not enter" & _
    " in your last name.<BR>"

end if

' Check to see if an address was entered
if chrAddress = "" then

  strError = strError & "You did not enter" & _
    " in your address.<BR>"

end if

' Check to see if a city was entered.
if chrCity = "" then

  strError = strError & "You did not enter" & _
    " in your city.<BR>"

end if

' Check to see if the state was entered
' of if the length is more than two
' characters.
if chrState = "" or len(chrState) > 2 then

  strError = strError & "You did not enter" & _
    " in a valid state.<BR>"

end if

' Check to see if a zip code was entered.
if chrZipCode = "" then

  strError = strError & "You did not" & _
    " enter in your zip code.<BR>"

end if

' Check to see if the card name was entered.
```

```
if chrCardName = "" then

   strError = strError & "You did not enter" & _
     " in the name on your credit card.<BR>"

end if

'  Check to see if the card number was entered
if chrCardNumber = "" then

   strError = strError & "You did not enter" & _
     " in your credit card number.<BR>"

end if

'  Check to see if the card expiration
'  date was entered
if (chrExpDate = "") or _
   (isdate(chrExpDate) = false) then

   strError = strError & "You did not enter" & _
     " in a valid credit card" & _
     " expiration date.<BR>"

end if
```

Now that the data is validated, we are ready to take appropriate action. We can check the strError variable to see if it is set. If it is, then there was an error. If not, then there was no error.

```
'  Now we check to see if there are any errors.
if strError <> "" then


%>
```

If there is an error, we simply display the appropriate message and write out the error string. The key though is ensuring we have the data from the form stored so that it can be retrieved and displayed when the user returns to the form. The best way to do this is with session variables, which will stay *alive* while the user's session is still in progress (see Listing 10.9). Then on the subscription form we can retrieve those values and display them.

Listing 10.9: ProcessSub.asp **Continued**

```
    <!-- Note the error -->
    <B><font color="red">
    There is an error in your
    subscription request:<BR><BR>
    </b></font>

<%

    '  Write out the error messages
    Response.Write strError

%>

    <!--  Link back to the subscription page -->
    <BR>
    Click <a href="subscription.asp">here</a>
    to update.

<%

    '  Set session variables to the
    '  subscription form can be re-populated
    Session("intLength") = _
      Request("intLength")
    Session("chrFirstName") = _
      Request("chrFirstName")
    Session("chrLastName") = _
      Request("chrLastName")
    Session("chrAddress") = _
      Request("chrAddress")
    Session("chrCity") = _
      Request("chrCity")
    Session("chrState") = _
      Request("chrState")
    Session("chrZipCode") = _
      Request("chrZipCode")
    Session("chrPhone") = _
      Request("chrPhone")
    Session("chrEmail") = _
      Request("chrEmail")
    Session("chrCardName") = _
```

```
      Request("chrCardName")
    Session("chrCardType") = _
      Request("chrCardType")
    Session("chrCardNumber") = _
      Request("chrCardNumber")
    Session("chrExpDate") = _
      Request("chrExpDate")

  else

  %>
```

If all of the data was valid, then we are ready to process the subscription form. An appropriate thank you message is displayed and then a recap of the form data is displayed (see Listing 10.10).

Listing 10.10: `ProcessSub.asp` **Continued**

```
    <!--  Thank the customer for the order -->
    <font size="4" color="blue">
    Thank you for your order!
    It will be processed immediately.</font>

    <!--  Redisplay the data entered into
    the subscription -->
    <BR><BR>
    <Table>
      <tr><td align="right">
        <B>Name:</b></td>
        <td><i>
        <% = chrFirstName & " " & chrLastName %>
        </i></td></tr>

      <tr><td align="right">
        <B>Address:</b></td>
        <td><i>  <% = chrAddress %></i>
        </td></tr>

      <tr><td align="right">
        <B>City:</b></td>
        <td><i>  <% = chrCity %></i>
        </td></tr>

      <tr><td align="right">
```

```
    <B>State:</b></td>
    <td><i>  <% = chrState %></i>
    </td></tr>

  <tr><td align="right">
    <B>Zip Code:</b></td>
    <td><i>  <% = chrZipCode %></i>
    </td></tr>

  <tr><td align="right">
    <B>Phone:</b></td>
    <td><i>  <% = chrPhone %></i>
    </td></tr>

  <tr><td align="right">
    <B>Email:</b></td>
    <td><i>  <% = chrEmail %></i>
    </td></tr>

  <tr><td align="right">
    <B>Card Name:</b></td>
    <td><i>  <% = chrCardName %></i>
    </td></tr>

  <tr><td align="right">
    <B>Card Type:</b></td>
    <td><i>  <% = chrCardType %></i>
    </td></tr>

  <tr><td align="right">
    <B>Card Number:</b></td>
    <td><i>  <% = chrCardNumber %></i>
    </td></tr>

  <tr><td align="right">
    <B>Expiration Date:</b></td>
   <td><i>  <% = chrExpDate %></i>
    </td></tr>
```

Now we are ready to do the important step of inserting the data into the database. The first step is to create an ADO connection object to the database. You will need an ODBC DSN to connect to the database. Be sure to create the DSN. Note that in Listing 10.11 a file DSN is being utilized, but a system DSN could be created instead. Be aware that user DSNs operate only under the context of the user for which they were created, rendering them unsuitable for use within IIS.

Next we have to sanitize the data for insertion into the database. We have to ensure that any single quotes that may be entered are doubled up so they can be inserted and not confused as delimiters. Examples of this problem would include last names (e.g., O'Brien), cities, addresses, etc. Using the Replace command makes it easy to replace these single quotes with doubles. In this case we will check the First Name, Last Name, Address, Card Name, and City.

TIP

SQL server will interpret two single quotes together ('') as only one single quote. We will need to double up all single quotes that are part of the data to be stored in a field. Our values that are being inserted should start with a single quote and end with one as well.

Once the data is ready, we can build a SQL statement for inserting the data into the database. And then we are ready to execute the SQL statement (see Listing 10.11).

Listing 10.11: `ProcessSub.asp` **Continued**

```
<%

   ' Create an ADO database connection
   set dbSubs = server.createobject _
     ("adodb.connection")

   ' Open the connection using our
   ' ODBC file DSN
   dbSubs.open("filedsn=SubForm")

   ' If any of our names have a single
   ' quote, we will need to double it to
   ' insert it into the database
   chrFirstName = _
     replace(chrFirstName, "'", "''")
   chrLastName = _
     replace(chrLastName, "'", "''")
   chrAddress = _
```

```
      replace(chrAddress, "'", "''")
    chrCardName = _
      replace(chrCardName, "'", "''")
    chrCity = replace(chrCity, "'", "''")

    '  SQL insert statement to insert
    ' the subscription data into the database
    sql = "insert into subscriptions(" & _
            "chrFirstName, " & _
            "chrLastname, " & _
            "chrAddress, " & _
            "chrCity, " & _
            "chrState, " & _
            "chrZipCode, " & _
            "chrPhone, " & _
            "chrEmail, " & _
            "chrCardName, " & _
            "chrCardType, " & _
            "chrCardNumber, " & _
            "chrExpDate, " & _
            "intLength) " & _
            "values (" & "'" & _
             chrFirstName & "', '" & _
             chrLastName & "', '" & _
             chrAddress & "', '" & _
             chrCity & "', '" & _
             chrState & "', '" & _
             chrZipCode & "', '" & _
             chrPhone & "', '" & _
             chrEmail & "', '" & _
             chrCardName & "', '" & _
             chrCardType & "', '" & _
             chrCardNumber & "', '" & _
             chrExpDate & "', " & _
             intLength & ")"

    ' Execute the SQL statement
    dbSubs.execute(sql)

  end if

  %>
```

```
</body>
</html>
```

That's it for the user-side programming. In the next section, we will explore how we can use Web-based reporting to retrieve the subscriptions.

TESTING THE APPLICATION

Now we are ready to begin testing. Calling the `subscription.asp` page from your Web server accesses the Web page shown in Figure 10.1.

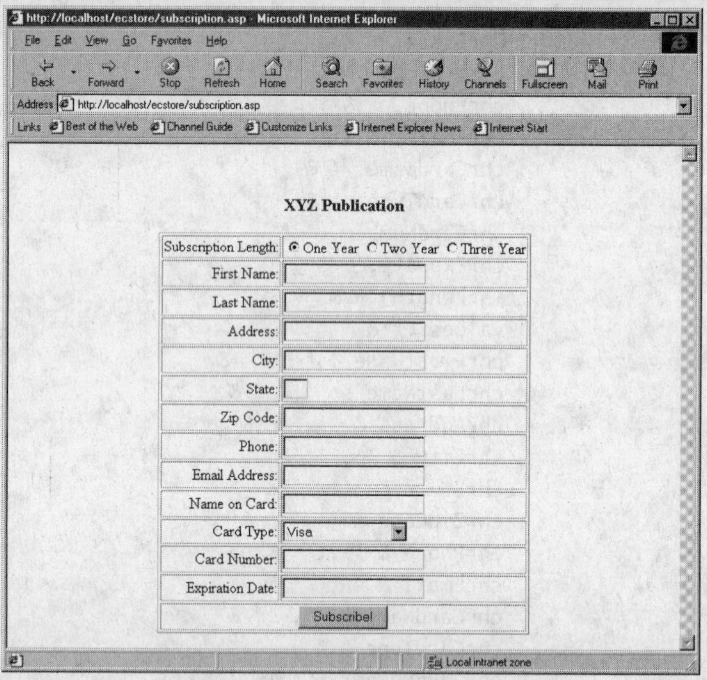

FIGURE 10.1: The `subscription.asp` page

Now we need to go ahead and enter data into the form. We will want to enter in some invalid data so that we can test the error handling. Figure 10.2 shows the form filled out with sample data. Note that the expiration date is invalid. When done, we need to submit the form to the `ProcessSub.asp` page.

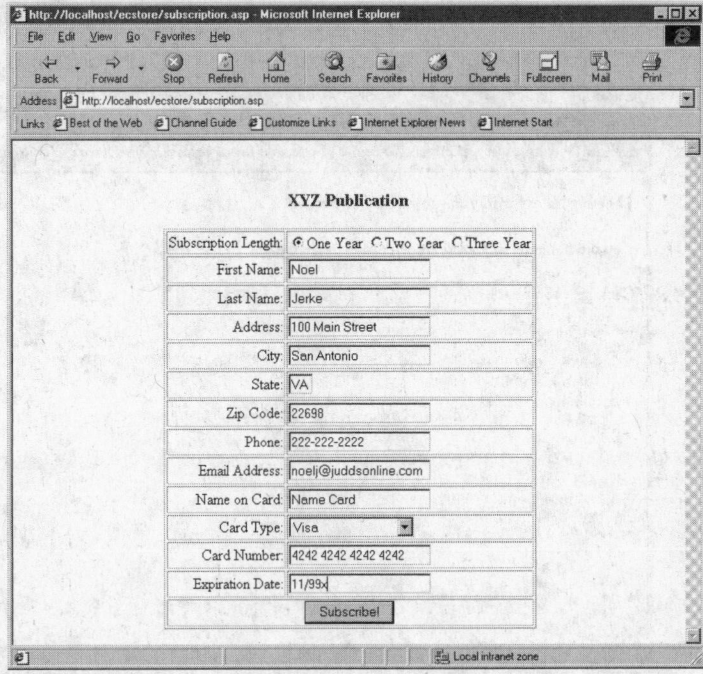

FIGURE 10.2: Entering invalid data into the subscription page

The ProcessSub.asp page will process the data. And, in fact, if all is working properly, we should see an error message indicating that the expiration date is invalid. Figure 10.3 shows the error message.

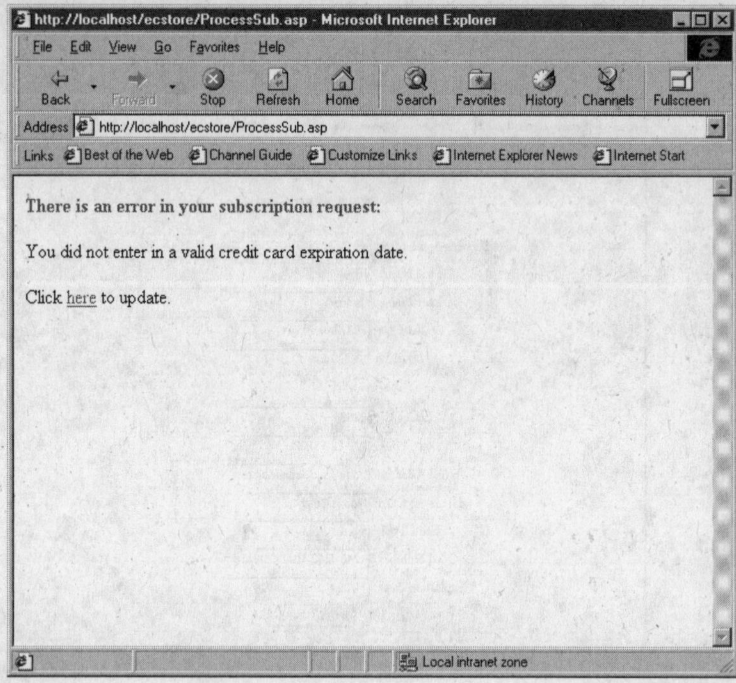

FIGURE 10.3: Error page with invalid expiration date

Now we can click on the error link and go back to the subscription page. When we do so, the data form should be re-populated with our subscription data, error messages, and all. Figure 10.4 shows a correctly entered subscription.

TIP

You may want to have the field name highlighted in red to help indicate on the subscription form which field is invalid.

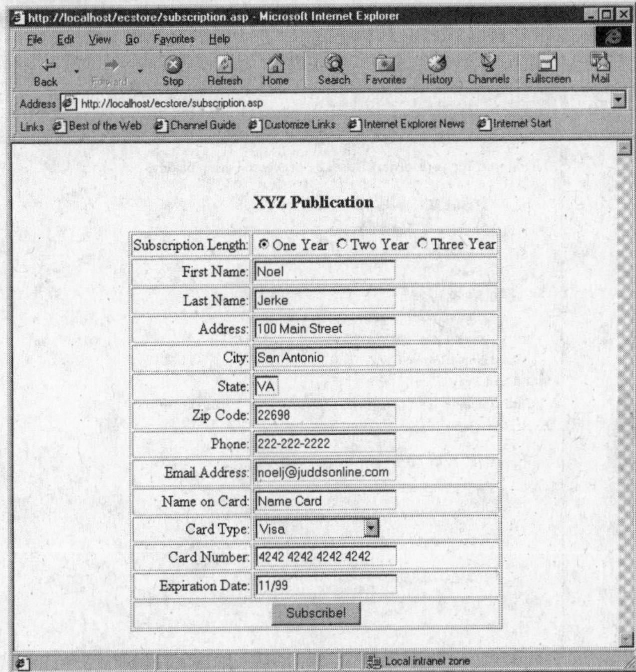

FIGURE 10.4: Entering valid data into the subscription page

Now we can correct the data and then resubmit the subscription data. When we do, the thank you response is displayed with a recap of the data. Figure 10.5 shows the thank you page. We should also be able to verify that the data went into the database.

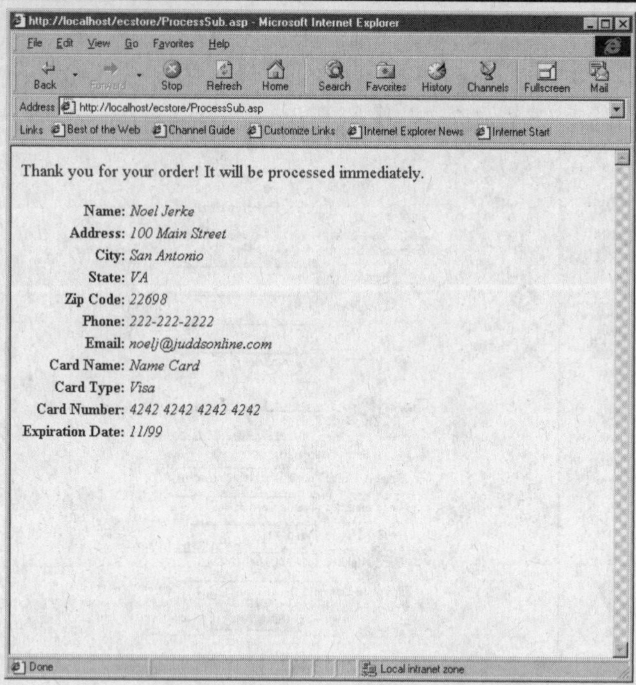

FIGURE 10.5: Thank you message after a successful subscription

Now that we have completed the user experience, we need to worry about the back-end management of the subscription data. We will need a way to retrieve the subscriptions.

MANAGING THE APPLICATION

The last piece of our e-commerce sample application is the reporting form. The purpose of the form is to report out the subscription data entered since the last subscriptions were processed. It will also give an option for the user to mark the current listing of subscriptions as processed. Listing 10.12 shows the code for the `SubReport.asp` page.

Listing 10.12: `SubReport.asp`

```
<%@ Language=VBScript %>
<HTML>
<HEAD>
```

```
<META NAME="GENERATOR"
  Content="Microsoft Visual Studio 6.0">
</HEAD>
<BODY>
```

The first step is to create our database connection. Then we need to check and see if we are to mark subscriptions as processed. If so, then there will be an `idSubscription` parameter on the URL. This is set later in the code when the clear option is selected. If the parameter is set, then all of the subscriptions that have an ID less than or equal to the subscription ID will be cleared. Anything above that will remain unprocessed and will be displayed (see Listing 10.13).

Listing 10.13: SubReport.asp **Continued**

```
<%

    ' Create an ADO database connection
    set dbSubs = server.createobject _
      ("adodb.connection")
    set rsSubs = server.CreateObject _
      ("adodb.recordset")

    ' Open the connection using our
    ' ODBC file DSN
    dbSubs.open("filedsn=SubForm")

    ' Retrieve any subscription IDs on the URL
    idSubscription = Request("idSubscription")

    ' Check to see if there is a value.
    if idSubscription <> "" then

      ' Built an SQL update statement
      ' to process the subs.
      sql = "update subscriptions set" & _
        " intProcessed = 1 where" & _
        "idSubscription <= " & _
        idSubscription

      ' Execute the SQL statement
      dbSubs.execute sql

    end if
```

Next we are ready to retrieve all of the subscriptions in the system that have not been processed. A SQL statement is built with the appropriate *where* clause, and then the SQL statement is executed with a record set returned.

```
  '  Create a SQL statement to retrieve
  '  any unprocessed subscriptions
  sql = "select * from subscriptions" & _
    " where intProcessed = 0"

  '  Execute the statement and retrieve
  '  the record set
  set rsSubs = dbSubs.Execute(sql)

%>
```

Next we are ready to begin the structure of the table that will be used to display the unprocessed subscriptions. The formatting is fairly simple, with field names on the left and the data on the right (see Listing 10.14).

TIP

You might want to put some logic in place to have the subscriptions listed in several columns instead of just one. If you are processing many subscriptions, that will reduce the number of pages that will be displayed.

Listing 10.14: SubReport.asp **Continued**

```
<!--  Start the table to display the subs. -->
<Table border="1">

<%

  '  Check to see if no subs are returned
  if rsSubs.EOF then

    '  If so, then write
    Response.Write _
      "No subscriptions to report."

  else
```

```
    '  Loop through the subs
    do until rsSubs.eof

%>

    <!--  Display the subscription data -->
    <TR>
    <TD align="right">First Name:</TD>
    <TD>    <%=rsSubs("chrFirstName")%></TD>
    </TR>

    <TR>
    <TD align="right">Last Name:</TD>
    <TD>    <%=rsSubs("chrLastName")%></TD>
    </TR>

    <TR>
    <TD align="right">Address:</TD>
    <TD>    <%=rsSubs("chrAddress")%></TD>
    </TR>

    <TR>
    <TD align="right">City:</TD>
    <TD>    <%=rsSubs("chrCity")%></TD>
    </TR>

    <TR>
    <TD align="right">State:</TD>
    <TD>    <%=rsSubs("chrState")%></TD>
    </TR>

    <TR>
    <TD align="right">Zip Code:</TD>
    <TD>    <%=rsSubs("chrZipCode")%></TD>
    </TR>

    <TR>
    <TD align="right">Phone:</TD>
    <TD>    <%=rsSubs("chrPhone")%></TD>
    </TR>

    <TR>
    <TD align="right">Email:</TD>
```

```
<TD>     <%=rsSubs("chrEmail")%></TD>
</TR>

<TR>
<TD align="right">Card Name:</TD>
<TD>     <%=rsSubs("chrCardName")%></TD>
</TR>

<TR>
<TD align="right">Card Number:</TD>
<TD>     <%=rsSubs("chrCardNumber")%></TD>
</TR>

<TR>
<TD align="right">Expiration Date:</TD>
<TD>     <%=rsSubs("chrExpDate")%></TD>
</TR>

<TR>
<TD align="right">Date Entered:</TD>
<TD>     <%=rsSubs("dtEntered")%></TD>
</TR>

<TR>
<TD align="right">Subscription Length:</TD>
<TD>     <%=rsSubs("intLength")%></TD>
</TR>

<TR>
<TD> </TD>
<TD> </TD>
</TR>
```

In order to be able to clear the listed subscriptions, we need to save the ID of the last subscription displayed so that it can be passed back to this page. The ID of the subscription is stored in the `idSubscription` variable. Then we advance the record set (see Listing 10.15).

Listing 10.15: `SubReport.asp` **Continued**

```
<%

    '  Store the last subscription id
    idSubscription = rsSubs("idSubscription")

    '  Move to the next sub
    rsSubs.MoveNext

    loop

  end if

%>

</table>

<BR><BR>
```

Finally we build a link back to this page with the ID of the last subscription so this report can be cleared. Note that the ID of the subscription is stored on the URL with the `idSubscription` parameter (see Listing 10.15).

Listing 10.16: `SubReport.asp` **Continued**

```
<!-- Link to this page with the last
     subscription ID -->
Click <a href="SubReport.asp?idSubscription=
  <%=idSubscription%>">here</a>
  to clear this report.

</BODY>
</HTML>
```

The page is then ready to be run. Make sure the database is seeded with some sample subscriptions. Figure 10.6 shows the report page with the sample data. Note the link to clear the report.

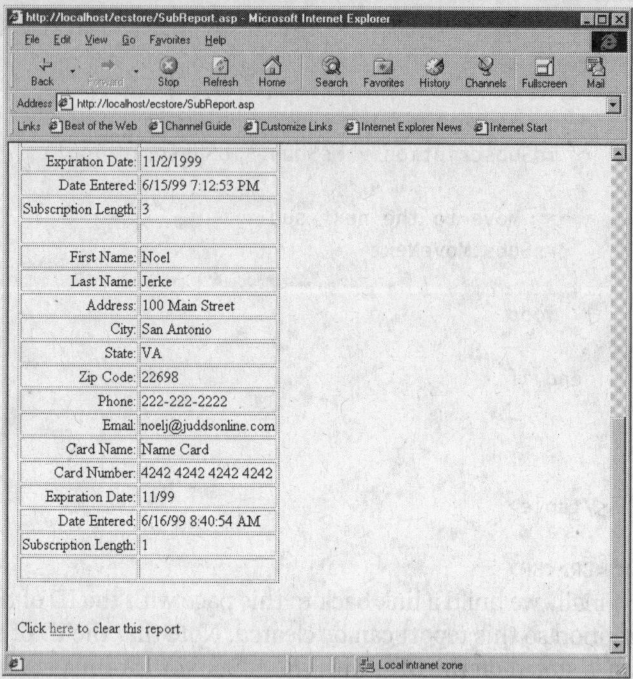

FIGURE 10.6: Subscriptions report page

Go ahead and click on the link to clear the subscriptions. When you do so, the page is re-called with the ID of the last subscription on the URL. Then the section of code is run to mark these subscriptions as processed. You should be able to check the processed fields in the database to verify they are set to 1. Any new subscriptions will be displayed, or a message is displayed indicating that no more subscriptions are available to be displayed. Figure 10.7 shows the processed page.

We might want to provide a richer interface for searching for subscriptions, processed and unprocessed. Date entered, length of subscription, etc., may be offered as options to search by.

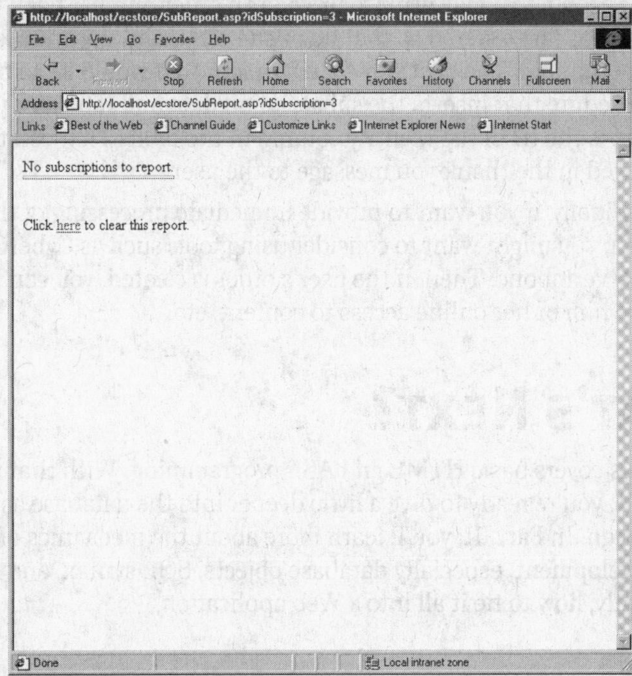

FIGURE 10.7: Cleared subscriptions report page

FINAL CONSIDERATIONS

Our sample application hits on the key tools we will be using for development—ASP, SQL Server, HTML, and a browser. For a site that needs a simple way to request subscriptions, memberships, or other data, this type of form will be more than adequate.

A few things should be considered when implementing this type of form. The first is security. Certainly the form should be encrypted with Secure Sockets Layer (SSL) to ensure the data cannot be easily *sniffed* on the Internet. You should also make sure that your usernames and passwords to access the database are not readily guessed or easily found out. The manager page should not be readily accessible to just anyone. You will want to secure it either with a password-protected form using SQL, or else by using Windows NT Authentication and an Access Control List (ACL) on the directory where the manager page exists.

Second, you may want to provide an order number back to the person who has just ordered so that he or she can make any queries referencing that number. The best way to implement that would be to build a stored procedure that inserts the subscription data and returns a parameter that is the ID of the identity column in the table. That can then be displayed in the thank you message to the user.

Finally, if you want to provide immediate processing of the credit card data, you might want to consider using tools such as CyberCash or HP/Veriphone. Then, if the user's order is cleared, you can immediately give him or her online access to content, etc.

What's Next?

This covers basic HTML and ASP programming. With that under your belt, you're ready to dive a little deeper into the database aspect of site design. In Part III, you'll learn more about the mechanics of database development, especially database objects, SQL syntax, and most importantly, how to tie it all into a Web application.

PART iii

Database Development

Chapter 11

Database Access: Architectures and Technologies

The power and versatility of a Web application often come from the database behind it. A skillfully designed database architecture becomes the engine that drives a robust and personalized experience for your visitor. But databases are the broadest and most diverse area of computer programming. Before I can give you very much detail on what a database is, how to design one, and then how to program it, I must explain some of the key concepts in this field and the numerous acronyms that are used throughout this book.

In my attempt to explain all the data access–related technologies in a single chapter, I may oversimplify things. This chapter is for readers who are not comfortable with the various acronyms, such as OLE DB and ADO, and terms such as n-tiers,

Adapted from *Mastering™ Database Programming with Visual Basic® 6*, by Evangelos Petroutsos

ISBN 0-7821-2598-0 896 pages $39.99

and so on. If you know the difference between OLE DB and ADO, you can skip this chapter and jump to the next chapter, where I discuss the structure of databases.

Databases and Database Management Systems

A *database* is a complex object for storing structured information, which is organized and stored in a way that allows its quick and efficient retrieval. We put a lot of effort into designing a database so that we can retrieve the data easily. The information is broken into *tables*, and each table stores different entities (one table stores customer information, another table stores product information, and so on). We break the information into smaller chunks so that we can manage it easily (divide and conquer). We can design rules to protect the database against user actions and ask the database management system (DBMS) to enforce these rules (for example, to reject customers without a name). These rules apply to all the items stored in the Customers table; the same rules don't apply to the Products table and the Orders table, of course.

In addition to tables, we define *relationships* between tables. Relationships allow users to combine information from multiple tables. Let's say you store customer information in one table and sales information in another table. By establishing a relationship between the two tables, you can quickly retrieve the invoices issued to a specific customer. Without such a relationship, you would have to scan the entire Invoice table to isolate the desired invoices. This view of a database, made up of tables related to one another, is a *conceptual* view of the database. And the database that relies on relationships between tables is called *relational*.

The actual structure of the database on the disk is quite different. In fact, you have no idea how data is stored in the database (and you should be thankful for this). The information is physically stored into and recalled from the database by a special program known as a DBMS. DBMSs are among the most complicated applications, and a modern DBMS can instantly locate a record in a table with several million records. While the DBMS maintains all the information in the database, applications can access this information through statements made in *Structured Query Language (SQL)*, a language for specifying high-level operations. These operations are called *queries*, and there are two types of queries: selection queries, which extract information from the database, and action queries, which update the database. How the DBMS maintains, updates, and retrieves this information is something the application doesn't have to deal with.

Specifically, a DBMS provides the following functions:

- A DBMS allows applications to define the structure of a database with SQL statements. The subset of SQL statements that define or edit this structure is called Data Definition Language (DDL). All DBMSs use a visual interface to define the structure of a database with simple point-and-click operations, but these tools translate the actions of the user into the appropriate DDL statements. SQL Server, for example, allows you to create databases with a visual tool, the Enterprise Manager, but it also generates the equivalent DDL statements and stores them into a special file, called a *script*.
- A DBMS allows applications to manipulate the information stored in the database with SQL statements. The subset of SQL statements that manipulate this information is called Data Manipulation Language (DML). The basic data-manipulation actions are the insertion of new records, modification and deletion of existing ones, and record retrieval.
- A DBMS protects the integrity of the database by enforcing certain rules, which are incorporated into the design of the database. You can specify default values, prohibit certain fields from being empty, forbid the deletion of records that are linked to other records, and so on. For example, you can tell the DBMS not to remove a customer if the customer is linked to one or more invoices. If you could remove the customer, that customer's invoices would be "orphaned." In addition, the DBMS is responsible for the security of the database (it protects the database from access by unauthorized users).

NOTE

The terms "records" and "fields" are not used in the context of relational databases. We now talk about "rows" and "columns." I'm using the old-fashioned terms because most readers who are new to relational databases are probably more familiar with records and fields. If you have programmed older ISAM databases, or even random-access files, you're probably more familiar with records and fields. I will drop the older terms shortly.

SQL Server is a database management system and not a database. A SQL Server database is a database maintained by SQL Server. *SQL* is a universal language for manipulating databases and is supported by all DBMSs—we'll examine it in detail in Chapter 13. SQL retrieves selected records from the database and returns them to the client. The set of records returned by an SQL statement is called a *cursor*. If another user changes some records in the database, those changes will not be reflected in the existing cursors. We need a more complicated mechanism that will synchronize the data in the database and the client computer, and this mechanism is *ADO (ActiveX Data Objects)*. We'll get to ADO soon, but first let's discuss Microsoft's view of data access. We'll look at the big picture first, and then at the individual components.

Windows DNA

The one term you'll be hearing and reading about most frequently in association with Windows 2000 is DNA. *DNA* stands for *Distributed interNet Architecture*, and it's a methodology for building distributed applications. A methodology is a set of rules, or suggestions, and not a blueprint for developing applications; it's a recommendation on how to build distributed applications. Since this recommendation comes from Microsoft, you can consider it a very clear hint of the shape of things to come. Follow these recommendations and your applications will not be outdated soon.

A *distributed application* is one made up of multiple components that run on different machines. These machines can be interconnected through a local area network (LAN)—or a few machines on a LAN and a few more machines on the Internet. To make things even more interesting, throw into the mix a second LAN, located a few thousand miles away. So, in effect, DNA is about building applications for the Internet. If you want to understand how all the pieces fit together, why Microsoft is introducing new access technologies, and why it chooses weird acronyms to describe them, you should start with the big picture.

The big picture starts with the realization that not all information is stored in databases. When most of us are talking about data, we think of databases, rows, and columns—well-structured data that can be easily retrieved. But not all information can be stored in databases. A lot of information is stored in e-mail folders, text documents, spreadsheets, even audio and video files. The ultimate data-access technology is one that can access any information, from anywhere, whether from a database, an electronic mailbox, a text file, even a handheld device. Ideally, we should be able to access information in a uniform way, no matter where this information resides. And we should also be able to access it from anywhere, meaning the Internet.

Universal Data Access

Microsoft uses the term *Universal Data Access* to describe this idea. The premise of Universal Data Access is to allow applications to efficiently access data where it resides, through a common set of tools. There's nothing new about accessing diverse sources of information today, but how is it done? In most cases, we replicate the information. Quite often, we transform the information as we replicate it. The problem with this approach is that we end up with multiple copies of the same information (a highly expensive and wasteful practice).

At a high level, Universal Data Access can be visualized as shown in Figure 11.1. *Data providers*, or *data stores*, store information, and their job is to expose the data through data services. *Data consumers* receive and process the data. Finally, *business components* provide common services that extend the native functionality of the data providers.

FIGURE 11.1: Universal Data Access

A data provider can be a database management system like SQL Server, but it doesn't need to be. Eventually, every object that stores data will become a data provider.

ADO 2.5, which is currently distributed with Windows 2000, supports a few special objects for accessing semi-structured data. Semi-structured data are the data you retrieve from sources other than database rows, such as folders and their files, e-mail folders, and so on.

For the purposes of this book, data providers are DBMSs. The data consumer is an application that uses the data. This application is usually called a *client* application, because it is being served by the data provider. The client application makes requests to the DBMS, and the DBMS carries out the requests. The data consumer need not be a typical client application with a visible interface. In this book, however, you'll learn how to build client applications that interact with the user. Finally, the service components are programs that read the data from the data source in their native format and transform it into a format that's more suitable for the client application. Universal Data Access requires four basic service components:

Cursor Service The UDA cursor is a structure for storing the information returned by the data source. The cursor is like a table, made up of rows and columns. The cursor service provides an efficient, client-side cache with local scrolling, filtering, and sorting capabilities. The cursor is usually moved to the client (that is, the address space where the client application is running), and the client application should be able to scroll, filter, and sort the rows of the cursor without requesting a new cursor from the DBMS. Figure 11.2 shows a client application for browsing and editing customer data. A cursor with all customers (or selected ones) is maintained on the client. The scrollbar at the bottom of the Form, which is a Visual Basic control, allows the user to move through the rows of the cursor. The fields of the current row in the cursor are displayed on the Form and can be edited.

NOTE

For readers who are already familiar with SQL Server, I must point out that the cursors you create with T-SQL statements are different than UDA cursors. The SQL Server cursor contains raw information (the rows extracted from the database with the SQL statement). The UDA cursor contains not only data, but also the functionality to manipulate the data. This functionality is implemented mostly with methods for sorting and filtering the rows, navigational methods, and so on.

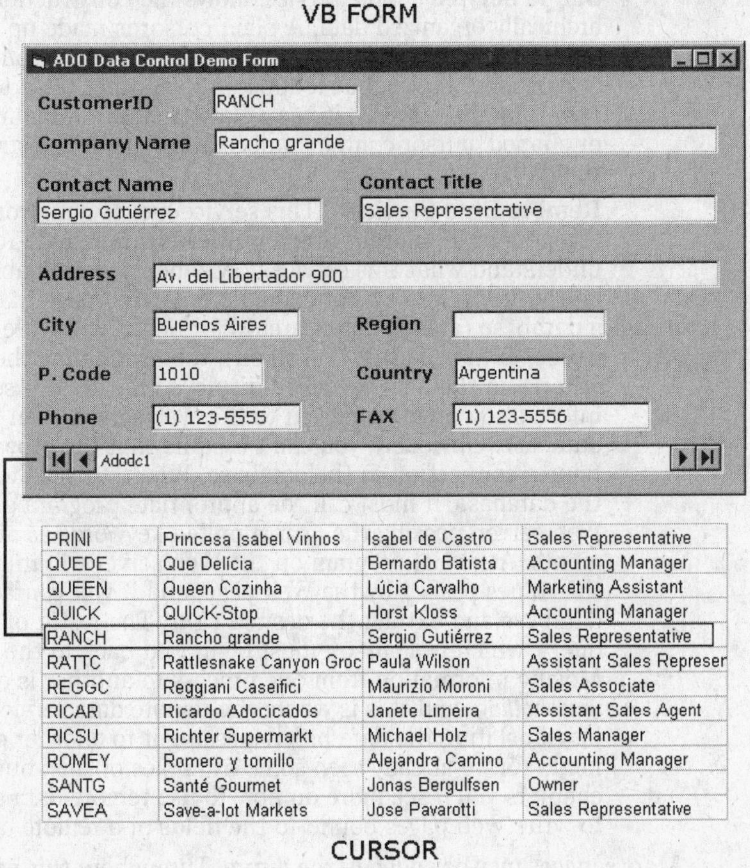

VB FORM

ADO Data Control Demo Form

CustomerID RANCH

Company Name Rancho grande

Contact Name Sergio Gutiérrez

Contact Title Sales Representative

Address Av. del Libertador 900

City Buenos Aires

Region

P. Code 1010

Country Argentina

Phone (1) 123-5555

FAX (1) 123-5556

Adodc1

PRINI	Princesa Isabel Vinhos	Isabel de Castro	Sales Representative
QUEDE	Que Delícia	Bernardo Batista	Accounting Manager
QUEEN	Queen Cozinha	Lúcia Carvalho	Marketing Assistant
QUICK	QUICK-Stop	Horst Kloss	Accounting Manager
RANCH	Rancho grande	Sergio Gutiérrez	Sales Representative
RATTC	Rattlesnake Canyon Groc	Paula Wilson	Assistant Sales Represer
REGGC	Reggiani Caseifici	Maurizio Moroni	Sales Associate
RICAR	Ricardo Adocicados	Janete Limeira	Assistant Sales Agent
RICSU	Richter Supermarkt	Michael Holz	Sales Manager
ROMEY	Romero y tomillo	Alejandra Camino	Accounting Manager
SANTG	Santé Gourmet	Jonas Bergulfsen	Owner
SAVEA	Save-a-lot Markets	Jose Pavarotti	Sales Representative

CURSOR

FIGURE 11.2: Showing how the cursor service is encapsulated into the control at the bottom of the Form

Synchronization Service This service updates the database with the data in the local cursor. This service must be able to update the database instantly, as the user edits the data in the cursor, or in batch mode. As you will see in Chapter 15, there are two major types of cursors: those that reside on the server and those that reside on the client. The rows of a client-side cursor are moved to the client and can't be synchronized to the database at all times. It is possible for another user to edit the same rows in the database while the client application is processing those rows in the client-side cursor.

Shape Service This service allows the construction of hierarchically organized data. A plain cursor is made up of rows extracted from the database. The data may have come from one or more tables, but it appears as another table to the client; in other words, it has a flat structure. A hierarchical, or shaped, cursor contains information about the structure of the data.

Remote Data Service This service moves data from one component to another in a multitier environment. You'll understand what this service does when you read about tiers, later in this chapter. For example, in a Web page that queries a database (a page that searches for books with title keywords, author names, and so on), the user enters the search criteria on the page, which is displayed in the browser. This information must be moved to the Web server, then to the database. Obviously, you can't assume that the browser maintains a connection to the database. When it needs to query the database, it must call the appropriate program on the Web server, passing the user-supplied keywords as arguments. A special program on the Web server will intercept the values passed by the Web page, and it will contact the database and extract the desired rows. The result of the query, which is a cursor, must be moved back to the client. Moving information from one process to another is called *marshalling,* and this is where the remote data service comes in, translating the data before passing it to another component. You've already seen some examples of this, but in later chapters you'll see more on how to use remote data services to write Web pages bound to the fields of a remote database.

More services may be added in the future. Throughout this book, we discuss how these services enable you to write client-server applications. The cursor service, for example, is implemented in the Recordset object, which is a structure for storing selected records. You can use the Recordset object's properties and methods to navigate through records and manipulate them. To navigate through the Recordset, for example, you use the MoveNext method:

```
RS.MoveNext
```

RS is a Recordset object variable that represents the cursor on the client.

To change the Address field of the current record in the cursor, you use a statement like the following one:

```
RS.Fields("Address") = "10001 Palm Ave"
```

The cursor service is responsible for scrolling and updating the local cursor (the copy of the data maintained on the client). Depending on how you've set up the Recordset object, the changes can be committed immediately to the database, or you can commit all edited records at a later point. To commit the changes to the database, you can call either the Update method (to commit the current record) or the UpdateBatch method (to commit all the edited records in batch mode). Updating the database takes place through the synchronization server. The component services are totally transparent to you, and you can access them through the ADO objects (the Recordset object being one of them).

To summarize, Universal Data Access is a platform for developing distributed database applications that can access a diverse variety of data sources across an intranet or the Internet. You can think of Universal Data Access as the opposite of a universal database that can hold all types of information and requires that users actually move the information from its original source into the universal database. Let's see how this platform is implemented.

ADO and OLE DB

The two cornerstones of Universal Data Access are ActiveX Data Objects (ADO) and OLE for Databases (OLE DB). OLE DB is a layer that sits on top of the database. ADO sits on top of OLE DB and offers a simplified view of the database. Because each database exposes its functionality with its own set of API (application programming interface) functions, to access each database through its native interface, you'd have to learn the specifics of the database (low-level, technical details). Porting the application to another database would be a major undertaking. To write applications that talk to two different databases at once (SQL Server and Oracle, for instance), you'd have to learn two different APIs and discover the peculiarities of each database, unless you use OLE DB and ADO.

OLE DB offers a unified view of different data providers. Each database has its own set of OLE DB service providers, which provide a uniform view of the database. ADO hides the peculiarities of each database and gives developers a simple conceptual view of the underlying database. The difference between ADO and OLE DB is that OLE DB gives you more control over the data-access process, because it's a low-level interface. As far as Visual Basic is concerned, OLE DB uses pointers and other C++ argument-passing mechanisms, so it's substantially more difficult to use than ADO. Actually, most C++ programmers also use ADO to access databases because it offers a simpler, high-level view of the database.

Figure 11.3 shows how your application can access various databases. The most efficient method is to get there directly through OLE DB. This also happens to be the most difficult route, and it's not what VB programmers do. The next most efficient method is to go through ADO, which makes the OLE DB layer transparent to the application. You can also get to the database through ODBC (Open DataBase Connectivity), which is similar to OLE DB, but it's an older technology. If you can program ODBC, then you can program OLE DB, and there's no reason to use ODBC drivers. Many of you are already familiar with DAO (Data Access Objects) and RDO (Remote Data Objects). These are older technologies for accessing databases through ODBC. In a way, they are equivalent to ADO. These components, however, will not be updated in the future, and you should use them only if you're supporting database applications that already use DAO or RDO.

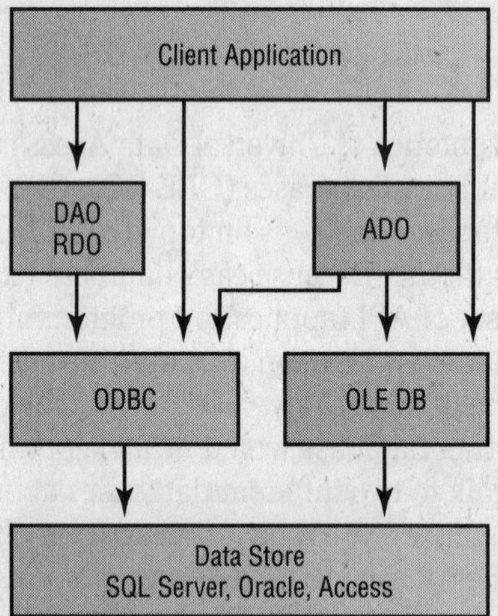

FIGURE 11.3: How client applications communicate with databases

There was a time when DAO was the only way for VB programmers to program databases, and as a result, too many DAO-based applications are in use today (and will remain in use for a while). In fact, most VB books in the market still focus on DAO in discussing Visual Basic's data-access capabilities. However, it's an outdated technology, and you should not base any new project on DAO. I wouldn't be surprised if the ADO data control takes the place of the DAO data control in the toolbox of the next version of Visual Basic.

The ADO Objects

Let's switch our attention to the ADO objects. You'll find all the information you need about ADO in the following chapters, so this is a very brief overview to show you how the ADO object model reflects the basic operations we perform on databases. A client application performs the following:

1. Establishes a connection to the database
2. Executes commands against the database
3. Retrieves information from the database

ADO's basic objects correspond to these operations, and they are appropriately named Connection, Command, and Recordset. The Connection object represents a connection to the database. To specify the database you want to connect to, set the Connection object's properties and then call the Open method to actually establish the connection. With the visual database tools, you don't even have to set any properties. You specify the database you want to connect to with point-and-click operations, and VB will prepare the appropriate Connection object for you.

Connection objects are expensive in terms of resources, and establishing a new connection is one of the most resource-intensive operations. It's crucial, therefore, to create a single Connection object in your application and use it for all the operations you want to perform against the database. If you need to connect to multiple databases, however, you must create one Connection object for each database. (This statement isn't universally true. There are situations, as in Web applications, where you can't afford to maintain a Connection object for each viewer. As far as client applications are concerned, however, the rule is to establish a connection and maintain it during the course of the application.)

Once you've established a connection to the database, you can execute commands against it. A command can be an SQL statement or the name of a stored procedure. *Stored procedures* are applications written in Transact-SQL (T-SQL, the programming language of SQL Server) and are usually called with arguments. To execute an SQL statement or a stored procedure, you must set up a Command object and then call its Execute method to execute the command. The Command object contains the SQL statement or the name of the stored procedure as well as the required arguments. If the command retrieves information from the database, the results are stored in a Recordset object, and you can access them from within your application through the methods and properties of the Recordset object.

Now that you've seen how an application communicates with the database, we'll turn our attention to the formerly ubiquitous client-server architecture. This architecture is different than DNA, but you need a solid understanding of client-server architecture before you adopt more complicated architectures for your applications. If you're developing database applications to run on a LAN, client-server architecture is adequate.

Client-Server Architecture

Client-server architecture is based on a simple premise: Different computers perform different tasks, and each computer can be optimized for a particular task. It makes sense, therefore, to separate the DBMS from the client application. In a networked environment, the DBMS resides on a single machine. However, many applications access the database, and all clients make requests from the same database. The program that accepts and services these requests is the DBMS, and the machine on which the DBMS is running is the database server. The client applications do not know how the data is stored in the database, nor do they care.

In client-server architecture, the application is broken into two distinct components, which work together for a common goal. These components are called *tiers*, and each tier implements a different functionality. The client-server model involves two tiers. As you will see later in this chapter, you can—and often should—build applications with more than two tiers.

Client-server became very popular because much of the processing is done on the client computer, which can be an inexpensive desktop computer. The more powerful the client is, the more processing it can do. Two clients may receive the same data from the client—sales by territory, for instance. One computer can do simple calculations, such as averages, while another, more powerful, client might combine the data with a mapping application to present complicated charts.

The Two-Tier Model

The first tier of a client-server application is the client tier, or *presentation tier*, which runs on the client. This tier contains code that presents data and interacts with the user, and it is usually a VB application. You can also build client tiers that run in a browser–these are Web pages that contain controls, which are similar to the basic VB controls and allow the user to interact with the database. Figure 11.4 shows a simple client application for browsing and editing customers. This is a VB Form with TextBox controls that display the current customer's fields. Figure 11.5 shows a Web page that does the same. It contains Text controls, which are bound to the customer fields in the database. The VB client application relies on the cursor service, while the Web page relies on the remote data service.

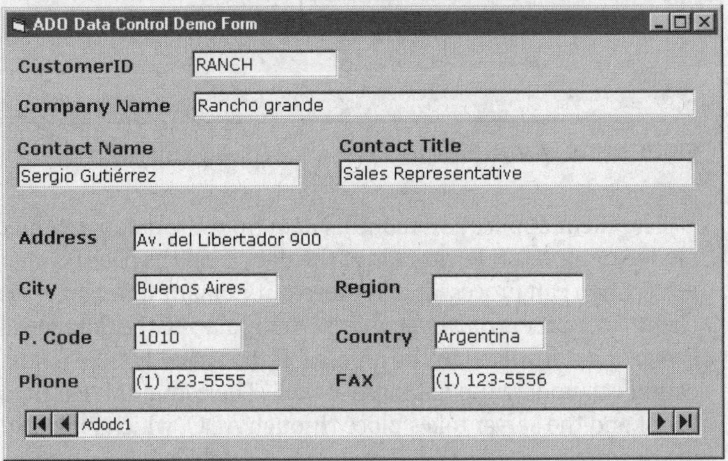

FIGURE 11.4: A VB client application for viewing and editing customers

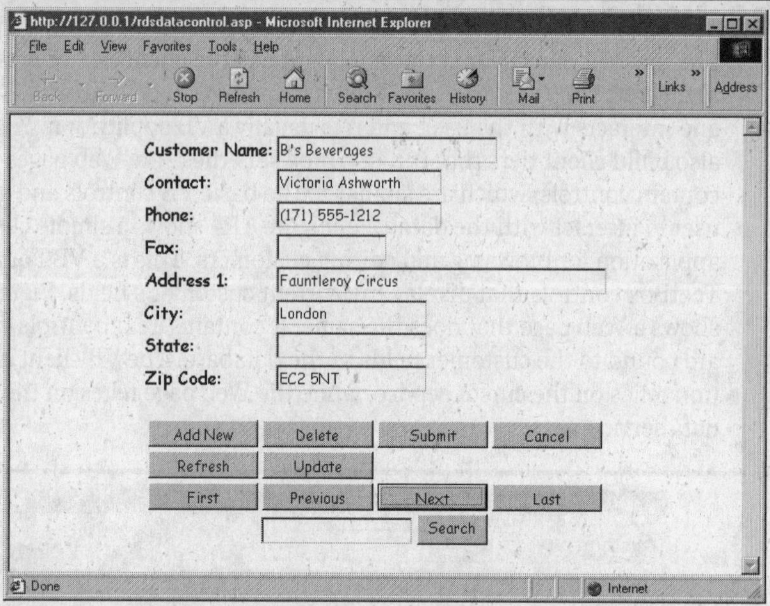

FIGURE 11.5: A Web page for viewing and editing customers

The client application requests data from the database and displays it on one or more VB Forms. Once the data is on the client computer, your application can process it and present it in many different ways. The client computer is quite capable of manipulating the data locally, and the server is not involved in the process. If the user edits the fields, the application can update the database as well. The communication between the client and the server takes place through ADO, which makes it really simple to extract data from and update the database.

The second tier is the *database server*, or DBMS. This tier manipulates a very complex object, the database, and offers a simplified view of the database through OLE DB and ADO. Clients can make complicated requests like "Show me the names of the customers who have placed orders in excess of $100,000 in the last three months," or "Show me the best-selling products in the state of California." The DBMS receives many requests of this type from the clients, and it must service them all. Obviously, the DBMS can't afford to process the data before passing it to the client. One client might map the data on a graph, another client might display the same data on a ListBox control and so on. The server's job is to extract the required data from the tables and furnish them to the client in the form of a cursor. It simply transmits a cursor to the client and lets the client process the information. The more powerful the client, the more it can do with the data. (As you will see later in this chapter, in the discussion of stored procedures, certain operations that are performed frequently, or that require the transmission of a very large number of rows to the client, can be carried out by the server.)

By splitting the workload between clients and servers, we allow each application to do what it can do best. The DBMS runs on one of the fastest machines on the network. The clients don't have to be as powerful. In fact, there are two types of clients: *thin* and *fat clients*.

Thin and Fat Clients

Thin clients are less-powerful computers that do very little processing on their own. A browser is a thin client: its presentation capabilities are determined by the current version of HTML. The benefits of thin clients are their cost (any computer that runs Internet Explorer or Netscape Navigator is good enough) and their connectivity (they can access the database server from anywhere). Another very important—and often overlooked—feature of thin clients is that their presentation capabilities don't vary. A client application that runs within a browser will run on virtually all computers. Thin clients are easy to maintain, too, a fact that can lower the cost of deployment of the application.

A *fat client* is a desktop computer with rich presentation features. Because client applications that run on fat clients are far more flexible and powerful, they require more expensive computers to run, and their interfaces can't be standardized. You can make them as elaborate as the available hardware permits.

The Three-Tier Model

The two-tier model is a very efficient architecture for database applications, but not always the best choice. Most programmers develop two-tier applications that run on small local area networks. The most complete form of a database application, however, is one that involves three tiers.

In two-tier or client-server architecture, the client talks directly to the database server. Every application that connects to SQL Server or Oracle, and retrieves some information, like customer names or product prices, is a client-server application. The role of the database server is to access and update the data. Everything else is left to the client. In other words, the client is responsible for presenting the data to the user, parsing user input, preparing the appropriate requests for the database server, and finally implementing the so-called business rules. A *business rule* is a procedure specific to a corporation. Your corporation, for example, may have rules for establishing the credit line of its customers. These rules must be translated into VB code, which will be executed on the client. It is also possible to write procedures that will be executed on the server, but you can't move all the processing back to the server.

Business rules change often, as they reflect business practices. New rules are introduced, existing ones are revised, which means that the code that implements them is subject to frequent changes. If you implement business rules on the client, you must distribute new executables to the workstations and make sure all users on the network are using the latest version of the client software (that is, your applications). If business rules are implemented on the server, you don't have the problem of redistributing the application, but you place an additional burden to the server, tying it up with calculations that it's not optimized for or that could be performed on another machine.

This leads naturally to the introduction of a third tier, the middle tier. The *middle tier* is an object that sits between the client application and the server. It's a Class (or multiple Classes) that exposes several methods and isolates the client from the server. If many clients need to calculate insurance premiums, you can implement the calculations in the middle tier. Client applications can call the methods of the objects that reside on the middle tier and get the results. The client application need not know how premiums are calculated or whether the calculations involve any database access. All they need to know is the name of one or more methods of the objects that run on the middle tier.

The main advantage of the middle tier is that it isolates the client from the server. The client no longer accesses the database. Instead, it calls the methods exposed by the objects in the middle tier. A client application will eventually add a new customer to the database. Even this simple operation requires some validation. Is there a customer with the same key already in the database? Did the user fail to supply values for the required fields (we can't add a customer without a name, for example)? Adding orders to a database requires even more complicated validation. Do we have enough items of each product in stock to fill the order? And what do we do if we can fill only part of the order?

A well-structured application implements these operations in the middle tier. The client application doesn't have to know how each customer is stored in the database if it can call the AddCustomer() method passing the values of the fields (customer name, address, phone numbers, and so on) as arguments. The middle tier will actually insert the new information to the database and return a True value if all went well, or an error message if an error occurred.

Likewise, the client application can pass all the information of the invoice to the middle-tier component and let it handle the insertion of the new invoice. This action involves many tables. We may have to update the stock, the customer's balance, possibly update a list of best-selling products, and so on. The middle-tier component will take care of these operations for the client. As a result, the development of the client application is greatly simplified. The client will call the NewInvoice member passing the ID of the customer that placed the order, the products and quantities ordered, and (optionally) the discount. Or, you may leave it up to the middle tier to calculate the discount based on the total amount, or the items ordered.

The NewInvoice method must update multiple tables in a transaction. In other words, it must make sure that all the tables were updated, or none of them. If the program updates the customer's balance, but fails to update the stock of the items ordered (or it updates the stock of a few items only), then the database will be left in an inconsistent state. The program should make sure that either all actions succeed, or they all fail. You can execute transactions from within your VB code, but it's a good idea to pass the responsibility of the transaction to a middle-tier component.

As a side effect, the middle tier forces you to design your application before you actually start coding. If you choose to implement business rules as a middle tier, you must analyze the requirements of the application, implement and debug the middle-tier components, and then start coding the client application. While this is "extra credit" if you're only learning how to program databases with VB, or you write small applications to be used by a workgroup in your company, it's more of a necessity if you're working as a member of a programming team. By designing and implementing the middle tier, you are in effect designing the client application itself, and the work you do in the middle tier will pay off when you start coding the client application.

The middle tier can also save you a good deal of work when you decide to move the application to the Web. Sooner or later, you'll be asked to develop a site for your company. If the middle tier is already in place, you can use its components with a Web application. Let me describe a sample component: A client application needs a function to retrieve books based on title keywords and/or author name(s). If you specify which of the search arguments are title keywords and which ones are author names, the operation is quite simple. As I'm sure you know, all electronic bookstores on the Web provide a box where you can enter any keyword and then search the database. The database server must use the keywords intelligently to retrieve the titles you're interested in. If you think about this operation, you'll realize that it's not trivial. Building the appropriate SQL statement to retrieve the desired titles is fairly complicated. Moreover, you may have to revise the search algorithm as the database grows.

The same functionality is required from within both a client application that runs on the desktop and a client application that runs on the Internet (a Web page). If you implement a SearchTitles() function for the client application, then you must implement the same function in VBScript and use it with your Web application. If you decide to change implementation of the function, you must recompile the desktop application, redistribute it, and then change the scripts of the Web application accordingly. Sooner or later the same arguments will retrieve different titles on different machines.

If you implement the SearchTitles() function as a middle-tier component, the same functionality will be available to all clients, whether they run on the desktop or the Web. You may wish to extend the search to multiple databases. Even in this extreme case, you will have to revise the code in a single place, the middle tier, and all the clients will be able to search both databases with the existing code. As long as you don't add any new arguments to the SearchTitles() function, the client will keep calling the same old function and be up-to-date.

It is actually possible to write client applications that never connect to the database and are not even aware that they're clients of a database server. If all the actions against the database take place through the middle tier, then the client's code will be regular VB code and it could not contain any database structures. As you can understand, it's not feasible to expect that you can write a "database application without a database," but the middle tier can handle many of the complicated tasks of accessing the database and greatly simplify the coding of the client application.

The Layers of a Three-Tier Application

The three-tier model breaks the components of the application into three categories, or layers, described below. Figure 11.6 shows a diagram of a three-tier application.

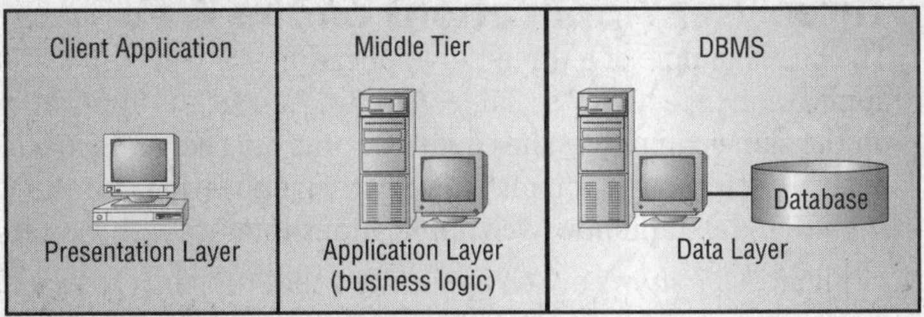

FIGURE 11.6: A three-tier application

Presentation Layer This program runs on the client and interacts with the user, primarily presenting information to the user. You will usually develop applications for the presentation layer (unless you're on the business services team), and these applications are frequently called *user services*. By the way, user services are not trivial. They can include advanced data-bound controls and, in many cases, custom data-bound controls. Data-bound controls are bound to a field in the database and change value to reflect the field's current value, as the user navigates through the Recordset. When a data-bound control is edited, the new value is committed automatically to the database (unless the control is not editable).

Application Layer Also known as the business layer, this layer contains the logic of the application. It simplifies the client's access to the database by isolating the user services from the database. In addition, you can insert business rules here that have nothing to do with the presentation logic. This layer is designed before you start coding the client application. The components of the application or business layer are frequently called *business services*.

Data Layer This layer is the database server, which services requests made by the clients. The requests are usually queries, like "Return all titles published by Sybex in 1999" or "Show the total of all orders placed in the first quarter of 2000 in California." Other requests may update the database by inserting new customers, orders, and so on. The database server must update the database and at the same time protect its integrity (for example, it will refuse to delete a customer if there are invoices issued to that specific customer).

Three-Tier Applications on the Web

The best example of a three-tier application is a Web application. Web applications are highly scalable, and two tiers of the application may run on the same computer (the client tier runs on a separate machine, obviously). Even though you may never write applications for the Web, you should understand how Web applications interact with viewers.

Figure 11.7 shows a Web application that runs in a browser and contacts a Web server and a database server to interact with the user. The first tier–the presentation layer–is the browser, which interacts with the user through HTML documents (Web pages). A Web page may contain controls where the user can enter information and submit it to the server. The Web page, therefore, is the equivalent of a VB Form. Where your VB application can read the controls' values the moment they're entered, the values of the controls on a Web page must be passed to the server before they can be processed.

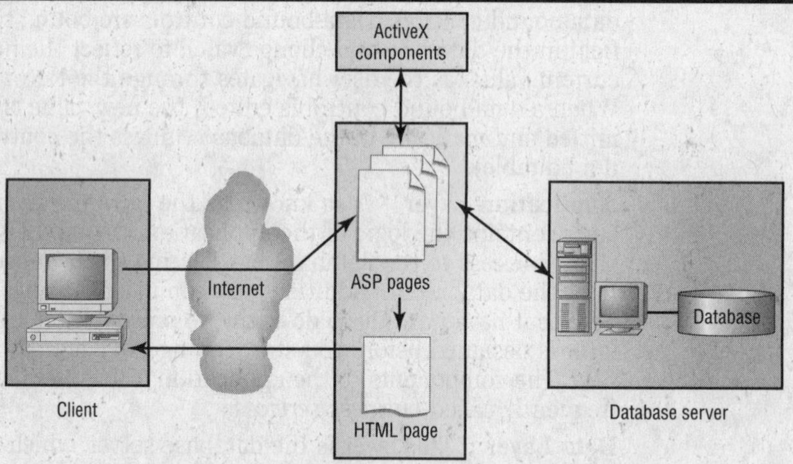

FIGURE 11.7: A Web application, which is a typical example of a three-tier application

All requests are channeled by the browser to the Web server. Internet Information Server (IIS) is Microsoft's Web server and requires Windows NT or Windows 2000, Server edition. Most of the examples in this book will work with the Personal Web Server, which comes with Windows 98. IIS is the middle tier (the application layer). The Web server's role is to generate HTML documents and send them to the client. If the Web server needs to access a database, it must contact a DBMS through an

ActiveX component. The programs on the Web server are active server pages, written in VBScript.

The DBMS, finally, is the data layer of the application.

Notice that the tiers of a Web application need not reside and execute on different machines. The DBMS may be running on the same machine as the Web server. For testing purposes, you can run all three tiers on the same computer, but when you deploy the application, you will install the client application on multiple workstations. The Web server and the DBMS are frequently installed on the same machine, but they run as two separate processes. Even though they're on the same computer, the DBMS will authenticate the Web server and will not allow it to view information or invoke procedures unless it has the appropriate privileges. As the site grows, you may have to use multiple databases and/or multiple Web servers.

SQL Server

Quite a few of you are familiar with Access, and you may have even developed database applications with Access. As I mentioned earlier, however, Access is a desktop database. It can't be scaled up, and it can't accommodate many simultaneous users. To develop real database applications, you should move to SQL Server. SQL Server is Microsoft's DBMS. It's highly scalable and you can use it to develop applications for everything from small networks to thousands of users.

Until recently, Microsoft was pushing Access databases with Visual Basic. Now VB 6 comes with all the drivers and tools you need to access SQL Server databases, and the next version of VB will probably rely heavily on SQL Server. So, this is an excellent time to move up to SQL Server. The current version of SQL Server (version 7) runs under Windows 98 and can be easily deployed in a small network. Even if you have no prior experience with SQL Server, I urge you to install the Evaluation Edition of SQL Server on your computer and use the same machine for development and as a database server.

NOTE

Nearly all of this book's examples will work on a stand-alone computer running Windows 98, but I recommend using Windows NT or Windows 2000.

There are two ways to use SQL Server: as a powerful substitute for Access or as a powerful DBMS (which is what SQL Server is). You can write an application that works with Access, then change its connection to the same database on SQL Server, and the application will work. I know some programmers who upsized their Access database to SQL Server and then changed their DAO-based VB code to work with SQL Server. By the way, converting an application based on DAO to work with ADO is not trivial, but if you write applications based on ADO, you can manipulate Access and SQL Server databases with nearly the same code.

SQL Server has a few unique features that you can't ignore. To begin with, SQL Server has its own programming language, called Transact-SQL (T-SQL). T-SQL is an extension of SQL and it's so powerful that it can do just about everything you can do with VB. T-SQL has no user interface but it supports many data-manipulation functions (similar to the functions of VB) and flow-control statements. It can also access the tables of a database through SQL. In essence, T-SQL combines the power of SQL with the structure of more traditional programming languages. If you don't care about a user interface, you can use T-SQL to implement all of the operations you'd normally code in VB. The advantage of T-SQL is that it's executed on the server and can manipulate tables locally. To do the same with VB, you'd have to move information from the server to the client and process it there. Stored procedures are faster than the equivalent VB code and they standardize client applications, since all clients will call the same procedure to carry out a task.

In effect, it's quite acceptable to implement business rules as stored procedures. I think stored procedures are one of the best reasons to switch from Access databases to SQL Server. A good VB programmer implements the basic operations of the application as functions and calls them from within the application. Practically, you can't implement every data-access operation as a stored procedure, and I urge you to do this. Stored procedures become part of the database and can be used by multiple applications, not just the client application.

WRITE BETTER CLIENT APPLICATIONS WITH STORED PROCEDURES

If you implement the NewInvoice stored procedure to add new invoices to a database, then you can call this stored procedure from within any VB application that needs to add invoices to the database. If you implement the same operation as a method of a middle-tier component, then you can call this method from within any application—including the Office applications. Because middle-tier components are implemented as Classes, they can be called by any COM-enabled application. In simple terms, this means that every programming language that supports the CreateObject() function can call the methods of the middle-tier component. You will see how to create a script to add orders to the database. If you distribute the application, users don't have to go through the visible interface of the application to add new invoices. They can write a short script to automate the process.

SQL Server also uses triggers. A *trigger* is a special stored procedure that is executed when certain actions take place. For example, you can write a procedure to keep track of who has deleted a record and when. Triggers are added to individual tables and can be invoked by three different actions: insertions, deletions, and updates.

SQL Server Tools

Many of you may not be familiar with SQL Server, so in the following sections I introduce you to its basic tools. If you don't have access to SQL Server on your company's network, you can install the desktop version on a local machine and use it as a development platform as well. For more information on ordering SQL Server 7, visit the Microsoft Web site at `www.microsoft.com/sql`.

NOTE

Although SQL Server 2000 is now available, SQL Server 7 is still used more often and so is referenced throughout this section of the book. If you're using SQL Server 2000, you may find new or optimized features not mentioned here, but the functionality of the examples will be the same.

SQL Server Service Manager

This tool allows you to start and stop SQL Server. To start SQL Server, select Start ➢ Programs ➢ SQL Server 7.0 ➢ Microsoft SQL Server 7.0 ➢ Service Manager, which opens a window where you can start and stop SQL Server. Select the MSSQLServer service in the Services box and then click the Start button. If you'd rather have SQL Server auto-start every time you turn on your computer, check the option "Auto-start Service when OS starts."

When SQL Server is running, a small icon with a green arrow is added to the system tray. If you attempt to connect to SQL Server from within a client application while SQL Server is not running, you will get an error message to the effect that there's a problem with your network. At this point you must stop the application, start SQL Server through the Service Manager, and then restart the VB application.

Enterprise Manager

The Enterprise Manager, shown in Figure 11.8, is a visual tool that allows you to view and edit all the objects of SQL Server. This is where you create new databases, edit tables, create stored procedures, and so on. You can also open a table and edit it, but the corresponding tools are not nearly as user-friendly as the ones that come with Access. SQL Server databases shouldn't be manipulated directly. Only the DBA should open tables and examine or edit their contents.

Visual Basic includes several visual database tools that allow you to view the structure of your databases, create and edit tables, create and debug stored procedures, and more. Much of what you can do with Enterprise Manager can be done with the visual database tools, except for adding new users, setting user rights, and similar operations. Again, these tasks are the responsibility of the DBA.

Expand the folder with the name of the server (TOSHIBA in Figure 11.8) in the left pane, and you will see five folders.

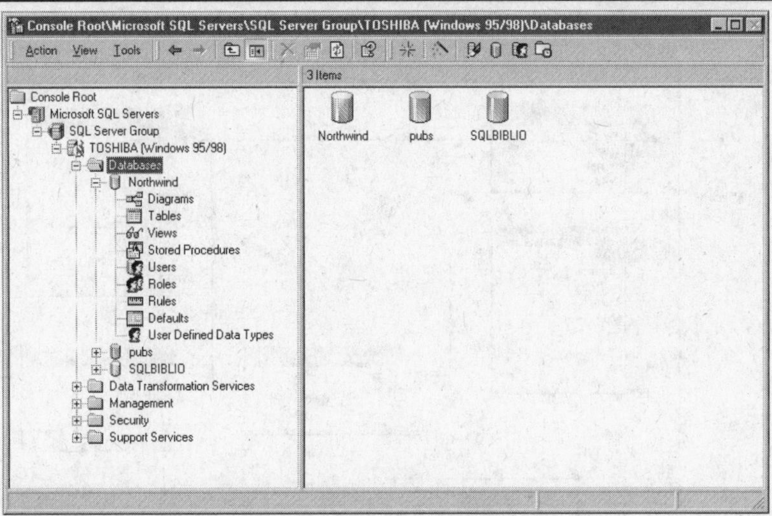

FIGURE 11.8: The SQL Server Enterprise Manager window

Databases

This folder contains a subfolder for each database. If you select a database here, you will see a list of objects, described below, that are specific to that database.

Diagrams A diagram is a picture of the database's structure, similar to the one shown in Figure 11.9. You can manipulate the very structure of the database from within this window, which shows how the various tables relate to each other. You can add new relationships, set their properties, add constraints for the various fields (for example, specify that certain fields must be positive), enforce referential integrity, and so on. Don't worry if you are not familiar with these terms; they are discussed in detail in the next few chapters of the book.

To create a new database diagram, right-click on the right window and select New diagram from the shortcut menu. A Wizard will prompt you to select the tables to include in the diagram, and then it will generate the diagram by extracting the information it needs from the database itself. You will find more information on creating tables and diagrams in Chapter 12.

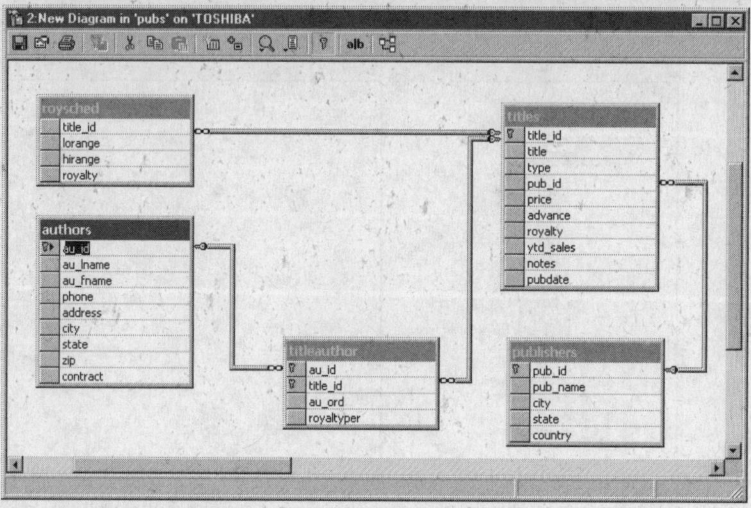

FIGURE 11.9: A database diagram showing the structure of its tables and the relationships between them

Tables A table consists of rows and columns where we store information. Databases have many tables and each table has a specific structure. You can edit the columns of each table through the Design window, shown in Figure 11.10. To open the Design window of a table, right-click the table's name and select Design from the shortcut menu.

2:Design Table 'titles'

Column Name	Datatype	Length	Precision	Scale	Allow Nulls	Default Value	Identity	Identity Seed	Identity Increment
title_id	tid (varchar)	6	0	0					
title	varchar	80	0	0					
type	char	12	0	0		('UNDECIDED')			
pub_id	char	4	0	0	✓				
price	money	8	19	4	✓				
advance	money	8	19	4	✓				
royalty	int	4	10	0	✓				
ytd_sales	int	4	10	0	✓				
notes	varchar	200	0	0	✓				
pubdate	datetime	8	0	0		(getdate())			

FIGURE 11.10: The Design window of the Titles table

Views A view is a section of a table, or a combination of multiple tables, and contains specific information needed by a client. If the Customers table contains salary information, you probably don't want every application to retrieve this information. You can define a view on the table that contains all the columns except for the salary-related ones. As far as the client application is concerned, the view is just another table. SQL Server's views are based on SQL statements and they're equivalent to Access queries.

Most views are editable (a view that contains totals, for example, can't be edited). To open a view, select Views in the left pane of the Enterprise Manager, then right-click the desired view's name in the right pane and select Return All Rows from the shortcut menu. The view's rows will appear on a grid, where you can edit their fields (if the view is updateable). To refresh the view, click the button with the exclamation mark in the window's toolbar.

Stored Procedures A stored procedure is the equivalent of a VB function, only stored procedures are written in T-SQL and they're executed on the server. In this folder, you see the list of stored procedures attached to the database and their definitions. You can create new ones as well, but you can't debug them. To edit and debug your stored procedures, use either the Query Analyzer (discussed in the next section) or the T-SQL Debugger, a tool that comes with VB. Actually, the Stored Procedure Properties window, which will appear if you double-click a procedure's name, contains the definition of the procedure and a button named Check Syntax. If you click this button, the Enterprise Manager will verify the syntax of the stored procedure's definition. It points out the first mistake in the T-SQL code, so it doesn't really qualify as a debugging tool.

Users In this folder, you can review the users authorized to view and/or edit the selected database and add new users. By default, each database has two users: the owner of the database (user *dbo*) and a user with seriously limited privileges (user *guest*). To view the rights of a user, double-click the user's name. On that user's Properties dialog box, you can assign one or more *roles* to the selected user (instead of setting properties for individual users, you create roles and then assign these roles to the users). If you click the Permissions button, you will see the user's permissions for every object in the database, as shown in Figure 11.11. It's a good idea to create a user called *application* (or something similar) and use this ID to connect to the database from within your application. This user will impersonate your application, and you can give this user all the rights your application needs.

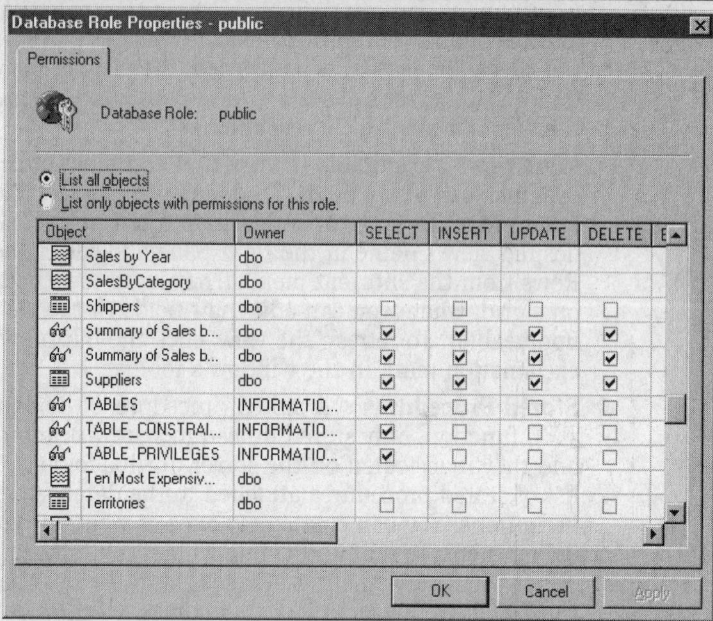

FIGURE 11.11: Setting user permissions for the various objects of a database

Roles When you select the Roles item in the right pane, you will see a list with the existing roles. A *role* is nothing more than a user profile. If multiple users must have common privileges, create a new role, set permissions to this role, and then use it to specify the permissions of individual users.

Rules SQL Server allows you to specify rules for the values of individual fields of a table. These rules are called CHECK constraints and they are specified from within the Database Diagram window. There's no reason to use this window to specify rules, but it's included for compatibility reasons.

Defaults Here you can define the default values for any field. The default values are used when no value is supplied by the user, or the application, for the specific field. It is simpler to specify defaults during the design of the table than to provide the code that checks the user-supplied value and supplies a default value if the user hasn't entered a value for a field.

User-Defined Data Types This is where the *user-defined data types (UDTs)* are specified. SQL Server doesn't allow the creation of arbitrary data structures like Visual Basic does. A UDT is based on one of the existing data types, but you can specify a length (for character and binary types) and, optionally, a default value. For example, you can create a UDT, name it ZCODE, and set its type to CHAR and length to five. This is a shorthand notation rather than a custom data type. UDTs are useful when you allow developers to create their own tables. You can create data types like FNAME, LNAME, and so on, to make sure that all fields that store names, in all tables, have the same length. When you change the definition of a UDT, the table(s) change(s) accordingly without any action on your part.

Data Transformation Services (DTS)

This folder contains the utilities for importing data into SQL Server and exporting data out of SQL Server. The DTS component of SQL Server allows you to import/export data and at the same time transform it. In Chapter 12, you will see how to use the DTS component to upsize the Biblio sample database, which comes with both Access and Visual Basic.

Management

This folder contains the tools for managing databases. The most important tool is the Backup tool, which allows you to back up a database and schedule backup jobs. These tools are also meant for the DBA, and we are not going to use them in this book.

Security

This folder is where the DBA creates new logins and assigns roles to users. We are not going to use these tools in this book.

Support Services

This is where you configure two of SQL Server's support services: the Distributed Transaction Coordinator and SQL Server Mail. The Distributed Transaction Coordinator is a tool for managing transactions that span across multiple servers.

The SQL Server Mail service allows you to create mail messages from within SQL Server. These messages can be scheduled to be created and transmitted automatically and are used to notify the database administrator about the success or failure of a task. You can attach log files and exception files to the message.

The Query Analyzer

If there's one tool you must learn well, this is it. The Query Analyzer is where you can execute SQL statements, batches, and stored procedures against a database. To start the Query Analyzer, select Start ➢ Programs ➢ SQL Server 7.0 ➢ Microsoft SQL Server 7.0 ➢ Query Analyzer. The Query Analyzer uses an MDI interface, and you can open multiple windows, in which you can execute different SQL statements or stored procedures.

If you enter an SQL statement in the Query Analyzer window and click the Execute button (the button with the green arrow on the toolbar), the window will split into two panes. The result of the query will appear in the lower pane—the Results pane—as shown in Figure 11.12. The statement will be executed against the database selected in the DB box at the top of the window, so make sure you've selected the appropriate database before you execute an SQL statement for the first time. You can save the current statement to a text file with the File ➢ Save As command and open it later with the File ➢ Open command.

In addition to SQL statements, you can execute batches written in T-SQL. A *batch* is a collection of SQL and T-SQL statements. For example, you can enter multiple SQL statements and separate them with a GO statement. Each time a GO statement is reached, the Query Analyzer executes all the statements from the beginning of the file, or the previous GO statement. All the results will appear in the Results pane.

NOTE

SQL statements and batches are stored in text files with the extension .SQL. All of the SQL statements and stored procedures presented in this book can be found in a separate SQL file, each under the corresponding chapter's folder on the Sybex Web site. Go to `www.sybex.com` and search for this book (ISBN 2971).

By default, the Query Analyzer displays the row output produced by SQL Server: the results and any messages indicating the success or failure of the operation. Most people prefer the Grid view, which is shown in Figure 11.13. To activate this view, select Results in Grid from the Query menu. The advantage of this view is that you can change the width of the columns. The grid on the Results Grid tab contains the results of the query, and the messages returned by SQL Server are displayed on the Messages tab.

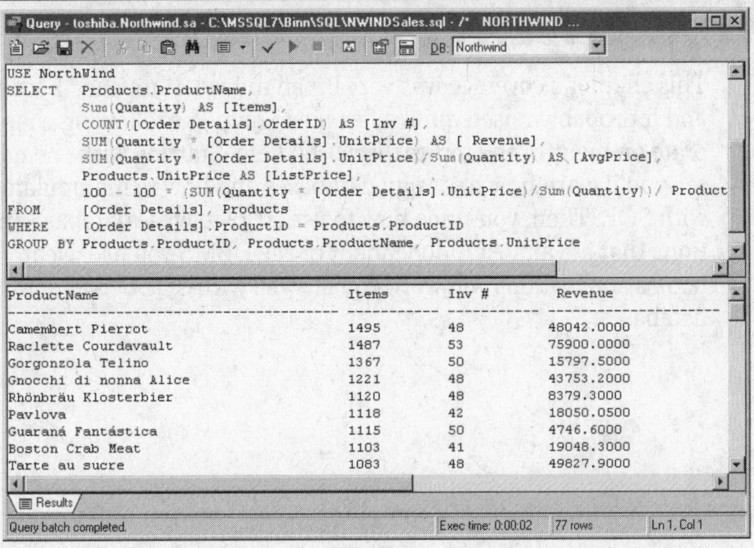
Query - toshiba.Northwind.sa - C:\MSSQL7\Binn\SQL\NWINDSales.sql - /* NORTHWIND ...
DB: Northwind
USE NorthWind
SELECT Products.ProductName,
Sum(Quantity) AS [Items],
COUNT([Order Details].OrderID) AS [Inv #],
SUM(Quantity * [Order Details].UnitPrice) AS [Revenue],
SUM(Quantity * [Order Details].UnitPrice)/Sum(Quantity) AS [AvgPrice],
Products.UnitPrice AS [ListPrice],
100 - 100 * (SUM(Quantity * [Order Details].UnitPrice)/Sum(Quantity))/ Product
FROM [Order Details], Products
WHERE [Order Details].ProductID = Products.ProductID
GROUP BY Products.ProductID, Products.ProductName, Products.UnitPrice
ProductName Items Inv # Revenue
Camembert Pierrot 1495 48 48042.0000
Raclette Courdavault 1487 53 75900.0000
Gorgonzola Telino 1367 50 15797.5000
Gnocchi di nonna Alice 1221 48 43753.2000
Rhönbräu Klosterbier 1120 48 8379.3000
Pavlova 1118 42 18050.0500
Guaraná Fantástica 1115 50 4746.6000
Boston Crab Meat 1103 41 19048.3000
Tarte au sucre 1083 48 49827.9000
Results
Query batch completed.
Exec time: 0:00:02
77 rows
Ln 1, Col 1

FIGURE 11.12: Executing SQL statements with the Query Analyzer

Query - toshiba.Northwind.sa - C:\MSSQL7\Binn\SQL\NWINDSales.sql - /* NORTHWIND ...

DB: Northwind

```
USE NorthWind
SELECT  Products.ProductName,
        Sum(Quantity) AS [Items],
        COUNT([Order Details].OrderID) AS [Inv #],
        SUM(Quantity * [Order Details].UnitPrice) AS [ Revenue],
        SUM(Quantity * [Order Details].UnitPrice)/Sum(Quantity) AS [AvgPrice],
        Products.UnitPrice AS [ListPrice],
        100 - 100 * (SUM(Quantity * [Order Details].UnitPrice)/Sum(Quantity))/ Product
FROM    [Order Details], Products
WHERE   [Order Details].ProductID = Products.ProductID
GROUP BY Products.ProductID, Products.ProductName, Products.UnitPrice
```

ProductName	Items	Inv #	Revenue	AvgPrice	ListPrice	Discount
Camembert Pierrot	1495	48	48042.0000	32.1351	34.0000	5.4850
Raclette Courdavault	1487	53	75900.0000	51.0423	55.0000	7.1959
Gorgonzola Telino	1367	50	15797.5000	11.5563	12.5000	7.5496
Gnocchi di nonna Alice	1221	48	43753.2000	35.8339	38.0000	5.7003
Rhönbräu Klosterbier	1120	48	8379.3000	7.4815	7.7500	3.4646
Pavlova	1118	42	18050.0500	16.1449	17.4500	7.4791
Guaraná Fantástica	1115	50	4746.6000	4.2570	4.5000	5.4000
Boston Crab Meat	1103	41	19048.3000	17.2695	18.4000	6.1441

Results Grid / Messages

Query batch completed. Exec time: 0:00:01 77 rows Ln 12, Col 1

FIGURE 11.13: The Query Analyzer's Grid view

What's Next?

This chapter's coverage was very broad indeed. It touched a lot of topics, and it probably raised quite a few questions. The following chapters elaborate on many of the topics discussed here. Starting with the next chapter, you'll learn how to design databases and how to manipulate them with SQL. Then, you'll see how to use ADO to write database applications that are almost independent of the DBMS you use. Nearly all of this book's applications will work equally well with SQL Server and Access databases.

Chapter 12

Basic Concepts of Relational Databases

This chapter explains the nature of relational databases, why we use a specific methodology to design them, and other related topics. An important part of this chapter is the discussion of the structure of the Northwind and Pubs sample databases, as well as the Biblio database. Northwind comes with both Visual Basic (the Jet version of the database) and SQL Server, and Pubs comes with SQL Server only. Biblio is a Jet sample database that comes with Visual Basic, and we'll import it into SQL Server so that we can use it in the examples of upcoming chapters from within both Access and SQL Server.

Adapted from *Mastering™ Database Programming with Visual Basic® 6*, by Evangelos Petroutsos

ISBN 0-7821-2598-0 896 pages $39.99

NOTE

To make this chapter easier to read, I will not get into the specifics of the tools that come with SQL Server, Access, or Visual Basic. You should use the tools that you know best to examine the sample databases discussed in this chapter.

Why examine the structure of existing databases instead of creating a new one from scratch? Because it's simpler to understand the structure of an existing database, especially a database designed by the people who have designed the data engines themselves. Besides, these databases are used in the examples of the following chapters, so you should make sure you understand their structures.

This chapter introduces the concepts of relational databases. Its purpose is not to teach you how to design corporate databases. The truth is that you needn't even be able to design databases before you start programming them. Quite the contrary: Your experience with database programming will help you develop a solid understanding of databases and their requirements and limitations. Then, you'll find it easier to develop a large database and even become an ER (entity/relationship) specialist–and make more money, too!

Relational Databases

In principle, designing databases is simple. More than anything else, it requires common sense. Databases are meant to solve practical problems faced by corporations on a daily basis: data storage and retrieval. Practical problems call for practical solutions, and databases are not based on mathematics or other abstract concepts.

The databases we're interested in are *relational*, because they are based on relationships among the data they contain. The data is stored in tables, and tables contain related data, or *entities*, such as persons, products, orders, and so on. The idea is to keep the tables small and manageable; thus, separate entities are kept in their own tables. If you start mixing customers and invoices, products and their suppliers, or books, publishers, and authors in the same table, you'll end up repeating information–a highly undesirable situation. If there's one rule to live by as a database designer and programmer, this is it: Do not duplicate information.

Of course, entities are not independent of each other. For example, orders are placed by specific customers, so the rows of the Customers table must be linked to the rows of the Orders table that store the orders of the customers. Figure 12.1 shows a segment of a table with customers (top left) and the rows of a table with orders that correspond to one of the customers (bottom right). The lines that connect the rows of the two tables represent *relationships*. I could discuss other, less efficient database structures, but this isn't a book on the history of databases. All modern databases are relational.

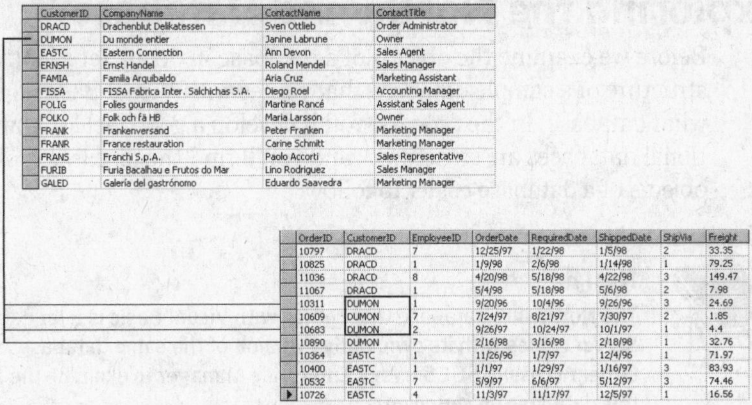

CustomerID	CompanyName	ContactName	ContactTitle
DRACD	Drachenblut Delikatessen	Sven Ottlieb	Order Administrator
DUMON	Du monde entier	Janine Labrune	Owner
EASTC	Eastern Connection	Ann Devon	Sales Agent
ERNSH	Ernst Handel	Roland Mendel	Sales Manager
FAMIA	Familia Arquibaldo	Aria Cruz	Marketing Assistant
FISSA	FISSA Fabrica Inter. Salchichas S.A.	Diego Roel	Accounting Manager
FOLIG	Folies gourmandes	Martine Rancé	Assistant Sales Agent
FOLKO	Folk och fä HB	Maria Larsson	Owner
FRANK	Frankenversand	Peter Franken	Marketing Manager
FRANR	France restauration	Carine Schmitt	Marketing Manager
FRANS	Franchi S.p.A.	Paolo Accorti	Sales Representative
FURIB	Furia Bacalhau e Frutos do Mar	Lino Rodriguez	Sales Manager
GALED	Galería del gastrónomo	Eduardo Saavedra	Marketing Manager

OrderID	CustomerID	EmployeeID	OrderDate	RequiredDate	ShippedDate	ShipVia	Freight
10797	DRACD	7	12/25/97	1/22/98	1/5/98	2	33.35
10825	DRACD	1	1/9/98	2/6/98	1/14/98	1	79.25
11036	DRACD	8	4/20/98	5/18/98	4/22/98	3	149.47
11067	DRACD	1	5/4/98	5/18/98	5/6/98	2	7.98
10311	DUMON	1	9/20/96	10/4/96	9/26/96	3	24.69
10609	DUMON	7	7/24/97	8/21/97	7/30/97	2	1.85
10683	DUMON	2	9/26/97	10/24/97	10/1/97	1	4.4
10890	DUMON	7	2/16/98	3/16/98	2/18/98	1	32.76
10364	EASTC	1	11/26/96	1/7/97	12/4/96	1	71.97
10400	EASTC	1	1/1/97	1/29/97	1/16/97	3	83.93
10532	EASTC	7	5/9/97	6/6/97	5/12/97	3	74.46
10726	EASTC	4	11/3/97	11/17/97	12/5/97	1	16.56

FIGURE 12.1: Linking customers and orders with relationships

Key Fields and Primary and Foreign Keys

As you can see in Figure 12.1, relationships are implemented by inserting rows with matching values in the two related tables; the CustomerID column is repeated in both tables. The rows with a common value in their CustomerID field are related. In other words, the lines that connect the two tables simply indicate that there are two fields, one on each side of the relationship, with a common value. These two fields are called *key fields*. The CustomerID field of the Customers table is the *primary key*, because it identifies a single customer. The CustomerID field of the Orders table is the *foreign key* of the relationship. A CustomerID value appears in a single row of the Customers table; it's the table's primary key. However, it may appear in multiple rows of the Orders table, because in this table the CustomerID field is the foreign key. In fact, it will appear in as many rows of the Orders table as there are orders for the specific customer. (You'll read more about keys a bit later in this chapter.)

NOTE

This simple idea of linking tables based on the values of two columns that are common to both tables is at the heart of relational databases. It allows us to break our data into smaller units, the tables, yet be able to combine rows in multiple tables to retrieve and present the desired information.

Exploring the Northwind Database

Before we examine the objects of a database in detail, let's look at the structure of a sample database that comes with Visual Basic, the Northwind database. In the process, you'll develop a good feel for how relational databases are structured, and you'll find the discussion of the objects of a database easier to follow.

NOTE

The Northwind database that comes with Visual Basic is a Jet database. SQL Server comes with its own, native version of the same database. You can use either Access or SQL Server's Enterprise Manager to examine the structure of this database on your own.

The Northwind database stores sales information: the customers and products of the Northwind Corporation and what products each customer has ordered, along with their prices, discounts, shipping information, and so on. A first attempt to record all of this information might be to enter long lines with every bit of information about each item ordered (and purchased): its price, the quantity ordered, the customer who placed the order, the employee who made the sale, where the item was shipped, and so on. With an exceptionally powerful computer, you'd probably be able to recall all kinds of information from this database. I need not describe why this scheme is inefficient. If a customer's phone number changes, you'll have to scan this long file and replace all instances of the old number with the new one. Clearly, the retrieval of information from this database is anything but efficient; you'd have to write code to scan an enormous table, from start to end, just to locate a few rows. Instead, we'll break the information we want to store in the database into separate tables. Let's start with the tables that make up the Northwind database, and then we'll look at the relationships between the tables.

Northwind Database Tables

The first step in database design is to break the information you want to store into smaller units, the tables, and establish relationships between them. To do so, identify the entities you want to store (products, customers, and so on) and create a table for each entity. A table is a grid: Each row corresponds to a different item, but all items have the same structure. The structure of the table is determined by its columns, and each column represents an attribute of the entity stored in the table. A table that stores products has a column for the product's name, another column for the product's price, and so on. Each product is stored in a different row. As products are added or removed from the table, the number of rows changes, but the number of columns remains the same; they determine the information we store about each product. You can add and remove columns to the table even after you have entered data in them.

The Products Table

The Products table stores information about the products sold by the Northwind Corporation. This information includes the product's name, packaging information, price, and other relevant fields. Additionally, each product in the table is identified by a unique ID number, as shown in Figure 12.2. Product names are easier to remember, but very difficult to enter on a Form. Besides, a product's name can change. Since the rows of the Products table are referenced by invoices (the Order Details table, which is discussed later), each product name change would entail a number of changes in the Order Details table, as well. The product ID that identifies each product need not change; it's a numeric value that carries no meaningful information about the product. Thus, by using a unique numeric value to identify each product, you can change the product's name without affecting any other tables.

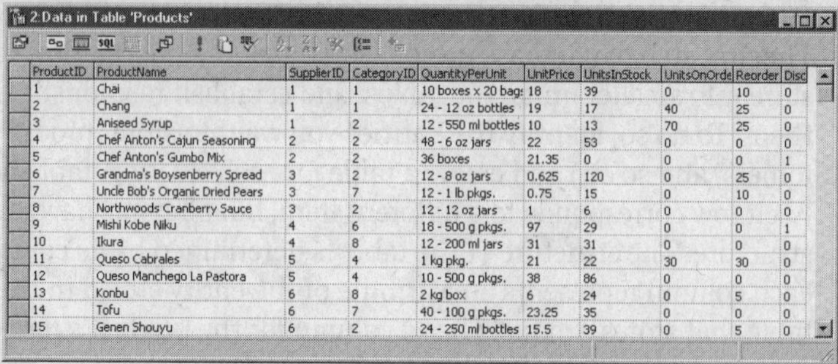

2:Data in Table 'Products'

ProductID	ProductName	SupplierID	CategoryID	QuantityPerUnit	UnitPrice	UnitsInStock	UnitsOnOrde	Reorder	Disc
1	Chai	1	1	10 boxes x 20 bag:	18	39	0	10	0
2	Chang	1	1	24 - 12 oz bottles	19	17	40	25	0
3	Aniseed Syrup	1	2	12 - 550 ml bottles	10	13	70	25	0
4	Chef Anton's Cajun Seasoning	2	2	48 - 6 oz jars	22	53	0	0	0
5	Chef Anton's Gumbo Mix	2	2	36 boxes	21.35	0	0	0	1
6	Grandma's Boysenberry Spread	3	2	12 - 8 oz jars	0.625	120	0	25	0
7	Uncle Bob's Organic Dried Pears	3	7	12 - 1 lb pkgs.	0.75	15	0	10	0
8	Northwoods Cranberry Sauce	3	2	12 - 12 oz jars	1	6	0	0	0
9	Mishi Kobe Niku	4	6	18 - 500 g pkgs.	97	29	0	0	1
10	Ikura	4	8	12 - 200 ml jars	31	31	0	0	0
11	Queso Cabrales	5	4	1 kg pkg.	21	22	30	30	0
12	Queso Manchego La Pastora	5	4	10 - 500 g pkgs.	38	86	0	0	0
13	Konbu	6	8	2 kg box	6	24	0	5	0
14	Tofu	6	7	40 - 100 g pkgs.	23.25	35	0	0	0
15	Genen Shouyu	6	2	24 - 250 ml bottles	15.5	39	0	5	0

FIGURE 12.2: Showing that each line in the Products table holds information about a specific product

The SupplierID and CategoryID columns contain integer values that point to rows of two other tables, the Suppliers and Categories tables, respectively. These two tables contain information about the Northwind Corporation's suppliers and various product categories.

NOTE

Supplier information can't be stored in the Products table, because the same supplier's name and address would be repeated in multiple products.

The Suppliers Table

Each product in the Northwind database has a supplier. Because the same supplier may offer more than one product, the supplier information is stored in a different table, and a common field, the SupplierID field, is used to link each product to its supplier. For example, the two products Mishi Kobe Niku and Ikura are purchased from the same supplier, Tokyo Traders. Their SupplierID fields point to the same row in the Suppliers table, as shown in Figure 12.3.

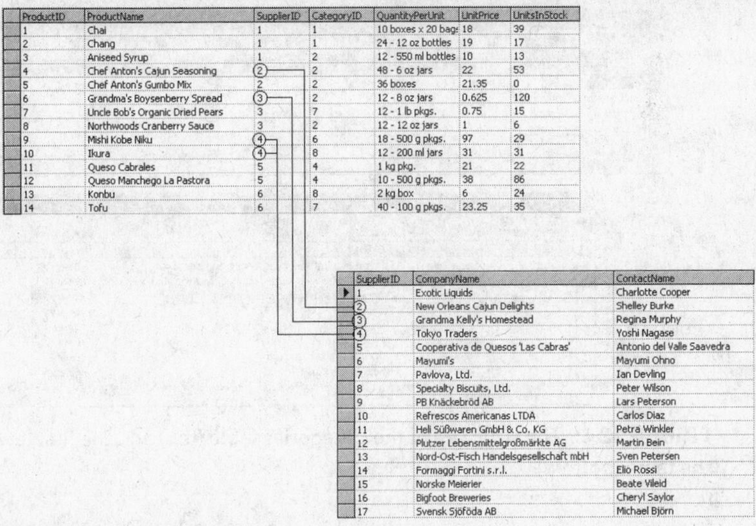

ProductID	ProductName	SupplierID	CategoryID	QuantityPerUnit	UnitPrice	UnitsInStock
1	Chai	1	1	10 boxes x 20 bag	18	39
2	Chang	1	1	24 - 12 oz bottles	19	17
3	Aniseed Syrup	1	2	12 - 550 ml bottles	10	13
4	Chef Anton's Cajun Seasoning	2	2	48 - 6 oz jars	22	53
5	Chef Anton's Gumbo Mix	2	2	36 boxes	21.35	0
6	Grandma's Boysenberry Spread	3	2	12 - 8 oz jars	0.625	120
7	Uncle Bob's Organic Dried Pears	3	7	12 - 1 lb pkgs.	0.75	15
8	Northwoods Cranberry Sauce	3	2	12 - 12 oz jars	1	6
9	Mishi Kobe Niku	4	6	18 - 500 g pkgs.	97	29
10	Ikura	4	8	12 - 200 ml jars	31	31
11	Queso Cabrales	5	4	1 kg pkg.	21	22
12	Queso Manchego La Pastora	5	4	10 - 500 g pkgs.	38	86
13	Konbu	6	8	2 kg box	6	24
14	Tofu	6	7	40 - 100 g pkgs.	23.25	35

SupplierID	CompanyName	ContactName
1	Exotic Liquids	Charlotte Cooper
2	New Orleans Cajun Delights	Shelley Burke
3	Grandma Kelly's Homestead	Regina Murphy
4	Tokyo Traders	Yoshi Nagase
5	Cooperativa de Quesos 'Las Cabras'	Antonio del Valle Saavedra
6	Mayumi's	Mayumi Ohno
7	Pavlova, Ltd.	Ian Devling
8	Specialty Biscuits, Ltd.	Peter Wilson
9	PB Knäckebröd AB	Lars Peterson
10	Refrescos Americanas LTDA	Carlos Diaz
11	Heli Süßwaren GmbH & Co. KG	Petra Winkler
12	Plutzer Lebensmittelgroßmärkte AG	Martin Bein
13	Nord-Ost-Fisch Handelsgesellschaft mbH	Sven Petersen
14	Formaggi Fortini s.r.l.	Elio Rossi
15	Norske Meierier	Beate Vileid
16	Bigfoot Breweries	Cheryl Saylor
17	Svensk Sjöföda AB	Michael Björn

FIGURE 12.3: Linking products to their suppliers

The Categories Table

In addition to having a supplier, each product belongs to a category. Categories are not stored along with product names, but in a separate table, the Categories table, whose structure is shown in Figure 12.4. Again, each category is identified by a numeric value and has a name (the CategoryID and CategoryName fields, respectively). In addition, the Categories table has two more columns: Description, which contains text, and Picture, which stores a bitmap.

The Products table (back in Figure 12.2) has a CategoryID column as well, which links each product to its category. By storing the categories in a separate table, you don't have to enter the actual name of the category (or its bitmap) along with each product. The CategoryID field of the Products table points to the product's category, and you can locate each product's category very quickly in the Categories table.

The CategoryID field in the Categories table is the primary key, because it identifies each row in the table. Each category has a unique CategoryID, which may be repeated many times in the Products table. The CategoryID field in the Products table is the foreign key.

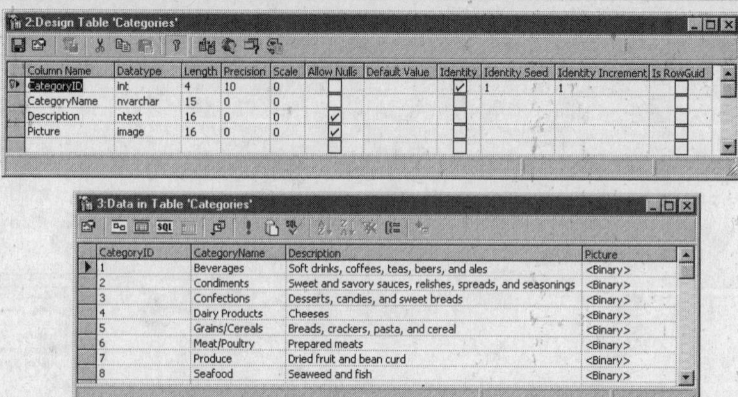

2:Design Table 'Categories'

Column Name	Datatype	Length	Precision	Scale	Allow Nulls	Default Value	Identity	Identity Seed	Identity Increment	Is RowGuid
CategoryID	int	4	10	0			✓	1	1	
CategoryName	nvarchar	15	0	0						
Description	ntext	16	0	0	✓					
Picture	image	16	0	0	✓					

3:Data in Table 'Categories'

CategoryID	CategoryName	Description	Picture
1	Beverages	Soft drinks, coffees, teas, beers, and ales	<Binary>
2	Condiments	Sweet and savory sauces, relishes, spreads, and seasonings	<Binary>
3	Confections	Desserts, candies, and sweet breads	<Binary>
4	Dairy Products	Cheeses	<Binary>
5	Grains/Cereals	Breads, crackers, pasta, and cereal	<Binary>
6	Meat/Poultry	Prepared meats	<Binary>
7	Produce	Dried fruit and bean curd	<Binary>
8	Seafood	Seaweed and fish	<Binary>

FIGURE 12.4: The structure of the Categories table (top) and the first few rows of the table (bottom)

But what do primary and foreign keys do in the Northwind database? When you look up products, you want to be able to locate quickly the category to which they belong. You read the value of the CategoryID field in the Products table, locate the row in the Categories table with the same value in the CategoryID column, and—voilà!—you have matched the two tables. You can also search the Products table for products that belong to a specific category. You start with the ID of a category and then locate all the rows in the Products table with a CategoryID field that matches the selected ID. The relationship between the two tables links each row of the first table to one or more rows of the second table, and you will see shortly how relationships are defined.

NOTE

The operation of matching rows in two (or more) tables based on their primary and foreign keys is called a *join*. Joins are very basic operations in manipulating tables, and they are discussed a little more in the next chapter.

The Customers Table

The Customers table, shown in Figure 12.5, stores information about the company's customers. Before we can accept an order, we must create a new row in the Customers table with the customer's data (name, phone number, address, and so on), if one doesn't exist already. Each row in the

Customers table represents a different customer and is identified by the CustomerID field. This field has a unique value for each row, similar to the ProductID field of the Products table. However, the CustomerID field is a five-character-long string, and not an integer.

CustomerID	CompanyName	ContactName	ContactTitle
DRACD	Drachenblut Delikatessen	Sven Ottlieb	Order Administrator
DUMON	Du monde entier	Janine Labrune	Owner
EASTC	Eastern Connection	Ann Devon	Sales Agent
ERNSH	Ernst Handel	Roland Mendel	Sales Manager
FAMIA	Familia Arquibaldo	Aria Cruz	Marketing Assistant
FISSA	FISSA Fabrica Inter. Salchichas S.A.	Diego Roel	Accounting Manager
FOLIG	Folies gourmandes	Martine Rancé	Assistant Sales Agent
FOLKO	Folk och fä HB	Maria Larsson	Owner
FRANK	Frankenversand	Peter Franken	Marketing Manager
FRANR	France restauration	Carine Schmitt	Marketing Manager
FRANS	Franchi S.p.A.	Paolo Accorti	Sales Representative
FURIB	Furia Bacalhau e Frutos do Mar	Lino Rodriguez	Sales Manager
GALED	Galería del gastrónomo	Eduardo Saavedra	Marketing Manager
GODOS	Godos Cocina Típica	José Pedro Freyre	Sales Manager
GOURL	Gourmet Lanchonetes	André Fonseca	Sales Associate
GREAL	Great Lakes Food Market	Howard Snyder	Marketing Manager
GROSR	GROSELLA-Restaurante	Manuel Pereira	Owner
HILAA	HILARION-Abastos	Carlos Hernández	Sales Representative

FIGURE 12.5: The Customers table

The Orders Table

The Orders table, shown in Figure 12.6, stores information (customer, shipping address, date of order, and so on) about the orders placed by Northwind's customers. The OrderID field, which is an integer value, identifies each order. Orders are numbered sequentially, so this field is also the order's number. As you will see in the "AutoNumber and Identity Fields" section later in this chapter, each time you append a new row to the Orders table, the value of the new OrderID field is generated automatically by the database. Moreover, this value can't be edited (this is a built-in mechanism for protecting the integrity of the database).

The Orders table is linked to the Customers table through the CustomerID field. By matching rows with identical values in their CustomerID fields in the two tables, we can recombine a customer with his orders.

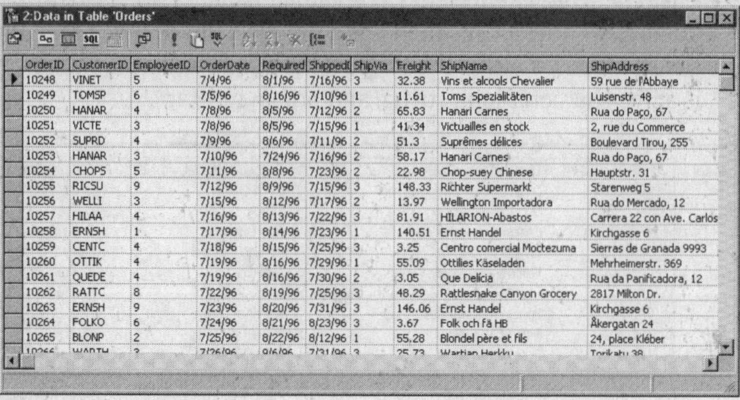

2:Data in Table 'Orders'

OrderID	CustomerID	EmployeeID	OrderDate	Required	Shipped	ShipVia	Freight	ShipName	ShipAddress
10248	VINET	5	7/4/96	8/1/96	7/16/96	3	32.38	Vins et alcools Chevalier	59 rue de l'Abbaye
10249	TOMSP	6	7/5/96	8/16/96	7/10/96	1	11.61	Toms Spezialitäten	Luisenstr. 48
10250	HANAR	4	7/8/96	8/5/96	7/12/96	2	65.83	Hanari Carnes	Rua do Paço, 67
10251	VICTE	3	7/8/96	8/5/96	7/15/96	1	41.34	Victuailles en stock	2, rue du Commerce
10252	SUPRD	4	7/9/96	8/6/96	7/11/96	2	51.3	Suprêmes délices	Boulevard Tirou, 255
10253	HANAR	3	7/10/96	7/24/96	7/16/96	2	58.17	Hanari Carnes	Rua do Paço, 67
10254	CHOPS	5	7/11/96	8/8/96	7/23/96	2	22.98	Chop-suey Chinese	Hauptstr. 31
10255	RICSU	9	7/12/96	8/9/96	7/15/96	3	148.33	Richter Supermarkt	Starenweg 5
10256	WELLI	3	7/15/96	8/12/96	7/17/96	2	13.97	Wellington Importadora	Rua do Mercado, 12
10257	HILAA	4	7/16/96	8/13/96	7/22/96	3	81.91	HILARION-Abastos	Carrera 22 con Ave. Carlos
10258	ERNSH	1	7/17/96	8/14/96	7/23/96	1	140.51	Ernst Handel	Kirchgasse 6
10259	CENTC	4	7/18/96	8/15/96	7/25/96	3	3.25	Centro comercial Moctezuma	Sierras de Granada 9993
10260	OTTIK	4	7/19/96	8/16/96	7/29/96	1	55.09	Ottilies Käseladen	Mehrheimerstr. 369
10261	QUEDE	4	7/19/96	8/16/96	7/30/96	2	3.05	Que Delícia	Rua da Panificadora, 12
10262	RATTC	8	7/22/96	8/19/96	7/25/96	3	48.29	Rattlesnake Canyon Grocery	2817 Milton Dr.
10263	ERNSH	9	7/23/96	8/20/96	7/31/96	3	146.06	Ernst Handel	Kirchgasse 6
10264	FOLKO	6	7/24/96	8/21/96	8/23/96	3	3.67	Folk och fä HB	Åkergatan 24
10265	BLONP	2	7/25/96	8/22/96	8/12/96	1	55.28	Blondel père et fils	24, place Kléber
10266	WARTH	3	7/26/96	9/6/96	7/31/96	3	25.73	Wartian Herkku	Torikatu 38

FIGURE 12.6: The Orders table

The Order Details Table

You've probably noticed that the Northwind database's Orders table doesn't store any details about the items ordered. This information is stored in the Order Details table (see Figure 12.7). Each order is made up of one or more items, and each item has a price, a quantity, and a discount. In addition to these fields, the Order Details table contains an OrderID column, which holds the order number to which the detail line belongs. In other words, the details of all invoices are thrown into this table and are organized according to the order to which they belong.

The reason details aren't stored along with the order's header is that the Order and Order Details tables store different entities. The order's header, which contains information about the customer who placed the order, the date of the order, and so on, is quite different from the information you must store for each item ordered. Try to come up with a different design that stores all order-related information in a single table, and you'll soon realize that you end up duplicating information. Figure 12.8 shows how three of the tables in the Northwind database—Customers, Orders, and Order Details—are linked to one another.

I should probably explain why the order's total doesn't appear in any table. To calculate an order's total, you must multiply the quantity by the price, taking into consideration the discount. If the order's total were stored in the Orders table, you'd be duplicating information. In other words, you'd be able to retrieve the same information from two different tables, and there's no guarantee that the values will always be the same.

2:Data in Table 'Order Details'

OrderID	ProductID	UnitPrice	Quantity	Discount
10331	54	5.9	15	0
10332	18	50	40	0.2
10332	42	11.2	10	0.2
10332	47	7.6	16	0.2
10333	14	18.6	10	0
10333	21	8	10	0.1
10333	71	17.2	40	0.1
10334	52	5.6	8	0
10334	68	10	10	0
10335	2	15.2	7	0.2
10335	31	10	25	0.2
10335	32	25.6	6	0.2
10335	51	42.4	48	0.2
10336	4	17.6	18	0.1
10337	23	7.2	40	0
10337	26	24.9	24	0
10337	36	15.2	20	0
10337	37	20.8	28	0
10337	72	27.8	25	0

FIGURE 12.7: The Order Details table

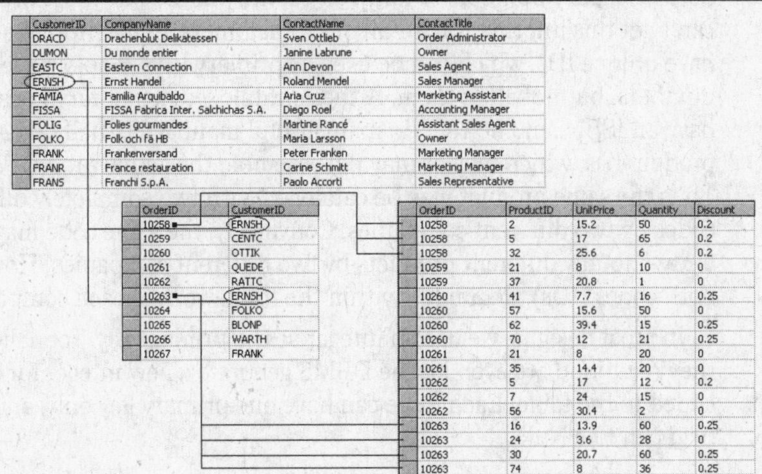

CustomerID	CompanyName	ContactName	ContactTitle
DRACD	Drachenblut Delikatessen	Sven Ottlieb	Order Administrator
DUMON	Du monde entier	Janine Labrune	Owner
EASTC	Eastern Connection	Ann Devon	Sales Agent
ERNSH	Ernst Handel	Roland Mendel	Sales Manager
FAMIA	Familia Arquibaldo	Aria Cruz	Marketing Assistant
FISSA	FISSA Fabrica Inter. Salchichas S.A.	Diego Roel	Accounting Manager
FOLIG	Folies gourmandes	Martine Rancé	Assistant Sales Agent
FOLKO	Folk och fä HB	Maria Larsson	Owner
FRANK	Frankenversand	Peter Franken	Marketing Manager
FRANR	France restauration	Carine Schmitt	Marketing Manager
FRANS	Franchi S.p.A.	Paolo Accorti	Sales Representative

OrderID	CustomerID
10258	ERNSH
10259	CENTC
10260	OTTIK
10261	QUEDE
10262	RATTC
10263	ERNSH
10264	FOLKO
10265	BLONP
10266	WARTH
10267	FRANK

OrderID	ProductID	UnitPrice	Quantity	Discount
10258	2	15.2	50	0.2
10258	5	17	65	0.2
10258	32	25.6	6	0.2
10259	21	8	10	0
10259	37	20.8	1	0
10260	41	7.7	16	0.25
10260	57	15.6	50	0
10260	62	39.4	15	0.25
10260	70	12	21	0.25
10261	21	8	20	0
10261	35	14.4	20	0
10262	5	17	12	0.2
10262	7	24	15	0
10262	56	30.4	2	0
10263	16	13.9	60	0.25
10263	24	3.6	28	0
10263	30	20.7	60	0.25
10263	74	8	36	0.25

FIGURE 12.8: Linking customers to orders and orders to their details

The Employees Table

This table holds employee information. Apparently, the employees of the Northwind Corporation work on commission, and we need to know what sales they have made. When a sale is made, the ID of the employee who made the sale is recorded in the Orders table.

The Shippers Table

Finally, Northwind Corporation uses three different shippers. The Shippers table holds information about the shippers, and each shipper's ID appears in the Orders table, along with the order date, shipment date, address, and so on.

Understanding Relations

In a database, each table has a field with a unique value for every row. This field is marked with the icon of a key in front of its name, as you can see back in Figure 12.4, and it's the table's primary key.

The primary key does not have to be a meaningful entity, because in most cases there's no single field that's unique for each row. The primary key need not resemble the entity it identifies. The only requirement is that primary keys are unique in the entire table. The IRS probably uses Social Security numbers to uniquely identify us all, but your corporation can't get this information for all of its customers. Some products may have unique IDs, which can be used as primary keys. Books have ISBN numbers, but not all of them. A thesis cataloged in a library does not have an ISBN, and neither do many useful manuals. Usually, we make up product IDs, which may or may not resemble the actual product's name. Thus the same product may be cataloged with two completely different codes by two different companies. Conversely, the same code may be used for two totally different products by two different companies. However, both codes (IDs) are unique within the framework of each company.

In most designs, we use an integer as the primary key. To make sure they're unique, we even let the DBMS generate a new integer for each row added to the table. Each table can have one primary key only, and this field can't be Null.

NOTE

Most primary keys are made up (either by the user, or by the DBMS itself). Some people make up semi-real keys. For example, I've seen databases that use ISBN values to uniquely identify most of the books, and fake ISBNs (they start with the digits 000, or 999) to represent the few books that have no ISBNs. This approach will work for a while, especially if you know how to make up ISBNs, but you never know when it will fail. What if another bookseller had the same idea and eventually you have to do business with this bookseller? There's a chance that the two "unique" identification systems will collide with each other. If you can't use a real entity as the primary key, leave it to the system to make unique keys for you. (You'll see how this is done in the upcoming "AutoNumber and Identity Fields" section.) The numeric keys will not help the problem of conflicting IDs, but they do not pretend to be globally unique, like ISBNs.

The related rows in a table repeat the primary key of the row they are related to, in another table. The copies of the primary keys in all other tables are called *foreign keys*. Foreign keys need not be unique (in fact, they aren't) and any field can serve as a foreign key. What makes a field a foreign key is that it matches the primary key of another table. The CategoryID field is the primary key of the Categories table, because it identifies each category. The CategoryID field in the Products table is the foreign key, because the same value may appear in many rows (many products may belong to the same category). When you relate the Products and Categories tables, for example, you must also make sure that:

- Every product added to the foreign table points to a valid entry in the primary table. If you are not sure about the category to which the product belongs, you can leave the CategoryID field of the Products table empty. The primary keys, however, can't be Null.
- No rows in the Categories table are removed if there are rows in the Products table pointing to the specific category. This will make the corresponding rows of the Products table point to an invalid category.

These two restrictions would be quite a burden on the programmer if the DBMS didn't protect the database against actions that could impair its integrity. The integrity of your database depends on the validity of the relations. Fortunately, all DBMSs can enforce rules to maintain their integrity. You'll learn how to enforce rules that guarantee the integrity of your database in the "Database Integrity" section later in this chapter.

Querying Relational Databases

Now let's consider the most common operations you'd like to be able to perform on the Northwind database's tables. The process of retrieving data from the tables is known as *querying*, and the statements you execute against a database to retrieve selected rows are called *queries*. These statements are written in SQL (Structured Query Language), which is discussed in detail in the next chapter. In this section, we'll look at a few simple queries and how the DBMS combines rows from multiple tables to return the data we're interested in.

Retrieving a Customer's Orders

This is probably the most common operation one would perform on a database like Northwind. To retrieve a customer's orders, start with the customer's ID and locate all the lines in the Orders table whose CustomerID field matches the CustomerID field of the selected row in the Customers table. To retrieve the customer's orders, the DBMS must search the Orders table with its foreign key. To help the DMBS with this operation, you should index the Orders table on its CustomerID field. Both versions of the Northwind database define an index on this field.

Calculating the Total for Each Order

The Orders table doesn't contain the total for each order–and it shouldn't. The totals must be calculated directly from the details. As mentioned earlier, databases shouldn't duplicate information, and storing the totals in the Orders table would be a form of duplication; you'd duplicate the information that's already present in another table. Had you stored the totals along with each order, then every time you changed a detail line, you'd also have to change a row in the Orders table.

To calculate an order's total, the DBMS must search the Order Details table with its foreign key (OrderID) and the quantities times prices for all rows that belong to the specific order (it must also take into consideration the discount). To help the DBMS with this operation, you should index the Order Details table on its OrderID field. Both versions of the Northwind database define an index on the OrderID field.

Calculating the Total for Each Customer

This operation is similar to totaling an order, but it involves three tables. Start with the customer's ID and select all the rows in the Orders table whose CustomerID field matches the ID of the specific customer. This is a list with the IDs of the orders placed by the selected customer. Then scan all the rows of the Order Details table whose OrderID field is in this list and sum the products of quantities times prices.

Performing More Complicated Queries

The kind of information a manager may require from a database can't always be classified or enumerated. You can perform complicated queries, such as locating the state in which a specific product is very popular, the best-selling product for each month or quarter, and so on. All the information is in the database, and it's a question of combining the proper fields of the various tables to extract the information you need in order to make better decisions.

Most practical queries involve multiple tables and their relationships. Primary and foreign keys are central concepts in querying databases and, as such, are one of the most important aspects of the design process. Sometimes, the most difficult aspect of SQL is joining multiple tables based on their relationships.

Database Objects

Now that you've been introduced to the basic concepts (and objects) of a relational database by means of examples, you should have a good idea of what a relational database is. You understand how data is stored in separate tables in the database and how the tables are linked to one another through relationships. You also know how relationships are used to execute complicated queries that retrieve data from multiple tables. I'm sure you have questions about specific attributes and techniques, which are addressed in the following sections of this chapter. Let's begin our detailed discussion of the objects of a relational database with the most basic of objects: tables.

Tables

A *table* is a collection of rows with the same structure that stores information about an entity such as a person, an invoice, a product, and so on. Each row contains the same number of columns, and each column can store data of the same data type. You can think of a table as a grid or a random access file that stores records. As you know, each record in a random-access file has the same structure, and you can't read or write data to the file unless you know the structure of the records it holds. I probably need not mention this, but any resemblance between tables and random access files ends here.

A DBMS like SQL Server or Access doesn't store tables in separate files. All of the data reside in a single file, along with auxiliary information required by the DBMS to access them quickly. In reality, the DBMS uses more space to store the auxiliary information than for the data itself. The tables in a database are an abstraction; they form a conceptual model of the data. This is how we humans view the database. Tables don't reflect the actual structure of the data in the database. Instead, they reflect the entities in our database, and the relations between tables reflect actions (products are *purchased*, customers *place* orders, and so on).

Internally, every DBMS stores information in a proprietary format, and we need not know anything about this format. In effect, this is one of the requirements of the relational database model: *The physical structure may change, but these changes shouldn't affect how we see the database.* Microsoft may change the physical structure of the data in an MDB file, but Access will still see tables and indexes, it will still be able to relate tables to each other using common field values (the primary and foreign keys), and your applications will keep working. You will see the same tables, the same SQL statements will retrieve the same data, and you won't even notice the difference (there will be new features, of course, but existing applications will continue to work without any modifications).

CUSTOMERS AND SUPPLIERS: SAME ENTITIES, DIFFERENT FUNCTION

You will notice that the Northwind database's Customers and Suppliers tables have the exact same structure. As far as the operations of an application are concerned, customers and suppliers are two separate entities, and there's no overlap between the two. This is a rather unusual situation, where two different entities have the same (or nearly the same) structure.

Keep in mind that Northwind is a sample database. In a real-world situation, the two tables may not be totally isolated, as the same company may act both as a supplier and as a customer. In other words, it may not only sell to your company, but buy from it as well.

CONTINUED →

In my applications, I use a single table for customers and suppliers. This approach may complicate the programming a little, but it simplifies operations from a user's point of view. If you don't know that a supplier is also a customer, you may end up paying for the items you purchase regularly and never know that the other party is not keeping up with their obligations. There are other practical reasons for treating both customers and suppliers as a single entity, such as preferring a supplier who is also a good customer of yours.

Creating Tables

To create a table, you must specify its structure by declaring its columns: specify how many columns the table has, their names, and their types. No matter what DBMS you're using, follow these steps to create tables:

1. Make up a name for the table. Table names can be quite long, so you should name them after the entity they represent. Table names, as well as field names, can include spaces as long as you remember to enclose them in a pair of square brackets ([Order Details], [Sales in Europe], and so on) in your code.

2. Make up a name for each column (or field) of the table. Columns are the attributes of the entity represented by the table. The columns of a table that stores customers should probably contain a customer's name, address, phone numbers, electronic address, and so on. The columns of a table that stores invoices should contain an invoice's number, the date of the invoice, shipping address, and so on.

3. Decide the data type for each column. Since different columns store different items of information, their types should match. A column that stores quantities should be defined as integer, while a column that stores prices should be defined as currency. Likewise, a column that stores dates should be defined accordingly.

NOTE

Different DBMSs use different names for the data types they support, but they support all the basic data types. When you program databases through the ADO component, however, you can use ADO constants for each type, regardless of the name used by the DBMS to describe each type. Table 12.1, later in this chapter, shows the data types supported by Access and SQL Server and the ADO constant for each data type.

That's all it takes to design a table. If later you decide that you need an additional column, you can always add one without affecting the structure, or the content, of the existing ones. You will see the tools for creating a new database from scratch, or edit existing databases, in the following chapter.

When you create a new table, a grid with the names and the attributes of the fields is displayed. Figure 12.9 shows the table design grid for SQL Server. Each row in the grids corresponds to a table column.

2:Design Table 'Customers'

Column Name	Datatype	Length	Precision	Scale	Allow Nulls	Default Value	Identity	Identity Seed	Identity Increment	Is RowGuid
CustomerID	nchar	5	0	0	☐		☐			☐
CompanyName	nvarchar	40	0	0	☐		☐			☐
ContactName	nvarchar	30	0	0	☑		☐			☐
ContactTitle	nvarchar	30	0	0	☑		☐			☐
Address	nvarchar	60	0	0	☑		☐			☐
City	nvarchar	15	0	0	☑		☐			☐
Region	nvarchar	15	0	0	☑		☐			☐
PostalCode	nvarchar	10	0	0	☑		☐			☐
Country	nvarchar	15	0	0	☑		☐			☐
Phone	nvarchar	24	0	0	☑		☐			☐
Fax	nvarchar	24	0	0	☑		☐			☐

FIGURE 12.9: Designing a table in SQL Server's Enterprise Manager

Each column must have a name with a maximum length of 64 characters (for Access and SQL Server databases). The column's data type can be selected from a drop-down list and can have one of the values shown in Table 12.1. Notice that Access and SQL Server don't recognize the same data types (the most common data types, however, are common to both). You won't see the constants listed in Table 12.1 when you design tables with Access or SQL Server, but this is the value you must specify when you program databases with ADO.

TABLE 12.1: Access and SQL Server Data Types

CONSTANT	ACCESS	SQL SERVER
adBinary		binary
adBoolean	Yes/No	bit
adChar		char
adCurrency	Currency	money, smallmoney
adDate	Date/Time	datetime, smalldatetime
adDBTimeStamp	Date/Time	timestamp
adDecimal		decimal, numeric
adDouble	Double	float
adGUID	ReplicationID	uniqueidentifier
adInteger	Long Integer, AutoNumber	int, Identity
adLongVarBinary	OLE Object	image
adLongVarChar	Memo	text
adNumeric		decimal, numeric
adSingle	Single	real
adSmallInt	Integer	smallint
adTinyInt		tinyint
adVarBinary		varbinary
adVarChar		varchar

NAMING CONVENTIONS

Sooner or later, someone will need to revise your database. To make things easier for that person, whether it's you or someone else, consider using a naming convention consistent with all of your design work. Though not used in the sample databases included with SQL Server and Access, most developers use a common standard, such as the Leszynski/Reddick naming convention, which simply incorporates a description of an object into the name itself. This makes

CONTINUED ➞

it easier to identify and organize objects at a glance, as well as to follow the code you wrote six months ago. The specific guidelines of this particular protocol can be found at `http://msdn.microsoft.com/library/backgrnd/html/msdn_20naming.htm`.

Entering Data into Tables

There are many ways to enter data into a database's tables. You can use SQL statements: The INSERT statement appends a new row to a table and sets its fields to the value specified with the command. You can also open the actual table and edit it. Both Access and SQL Server support this type of direct editing. Just double-click the name of an Access table, or right-click the name of a SQL Server and select Open Table ➢ Return All Rows from the shortcut menu. By the way, SQL Server is a DBMS and not a visual environment for accessing and manipulating data. Access is primarily a front-end application, so it's easier to edit Access tables than SQL Server tables. Finally, you can write VB applications that allow users to edit tables through the proper interface. Obviously, this is the recommended method, since it allows you to validate the data and protect the database against user mistakes.

Null Values

If you're not familiar with database programming, you probably haven't used Null values yet, and you'll be surprised how important Null values are to databases. A *Null value* means that the actual field value is unknown. A numeric field with a zero value is not a Null value. Likewise, a blank string is not a Null value either. Nulls were introduced to handle incomplete or exceptional data, and they should be handled in a special manner. A field that has not been assigned a value is considered incomplete. If this field is involved in an operation, the result of the operation is considered exceptional, since it's neither zero nor a blank string. When a new row is created, all of its columns are set to Null, and unless you specify a value, they remain Null. You can modify this default behavior by requesting that certain columns can't be Null. If you attempt to add a new row with a Null value in a column that's not allowed to accept Nulls, the database will reject the insertion. The same will happen if you edit a row and set to Null the value of a column that's not allowed to accept Nulls.

Primary key fields (the fields that link tables to one another), for example, can never be Null. To specify that any other field may not accept the Null value, you must set the Required property in Access to True or the Allow Nulls property in SQL Server to False.

If your tables contain Null values, you should be aware of how the DBMS handles them. When you sum the values of a column with the SUM() function, Null values are ignored. If you count the rows with the COUNT() function, the Null fields are also ignored. The same is true for the AVG() function, which calculates the average value. If it treated the Null values as zeros, then the average would be wrong. The AVG() function returns the average of the fields that are not Null. If you want to include the Null values in the average, you must first replace them with the zero numeric value. These rules apply to both Access and SQL Server.

Null values are so important in working with databases that SQL recognizes the keywords IS NULL and IS NOT NULL (SQL statements are not case-sensitive, but this book uses uppercase so that you can quickly spot the SQL keywords in the examples). To exclude the Null values in an SQL statement, use the clause:

```
WHERE column_name IS NOT NULL
```

Here's a simple example of an SQL statement that retrieves the titles that have a price and ignores the rest of them:

```
SELECT Title, Price
FROM Books
WHERE Price IS NOT NULL
```

To retrieve the titles without a price, use a statement similar to this:

```
SELECT Title
FROM Books
WHERE Price IS NULL
```

Indexes

So now you've created a few tables and have actually entered some data into them. Now the most important thing you can do with a database is extract data from it (or else, why store the information in the first place?). And I don't mean view all the customers or all the products. We rarely browse the rows of a single table. Instead, we're interested in summary information that will help us make business decisions. We need answers to questions like "What's the most popular product in California?" or "What's the month with the largest sales for a specific product?" and so on. To retrieve this type of information, you must combine multiple tables. As you can guess, a DBMS must be able to scan the tables and locate the desired rows quickly. An index is nothing more than a mechanism for speeding up lookup operations.

Computers use a special technique, called *indexing*, to locate information very quickly. This technique requires that the data be maintained in some order. As you will see, the indexed rows need not be in a specific physical order, as long as we can retrieve them in a specific order.

Fortunately, you don't have to maintain the rows of the tables in any order yourself. The DBMS does it for you. You simply specify that a table be maintained in a specific order according to a column's value, and the DBMS will take over.

Indexes are manipulated by the DBMS, and all you have to do is define them. Every time a new row is added, or an existing row is deleted or edited, the table's indexes are automatically updated. You can use the index at any time to locate rows very quickly. Practically, indexes allow you to select a row based on an indexed field instantly. When searching for specific rows, the DBMS will take into consideration automatically any index that can speed the search.

EFFICIENCY ISSUES

Tables are not static objects. Most tables in a database change constantly: new rows are added and existing rows are deleted or edited. This also means that the DBMS must constantly update the table indexes. This process can become quite a burden, so you shouldn't create too many indexes. On the other hand, indexes speed up lookup operations enormously. So, where do you draw the line?

If you're using Access, you must tune the performance of the database manually. If a table is updated heavily on a daily basis, try to minimize the number of indexes on that table. If a table isn't updated as frequently, but it's used by many queries, you can add many indexes to speed up the queries. Unfortunately, the tables

CONTINUED →

that are used most often in queries are also updated heavily. At any rate, if you're putting too much effort into squeezing every drop of performance out of your Access database, it's probably time to move up to SQL Server.

One of the many tools that come with SQL Server 7 is the Index Tuning Wizard, which helps you decide which indexes to keep and which ones to drop. The Index Tuning Wizard monitors the performance of the database, logs the necessary statistics, and tells you which indexes are responsible for most of the performance. These are the indexes you need in your database; the rest can be dropped at the price of slowing down some queries that are not used as frequently. The Wizard can also create a script with the changes it suggests and implement them immediately. For more information on the Index Tuning Wizard, see SQL Server's online books on the SQL Server CD.

Views

In addition to tables, most databases support views. A *view* is a virtual table: It looks and behaves just like a table—it can be updated, too—but it's not an object that exists in the database. It's based on query. Views come to life when they're requested, and they're released when they're no longer needed. Any operations you perform on a view are automatically translated into operations on the table(s) from which the view is derived.

Views enhance the security of the database. Consider a Personnel table, which stores information about employees, including their salaries and other sensitive information. While most of the information is public (names, telephone extensions, departments, the projects each employee is involved with, and so on), some fields should be restricted to authorized users only. While you could split the table into smaller ones, SQL Server allows you to create unique views and assign access rights to those views to selected user groups.

You can also use views to hide the complexity introduced by the normalization process and the relations between tables. Users don't really care about normalization rules or relationships. They would rather see a list of customer names, their orders, and the actual product names. This information exists in the database, but it's scattered in four different tables: Customers, Orders, Order Details, and Products. By defining a view on the database, you can maintain a structure that eases your development, yet gives the users the "table" they would rather see.

Updating Tables and Views

Changes in the view are reflected immediately in the underlying table(s). When the underlying tables change, however, these changes are not reflected immediately to the views based on them. Views are based on the data in the tables the moment the query was executed. A view that's based on a table and hides a few of its rows (or columns) is always updateable, as long as it contains the primary key of the table. (As mentioned already, the primary key uniquely identifies a table's row. Without this piece of information, SQL Server wouldn't know which row to update.)

Some views cannot be updated. Views based on SQL statements that combine multiple tables may not be, and views that contain totals can't be updated. Totals are based on many rows and SQL Server doesn't know which order or detail line it must change to affect the total.

Figure 12.10 shows a section of the Invoices view (I have hidden many of the columns by setting their width to zero). Start SQL Server's Enterprise Manager, open the Northwind database folder in the left pane, and click Views under the Northwind database name. The names of all the views defined for the database will be displayed in the right pane. To open a view, right-click on its name and select Open ➢ Return All Rows from the shortcut menu.

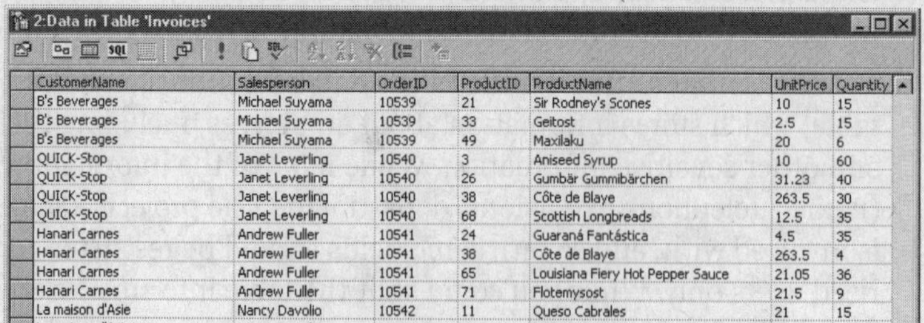

2:Data in Table 'Invoices'

CustomerName	Salesperson	OrderID	ProductID	ProductName	UnitPrice	Quantity
B's Beverages	Michael Suyama	10539	21	Sir Rodney's Scones	10	15
B's Beverages	Michael Suyama	10539	33	Geitost	2.5	15
B's Beverages	Michael Suyama	10539	49	Maxilaku	20	6
QUICK-Stop	Janet Leverling	10540	3	Aniseed Syrup	10	60
QUICK-Stop	Janet Leverling	10540	26	Gumbär Gummibärchen	31.23	40
QUICK-Stop	Janet Leverling	10540	38	Côte de Blaye	263.5	30
QUICK-Stop	Janet Leverling	10540	68	Scottish Longbreads	12.5	35
Hanari Carnes	Andrew Fuller	10541	24	Guaraná Fantástica	4.5	35
Hanari Carnes	Andrew Fuller	10541	38	Côte de Blaye	263.5	4
Hanari Carnes	Andrew Fuller	10541	65	Louisiana Fiery Hot Pepper Sauce	21.05	36
Hanari Carnes	Andrew Fuller	10541	71	Flotemysost	21.5	9
La maison d'Asie	Nancy Davolio	10542	11	Queso Cabrales	21	15
La maison d'Asie	Nancy Davolio	10542	54	Tourtière	7.45	24
LILA-Supermercado	Laura Callahan	10543	12	Queso Manchego La Pastora	38	30
LILA-Supermercado	Laura Callahan	10543	23	Tunnbröd	9	70
Lonesome Pine Restaurant	Margaret Peacock	10544	28	Rössle Sauerkraut	45.6	7
Lonesome Pine Restaurant	Margaret Peacock	10544	67	Laughing Lumberjack Lager	14	7
Lazy K Kountry Store	Laura Callahan	10545	11	Queso Cabrales	21	10

FIGURE 12.10: The Invoices view displaying the order details along with customer names and product names

Try editing the Invoices view to see how it behaves. Bring the CustomerName column into view, change the name *Hanari Carnes* into uppercase, and then move to another cell. The customer's name has been changed already, not only in the open view, but in the database as well. If you opened the Customers table, you would see that the changes have already been committed to the database. Yet, the remaining instances of the same name on the view didn't change. That's because the view isn't updated constantly. SQL Server doesn't maintain a "live" link to the database, and it can't update the view every time.

Things can get even worse. Locate another instance of the same customer in the view and change the name to *HANARI CARNES1*. As soon as you move to another cell, the following message will pop up:

```
Data has changed since the Results pane was
    last updated. Do you want to save your
    changes now?
Click Yes to save your changes and update
    the database
Click No to discard your changes and refresh
    the Results pane
Click Cancel to continue editing
```

What's happened here? The name of the customer you read from the database was Hanari Carnes, and you changed it to uppercase. This change was committed to the Customers table. Then you attempted to change the name Hanari Carnes into something else again, and SQL Server attempted to update the Customers table for a second time. This time, SQL Server didn't find the name Hanari Carnes there; it had already been changed (to HANARI CARNES). And that's exactly what the message tells you. You have attempted to change a field, but its original value is no longer the same as when it was read.

Of course it isn't. You just changed it, right? But SQL Server doesn't keep track of who's changing what in the database. For all it knows, the changes could have been made by another user, so it simply tells you that the record you're about to change is no longer the same. Imagine if this was a seat reservation application. You'd assign the same seat to two different customers. When you change a row in a table, you must be sure that the row hasn't changed since you last read it.

Confusing? Welcome to the world of database programming! As you can understand, this behavior is not unique to views. It's a major issue in database programming known as *concurrency control*. In a multiuser environment, there's always a risk of two or more people attempting to update the same information at once. The behavior you just witnessed is actually a feature of the database: It lets you know that someone else has already changed the row you read. Otherwise, you'd have to implement the same logic from within your application. I didn't mean to scare you; I just wanted to introduce you to one of the most troublesome aspects of database programming so you'll be aware of it as you develop databases of your own.

NOTE

You can't repeat this experiment with Access. Access may not be as powerful a DBMS as SQL Server, but it has a very flexible user interface, meant to be used by people with little database experience. The CompanyName field is displayed as an element of a ComboBox control. You're forced to select another valid company name from a list with all customer names, but you can't edit the company name directly—unless you're editing the Customers table.

Access Views

Access's views are called queries, and they are basically the same thing. You write a query (an SQL statement) that retrieves selected rows from one or more tables and attach its definition to the database. To work with a query, double-click its name in the Queries window to view a grid with the qualifying rows. There's one major difference between SQL Server views and Access queries. If the query is updateable, the changes you make are committed immediately to the database, and they also update the query's grid. This instant feedback is a nice feature that makes working with Access queries very convenient. Even if another user changes one of the rows you're viewing, your grid will be updated immediately.

NOTE

If you're wondering why the two products behave so differently, the answer is that Access is a not-so-powerful DBMS with a user-friendly interface. SQL Server, on the other hand, is a very powerful DBMS, but not a front-end application. You must write applications to access SQL Server's tables and views and not edit them directly. When you fetch a row with your application, SQL Server provides the most recent version of the row. If another user changes the row after you have read it, an error will be generated, and you can handle the conflict from within your code.

Establishing Relationships

Once the information has been broken up logically into separate tables, you must establish relationships between the tables, which is the essence of the relational database model. To relate tables to each other, you use fields with common values. In this section, you'll see how primary and foreign keys are used to establish relationships between tables.

Primary and Foreign Keys

The Categories table has a CategoryID field, which holds a value that identifies each category. This value must be unique for each row of the Categories table, and it's the table's primary key. The Products table also has a CategoryID field, which is set to the ID of the product's category. The two fields have the same name, but this is not a requirement. It's just a convenience for us. The mere existence of the two fields doesn't mean that the two tables are related to each other. You must specify how the tables will be related, as well as which field is the primary key and which field is the foreign key. The primary key is unique to each row, while the foreign key may appear in more than one row. This relationship is called one-to-many, because a single row of the Categories table is usually pointed to by multiple rows of the Products table.

Figure 12.11 shows how SQL Server depicts relationships between tables. To view the relationships between the tables of a database, start the Enterprise Manager and open the desired database in the left pane. Click the Diagrams icon under the database's name and when the Relationships icon appears in the right pane, double-click it. The Relationships diagram will appear in a new window. Each table is represented by a ListBox with the table's field names, and the relationships between tables are represented with arrows. On one end of the arrow is the icon of a key, which indicates the primary key. On the other end of the arrow is the infinity symbol, which indicates the table with the foreign key. The infinity symbol means that there may be many rows pointing to the row with the primary key.

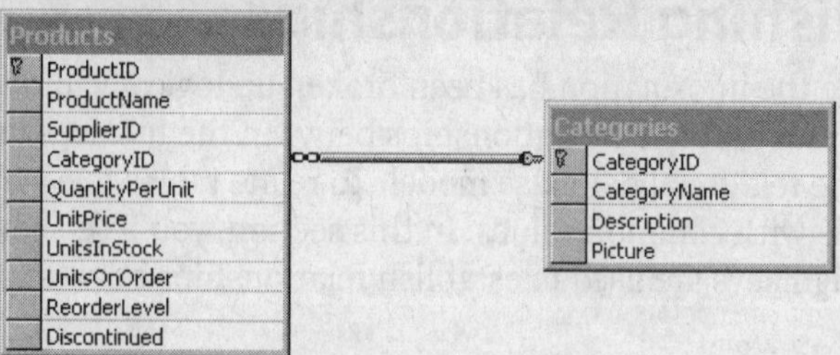

FIGURE 12.11: The CategoryID field in the Products table is the foreign key, which points to the primary key in the Categories table

A last note on keys: primary key fields are not used for custom searches. It doesn't make sense to retrieve all customers with an ID of 1000 or less, or the products with an ID between 50 and 75. Primary key fields are used to connect two tables, so we are never interested in their actual value. Here's a simple SQL statement that retrieves the orders placed by the customer Alfreds Futterkiste:

```
SELECT * FROM Orders
WHERE Customers.CompanyName =
      'Alfreds Futterkiste' AND
      Orders.CustomerID = Customers.CustomerID
```

This statement tells the DBMS to retrieve the rows of the Orders table that match the following criteria:

- The customer's CompanyName field is the customer's name, *and*
- The foreign key in the Orders table matches the primary key in the Customers table.

This query will return all the rows of the Orders table whose CustomerID field is the same as the CustomerID field of the specified customer's row. Primary and foreign keys are used to match rows in two tables, and their actual values are of no interest to us. (The asterisk is a special character that means "all the fields." You could have specified a comma-separated list of the desired fields in the place of the asterisk.)

Viewing and Editing Relationships

To view the relationships of an Access database, switch to the Tables view and select Relationships from the Tools menu. The window shown in Figure 12.12 will appear on your screen, which is quite similar to the

Relationships diagram of SQL Server. The relationships between tables are represented with lines, which have the digit *1* on the primary key's side and the infinity symbol on the foreign key's side. In addition, the primary key in each table is printed in bold to stand out.

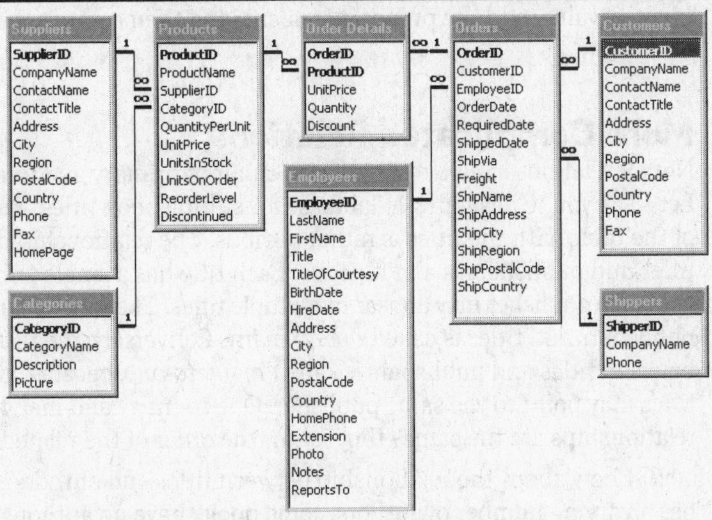

FIGURE 12.12: Viewing the relationships in an Access database

To delete a relationship, right-click its name and select Delete from the shortcut menu (in SQL Server, select Delete Relationship from Database). To view or edit the properties of the relationship, select Edit (or Properties in SQL Server) from the same shortcut menu. The Properties window should specify the primary and foreign keys, and in SQL Server each relationship has a name. Notice that Access relationships are not named.

AutoNumber and Identity Fields

The actual values of the primary key fields are so irrelevant that in most cases we let the DBMS generate their values for us. The DBMS can automatically generate an integer value for a primary key field every time a new row is added. SQL Server uses the term *Identity* for this data type, while Access uses the term *AutoNumber*. If you specify an AutoNumber field in Access, you can specify whether it will be increased by one or by a random value. In SQL Server, you can specify the initial value of an Identity field and its increment.

To create the new value for an AutoNumber or Identity field, the DBMS adds a value (usually one) to the last value of this field in the same table. This operation is simple in principle, but it would be quite a task if you had to implement it on your own. With many users adding rows to the same table, you'd have to lock the table, read the last row's Identity value, add the proper increment, and then commit the newly added row.

More Complicated Relations

Not all relations can be resolved with a pair of primary and foreign keys. Let's say you're designing a database for storing book titles. The structure of the table with the titles is rather obvious. The relationship between titles and publishers is also obvious: Each title has a single publisher and the same publisher may appear in multiple titles. The relationship between publishers and titles is called *one-to-many.* Conversely, the relationship between titles and publishers is called *many-to-one*, because multiple titles may point to the same publisher. One-to-many and many-to-one relationships are the same—they follow the order of the related tables.

But how about the relationship between titles and authors? Each book has a varying number of authors; some books have no author, others may have six authors. Likewise, the same author may have written more than one title. The relationship between titles and authors is called *many-to-many.* To establish a direct relationship between the Titles and Authors tables, some rows in the Titles table should point to many rows in the Authors table. Likewise, some rows in the Authors table should point to many rows in the Titles tables. To avoid this type of relationship in your design, introduce a new table, which is linked with a one-to-many relationship to the Titles table and a many-to-one relationship to the Authors table.

In our example, we introduced an intermediate table between the Titles and Authors tables: the TitleAuthor table, which contains one row per title-author pair, as shown in Figure 12.13. This table has a very simple structure (you could say that it doesn't even contain any original information). It simply maps books to authors. If a book has three authors, we add three rows to the Title Author table. All rows have the same ISBN (the title's key) and the authors' ID keys.

Intermediate tables like the TitleAuthor table are very common in database design. Practically, there's no other method of implementing many-to-many relations between tables.

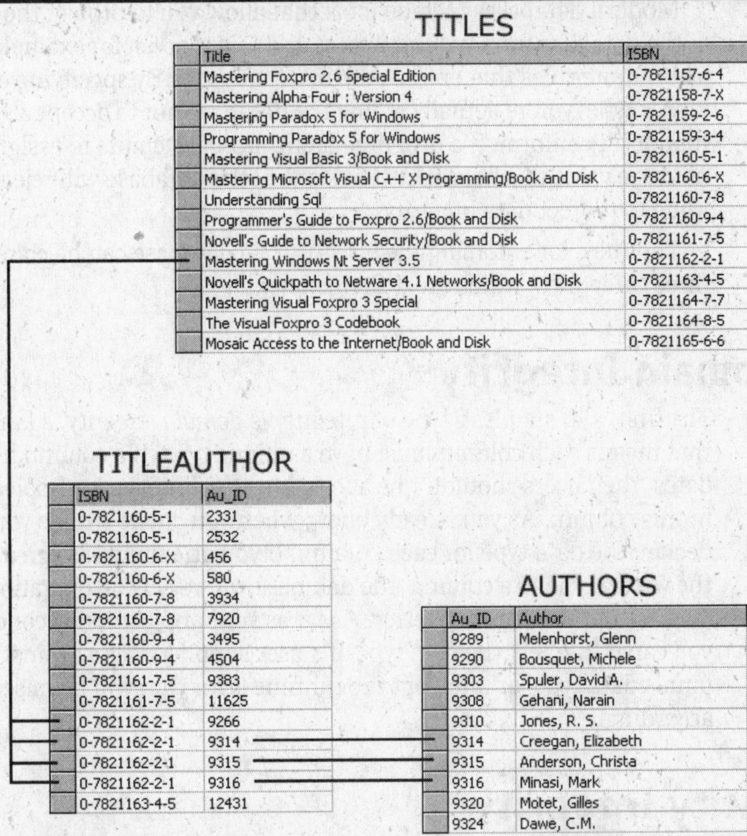

TITLES

Title	ISBN
Mastering Foxpro 2.6 Special Edition	0-7821157-6-4
Mastering Alpha Four : Version 4	0-7821158-7-X
Mastering Paradox 5 for Windows	0-7821159-2-6
Programming Paradox 5 for Windows	0-7821159-3-4
Mastering Visual Basic 3/Book and Disk	0-7821160-5-1
Mastering Microsoft Visual C++ X Programming/Book and Disk	0-7821160-6-X
Understanding Sql	0-7821160-7-8
Programmer's Guide to Foxpro 2.6/Book and Disk	0-7821160-9-4
Novell's Guide to Network Security/Book and Disk	0-7821161-7-5
Mastering Windows Nt Server 3.5	0-7821162-2-1
Novell's Quickpath to Netware 4.1 Networks/Book and Disk	0-7821163-4-5
Mastering Visual Foxpro 3 Special	0-7821164-7-7
The Visual Foxpro 3 Codebook	0-7821164-8-5
Mosaic Access to the Internet/Book and Disk	0-7821165-6-6

TITLEAUTHOR

ISBN	Au_ID
0-7821160-5-1	2331
0-7821160-5-1	2532
0-7821160-6-X	456
0-7821160-6-X	580
0-7821160-7-8	3934
0-7821160-7-8	7920
0-7821160-9-4	3495
0-7821160-9-4	4504
0-7821161-7-5	9383
0-7821161-7-5	11625
0-7821162-2-1	9266
0-7821162-2-1	9314
0-7821162-2-1	9315
0-7821162-2-1	9316
0-7821163-4-5	12431

AUTHORS

Au_ID	Author
9289	Melenhorst, Glenn
9290	Bousquet, Michele
9303	Spuler, David A.
9308	Gehani, Narain
9310	Jones, R. S.
9314	Creegan, Elizabeth
9315	Anderson, Christa
9316	Minasi, Mark
9320	Motet, Gilles
9324	Dawe, C.M.

FIGURE 12.13: Connecting the Titles table to the Authors table with an intermediate table, the TitleAuthor table

Database Integrity

The major challenge in database design is maintaining the integrity of the database. Designing a database is only the beginning; you must also make sure that the database is kept in good shape at all times. The burden of keeping a database in good shape is shared by the database administrator (DBA) and the programmers. As a programmer, you must make sure that all the data your code places into the database are valid. This is quite a task and would require an enormous amount of validation, but, as you'll learn in this section, the database itself can help.

Modern databases include tools that allow you to protect the integrity of the database from within. Access and SQL Server, for example, let you incorporate rules that enforce database integrity. By specifying each column's type, you're actually telling the database not to accept any data that don't conform. If a user or an application attempts to assign a numeric value to a field that stores dates, the database will reject the value to protect data integrity.

The rules for enforcing the integrity of a database can be classified into three categories, which are described next.

Domain Integrity

The first, and simplest, type of integrity is *domain integrity*, a fancy term that means each column must have a unique type. If a column holds dates, then users shouldn't be allowed to store integers or Boolean values in this column. As you already know, when you create a table you must declare the data type for each column. If you attempt to assign a value of the wrong type to a column, the database will reject the operation and raise a trappable runtime error. As far as your application is concerned, you can either test the data type of a user-supplied value against the column's data type, or intercept the runtime error that will be raised and act accordingly.

Entity Integrity

The second type of integrity is *entity integrity*, which means that an entity (a customer, product, invoice, and so on) must have a valid primary key. If a table's primary key is Null, no rows in other tables can be connected to this row. All DBMSs can enforce this type of integrity by not allowing the insertion of rows with Null keys, or by preventing changes that would result in a Null value for a primary key. All you have to do to enforce this type of integrity is set the Nullable property of the column that's used as primary key to False. Actually, you don't even have to set the Nullable property, because neither Access nor SQL Server will accept Null values for primary key fields.

Referential Integrity

This is one of the most important topics in database design. Designing the database is a rather straightforward process, once you have understood the requirements of the corporation (the information that will be stored in the database, how it will be recalled, and the relations among the various tables). Just as important, if not more important, is ensuring that the various relationships remain valid at all times.

Relationships are based on primary and foreign keys. What will happen if the primary key in a relationship is deleted? If you delete a row in the Customers table, for instance, then some orders will become orphaned; they will refer to a customer who doesn't exist. Your applications will keep working, but every now and then you'll get incorrect results. Nothing will go wrong in calculating the total for an existing customer, for example.

If you calculate the grand total for all customers, you'll get one value. If you calculate the grand total for all the detail lines, you'll get a different value. This inconsistency shouldn't exist in a database. Once you realize that your database is in an inconsistent state, you must start examining every table to find out why and when it happened and what other reports are unusable. This is a major headache that you want to avoid. And it's simple to avoid such problems by enforcing the database's referential integrity.

Problems related to the referential integrity of the database can be intermittent, too. If the deleted customer hasn't placed an order in the last 12 months, all the totals you calculate for the last 12 months will be correct. If you receive a (very) late payment from this customer, however, you won't be able to enter it into the database. There's no customer to link the payment to!

Enforcing Referential Integrity

Both Access and SQL Server can be programmed to enforce referential integrity. If you enforce the integrity of the relationship between Customers and Orders, for example, when an application attempts to delete a customer, the database will raise a runtime error and not allow the deletion of the record. If the customer has no orders in the Orders table, the application will be allowed to delete the customer. This action will not impair the integrity of the database because there are no related rows.

The good news is that you don't need to write any code to enforce referential integrity. When you specify a relationship, you can also specify that the integrity of the relationship be enforced. In Access, select a relationship in the relational diagram, right-click it, and select Edit from the shortcut menu to open the Edit Relationships window shown in Figure 12.14. Select the primary and foreign keys in the two related tables, then check the Enforce Referential Integrity option, which tells the Jet engine that it shouldn't change (or delete) the primary key if there are foreign keys referencing it.

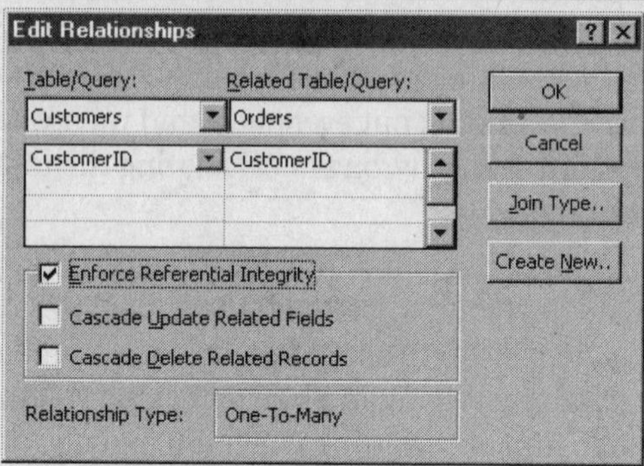

FIGURE 12.14: Edit Relationships window showing that Access can enforce referential integrity as well as cascade updates and deletes

SQL Server can also enforce referential integrity, rejecting any changes in the primary key if this key is referenced by another table. Open the Properties window of a relationship by right-clicking the arrow that represents the relationship between two tables in the Relationships diagram, then selecting Properties from the shortcut menu. Click the Relationships tab and check Enable Relationship for INSERT and UPDATE (see Figure 12.15). The Check Existing Data on Creation option is valid when you create a new relationship between two tables that contain data already. It tells SQL Server to make sure that existing data does not violate the new relationship.

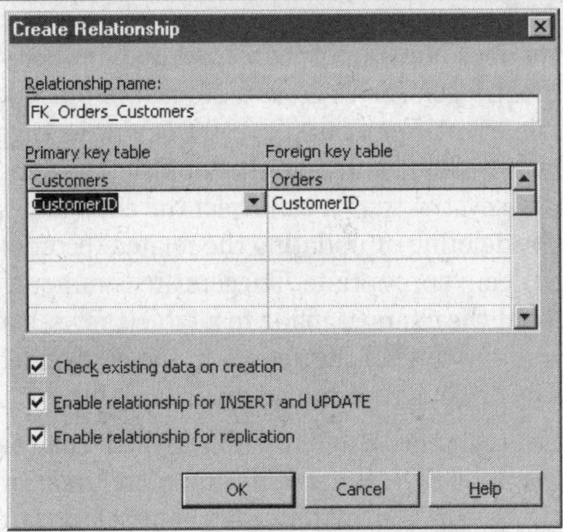

FIGURE 12.15: Specifying the properties of a relationship in a SQL Server database

Cascade Updates and Deletes

In Access, you can also use *cascade updates* and *cascade deletes*. These options are not available in SQL Server. When the Cascade Delete option is in effect, you can delete a customer, but all related rows in every table in the database will also be deleted. If you use cascade deletes to enforce referential integrity, then all the orders placed by the specific customer in the Orders table must also be deleted. As each row in the Orders table is deleted, it must take with it all the related rows in the Order Details table as well.

Cascading updates are a less drastic method of enforcing referential integrity. When you change the value of a primary key, Access changes the foreign keys in all tables related to the updated table. If you change a customer's ID, for example, Access will change the OrderID field in the Orders table for all orders placed by that customer.

NOTE

If the primary key is an AutoNumber field, you need not turn on cascading updates, since AutoNumber fields can't change. Cascading deletes are valid, because AutoNumber fields can be deleted.

Triggers

SQL Server does not support cascaded updates because it uses a better mechanism: triggers. A *trigger* is a procedure that's invoked automatically, like an event. For example, you can write a trigger that runs every time a row is updated and takes the appropriate action. If a user changes the primary key, the trigger can reject the changes, cascade deletes and updates (by deleting or updating the related records), or take any other action you deem appropriate. Triggers are commonly used to store information about the changes made to a table's rows, such as the name of the user and the time of the action. In the case of deletions, the trigger can save the original row into an auxiliary table.

Triggers are implemented in T-SQL, which is an extension of SQL. T-SQL is a mix of SQL statements and more traditional programming statements such as control flow statements, loop structures, and so on. A good example of a trigger is one that is invoked automatically each time a row is deleted in the Customers table. This trigger deletes all the rows in the Order Details table that correspond to customer orders being deleted. After the detail lines have been deleted, the trigger deletes the rows of the Orders table that correspond to orders placed by the same customer. Since the details of these orders no longer exist, you can delete the order without violating the integrity of the database. Finally, the trigger deletes a row from the Customers table.

In the description of the Northwind database earlier in this chapter, I mentioned that the order totals are not stored in the Orders table, because this design would duplicate information. If your applications spend a lot of time calculating order totals, you may consider saving each order's total in a field of the Orders table. If you do so, you must write a trigger that's invoked every time a row in the Order Details table is added or edited. This trigger must calculate the total of the order and update the corresponding field in the Orders table. The trigger will be fired no matter how the row is added or edited, and it ensures that the Orders table reflects the changes in the Order Details table at all times.

THE PUBS DATABASE

The Pubs database is a sample database that comes with SQL Server, and it is used almost exclusively in the examples of SQL Server's online help. The tables of the Pubs database contain very few rows, but they were designed to demonstrate many of the operations we perform on databases. I use this database in some of the examples in this book. The tables of the Pubs database include Titles, Authors, TitleAuthor, Roysched, Pub_Info, Stores, Sales, and Discounts. Figure 12.16 shows the relationships between the tables of the Pubs database involved in calculating royalties. The royalty breakpoints are shown in Figure 12.17.

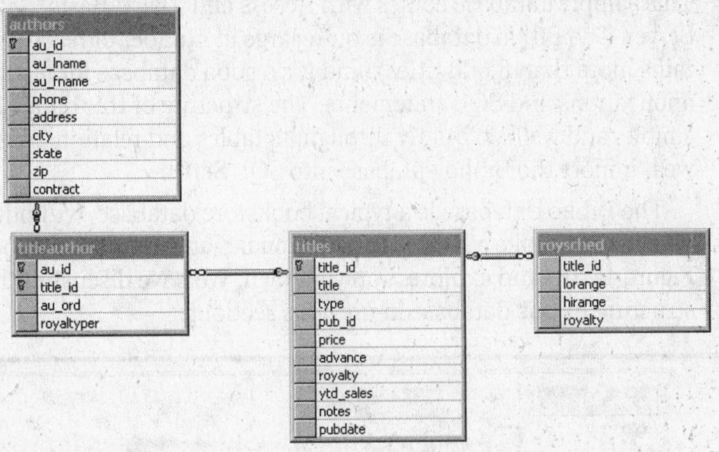

FIGURE 12.16: Linking titles, authors, and royalties in the Pubs database

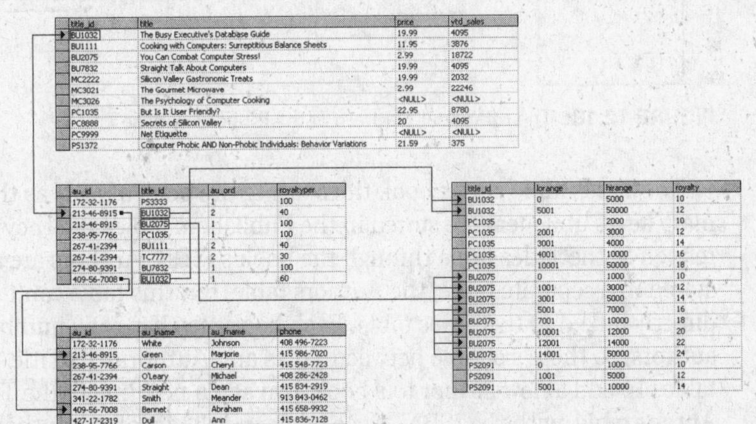

title_id	title	price	ytd_sales
BU1032	The Busy Executive's Database Guide	19.99	4095
BU1111	Cooking with Computers: Surreptitious Balance Sheets	11.95	3876
BU2075	You Can Combat Computer Stress!	2.99	18722
BU7832	Straight Talk About Computers	19.99	4095
MC2222	Silicon Valley Gastronomic Treats	19.99	2032
MC3021	The Gourmet Microwave	2.99	22246
MC3026	The Psychology of Computer Cooking	<NULL>	<NULL>
PC1035	But Is It User Friendly?	22.95	8780
PC8888	Secrets of Silicon Valley	20	4095
PC9999	Net Etiquette	<NULL>	<NULL>
PS1372	Computer Phobic AND Non-Phobic Individuals: Behavior Variations	21.59	375

au_id	title_id	au_ord	royaltyper
172-32-1176	PS3333	1	100
213-46-8915	BU1032	2	40
213-46-8915	BU2075	1	100
238-95-7766	PC1035	1	100
267-41-2394	BU1111	2	40
267-41-2394	TC7777	2	30
274-80-9391	BU7832	1	100
409-56-7008	BU1032	1	60

title_id	lorange	hirange	royalty
BU1032	0	5000	10
BU1032	5001	50000	12
PC1035	0	2000	10
PC1035	2001	3000	12
PC1035	3001	4000	14
PC1035	4001	10000	16
PC1035	10001	50000	18
BU2075	0	1000	10
BU2075	1001	3000	12
BU2075	3001	5000	14
BU2075	5001	7000	16
BU2075	7001	10000	18
BU2075	10001	12000	20
BU2075	12001	14000	22
BU2075	14001	50000	24
PS2091	0	1000	10
PS2091	1001	5000	12
PS2091	5001	10000	14

au_id	au_lname	au_fname	phone
172-32-1176	White	Johnson	408 496-7223
213-46-8915	Green	Marjorie	415 986-7020
238-95-7766	Carson	Cheryl	415 548-7723
267-41-2394	O'Leary	Michael	408 286-2428
274-80-9391	Straight	Dean	415 834-2919
341-22-1782	Smith	Meander	913 843-0462
409-56-7008	Bennet	Abraham	415 658-9932
427-17-2319	Dull	Ann	415 836-7128

FIGURE 12.17: Applying the relationships of Figure 12.16 to some actual data

The remaining tables of the Pubs database have to do with employees and jobs and are not used in this book's examples. The Employees table holds personnel information and the Jobs table holds job descriptions.

THE BIBLIO DATABASE

This sample database comes with Access and Visual Basic, but not SQL Server. The Biblio database is quite large in number of records (it contains more than 8,000 titles), and it's a good database for testing your applications and SQL statements. The structure of this database is quite simple, and we'll go briefly through its tables and relationships. Then we'll import the Biblio database into SQL Server.

The Biblio database is a typical bookstore database, without sales information. Take a look at the relational diagram of the database (see Figure 12.18) and explore it on your own. We have discussed the basic structure of this database in previous sections.

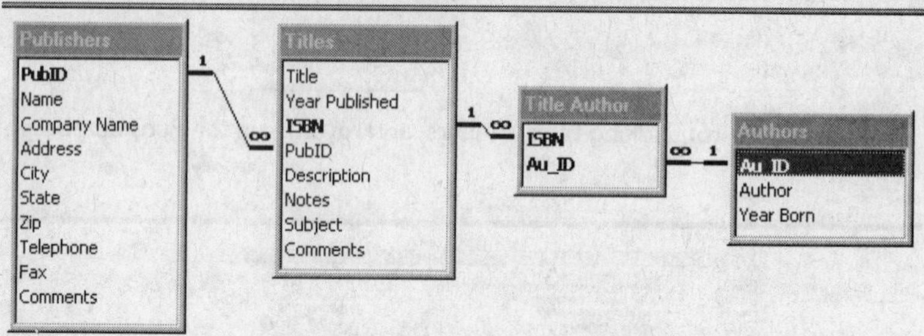

FIGURE 12.18: The relational diagram of the Biblio database

The Titles table stores book titles, using the book's ISBN as the primary key. Publishers are stored in the Publishers table, and they are related to the Titles table through the book's ISBN. Authors are also stored in a separate table, the Authors table, but this table can't be directly linked to the Titles table. Each book may have any number of authors, so there's a table between Titles and Authors, the TitleAuthor table. To add a new author to a book, you add a new line to the Title-Author table, with the ISBN of the book and the ID of the author.

SHOULD PRIMARY KEYS BE INTEGERS?

This database uses the book's ISBN as the primary key. You'll probably read that primary keys should be integers, because the DBMS can handle them faster than strings. This is true, but SQL Server is extremely efficient when it comes to indexing. If it makes sense to use a meaningful field in the table as the primary key, do it. As long as the field's length doesn't exceed 50 characters, you will not notice any delay. I'm not sure this is the case for a table with a billion rows, but for a moderately sized database, it's okay to use noninteger primary keys. You may not have noticed it, but all of the sample databases that come with either VB or SQL Server include tables that use noninteger primary keys. I can't see why the folks at Redmond would have gone to the trouble of making up keys if an AutoNumber or Identity field makes a more efficient primary key.

Importing the Biblio Database into SQL Server

In Chapter 15, I will use the Biblio database in SQL Server, as well as the other sample databases that come with VB and SQL Server, so it would be a good idea to port the database from Access into SQL Server (or *upsize* it, to use a trendy expression). If you have used Access in the past and plan to switch to SQL Server, you may wish to upsize some of your own databases too.

This last section takes you through the steps of importing an Access database into SQL Server. While you'd usually leave this type of operation to the database administrator, it's fairly simple and you should be able to perform it on your own. Besides, importing the database into SQL Server can be scripted in VBScript, and you may wish to learn a little more about the process.

NOTE

VBScript is Microsoft's scripting language and is incorporated into many of its products. As a VB programmer, you can add scripting capabilities to your own applications with the help of the Scripting control. VBScript is identical to Visual Basic, but it lacks a visual user interface.

To import data from another database into SQL Server, use the Data Transformation Services (DTS). DTS is a component of SQL Server that allows you to import data from different databases and text files, as well as export data to other databases. To import the Biblio database from Access, follow these steps:

1. To start the DTS Import Wizard, right-click the Databases folder and select All Tasks ➢ Import Data from the shortcut menu. Click Next to skip the welcome screen.
2. In the Choose a Data Source screen, specify the source of the data (the Biblio Access database). In the Source box, select Microsoft Access, and in the File Name box enter the path to the `Biblio.mdb` file. Or click the button next to the File Name box and locate the database file through the File Open dialog box. Click Next.
3. In the Choose a Destination screen, choose the database that will accept the data. The destination must be the Microsoft OLE DB Provider for SQL Server. Specify the name of the server on your network—or `(local)`, if you're running SQL Server on the same machine—as well as the authentication type. In the Database box, select New to create a new database that will accept the Biblio database. As soon as you select the New entry in the Database drop-down list, the Create Database dialog box will appear (see Figure 12.19). The same dialog box appears when you create a new SQL Server database.

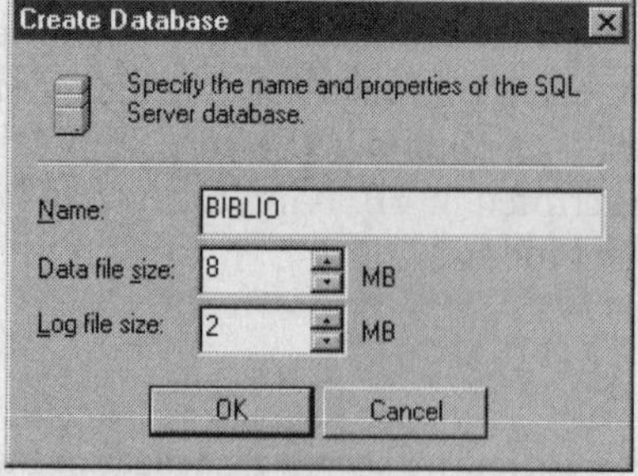

FIGURE 12.19: The Create Database dialog box

4. In the Create Database dialog box, specify the name of the new database and its initial size. Eight megabytes are more than enough for the Biblio database, and a log file size of 2MB is also plenty. Click OK, and SQL Server will create the new database and return to the Choose A Destination screen. Click Next to move on.
5. In the Specify Table Copy or Query screen (see Figure 12.20), specify whether to copy the Access database's tables into the new database, or to select specific rows from the database's tables with one or more queries. You'll want to copy all the rows of the Biblio tables in the new database, so check the first option and click Next.
6. In the Select Source Tables screen (see Figure 12.21), specify which tables will be transferred. Each time you select a table by clicking in front of its name, a similarly named table is added to the Destination Table column. Check all source tables in the first column. You can also change the name of the destination table, but there's no need to change the names of the Biblio database.

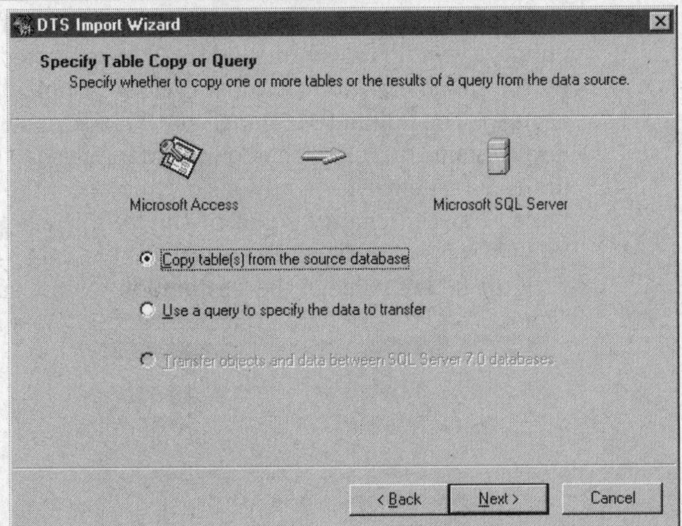

FIGURE 12.20: The Specify Table Copy or Query screen of the Wizard

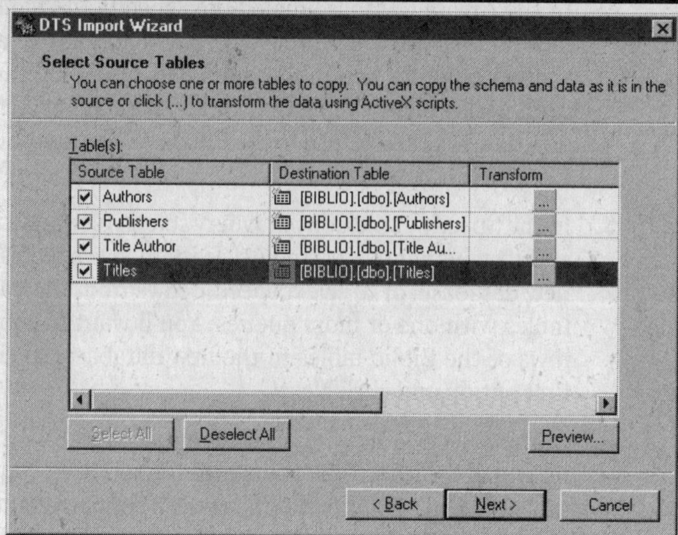

FIGURE 12.21: The Select Source Tables screen of the Wizard

7. The buttons in the Transform column of the Select Source Tables screen let you specify transformations on the data as it is imported into SQL Server. Click the button of the column you want to transform, and you'll be prompted to specify the transformation (in most cases, a simple data type change). The Column Mappings and Transformations window contains two tabs. The Column Mappings tab (see Figure 12.22) shows the definitions of the rows of the selected table. You can change some of the definitions, or even exclude some of the columns. If you want to omit a column, click the table's name in the Destination column and select "ignore."

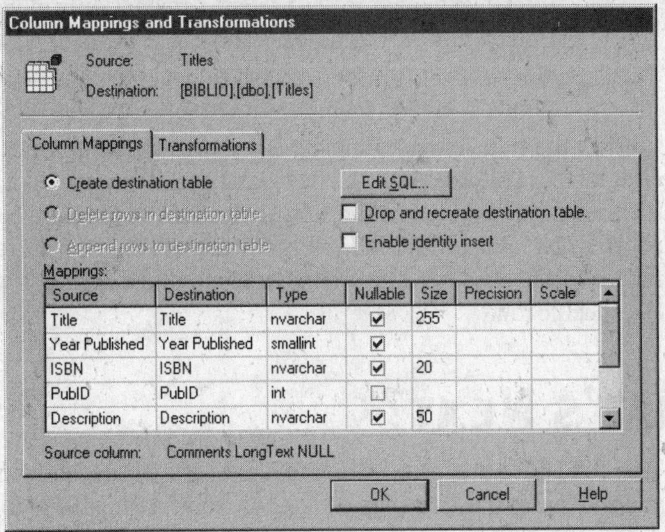

FIGURE 12.22: The Column Mappings and Transformations window

8. On the Transformations tab, you can specify whether the source columns will be copied directly or transformed as they are copied into the destination columns. If you check the second option, the text box on the window will be enabled. Here you can enter a script to transform the data as it's transferred. The script is a short program written in VBScript that manipulates the fields of the source and destination fields.

9. Click OK to return to the Column Mappings and Transformation Wizard. There's no need to specify any transformations, so let the Wizard translate the table definitions and transfer all rows for you.

10. Click OK to return to the DTS Wizard, and click Next to specify when the data import will take place. Select Run Immediately to import the database immediately. If you plan to import the same data in the future, check Save DTS Package. SQL Server will create a script automatically so that you won't have to go through all the screens of the Import Wizard again. If you choose to save the DTS package, you'll be prompted to enter a name for the package.

11. Click Next again to see the last screen. Confirm your intention to import the database and click Finish. SQL Server will start transferring data asynchronously, and it will display the progress of the operation on the Data Transferring screen.

After the transfer has completed, you will see the number of rows of each table transferred into the new database. If any errors occur during the transfer, the process of importing the corresponding table will be aborted. The Wizard will tell you how many rows it transferred successfully, and you can open the original table to find out what's wrong with the specific row.

What's Next?

This concludes the introduction to databases. In the following chapter, you will learn to use the visual database tools. Using these tools, you can design databases right in Visual Basic's IDE. These tools also allow you to manipulate SQL Server and Oracle databases (edit tables, establish relationships, and create queries) as if you were working with Access databases. I know you're eager to write some VB code, but these tools will make things a whole lot simpler.

Chapter 13

Introduction to Relational Databases and SQL

Understanding the concepts behind good design gives you a solid foundation for building a database. In this chapter, you'll learn more about specific database structures, as well as some of the SQL syntax you'll need to know when building your Web application. All of the database access code and discussion in this book centers around Open Database Connectivity (ODBC) databases—primarily SQL Server, since that's the database with which I'm most familiar—but you can apply the information just as effectively to Oracle, Sybase, or any relational SQL database.

Adapted from *Mastering™ Active Server Pages 3*, by A. Russell Jones

ISBN 0-7821-2619-7 928 pages $49.99

Databases vs. Files

Unless you're a new developer, you've probably seen how to use sequential files to save data. You probably also realize that sequential files aren't always the most efficient way to store data—especially large data sets. Whenever someone begins to discuss efficiency, you should immediately become skeptical. But why aren't files efficient? I'm not saying that files in general are inefficient, or even that sequential files in general are inefficient. I'm saying that data sets (especially large ones) stored in sequential files are inefficient.

If you're streaming data to a browser, as Web servers stream HTML files, then sequential files are the most efficient method for storing data long-term. But if you only need a single item of information, sequential files are inefficient. One reason they're inefficient is that you can't jump directly to a single item within the file. You must either read the file sequentially up to the point where the requested data resides for each request, or read the entire file at application or session startup and store the information at application scope, which wastes memory. Another reason sequential files are inefficient is that you can't write data to the middle of the file without rewriting the entire file.

With a sequential file, fixed field lengths or delimiters define the separation between individual items, called fields. The most common type of delimited file is the comma-delimited file, which uses the comma character to separate fields. You don't have to use a comma—although commas are the most common separator character, they're not always the most efficient. Commas appear in most text. Therefore, text fields containing commas always present a problem: how can the computer tell the difference between a comma that acts as a field delimiter and delimits a field, and a comma that's part of the data?

Delimiters provide separation between fields, but they don't specify the length for any particular field. Delimiters separate variable-length fields. But for many field types, you know exactly how long the field needs to be to contain the data. A date/time field, for example, formatted in `mm/dd/yyyy hh:mm:ss am/pm` form, is always exactly 22 characters long. A name field, on the other hand, may vary between 2 and 20 characters in length. Comma-delimited files work extremely well when you're working with streaming data, but don't work nearly as well when you need to access or alter individual items in the middle of the file.

For example, suppose I have a sequential file containing names and addresses and I want to change the address for the first person in the file. If the new address is longer than the existing address, I can't overwrite the information without also potentially overwriting critical information that follows the address. For example:

```
' Original File contents

Doe,John,15440 St. Paul Ave,Minneapolis,MN,99820

' New Address
98029 Livonia Ave #205,Minneapolis,MN,99820
```

The new address is longer than the old address. If I simply start at the current beginning-of-address position and write the new data, the file will look like this:

```
' Overwritten File contents

Doe,John,98029 Livonia Ave #205,neapolis,MN,99820
```

As you can see, the new address line overwrites part of the city field. Similarly, if the new address were shorter than the old address, overwriting the data would leave extraneous characters from the previous address, and I would need to pad the new data with blanks to completely erase the old data. Therefore, I need to rewrite the file to replace the address. Rewriting the entire file to change a value is not a problem when a sequential file contains a small number of items, but as the file grows to hundreds, thousands, or millions of items, it takes longer and longer to write the data. To avoid such problems, programmers invented the concept of random access files. With a random access file you aren't concerned with separator characters; instead, your primary concern becomes field length.

With a random access file, you store data in records. Each record consists of fields, and each field is a pre-selected size. For example, you can store a date in six bytes—as six text characters, e.g., 041299; as a number that's an offset from a single known date; or as two one-byte values for the month and day combined with a two-byte value for the year. All these date-storing schemes rely on the fact that the program storing the data and the program reading the data both understand and agree on the format in which dates are stored.

Similarly, you could arbitrarily assume that last names are never longer than 30 characters; therefore, you could create a 30-character field to store last names. Unfortunately, the size you select is critical. Having decided that last names are 30 characters, you may not be able to change that length easily. When you find a last name longer than 30 characters, you won't be able to accommodate it. In other words: random access files waste storage space.

The advantage of the random access file is that you can replace data in the middle of the file without rewriting the entire file. As long as the new data conforms to the field type and size of the existing data, you can overwrite the old data without a problem.

Because all of the fields in each record are the same length, all of the records are also the same length. You can also think of the data as a set of records, or a record set. Each record set consists of an arbitrary number of records, each of which contains the same number and type of fields. That conveniently lets you think of random access files in terms of tables. A *table* is a set of records in which the data in a given column is always the same type and size. Therefore, a record set and a table are essentially the same thing.

With a random access file, you can do much more than replace records; you can sort records as well. For example, suppose I have a list of grammar-school children. Each child belongs in a specific grade and several teachers teach each grade. I want to divide the children into classes such that each teacher gets roughly the same number of children. I want a final listing by grade, teacher, and child.

To obtain my final list, I'm going to need to sort the data. I need to separate the children into classes and group the class records together. Assume that the records are originally on disk as shown in Table 13.1.

TABLE 13.1: Sample Class Records—Students

ID	GRADE	TEACHER	LASTNAME	FIRSTNAME
1	1	NA	Jones	Barry
2	2	NA	Templeton	Bill
3	2	NA	Jones	Meredith
4	1	NA	McArthur	Isabel
5	3	NA	Said	Mohammed
6	3	NA	Chen	Xiulian
7	2	NA	Barker	Charles

To determine how many teachers I need for each grade, I first need to count the number of students in each grade. To do that, I need to loop through the file, reading each record and keeping a separate counter for each grade. At the end of the loop, I will know the number of students in each grade.

Next, I can assign teachers by desired class size. For example, if I have 160 first-grade students, I will need 8 teachers if the average class size is 20, but only 6 teachers if the average class size is 25. I could now loop back through the file and assign a teacher to each student.

The data is complete, but I still have a problem: how am I going to display the data? On disk, the records are still in their original sequence. To display the data in order, I'll need to sort it. I could rewrite the file in the correct sequence, moving each record to its sorted position, but that's inefficient. If I add a student, I'll have to rewrite the data again, and if I have to rewrite all the data to add a record, a random access file provides very little advantage over a sequential file!

Suppose that instead of rewriting the data in the proper sequence, I keep a separate list of the IDs as a file on disk. Each ID in the separate file is associated with the record number of the complete file. I can now say that the list of IDs is an index into the data file—let's call it the Grade-Teacher-Name (GTN) index. If I can find an ID in the index file, I can obtain the record number of the data in the main file.

Using the index, I can retrieve the list in GTN sequence without altering the physical position of the data. Similarly, if I add a new student record to the end of the main file, I can loop through my GTN index to find out where the new student belongs, then insert the new student ID number at that location. The index file is a sequential file, but it's relatively small compared to the data file. It's much faster to rewrite the index file than to rewrite the data file.

I still have some problems, though. Suppose a teacher gets married during the school year. I now need to update each student's record with the teacher's new name. Not only that, I probably need to go back to the data from previous years and replace that teacher's name throughout my data set. It would be much simpler if I could keep the teacher names in one file and the student names in another and join them when I needed a report.

For example, suppose that instead of using up valuable space to put a teacher name in each row, I changed the data design so each row contains a `TeacherID` column as shown in Table 13.2.

TABLE 13.2: Sample Class Records—Students

ID	GRADE	TEACHERID	LASTNAME	FIRSTNAME
1	1	32	Jones	Barry
2	2	86	Templeton	Bill
3	2	87	Jones	Meredith
4	1	21	McArthur	Isabel
5	3	45	Said	Mohammed
6	3	45	Chen	Xiulian
7	2	86	Barker	Charles

Now, rather than changing each row associated with that teacher, I can change a single row in another, related table called `Teachers`, as shown in Table 13.3.

TABLE 13.3: Sample Class Records—Teachers

TEACHERID	LASTNAME	FIRSTNAME
32	Franklin	Marsha
86	Barstow	Emily
21	Bannister	Henry
87	McAllister	Ian
45	Pinker	Dorothy

Now, no matter how many teacher changes I make, I can either update a single row in the `Teachers` table or the `TeacherID` column in the `Students` table. A data design like this consists of relationships. The `TeacherID` column in the `Teachers` table is a primary key, meaning one and only one row may be associated with a single value. The related `TeacherID` column in the `Students` table is a foreign key because it contains data that originates from outside the table—in other words, from a foreign table. Because one teacher may teach many students, there is a one-to-many relationship between the tables.

Extend this idea a little bit. Imagine that in this school, each student takes many classes during the day and that those classes aren't all the same each day. In other words, each student may have many teachers and classes, which changes the relationship between teachers and students from one-to-many into a many-to-many relationship. If you can imagine that, then you can also imagine that managing the key relationships and indexes isn't an easy task. You probably wouldn't want to write that code yourself. Well, fortunately, you don't have to. Managing relationships like this is exactly what relational databases were meant to do.

Part of managing data relationships involves ensuring that the data you're putting into the database is the right data. With a file, you must write the data validation code yourself. Databases simplify that process by refusing to store data that doesn't meet the requirements (field types and sizes) specified when you created the database. But modern databases go far beyond simple data type validation. You can define complex data types, such as combinations of numeric and string values, as well as rules about how the data in columns must relate. For example, you could create a data type called `ORDER_ID`. An `ORDER_ID` consists of two characters identifying the product, a dash, a four-character product subtype number, a dash, and the order date in `MMDDYYYY` format. For example:

```
FB-8382-12041999
```

When you assign the `ORDER_ID` data type to a column, the database enforces validity on that column. If your company subsequently changes the rules, you can theoretically revise the `ORDER_ID` data type and change the data in the database to fit the new rules without having to change the code in all the applications that access the data.

Databases can also enforce data-relationship rules. The simplest example involves a one-to-many primary-foreign key relationship between two tables. Each row in the table on the many side of the relationship must have a matching row in the table on the one side of the relationship. The database rejects data that doesn't fit those requirements. Similarly, the database would not let you delete a row from the one side that had matching rows on the many side.

Indexes, primary keys, and foreign key relationships are all part of a larger concept called constraints. A constraint is a limitation, a way to prevent error conditions from occurring. For example, a primary key has unique value for each row in a table. Primary keys may not be null. The database enforces five types of constraints:

Not null Means that the field may not contain a null value.

Unique Means that the field must be unique within its column.

Primary key Is a combination of unique and not null. A table may have only one primary key.

Foreign key Defines a relationship between two tables, either one-to-one, one-to-many, or many-to-many.

Check Enforces rules concerning data values; for example, an `Employee_Age` column must be between 18 and 70.

Databases have one more huge advantage over files—they can run queries. A query is a request to retrieve, alter, or add data to a database. You write queries in a special language called Structured Query Language (SQL, pronounced "sequel"). Because most databases store the database objects themselves in standard tables, you can use SQL to modify the database itself.

SQL Code Conventions

By convention, I will show SQL keywords in uppercase in the book, even though SQL is not case-sensitive. As with VBScript code, I have not been as careful to adhere to any case conventions in the code itself.

SQL doesn't have line termination characters or line continuation characters, so I've broken the lines to fit the layout of this book. You don't have to do that. SQL lets you format the code however you like—including one long line (but don't do that). Indent SQL code as you would indent your VBScript code; that is, make it readable.

SQL has two types of comments: inline comments, which begin with a double-dash (–) and continue to the end of the line, and block comments, which, like Java or C, begin with a slash-star (/*) and end with the reverse—a star-slash (*/). For example:

```
- This is an inline comment.
/*
This is a block comment.
*/
```

You can freely nest inline comments within block comments. For example:

```
/* The following SELECT statement has been commented out
- SELECT * FROM SomeTable
*/
```

You may not continue a code line after a comment. For example, the following statement is invalid:

```
SELECT - This is a select statement - * FROM ...
```

SQL Server ignores all but the first double-dash on any line.

Introduction to SQL

Structured Query Language (SQL) is a straightforward subject, partly because it doesn't do much, and partly because the language is standardized. Most modern databases use a variant of SQL that, for the most part, conforms to the American National Standards Institute (ANSI) 92 standard. That standard means you can use similar, although not quite identical, SQL code to access many different databases. Fortunately, for basic operations, there's no difference between most common databases.

SQL lets you perform four basic operations:

SELECT – Retrieve data

INSERT – Add data

UPDATE – Change data

DELETE – Remove data

The *SELECT* Statement

The SELECT statement retrieves data from the database. To retrieve the data, you specify a field list, a table list, a list of fields to sort by, and the sort order.

The parts of a SQL statement are called clauses. A basic SELECT statement has up to four clauses. For example:

```
SELECT (field1, field2, etc.)
FROM (table list)
WHERE (condition)
ORDER BY (field1 [ASC|DESC],
  field2 [ASC|DESC], etc.)
```

The WHERE and ORDER BY clauses are optional. If you omit the WHERE clause, the query returns all rows from the specified tables. If you omit the ORDER BY clause, SQL retrieves rows in the sequence in which they're

Part iii

stored in a table. By default, when you retrieve data from multiple tables, SQL uses the row order from the first specified field.

At the most basic level, you can obtain all the information from a table using an asterisk (*) as a shorthand way of specifying all fields. For example:

```
SELECT * FROM Teachers
```

This query returns all the columns in all rows of the `Teachers` table:

TeacherID	LastName	FirstName
32	Franklin	Marsha
86	Barstow	Emily
21	Bannister	Henry
87	McAllister	Ian
45	Pinker	Dorothy

Of course, you don't have to select all fields; you can specify the exact fields and field order that you wish. For example:

```
SELECT LastName, TeacherID FROM Teachers
```

This query returns a different result:

LastName	TeacherID
Franklin	32
Barstow	86
Bannister	21
McAllister	87
Pinker	45

Programmers moving from file-based databases to relational databases often make the mistake of thinking that the simple `SELECT` statement is all they need. They are accustomed to scrolling (moving sequentially from field to field) through a set of records to find the ones they need. That's absolutely the wrong way to approach relational databases. Don't search for records yourself—let the database do the work. That's what the `WHERE` clause does—it limits the returned records to exactly the ones you need.

For example, to find only the teachers with last names starting with M, you add a `WHERE` clause to the `SELECT` statement:

```
SELECT * FROM Teachers WHERE LastName LIKE 'M%'
```

This query returns one row:

TeacherID	LastName	FirstName
87	McAllister	Ian

The ORDER BY clause of the SELECT statement controls the order of the records returned by the query. For example, to select all students by grade, you could use the following SELECT statement:

```
SELECT * FROM Students ORDER BY Grade,
LastName, FirstName
```

The fields in the ORDER BY clause do not have to appear in the selected field list. The default sort order is ascending (ASC), but you can retrieve fields in reverse order by specifying the DESC keyword after the appropriate field name. You don't have to select all the fields, and you may select them in any order you desire. The following SELECT statement includes all the basic SELECT clauses:

```
SELECT StudentID, LastName, FirstName
FROM Students ORDER BY Grade DESC
```

If you run the query and compare the results to the Grade column in the Students table, you can see that the query does indeed return the data sorted in reverse Grade order.

INNER and *OUTER JOIN* Statements

You can use the SELECT statement to retrieve data from more than one table at a time. SQL statements referencing more than one table typically (but not necessarily) use a JOIN statement to connect the tables on a common field or value.

For example, suppose you want a list of all students taught by Marsha Franklin. To obtain the list, you need to join the Teachers table to the Students table on the common TeacherID field. In the Teachers table, the TeacherID field is a primary key; in the Students table the TeacherID field is a foreign key. Because the primary key in a table is always unique and not null, you know that the TeacherID exists in each row of the Teachers table. For this example, assume you know that every student has been assigned a teacher.

There's a many-to-many relationship between teachers and students. That's because one teacher teaches many students, and each student has several teachers. That relationship appears in the TeacherStudent table.

Therefore, you need to join the Teachers table with the TeacherStudent table to find the students assigned to a particular teacher. For example:

```
SELECT StudentID
FROM TeacherStudent INNER JOIN Teachers
ON TeacherStudent.TeacherID=Teachers.TeacherID
WHERE Teachers.LastName='Franklin'
  AND Teachers.FirstName='Marsha'
```

When you run the query, the result is a single column of StudentIDs:

StudentID
1
3
5

Although accurate, a list of StudentID values is not a satisfactory solution because you still don't know the names of the students assigned to the teacher. The TeacherStudent table contains the StudentIDs, but not the students' names. To get the names of the students, you need to include the Students table in the query. You can create multiple joins in a single SELECT statement.

To retrieve the names, you need two INNER JOIN statements, because there's no direct relationship between teachers and students. For example:

```
SELECT Students.*
FROM Students INNER JOIN
(TeacherStudent INNER JOIN Teachers
  ON Teachers.TeacherID=TeacherStudent.TeacherID)
ON Students.StudentID=TeacherStudent.StudentID
WHERE Teachers.LastName='Franklin'
ORDER BY Students.LastName
```

The preceding statement has several interesting features. First, when you use two tables, you can't use the asterisk shorthand to retrieve all the fields from only one of the tables (although you can use it to retrieve all the fields in both tables). In such cases, the Tablename.* syntax selects all the fields from the named table. Second, the INNER JOIN statement requires that you specify which tables and fields the database should join to produce the query. Finally, when you work with more than one table you must specify the table name as well as the column name for each field where the field name appears in more than one table. The `LastName` and `TeacherID` fields appear in both the `Teachers` and `TeacherStudent` tables. In other words, if the column name is not unique among all fields in all tables in the `FROM` clause, the server will raise an error, because it can't distinguish the table from which to extract the data.

Now suppose some students haven't been assigned a teacher. In this case, the `INNER JOIN` clause still works, but the resulting record set will omit the rows in the `Students` table for which the `TeacherID` column value is `Null`. For example:

```
SELECT Teachers.*, Students.*
FROM Students INNER JOIN
(TeacherStudent INNER JOIN Teachers ON
  Teachers.TeacherID=TeacherStudent.TeacherID)
ON Students.StudentID=TeacherStudent.StudentID
ORDER BY Students.LastName
```

When you know that a foreign key may not exist, or may not match a key value in the joined table, you can perform a `LEFT (OUTER) JOIN` or a `RIGHT (OUTER) JOIN`. The `OUTER` keyword is optional. Outer joins return all the values from one of the tables even if there's no matching key. For example, if you run the following statement, you'll find that it displays more rows than the previous `SELECT` example:

```
SELECT Teachers.*, Students.*
FROM Students LEFT JOIN
(TeacherStudent INNER JOIN Teachers ON
  Teachers.TeacherID=TeacherStudent.TeacherID)
ON Students.StudentID=TeacherStudent.StudentID
ORDER BY Students.LastName
```

That's because the `LEFT JOIN` selects all the students, regardless of whether they have been assigned a teacher. Similarly, you could list all the teachers even if no students had been assigned to them. `RIGHT JOIN` works the same way, but returns all the rows from the right-hand side of the join. One other variation supported by some databases (including SQL Server), the `FULL (OUTER) JOIN`, retrieves unmatched rows from tables on both sides of the join.

Calculated Values and the *GROUP BY* Clause

Transact-SQL (T-SQL) contains a number of functions to calculate values. A calculated value is a result of an operation on one or more columns in multiple rows; for example, a sum, average, or total. In T-SQL, calculated values are called aggregates, and the functions are aggregate functions because they aggregate, or collect a number of values into a single value using a calculation. For example, you can retrieve the total number of rows in any table with the following SELECT statement, substituting an appropriate table name in the FROM clause:

```
SELECT count(*) FROM <tablename>
```

A count of the Students table returns 7.

Counting is even more useful when you group results by another column. For example, if you want to know the total number of students taught by each teacher, you could obtain a count of students and group the results by teacher. The results look like Table 13.4.

TABLE 13.4: Count of Students by Teacher

TeacherID	LastName	FirstName	TotalStudents
21	Bannister	Henry	1
86	Barstow	Emily	1
32	Franklin	Marsha	3
87	McAllister	Ian	1
45	Pinker	Dorothy	1

The SELECT statement to obtain the results in Table 13.4 includes a new clause, the GROUP BY clause. The syntax is:

```
SELECT (field1, field2, etc.)
FROM (table list)
WHERE (condition)
GROUP BY (field1, field2, etc.)
HAVING (condition)
ORDER BY (field1 [ASC|DESC],
  field2 [ASC|DESC], etc.)
```

Here's the statement to select the data in Table 13.4.

```
SELECT Teachers.TeacherID, Teachers.LastName,
  Teachers.FirstName,
  COUNT(TeacherStudent.StudentID)
    AS TotalStudents

FROM Students INNER JOIN (TeacherStudent
  INNER JOIN Teachers
  ON Teachers.TeacherID =
    TeacherStudent.TeacherID)
  ON Students.StudentID =
    TeacherStudent.StudentID

GROUP BY Teachers.TeacherID,
  Teachers.LastName, Teachers.FirstName
HAVING count(TeacherStudent.StudentID) > 0

ORDER BY Teachers.LastName
```

That's an intimidating statement at first, but take each clause separately and it's quite straightforward. The first clause—the column list—simply lists the names of the columns you want the query to return. Note that you can provide a name for the calculated column using the AS keyword followed by the name to use. Actually, the AS keyword lets you rename any column or table in SQL statements. The FROM clause lists the table names and the relationships between them, using joins to tell the database how to combine the tables. The GROUP BY clause controls the groupings. You must include all referenced columns in the GROUP BY clause except the calculated columns. Put the columns in the sequence you want the database to group them by. In this case, I put the TeacherID column first because I want to obtain the count of students for each teacher. The order of the rest of the fields in the GROUP BY statement is immaterial, but they must appear.

The HAVING statement lets you add conditions—just like the WHERE clause. The difference is that the WHERE clause selects records before the grouping occurs, whereas the HAVING clause selects records after the grouping. If you don't include a WHERE clause, the HAVING clause acts the same as a WHERE clause.

T-SQL can also perform other, more familiar functions. For example, you can add or concatenate values using the + operator. If you want to retrieve the list of teachers as a single first-last formatted string, you could write a query like this:

```
SELECT Teachers.FirstName + ' ' +
  Teachers.LastName AS Name
ORDER BY Teachers.LastName
```

Running the query produces a list of teacher names in first-last format:

Name

Henry Bannister

Emily Barstow

Marsha Franklin

Ian McAllister

Dorothy Pinker

You've seen the rudiments of how to select data. Selecting data doesn't change it, so selecting is a safe operation. All the other statements change data in some way. You'll be happy to know that the other statements are considerably less complex than the SELECT statement. I suggest you make a backup copy of your database before you continue.

The *INSERT* Statement

SQL INSERT statements add one or more new rows to a table. The INSERT statement has two variations. The first variation adds one row by assigning values to a specified list of columns in a specified table. The values you want to insert follow a VALUES statement. You put parentheses around both the `field list` and the `values list`. For example:

```
INSERT INTO table name (field list)
VALUES (values list)
```

You must provide a value for all fields that cannot accept a null value and do not have a default value. You do not have to provide values for identity columns. For example, to insert a row into the Teachers table, you must provide a last name and a first name:

```
INSERT INTO Teachers (LastName, FirstName)
VALUES('Swarthmore', 'John')
```

The second variation lets you add multiple rows using a SELECT query in place of the VALUES list, as follows:

```
INSERT INTO table name (field list)
SELECT query
```

For example, suppose you had a list of students waiting to be enrolled. You could add all the students simultaneously to the Students table. There's a StudentsWaitingList table you can use to test this query. For example:

```
INSERT INTO Students
   (Grade, LastName, FirstName)
SELECT Grade, LastName, FirstName
FROM StudentsWaitingList
```

If you're inserting data into all the columns in the target table, you can omit the field list. The SELECT statement you use to obtain the data you want to insert can include any clause or condition discussed in the previous section, including calculated fields and a GROUP BY clause.

The *UPDATE* Statement

UPDATE statements change data in one or more columns and in one or more rows. The UPDATE statement is dangerous, because if you forget to specify conditions, your database will happily update all the rows in the table. You should always specify a WHERE condition when updating data. The UPDATE statement has the following syntax:

```
UPDATE (table name)
SET field1 = (value/expression),
   field2 = (value/expression), ...
FROM (table/query source)
WHERE (condition)
```

The UPDATE statement has four clauses. In the UPDATE clause, you must specify a table name containing the fields to update. You may not update multiple tables simultaneously.

The SET clause contains the list of fields you wish to update. You separate the list with commas. Each item in the list consists of a field name, an equals sign, and a new value. You can use a constant, a variable, a field from another table, or an expression for the value on the right-hand side of the equals sign.

The FROM clause is optional. If you're updating a single row with constant values, you can omit the FROM clause. You need the FROM clause when you're updating data in one table from values stored in a different table (or in another place in the same table). Fortunately, the FROM clause is identical to the FROM clause you saw earlier in this chapter in "The SELECT Statement" section. You may update from multiple tables using JOIN statements as appropriate.

The WHERE clause (don't forget the WHERE clause!), again, is a condition that identifies the rows in the target table you wish to update. For example, suppose the student Isabel McArthur announces that she is changing her name to Serena McArthur. You can update her student record with the following SQL statement:

```
UPDATE Students SET FirstName = 'Serena' WHERE
Students.LastName='McArthur'
  AND Students.FirstName='Isabel'
```

The *DELETE* Statement

The DELETE statement is the simplest of all, but quite powerful. You can use the DELETE statement to delete one or more rows in one or more tables. For example, after inserting all the records from the Students-WaitingList table, you can delete all the records in the table using the following statement:

```
DELETE FROM StudentsWaitingList
```

The DELETE statement is just as dangerous as the UPDATE statement, as you can see, because it cheerfully deletes data without prompting. If you accidentally run a DELETE statement it's difficult to recover your data. You should rarely use a DELETE statement without a WHERE clause. If you want to delete all the data from a table, it's much more efficient to use a different type of statement, one of a group of statements that alters the database itself—the TRUNCATE TABLE statement. Truncating a table removes all the data and resets the identity column value to its default—usually 1. For example, to delete all the data in the StudentsWaitingList table, you can write:

```
TRUNCATE TABLE StudentsWaitingList
```

I said you should rarely use DELETE without a WHERE clause. There is one reason to do so. The TRUNCATE statement is not logged—that means you can't recover if you use it automatically, whereas the DELETE statement is a logged operation. That's the reason TRUNCATE is so much more efficient—it avoids the log operations, but it also means the data is unrecoverable from the transaction log.

The DELETE statement becomes slightly more complex when you want to delete data based on values from another table. For example, suppose you decide to delete all the students who have no assigned teachers. You need to join the TeacherStudent table to the Students table, find the rows where the TeacherID columns contain Null values in the TeacherStudent table, and then delete those rows in the Teachers table. This may sound like a two-step operation, but you can accomplish it in SQL in a single step, as follows:

```
DELETE FROM Students
WHERE StudentID NOT IN
   (SELECT DISTINCT StudentID
FROM TeacherStudent)
```

The previous statement uses the NOT IN keywords to test for the existence of a StudentID in a subquery (the portion of the previous query contained in parentheses). A subquery is a separate query that returns data. In this case, the subquery returns the list of all StudentIDs that appear in the TeacherStudent table. Any StudentIDs that do not appear in that table have no assigned teachers, and can be deleted.

When you want to delete data from one table in a join, you must specify the name of the table after the DELETE keyword. For example, suppose you add all the rows in the StudentsWaitingList table to the Students table, then decide to remove them:

```
DELETE Students
FROM Students
INNER JOIN StudentsWaitingList
  ON Students.LastName =
    StudentsWaitingList.LastName AND
    Students.FirstName =
    StudentsWaitingList.FirstName
```

Without the DELETE Students clause, the database cannot decide which table to delete the data from.

Generating Unique IDs

As previously discussed, you have several ways to uniquely distinguish one row from another. Identity fields work wonderfully within a table, but have serious weaknesses when you're working between tables, or worse, between databases, because the database only guarantees the uniqueness of an identity value for new rows.

Going back to the previous example, suppose your company has a mobile sales force using laptops. Each salesperson generates a few dozen orders per day. The salespeople enter these orders into a local Access database on their laptops. Periodically, the salespeople connect to the central office to upload the orders.

Further, suppose you were given the task of writing both the local order-entry application and an ASP page to accept the orders via a secured connection. You must contrive a means to create a table that can accept the rows from many remote databases—and you're not allowed to change the data from the laptops.

This is a tough problem because you must avoid identical `OrderID` values from any two machines. To solve it, you can use Globally Unique IDs (GUIDs). As you can imagine, these numbers are long. Microsoft Windows uses GUIDs to identify COM objects. If you look in the Windows Registry, you'll find that the `HKEY_CLASSES_ROOT\CLSID` key contains a large number of GUIDs, which look like this:

```
{098f2370-bac0-11ce-b579-08012b30bfeb}
```

GUIDs are globally unique because they depend on the local machine's network card MAC address, the local date and time, and for all I know, the internal ID of your microprocessor and the phase of the moon. It doesn't matter—believe me, the chances of another computer being able to generate a GUID that matches any GUID produced on any other computer in the world is vanishingly small.

SQL Server 7 and higher support GUIDs natively, but earlier versions do not. You can create a custom VB or C++ DLL to generate GUIDs, but that's beyond the scope of this book. There's a great deal more to know about SQL and SQL Server, but the information in this chapter gives you a good start.

I strongly suggest you spend some more time exploring SQL's capabilities. The Transact-SQL help files (press Shift+F1 from within Query Analyzer) and the SQL Server Books Online contain an enormous amount of information. In addition, there are many excellent reference and tutorial works on SQL.

WHAT'S NEXT?

Before you can use a database in your application, it would help to know how to administer it. The next chapter will introduce you to the Visual Database Tools included with many Microsoft development products, including the latest Visual Basic IDE. You'll see how to hook up your database to your development environment. You'll also learn how to view and query data, as well as work with stored procedures and triggers.

Chapter 14

Exploring Data from Visual Basic

In previous chapters, you got a sample of the ADO object model and have some sense of what you can do with ADO. Now it's time to start working with data. A few years ago, this would have meant writing a lot of code to connect to data sources, retrieve information about the data, examine the data, and update it. You can still do all these operations in code, but that's not the best way to go if you want to get up and running with data quickly.

Starting with Visual Basic 5, the developers at Microsoft began working hard to make basic database operations easier to perform. You can now do a wide variety of database operations using visual tools without ever having to write a line of code. This makes it possible for you to be vastly more productive as a database developer. If you need to be a database administrator as well, you'll still need to use your database's native tools for

Adapted from *Visual Basic® Developer's Guide to ADO*, by Mike Gunderloy

ISBN 0-7821-2556-5 480 pages $39.99

some operations. For example, these tools don't offer any support for creating users or performing other security operations.

In this chapter, you'll learn about the Data View window and the tools that you can call from this window. These tools are collectively known as the Visual Database Tools, and they're shared by many Microsoft products, including Visual Basic, Visual C++, Visual J++, Visual Interdev, and even Microsoft Office 2000. In addition, these tools can work with data from any OLE DB or ODBC provider. The net effect is that they let you concentrate on what you want to do instead of on the tedious syntax of how to do it. Let's start by looking at the Data View window itself.

USING THE DATA VIEW WINDOW

To open the Data View, choose View ➢ Data View Window from the Visual Basic menus, or click the Data View Window button on the Visual Basic Standard Toolbar. Figure 14.1 shows the default state of the Data View window. As you can see, it's a TreeView-based interface, similar to the left pane of Windows Explorer.

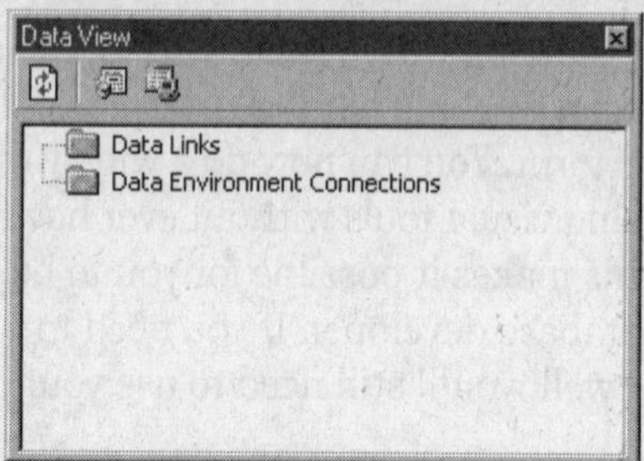

FIGURE 14.1: The Data View window

The Data View includes two top-level nodes:

Data Links Represent connections to individual databases. These connections are stored independently of any particular Visual Basic project. You'll see the same set of connections reappear if you close your Visual Basic project and open another project, or close and reopen Visual Basic itself. Data links are useful for data that you need to have available all or most of the time.

NOTE

Don't confuse data links in the Data View with Microsoft Data Link files that you'll find in Windows Explorer. A Microsoft Data Link file contains the information needed to open an OLE DB connection to a data source.

Data Environment Connections Represent connections made through the Visual Basic Data Environment Designer. These connections are specific to a particular Visual Basic project.

An empty Data View isn't particularly useful. Figure 14.2 shows what the Data View might look like after adding a couple of data links and expanding parts of the TreeView. In the next section, you'll learn how to add new data links to the Data View.

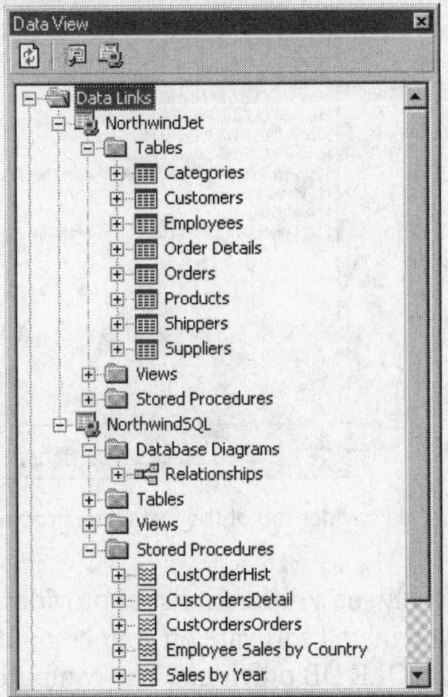

FIGURE 14.2: Data View window with some data links

Connecting to Data

The simplest way to connect the Data View to actual data is to create a new data link. You can do this by right-clicking in the Data View window and choosing Add A Data Link, or by clicking the Add A New Data Link button on the Data View toolbar.

When you add a new data link, the Data View will display the Data Link Properties dialog box shown in Figure 14.3. You'll get very familiar with this dialog box as you work with ADO data sources; it's used any time you need to connect something to an OLE DB provider. As you can see, the first tab allows you to choose a particular OLE DB provider to use for the current data link. Once you select a provider, you can navigate through the other tabs of this dialog box to set provider-specific information.

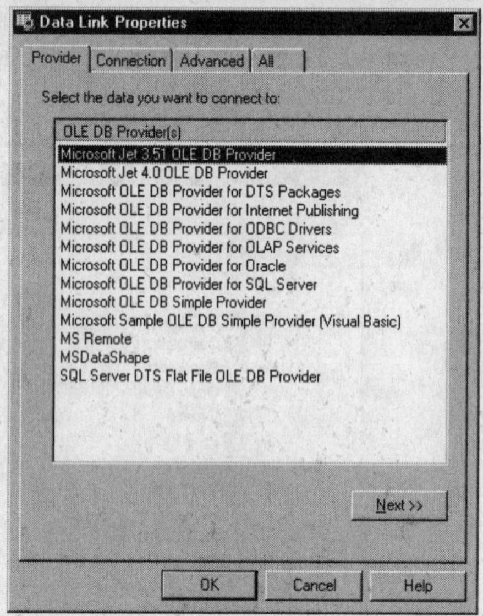

FIGURE 14.3: The Provider tab of the Data Link Properties dialog box

You'll probably see a different list of providers than that shown in Figure 14.3. As you install software on your computer, you'll end up with more and more OLE DB providers. The computer from which this screenshot was taken has had Visual Basic 6, SQL Server 7, ADO 2.5, the OLE DB Simple Provider Toolkit, Internet Explorer 5, and Microsoft Internet Information Server 4 installed. Here's a brief rundown of the OLE DB providers shown in this example:

- The Microsoft Jet 3.51 and Microsoft Jet 4 providers are used to read data from Microsoft Access databases and other databases that rely on the Jet database engine. The 4 driver doesn't remove the 3.51 driver, because they have slightly different default behaviors and the provider developers are wary of breaking existing applications.

- The Provider for DTS Packages and the SQL Server DTS Flat File OLE DB Provider are used to connect to SQL Server 7 Data Transformation Services packages. These packages are used in data warehousing applications to convert data from one format to another. We won't cover DTS in this book, but there's a summary in *SQL Server 7 In Record Time* (by Mike Gunderloy and Mary Chipman, ISBN 0-7821-2155-1, Sybex, 1998).
- The Provider for Internet Publishing is used to retrieve information from Web and FTP servers on the Internet or (more likely) your corporate intranet. It's installed by Office 2000 or Internet Explorer 5.
- The Provider for ODBC Drivers gives you a handy way to use ADO to connect to older data sources for which you do not yet have an OLE DB provider. You'll recall that Open Database Connectivity, or ODBC, was the old standard for connecting to heterogeneous databases. This provider allows you to use existing ODBC drivers to retrieve data, at the cost of some performance. If you have a native OLE DB provider specifically for your target data, you should use it instead of this provider.
- The Provider for OLAP Services retrieves data from the Microsoft Online Analytical Processing (OLAP) Server. This server ships with SQL Server 7, and is used to generate summary data from large databases.
- The Provider for Oracle is used to retrieve data from Oracle databases. There are examples of using this provider later in this chapter.
- The Provider for SQL Server can retrieve data from Microsoft SQL Server versions 6.5 and 7. Many of the examples in this book use this provider.
- The Simple Provider implements a reduced set of OLE DB interfaces designed to present tabular data on Web pages.
- The Sample OLE DB Simple Provider (Visual Basic) is an example from Microsoft that demonstrates the use of the Simple Provider interfaces from Visual Basic.

- The MS Remote provider is used to send data requests across the Internet to a remote database. This provider is an essential part of the Remote Data Service.
- The MSDataShape provider is designed to retrieve hierarchical recordsets.

Connecting to SQL Server Data

After choosing the SQL Server provider, you need to fill in the information on the Connection tab of this dialog box. This information tells OLE DB where to find the data you'd like to connect to. Each provider can control which prompts appear on this tab—you'll notice that they change depending on which provider you choose. Figure 14.4 shows the information that the SQL Server provider prompts for. In this case, the information is already filled in to connect to the Northwind database on a server named Beaver. The Test Connection button on this tab allows you to make sure that you've filled in all the required information correctly. With the SQL Server provider, no database names appear in the combo box until you've been authenticated by the server. If your network uses SQL Server 7 with integrated security, this authentication will happen based on your Windows NT login identity. Otherwise, you'll need to fill in a SQL Server username and password to see the list of available databases.

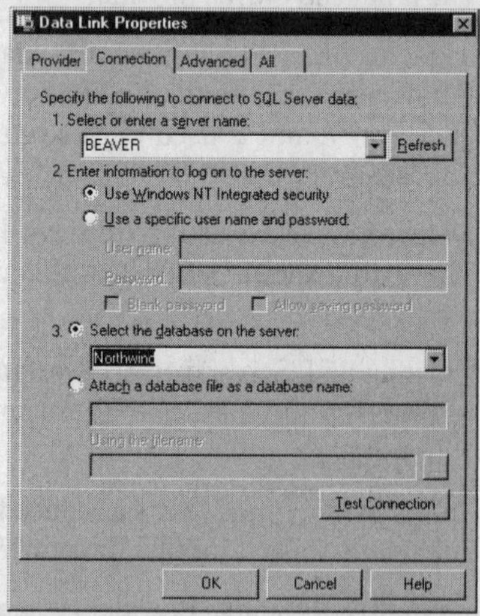

FIGURE 14.4: The Connection tab of the Data Link Properties dialog box for a SQL Server database

The other two tabs of this dialog box (Advanced and All) contain settings that you probably won't need to touch. The All tab in particular allows you to tweak any of the initialization properties for the OLE DB connection. Figure 14.5 shows what this tab might look like in the case of the SQL Server OLE DB provider.

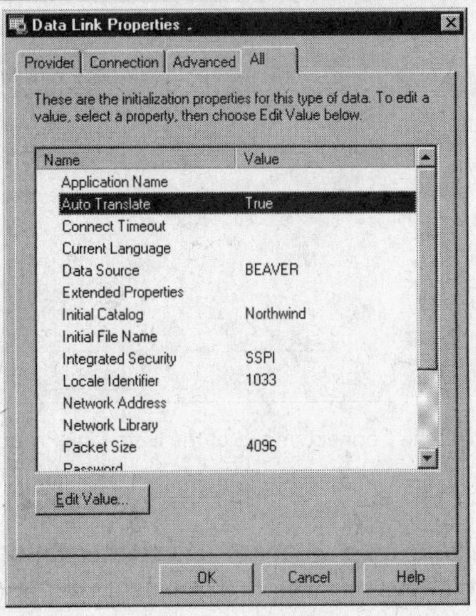

FIGURE 14.5: The All tab of the Data Link Properties dialog box for a SQL Server database

When you click the OK button on the Data Link Properties dialog box, the Data View will create the new link and assign it a default name such as DataLink1. You can change this name immediately, or change it at any time by right-clicking the name and choosing Rename from the context menu.

Connecting to Jet or Oracle Data

Adding a Jet or Oracle database (or a database from any other OLE DB provider, for that matter) follows the same steps. The only difference is that the tabs of the dialog box after the first one will contain information specific to the chosen provider. Figure 14.6, for example, shows the Connection tab for a Jet database.

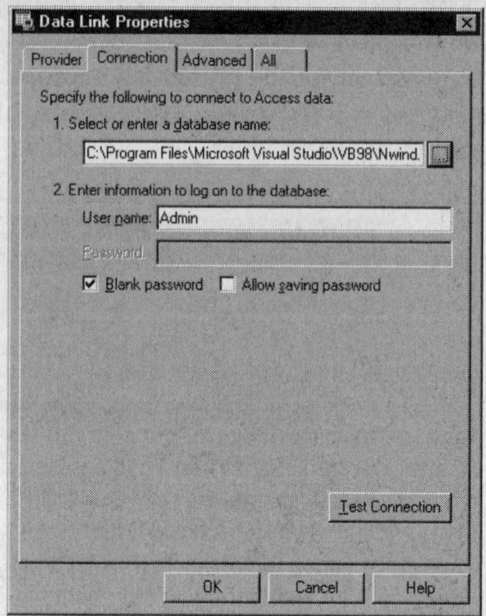

FIGURE 14.6: The Connection tab of the Data Link Properties dialog box for a Jet database

To connect to a Jet database using either the 3.51 provider or the 4 provider, you'll have to supply three pieces of information:

- The database path and name
- The username
- The password (which may be blank)

If the database requires a password, you have the option of whether or not to save the password with the connection information.

WARNING

Passwords are saved in plain text in the Windows Registry, so saving passwords can represent a significant security risk.

Figure 14.7 shows the Connection tab for an Oracle database.

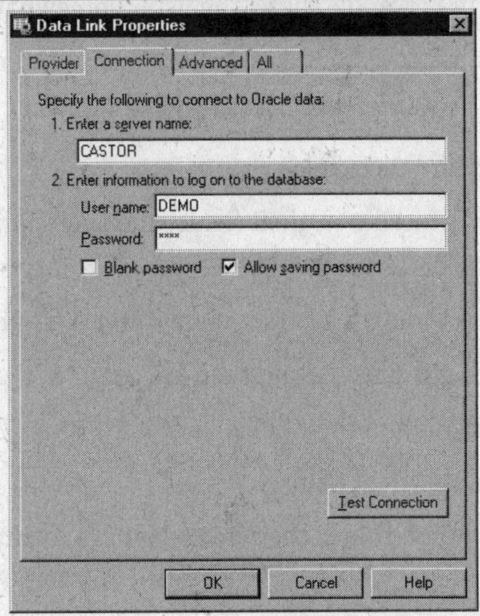

FIGURE 14.7: The Connection tab of the Data Link Properties dialog box for an Oracle database

Again, you'll have to supply three pieces of information to connect to an Oracle database:

- The server name
- The username
- The password (which may be blank)

Once again, the password is stored in plain text if you allow it to be saved.

Information in the Data View

The information shown in the Data View varies depending on the type of OLE DB provider you're using. For a Jet database, the Data View will show you:

- Tables and their fields
- Views and their fields
- Stored procedures, their fields, and their parameters

For a SQL Server database, the list is somewhat more extensive:

- Database diagrams, their tables, and their fields
- Tables, their fields, and their triggers
- Views and their fields
- Stored procedures, their fields, and their parameters

An Oracle database has an even more extensive list:

- Database diagrams, their tables, and their fields
- Tables, their fields, and their triggers
- Synonyms and their fields
- Views and their fields
- Stored procedures, their fields, and their parameters
- Functions and their parameters

When you use the Data View, you're actually using ADO and OLE DB for everything. Behind the scenes, the Visual Database Tools are generating SQL statements and sending them off to the database. You don't have to worry about the details, though; you can just point and click in the Data View interface. In the rest of this chapter, you'll learn about some of the operations that you can perform with the Data View.

Data Link Storage

Since connection information in the Data View persists between Visual Basic sessions, it obviously must be stored somewhere. Although the method of storage is undocumented, an understanding of it is helpful for a couple of reasons. First, you may need to manually inspect the OLE DB connection string for a particular data link if something has changed, or for troubleshooting purposes. Second, you may wish to transfer or propagate the persistent link information from one computer to another, perhaps to share it with other developers in your organization.

Not surprisingly, this information is stored in the Windows Registry. You can use the Registry Editor to inspect or edit the information contained in the key

```
HKEY_CURRENT_USER\Software\VB
   and VBA Program Settings\Microsoft
   Visual Basic AddIns\VBDataViewWindow
```

This key contains a list of pairs of values. Each pair contains the name and OLE DB connection string for a single node in the Data Links section of the Data View window. For example, if you have the two links shown in Figure 14.2 in your Data View, you'd have this data in the Registry (this is the format that the Registry will export it to as text):

```
"DisplayOnConnect"="0"
"DataLinkName1"="NorthwindSQL"
"DataLinkString1"="Provider=SQLOLEDB.1;
    Integrated Security=SSPI;
    Persist Security Info=False;
    Initial Catalog=Northwind;Data Source=BEAVER"
"DataLinkName2"="NorthwindJet"
"DataLinkString2"="Provider=Microsoft.Jet.OLEDB.4;
    Persist Security Info=False;
    Data Source= C:\\Program Files\\Microsoft Visual
    Studio\\ VB98\\Nwind.mdb"
```

The DataLinkName and DataLinkString values contain the information for each persistent data link in the Data View. The DisplayOnConnect value controls whether the Data View window is shown (the data in the value will be 1 in this case) or hidden (the data in the value will be 0) when Visual Basic is first launched.

Creating and Using Database Diagrams

One good use for the Visual Database Tools is to explore the structure of a database. Microsoft Access developers are used to the Relationships window in Access, which graphically displays tables and their relationships. Starting with the Data View, you can build such a view for other databases, such as SQL Server databases.

To create a database diagram in a SQL Server database, for example, right-click the Database Diagrams folder and choose New Diagram. This will give you a blank window within the Visual Basic design space. Now you can populate this window with tables. The easiest way to start this process is by simply dragging a table from a Data Link or Data Environment connection in the Data View into your new database diagram. By default, it will be displayed as a list of column names. The view used for the Customers table is shown in Figure 14.8. There are four other views available, which you can select by right-clicking the table in the database diagram.

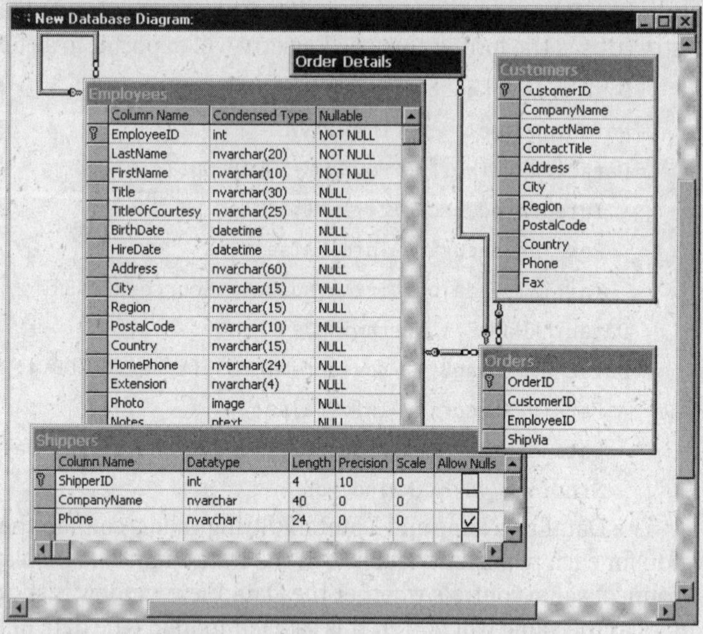

FIGURE 14.8: A database diagram for part of the SQL Server Northwind database

The four other views are as follows:

Column Properties Displays all the properties of the columns in the table. The Shippers table in Figure 14.8 uses this view.

Keys Shows only column names for primary and foreign keys in the table. The Orders table in Figure 14.8 uses this view.

Name Only Shrinks the table display to a title bar only. The Order Details table in Figure 14.8 uses this view.

Custom Shows a selection of the properties for the column in the table (you can change the properties shown by choosing Modify Custom View from the shortcut menu for the table). The Employees table in Figure 14.8 is displayed using this view.

No matter which view you choose, the database diagram will show the relationships between the tables in the view. These are the "pipes" between the tables. The key symbols identify primary keys, while the infinity symbols identify foreign keys. In a self-join, the pipe will make a loop, as shown for the Employees table in Figure 14.8.

Shortcut menus within the database diagram let you control its appearance. You can add text annotations to the diagram, show or hide the names of the relationships, set up the page for printing, automatically arrange the tables, and control the zoom of the display. You can also right-click any table or relationship to view its properties.

The database diagram is not simply a display; it's also a workspace for designing databases. You can create new relationships by dragging and dropping a foreign key field to a primary key field. You can delete relationships using the shortcut menu for the relationship. You can even create new tables by right-clicking in the diagram and selecting New Table. This will open a blank table designer. The next section covers the use of the table designer.

Working with Tables

Working with the data in tables from the Data View is simple. Choose the appropriate database, expand the tree until you can see the table in question, and double-click it (or right-click and choose Open). This will open the table in a datasheet. You can add, edit, and delete data just by typing within this datasheet.

Depending on the provider, you can also do design work on the tables in your database. Right-click the table in the Data View window and choose Design. (If there's no Design choice, then the OLE DB provider for this data link doesn't support designing tables.) Figure 14.9 shows a table from a SQL Server database open in the table designer.

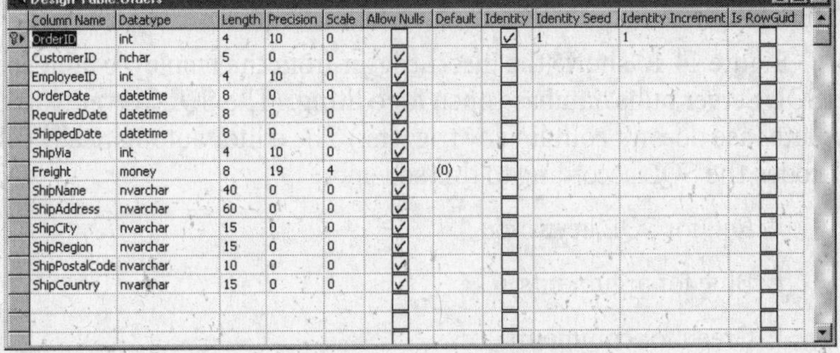

Design Table:Orders

Column Name	Datatype	Length	Precision	Scale	Allow Nulls	Default	Identity	Identity Seed	Identity Increment	Is RowGuid
OrderID	int	4	10	0			✓	1	1	
CustomerID	nchar	5	0	0	✓					
EmployeeID	int	4	10	0	✓					
OrderDate	datetime	8	0	0	✓					
RequiredDate	datetime	8	0	0	✓					
ShippedDate	datetime	8	0	0	✓					
ShipVia	int	4	10	0	✓					
Freight	money	8	19	4	✓	(0)				
ShipName	nvarchar	40	0	0	✓					
ShipAddress	nvarchar	60	0	0	✓					
ShipCity	nvarchar	15	0	0	✓					
ShipRegion	nvarchar	15	0	0	✓					
ShipPostalCode	nvarchar	10	0	0	✓					
ShipCountry	nvarchar	15	0	0	✓					

FIGURE 14.9: The Visual Database Tools table designer

You can design entirely new tables with this interface or alter existing tables. If you've worked with server databases in the past, you'll be pleasantly surprised at the ease with which you can alter existing tables. For example, to change the length of an `nvarchar` field in a SQL Server database, just highlight the existing length and type the new value. When you close the designer, the Visual Database Tools will commit the changes.

WARNING

Whether the designer displays them on screen or not, changes are not saved until you close the designer and confirm that you want to make changes. If your computing environment is unstable, you'll want to take this step often.

By right-clicking in the table designer and choosing Properties, you can also alter table-level properties. Again, the available selection will vary with the OLE DB provider you're using to get to the table. For a SQL Server table, for example, you can perform these operations in the property sheet:

- Add and remove CHECK constraints.
- Edit the table's relationships.
- Set or remove a primary key.
- Create and delete indexes.

Using Triggers

Client-server databases (such as SQL Server and Oracle, but not Jet) typically support triggers. The Data View lets you edit existing triggers or add new triggers to a table, provided the underlying database supports this functionality.

Figure 14.10 shows the insert trigger from the employee table in the SQL Server pubs database open for editing. (The SQL Server Northwind database doesn't contain any triggers.) The editor automatically color-codes the SQL according to this scheme:

- Red for SQL keywords
- Blue for arguments
- Green for comments
- Light blue for punctuation

- Black for other text
- Orange for functions

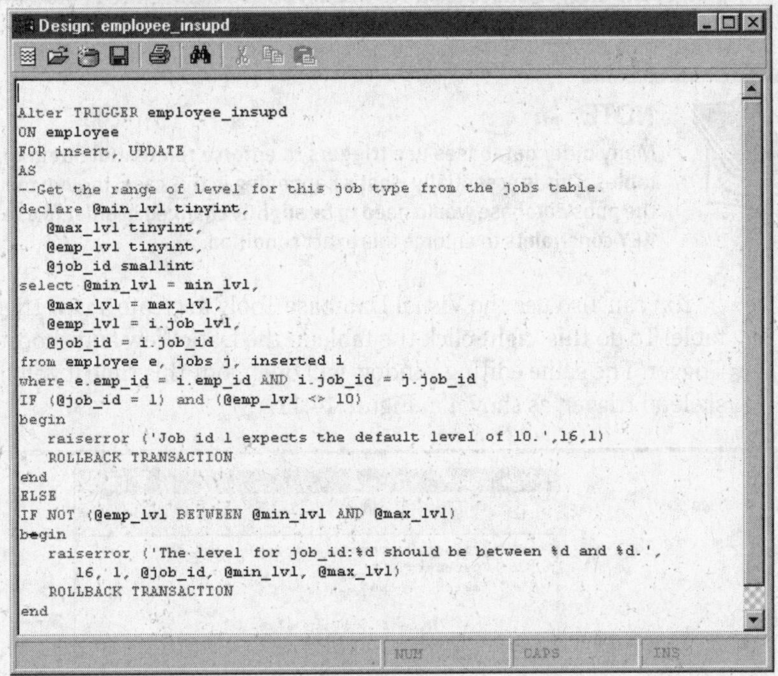

Design: employee_insupd
Alter TRIGGER employee_insupd
ON employee
FOR insert, UPDATE
AS
--Get the range of level for this job type from the jobs table.
declare @min_lvl tinyint,
@max_lvl tinyint,
@emp_lvl tinyint,
@job_id smallint
select @min_lvl = min_lvl,
@max_lvl = max_lvl,
@emp_lvl = i.job_lvl,
@job_id = i.job_id
from employee e, jobs j, inserted i
where e.emp_id = i.emp_id AND i.job_id = j.job_id
IF (@job_id = 1) and (@emp_lvl <> 10)
begin
raiserror ('Job id 1 expects the default level of 10.',16,1)
ROLLBACK TRANSACTION
end
ELSE
IF NOT (@emp_lvl BETWEEN @min_lvl AND @max_lvl)
begin
raiserror ('The level for job_id:%d should be between %d and %d.',
16, 1, @job_id, @min_lvl, @max_lvl)
ROLLBACK TRANSACTION
end
NUM
CAPS
INS

FIGURE 14.10: Editing a SQL Server trigger

You may not be familiar with the syntax for triggers, but this one is fairly straightforward. The ALTER TRIGGER statement at the top is inserted by the editor. This is the SQL statement that changes an existing trigger when you run it so that the effect of running this statement (using the Save To Database toolbar button) is to modify the existing trigger. ALTER TRIGGER isn't part of the saved trigger, but rather an editing convenience.

The declare section specifies four variables used in the trigger and sets their datatypes. The SELECT statement (which includes FROM and WHERE clauses) then fills in these variables with values based on the current row. Note the use of the special table named "inserted" (here aliased to the name "i"), which contains the row that caused this trigger to be invoked.

The trigger then uses logic in a pair of IF statements to determine whether the `job_lvl` field for the newly inserted employee is within an acceptable range, determined from the jobs table. If it is outside this range, the trigger executes a ROLLBACK TRANSACTION statement, which has the effect of discarding the attempted insertion.

NOTE

Many older databases use triggers to enforce referential integrity between tables. This is essentially what's happening in this case, though the design of the pubs database would need to be slightly changed in order to use FOREIGN KEY constraints to enforce this exact condition.

You can also use the Visual Database Tools to create a new trigger for a table. To do this, right-click the table in the Data View and choose New Trigger. The same editing window will open, but this time it will have a skeletal trigger, as shown in Figure 14.11.

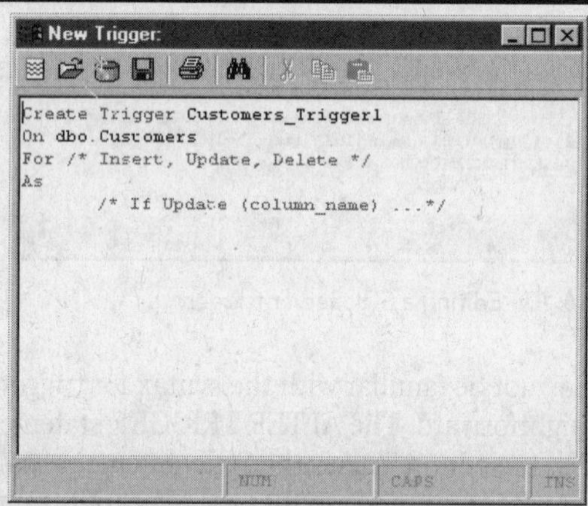

FIGURE 14.11: Creating a new trigger for the Customers table

Here the only thing provided by the editor is the CREATE TRIGGER statement, which is used to save a new trigger to the database. The text in green between the /* and */ symbol pairs is ignored by SQL Server when it interprets the trigger.

Using the Query Designer

Probably the most important job of ADO is to retrieve data from a database. In most cases, you'll do this by running a query, a collection of SQL commands that tell the database which data you want. (Some products call these *views* instead of queries.) The Visual Database Tools include a powerful Query Designer that lets you design new queries and modify or run existing queries through a graphical interface, instead of by writing SQL statements directly. Whatever job you're doing with ADO, you'll find the Query Designer, launched from the Data View, to be a quick and easy way to build the queries you need. Even if you're planning to execute queries in code, instead of persisting them to the database, you'll find that the Query Designer's ability to generate the SQL statements you need is very helpful. The Query Designer is limited to generating SELECT queries.

Designing a Query

To open a query, locate the appropriate object in the Data View TreeView (usually it will be under Views), right-click it, and choose Design. You'll see the Query Designer open, displaying the design of this query. If you then right-click in the query and choose Run, the Query Designer will retrieve the records specified by the query. Figure 14.12 shows a query open in the Query Designer.

NOTE

If you don't see Design on the right-click menu for a particular view, it means one of two things: either the OLE DB provider for that data link doesn't support the interfaces required by the Query Designer or the particular query cannot be represented within the Designer. In this case, there's no alternative to using the native tools supplied with the database to inspect this particular view.

The Query Designer shows you four different views of your query. From top to bottom, these are:

The Diagram Pane Provides a graphical representation of the tables and fields used as the sources of data for your query. Lines show how the tables are joined, and check marks show the fields included in the resultset of the query.

The Grid Pane Provides a way to further control the fields that are included in the query. Here you can specify sorting, grouping, and searching conditions, the results of action queries, or the names of aliases.

The SQL Pane Shows you the SQL statement that represents this query in the database. You can verify the syntax of this statement or edit it by hand.

The Results Pane Shows you the data retrieved by running the query. You can both view and edit data in the Results pane.

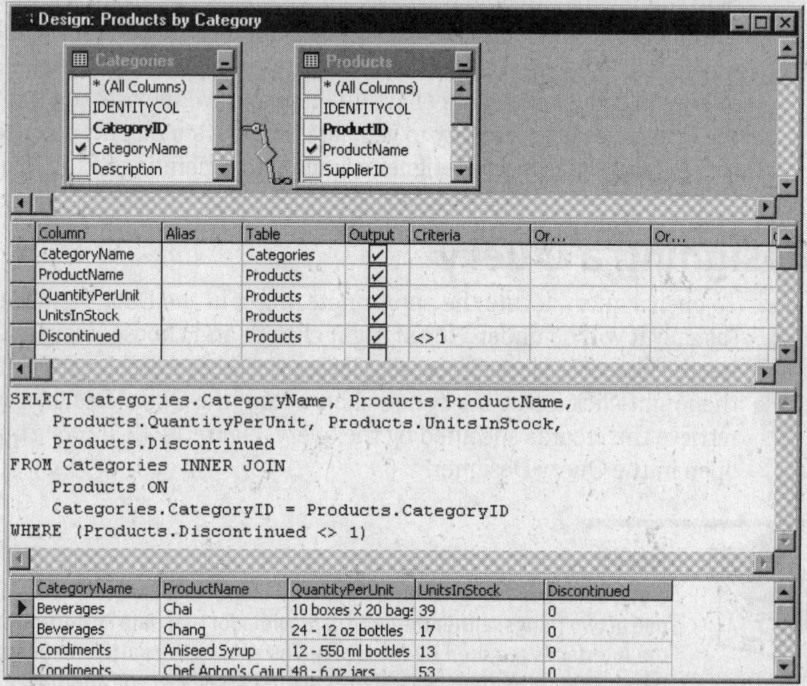

FIGURE 14.12: Query open in the Query Designer

The Query Designer keeps the information in all four panes synchronized. For example, if you check a new field in the Diagram pane, it will appear in the Grid and SQL panes and show up in the Results pane the next time that the query is executed.

The Diagram Pane

Usually, you'll start designing queries in the Diagram pane. To create a new, blank query, just right-click the Views node in a data link and choose New View.

To add a new table to the query, drag the table from the Data View. With certain types of data sources, you'll need to limit yourself to tables from a single data link. However, if you're using SQL Server 7, which supports distributed queries, you can drag in a table from just about any data source and add it to your query. To remove a table, right-click within the table and choose Remove.

To add or remove a column from the query's output, check or uncheck the check box to the right of the field. In addition to individual columns, you can check the box for "* (All Columns)" to include all the columns from this table in the resultset. Some databases, such as SQL Server, include an additional choice named IDENTITYCOL. This column will include the column with its Identity property set to True (if there is one) from this table in the query's output.

To see the datatype of a column, just hover your cursor over that column name in the Diagram pane, and the information will appear in a ToolTip.

If your query includes multiple tables, you'll almost certainly want to specify a join between the tables. If the database includes referential integrity information (PRIMARY KEY and FOREIGN KEY constraints), the Query Designer will automatically include these joins when you drop related tables. Otherwise, you can create joins by dragging a column from the many-side table and dropping it on the corresponding one-side column. The Query Designer also makes it easy to create non-equijoins (joins that include something other than the matching data from both tables) and outer joins. To create a join other than an equijoin, first create the equijoin and then right-click the join line and choose Properties. This will open the Join Properties dialog box shown in Figure 14.13.

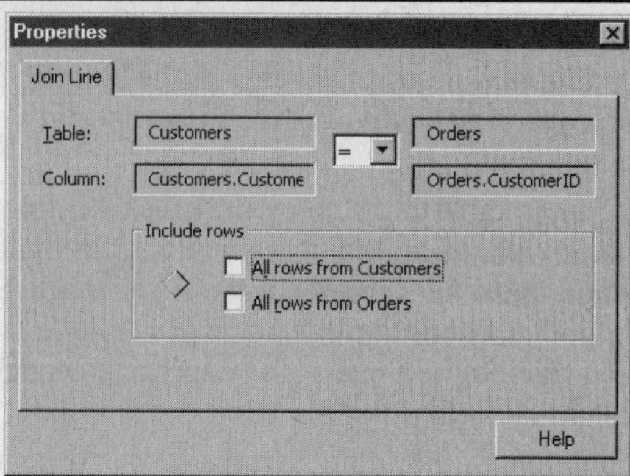

FIGURE 14.13: Editing join properties

To create a non-equijoin, select a different join criterion from the combo box. To create an outer join, select one of the two check boxes in the Include Rows section of the dialog box. In either case, the Query Designer will alter the appearance of the graphic on the join line, so you can determine the type of join without looking at the join properties.

If there's a criterion set on a field, you can remove it by right-clicking the field and choosing "Remove Filter." This isn't all that useful, since there's no way to put the criterion back in this pane. Usually, you'll want to make filtering changes in the Grid pane instead.

Finally, by right-clicking and selecting Properties within the Diagram pane, you can select options for the query as a whole. The most common of these is the TOP option, which allows you to limit the size of the resultset returned by the query.

The Grid Pane

The Grid pane allows you to fine-tune the resultset of the query. This includes creating aliases for columns, setting criteria used to filter the query, and selecting grouping options.

To add a new column to the resultset, select the column and table names from the combo boxes in a blank row of the Grid pane. The drop-down arrows for these boxes are hidden until you click in the grid, but they're always there.

To create an alias for a column, just type the new name into the Alias column of the grid on that column's row. An alias specifies the name used to refer to that column within the query's resultset.

To create a calculated column, type an arbitrary name into the Alias column and type the expression itself into the Column column. Remember that you need to use the syntax that the underlying OLE DB provider uses for this data source. For example, with a Jet database you might use `[Company] & [Contact]` to define a concatenated field, while with a SQL Server database you'd use `Company + Contact`.

To set a criterion used to filter the resultset (part of a SQL WHERE clause), type the appropriate restriction in the Criteria column of the Grid on the row with the column you want to restrict. You can set multiple criteria by using more of the grid. To connect two criteria on the same field with an OR, type the criteria into successive columns on the same row. To connect them with an AND, create a second row for the same field and enter the criteria on successive rows.

To transform your query into a grouping query, right-click in the Grid pane and select Group By. This will add a Group By column to the grid. You can then select an appropriate aggregate expression for each row in the grid by clicking in this column and choosing from the drop-down list that is displayed.

The SQL Pane

The SQL pane is primarily there as a reference for new users and a tool for advanced SQL authors. You can use it as a tool to learn SQL by constructing a query with the Diagram and Grid panes and watching to see what the Query Designer does with it. Alternatively, if you already know SQL well, you can make changes in this pane and they'll be propagated back to the other panes. You can also use the Query Designer to create queries graphically, and then cut and paste the generated SQL to other places where you need it, such as in code.

If you make a change in the SQL pane, it's not reflected in the other panes until you move out of the SQL pane. This allows you to edit and revise without worrying about extraneous error messages.

Although not all SQL statements are supported by the Query Designer, there are some statements that are supported in the SQL pane but not in the Diagram and Grid panes—for example, the basic union query:

```
SELECT CompanyName
```

```
FROM Customers
UNION
SELECT CompanyName
FROM Suppliers
```

This query can be successfully designed and executed by the Query Designer, but only by starting in the SQL pane. When you move out of that pane, the Query Designer warns you that the query cannot be displayed graphically. If you choose to continue, the Diagram and Grid panes will be grayed out, but you can still work with the query's data.

The Results Pane

At first glance, the Results pane might seem straightforward: just a place where the results of executing your query are displayed. But this pane is more than just a static display. Within certain broad limits (discussed below) you can edit the data shown in this pane as well.

To edit data in the Results pane, just navigate to the cell containing the value you wish to change, using the arrow keys, scroll bars, or mouse. Highlight the value and type in the new data. To enter a null, type **Ctrl+0**. When you leave the row that you're editing, the Query Designer will attempt to save the data back to the database.

Of course, the Designer might not succeed for a variety of reasons. Here are some of the limits on what you can edit using the Results pane:

- You can only edit memo and other long text columns that contain fewer than 900 characters of data.
- You cannot edit binary large object (BLOB) data.
- You must have the appropriate permissions to change data in the database.
- The resultset must contain the primary key of the output, or enough other information to uniquely identify the source rows for the data being edited.
- You cannot edit data if the query contains a table that isn't joined to the other tables in the query.
- You cannot edit data if the query displays multiple tables in a many-to-many relationship.
- You cannot edit aggregate queries.

- You cannot edit queries that use the DISTINCT keyword.
- You cannot edit columns based on expressions.
- You cannot edit timestamp columns.

In addition, there are differences between the support that the various OLE DB providers offer for updating. So changes that can be made when you're connected to one provider might not work with a different provider.

Creating and Debugging Stored Procedures

The last major class of objects in the Data View is stored procedures. *Stored procedures* are pieces of compiled SQL code that run exclusively on the server, and that may or may not deliver a resultset to the client. This powerful tool is often overlooked by Visual Basic developers who are accustomed to file-server databases instead of client-server databases.

NOTE

Debugging stored procedures is supported only for Microsoft SQL Server 6.5 Service Pack 3 or higher, or Microsoft SQL Server 7.

The Data View offers the ability to view the design of stored procedures, execute them, and (if you've installed Microsoft SQL Server) debug them. Each of these features is covered in this section.

WARNING

By default, SQL Server installation does not include the necessary support for the Visual Database Tools stored procedure debugger. If you're using SQL Server 6.5, there's a setup program named `sdi_nt4.exe` on the SQL Server CD-ROM. If you're using SQL Server 7, be sure to check "Development Tools" when you're selecting the components to include.

Viewing Stored Procedure Definitions and Resultsets

To view the definition of a stored procedure, navigate to the stored procedure node in the appropriate data link, expand it, right-click the stored procedure, and select Design. (As always, if this choice doesn't appear on the shortcut menu, either the OLE DB provider or the underlying database doesn't support designing stored procedures.) This will open the stored procedure in an editing window that uses the same color-coding as the trigger editor, covered earlier in the chapter. Figure 14.14 shows an example of a stored procedure open in this editor.

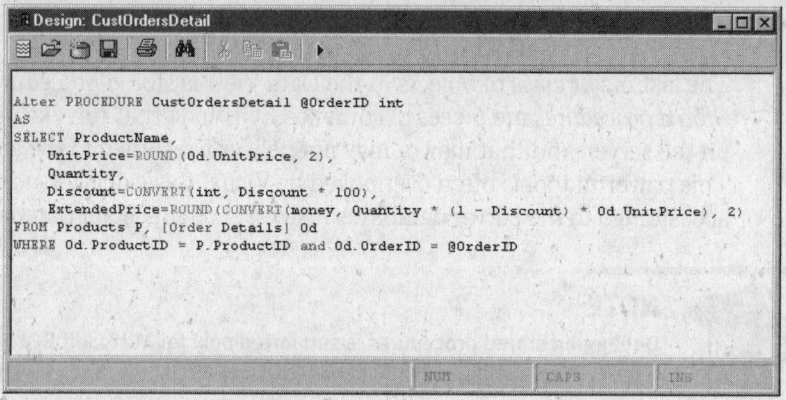

Design: CustOrdersDetail

```
Alter PROCEDURE CustOrdersDetail @OrderID int
AS
SELECT ProductName,
    UnitPrice=ROUND(Od.UnitPrice, 2),
    Quantity,
    Discount=CONVERT(int, Discount * 100),
    ExtendedPrice=ROUND(CONVERT(money, Quantity * (1 - Discount) * Od.UnitPrice), 2)
FROM Products P, [Order Details] Od
WHERE Od.ProductID = P.ProductID and Od.OrderID = @OrderID
```

NUM CAPS INS

FIGURE 14.14: Editing a stored procedure

Seeing the data (if any) returned by the stored procedure is a bit harder. You might think you could just right-click and choose Run, but that's not a choice when the Visual Database Tools are hosted inside of Visual Basic (though, oddly, that choice is available when the same tools are hosted inside of Visual C++). Instead, you have to load the stored procedure into the T-SQL Debugger and run it from there. I'll cover the T-SQL Debugger in the next section.

The T-SQL Debugger

T-SQL stands for Transact SQL, Microsoft's flavor of Structured Query Language. Although you can use the T-SQL Debugger directly from the Data View, for maximum flexibility you'll also want to install it as a Visual Basic Add-In. To do this, choose Add-Ins ➢Add-In Manager from the Visual Basic menus, scroll down the list until you find "VB T-SQL Debugger," and change the Load Behavior to Loaded. (If you're going to use it frequently, you should also check the Load On Startup check box.) This will add two items to the Visual Basic menus. Add-Ins ➢ T-SQL Debugger will let you launch the debugger at any time. Tools ➢ T-SQL Debugging Options will open the dialog box shown in Figure 14.15.

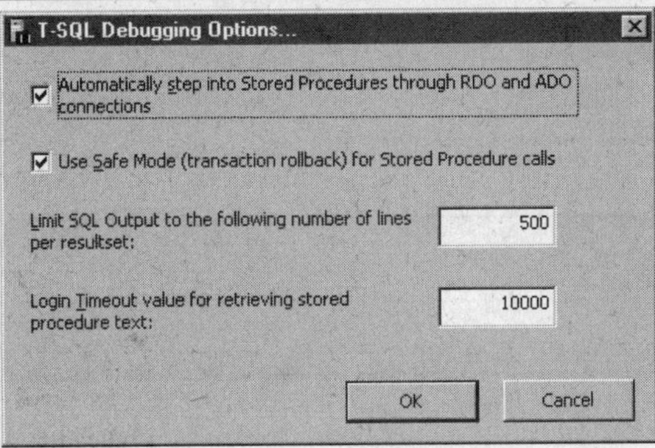

FIGURE 14.15: T-SQL Debugging Options dialog box

This dialog box offers four options:

- Checking Automatically Step Into Stored Procedures Through RDO And ADO Connections will bring up the debugger whenever you invoke a stored procedure. This option is useful if you're testing an application that makes some use of stored procedures and you suspect an error in their use.
- Checking Use Safe Mode (Transaction Rollback) For Stored Procedure Calls automatically rolls back any testing you do at design time.
- The Limit SQL Output To The Following Number Of Lines Per Resultset controls the maximum number of rows that will be shown in the debugger itself. It does not limit the data actually returned from the stored procedure.
- The Login Timeout Value For Retrieving Stored Procedure Text value keeps the debugger from hanging forever in case you don't have design permissions for the stored procedure in question.

To invoke the debugger, you can right-click a stored procedure in the Data View and choose Debug. The debugger will prompt you to fill in values for any input parameters that the stored procedure requires to do its work. Once any input parameters are supplied, the debugger window opens. This window is shown in Figure 14.16.

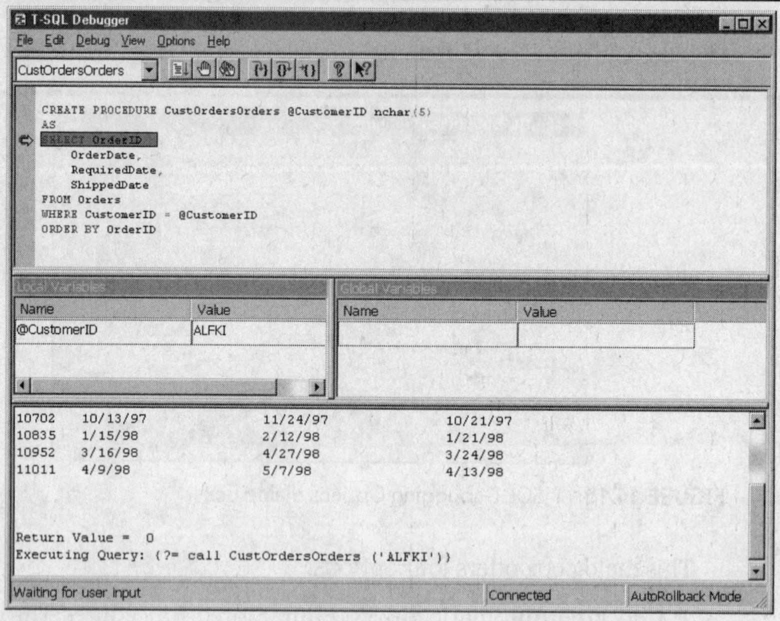

FIGURE 14.16: The T-SQL Debugger

The T-SQL Debugger includes many of the standard features of other debuggers. The topmost pane shows you the text of the stored procedure that you're working with. The middle two panes give the values of local and global variables in the stored procedure, if any. The lower pane shows the results as you execute the stored procedure.

WHAT'S NEXT?

Now that you have a better understanding of the Visual Basic IDE as it relates to using ADO, it's time for a closer look at incorporating ADO objects into your code. The next chapter covers ADO 2.5 and how you can use it in your ASP pages to make use of your new database.

Chapter 15

ADO 2.5 for Web Developers

ActiveX Data Objects (ADO) was created as a means for programmers to access a database using just a few simple objects and collections. Though it can be used with many different programming languages, this chapter discusses ADO 2.5 from a Web developer's point of view. ADO supports features you can't harvest from within ASP scripts, such as asynchronous execution of commands, as well as other features that are very useful in building interactive desktop applications, but are not used in Web development.

As far as Web applications go, most developers use ADO to:

1. Query a database and format the results of the query as HTML documents. If a query returns too many rows, you'll probably want to display them on

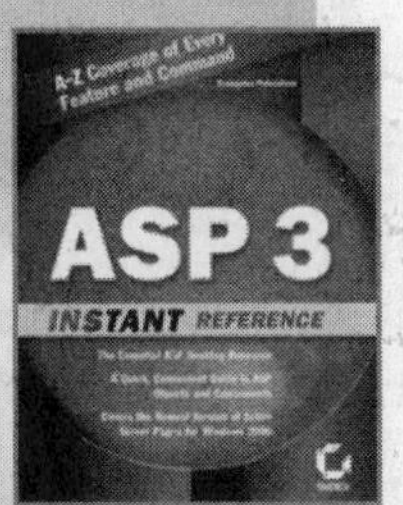

Adapted from *ASP 3 Instant Reference*, by Evangelos Petroutsos

ISBN 0-7821-2781-9 496 pages $24.99

multiple pages with the usual Next/Previous buttons at the bottom of the Form.

2. Update tables by adding new rows or editing and deleting existing rows.

Web applications are not nearly as interactive as desktop applications. Usually, we don't allow users to view records on their browser, edit them, and then commit the changes to the database. A typical Web application isn't concerned with concurrency issues, either; a customer can't edit another customer's fields, and two customers are not allowed to edit (or even view) the same order. Any changes made to the database through the browser overwrite the existing data. This assumption is much more reasonable in Web applications than in desktop applications. The material in this chapter addresses the needs of a typical Web application that maintains a list of customers (each customer can view and edit their own data), sales and delivery information, and so on. If you want to allow the editing of the products table, for example, from within a browser, you should look into other technologies, like RDS (Remote Data Services).

Using the ADO Objects

The list below includes the objects exposed by ADO 2.5. The Record and Stream objects are new to ADO 2.5 and are used in accessing semi-structured data stores such as e-mail and file systems. They're not commonly used in developing Web applications, but they're covered here for the sake of completeness.

- **Connection object**
  - Errors collection
- **Command object**
  - Parameters collection
- **Recordset object**
  - Fields collection
- **Record object**
  - Fields collection
- **Stream object**

The Connection object represents a connection from your script to the database. All of the actions you want to perform on the database must use this object to access the database. Usually, we set up a Connection object at the beginning of the script and release it when we're done. Most of the scripts in a Web application will probably connect to the same database, and you may be tempted to create a Connection variable in the Session level so that all scripts can use the same Connection object. You should never create Connection objects in the Session level. None of these objects will be released before the end of the session, and you may have hundreds or thousands of concurrent sessions. Moreover, any object involved in a transaction is automatically released at the end of the transaction.

The Command object represents a command to be executed against the database. This object contains the SQL statement or the name of the stored procedure to be executed and the values of any parameters expected by the stored procedure. The parameters of a stored procedure are stored in the Parameters collection of the Command object, each in a different Parameter object. You assign values to input parameters before calling the procedure, and you read the values of output parameters after the execution of the stored procedure. If the stored procedure returns a cursor, you can assign it to a Recordset variable through the Command.Execute method.

The ADO object you'll be using most often in your ASP scripts is the Recordset object, which contains the cursor returned by a stored procedure or SQL statement, and it exposes the functionality you need to read and edit the rows of the cursor. For example, you can scan the rows of the cursor through the navigational methods of the Recordset object, or edit the fields of a row, and commit the changes to the database. All of the functionality for accessing the cursor is exposed by the Recordset object. A Record object represents an item in a Recordset of semi-structured rows. A Recordset that contains rows from one or more tables in a database is not made up of Record objects. Record objects are used to represent files or directories, messages, or other information that's not as rigidly structured as a table row.

The Stream object, finally, lets you access the contents of a Record. If the Record represents a text file, for example, the Stream object lets you read (or edit) the file. If the Record object represents an e-mail message, the corresponding Stream object gives you access to the actual message (its body, attachments, and so on). The Record and Stream objects are part of Microsoft's Universal Data Access. I'm not going to discuss them in detail here; rather, I'll discuss only the methods of these objects needed to support data access operations in Web development. If you're familiar with ADO, you will notice that a few members are missing. The methods used to perform asynchronous operations, for example, are not discussed here; asynchronous operations are not used in scripts. Some of the ADO objects raise events, which are also not discussed here, because scripts can't handle events.

The Properties Collection

Most objects support the Properties collection, which is made up of Property objects. This collection contains provider-specific information, through properties that are not part of ADO. We use this property to query the provider about specifics, such as the maximum number of columns it can return in a cursor, whether it supports outer joins, and so on. Most developers never use the Properties collection—you may have to query a provider if you're writing applications that might contact several providers, or if you want to take advantage of a specific feature of a provider. For example, Access doesn't support the outer join operation, but SQL Server does.

ADO objects expose a number of properties and methods, which all providers must support. Because ADO is designed to handle different databases, it should be able to cope with features that are specific to a provider. The Properties collection is the mechanism to determine the features that are specific to a provider. The Properties collection contains a very large number of members. Please consult the ADO documentation for more information on the members of the Properties collection.

In the following sections, you will find detailed descriptions of each ADO object's methods and properties. The most important members are demonstrated with examples. However, this is reference material, and if you're totally unfamiliar with database programming, you should probably read a book with a tutorial structure, such as the *Visual Basic Developer's Guide to ADO* or *Mastering Database Programming with Visual Basic 6*, both published by Sybex. Please keep in mind that certain members that can't be used in Web applications were omitted here.

NOTE

Most of the arguments of the ADO objects' methods have a limited set of possible values, which are called enumerated types. The members of the various enumerated types are listed in the ADO documentation.

THE CONNECTION OBJECT

The Connection object represents a connection to a data source. The Connection object is used to indicate the database against which a command will be executed, or the database from which the rows of a Recordset object will come; it contains all the information needed to establish a connection to the database server and access the specified database.

You usually set up a Connection object and then use it as an argument to the methods of the Command and Recordset objects that access the database. However, you can use the Connection object's Execute method to execute a Command object directly against the database, as long as the command doesn't pass any parameters to the query or stored procedure. In addition, you must use the Connection object to execute multiple commands in a transaction—only the Connection object supports transactions.

Finally, you can use the Connection object's OpenSchema method to retrieve schema information about your database. This operation isn't common in Web applications, however.

To execute a command through the Connection object, declare a Connection object and a Recordset object where the result of the query will be stored. Then, call the Connection object's Execute method to execute a SQL statement or a stored procedure against the database. The following statement retrieves the ISBN and Title columns of all the rows in the Titles table of the Pubs database:

```
<%
Dim CN
Dim RS
Set CN=Server.CreateObject("ADODB.Connection")
CN.Open "Provider=SQLOLEDB.1;uid=sa;" & _
  "password=;Initial Catalog=Pubs"
Set RS = CN.Execute _
  ("SELECT Title_ID, Title FROM Titles")
%>
```

If you're using Access, use the following statements to retrieve a few fields of the Titles table of the BIBLIO database:

```
<%
Dim CN
Dim RS
```

```
Set CN=Server.CreateObject("ADODB.Connection")
CN.Open "DSN=BIBLIO"
Set RS = CN.Execute _
  ("SELECT ISBN, Title, Notes FROM Titles")
%>
```

To execute the "Ten Most Expensive Products" stored procedure of the NorthWind database through the Connection object, use the following statements in your script:

```
<%
Dim CN
Dim RS
Set CN=Server.CreateObject("ADODB.Connection")
CN.Open "provider=SQLOLEDB.1;uid=sa;" & _
  "password=;Initial Catalog=NorthWind"
Set RS = CN.Execute _
  ("[Ten Most Expensive Products]")
%>
```

Notice that the CN object variable must be created explicitly. The RS object variable is declared, but not created. ASP knows that the Connection.Execute method returns a Recordset and it automatically creates a Recordset object to accept the cursor returned by the Execute method.

The last example opens the NorthWind database, retrieves the specified rows, and stores them. To iterate through the rows of the Recordset, use a loop like this:

```
While Not RS.EOF
  Response.Write "<TR>"
  Response.Write "<TD>" & _
    RS.Fields("ProductName") & "</TD>"
  Response.Write "<TD>" & _
    RS.Fields("UnitPrice") & "</TD>"
  Response.Write "</TR>"
  RS.MoveNext
Wend
```

You will find more information on manipulating the rows of a Recordset in the section "The Recordset Object" later in this chapter. In the following sections you'll find detailed information on the members of the Connection object.

Properties

Attributes

This property represents the characteristics of a Connection object. For example, you can use Attributes to find out whether the Connection object can perform "retaining commits" and "retaining aborts."

CommandTimeout

This property indicates how long to wait for a command to be executed on the Connection object. This value is expressed in seconds, and its default value is 30 seconds. This property is different from the ConnectionTimeout property, which determines how long to wait for a connection to be established. The CommandTimeout property applies to open connections.

ConnectionString

This property contains the information required to establish a connection to a data source. The information is stored in a string, and it consists of a series of `argument = value` statements, separated by semicolons, as in the following example:

```
CN.ConnectionString = _
    "Provider=Microsoft.Jet.OLEDB.4.0;" & _
    "Data Source=C:\VB\NWind.mdb"
```

You must pass some or all of the following five items to a Connection object to establish a connection to the database:

Provider = <provider name> This is the name of a provider: "OLEDBSQL" for SQL Server, "Microsoft.Jet.OLEDB" for the OLE DB driver for Access databases, and so on.

File Name = <file name> This item is used for Recordsets that have been persisted to the file *<file name>*.

Remote Provider = <remote provider name> This item specifies the name of a provider to be used with a client-side connection (Remote Data Source only).

Remote Server = <remote server name> This specifies the path name of the server to use when opening a client-side connection (Remote Data Service only).

URL=<absolute URL> This item specifies the connection string as an absolute URL identifying a resource, such as a file or directory.

The ConnectionString property automatically inherits the value used for the `ConnectionString` argument of the Open method, and you can override the current ConnectionString property during the Open method call.

If you specify the `File Name` item in the ConnectionString, ADO will load the associated provider and will ignore the `Provider` setting. You can't pass both the `Provider` and `File Name` items in the connection string.

Most developers set up a Data Source Name (DSN) for the database and assign the following value to the ConnectionString property:

```
CN.ConnectionString = "DSN=AllBooks"
```

where `AllBooks` is the database's DSN. To set up a DSN for a database, use the ODBC Data Sources tool in the Control Panel. This tool is a wizard that lets you specify the provider (OLEDB drivers for SQL Server, for instance) and the database. If you set up a DSN for a SQL Server database, you must also provide a username and password, as in the following example:

```
CN.Open "DSN=SQLNWIND;uid=sa;password=;"
```

ConnectionTimeout

This property indicates how long to wait while establishing a connection before terminating the attempt and generating an error. The default value is 15 seconds.

CursorLocation

This property sets or returns the location of the cursor. Any Recordset created through a Connection object inherits the CursorLocation setting of the Connection object.

ADO supports server-side and client-side cursors. Server-side cursors reside on the server and with them, every time your application requests another row of the Recordset, the row has to be fetched from the server. Server-side cursors are used by applications that need access to "live" data. When the cursor resides on the server, changes to the underlying tables can be posted immediately to the cursor. Client-side cursors are transmitted to the client at once and, as a result, any changes made to the underlying tables are not automatically reflected to the client cursor. Server-side cursors are much more flexible than client-side cursors, but this flexibility comes with a price. Moreover, not all applications need "live" cursors. A client-side cursor is quite adequate for a typical Web application. Web applications use small cursors, and it makes sense to move the entire cursor to the client before processing it. Notice that the "client" here is the Web server (the machine that executes the script) and not the Web client (the machine on which the browser runs). For small sites, the Web server and the database server may run on the same computer.

The most common operation for Web applications is to fetch data from the server, format them as HTML pages, and send them to the client. Not only that, these applications limit the number of rows sent to the client at a time. If the user has requested more than a few dozen rows, the application will usually generate HTML pages with only 10 or 20 rows, and the usual Next/Previous buttons. See the section "Implementing Paged Recordsets," later in this chapter, for more information on this technique.

DefaultDatabase

This is the default database for a Connection object. If there is a default database, SQL strings may use an unqualified syntax to access objects in that database (i.e., you can omit the database name). If you have not defined a default database, you must prefix the database object names with the name of the database.

Errors Collection

Any errors that may occur during the execution of a command against a database are stored in the Errors collection of the Connection object. The members of the collection are Error objects, and the Error object's members are described in the last section of this chapter.

IsolationLevel

This property indicates the level of isolation for a Connection object. This property is set to an IsolationLevelEnum constant and its default type is adXactChaos. The isolation level determines how other transactions interact with yours, whether your application is allowed to see changes made by other transactions, and whether other transactions can see changes made by your transaction. If your script needs such fine control over transactions, you should implement the transactions with stored procedures, or develop custom components with Visual Basic, or Visual C++.

Mode

The Mode property indicates the available permissions for modifying data in a Connection, Record, or Stream object; its setting is one of the ConnectModeEnum constants. The default value for a Record object is adModeRead. The default value for a Stream associated with an underlying source (opened with a URL as the source or as the default Stream of a Record) is adReadOnly. The default value for a Stream not associated with an underlying source (instantiated in memory) is adReadWrite.

Properties Collection

This is a collection of Property objects that contain provider-specific information about the Connection object. See the section "The Properties Collection," at the beginning of the chapter for more information.

Provider

The Provider property returns the name of the provider used with the Connection object. When you set the ConnectionString property, or the `connectionString` argument of the Connection object's Open method, the Provider property is set automatically. The default provider is MSDASQL. This is the OLE DB provider for ODBC, and you use it to access all ODBC-compliant databases that don't have a native OLE DB provider. The value of the provider is

MSDASQL for ODBC

Microsoft.Jet.OLEDB.4.0 for Access

SQLOLEDB for SQL Server

MSDAORA for Oracle

MSDataShape for the Microsoft Data Shape driver, which returns hierarchical Recordsets

State

This read-only property indicates whether a Connection object is open, and the property's value is an ObjectStateEnum constant. If a Connection is open, you can't call its Open method again to establish a connection to a different database. You must first close it, and then open it with a new connection string.

Version

This read-only property returns the version of ADO in use.

Methods

BeginTrans, CommitTrans, RollbackTrans

These methods manage transactions. To initiate a transaction, use the BeginTrans method. Then, code all the actions involved in the transaction. Finally, call the CommitTrans method to complete the transaction, or call the RollbackTrans method to abandon the transaction and undo the changes made so far in the transaction. The syntax of the BeginTrans method is `level = BeginTrans`. The other two methods don't accept any arguments and they don't return a value either.

The BeginTrans method returns a value that indicates the nesting level of the transaction. The top transaction's level is 1. If you're executing nested transactions by initiating a new transaction before another one has completed, then the BeginTrans method that initiates the nested transaction will return the value 2, and so on.

Not all providers support transactions. Verify that the provider-defined property "Transaction DDL" appears in the Connection object's Properties collection, indicating that the provider supports transactions. If the provider does not support transactions, calling one of these methods will return an error. Both Access and SQL Server support transactions.

The statements in Listing 15.1 add an order to the NorthWind database. First, a new row is added to the Orders table. Then a few rows are added to the Order Details table. The ID of the order added to the Orders table is assigned automatically by the database. This value is stored in the OrderID variable and is used in the new rows of the Order Details table. All actions take place in a transaction, so if one of them fails, the transaction is aborted and any changes made to the database are rolled back.

Listing 15.1: The `Transact1.asp` **Script**

```
<!- #include file="adovbs.inc" ->
<%
Dim CN
Dim RSOrders
Dim RSDetails

Set CN=Server.CreateObject("ADODB.Connection")
CN.Open "DSN=SQLNWIND;uid=sa;password=;"

On Error Resume Next
CN.BeginTrans
Set RSOrders = Server.CreateObject _
  ("ADODB.Recordset")
Set RSOrders.ActiveConnection = CN
RSOrders.LockType = adLockOptimistic
RSOrders.CursorLocation = adUseServer
RSOrders.CursorType = adOpenKeyset
RSOrders.Open "Orders"

RSOrders.AddNew
RSOrders.Fields("CustomerID")="ALFKI"
RSOrders.Fields("OrderDate")=Date
RSOrders.Update

OrderID = RSOrders.Fields("OrderID")
Response.write "Order " & OrderID & _
  " added successfully"
RSOrders.Close
Set RSOrders = Nothing

Set RSDetails = Server.CreateObject _
  ("ADODB.Recordset")
Set RSDetails.ActiveConnection = CN
RSDetails.LockType = adLockOptimistic
RSDetails.CursorLocation = adUseServer
RSDetails.CursorType = adOpenKeyset
RSDetails.Open "[Order Details]"
RSDetails.AddNew
RSDetails.Fields("OrderID") = OrderID
RSDetails.Fields("ProductID") = 14
RSDetails.Fields("Quantity") = 2
```

```
RSDetails.Fields("UnitPrice") = 23.25
RSDetails.Update
Response.Write "<BR>Item 14 added to order"
RSDetails.AddNew
RSDetails.Fields("OrderID") = OrderID
RSDetails.Fields("ProductID") = 18
RSDetails.Fields("Quantity") = 5
RSDetails.Fields("UnitPrice") = 14
RSDetails.Update
Response.Write "<BR>Item 18 added to order"
Response.Write "<B>Transaction" & _
  " committed successfully</B>"
CN.CommitTrans
Response.End
%>
```

Notice that the CN.AbortTrans method is not called explicitly. If an error occurs in the script, the script's execution will be terminated and the transaction will be aborted automatically. To make the transaction fail, comment out the line that sets the ProductID field of the second detail line. The database requires that each row added to the Order Details table have a valid ProductID field (it won't accept Null values in this field). If you execute the script again, the following message will appear:

```
Order 11107 added successfully
    Item 14 added to order
Microsoft OLE DB Provider for ODBC Drivers error '80040e2f'
   [Microsoft][ODBC SQL Server Driver][SQL Server]Cannot
insert
   the value NULL into column 'ProductID', table
    'Northwind.dbo.Order Details'; column does not allow
nulls.
    INSERT fails.
/ado/transact.asp, line 62
```

This page informs you initially that a new row was added to the Orders table and that a new row was added to the Order Details row. The insertion of the second row failed, as expected. If you open the Orders and the Order Details tables, you'll see that the rows reported as being added successfully cannot be found in the corresponding tables. The transaction failed, and any changes made to the database were rolled back automatically.

This method for handling transactions works, but the output it produces isn't quite user-friendly. This message isn't what you want your viewers to see. In a high-level language like VB, you could intercept the error and display your own message. With VBScript, you can't use the statement `On Error GoTo TransactionError`. Listing 15.2 is a revised version of the same script that handles each error as it occurs. This script uses the `On Error Resume Next` statement to handle errors. After each call that may fail, the code examines the value of the Err.Number property. If an error has occurred, the script displays the appropriate message, calls the RollbackTrans method, and terminates.

Listing 15.2: The `Transact2.asp` Script

```
<!- #include file="adovbs.inc" ->
<%
Dim CN
Dim RSOrders
Dim RSDetails

Set CN=Server.CreateObject("ADODB.Connection")
CN.Open "DSN=SQLNWIND;uid=sa;password=;"

On Error Resume Next
CN.BeginTrans
Set RSOrders = Server.CreateObject _
  ("ADODB.Recordset")
Set RSOrders.ActiveConnection = CN
RSOrders.LockType = adLockOptimistic
RSOrders.CursorLocation = adUseServer
RSOrders.CursorType = adOpenKeyset
RSOrders.Open "Orders"

RSOrders.AddNew
RSOrders.Fields("CustomerID")="ALFKI"
RSOrders.Fields("OrderDate")=Date
RSOrders.Update
If Err.Number <> 0 Then
    Response.Clear
    Response.Write "Could not add order." & _
      " Transaction aborted."
    CN.RollBackTrans
    Response.End
End If
```

```
OrderID = RSOrders.Fields("OrderID")
Response.write "Order " & OrderID & _
  " added successfully."
RSOrders.Close
Set RSOrders = Nothing

Set RSDetails = Server.CreateObject _
  ("ADODB.Recordset")
Set RSDetails.ActiveConnection = CN
RSDetails.LockType = adLockOptimistic
RSDetails.CursorLocation = adUseServer
RSDetails.CursorType = adOpenKeyset
RSDetails.Open "[Order Details]"
RSDetails.AddNew
RSDetails.Fields("OrderID") = OrderID
RSDetails.Fields("ProductID") = 14
RSDetails.Fields("Quantity") = 2
RSDetails.Fields("UnitPrice") = 23.25
RSDetails.Update
If Err.Number <> 0 Then
    Response.Clear
    Response.Write "Could not add item" & _
      " (1). Transaction aborted."
    CN.RollBackTrans
    Response.End
Else
    Response.Write "<BR>Item 14 added" & _
      " to order."
End If

RSDetails.AddNew
RSDetails.Fields("OrderID") = OrderID
'RSDetails.Fields("ProductID") = 18
RSDetails.Fields("Quantity") = 5
RSDetails.Fields("UnitPrice") = 14
RSDetails.Update
If Err.Number <> 0 Then
    Response.Clear
    Response.Write "<BR>Could not add item" & _
      " (2). <B>Transaction aborted</B>."
    CN.RollBackTrans
    Response.End
Else
```

```
        Response.Write "<BR>Item 18 added" & _
          " to order."
    End If
    Response.Write "<B>Transaction committed" & _
      " successfully.</B>"
    CN.CommitTrans
    Response.End
    %>
```

To test the revised script, comment out the line that adds the ID of the second detail line and run it. This time the revised script will display a more descriptive message, as shown below:

```
Order 11108 added successfully.
Item 14 added to order.
Could not add item (2). Transaction aborted.
```

You can also implement transactions through the ObjectContext object. The best method of implementing transactions is to write middle-tier components that accept the appropriate arguments, attempt to update the database, and return a True/False result, indicating the success or failure of the transaction. This topic is beyond the scope of a reference book like this, but you can find more information on implementing transactions with middle-tier components in Sybex's *Visual Basic Developer's Guide to SQL Server.*

Close

This method closes an open Recordset (or Connection, Record, or Stream) object. Closing an object does not remove it from memory, but it frees the resource allocated to it by the system. You can change the object's properties and open it again later. To completely eliminate an object from memory, set the object variable to `Nothing`.

When you close a Connection object, any active Recordset objects associated with the connection will also be closed. When you close a Recordset, Record, or Stream object, the system releases the associated data. One of the most common runtime errors is that the requested operation can't be performed on a closed object. You may have forgotten to open a connection for a Recordset, or call a method of the Recordset object before opening it. See the discussion of the Open method for more information on opening and closing objects.

Execute

This method executes the specified SQL statement or stored procedure. If the command returns a Recordset, then use the following syntax:

```
Set RS = CN.Execute _
  (commandText, recordsAffected, options)
```

where CN is a Connection object. `commandText` is a string holding the name of the SQL statement, table name, or stored procedure; `recordsAffected` is a variable that returns the number of rows affected by the action queries. The `options` argument indicates how the provider will interpret the `commandText` argument. Its value is the CommandTypeEnum constant.

The Recordset returned by the Connection.Execute method is a server-side, read-only, forward-only Recordset. This cursor is quite flexible for typical Web applications, which scan the rows of a cursor forward-only, but you can't use its RecordCount property to find the number of qualifying rows. If you want to know the number of rows before processing the rows of the cursor, use the Recordset object's Open method to set up a static client-side cursor.

To execute a SQL statement against a database through the Connection object's Execute method, pass the statement to be executed as an argument:

```
<%
Set CN = Server.CreateObject _
  ("ADODB.Connection")
Set RS = Server.CreateObject _
  ("ADODB.Recordset")
CN.ConnectionString = "DSN=BIBLIO"
CN.Open
SQL = "SELECT Title FROM Titles" & _
  " WHERE ISBN LIKE '0-672%'"
Set RS = CN.Execute(SQL)
%>
```

This statement retrieves the titles with the specified digits at the beginning of their ISBN and stores the qualifying titles in the RS Recordset object variable.

To retrieve an entire table, use the table's name as argument to the Execute method. Likewise, to execute a stored procedure, pass the procedure's name as an argument. If the procedure expects any arguments or returns values other than a cursor, you can't use the Connection object's Execute method; use the Command.Execute method instead.

Open

This method opens a connection to a data source and its syntax is:

```
Open [connectionString, userID, password, options]
```

The `connectionString` argument contains connection information. `userID` and `password` will be used to verify the user against the database; these arguments overwrite the equivalent settings in the `connectionString` argument. The last argument, `options`, is a ConnectOptionEnum constant that determines whether this method runs synchronously or asynchronously. You can't use asynchronous operations in scripts, so you can ignore this argument.

When you no longer need the connection, call its Close method to free any associated system resources. Closing an object does not remove it from memory. To completely eliminate an object from memory, set the object variable to `Nothing`.

The following statements establish a connection to the BIBLIO database, through the `CN` object variable. This object variable is assigned to a Recordset's ActiveConnection property, so that you can execute SQL statements against the database through the Recordset's Open method:

```
<%
Set CN = Server.CreateObject _
  ("ADODB.Connection")
Set RS = Server.CreateObject _
  ("ADODB.Recordset")
CN.ConnectionString = "DSN=BIBLIO"
CN.Open
' MORE STATEMENTS
Set RS.ActiveConnection = CN
%>
```

BIBLIO is an access database, and you don't need a user ID and password to log on. To connect to a SQL Server database with a DSN, specify the additional arguments, inserting your user ID and password:

```
"DSN=BIBLIO;uid=;password=;"
```

OpenSchema

The OpenSchema method returns database schema information from the provider—information such as the tables in the database: their columns, data types, and so on. It is called as follows:

```
Set Recordset = Connection.OpenSchema _
  (queryType [, criteria, schemaID])
```

The information is returned in a Recordset object, and the exact contents of the Recordset depend on the `queryType` argument, which is a SchemaEnum constant. The `criteria` optional argument is an array of query constraints. The constraints for each `queryType` constant are listed in the same table with the SchemaEnum constants.

The `schemaID` argument is used with providers that support schema queries not defined in the OLE DB specification. This argument is ignored if the `queryType` is set to a value other than adSchemaProviderSpecific. Use the adSchemaProviderSpecific constant if the provider defines its own nonstandard schema queries.

The code in Listing 15.3 will display the names of all the tables in a database on a new page. Notice that the script uses the Access version of the BIBLIO database, but you can change the value of the ConnectionString property accordingly to make it work with a SQL Server database. This script doesn't refer implicitly to any of the tables in the database; it simply maps the structure of the database.

Listing 15.3: The `ShowTables.asp` Script

```
<%
Const adSchemaTables = 20
Set CN = Server.CreateObject _
  ("ADODB.Connection")
CN.ConnectionString = "DSN=BIBLIO"
CN.Open
Set RSTables = CN.OpenSchema(adSchemaTables)
Response.Write "<B>The database contains" & _
  " the following tables</B>"
While Not RSTables.EOF
  If RSTables.Fields("TABLE_TYPE") <> _
    "SYSTEM TABLE" Then
      Response.Write "<BR>  " & _
        "   "
      Response.Write _
```

```
            RSTables.Fields("TABLE_NAME")
      End If
      RSTables.MoveNext
   Wend
   %>
```

To retrieve the names of the columns of all tables, use the statements in Listing 15.4.

Listing 15.4: The `ShowColumns.asp` **Script**

```
   <%
   Const adSchemaColumns = 4
   Set CN = Server.CreateObject _
      ("ADODB.Connection")
   CN.ConnectionString = "DSN=BIBLIO"
   CN.Open
   Set RSCols = CN.OpenSchema _
      (adSchemaColumns)
   currCatalog = RSCols.Fields("TABLE_NAME")
   Response.Write "<TABLE>"
   Response.Write "<TR><TD COLSPAN=2>" & _
      "TABLE NAME " & currCatalog
   RSCols.MoveNext
   Do While RSCols.Fields("TABLE_NAME") = _
      currCatalog
      Response.Write "<TR><TD WIDTH=50></TD><TD>"
      Response.Write "<B>" & RSCols.Fields _
         ("COLUMN_NAME") & "</B>"
      Response.Write "</TD></TR>"
      RSCols.MoveNext
      If RSCols.EOF Then Exit Do
      If currCatalog <> _
         RSCols.Fields("TABLE_NAME") Then
            currCatalog = RSCols.Fields("TABLE_NAME")
            Response.Write _
               "<TR><TD COLSPAN=2>TABLE<B> " & _
               currCatalog & "</B>"
            Response.Write "<TR><TD></TD><TD>"
            Response.Write _
               RSCols.Fields("COLUMN_NAME")
            Response.Write "</TD></TR>"
      End If
   Loop
```

```
Set RSCols = Nothing
%>
```

Part of the output produced by the ShowColumns.asp script is shown next. Notice that this script will display the structure of the views too. You can edit the code to view the columns of selected tables.

```
TABLE Orders
        OrderID
        OrderID
        UserID
        OrderDate
        BookISBN
        BookQTY
TABLE Publishers
        PubID
        PubID
        Name
        Company Name
        Address
        City
        State
        Zip
        Telephone
        Fax
        Comments
```


The Command Object

A Command object is a definition of a specific command that you intend to execute against a data source. The commands can be SQL statements or stored procedures, which either retrieve rows from a database or update it.

To execute a command, you must set up a Connection object and a Command object. If the Command object invokes a stored procedure, you may have to create a Parameters collection and add Parameter objects to this collection. Each Parameter object corresponds to a different parameter of the stored procedure.

The following statements execute a simple SQL statement against the NorthWind database through a Command object:

```
Set CMD = Server.CreateObject("ADODB.Command")
Set CMD.ActiveConnection = CN
CMD.CommandText = "SELECT CompanyName" & _
  " FROM Publishers"
CMD.CommandType = adCmdStoredProc
Set RS = CMD.Execute
```

The CN Connection object represents an existing connection to the database. You have already seen how to establish connections to databases.

The following statements execute the "Ten Most Expensive Products" stored procedure. Again, CN is the name of an existing Connection object:

```
Set CMD = Server.CreateObject("ADODB.Command")
Set CMD.ActiveConnection = CN
CMD.CommandText = "[Ten Most Expensive Products]"
CMD.CommandType = adCmdText
Set RS = CMD.Execute
```

The cursor with the rows returned by the Command.Execute method is a forward-only cursor. Even if you set the properties of the RS object variable in your code differently, the Command.Execute method will reset the Recordset object's properties.

Finally, you can use the Command object to execute a stored procedure with parameters. The simplest form to pass parameters to the Command .Execute method is the following:

```
Set CMD = Server.CreateObject("ADODB.Command")
Set CMD.ActiveConnection = CN
CMD.CommandText = "[Sales By Year]"
CMD.CommandType = adCmdStoredProc
Set RS = CMD.Execute _
    (, Array("1/1/1996", "31/1/1996")
```

The first, optional, argument is the number of rows affected by action queries, as you will see in the description of the Execute method. You can also set up Parameter objects and append them to the Parameters collection of the Command object before calling the Execute method. See the section titled "The Parameter Object" for more information.

Properties

ActiveConnection

This property indicates the Connection to which the Command object belongs. You can assign to this property either a Connection object or a string that contains the connection's ConnectionString property. You should prefer the first method, if a Connection object is available, because it allows you to reuse an existing connection. When you specify the connection's properties with a connection string, ADO creates a new Connection object.

```
<%
Dim CN
Dim CMD
Set CN = Server.CreateObject _
  ("ADODB.Connection")
CN.ConnectionString = "DSN=BIBLIO"
Set CMD = Server.CreateObject("ADODB.Command")
Set CMD.ActiveConnection = CN
Set RS = CMD.Execute "SELECT CompanyName" & _
  " FROM Publishers"
' Insert here the statements to
' process the Recordset
%>
```

CommandText

This property contains a string with the text of a command that you want to issue against a database. The value of this property is a string that contains an SQL statement, a table name, a relative URL, or a stored procedure name. See the section "The Command Object" above for an example.

CommandTimeout

CommandTimeout indicates how long to wait while executing a command before terminating the attempt and generating an error. Its default value is 30 seconds. Notice that the Connection object's Timeout property has no effect on the CommandTimeout property of the Command objects on this connection. Moreover, the CommandTimeout property shouldn't be longer than the script's timeout interval.

CommandType

This property sets/returns the type of a Command object and is a CommandEnumType constant. Use the adExecuteNoRecords constant (this is an ExecuteOptionEnum constant) to specify that you don't care about the number of rows affected by the command. Although ADO will figure out the command's type, you can optimize the execution of the command by specifying its type (this minimizes the internal processing). If you don't set this property or set it to adCmdUnknown (the default value), ADO will attempt to execute it first as a SQL statement, then as a stored procedure, and finally as a table name. In other words, ADO uses a trial-and-error technique to resolve the command's type.

Name

This is the name of the Command object. The Name property is rarely used in programming, and certainly not in ASP programming.

Parameters Collection

This collection is made up of Parameter objects. Each Parameter object contains information about a parameter of the query or stored procedure you will execute through the Command object. For a discussion of the members of a Parameter object, see the description of the Parameters collection.

The following loop (Listing 15.5) reads the definition of the Sales By Year stored procedure from the database, goes through the Parameters collection, and displays each parameter's name, type, and direction. The script calls the Refresh method of the Parameters collection to retrieve information about the parameters.

Listing 15.5: The `Params.asp` Script

```
<!- #include file="adovbs.inc" ->
<%
Set RS = Server.CreateObject("ADODB.Recordset")
Rs.CursorLocation=adUseClient
RS.CursorType=adOpenStatic
Set CMD = Server.CreateObject("ADODB.Command")
Set CN=Server.CreateObject("ADODB.Connection")
```

```
CN.Open "DSN=SQLNWIND;uid=sa;password=;"

CMD.ActiveConnection=CN
CMD.CommandType = adCmdStoredProc
CMD.CommandText = "Sales by year"

CMD.Parameters.Refresh
Response.Write "<TABLE BORDER><TR>"
Response.Write "<TD><B>Name</B></TD>"
Response.Write "<TD><B>Type</B></TD>"
Response.Write "<TD><B>Direction</B></TD><TR>"
For Each param In CMD.Parameters
    Response.Write "<TD>" & param.Name
    Select Case param.Direction
        Case adParamInput:
            Response.Write "<TD>Input"
        Case adParamOutput:
            Response.Write "<TD>Output"
    ' INSERT CODE FOR MORE CASES HERE
    End Select
    Select Case param.Type
        Case adCurrency:
            Response.Write "<TD>Currency</TD>"
        Case adDate, adTime, adDBDate, _
        adDBTime, adDBTimeStamp:
            Response.Write _
            "<TD>Date/Time</TD>"
    ' INSERT CODE FROM MORE CASES HERE
    End Select
    Response.Write "</TR>"
Next
Response.Write "</TABLE>"
%>
```

The output produced by the ShowParams.asp script is a table, like the following one:

Name	Type	Direction
RETURN_VALUE	Return Value	Other
@Beginning_Date	Input	Date/Time
@Ending_Date	Input	Date/Time

Prepared

This property returns a Boolean value that determines whether to save a compiled version of a command before executing it. If you save the compiled version of the command before executing it (by setting its Prepared option to True), the command will take longer to execute the first time. Subsequent calls to the same command will return sooner, however, because the compiled version is already available. If the property is False, the provider will execute the Command object directly without creating a compiled version.

Properties Collection

This is a collection of Property objects that contain provider-specific information about the Command object.

State

This is a read-only property that returns an ObjectStateEnum constant. This constant specifies whether the object is executing a command, fetching rows, or attempting to connect.

For example, you can examine the State of a Recordset object before attempting to access its rows, to make sure the Recordset has been populated. If its State property is not adStateOpen, then any attempt to manipulate its rows will result in a runtime error. I mentioned that scripts don't perform asynchronous operations.

The State property of the Command object is used to find out whether an asynchronous command has completed its execution. Technically, it is possible to initiate a connection or the execution of a command asynchronously from within a script, but then you'd have to constantly monitor the State of the object to find out whether the operation has completed. This defeats the purpose of asynchronous operations, and that's why we don't use asynchronous operations in scripting. Asynchronous operations are used in environments that can handle events. Only then can we initiate an asynchronous operation, continue with some other task, and be notified through an event about the completion of the operation.

Methods

Cancel

Call this method to cancel an asynchronous Open operation. A runtime error will be generated if the operation you're attempting to cancel is not asynchronous.

CreateParameter

Use this method to create a new Parameter object, passing the parameter's attributes as arguments to the method, as shown here:

```
Set parameter = Command.CreateParameter _
  ([name, type, direction, size,        value])
```

The new Parameter object must be appended to a Command object's Parameters collection with the Append method. The `name` argument is the parameter's name, `type` is its data type, and its `size` is in bytes or characters. The `direction` argument is equivalent to the parameter's Direction property, and it specifies whether it's an input or output parameter. The last argument, `value`, is the parameter's value.

As you can see from the syntax of the method, all arguments are optional. You can create a Parameter object and then set all its properties as follows:

```
<%
Set oParam = CMD.CreateParameter
oParam.Name = "parameter1"
oParam.Type = adTypeInteger
oParam.Direction = adParameterDirectionInput
oParam.Value = 1001
%>
```

This code segment assumes you have set up a Command object (the CMD variable) and creates a new parameter for the Command object. The new parameter's name is `parameter1`, its type is integer, and it will be used to pass a value to the stored procedure. Since integers have a fixed size, you need not set the Parameter object's Size property. If you do, the setting will be ignored.

After setting up a Parameter object, you can add it to the Parameters collection with the following statement:

```
CMD.Parameters.Add oParam
```

After creating all necessary Parameter objects and attaching them to the Parameters collection, you can execute a stored procedure with the Execute method. The parameters you specified will be matched to the stored procedure's parameters automatically.

All stored procedures return a value, but you need not set up a Parameter object for this parameter, if you don't care about its value. If you want to specify a Parameter object for the procedure's return value, its Direction property must be set to adParamReturnValue. For more information on setting up and using parameters, see the section titled "The Parameter Object."

Execute

The Execute method executes a SQL statement or stored procedure, as specified by the CommandText property. If the command retrieves a cursor, the Execute command will return a Recordset object, using the following statement:

```
Set RS = Command.Execute _
   ([recordsAffected, parameters, options])
```

The provider sets the `recordsAffected` optional argument; it's the number of rows affected by the command. This argument is set only for action queries or stored procedures. `recordsAffected` does not return the number of records returned by a result-returning query or stored procedure. The `parameters` argument is also optional, and it's an array of parameter values passed to a SQL statement. You can't retrieve output parameters when passing parameters with this method. Most developers set up a Parameters collection and attach it to the Command object. The last argument, `options`, is also optional and specifies how the provider should evaluate the CommandText property of the Command object. This property can be one or more CommandTypeEnum constants.

If the CommandText property specifies a cursor-returning query, the results of the query are stored in a new Recordset object. If the command is not a cursor-returning query, the provider returns a closed Recordset object.

See the section "The Command Object" earlier in this chapter for an example of how to execute a command through the Command object.

The Recordset Object

A Recordset object represents a cursor retrieved from a database by executing a Command (usually a SELECT SQL statement). The Recordset has the structure of a grid. The columns map fields, and the rows map records. However, you can't access a row with an index; you must first move to the desired row, which is referred to as *current row*, and then access this row's fields.

Properties

AbsolutePage

This property specifies the page on which the current row resides. The size of the page can be set with the PageSize property. See the description of the PageSize property for an example of using the AbsolutePage property to display paged Recordsets.

AbsolutePosition

AbsolutePosition specifies the position of the current row in a Recordset object; it's an ordinal number between 1 and the number of rows in the Recordset (which is given by the RecordCount property). The AbsolutePosition and the RecordCount properties are reported correctly with static, client cursors only. Do not use server-side cursors if you plan to use the AbsolutePosition property in your script.

ActiveCommand

This property returns the Command object that created the Recordset object. If the Recordset is not based on a command, the ActiveCommand property returns an empty string.

ActiveConnection

The ActiveConnection property sets or returns the Connection object used by a Recordset to connect to the database. The property applies to Command and Recordset objects as well. It does not return an object; instead, it returns a string with the definition of the connection (the

ConnectionString property). To set the ActiveConnection property, use a Connection object:

```
RS.ActiveConnection = CN
```

When you request the value of this property, a string like the following will be returned (all in one line):

```
Provider=SQLOLEDB.1;Persist Security Info=False;User
 ID=sa;Initial Catalog=Northwind
```

BOF, EOF

The BOF property returns True if the current row is ahead of the first row in the Recordset. The EOF property returns True if the current row is after the last row in the Recordset. If both BOF and EOF are True, then the Recordset is empty. The EOF property is also set to True by the Find and Seek operations to indicate that there's no matching row in the Recordset. Here's how you determine whether a row was located:

```
RS.Find "CompanyName LIKE 'SYBEX%'"
If RS.EOF Then
Response.Write "No rows were found"
Else
    {process row}
End If
```

The EOF property is used frequently in loops that iterate through the rows of a Recordset:

```
While Not RS.EOF
    ' process current row's fields
    RS.MoveNext
Wend
```

Bookmark

This property returns a bookmark that uniquely identifies the current row in a Recordset. You can also set this property to move to another row. To bookmark a row, use the statement

```
thisRow = RS.Bookmark
```

You can return to a bookmarked row by assigning an existing bookmark to the Recordset's Bookmark property:

```
RS.Bookmark = thisRow
```

Do not compare bookmarks with the usual relational operators. Use the CompareBookmark method instead.

CacheSize

This property specifies how many rows are stored in the cache. If a row exists in the cache, ADO doesn't fetch it from the database. The CacheSize property is changed when we create paged Recordsets, to match the PageSize property. See the section "Creating Paged Recordsets with PageSize," later in this chapter for more information.

CursorLocation

CursorLocation sets or returns the location of a cursor, which may reside either on the client or on the server; the property's value is one of the CursorLocationEnum constants. The client is not the remote machine; it's the machine on which the script is executing. The Web client can't access the database remotely. All it can do is request the execution of a script on the server. The script, in turn, will contact the database server (a machine running SQL Server, for example), retrieve the information, and send it to the client in HTML format. Client-side cursors are transmitted to the client. The advantage of client-side cursors is that they report the number of rows in the cursor and they allow your script to specify the absolute position in the Recordset. Server-side cursors don't report this value; their rows are moved to the client as needed. In Web applications, the size of the cursors is quite small, and we prefer to download them to the client, where they can be processed without further trips to the server. Again, these trips are between the database server and the Web server (and in many cases the two servers run on the same machine).

The CursorLocation, as well as the CursorType property, must be set before the Recordset is opened. Notice that you can't set the location and type of a cursor returned by the Command.Execute method; this cursor is always client-side and forward-only. Use the Recordset.Open method to specify the kind of cursor you want to open.

CursorType

This property sets or returns the type of a cursor, and its value is one of the CursorTypeEnum constants. The default value is adOpenForward-Only. The various cursor types support the different features listed here, and you should use the Supports method to find out whether a Recordset supports a specific property. The cursor can be one of the following types:

Forward-Only This is the simplest type of cursor, but also the least flexible cursor. It can only be scanned forward and its membership is fixed. This means that you can't see additions and changes made to the same rows by other users. Always use forward-only cursors in situations when you need to make only a single pass through a Recordset.

Static The static cursor contains an image of the rows the moment it was created. Like the forward-only cursor, the static cursor doesn't allow you to see additions made by other users. However, you can see the changes made to the cursor's rows by other users (as long as it's a server-side cursor). It supports adBookmark, adHoldRecords, adMovePrevious, and adResync features.

KeySet Changes and deletions made by other users are visible. All types of movement through the Recordset are allowed except for bookmarks, if the provider doesn't support them. It supports adBookmark, adHoldRecords, adMovePrevious, and adResync features.

Dynamic Dynamic cursors are the most flexible cursors. As their name implies, the membership is dynamic. You can see not only changes to the cursor's rows, but also to the rows added by other users (as long as they qualify for inclusion to the cursor). It supports all types of movement, and it's the most expensive cursor in terms of server resources.

If the cursor resides on the client, its type is Static, regardless of the value you set in the code. If a provider does not support the requested cursor type, the provider may return another cursor type.

Fields Collection

This collection is made up of Field objects, and each Field object contains information about a column of the Recordset (the column's type, its value, and so on). For a discussion of the members of a Field object, see the section titled "The Field Object," later in this chapter.

Filter

This property specifies a filter for a Recordset. The rows that do not match the filter's specification are screened out. You can restore the original Recordset by setting its filter property to adFilterNone.

This property can be set to a FilterGroupEnum constant or a criterion that combines field names, values, and relational operators. In addition to the usual relational operators (<, <=, >, >=, =, and <>), you can use the LIKE operator, as well as the logical operators AND and OR. To use literals in a Filter expression, use single quotes. Use the pound sign (#) to delimit dates.

The filter constants allow you to identify the pending rows before a batch update or the conflicting rows after a batch update. Setting the Filter property to a zero-length string ("") has the same effect as using the adFilterNone constant.

Whenever the Filter property is set, the first row of the filtered Recordset becomes the current row. You can also create an array of bookmarks and use it to screen out undesired rows. This allows you to create groups that can't be declared with formal filter expressions. If no row matches the specified criteria, then the Recordset.EOF property is set to True.

The Filter property is used to implement multiple operations on the same Recordset. You can create a single Recordset with all the rows you need for a few operations (as long as all the operations will be performed in the context of the same page) and then isolate the rows you need for each operation and act on them. For example, you can retrieve the orders of all customers who have placed more than 10 orders in the last month. Then you can filter this Recordset to locate customers in certain states, or customers with total sales that exceed a certain amount, and so on. Without the Filter property, you'd have to go through the entire Recordset, isolate the desired rows with an If statement, and then act on these rows.

The following script (Listing 15.6) retrieves the order totals for each customer in the NorthWind database. The rows are stored in a client-side, static Recordset. Then, the script filters the Recordset to display the number of orders placed by customers in selected countries, applying a different filter for each country. After that, it counts the number of orders in different ranges; again, it applies three filters, one for each range. The output produced by the script is shown in Figure 15.1. Without the Filter property, you'd have to execute six different SQL statements against the database, or iterate through the Recordset at least once with a fairly complicated loop, which should maintain several counters.

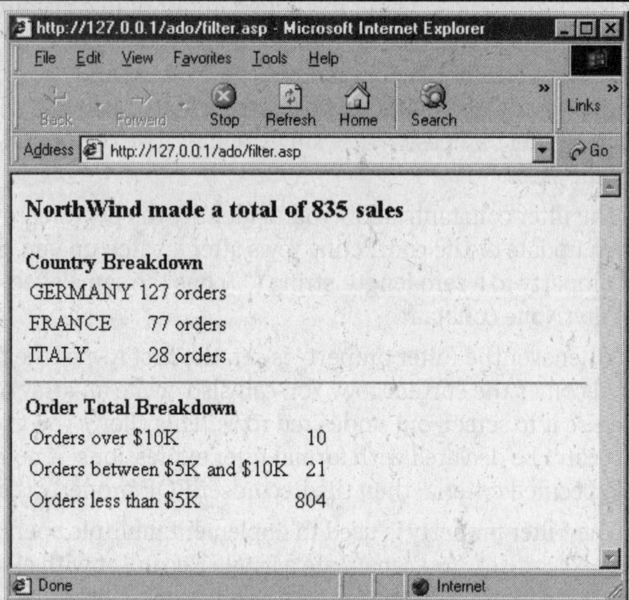

FIGURE 15.1: The output of the `Filter.asp` script

Listing 15.6: The `Filter.asp` Script

```
<!- #include file="adovbs.inc" ->
<%
Dim CN
Dim RS

SQL="SELECT Customers.CompanyName," & _
   " Customers.Region, Customers.Country," & _
   " Orders.OrderID, SUM(Quantity*" & _
   "(1-Discount)*[Order Details].UnitPrice)" & _
   " As OrderTotal FROM Customers" & _
   " INNER JOIN Orders ON Customers." & _
   "CustomerID=Orders.CustomerID" & _
   " INNER JOIN [Order Details] ON" & _
   " [Order Details].OrderID=" & _
   "Orders.OrderID GROUP BY" & _
   " Customers.CompanyName," & _
   " Customers.Region," & _
   " Customers.Country, Orders.OrderID" & _
```

```
    " ORDER BY Customers.CompanyName," & _
    " OrderTotal DESC"
  Set CN=Server.CreateObject("ADODB.Connection")
  CN.Open "DSN=SQLNWIND;uid=sa;password=;"
  Set RS = Server.CreateObject("ADODB.Recordset")
  RS.CursorLocation = adUseClient
  RS.CursorLocation = adOpenStatic

  Set RS.ActiveConnection = CN
  RS.Open(SQL)
  Response.Write "<H3>NorthWind made a total" & _
    " of RS.RecordCount & " sales" & "</H3>"
  Response.Write "<B>Country Breakdown</B>"
  Response.Write "<TABLE>"
  RS.Filter = "Country='Germany'"
  Response.Write "<TR><TD>GERMANY</TD>"
  Response.Write "<TD ALIGN=right>" & _
    RS.RecordCount & " orders</TD></TR>"

  RS.Filter = "Country='France'"
  Response.Write "<TR><TD>FRANCE</TD>"
  Response.Write "<TD ALIGN=right>" & _
    RS.RecordCount & " orders</TD></TR>"

  RS.Filter = "Country='Italy'"
  Response.Write "<TR><TD>ITALY</TD>"
  Response.Write "<TD ALIGN=right>" & _
    RS.RecordCount & " orders</TD></TR>"
  Response.Write "</TABLE>"

  Response.Write "<HR>"
  Response.Write "<B>Order Total Breakdown</B>"
  Response.Write "<TABLE>"
  RS.Filter = "OrderTotal > 10000"
  Response.Write "<TR><TD>Orders over $10K</TD>"
  Response.Write "<TD ALIGN=right>" & _
    RS.RecordCount & "</TD></TD>"

  RS.Filter = "OrderTotal <= 10000 And" & _
    " OrderTotal > 5000"
  Response.Write "<TR><TD>Orders between" & _
    " $5K and $10K</TD>"
```

```
Response.Write "<TD ALIGN=right>" & _
  RS.RecordCount & "</TD></TR>"

RS.Filter = "OrderTotal <= 5000"
Response.Write "<TR><TD>Orders less" & _
  " than $5K</TD>"
Response.Write "<TD ALIGN=right>" & _
  RS.RecordCount & "</TD></TR>"
Response.Write "</TABLE>"
%>
```

Index

The Index property sets or returns the name of the index currently in use and its syntax is:

```
Recordset.Index = indexName
```

where `indexName` is the name of an index. This property is used in conjunction with the Seek method, which locates rows instantly based on an existing index. The index is part of the database and you can't create an index on-the-fly for the needs of a specific script. If a table column is used frequently in searches, create an index based on this column's values and use it with the Seek method. See the Seek section for an example.

LockType

This property sets or returns the type of locks placed on the rows in a Recordset, and its value must be a LockTypeEnum constant. The default value is adLockReadOnly, which eliminates concurrency problems altogether by making the application unable to edit a row. This property must be set before you open the Recordset.

The most flexible locking mechanism is *optimistic locking*. This allows other programs to view the rows you're editing. As far as Web applications go, we don't allow viewers to edit rows in a highly interactive mode (not yet, at least). Web applications retrieve a very small number of rows from one or more tables, download them to the client, and return the edited rows to the server, where a script updates the database. Moreover, each viewer doesn't edit a large section of the database. Typically, viewers can edit their own orders or other information that doesn't apply to other viewers. So, use the read-only locking mechanism when you retrieve rows from the database and call a stored procedure to update the database.

MarshalOptions

This property is used with disconnected Recordsets. The user can edit a disconnected Recordset for a long time before committing the changes to the database. The changes you make to a disconnected Recordset are not posted until you call the Recordset's UpdateBatch method. When the update method is called, you may not wish to send all the rows to the database. It is possible to send only the rows that have changed (including added and deleted rows) since the disconnected Recordset was opened. The MarshalOptions property determines which rows are sent to the client and it can have one of the values adMarshalAll (0) and adMarshalModifiedOnly (1).

MaxRecords

The MaxRecords property specifies the maximum number of records to be returned into a Recordset from a query. Use this property to limit the number of rows returned by the Recordset. This property is equivalent to including the TOP N clause in the SQL statement.

PageCount

PageCount indicates how many pages are contained in the Recordset object. The value of this property is set by the number of rows in the Recordset and the setting of the PageSize property. A *page* is a group of rows whose size equals the PageSize property setting.

PageSize

This property indicates how many records constitute one page in the Recordset. Use PageSize to determine how many records make up a logical page of data. Use the AbsolutePage, PageCount, and PageSize properties to create paged output for display on a browser.

Creating Paged Recordsets with PageSize

There are hardly any Web applications that use a database but *don't* have to display the rows of large cursors on multiple pages. When a viewer looks up information in a database, the search may return a few dozen or a few hundred rows. Obviously, you can't display all the information on a single page. Instead, you must display the rows in groups of 10 or 20 at a time and allow viewers to select any group in this cursor. Because each group is displayed on the same page, this technique is known as *paged cursors*, or *paged Recordsets*. Because paged Recordsets are so important in building Web applications, I present a rather lengthy example to demonstrate this technique.

Let's start with the core VBScript code for displaying, not all the rows in the entire Recordset that match specific requirements, but a specific group of these rows (the third group of 20 matching rows, for example). If you set the PageSize to 20, you can execute the following statements to display the third group of 20 matching rows (rows 41 through 60).

```
Set SelTitles=Server.CreateObject _
  ("adodb.Recordset")
SelTitles.CursorLocation = adUseClient
SelTitles.CursorType = adOpenStatic
SelTitles.CacheSize=20
SelTitles.PageSize=20
SelTitles.Open SQLArgument, connectString
SelTitles.AbsolutePage = 3
While Not SelTitles.EOF
    ' statements to display the fields
Wend
```

Figure 15.2 shows a Form that prompts the viewer to enter a part of a book's title. The script that processes this Form, `TitleSearch.asp` (Listing 15.8), searches the database to locate rows that contain this string in their title.

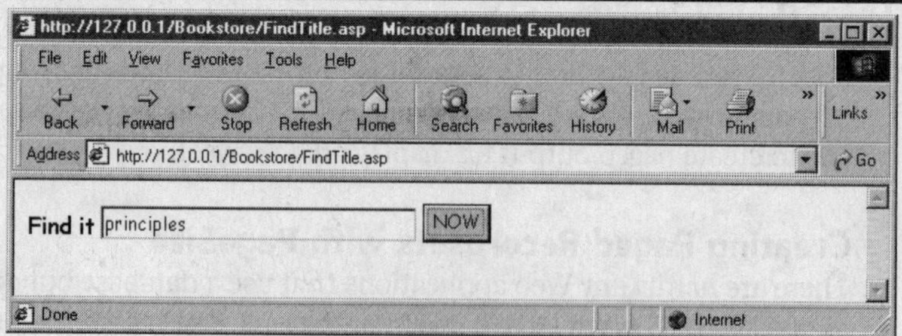

FIGURE 15.2: The `FindTitle.asp` script

Listing 15.7: The `FindTitle.asp` Script

```
<HTML><FONT FACE='MS Sans Serif'>
```

```
<FORM ACTION="TitleSearch.ASP"
  METHOD="GET" NAME="SRCHFORM">
    <P>
    <FONT size="3" FACE="Comic Sans MS">
    Find it</FONT>
    <FONT FACE="Comic Sans MS"> </FONT>
    <INPUT TYPE="text" SIZE="35"
      NAME="SRCHARG">
    <INPUT TYPE="submit" NAME="Search"
      VALUE="NOW">
</FORM>
</FONT>
</BODY>
</HTML>
```

The FindTitle script (Listing 15.7) includes a reference to a second script, `TitleSearch .asp`. It's a fairly complicated script (Listing 15.8), so focus on its main operations, which are outlined after the listing. As you can see in Figure 15.3, the `TitleSearch.asp` script displays the qualifying rows in groups of 20. Each page contains 20 rows, while the user can select any group of 20 rows by clicking the appropriate hyperlink at the bottom of the page. You can't see the navigational hyperlinks in Figure 15.3, but you can see the total number of rows that match the search criteria and the number of the pages on which they're displayed.

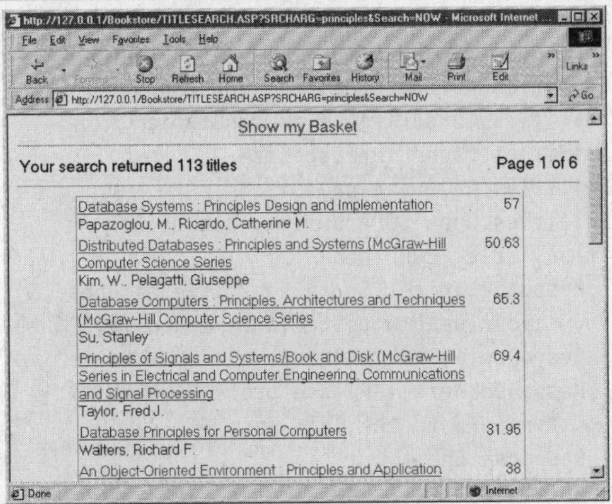

FIGURE 15.3: Displaying paged Recordset

Listing 15.8: The `TitleSearch.asp` Script

```
<!- #include file="adovbs.inc" ->
<HTML><FONT FACE='MS Sans Serif'>
<body BGCOLOR="#F0F0B0">
<%
currentPage=Request.QueryString("whichpage")
If currentPage="" Then
  currentPage=1
End If
pageSize=Request.QueryString("pagesize")
If pageSize="" Then
  pageSize=20
End If

ReqTitle = Request.QueryString("SRCHARG")
SQLArgument = "SELECT Titles.ISBN," & _
  " Titles.Title, Titles.Description" & _
  " As Price, Authors.Author" & _
  " FROM Titles, [Title Author]," & _
  " Authors WHERE Titles.Title LIKE '%" & _
  UCase(ReqTitle) & "%'" & _
  " AND Titles.ISBN = [Title Author].ISBN" & _
  " AND [Title Author].Au_ID = Authors.Au_ID"
connectString="DSN=BIBLIO"
Set SelTitles=Server.CreateObject _
  ("adodb.Recordset")
SelTitles.CursorLocation = adUseServer
SelTitles.CursorType = adOpenStatic
SelTitles.CacheSize=pageSize
SelTitles.PageSize=pageSize
SelTitles.Open SQLArgument, connectString
If SelTitles.EOF Then
  Response.Write "Sorry, no title matches" & _
    " your search criteria (" & ReqTitle & ")."
  Response.Write "<BR>"
  Response.Write "Please press Back to" & _
    " return to the main page."
  Response.End
End If
SelTitles.MoveFirst
PageCount = CInt(SelTitles.PageCount)
maxCount=20
```

```
maxRecordsAllowed=200
If PageCount > _
  Int(maxRecordsAllowed / PageSize) Then
  maxCount = Int(maxRecordsAllowed / _
    PageSize + 0.5)
Else
  maxCount = PageCount
End If
SelTitles.AbsolutePage=currentPage
totRecords=0
BooksTotal=SelTitles.RecordCount
Response.Write "<BR>" & BooksTotal
Response.Write "<CENTER ALIGN=LEFT" & _
  " BGCOLOR=cyan><FONT SIZE=+1>" & _
  "<A HREF=BASKET.ASP>" & _
  "Show my Basket</A></FONT></CENTER>"
Response.Write "<HR>"
Response.Write "<TABLE WIDTH=100%>" & _
  "<TR><TD ALIGN=LEFT>"
Response.Write "<FONT SIZE=4>" & _
  "Your search returned " & _
  booksTotal & " titles</FONT>"
Response.Write "<TD ALIGN=RIGHT>"
Response.Write "<FONT SIZE=4> Page " & _
  currentPage & " of " & maxcount & "<br>"
Response.Write "</TABLE>"
Response.Write "<HR>"
%>
<CENTER>
<TABLE RULES=none WIDTH=80%>
<%
  BooksFound = False
  bcolor = "lightyellow"
  Do While Not SelTitles.EOF And _
  totRecords < SelTitles.PageSize
    If bcolor = "lightyellow" Then
      bcolor = "lightgrey"
    Else
      bcolor = "lightyellow"
    End If
%>
<TR BGCOLOR = <% =bcolor %>>
<TD><A HREF="BookISBN.asp?ISBN=
```

```
<% =SelTitles("ISBN") %>">
<% =SelTitles("Title") %></A>
<%
currentISBN=SelTitles.Fields("ISBN")
currentPrice=SelTitles.Fields("Price")
BookISBN=SelTitles.Fields("ISBN")
Authors=""
Do
  If Not _
  IsNull(SelTitles.Fields("Author")) Then _
  Authors=Authors & SelTitles.Fields _
  ("Author") & ", "
  SelTitles.MoveNext
  If SelTitles.EOF Then
    currentISBN=""
  Else
    currentISBN = SelTitles.Fields("ISBN")
  End If
Loop While currentISBN = BookISBN
Authors = Left(Authors, Len(Authors)-2)
%>
<BR> <% =Authors %>
<TD ALIGN=RIGHT VALIGN=TOP> <% =currentPrice %>
<%
    BooksFound = True
    If Not SelTitles.EOF Then _
      SelTitles.MoveNext
    totRecords = totRecords + 1
  Loop
%>
</TABLE>
<%
  If BooksFound=False Then
    Response.Write "No books were found."
  End If
  Set SelTitles = Nothing
%>
<P>
<%
  pad = "0"
  Scriptname = Request.ServerVariables _
    ("script_name")
  For pgCounter=1 to maxcount
```

```
      If pgCounter>=10 then pad=""
      ref="<a href='" & Scriptname & _
        "?whichpage=" & pgCounter & _
        "&SRCHARG=" & ReqTitle & _
        "&pagesize=" & pageSize & _
        "'>" & pad & pgcounter & _
        "</a>  "
      response.write ref & " "
    Next
    If PageCount > maxCount Then
      Response.Write "<HR>"
      Response.Write "<FONT SIZE=3>" & _
        "Your search for [" & _
        ReqTitle & "] returned " & _
        booksTotal & " titles, "
      Response.Write "but you will see" & _
        " only the first " & _
        maxRecordsAllowed & " of them. "
      Response.Write "Please specify" & _
        " better the titles " & _
        "you're interested in, or "
      Response.Write "use the Detailed" & _
        " Search Form.</FONT>"
      Response.Write "<HR>"
    End If
  %>
  </HTML>
```

The TitleSearch script selects the rows to be displayed by setting the AbsolutePage property of the Recordset object. The PageSize property is set to 20 (the number of rows per page), and the CacheSize property is also set to the same value. There's no reason to keep more rows in the cache, and keeping fewer rows in the cache means more trips to the server.

After displaying the current group of 20 rows, the script prepares hyperlinks at the bottom of the page. Each hyperlink corresponds to another page, and its destination is something like:

```
<A HREF='TitleSearch.asp'?whichpage=4&
SRCHARG='principles'&pageSize=20>04</A>
```

The destination of the hyperlink 04 (which leads to the fourth group of 20 rows) calls the same script, passing as parameters the desired group's number, the search argument (because it can no longer be retrieved from the Request collection), and the size of the page.

RecordCount

This property returns the number of rows in a Recordset. The property returns −1 when ADO cannot determine the number of records, or if the provider or cursor type does not support RecordCount. Only client-side Recordsets (which are static by definition) and keyset cursors return the correct number of rows.

Sort

The Sort property allows you to sort the rows of a Recordset. Its value is one or more field names on which the Recordset is sorted. You can also specify whether the Recordset will be sorted in ascending or descending order. Multiple field names are separated by a comma. A space and the keyword ASC, which sorts the field in ascending order, or DESC (descending order), optionally follow them. By default, the field is sorted in ascending order. Use the following syntax:

```
Sort fieldname [ASC|DESC]
   [, fieldname [ASC|DESC]]
```

The Sort operation is quite fast because the rows are not physically rearranged; they're simply accessed in the specified order. If the Recordset resides on the client, a temporary index will be created for each field specified in the Sort property. To reset the rows to their original order and delete temporary indexes, set the Sort property to an empty string.

The `fieldname` argument cannot be named "ASC" or "DESC" because those names conflict with the keywords ASC and DESC. Give a field with a conflicting name an alias by using the AS keyword in the query that returns the Recordset.

Source

Source indicates the source for the data in a Recordset object (Command object, SQL statement, table name, or stored procedure). To set this property, assign a string value with the name of the Command object or the Command object itself.

State

The State property indicates whether a Recordset object is open. If a Recordset is open, you can't call its Open method again to populate it with a different cursor. You must first close it and then open it with a new SQL statement or stored procedure.

You can also use the same property with asynchronous operations to find out whether the Recordset is fetching rows or whether it has read the entire cursor. The State property applies to Connection objects (it indicates whether a connection has been established) and to Command objects (it indicates whether the command is still executing or whether it has completed its execution).

The State property is read-only and returns an ObjectStateEnum constant. Because this property may return multiple constants, you must use the AND operator to find out a specific state. While a Recordset is being opened, the State property will return the constant adStateOpen + adStateExecuting.

Status

The Status property of the Recordset object is a read-only value that indicates the status of the current row, and its value is a RecordStatusEnum type. The value adRecModified (2), for example, indicates that the current row has been modified. If you're on a new row, added with the AddNew method, the Status property is adRecNew (1).

StayInSync

The StayInSync property is read-only and it applies to hierarchical Recordsets. It indicates whether a change in one or more child rows implies a change in the parent row. If so, you must refresh the hierarchical Recordset by calling the Resync method.

Methods

AddNew

This method creates a new row and appends it to the Recordset (provided that the Recordset is updateable). The syntax of the AddNew method is:

```
AddNew [fieldList, values]
```

You can edit the fields and then commit the changes to the database with the Update method or by moving to another row. Alternatively, you can specify a list of field names and values to be inserted into the new row, similar to the INSERT SQL statement. If you use the second form of the method, be sure that the order of field names matches the order of field values.

Here's how to add a new row with the AddNew/Update methods:

```
RS.AddNew
RS.Fields(0) = <value>
RS.Fields(1) = <value>
. . .
RS.Update
```

Here's how to add a new row with a single statement:

```
RS.AddNew Array("field1", "field2", _
  …, "fieldN"), Array(value1, value2, _
  …, valueN)
```

When you use the second method, ADO submits the changes immediately to the database; there's no need to call the Update method.

Cancel

Call this method to cancel an asynchronous Open operation. A runtime error will be generated if the operation you're attempting to cancel is not asynchronous.

CancelBatch

Call this method to cancel a pending batch update and its syntax is:

```
CancelBatch [affectRecords]
```

The `affectRecords` optional argument determines which records will be affected and can be an AffectEnumType constant. Batch updates are not used commonly in Web applications.

CancelUpdate

This method cancels an AddNew operation, as well as any changes made to the current row. You call this method to restore the original field values of a row in data-editing applications. This method isn't used commonly in Web applications; use stored procedures to update rows in the database from within your script.

Clone

The Clone method creates a copy of a Recordset object, through the syntax

```
Set RS2 = RS1.Clone (lockType)
```

The `lockType` argument specifies whether the clone is read-only and must be a LockTypeEnum constant.

Clone Recordsets are used when you want to maintain two identical Recordsets (usually when you need two current rows at once). The Clone method is more efficient than creating and opening a new Recordset object with the same definition. Changes you make to one Recordset object are visible in all of its clones, regardless of cursor type. However, once you execute Requery on the original Recordset, the clones will no longer be synchronized to the original.

You can only clone a Recordset object that supports bookmarks. Bookmarks are identical in the original and the cloned Recordset, so you can locate a row in any Recordset. Cloned Recordsets can be sorted differently, and this is a good reason to clone a Recordset.

Close

This method closes an open Recordset (or Connection, Record, or Stream) object. Closing an object does not remove it from memory, but it frees the resources allocated to it by the system. You can change the object's properties and open it again later. To completely eliminate an object from memory, set the object variable to `Nothing`.

When you close a Connection object, any active Recordset objects associated with the connection will also be closed. When you close a Recordset, Record, or Stream object, the system releases the associated data. One of the most common runtime errors is that the requested operation can't be performed on a closed object. You may have forgotten to open a connection for a Recordset or even the Recordset itself. See the discussion of the Open method for more information on opening and closing objects.

CompareBookmarks

This method compares two bookmarks and returns an indication of their relative values. The syntax of the CompareBookmarks property is:

```
CompareBookmarks (bookmark1, bookmark2)
```

The value returned is a CompareEnum constant, which indicates the relative order of the two rows in the Recordset.

Delete

This method deletes the current record or a group of records; its syntax is:

```
Delete [affectRecords]
```

The `affectRecords` optional argument determines which records will be affected and can be an AffectEnumType constant.

After deleting the current record, the deleted record remains current until you move to a different record. If you attempt to access the value of these fields, however, an error will be generated. Once you move away from the deleted record, it is no longer accessible.

If the attempt to delete records fails because of a conflict with the underlying data (for example, if a record has already been deleted by another user), ADO will set the Error object, but it will not set the Err object (the two objects are different). As a consequence, it will not halt the execution of the script. You can set the Filter property to adFilter-ConflictingRecords to isolate the conflicting rows.

Find

The Find method searches a Recordset to locate the first row that matches the specified criteria. Its syntax is:

```
Find criteria [, skipRows, _
  searchDirection, start]
```

If no row matches the criteria, the Find method sets the EOF property to True (or the BOF property, if you're searching backward). The `criteria` argument is a string that contains a column name, a comparison operator, and a value to be used in the search. Notice that you can't combine multiple criteria with the logical operators (AND/OR). The second argument, `skipRows`, specifies an offset from the current row (or the `start` bookmark) where the search will begin. By default, the search starts on the current row. Most applications call the MoveFirst method before calling the Find method. The `searchDirection` argument specifies whether the search should begin on the current row or the next available row in the direction of the search, and its value can be a DirectionEnumType constant. The last argument, `start`, is the bookmark of the row that will be used as the starting position for the search.

The `criteria` argument may contain relational operators (<, <=, >, >=, =, <>) as well as the LIKE operator.

GetRows

The GetRows method retrieves multiple records of a Recordset object into an array. The method returns a variant that evaluates to a two-dimensional array when called as:

```
array = RS.GetRows ([rows, start, fields])
```

The rows optional argument is a GetRowsOptionEnum constant that indicates the number of records to retrieve. The `start` optional argument is a string or variant value that evaluates to the bookmark of the record from which the GetRows operation should begin. You can also use a BookmarkEnum constant. The last argument, `fields`, is the name of a field (or an array of field names) that specifies which columns will be retrieved. If you omit the `fields` argument, then all columns will be returned.

To manipulate the array from within your code, keep in mind that the first subscript corresponds to the columns of the Recordset (fields), and the second index corresponds to the rows of the Recordset. The array is dimensioned automatically to fit the size of the Recordset.

To specify which fields you want the GetRows method to return, you can pass either a single field name (or ordinal position) or an array of field names (or ordinal numbers) in the `fields` argument.

GetString

This method returns the Recordset as a string. Call it as:

```
Set Variant = RS.GetString _
  ([stringFormat, numRows, columnDelimiter, _
  rowDelimiter, nullExpr])
```

The `stringFormat` argument specifies how the Recordset will be converted to a string, and its value is a `StringFormat` constant. The `rowDelimiter`, `columnDelimiter`, and `nullExpr` parameters are used only when the stringFormat is adClipString. The `numRows` argument is also optional, and you can use it to specify the number of rows to be converted. If you omit this argument, all the rows in the Recordset are converted. The last argument is the delimiter that will be used between columns. The default delimiter is the TAB character. The `nullExpr` parameter is a value to be used in the place of Null fields.

The GetString method is a very convenient method to convert a cursor into an HTML table. All you have to do is define the <TR><TD> tag as row delimiter and the <TD> tag as column delimiter. The Cursor2Table script (Listing 15.9) displays a table with the first 20 ISBN and Title fields of the Titles table of the BIBLIO database.

Listing 15.9: The `Cursor2Table.asp` Script

```
<%
Set CN = Server.CreateObject _
   ("ADODB.Connection")
Set RS = Server.CreateObject _
   ("ADODB.Recordset")
CN.ConnectionString = "DSN=BIBLIO"
CN.Open
Set RS.ActiveConnection = CN
RS.Open "SELECT TOP 20 ISBN, Title" & _
   " FROM Titles"
TBL = RS.GetString(, , "<TD>", _
   "<TR><TD>" & vbCrLf)
Response.Write "<TABLE>" & TBL & "</TABLE>"
%>
```

Move

The Move method moves `numRecords` rows ahead of the current row or of the row number specified by the `start` argument. If the `numRecords` argument is negative, the Move method moves toward the beginning of the Recordset. The syntax of the Move method is:

```
Move numRecords [, start])
```

If your code attempts to move to a row before the first record, ADO sets the current record to the position before the first record in the Recordset and sets the BOF property to True. An attempt to move backward when the BOF property is already True generates an error. Likewise, with an attempt to move to a row after the last row, ADO sets the current record to the position after the last record in the Recordset and sets the EOF property to True. Calling the Move method from an empty Recordset object generates an error.

This is the only navigational method supported by forward-only Recordsets. You can specify a negative value for the `numRecords` argument to move backward, provided that the destination row is in the cache. Use a large value for the CacheSize property to support full scrolling with a forward-only cursor.

MoveFirst, MoveLast, MoveNext, and MovePrevious

These are the Recordset object navigational methods: they move to the first, last, next, or previous row in a Recordset, respectively. Forward-only cursors support the MoveFirst and MoveNext methods only.

NextRecordset

The statement `Set RS2 = RS1.NextRecordset` returns the next Recordset. Some SQL statements may return multiple Recordsets (a T-SQL batch with multiple SELECT statements, for example). After you have iterated through the rows of the first Recordset, you can call the NextRecordset method to move to the next Recordset. At any given time, you can see only one Recordset.

Multiple Recordsets are generated by compound statements, which must be executed with the Execute method of the Command object or the Open method of the Recordset object. The NextRecordset method can be called many times; as long as there are Recordsets, NextRecordset returns a new one. When it runs out of Recordsets, it will return an empty Recordset. To test empty Recordsets, examine the EOF and BOF properties. If they're both True, then the Recordset is empty.

If one of the statements in the compound command does not return a Recordset, the NextRecordset method will be closed. You can examine its State property to test for this case.

When you call the NextRecordset method, ADO executes only the next command in the statement. If you explicitly close the Recordset object before stepping through the entire command statement, ADO never executes the remaining commands.

The NextRecordset method is used with non-uniform Recordsets, which are usually the result of SQL statements that include COMPUTE clauses. The following SQL statement returns each order's details followed by their totals. The customer total follows the customer's orders.

```
SELECT
   CompanyName,
   Orders.OrderID,
   ProductName,
   UnitPrice=
     ROUND([Order Details].UnitPrice, 2),
```

```
    Quantity,
    Discount=CONVERT(int, Discount * 100),
    ExtendedPrice=
      ROUND(CONVERT(money,
      Quantity * (1-Discount)*
      [Order Details].UnitPrice), 2)
  FROM
    Products,
    [Order Details],
    Customers,
    Orders
  WHERE
    [Order Details].ProductID=Products.ProductID
      And [Order Details].OrderID=Orders.OrderID
      And Orders.CustomerID=Customers.CustomerID
  ORDER BY
    Customers.CustomerID,
    Orders.OrderID
  COMPUTE
    SUM(ROUND(CONVERT(money,
      Quantity * (1 - Discount) *
      [Order Details].UnitPrice), 2))
    BY Customers.CustomerID, Orders.OrderID
  COMPUTE
    SUM(ROUND(CONVERT(money,
      Quantity * (1 - Discount) *
      [Order Details].UnitPrice), 2))
    BY Customers.CustomerID
```

The structure of this Recordset is not uniform. The first few lines contain the details of the first order, followed by the order's total. The other orders of the same customer follow and after the last order for each customer, the customer's total appears, as shown in Figure 15.4 (this is how a script renders the information in the Recordset on a Web page, but you get an idea of the Recordset's structure). This statement returns a peculiar Recordset: its rows do not have the same structure. Some rows contain many columns, some rows contain a single value. Technically, this isn't a single Recordset. It's a set of Recordset objects and each one of them has the same structure. To scan this Recordset, you must start as usual, but the first Recordset will be exhausted as soon as you hit the first row with a different structure. This marks the beginning of a new Recordset, and you must call the NextRecordset method to retrieve the next Recordset and scan its rows.

The script in Listing 15.10 scans the multiple Recordsets returned by the previous SQL statement. The output it produces is shown in Figure 15.4.

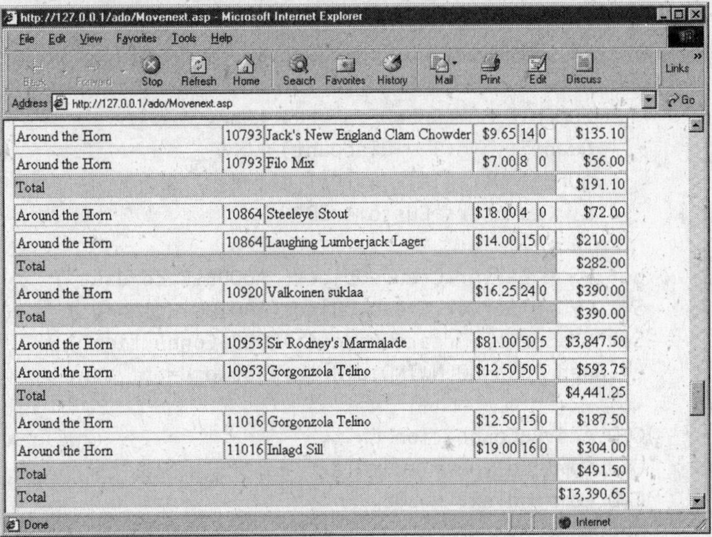

Around the Horn	10793	Jack's New England Clam Chowder	$9.65	14	0	$135.10
Around the Horn	10793	Filo Mix	$7.00	8	0	$56.00
Total						$191.10
Around the Horn	10864	Steeleye Stout	$18.00	4	0	$72.00
Around the Horn	10864	Laughing Lumberjack Lager	$14.00	15	0	$210.00
Total						$282.00
Around the Horn	10920	Valkoinen suklaa	$16.25	24	0	$390.00
Total						$390.00
Around the Horn	10953	Sir Rodney's Marmalade	$81.00	50	5	$3,847.50
Around the Horn	10953	Gorgonzola Telino	$12.50	50	5	$593.75
Total						$4,441.25
Around the Horn	11016	Gorgonzola Telino	$12.50	15	0	$187.50
Around the Horn	11016	Inlagd Sill	$19.00	16	0	$304.00
Total						$491.50
Total						$13,390.65

FIGURE 15.4: Scanning multiple Recordsets

Listing 15.10: The `MultiRecordset.asp` Script

```
<!- #include file="adovbs.inc" ->
<%
SQL = "SELECT TOP 100 CompanyName," & _
  " Orders.OrderID, ProductName," & _
  " UnitPrice=ROUND([Order Details]." & _
 "UnitPrice, 2), Quantity," & _
  " Discount=CONVERT(int, Discount * 100)," & _
  " ExtendedPrice=ROUND(CONVERT(money," & _
  " Quantity * (1-Discount)*" & _
  " [Order Details].UnitPrice), 2)" & _
```

```
    " FROM Products, [Order Details]," & _
    " Customers, Orders" & _
    " WHERE [Order Details].ProductID =" & _
    " Products.ProductID And" & _
    " [Order Details].OrderID=" & _
    "Orders.OrderID And Orders.CustomerID=" & _
    "Customers.CustomerID" & _
    " ORDER BY Customers.CustomerID," & _
    " Orders.OrderID" & _
    " COMPUTE SUM(ROUND(CONVERT(money," & _
    " Quantity * (1 - Discount) *" & _
    " [Order Details].UnitPrice), 2))" & _
    " BY Customers.CustomerID," & _
    " Orders.OrderID" & _
    " COMPUTE SUM(ROUND(CONVERT(money," & _
    " Quantity * (1 - Discount) *" & _
    " [Order Details].UnitPrice), 2))" & _
    " BY Customers.CustomerID"

Set RS = Server.CreateObject("ADODB.Recordset")
Set CMD = Server.CreateObject("ADODB.Command")
Set CN=Server.CreateObject("ADODB.Connection")
CN.Open "DSN=SQLNWIND;uid=sa;password=;"

CMD.ActiveConnection=CN
CMD.CommandType = adCmdText
CMD.CommandText = SQL
Set RS = CMD.Execute
Response.Write _
  "<TABLE BORDER=Frame CELLSPACING=0>"
While Not RS.EOF
  If RS.Fields.Count=1 Then
    Line= "<TR><TD COLSPAN=6" & _
      " BGColor=yellow>Total "
  End If
  For i=0 To RS.Fields.Count-1
    If RS.Fields(i).Type = adCurrency Then
      Line = Line & "<TD ALIGN=right>" & _
      FormatCurrency(RS.Fields(i)) & "</TD>"
    Else
      Line = Line & "<TD>" & _
        RS.Fields(i) & "</TD>"
```

```
        End If
        Response.Write "</TR><TR>"
      Next
      Response.Write Line
      Response.Write "</TR>"
      Line = ""
      RS.MoveNext
      If RS.EOF Then
        Set RS = RS.NextRecordset
        If RS Is Nothing Then
          Response.End
        End If
      End If
    Wend
    %>
```

Open

The Open method opens a Recordset by executing a cursor-returning command against the database or by opening a table, and its syntax is:

```
Open [source, activeConnection, cursorType, lockType,
options]
```

The `source` argument is a Command object, a SQL statement, a table's name, or a stored procedure's name. It can also be a URL, the name of a file where a persisted Recordset has been stored (most likely with the Save method), or a Stream object. The `activeConnection` argument is a Connection object.

The `cursorType` argument (a CursorTypeEnum constant) specifies the type of the cursor, and the `lockType` argument (a LockTypeEnum constant) specifies the cursor's locking mechanism. The default cursor is forward-only and read-only. The `options` argument indicates how the `source` argument should be interpreted (i.e., whether it's something different from a Command object, or whether the Recordset should be read from a file, where it was previously stored with the Save method).

If the `source` argument is not a Command object, you can use the `options` argument to specify the type of the *source*. This will optimize performance because ADO will not have to figure on its own the type of command it must execute against the database.

If the data source returns no records, the data store returns an empty Recordset by setting both its BOF and EOF properties to True.

If you want to create a custom Recordset, you must first set its Fields (by populating the Fields collection with Field objects) and then call Open with no arguments.

The simplest method to create a Recordset is the Recordset object's Open method. The following statements create a Recordset with the rows of the Titles of the BIBLIO database. It also sets the cursor's location and type. The CursorLocation and CursorType properties must be set before the Recordset is opened:

```
<%
SQLArgument = "Titles"
connectString="DSN=BIBLIO"
Set SelTitles=Server.CreateObject _
  ("adodb.Recordset")
SelTitles.CursorLocation = adUseClient
SelTitles.CursorType = adOpenStatic
SelTitles.Open SQLArgument, connectString
Response.Write "The cursor contains " & _
               SelTitles.RecordCount & " rows"
%>
```

The `SQLArgument` argument is the name of a table. To retrieve selected rows, use a SQL statement instead. The following is a lengthy SQL statement that retrieves all the orders in the NorthWind database. This information isn't stored in any single table. Instead, we must calculate each order's total by summing the products of the units of each item times their prices:

```
SQL = "SELECT Customers.CompanyName," & _
   " Customers.Region, Customers.Country," & _
   " Orders.OrderID, SUM(Quantity*(1-" & _
   "Discount)*[Order Details].UnitPrice)" & _
   " As OrderTotal" & _
   " FROM Customers" & _
   " INNER JOIN Orders ON" & _
   " Customers.CustomerID=Orders.CustomerID" & _
   " INNER JOIN [Order Details] ON" & _
   " [Order Details].OrderID=Orders.OrderID" & _
```

```
" GROUP BY Customers.CompanyName," & _
" Customers.Region, Customers.Country," & _
" Orders.OrderID" & _
" ORDER BY Customers.CompanyName," & _
" OrderTotal DESC"
```

To retrieve the qualifying rows in a Recordset, use the following statements. This time we set the Recordset's ActiveConnection property to an existing Connection object:

```
<%
Set CN=Server.CreateObject("ADODB.Connection")
CN.Open "DSN=SQLNWIND;uid=sa;password=;"
Set RS = Server.CreateObject("ADODB.Recordset")
RS.CursorLocation = adUseClient
RS.CursorLocation = adOpenStatic
Set RS.ActiveConnection = CN
RS.Open(SQL)
%>
```

Requery

The Requery method updates the data in a Recordset object by executing the query on which the Recordset is based. In `Requery [options]`, the `options` argument is an ExecuteOptionEnum constant that affects how the operation is performed. The Requery method is equivalent to calling the Close method and then the Open method of the Recordset. The number of rows in the Recordset may change after calling the Requery method.

Resync

This method synchronizes the data in the Recordset with the underlying database, and it's called with the following syntax:

```
Resync [affectRecords, resyncValues]
```

The `affectRecords` argument is an AffectEnumType constant that specifies which records will be updated. The `resyncValues` argument is a ResyncEnum type that specifies whether the underlying values will be overwritten.

The Resync method does not execute the query on which the Recordset was based. As a result, the Resync method doesn't see any new rows inserted since the Recordset was created. If one or more of the underlying rows were deleted, ADO will return warnings in the Errors collection. You can set the Filter property to adFilterConflictingRecords to isolate the conflicting rows. The Resync property is not commonly used in Web development.

Save

This method saves (persists) the Recordset to a file or Stream object, using the syntax

```
Save destination [, persistFormat]
```

The `destination` argument is the path name of the file where the Recordset will be saved or a reference to a Stream object. The `persistFormat` argument specifies the format in which the Recordset will be saved, and its value can be a PersistFormatEnum constant. The Recordset can be saved either in a proprietary format (adPersistADTG) or in XML format (adPersistXML).

If a filter is in effect, only the rows accessible under the filter are saved. If the Recordset is hierarchical, then the current child Recordset and its children are saved, including the parent Recordset. If the Save method of a child Recordset is called, the child and all its children are saved, but the parent is not.

You must specify a destination argument only the first time you call the Save method. If you call the Save method with a different destination, then both destinations will remain open.

Seek

The Seek method searches the index of a Recordset to quickly locate the row that matches the specified values, and changes the current row position to that row. The Seek method works with server-side cursors only. Its syntax is:

```
Seek keyValues [, seekOption]
```

The `keyValues` argument is an array representing one or more columns; the array contains a value to compare against each corresponding column. The second argument specifies the comparison to be executed between the index columns and the corresponding `keyValues`.

If the Seek method does not find the desired row, no error occurs and the Recordset is positioned at EOF.

Supports

The Supports (cursorOption) method determines whether a specified Recordset object supports a particular cursor-related feature; it returns True if the feature is supported, False otherwise. The `cursorOption` argument is a CursorOptionEnum constant.

Usually, you know whether your Recordset object supports a feature at design time. If you want to find out whether an open Recordset supports a specific feature, call the Supports method with the appropriate argument.

Update

This method commits any changes made to the current row of a Recordset in the underlying tables. To commit all the fields, set their values first and then call the Update method without arguments. If you want to change the values of selected fields, use `Update [fields, values]`, passing the field names and their new values as two matched-order arrays.

You use the Update method to save a new row after calling the AddNew method or after the user makes changes on data-bound controls on a Form. If you move to another row with one of the Move methods, or if you close the Recordset with the Close method, any changes in the current row are committed to the database automatically.

To update selected fields of the current row, call the Update method, as follows:

```
RS.Update Array("Phone", "FAX"), _
   Array("555-1234", "555-2233")
```

or

```
RS.Fields("Phone") = "555-1234"
RS.Fields("FAX") = "555-2233"
RS.Update
```

You don't have to call the Update method in the second code segment. The changes will be committed to the database once you move to a different row with one of the Move methods.

The following statements add a new row to the Recordset and set the values of a few of the fields of the new row through the Fields collection. Then, the Update method is called to commit the changes:

```
RS.AddNew
RS.Fields("CustomerID") = "NCMPY"
RS.Fields("CompanyName") = "New Company Name"
RS.Update
```

UpdateBatch

This method writes all pending updates to disk in batch mode and its syntax is:

```
UpdateBatch [affectRecords]
```

The optional argument determines which rows of the Recordset will be transmitted to the database server, and its value must be an adAffect-EnumType constant. Batch updates are possible with keyset or static cursors only.

If the attempt to transmit changes fails for any or all records because of a conflict with the underlying data (for example, if a record has already been deleted by another user), the provider returns warnings to the Errors collection and a runtime error occurs. Set the Filter property to adFilterAffectedRecords to screen the conflicting rows.

The Record Object

The Record object represents a row in a semi-structured Recordset. A folder, for example, can be represented as a Recordset, and individual files are represented by Record objects. Notice that the Record object isn't the row of a typical Recordset, like the ones presented earlier in this chapter. The Stream and Record objects are used to access semi-structured data sources, but not databases.

The Record object also represents an alternative way to navigate hierarchically organized data. A folder may be represented with a Record, which has subordinate Records that represent its files and folders.

A folder is uniquely identified by an absolute URL, so you can open a Record object by specifying an absolute URL. A Connection object is implicitly created and set to the Record object when the Record is opened with an absolute URL (see the description of the Open method for more details).

Properties

ActiveConnection

This property identifies the Connection object to which the specified Record belongs.

Fields Collection

Each Record object has a Fields collection that contains information about the Record's fields. See the section titled "The Field Object" for more information on the members of the individual fields.

Mode

This property indicates the permissions for modifying data in a Record object; its value is a ConnectModeEnum constant.

ParentURL

The ParentURL property returns an absolute URL string that points to the parent Record of the current Record object. This property is Null if there is no parent for the current object (for example, if the Record object represents the root of a directory). It is also Null if the Record object represents an entity that cannot be specified with a URL.

RecordType

This property indicates the type of a Record and returns a RecordTypeEnum constant.

Source

This property indicates the entity represented by a Record object. The Source property returns the Source argument of the Record object's Open method. It can be a string with an absolute or relative URL, or a reference to an already open Recordset object.

State

The State property indicates whether a Record object is opened or closed, and it returns an ObjectStateEnum constant.

Methods

Cancel

This method cancels an asynchronous operation on a Record object. The asynchronous operation can be a call to the following methods: CopyRecord, DeleteRecord, MoveRecord, or Open.

Close

Use the Close method to close a Record object. All related data are released, and you must reopen the Record if you need it.

CopyRecord

The CopyRecord method copies a file or directory, and its contents, to another location. In the syntax

```
CopyRecord source, destination [, _
   userName, password, options, async]
```

`source` is a URL that identifies the file or directory to be copied. If the `source` argument is omitted (or if it's set to an empty string), the method will copy the file or directory represented by the Record object on which the method is applied. The `destination` argument is the URL of the destination (where the source will be copied), and it must be different from the `source` argument. The `userName` and `password` arguments may be needed to authorize the user's access to the destination.

The `options` argument is a CopyRecordOptionsEnum constant that specifies the behavior of this method. The last argument, `async`, determines whether the operation should take place asynchronously (if True) or synchronously (if False). All subdirectories in the source are copied recursively, unless the adCopyNonRecursive option is specified. In a recursive operation, `destination` must not be a subdirectory of `source`.

DeleteRecord

The DeleteRecord method deletes a file or directory, and all its subdirectories, using the syntax

```
DeleteRecord source [, async]
```

The `source` argument specifies a URL that identifies the object to be deleted (a file or directory). If the `source` argument is omitted, then the

DeleteRecord method will remove the file or directory represented by the Record on which the method is applied. The `async` argument specifies whether the operation will take place synchronously (if False) or asynchronously (if True).

GetChildren

The statement

```
Set Recordset = Record.GetChildren
```

returns a Recordset whose rows represent the files and subfolders in the folder represented by the stated Record object.

MoveRecord

This method moves a file, or a directory and its contents, to another location. Call it with the syntax:

```
MoveRecord (source, destination _
    [, userName, password, options, async])
```

The `source` argument is a URL that identifies the Record object to be moved. This argument is usually omitted, and the operation is applied on the Record object on which the method is applied. The `destination` argument is the URL of the location where the Record will be moved. The `source` and `destination` arguments must be different, or else a runtime error is generated. The `userName` and `password` arguments are used to verify the user's rights.

The `options` argument is a MoveRecordOptionsEnum constant, which specifies the method's behavior. If the destination exists already, you can overwrite it by setting the adMoveOverWrite option. You can specify multiple options by combining the individual options with the OR operator.

The last argument, `async`, determines whether the operation will be executed asynchronously (if True) or synchronously (if False).

Open

The Open method opens a Record object. Its full structure is:

```
Open [source, ActiveConnection, mode, _
    createOptions, options, userName, password]
```

The `source` argument is the URL of the entity represented by the Record object. For the simplest type of Record, which represents a row, Record can be a row of an open Recordset object. For Recordset-related Records, the `ActiveConnection` argument is a connection string or a valid Connection object. If the Record is associated to a file system, then `source` can be a relative or an absolute URL. In the second case, it specifies the file or folder over which subsequent operations will apply. The mode argument is a ConnectModeEnum constant that specifies the access mode for the Record object that will be opened.

The `createOptions` argument is a RecordCreateOptionsEnum constant that specifies whether an existing file or folder should be opened, or a new one should be created. The `options` argument is a Record-OpenOptionsEnum constant that specifies options for opening the Record. The last two arguments are used to validate the user's rights to the files or folders that will be accessed through the Record object.

The following statements open a Record from the URL of an existing folder.

```
Dim RecSet Rec = Server.ObjectVariable("ADODB.Record")
Rec.Open "http://127.0.0.1/PublicDocs/"
```

A relative URL is the URL of a document in the context of the Connection object:

```
Dim CN
Set CN = Server.CreateObject("ADODB.Connection")
Dim Rec
Set Rec = Server.CreateObject("ADODB.Record")
CN.Open "http://127.0.0.1/PublicDocs/"
Rec.Open "Resume.doc", aConnection
```

The Stream Object

A Stream object represents a Stream of binary data or text. ADO can access semi-structured data stores, such as a file system or an e-mail system. A Stream object consists of Records that correspond to the contents of a file or the items in an e-mail system.

A Stream object can be obtained in these ways:

- From a URL pointing to an object (typically a file) containing binary or text data. This object can be a simple document, in which case a Record object represents a document or a folder. Accessing files and folders through a Stream object is similar to using the FileSystemObject (this is an object of the Windows Scripting Host).

- From a Record object. After you have opened a Record object, you can obtain its default Stream.
- By creating a Stream object with the appropriate declaration. This Stream can be used to store data, which you can manipulate from within your code.

You can use the Stream object's methods and properties to access its Records (the subfolder of a folder, the contents of a file, the messages stored in an e-mail system, and so on). You can also save information to a folder or file by using the Stream object. The Stream object allows you to access non-traditional data stores (non-relational databases) through the ADO object. This capacity of ADO doesn't apply to databases and their programming, and it's not discussed in this book.

Properties

Charset

This property specifies the character set into which the contents of a text Stream should be translated. The default value is "Unicode." Other values are the character set strings used in the HTML <META> tag (Windows-1252, etc.). For a list of the character sets available on your system, see the following branch of the Registry:

```
HKEY_CLASSES_ROOT\MIME\Database\Charset
```

EOS

The EOS (End Of Stream) property is the equivalent of the EOF property for Stream objects. It returns True if the current position is the end of the Stream. Unlike the EOF property, the EOS property can be set. When you set the EOS property to True, you specify that the current position becomes the end of the Stream. Any additional characters or bytes in the Stream are discarded.

LineSeparator

This property specifies the character to be used as the line separator in a text Stream, and its value must be a LineSeparatorEnum constant. The default value is adCRLF. The LineSeparator must be used with text Streams only; it's ignored if specified with a binary Stream.

Mode

The Mode property indicates the permissions for modifying data in a Stream object. The same property applies to Connection objects and Record objects as well.

Position

This property identifies the current position in a Stream object. It sets a long integer value, which is the offset (in characters or bytes) of the current position from the beginning of the Stream. The value zero corresponds to the first byte in the Stream.

Size

This property returns the size of a Stream object in number of bytes. If the size of the Stream object is not known, the Size property will return the value −1, similar to the RecordCount property.

State

Like the State property of all other objects, the Stream.State property indicates whether the Stream object is open or closed, as well as the status of an asynchronous operation. Its value is an ObjectStateEnum constant. If the Stream object is open, the State property may also indicate the status of an asynchronous operation. If the operation hasn't completed, the value of the State property will be adStateOpen + adStateExecuting.

Type

The Type property identifies the type of the data stored in a Stream object, and it can be a StreamTypeEnum constant. The default value is adTypeText. This property can be set only while you're on the first byte of the Stream; at any other position, the Type property is read-only.

Methods

Cancel

Call this method to cancel an asynchronous Open operation. A runtime error will be generated if the operation you're attempting to cancel is not asynchronous.

Close

This method closes an open Stream object. Closing a Stream object does not remove it from memory. To remove the object from memory and release its resources, set it to `Nothing`. The Close method releases the data associated with the Stream object.

CopyTo

The CopyTo method copies `numChars` characters or bytes from one Stream object to another, and its syntax is:

```
CopyTo destStream [, numChars]
```

The `destStream` argument is a reference to an open Stream object, into which the characters or bytes will be copied. If you omit the `numChars` argument, the method will copy all the characters or bytes from the current location to the end of the Stream.

Flush

This method flushes the Stream to the object (a file, for example) to which the Stream object is associated. This method need not be called frequently because the Stream object flushes its buffer as frequently as possible in the background. When a Stream object is closed, its contents are automatically flushed.

LoadFromFile

This method loads the contents of an existing file into a Stream; its only argument is the source filename. The Stream object must be already open before its LoadFromFile method can be called. Any existing bytes in the Stream are overwritten by the contents of the file. Any existing bytes after the EOS created by LoadFromFile are truncated.

Open

The Open method opens a Stream object. Its syntax is:

```
Open [source, mode, openOptions, _
  userName, password]
```

The source argument specifies the source of the Stream's data. It may be an absolute URL or a string pointing to a structured data source, such as a file system of an e-mail storage. Alternately, source may contain a reference to an already open Record object, which opens the default Stream associated with the Record. The mode argument specifies the access mode for the Stream. The openOptions argument is a StreamOpen-OptionsEnum constant and specifies whether the Stream's data will come from a URL or a file. The userName and password arguments contain information required to validate access to the Stream object.

Read

The Read method is called by

```
variant = Stream.Read (numBytes)
```

and reads numBytes bytes from a Stream object. The data read from the Stream are stored in a variant. The numBytes argument can be a Stream-ReadEnum constant; its default value is adReadAll.

ReadText

To read the beginning of a text Stream, use

```
String = Stream.ReadText (numChars)
```

This method reads numChars characters from a text Stream object. The text read from the Stream is stored in a string variable. The numChars argument can be a StreamReadEnum constant, and its default value is adReadAll.

SaveToFile

This method saves the binary contents of a Stream to a file by means of

```
SaveToFile filename [, saveOptions]
```

The filename argument is the name of the file to which the contents of the Stream will be saved. The saveOptions argument is a Save-OptionsEnum constant that specifies whether a new file should be created by SaveToFile if it does not already exist. The default value is adSaveCreateNotExists.

SetEOS

This method defines the end of the Stream. SetEOS updates the value of the EOS property by making the current Position the Stream end; any bytes or characters following the current Position are truncated.

SkipLine

This method skips one entire line when reading a text Stream. The SkipLine method is used with text Streams only.

Write

This method writes binary data to a Stream object. Its argument contains an array of bytes that will be written to the Stream. The current Position is set to the byte following the written data. The Write method does not truncate the rest of the data in a Stream. If you want to truncate these bytes, call SetEOS.

WriteText

The WriteText method writes a specified text string to a Stream object when called as

```
WriteText data [, options]
```

The `data` argument contains the text to be written to the Stream. The `options` argument is a StreamWriteOptionsEnum constant, and it specifies whether a line separator must be written to the end of the string.

The WriteText method does not truncate the rest of the data in a Stream. If you want to truncate these characters, call SetEOS. If you WriteText past the current EOS position, the size of the Stream will be increased to contain any new characters, and EOS will move to the new last byte in the Stream.

A simple example follows of using the Stream object in a Web application. The same functionality can be achieved through the FileAccess component, but I'll use the Stream object to demonstrate how you can access semi-structured information using the Stream object. The essence of Universal Access is a uniform set of tools for accessing not only databases, which are rigidly structured, but semi-structured data sources, like folders and files, inboxes, and so on.

The example displays the contents of a text file in a TextArea control on a Web page. The viewer can edit the information and submit the revised text to the server.

The EditText.htm file is shown in the following listing. Instead of placing some text between the two <TEXTAREA> tags, it uses a script to read the contents of a file from a Stream object. You could have used the FileSystemObject object to read the file, but this is a simple example to demonstrate the use of the Stream object.

```
<HTML>
<FORM ACTION="GetText.asp" METHOD=GET>
<TEXTAREA NAME=MyText
   STYLE='WIDTH=90%; HEIGHT=250'>
<%
Const adOpenFromURL=8
Set objStream = Server.CreateObject _
   ("ADODB.Stream")
objStream.Open _
   "URL='http://127.0.0.1/ADO/test.txt', _
   adModeRead, adOpenStreamFromURL"
Response.Write objStream.ReadText
%>
</TEXTAREA>
<BR>
<INPUT TYPE=Submit>
</FORM>
</HTML>
```

The Submit button sends the contents of the TextArea control to the Web server, where it's processed by the GetText.asp script. This script overwrites the original file (test.txt), creates a new Web page with the revised text, and sends that back to the client as a confirmation. Here's the listing of the GetText.asp script:

```
<%
Const adOpenFromURL=8
Const adModeReadWrite = 4
Set objStream = Server.CreateObject _
```

```
    ("ADODB.Stream")
objStream.Open _
   "URL='http://127.0.0.1/ADO/test.txt'," & _
   " adModeReadWrite, adOpenStreamFromURL"
objStream.Position=0
objStream.SetEOS
newText = Request.Form("MyText")
objStream.WriteText newText
objStream.Close
Response.Write "<HTML>"
Response.Write newText
Response.Write "</HTML>"
%>
```

By setting the Stream object's Position property to 0, the script moves to the beginning of the file, so that the write operation will overwrite the original file. The SetEOS method resets the file; it sets the end of the Stream to the current location, which is the beginning of the file. Then the script writes the contents of the TextArea control to the file and closes the Stream object. It's not the most exciting example, but it shows how you can use ADO to manipulate text files.

The Field Object

A Field object represents a column of a table in the database. Each table exposes the Fields collection, which contains a Field object for each column in the table. Use the items of the Fields collection to find out information about the table's columns. Most of the members of the Field object are the same as the properties of the Parameter object.

Properties

ActualSize

This property returns the actual length of the data stored in a field. Use ActualSize with variable length fields to find out the length of the data stored in the field. For fixed-length fields, the ActualSize property is the same as the DefinedSize property.

Attributes

This property indicates one or more characteristics of a Field object, and its value is a FieldAttributeEnum constant. To find out whether an attribute is set, AND the Attributes property value with the desired constant:

```
If (Field.Attribute And adFldLong) = _
  adFldLong Then
    {can call the AppendChunk method on
     this field}
End If
```

DefinedSize

This property indicates the defined size of a Field object (the size that appears in the table's definition). You can set a size for only varchar and binary fields.

Name

This property returns or sets the field's name. You must set this property in a custom Recordset and read it in a Recordset, based on a query.

NumericScale

This property indicates the scale of a numeric field (the number of digits to the right of the decimal point).

OriginalValue

This is the value of a field the moment it was read from the database; it doesn't change when you edit the field.

Precision

This property specifies the precision of a field that holds a numeric value (the same property applies to the Parameter object as well). A numeric value's precision is the maximum number of digits used to represent the field's value.

Status

The Status property indicates whether a Field object has been added to the Fields collection, or whether an existing field has changed value. Its value is a FieldStatusEnum constant.

Type

This is the field's (column's) data type, and it can a DataTypeEnum constant.

UnderlyingValue

This is the value of a field in the database. If the user has edited the field, then the UnderlyingValue is different from the Value property. If another user has edited the field in the database, then the underlying value is different from the Value and OriginalValue properties.

Reading a field's UnderlyingValue property is similar to calling the Resync method for a specific field. The UnderlyingValue and OriginalValue properties are used to resolve conflicts in batch updates.

Value

This is the current value of a Field object. This value is different from the UnderlyingValue property if the field has been edited since it was read on the client. The Value is the default property of the Field object and you can omit its name. The following expressions are equivalent:

```
RS.Fields("Name").Value
RS.Fields("Name")
```

Because the Fields property is the default property of the Recordset object, the previous expressions are also equivalent to the following one:

```
RS("Name")
```

Methods

AppendChunk

The AppendChunk method appends data to a large text or binary field. Its only argument is a variant holding the data to be appended to the Field object. The first time you call the AppendChunk method, it overwrites any existing data. Subsequent calls to this method append to the data already written to the field. If you switch to another field, the AppendChunk method assumes that you're done appending data. The next time you call the AppendChunk method on the same field, it will overwrite.

GetChunk

This method returns a large text or binary field, or part of it, via `variable = GetChunk(size)`. The `size` argument is the number of characters or bytes you want to retrieve. In situations where system memory is limited, you can use the GetChunk method to manipulate long values in portions, rather than in their entirety.

The first call to the GetChunk method retrieves data from the beginning of the field. Each successive call of the GetChunk method retrieves data starting from where the previous call left off.

Fields Collection Methods

Append

This method appends a Field object to the Fields collection with the syntax

```
Append fieldname, type _
    [, definedSize, Attributes]
```

where `fieldname` is the field's name and `type` is its data type (a DataTypeEnum constant). The optional argument `definedSize` is used with character and binary fields to denote the maximum length of data that can be stored in the field. `Attributes` is another optional argument (a FieldAttributeEnum constant) that specifies additional field attributes.

Delete

This method deletes a Field object from the Fields collection. The sole argument is the name of the Field object to be deleted, and this cannot be the ordinal position of the object in the Fields collection. This method should be used with custom Recordsets. You can't manipulate the structure of a table by adding or deleting fields in the Fields collection.

Refresh

The Refresh method reads the field definitions in the Fields collection directly from the database.

The Parameter Object

A Parameter object represents a parameter or argument associated with a Command object, based on a parameterized query or stored procedure. To call a stored procedure with input/output parameters, you must create a Parameter object for each of the stored procedure's parameters, and then append it to the Command object's Parameters collection. After you have populated the Parameters collection, you can call the stored procedure with the Command object's Execute method. The members of the Parameter object described in the following section allow you to manipulate the parameters of the stored procedures, set the values of the input parameters, and read the values of the output parameters.

Properties

Attributes

This property sets or returns one or more characteristics of a Parameter object. It is a ParameterAttributesEnum constant, or a combination of two or more constants. To assign a new attribute, you must OR the appropriate constant with the existing attributes:

```
param.Attributes = param.Attributes _
  OR adParamNullable
```

To find out whether an attribute is set, use a statement like the following:

```
If (param.Attributes AND adParamNullable) Then
  . . .
```

Direction

The Direction property represents an input parameter, an output parameter, or both. Its value is a ParameterDirectionEnum constant.

Name

The name of the Parameter object is used to identify the object in the Parameters collection. The Parameter object's Name property need not be the same as the name of the parameter in the stored procedure.

NumericScale

This property determines the numeric scale (the number of digits to the right of the decimal point) of the numeric value stored in the Parameter object.

Precision

This property specifies the precision of a parameter that holds a numeric value (the same property applies to the Field object as well). A numeric value's precision is the maximum number of digits used to represent the parameter's value.

Size

This property indicates the maximum size, in bytes or characters, of a Parameter object (or a Field object). This property must be used with variable-length data types (varchar and binary types). Fixed-length data types have a Size property, but setting it doesn't affect the parameter's actual size.

Type

This property indicates the data type of a Parameter, Field, or Property object; it's a DataEnumType constant.

Value

This property sets or returns the Parameter object's value. You set this value for input parameters before calling a stored procedure through the Command object, and read this value for output parameters to retrieve the values returned by the stored procedure.

Method

CreateParameter

The CreateParameter method creates a new Parameter object with the properties specified in the following syntax:

```
Set parameter = _
  Command.CreateParameter ([name, type, _
  direction, size, value])
```

The new Parameter object must be appended to a Command object's Parameters collection with the Append method. The `name` argument is the parameter's name, `type` is its data type, and `size` is in bytes or characters (the last argument applies to variable-length fields only). The `direction` argument is equivalent to the parameter's Direction property and specifies whether the object is an input or output parameter. The last argument is the parameter's value.

As you can see from the syntax of the method, all arguments are optional. You can create a Parameter object and then set all its properties as follows:

```
Set oParam = CMD.CreateParameter
oParam.Name = "parameter1"
oParam.Type = adTypeInteger
oParam.Direction = adParameterDirectionInput
oParam.Value = 1001
```

Notice that the Size argument need not be set with data types of fixed size. Even if you set the Size property of an integer parameter, this setting will be ignored.

Parameters Collection

The Parameters collection supports three methods for adding and removing Parameter objects to the collection.

AppendChunk

AppendChunk appends a large section of text or binary data of the Value property of a Parameter object. It accepts a single argument, which is the text or the binary data to be appended.

Delete

This method deletes an object from the Parameters collection. Its argument is the name of the object you want to remove from the Parameters collection. You can also specify the parameter's order in the collection with an index value.

Append

The Append method appends a Parameter object to a Parameters collection. (The Fields collection supports the Append method, too, but in this case it appends a Field object to the Fields collection). The Append method accepts a single argument, which is an object variable. It represents a Parameter object that will be appended to the Parameters collection. To append a Parameter object to the Parameters collection of a Command object, create a Parameter object and set its properties, as discussed in the section "The Parameter Object." Then use the following statement to append the `oParam` object to the Parameters collection of the `CMD` object as follows:

```
CMD.Parameters.Append oParam
```

THE ERROR OBJECT

The Error object holds information about an error returned by the OLE DB provider. As such, it contains only data-access errors and provides additional information about an error to your application. The same condition may result in multiple errors, so you must scan the Errors collection of the Connection object to read them all.

Properties

Description

This property is a string with a short description of the error. The Description property is used to display additional information to the user when you can't handle the error from within your code.

HelpFile, HelpContext

These two properties determine the help file and the ContextID within this file, where the user can find additional information about the error. If you set these two properties, the corresponding help file will be opened automatically and the user will be positioned to the entry specified by the HelpContext property.

NativeError

This is an integer value that indicates the provider-specific error code for the current Error object.

Number

This property is a number that uniquely identifies an error. Use this property to find out which error occurred and handle it from within your code.

Source

This property is the name of the object (or application) that generated the error. The Source property is used in applications that make use of many different objects. For an ADO-generated error, for example, this property will be `ADODB.objName`, where objName is the name of the object that caused the error (Recordset, Command, and so on).

SQLState

This property indicates the SQL state for an Error object. This is a five-character string returned by the provider and identifies an error that occurred during the processing of an SQL statement. The error code S1109 means "invalid cursor location," and the error code 07001 means "wrong number of parameters." For a complete list of SQL Server's SQL-State codes, consult SQL Server's Books Online.

Methods

The Error object does not support any methods.

What's Next?

In the next section of the book, you'll delve into some of the more advanced aspects of designing Web applications, such as building your own ASP components and planning a project from start to finish. In the next chapter, you'll take a look at some of the tricks you can do with client-side scripting. You'll learn what it is, when you should use it, and what you should know before you do.

PART IV

ADVANCED ASP AND WEBCLASSES

Chapter 16

Client-Side Scripting

At this point, you've completed the task of learning about ASP itself. The rest of this book is devoted to raising your awareness level of peripheral technologies that can affect the depth and quality of your applications. The first, and probably most important of these, is client-side scripting. Through your server-side ASP scripts you have the ability to write code that executes within the client browser—in other words, you can use code to write code. The code you write can be dynamic—you can write browser-specific code. That's a difficult concept for beginning ASP programmers to master—that client-side code can consist of text generated from server-side code. Nevertheless, in this chapter you'll see how client-side code can improve the effectiveness and efficiency of your ASP applications.

Adapted from *Mastering™ Active Server Pages 3*,
by A. Russell Jones
ISBN 0-7821-2619-7 928 pages $49.99

VBScript vs. JScript/JavaScript/ECMAScript

Unfortunately, different browsers support different types of script. IE is the only browser (that I'm aware of) that supports VBScript, but almost all browsers support JavaScript. Therefore, if you're developing an Internet application, you probably need to write your client-side script in JavaScript. If you're deploying an application to an intranet where all the target users have IE, you can use VBScript.

The browser requirements make the VBScript vs. JavaScript decision for you–if you're going to use client-side script at all, it must be able to run in the target browsers, but again, unfortunately, it's not quite that simple. Not all browsers support all versions of JavaScript, the various versions of JavaScript differ in functionality, and the browsers themselves have different object models. That's equally true for all IE shops. Even if everyone has the same browser version, not everyone may have the same version of the scripting runtime. Therefore, code that runs perfectly well in one browser may not execute in another. You should plan to test extensively if you decide to use client-side script.

On a brighter note, the syntax for client- and server-side script is identical, with the exception that the ASP intrinsic objects aren't available through client-side script. However, you can obtain access to the values of the ASP object variables and properties on the client. I'll show you how to do that in the next section.

In this chapter, I'm going to provide some examples of both JavaScript (JScript) and VBScript, but I'll concentrate more heavily on the VBScript examples. If you're running Netscape, you can run the JavaScript examples without modification, except for those that demonstrate ActiveX functionality, but you'll need to translate the VBScript examples before they'll work. If you're using IE, both types of examples should work properly. I'm personally using IE 5, but all the examples in this chapter will work with IE 4 as well, and all but the DHTML examples will work with IE 3.

Sending Script to the Browser

From an ASP page, you send script to the browser just as if it were HTML. You place client-side script between `<script>` tags. For example:

```
<script language="VBScript">
</script>
```

Between the `<script>` tags, you place functions, subroutines, and global code and definitions. Just as with server-side script, the difference is that code within subroutines and functions executes only when called, whereas global code—script not placed within functions and subroutines—executes immediately after the script engine on the browser compiles it. Listing 16.1 shows an ASP file that writes a client-side script to display two Alert message boxes.

Listing 16.1: Client-Side Script to Display Alerts (`ch16i1.asp`)

```
<%@ Language=VBScript %>
<html>
<head>
</head>
<body>
This script creates two "alert" boxes
that execute on the client using JavaScript.
<script language="JavaScript">
   function showAlert() {
      alert("Hello from showAlert function!");
   }
   alert("Hello world");
   showAlert();
</script>
</body>
</html>
```

Note that there's a difference between `<script>` tags intended for server-side script, such as you've seen in the `global.asa` file, and `<script>` tags for client-side script. The ASP engine assumes you want the script to execute on the client unless you specifically mark it as server-side script using the `runat=server` attribute. You can include both server- and client-side `<script>` tags in the same ASP file, but there's a trick. Listing 16.2 shows an example.

Part iv

Listing 16.2: Combining Server and Client `<script>` Tags (ch16i2.asp)

```
<%@ Language=VBScript %>
<html>
<head>
<script language="VBScript" runat="server">
Sub writeShowAlertScript()
  With Response
    .Write "<scr" & _
      "ipt language='JavaScript'>" & vbCrLf
    .Write "function showAlert() {" & vbCrLf
    .Write "alert('Hello" & _
      " from showAlert function!');" & _
       vbCrLf
    .Write "}" & vbCrLf
    .Write "alert('Hello world');" & vbCrLf
    .Write "showAlert();" & vbCrLf
    .Write "</scr" & "ipt>"
  End With
End Sub
</script>
</head>
<body>
The script that shows the alert boxes on
the client were written dynamically with ASP.
<% call writeShowAlertScript()%>
</body>
</html>
```

Notice that the server script writes the client script. However, it breaks the client-side `<script>` tag itself into separate parts. If you don't do this, the ASP engine tries to compile the `<script>` tag meant for the client and generates a Nested Script Block error. To see this in action, change the first and last lines after the `With Response` statement to recombine the word `script` into a single word:

```
With Response
  .Write "<script" & _
    language='JavaScript'>" & vbCrLf
  .Write "function showAlert() {" & vbCrLf
  .Write "alert('Hello" & _
    from showAlert function!');" & _
```

```
    vbCrLf
  .Write "}" & vbCrLf
  .Write "alert('Hello world');" & vbCrLf
  .Write "showAlert();" & vbCrLf
  .Write "</script>" & vbCrLf
End With
```

Execute the file by requesting it from the browser. You should see the Nested Script Block error.

After each line of the client-side script, the server script writes a carriage return/linefeed character combination (the constant `vbCrLf`, also called the end-of-line character, although it's two characters in length—ASCII characters 13 and 10). End-of-line characters are optional with JavaScript, which uses the semicolon to delimit the ends of code lines, but they're required for VBScript, which relies on the end-of-line character to delimit the code lines. I usually write them for both languages, because in the browser, the end-of-line character makes the code easier to read for debugging purposes.

You can use script to pass information from the server to the client. One of the most common ASP questions is how a client-side page can gain access to the value of `Session` and `Application` variables. You do this by dynamically writing script to the browser. For example, Listing 16.3 shows how to assign the `Session.SessionID` variable to client-side script.

Listing 16.3: Transferring Server-Side Variables to Client-Side Scripts (`ch16i3.asp`)

```
<%@ Language=VBScript %>
<html>
<head>
<script language="VBScript">
  Dim SessionID
  MsgBox "Your SessionID is:" & _
    <%=Session.SessionID%>", _
    vbOK,"SessionID"
</script>
</head>
<body>
How to transfer ASP variable values
to a client script.
</body>
</html>
```

On the server, the ASP engine writes the string value of the code `<%=Session.SessionID%>` as part of the client-side script, which it sends to the client. The scripting engine running on the browser parses and compiles the script, then displays the message box. VBScript message boxes are more flexible than JavaScript alerts because you can control the number and content of buttons and display a title, whereas JavaScript alerts have no programmable title or button control capabilities. In addition, VBScript's `MsgBox` function returns which button the user clicked, which can be extremely useful.

You can use client-side script to force the browser to request other pages or to submit forms. For example, the Browser Capabilities component gives you the ability to determine which browser a client is using, and which scripting engine the browser supports, but doesn't provide the screen resolution. You can use a client-side script to obtain and send the screen resolution to your ASP program. Listing 16.4 uses the VBScript Screen object to determine the screen resolution width and height, then directs the browser back to the originating ASP page with the information stored in the `QueryString`.

Listing 16.4: Obtaining the Screen Resolution of the Client Computer (`ch16i4.asp`)

```
<%@ Language=VBScript %>
<% option explicit %>
<%
Dim screenWidth
Dim screenHeight
If Request.QueryString("ScreenWidth") = "" Then
  %>
  <script language="VBScript">
    Dim screenWidth
    Dim screenHeight
    screenWidth = Screen.Width
    screenHeight = Screen.Height
    document.location.href = _
      "ch16i4.asp?ScreenWidth=" & _
      screenWidth & "&ScreenHeight=" & _
      screenHeight
  </script>
  <%
Else
  screenWidth = _
```

```
        Request.QueryString("ScreenWidth")
    screenHeight = _
        Request.QueryString("ScreenHeight")
    %>
    <html>
    <head>
    </head>
    <body>
    Your screen resolution is <%=ScreenWidth%>
    x <%=ScreenHeight%>
    </body>
    </html>
    <%
End If
%>
```

The script first tests to see if the `Request.QueryString("ScreenWidth")` variable has a value. If not, it writes a client-side script to obtain the screen dimensions. The last line in the script sets the `document.location.href` property. The `document` is the current browser document. The `location` is a collection of properties containing information about the browser's location. The `href` property, like the equivalent HTML `href` attribute for <a> anchor tags, directs the browser to request a page. For example:

```
document.location.href = _
  "ch16i4.asp?ScreenWidth=" _
& screenWidth & "&ScreenHeight=" & screenHeight
```

The rest of the line concatenates the page request with the screen width and height that the script obtained from the Screen object to create a URL. After concatenation, the URL looks like this:

```
ch16i4.asp?ScreenWidth=800&ScreenHeight=600
```

When the browser submits the request to the server, the ASP engine fills the `QueryString` collection with the parameters appended to the URL—in this case, the `ScreenWidth=800` and `ScreenHeight=600` parameters. Because the variables now have a value, the `Else` portion of the ASP script executes, displaying the resolution in the browser window.

At this point, it should become obvious to you that there's another object model you need to learn if you want to work effectively with the objects exposed by the browser. The W3C Document Object Model (DOM) specification describes how browsers should expose the objects they contain. While no current browser completely meets the W3C DOM specifications, IE is far closer than Netscape and other browsers. IE's implementation of the DOM, and most recently its ability to use XML, have made it the most popular browser for development. I'll show you more about the DOM throughout this chapter.

You should begin thinking of all HTML as describing objects that have properties and methods rather than as tags with attributes, because the DOM describes all HTML tags as objects. For example, a <p> paragraph tag has properties describing its position, width, and height. It has border and background properties, and contains both HTML (all the markup between the <p> and </p> tags) and text (all the text between the <p> and </p> tags not inside angle brackets).

The Document Object Model

The Document Object Model (DOM) contains two central rules: all the tags in an HTML document must be accessible as objects and it must be possible to retrieve the HTML source from which those objects originate. As you can see, that means you should be able to use the DOM to obtain a reference to any object on an HTML page, change its properties, and call its methods (assuming it has any). You should also be able to delete DOM objects and create new DOM objects, thus dynamically changing the collection of objects on the page. These capabilities are at the heart of Dynamic HTML (DHTML). If you can change the properties of objects on the page, delete objects, and add new objects, then you can change the look and action of the page dynamically, with script.

As the browser HTML-parsing engine reads the incoming page, it creates objects and collections of objects. The top-level objects in this model are the navigator object (browser), the window object, the `frames` collection, and the document object. A window contains a document. Even if the browser hasn't fulfilled an HTML request, the window still contains a document—albeit one with no contents. A window may contain several child windows, each of which corresponds to a frame. The window object bundles the child windows together in a `frames` collection. Each frame is itself a window, with its own `frames` collection and its own document.

In this chapter, you'll work primarily with the document object, which contains the HTML on the page. As you may know, some tags are `block` elements, which can contain other tags. For example, a `<div>` tag may contain font, paragraph, and other formatting tags, as well as other `<div>` tags. These tags contained inside a `<block>` tag translate to collections in object parlance. Therefore, `block` elements all have an `all` property and a `children` property. The difference is that `all` refers to all contained tags, even tags where the end tag overlaps the containing tag's end tag. For example:

```
<p><b>This is bold text</p></b>
```

The `all` collection would include the first <b> tag. The `children` collection contains only tags entirely contained between the start and end tag of the `block` element. The `children` collection, in the preceding example, would not contain the <b> tag because it's an overlapped tag (and bad HTML practice, I should add).

Each tag has attributes, which translate to properties, although not always directly. For example, the `<p align="center">` tag has one attribute. The difference between the attributes of an HTML element and the properties of a DOM object are that the DOM object always has all its properties, even if they aren't explicitly set. Attributes that set visible characteristics, such as `align`, `color`, `size`, `visibility`, etc. are subsumed under the `style` property for each object. The `style` property itself is a character string containing the `style` attribute. An example that translates directly is the `bgcolor` attribute of a <body> tag. The body DOM object has a `bgColor` property whose value is the same type of value–a hex color string or named color–as the <body> tag itself.

As you work with the DOM, you'll begin to memorize the properties and capabilities of each object. Because they're generally similar, you'll find that your HTML experience translates easily into the DOM objects and properties.

Accessing the DOM from Script

To manipulate the DOM, you need to be able to reference the various element types. Because there may be many tags of the same type on a page, you need a way to identify the specific tag you want to reference. You can reference a tag by name, which is a translation from the name attribute in HTML 3.2, or you can reference it by ID. All DOM objects have an ID. You can create a specific ID by writing it into the HTML, but if an element doesn't contain an explicit ID, you may not be able to differentiate it from similar elements.

You obtain a reference to the document object automatically when you refer to the document object. For example, the following script changes the background color of the page using the VBScript `InputBox` function. The `InputBox` function displays a dialog at a specified location containing a prompt, a title, and a text field, and returns a user's input. The last two arguments to the `InputBox` function below contain the x and y positions for the upper-left corner of the dialog. Notice that you specify the location in *twips* (a twip equals 1/1440 in.), not pixels. The script assigns the user's input to the `document.bgColor` property. In this example, the default value for the `InputBox` is the current background color of the document. Listing 16.5 contains the code.

Listing 16.5: Using the `document` Object (`ch16i5.asp`)

```
<%@ Language=VBScript %>
<html>
<head>
</head>
<body bgcolor="lightblue">
</body>
</html>
<script language="VBScript">
  dim s
  s = Inputbox("Enter the background" & _
    color for the " & _
    "document.","Background Color", _
    document.bgColor,3000,2000)
  document.bgColor = s
</script>
```

When you run this script, you may enter either a hex-formatted color number, like `#ffffff`, or a named color, such as `red`. You'll see the background color of the document change instantly.

NOTE

It's important to understand that changes you make to the document's contents with script are not reflected in the background HTML for the document.

After changing the background color, if you right-click and select View Source from the context menu, you won't see the color value you entered in the <body> tag of the HTML. You'll see the original color value.

You can obtain references to child elements of the document using the `document.all("ID/name")` or you can omit the parentheses and quotes and use `document.all.ID`, where `ID` is the value of the `ID` attribute for the element you want to reference. For example, Listing 16.6 shows how to change the text of a paragraph.

Listing 16.6: Changing Paragraph Contents with Script (ch16i6.asp)

```
<%@ Language=VBScript %>
<html>
<head>
</head>
<body bgcolor="lightblue">
<p id="p1">This is a paragraph tag.</p>
</body>
</html>
<script language="VBScript">
   Dim el
   Set el = document.all("p1")
   el.innertext = "The text of this" & _
      paragraph was changed via script"
</script>
```

The paragraph tag has an ID of `p1`. The code inside the `<script>` tag sets a reference to the paragraph element using the following code:

```
Set el = document.all("p1")
```

Now, the `el` variable refers to the paragraph. Next it changes the `innerText` property of the paragraph. When the property changes, IE instantly updates the text on-screen so it reflects the new property value. Until IE 4, such client-side content changes were limited to the contents of input controls, but with DHTML, you can control the content and appearance of every element on the screen.

You can scroll the text across the screen by using absolute positioning. For example, Listing 16.7 extends the previous script by changing the `left` position attribute of the paragraph element's `style` property. To control the speed, the script uses a window method called `setTimeOut`. The `setTimeout` method accepts three arguments: the name of a function or subroutine, a time interval specified in milliseconds (one-thousandths of a second), and an optional language argument. You can use the language argument to call a JScript function from a `window.SetTimeout` method called from VBScript, or vice versa. When the specified interval has elapsed, the scripting engine calls the routine specified in the first argument.

Listing 16.7: Moving Objects On-Screen (ch16i7.asp)

```
<%@ Language=VBScript %>
```

```
<html>
<head>
</head>
<body bgcolor="lightblue">
<p id="p1"
  style="position: absolute; left: 640">
This text will move from right to left
across the screen.</p>
</body>
</html>
<script language="VBScript">
  Call window.setTimeout("moveText()", 50)
  Function moveText()
    Dim pos
    Set el = document.All("p1")
    pos = el.Style.Left
    If Right(pos, 2) = "px" Then
      pos = Left(pos, Len(pos) - 2)
    End If
    el.Style.Left = pos - 10
    If CLng(pos) >= -300 Then
      Call window.setTimeout("moveText()", 50)
    End If
  End Function
</script>
```

A proposed W3C specification called HTML+TIME, and an existing specification called SMIL, both address the problems of coordinating multiple simultaneous actions for on-screen elements. For example, if you wanted to coordinate the movement of a cartoon character's mouth with an audio clip, and at the same time coordinate the wind moving through computer-generated trees, you would have a difficult time doing it with timed scripts. Both the SMIL and HTML+TIME specifications provide a syntax to perform complex positioning and coordination actions.

If all you could do with client-side script were to change colors and text in the browser, it wouldn't be a subject for this book, but client-side script can do much more than that from an application perspective. You can use script to pre-validate user input, thus saving a round trip to the server; and you can use script to move server-side processing to the client, effectively partitioning your application. I'll show you how to validate user input and process data on the client in this chapter; and you'll see an example of partitioning in Chapter 19.

Client-Side Form Validation

One of the most useful tasks for client-side script is form validation. When a person fills out a form on the browser, there's little point in submitting all the information over the network if the data is incomplete or invalid. You can save server and network resources by validating the data on the client before sending the form data to the server for processing.

You use the DOM to gain script access to the contents of form input controls using the same syntax as for HTML elements. For example:

```
set myVar = document.all("controlName")
```

Suppose a user must enter a date. You provide an input text control and some directions, but you can't rely on the user to enter either a properly formatted date, a valid date, or, for that matter, any date at all before submitting the form. Therefore, you need to check the data. You've already seen how to validate data on the server, but you can save the round trip, improve your user interface, and make your users happier all at the same time by validating the data on the client. Listing 16.8 illustrates this example.

Listing 16.8: Client-Side Validation Example (ch16i8.asp)

```
<%@ Language=VBScript %>
<%
If request.Form("txtDate") <> "" Then
  response.write "You entered the" & _
    " valid date " & _
    request.Form("txtDate") & "."
  response.end
End If
%>

<html>
<head>
<script language="VBScript">
  Dim errMsg
  Dim submitVal
  Function frmDate_onSubmit()
    frmDate_onSubmit = doSubmit()
  End Function
  Function setErrorMsg(s)
    errMsg = s
```

```
      Call window.setTimeout("showErrorMsg", 100)
    End Function
    Function clearErrorMsg()
      errMsg = ""
      document.All("errMsg").innerText = _
        "Please re-enter the date in" & _
        " the form 'mm/dd/yyyy'."
    End Function
    Function showErrorMsg()
      document.All("errMsg").innerText = errMsg
      Call window.setTimeout _
        ("clearErrorMsg", 2000)
    End Function
    Function doSubmit()
      Dim dateVal
      Dim aDate
      Dim el
      Dim parts
      dateVal = document.All("txtDate").Value
      On Error Resume Next
      aDate = CDate(dateVal)
      If Err.Number <> 0 Then
         Call setErrorMsg(Err.Description)
         Call setErrorMsg _
           ("That doesn't appear to be " & _
           "a valid date.")
         doSubmit = False
         Exit Function
      ElseIf InStr(1, dateVal, "/", _
        vbBinaryCompare) = 0 Then
        Call setErrorMsg _
         ("You entered a date in the" & _
         " incorrect format. Use the" & _
         " format 'mm/dd/yyyy'.")
         doSubmit = False
         Exit Function
      End If
      parts = Split(dateVal, "/")
      If UBound(parts) < 2 Then
        Call setErrorMessage _
          ("You must enter a month, a " & _
          "day, and a year.")
```

```
        doSubmit = False
        Exit Function
      ElseIf (CLng(parts(0)) <> _
        CLng(Month(dateVal))) _
        Or CLng(parts(1)) <> _
        CLng(Day(dateVal)) _
        Or CLng(parts(2)) <> _
        CLng(Year(dateVal)) Then
        Call setErrorMsg _
          ("You entered an invalid date." & _
          "Use the format 'mm/dd/yyyy'.")
        doSubmit = False
        Exit Function
      End If
      document.frmDate.submit
      doSubmit = True
    End Function
  </script>
  </head>
  <body>
  <form name="frmDate" method="post">
  <div id="errMsg" style="color: red"></div><br>
  Enter a date in the form "mm/dd/yyyy"
  <input id="txtDate" type="text"
    name="txtDate" maxLength="10">
  </input> 
  <input type="button" value="Submit"
    onClick="doSubmit()">
  </form>
  </body>
  </html>
```

The data validation code aside, the script contains a few interesting points I haven't discussed yet. First, there are three ways to trap events in IE. The first way is to place the name of a script routine inside a tag as the value of an attribute whose name is the name of the event. For example:

```
<input type="button" name="btnSave"
  value="Save"
onClick="doClick()">
```

When the named event occurs—following the example, when the user clicks the Save button—IE calls the named routine.

The second method works like Visual Basic event procedures. You write a procedure named using the syntax controlName_eventName. For example:

```
<script language="VBScript">
Sub btnSave_onClick()
  ' code for event
End Sub
</script>
```

Using this method, IE automatically executes the routine when the user clicks the button.

The third method also works automatically. You provide the scripting language, the name of the object, and the event for which you want to write code. For example:

```
<script language="VBScript" for="btnSave"
  event="onclick">
  ' your code here
</script>
```

The first and third methods are generic because they work with any scripting language. All methods for executing a script when an event occurs are called *binding script to events*, or (usually) just *binding events*. In this page, to validate the input before the browser sends the data, you need to bind two events—the form submission event and the button click event.

You may notice that the script has two routines that deal with form submission—the automatically bound script frmDate_onSubmit and the doSubmit function called by the button, which validates the date. Interestingly, the frmDate_onSubmit also calls the doSubmit function. When I wrote this script, I originally bound just the button click event, reasoning that I would then submit the form through code. That worked fine as long as the user clicked the button. But if the user pressed Enter on the keyboard, the doSubmit event never fired—but the form still submitted its data to the server! It turns out that in IE, a form with a single input control submits automatically if you press the Enter key on the keyboard. The only solution to this feature is to bind the onSubmit event. Since the button and automatic form submission using the Enter key both call the doSubmit function, you can intercept the form submission, validate the data, and either submit the form or cancel submission and display an error message.

The only reason you can bind form submission at all is that form submission is a function; therefore the form object expects a return value. By returning the value `False` you can prevent the form from submitting. If you omit the return value or return any other value, the form submits normally.

USING ACTIVEX CONTROLS

Sometimes, even with DHTML, the capabilities available through HTML and a browser just aren't enough. For example, suppose you want to use a slider control to let a user control audio volume. You could create your own slider using lines or images and a great deal of code, but in doing so you would have recreated functionality that's already available on every Windows computer in the form of ActiveX controls. Recognizing this problem, Microsoft did two things to IE that made it the premier browser for development. First, IE is an ActiveX host. That means you can *site* (place) ActiveX controls within the browser and control them via script. Second, Microsoft made IE itself an ActiveX control. That means you can site IE within a window and instantly gain access to a custom browser for your own programs. In this section, you'll see how to use ActiveX controls inside IE.

WARNING

The examples in this section work only in Internet Explorer!

You've already seen how to instantiate ActiveX components on the server. The client-side analogues of ActiveX components are ActiveX objects or ActiveX controls. All three–ActiveX components, objects, and controls–are COM objects. The only difference is that ActiveX controls are usually visible so people can interact with them directly, whereas components and objects are usually invisible. To instantiate ActiveX controls within the browser, you use an `<object>` syntax that's similar to the syntax you've already used to create Application- and Session-scope components in the `global.asa` file. For example:

```
<object
  classid=
  "clsid:25bdf09d-ec8b-11cf-bd97-00aa00575603"
  codebase=
  "/Controls/MyContrl.cab#version=1,0,0,0"
```

Part iv

```
  id=myControl left: 40px; top: 10px;
  width: 385px; height: 42px; >
  <param name="property1">
  <param name="property1">
  <param name="property1">
</object>
```

The <object> tag tells the browser to:

1. Look up the classid in the registry.
2. Find the registry child key called InProcServer32, which contains the name of the OCX or DLL file that contains the code for the control.
3. If the control is not registered on the local computer, or if the version installed on the local computer is lower than the version specified in the optional codebase attribute, the browser can download and install the control from the URL specified in the codebase attribute.
4. The browser instantiates the control, sites it, resizes it, and finally displays the control.
5. The browser doesn't use the optional <param> tags—the control itself obtains the property values specified in the <param> tags and uses them to initialize its own properties.

The advantages of using ActiveX controls are:

- You gain instant access to a wide range of pre-built and tested code.
- You can perform tasks with ActiveX controls that are difficult or impossible through any other technology.

The disadvantages are:

- Only IE browsers can use ActiveX technology natively. Netscape users can obtain a third-party plug-in that extends Netscape so it can use ActiveX controls, with mixed results.
- ActiveX controls and objects have full access to the local machine, therefore they are a security risk. To help alleviate this problem, Microsoft introduced code signing, which lets you know the code producer. Code signing uses a third-party to provide a code authentication certificate stating that the code actually comes from the code producer. When the browser downloads an

unknown ActiveX control, the browser warns you that the page is trying to download new code. If the code is signed, you can follow a URL to the authentication site to read about and verify the code. You can then choose to continue or to ignore the download.

Sending ActiveX Objects to the Client

To instantiate an ActiveX control on the client, you simply include the <object> tag in the response. For example, the following ASP script creates a client-side slider control:

```
<%@ Language=VBScript %>
<html>
<head>
</head>
<body bgColor=#c0c0c0>
<object align=right
  classid=
  "clsid:373FF7F0-EB8B-11CD-8820-08002B2F4F5A"
  height=42 id=Slider style="COLOR: #c1c1cd;
  height: 42px; left: 40px; top: 10px;
  width: 385px; position: absolute;"
  width=385 valign="top">
  <param name="Enabled" value="1">
  <param name="Orientation" value="0">
  <param name="LargeChange" value="10">
  <param name="SmallChange" value="1">
  <param name="Min" value="0">
  <param name="Max" value="100">
  <param name="TickStyle" value="0">
  <param name="TickFrequency" value="10">
  <param name="Value" value="50">
</object>
</body>
</html>
```

The browser uses the `classid` attribute of the `<object>` tag to find and instantiate the slider object (part of the Windows Common Controls contained in the `mscomctl.ocx` file) on the client. You should note that the previous example does not include the optional `codebase` attribute. Because the browser won't know where to obtain the control, if it's not already registered on the client, the browser won't be able to create the control and errors will occur.

Accessing ActiveX Objects from Client-Side VBScript

Sending ActiveX controls to the browser would be of little use if you couldn't access their properties and respond to their events, but you can bind script to ActiveX control events in the same way you bind code to HTML elements. For example, Listing 16.9 instantiates the same slider control as the preceding example, but then binds two events to display the value of the control on-screen using DHTML.

Listing 16.9: Communicating with Client-Side ActiveX Controls (ch16i9.asp)

```
<%@ Language=VBScript %>
<html>
<head>
</head>
<body bgColor=#c0c0c0>
<div id="sliderValue" style=
  "position: absolute; top:
  10; left: 10"></div>
<object align=right
  classid=
  "clsid:373FF7F0-EB8B-11CD-8820-08002B2F4F5A"
  height=42 id=Slider style="COLOR: #c1c1cd;
  height: 42px; left: 40px; top: 10px;
  width: 385px; position: absolute;"
  width=385 valign="top">
  <param name="Enabled" value="1">
  <param name="Orientation" value="0">
  <param name="LargeChange" value="10">
  <param name="SmallChange" value="1">
  <param name="Min" value="0">
  <param name="Max" value="100">
```

```
   <param name="TickStyle" value="0">
   <param name="TickFrequency" value="10">
   <param name="Value" value="50">
</object>
<SCRIPT LANGUAGE=VBScript>
<!-
   dim slider
   sub document_onReadyStateChange()
     if document.readyState = "complete" then
       set slider = document.all("slider")
       document.all("sliderValue"). _
         innerText = slider.value
     end if
   end sub
   sub slider_Change()
     document.all("sliderValue").innerText = _
       slider.Value
   end sub
   sub slider_Scroll()
     document.all("sliderValue").innerText = _
       slider.Value
   end sub
//->
</script>
</body>
</html>
```

The script creates a global `slider` variable. The salient points in this script are that it binds to the document object and uses the `onReadyStateChange` event to test whether the document is complete. When the document is complete, the `onReadyStateChange` event code sets a reference to the slider object. The point is that if you try to set the reference without testing whether the document is complete, the slider object may not yet have been instantiated, thus causing an error.

The other two routines in the script are bound to the slider `Change` and `Scroll` events. Both of these scripts do exactly the same thing—they change the contents of a `<div>` tag based on the slider's `Value` property. These changes appear immediately, giving the user instant numeric feedback about the exact position of the slider control.

So far, you've seen how to use the `<object>` tag to create controls from the ASP page, but you can also use client-side VBScript directly to create non-visual ActiveX objects.

NOTE

You can create ActiveX controls as well as ActiveX objects without errors, but you can't site them with client-side VBScript code, so unless you need an invisible control for some reason, it won't do you much good.

For example, Listing 16.10 creates a Dictionary object, stores a few hundred items, then displays the dictionary contents in a `<div>` tag. You do, of course, need to ensure that the Microsoft Scripting Runtime (`scrrun32.dll`) is installed and registered on the client computer before trying to create a Dictionary object.

Listing 16.10: Creating Client-Side ActiveX Objects with Script (ch16i10.asp)

```
<%@ Language=VBScript %>
<html>
<head>
</head>
<body>
<script language="VBScript">
  Dim d
  Dim i
  Dim V
  Dim aDiv
  Dim s
  Call window.setTimeout("docComplete", 100)
  Sub docComplete()
    Do While document.readyState <> "complete"
      Call window.setTimeout _
      ("docComplete", 100)
    Loop
    Call showDictionary
  End Sub
  Sub showDictionary()
    Set d = Createobject _
    ("Scripting.Dictionary")
    For i = 1 To 500
      d.Add "Item" & CStr(i), i
    Next
    Set aDiv = document.All("dictionaryDiv")
    For Each V In d.Keys
      s = s & V & "=" & d(V) & "<br>"
```

```
      Next
      Set d = Nothing
      aDiv.innerHTML = s
    End Sub
  </script>
  <div id="dictionaryDiv"></div>
  </body>
  </html>
```

In this script, because the code references a `<div>` tag that appears *after* the script, you must wait until the document has created the `<div>`. This time, the code uses the `window.setTimeout` method to repeatedly test the document `readyState` property rather than binding a routine to the onReadyStateChange event. Which do you think is more efficient?

To end this section, here's a short observation on the relative merits of using the `<object>` tag syntax vs. using the `createObject` function in client-side script. The `<object>` syntax, while awkward and time-consuming, lets you specify the `codebase` from which the client can download the control if it's not already installed. You can use `createObject` only if you're delivering to clients when you know the ActiveX controls and objects have already been installed and registered on the client workstations.

Accessing ActiveX Objects from Client-Side JScript

You don't have to use VBScript to access ActiveX controls and objects—you can use JScript as well. To reference a client-side ActiveX control loaded with an `<object>` tag, you use an almost identical syntax as you do with VBScript. Listing 16.11 shows the slider control example from the previous section, rewritten in JScript.

Listing 16.11: Communicating with Client-Side ActiveX Controls, JScript Version (`ch16i11.asp`)

```
  <%@ Language=VBScript %>
  <html>
  <head>
  </head>
  <body bgColor=#c0c0c0>
  <div id="sliderValue" style="position:
    absolute; top: 10; left: 10"></div>
```

Part iv

```
<object align=right
  classid=
  "clsid:373FF7F0-EB8B-11CD-8820-08002B2F4F5A"
  height=42 id=Slider style="COLOR: #c1c1cd;
  height: 42px; left: 40px; top: 10px;
  width: 385px; position: absolute;"
  width=385 valign="top">
  <param name="Enabled" value="1">
  <param name="Orientation" value="0">
  <param name="LargeChange" value="10">
  <param name="SmallChange" value="1">
  <param name="Min" value="0">
  <param name="Max" value="100">
  <param name="TickStyle" value="0">
  <param name="TickFrequency" value="10">
  <param name="Value" value="50">
</object>
<script language="JScript" for="document"
  event="onreadystatechange">
  if (document.readyState == "complete")
    document.all("sliderValue").innerText =
      Slider.value;
</script>
<SCRIPT LANGUAGE=JScript FOR="Slider"
  defer EVENT="Change">
  document.all("sliderValue").innerText =
    Slider.value;
</script>
<SCRIPT LANGUAGE=JScript FOR="Slider"
  defer EVENT="Scroll">
  document.all("sliderValue").innerText =
    Slider.value;
</script>
</BODY>
</HTML>
```

Other than the scripting language used for the client-side script, there's no functional difference between Listing 16.11 and Listing 16.9—both show the value of the slider whether you change it by clicking or dragging the thumb.

JScript access to client-side ActiveX objects, like the `Scripting.Dictionary`, is slightly different. You don't have a `createObject` method as in VBScript; instead, you use the JScript `ActiveXObject` object to instantiate and create references to COM objects. Listing 16.12 shows the JScript equivalent of Listing 16.10—both create a Dictionary object, add 500 items, then display the key and item values in a <div> tag.

Listing 16.12: Accessing ActiveX Objects with JScript (ch16i12.asp)

```
<%@ Language=VBScript %>
<html>
<head>
</head>
<body>
<script language="JScript">
  var d, i, V, aDiv, s="";
  window.setTimeout("docComplete();",100);
  function docComplete() {
    while (document.readyState != "complete") {
      window.setTimeout("docComplete",100);
    }
    showDictionary();
  }
  function showDictionary() {
    var keys;
    var items;
    d = new
      ActiveXObject("Scripting.Dictionary");
    for (i=1; i <= 500; i++) {
      d.Add("Item" + i, i);
    }
    aDiv = document.all("dictionaryDiv");
    keys = new VBArray(d.Keys());
    keys = keys.toArray();
    for (i=0; i < keys.length; i++) {
      s = s + keys[i] + "=" +
        d.item(keys[i]) + "<br>";
    }
    aDiv.innerHTML = s;
    return("");
  }
</script>
<div id="dictionaryDiv"></div>
</body>
</html>
```

I've written this script specifically to show you a few differences. Microsoft has extended its version of JScript to be able to access ActiveX objects—the script will not work in any browser other than IE because the scripting language is IE-specific, even if it does look like JavaScript.

The script creates the variable d to hold the Dictionary reference. In JScript, you create the reference as follows:

```
d = new ActiveXObject("Scripting.Dictionary");
```

You add objects to the Dictionary in a manner similar to VBScript (but don't forget the parentheses—they're required in JScript). For example:

```
d.Add("Item" + i, i);
```

The major difference is how you gain access to the Dictionary's collections. JScript doesn't have a direct way of accessing ActiveX arrays or collections, such as the keys collection. Instead, you must create a VBArray object and assign it to a variable. For example:

```
keys = new VBArray(d.Keys());
```

After you have a reference to the VBArray object, you can convert it into a JScript array using the toArray function. For example:

```
keys = keys.toArray();
```

After conversion, you use the array normally. The remainder of the script concatenates a string (the variable s) and sets the innerHTML property of the <div> to the contents of the string variable, thus displaying all the keys and values contained in the Dictionary object.

Client-Side Data Access

You can use client-side script to handle data processing, thus effectively partitioning your application. The simplest solution is to use the Remote Data Service (RDS) Data Control, because it's almost exactly like a Connection object; it can use a Data Source Name (DSN) or a connection string as the connection source. Using the control is straightforward; you embed it into the response with an <object> tag. For example:

```
<OBJECT CLASSID=
  "clsid:BD96C556-65A3-11D0-983A-00C04FC29E33"
  ID="RDSDC1">
  <PARAM NAME="SQL"
    VALUE="{an SQL Statement"}>
  <PARAM NAME="CONNECT"
```

```
    VALUE="{your connectionstring}">
  <PARAM NAME="SERVER"
    VALUE=http://{yourServer}/>
</OBJECT>
```

NOTE

Replace the values between braces in the preceding example with the appropriate SQL statement, connection string, and server name for your needs.

The <param> tags set the initial properties of the control and include a SQL statement, a connection string, and the name of the `http` server that can supply the data. When the browser creates the object, it contacts the server, which automatically creates an instance of the `RDS.DataFactory` object. The `RDS.DataFactory` object retrieves the data and proxies the resulting record set over `http` (which means it transfers the data to the client). The mechanism by which this happens is beyond the scope of this book, but there are several excellent documents at the MSDN site that explain the process if you are interested. Search for the phrase `RDS.DataFactory` to find the documents.

The next two listings reference the `(local)` database server, which is SQL Server's default name for a database running locally, and the `http://localhost/` domain, which is the Web server's default local name. These may work for you if you're running a Web server and SQL Server on the same machine; otherwise, you should substitute your server and Web domain name when you run the code. Listing 16.13 contains a complete RDS Data Control example.

Listing 16.13: Client-Side Data Access with the RDS Data Control (`ch16i13.asp`)

```
<%@ Language=VBScript %>
<html>
<head>
<title>Retrieving Data With the
RDS.DataFactory Object</title>
</head>
<body>
<div id="students"></div>
<object classid="
  clsid:bd96c556-65a3-11d0-983a-00c04fc29e33"
```

Part iv

```
    id="RDSDC1">
    <param name="SQL" VALUE="SELECT StudentID,
      Grade, LastName, FirstName FROM Students
      ORDER BY Grade, LastName">
    <param name="CONNECT"
      value="Provider=SQLOLEDB.1;
      Persist Security Info=False;User ID=sa;
      Initial Catalog=ClassRecords;
      Data Source=(local)">
    <param name="SERVER" value=http://localhost/>
  </object>
  <script language="VBScript" for="RDSDC1"
    event="onDataSetComplete">
    Dim s
    Dim R
    Dim F
    Set R = RDSDC1.Recordset
    s = "<h2 align='center'>Students List</h2>"
    s = s & "<table border='1' align='center'
      width='100%'>"
    s = s & "<tr>"
    For Each F In R.fields
      s = s & "<td><b>" & F.Name & "</b></td>"
    Next
    s = s & "</tr>"
    While Not R.EOF
      s = s & "<tr>"
      For Each F In R.fields
        s = s & "<td>" & F.Value & "</td>"
      Next
      s = s & "</tr>"
      R.movenext
    Wend
    s = s & "</table>"
    R.Close
    document.All("students").innerHTML = s
  </script>
  </body>
  </html>
```

If you found this example exciting (and I do), then you should be even more excited by the fact that you can bind some DOM objects to the RDS Data Control. For example, you can bind a table by using a datasrc attribute in the <table> tag or by setting the property from script. You can then bind the table columns by setting a datafld attribute in the <td> tags (or by setting the property from script). Listing 16.14 shows an example.

Listing 16.14: Data-Binding Example (ch16i14.asp)

```
<%@ Language=VBScript %>
<html>
<head>
<title>Binding Data With the
  RDS.DataFactory Object</title>
</head>
<body>
<table id=Students DataSrc=#RDSDC1
  width=100% border=1>
<thead align=left>
  <tr>
    <th>StudentID</th>
    <th>Grade</th>
    <th>Last Name</th>
    <th>First Name</th>
  </tr>
</thead>
  <tr>
    <td><div datafld=StudentID></div></td>
    <td><div datafld=Grade></div></td>
    <td><div datafld=LastName></div></td>
    <td><div datafld=FirstName></div></td>
  </tr>
</table>
<object classid=
  "clsid:BD96C556-65A3-11D0-983A-00C04FC29E33"
  id="RDSDC1">
  <param name="SQL" value="select studentid,
    grade, lastname, firstname from students
    order by grade, lastname">
  <param name="CONNECT"
    value="provider=sqloledb.1;
    persist security info=false;user id=sa;
    initial catalog=classrecords;
    data source=(local)">
  <param name="SERVER" value=http://localhost/
    style="display: none">
```

```
</object>
</body>
</html>
```

By binding the table to the RDS Data Control object, you can automatically fill the table with the data. If you want to display one record at a time, you can place the Recordset object exposed by the RDS Data Control under script control and place buttons on the page connected to scripts that use the Move methods of the Recordset object. As the Recordset object moves from one record to another, the values of bound controls will update automatically.

There are some security risks associated with using the RDS Data Control with the server-side RDS.DataFactory. Because the client control must connect to a database, you expose the connection string, username, and password to the client machine. That can make the control unsuitable for use in secure applications because anyone can view the page source in the browser and acquire the username and password. You can improve the security somewhat by using a custom server-side business or data-access object—or an ASP page. The RDS Data Control sends an http request, and the RDS.Data connects to the specified object or page to obtain data rather than connecting directly to a database. That way you can limit the functionality of the connection rather than allowing the client free access to the database. Of course, you can also limit the actions a client can take via the database's internal security.

Table 16.1 shows the elements you can bind to data.

TABLE 16.1: Data-Bindable HTML Elements

Element	Updatable	Renders HTML	Bound Property
a	False	False	href
applet	True	False	property value via PARAM
button	False	True	innerText, innerHTML
div	False	True	innerText, innerHTML
frame	False	False	src
iframe	False	False	src
img	False	False	src
input type=checkbox	True	False	checked

CONTINUED ➞

TABLE 16.1 continued: Data-Bindable HTML Elements

Element	Updatable	Renders HTML	Bound Property
`input type=hidden`	True	False	value
`input type=label`	True	False	value
`input type=password`	True	False	value
`input type=radio`	True	False	checked
`input type=text`	True	False	value
`label`	False	True	innerText, innerHTML
`marquee`	False	True	innerText, innerHTML
`select`	True	False	obj.options (obj.selected Index).text
`span`	False	True	innerText, innerHTML
`textarea`	True	False	value

Sending Java Applets to the Client

Java applets—from the client-side scripting viewpoint—are much like ActiveX controls. Both are executable code and both are downloadable. You embed a reference to the code into an HTML response. ActiveX controls use the `<object>` syntax that you've already seen. Java applets use the `<applet>` syntax that you'll see in this chapter. Both tags have similar syntax. The big differences between the two happen invisibly. Internally, Java applets differ from ActiveX controls in several ways:

- Java applets are language-specific and operating-system neutral—they're written in the Java programming language and run on numerous operating systems, including Unix, Linux, Mac, and Windows systems. ActiveX controls are operating-system specific (for now) and language neutral. They run on Windows, but can be created with C, C++, VB, Delphi, and Java (J++).

- Java applets are relatively safe to download and run. They run in a sandbox, which means they have limited access to the local machine. ActiveX controls have complete access to the local machine, which is both good from a functional point of view, and bad from a security standpoint.
- Java applets require a virtual machine that translates the Java byte code to executable machine instructions as the program runs. ActiveX controls consist of (more or less) standalone code, although you usually need several supporting DLLs to run ActiveX controls created in any one language.

So why would you use one over the other? There isn't any hard-and-fast reason. ActiveX controls are usually faster than Java applets, primarily because they exist in executable form, while applets must be interpreted via the virtual machine. After you've downloaded an ActiveX control once, the control remains on your computer, ready to run almost instantly thereafter. Even after you've downloaded an applet, the virtual machine must load and translate the byte code each time the applet executes, which increases the startup time and is a major contributor to the difference in speed between applets and ActiveX controls.

If you're worried about security, Java applets can help solve your problems. Because they're unable to access most local machine resources, there are very few malicious applets; it's difficult to damage the computer if you can't write data to the disk or alter system files. In contrast, any novice can write an ActiveX control to reformat your hard drive or corrupt your registry files.

Using Java Applets

To download a Java applet to a browser, use an `<applet>` tag. Like the `<object>` tag, the `<applet>` tag specifies an embedded program that may or may not have a visual interface. If it does have a visible interface, the applet will commandeer part of the browser client window for its own display. You can include `width`, `height`, and `alignment` parameters to specify the physical screen space the applet requires.

The `<applet>` tag requires a `code` parameter specifying a Java `class` file. The optional `codebase` parameter specifies a URL from which the browser can obtain the code if it's not already resident on the client computer. For example:

```
<applet code="someApplet.class" codebase= _
```

```
  "http://mySite.com/applets/someApplet/"
  width="400" height="300" align="bottom">
</applet>
```

Like the <object> tag, applets can read initialization values from <param> tags included within the <applet> tag. For example, to initialize user-specific colors for an applet that accepts color names, you might write:

```
<applet code="someApplet.class" codebase= _
  "http://mySite.com/applets/someApplet/"
  width="400" height="300" align="bottom">
<param name=backgroundcolor
  value="blue"></param>
<param name="textcolor" value="white"></param>
</applet>
```

Both the code and codebase parameters accept either absolute or relative URLs. For example, Microsoft includes a sample applet called CoolHeadLines with IIS and the example ExAir site. The CoolHeadLines applet displays a list of headlines by scrolling them up the screen at a specified time interval. Listing 16.15 shows an HTML page that loads the applet with data.

WARNING

The code in listings 16.15 and 16.16 was adapted from the Microsoft Internet Information Server 4.0 online sample ExAir installed with IIS. If you don't have the ExAir sample application, you will receive an error when you click on the scrolling items in the CoolHeadLines applet, but you will still be able to see the headlines scroll.

Listing 16.15: Sample ExAir CoolHeadLines Applet (ch16i15.asp)

```
<html>
<head>
<title>CoolHeadLines</title>
</head>
<body>
<table border=1>
<tr><td>
<applet code="CoolHeadLines.class"
name="CoolHeadLines"
```

```
codeBase="applets"
width=170
height=76>
<PARAM NAME="BackColor" VALUE="255 255 255">
<PARAM NAME="TextColor" VALUE="0 0 0">
<PARAM NAME="HiliteTextColor"
  VALUE="60 179 113">
<PARAM NAME="ScrollDelay" VALUE="2">
<PARAM NAME="MessageDelay" VALUE="4">
<PARAM NAME="URLPrefix"
  VALUE="http://localhost/iissamples/exair">
<PARAM NAME="Text0"
  VALUE="EA Named Airline of the Year">
<PARAM NAME="URL0" VALUE="pr/970129a.asp">
<PARAM NAME="Text1"
  VALUE="We Match Blue Yonder!!!">
<PARAM NAME="URL1" VALUE="pr/970122a.asp">
<PARAM NAME="Text2"
  VALUE="Great Deals for the Holidays">
<PARAM NAME="URL2" VALUE="pr/961212a.asp">
<PARAM NAME="Text3"
  VALUE="Free Flights to Eugene">
<PARAM NAME="URL3" VALUE="pr/970312a.asp">
<PARAM NAME="Text4"
  VALUE="EA Donates $2 Million">
<PARAM NAME="URL4" VALUE="pr/970212a.asp">
<PARAM NAME="Text5"
  VALUE="New Domestic Routes">
<PARAM NAME="URL5" VALUE="pr/970222a.asp">
<PARAM NAME="Text6"
  VALUE="Free Flights to Chicago">
<PARAM NAME="URL6" VALUE="pr/970301a.asp">
<PARAM NAME="NumItems" VALUE="7">
</applet>
</td></tr>
</table>
</body>
</html>
```

Accessing Java Applets from Script

You might think that Java applets must be controlled programmatically from JavaScript, but that's not true. When you load a Java applet into IE,

Microsoft wraps a COM interface around the applet. The public methods and properties of the applet are then available to VBScript or any other Scripting Host-compatible scripting language. For example, the `CoolHeadLines` applet exposes a `MessageDelay` property. In Listing 16.15, the property was initialized (via a `<param>` tag) to 4. The script in Listing 16.16 resizes the applet using a timer, creating an accordion effect.

Listing 16.16: Controlling Applets from VBScript (`ch16i16.asp`)

```
<%@ Language=VBScript %>
<html>
<head>
</head>
<body>
<table border=1>
<tr><td>
<applet code="CoolHeadLines.class"
name="CoolHeadLines"
codeBase="applets"
width=170
height=76>
<PARAM NAME="BackColor" VALUE="255 255 255">
<PARAM NAME="TextColor" VALUE="0 0 0">
<PARAM NAME="HiliteTextColor"
  VALUE="60 179 113">
<PARAM NAME="ScrollDelay" VALUE="0">
<PARAM NAME="MessageDelay" VALUE="1">
<PARAM NAME="URLPrefix"
  VALUE="http://localhost/iissamples/exair">
<PARAM NAME="Text0"
  VALUE="EA Named Airline of the Year">
<PARAM NAME="URL0" VALUE="pr/970129a.asp">
<PARAM NAME="Text1"
  VALUE="We Match Blue Yonder!!!">
<PARAM NAME="URL1" VALUE="pr/970122a.asp">
<PARAM NAME="Text2"
  VALUE="Great Deals for the Holidays">
<PARAM NAME="URL2" VALUE="pr/961212a.asp">
<PARAM NAME="Text3"
  VALUE="Free Flights to Eugene">
<PARAM NAME="URL3" VALUE="pr/970312a.asp">
<PARAM NAME="Text4"
  VALUE="EA Donates $2 Million">
```

```
<PARAM NAME="URL4" VALUE="pr/970212a.asp">
<PARAM NAME="Text5"
  VALUE="New Domestic Routes">
<PARAM NAME="URL5" VALUE="pr/970222a.asp">
<PARAM NAME="Text6"
  VALUE="Free Flights to Chicago">
<PARAM NAME="URL6" VALUE="pr/970301a.asp">
<PARAM NAME="NumItems" VALUE="7">
</applet>
</td></tr>
</table>
<script language="VBScript">
  Dim direction
  direction = 0
  Call window.setTimeout("accordion", 1000)
  Sub accordion()
    Call window.setTimeout("accordion", 1000)
    Dim applet
    Set applet = document.All.Coolheadlines
    If Not direction Then
      applet.Width = applet.Width + 50
    Else
      applet.Width = applet.Width - 50
    End If
    direction = Not direction
  End Sub
</script></body>
</html>
```

You can see from the code that you access applets just as you would any other COM object. You've seen how to leverage your scripting language knowledge by partitioning your application—putting some of the logic on the client. As you grow your DHTML knowledge and improve your client-side scripting abilities, you'll begin to appreciate the power of a browser-based application model.

WHAT'S NEXT?

There are more opportunities to leverage your knowledge. In the next chapter, you'll see how to build your own COM components using Visual Basic.

Chapter 17

Building Your Own Components

In this chapter, you'll see how to build a server-side ActiveX component called `HTMLCalendar`. You'll code and compile the component into a DLL, then use it on a Web page. For the full benefit, you need to create and run the component yourself. Therefore, you'll need Visual Basic version 6 (or version 5 with the latest service pack).

Adapted from *Mastering™ Active Server Pages 3*, by A. Russell Jones

ISBN 0-7821-2619-7 928 pages $49.99

Interacting with ASP Objects

You can write stand-alone components that interact with different languages and environments. For example, you can use the Dictionary object from ASP, VB, C, C++, Delphi, FoxPro, Access, Office, or any other language, program, or environment that supports COM components. The reason the Dictionary object is so accessible is that it doesn't offer any special functionality. For example, it doesn't write HTML, doesn't return pointers to functions, doesn't access databases or use any database objects, and doesn't use the file system.

You can also write components that work very closely with a particular language or environment. The `HTMLCalendar` component belongs to this group. The component interacts with the ASP objects to output HTML and set `Session` values. To use ASP objects within your programs, you need to acquire references to the ASP intrinsic objects.

Referencing ASP Objects

ASP exposes two objects that you can use to obtain references to ASP objects from other COM-aware languages. The first is the ScriptingContext object and the second is the ObjectContext object. The ScriptingContext object is obsolete (although it still works) and you should not use it.

TIP

I'm mentioning the ScriptingContext object only because it is still included in the ASP object model. Microsoft recommends you use the ObjectContext object instead.

You can also gain access to ASP objects by passing them to other components as arguments—exactly as you might pass any other object as an argument.

Using the ScriptingContext Object

ASP raises two events for every page, the `OnStartPage` and `OnEndPage` events. ASP itself does not trap these events—it won't fire an `OnStartPage` or `OnEndPage` event routine in an ASP page (too bad), but you can trap them in an external ActiveX object. To use the ScriptingContext object from VB you must first set a reference to the Microsoft Active

Server Pages Object Library, and create the OnStartPage and OnEndPage event routines. Write the OnStartPage routine to accept a Scripting-Context object as its only argument. For example:

```
Sub OnStartPage(SC as ScriptingContext)
    ' your code here
End Sub
```

You use the ScriptingContext object to gain access to the other intrinsic ASP objects. For example:

```
Dim ASPResponse
Sub OnStartPage(SC as ScriptingContext)
    Set ASPResponse = SC.Response
    ASPResponse.Write "Hello from VB"
End Sub
```

As usual, if you create a variable that references an object, you should set it to Nothing when you no longer need the object reference. That's the purpose of the OnEndPage event:

```
Sub OnEndPage()
    Set ASPResponse = Nothing
End Sub
```

Despite the ease with which you can implement this method, you should no longer use it. When your ASP pages use transactions, this method does not let your components access the ASP object context and participate in the transaction. Use the ObjectContext object or pass references to the ASP objects explicitly, as arguments.

Using the ObjectContext Object

The ObjectContext object is more difficult to use, but works with all ASP pages, including those that are transactional. You must run your components in MTS (or as COM+ applications in Windows 2000) to gain access to the ASP ObjectContext object.

To acquire references to the ASP objects using the ObjectContext object, you add project references to the Microsoft Transaction Server Library (in Windows 2000, the COM+ Services Library), the Microsoft Active Server Pages Object Library, and the Microsoft Active Server Pages ObjectContext object. Next, register your component in a package (or

COM+ application), and set the appropriate security and role(s) for the package or application.

After completing that process, you can reference any other ASP object by using the getObjectContext function, and using the resulting reference to create references to the ASP objects. That sounds more complicated than it is; here's an example:

```
Dim oc as ObjectContext
Dim ASPResponse as Response
Set oc = getObjectContext()
Set ASPResponse = oc("Response")
```

Again, when you're done with the objects, release the references by setting the variables to Nothing. For example:

```
Set oc = Nothing
Set ASPResponse = Nothing
```

The simplest way to acquire the references is to implement the ObjectControl interface and add the code to set the references in the ObjectControl_Activate event procedure. The following example shows how to acquire a reference to the Response object each time MTS activates the component. The variables named oc and Response are module-level variables:

```
' code in component
Private oc as ObjectContext
Private Response as Response

Private Sub ObjectControl_Activate()
  On Error GoTo ErrObjectControl_Activate
  Dim methodname As String
  methodname = Classname & _
    ".ObjectControl_Activate"
  Set oc = GetObjectContext()
  If Not oc Is Nothing Then
    Set Response = oc("Response")
  Else
    Err.Raise 50000, methodname, _
      "Unable to set a" & _
```

```
      "reference to the Response object."
    End If
  ExitObjectControl_Activate:
    Exit Sub
  ErrObjectControl_Activate:
    Err.Raise Err.Number, methodname, _
      Err.Description
    Resume ExitObjectControl_Activate
  End Sub
```

Passing ASP Objects as Arguments

Perhaps the simplest method for gaining references to ASP objects is to have ASP pass the references as arguments. When you pass ASP object references in this manner, your component can use the objects, but cannot participate in transactions. For example:

```
' code in ASP page
Dim myObj
Set myObj = Server.CreateObject _
  ("SomeProject.SomeClass")
' the following method passes references
' to the ASP objects
myObj.setASPReferences _
  (Request, Response, Server, _
  Application, Session)

' code in the myObj component
Private mRequest as Request
Private mResponse as Response
Private mServer as Server
Private mApplication as Application
Private mSession as Session
Public Sub setASPReferences _
  (Request as Variant, _
  Response as Variant, _
```

```
    Server as Variant, _
    Application as Variant, _
    Session as Variant)
    Set mRequest = Request
    Set mResponse = Response
    Set mServer = Server
    Set mApplication = Application
    Set mSession = Session
End Sub
```

Having acquired the ASP object references, you may now use them within the component just as you use them from ASP. For example:

```
mResponse.Write "Hello from myObj!"
```

Remember to release the references before IIS destroys the component when the end of the ASP page completes. In VB, write the release code inside a procedure when you create the reference in the procedure, or in the `Terminate` event when you create the references as module-level variables.

VARIANTS VS. TYPED VARIABLES

In the preceding section, you may have noticed that the code in the `setASPReferences` routine defined all the arguments as Variants even though they were objects. When you're writing components for use with ASP, it's a good idea to accept `Variant` arguments because ASP has no typed variables—every variable in ASP is a `Variant`. If you write your routines to accept typed arguments, the ASP programmer must cast the variable to the correct type in the call, which is awkward. For example, here's a VB function that splits a name into its component parts. The function accepts only typed arguments:

```
' in component
Public Function SplitNames _-
    (aName as String) as Variant
    SplitNames = split(aName, " ")
End Function
```

To call the SplitNames function, an ASP programmer must use the CStr function to cast the Name variable to a String inside the calling code. For example:

```
Dim objSplitter
Dim aName
Dim arrNames
aName = "Ayn Rand"
set objSplitter = Server.CreateObject _
  ("NameSplitter.CNameSplitter")
arrNames = objSplitter.SplitNames(CStr(aName))
```

That might be acceptable if you're the only person using the component, but it's unacceptable—or at least unfriendly—if you're creating components for others to use.

Unfortunately, the corollary to accepting Variant arguments is that you need to test carefully in your component code to ensure that the arguments can be cast to the types you expect. For example, if you're expecting a string, test the subtype of the Variant argument using the VarType function:

```
' in component
Public Function SplitNames _
  (aName as Variant) as Variant
  If varType(aName) <> vbString Then
    Err.Raise 50000, _
    "NameSplitter.CNameSplitter", _
    "Invalid Argument Type—Expected String"
  Else
    SplitNames = split(aName, " ")
  End If
End Function
```

When you write your code this way, an ASP programmer can use your component easily. For example:

```
Dim objSplitter
Dim aName
Dim arrNames
aName = "Ayn Rand"
```

```
set objSplitter = Server.CreateObject _
   ("NameSplitter.CNameSplitter")
arrNames = objSplitter.SplitNames(aName)
```

If by accident the programmer sends an invalid `Variant` type, your function will catch the error and raise an error specifying exactly what the problem is.

Communication between ASP Pages and Components

When you create a component in Visual Basic for use with standard Windows programs, you typically create `Let` and `Get` properties, and, for objects, `Set` methods. People using your component can then set or retrieve these properties individually. That type of interface isn't as useful in an ASP environment for two reasons. First, each method you invoke on a component from ASP takes longer than making the same method call from within Visual Basic because VBScript objects are always late-bound; meaning VBScript uses the `IDispatch` interface rather than the more efficient COM (`Vtable`) interface. But more importantly, each property access takes time—and the one thing you don't have in Web applications is time. Because your goal is to service requests as fast as possible, you don't want to waste precious milliseconds setting properties. Therefore, you should write the components so that each method call accepts the arguments it needs to complete the method.

That's a rather abstract idea, so maybe a little code can help explain it better. Suppose you have an `Order` object, which has several properties: `CustomerID`, `ProductID`, `OrderDate`, `Price`, `Quantity`, `ShipToAddress`, `BillToAddress`, `ShipDate`, `DeliveryDate`, and `Returned`. You might normally create the object, then set its properties. For example:

```
Dim oOrder
Set oOrder = Server.CreateObject _
   ("MyCompany.Order")
With oOrder
   .CustomerID=458392
   .ProductID='T158G32'
   .OrderDate=now()
```

```
    .Price=14.99
    .Quantity=5
    .ShipToAddress="John Tucker," & _
      " 1414 Mebrun Cr., Kansas 01436"
    .BillToAddress="John Tucker," & _
      " 1414 Mebrun Cr., Kansas 01436"
    .DeliveryDate=DateAdd("d", 42, now())
    .Returned=0
    .SaveOrder
End With
```

When your program and the oOrder object are on the same machine, running in VB and executing on the same thread, that method is fine—the code executes extremely fast. However, when your VBScript and the oOrder object are on separate machines running in different threads, and all object accesses occur over the network, you will see severe performance degradation. The solution is to code the oOrder object so you only need to make a single call. For example:

```
Dim oOrder
Set oOrder = Server.CreateObject _
   ("MyCompany.Order")
oOrder.SaveOrder(458392, 'T158G32', _
   now(), 14.99, 5, "John Tucker," & _
   " 1414 Mebrun Cr., Kansas 01436", _
   "John Tucker, 1414 Mebrun Cr.," & _
   " Kansas 01436", _
   DateAdd("d", 42, now()), 0)
```

You might easily see a 100% improvement by using the concepts in the second example.

Let's take this idea one step further. Suppose you now want to keep track of the number of orders by this customer by storing them in memory for future reference, and that both the oOrder object and your page need to know that the customer has made a previous request. You can't store the data in the oOrder object because it has page-scope; it will be destroyed when the current page ends. You can't store the oOrder object itself in a Session variable because that would lock the Session down to a single thread. The answer is to store the properties of the oOrder object in `Session` variables, but not the object itself. Among several other choices, you could write a `getProperties` method for the `oOrder` object that returned the values as a `Variant` array, which you can store in a `Session` variable without the threading penalties imposed by storing the object itself.

The point of this discussion is that you can use `Application` and `Session` variables to communicate between one ASP page and another, between ASP pages and COM objects, and between COM objects and other COM objects.

Building the *HTMLCalendar* Component

The component you'll create displays a calendar in HTML. The calendar highlights the current date, lets people move forward or backward one month at a time, and provides a way for ASP or HTML pages to take a specific action when a user double-clicks any date.

The `HTMLCalendar` component contains only one public method: `showCalendar`. The `showCalendar` method requires a date argument, which it uses to determine which month and year to show. It accepts several other optional arguments controlling the width, height, and colors used for displaying and highlighting the calendar.

To create the component, start Visual Basic. From the New Project dialog, select the ActiveX DLL project type (see Figure 17.1).

VB creates a new project with one public class. Figure 17.2 shows the Project Explorer window after creating the new ActiveX DLL project.

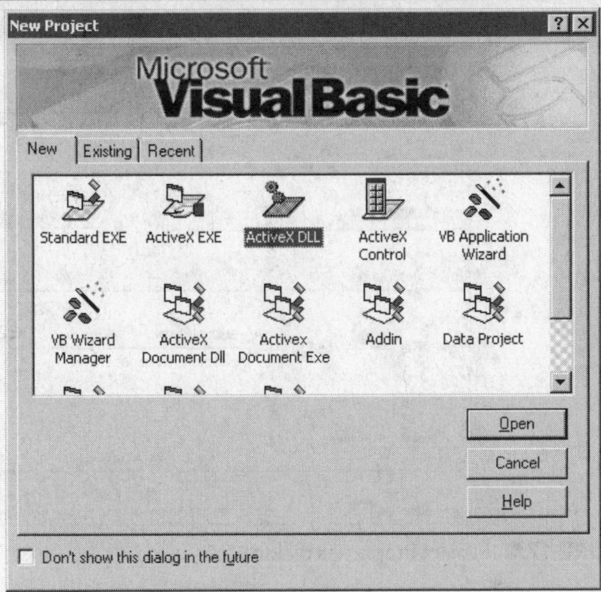

FIGURE 17.1: VB New Project dialog

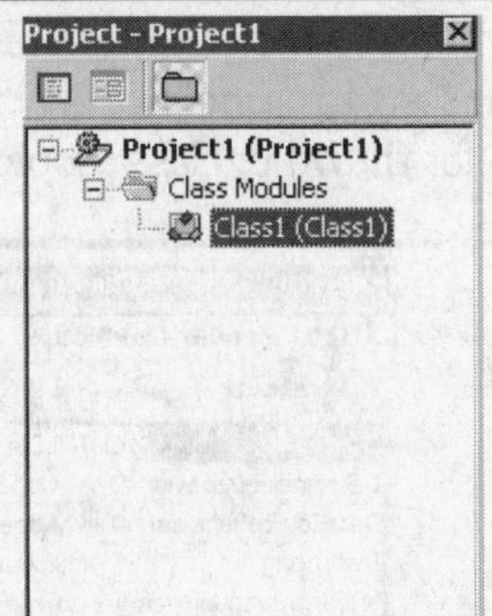

FIGURE 17.2: VB Project Explorer window showing the new ActiveX DLL project

Right-click on the project title (Project1) and select Project1 Properties from the context menu. You'll see the Project Properties dialog. Make sure you select the General tab, then change the name of the project to `HTMLCalendar` and check the Unattended Execution and Retained In Memory options (see Figure 17.3).

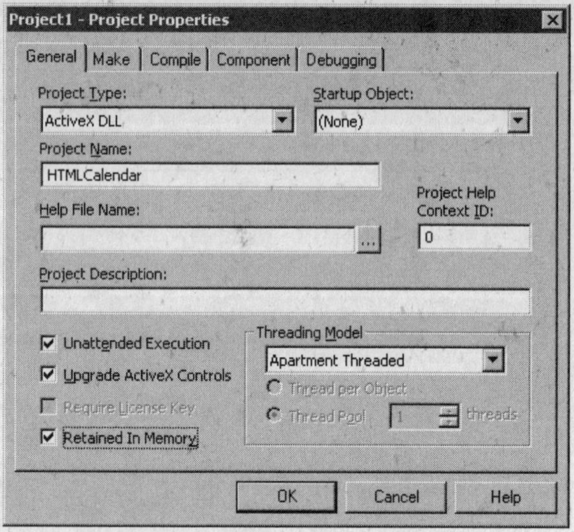

FIGURE 17.3: Project Properties dialog

Click OK to save your changes.

Right-click on the `Class1` class entry in the Project Explorer window and select Properties from the context menu. The class properties appear in the Properties window. Change the name of the class to `CHTMLCalendar`, change the `MTSTransactionMode` property to `No Transactions`, and accept the defaults for the other class properties as shown in Figure 17.4.

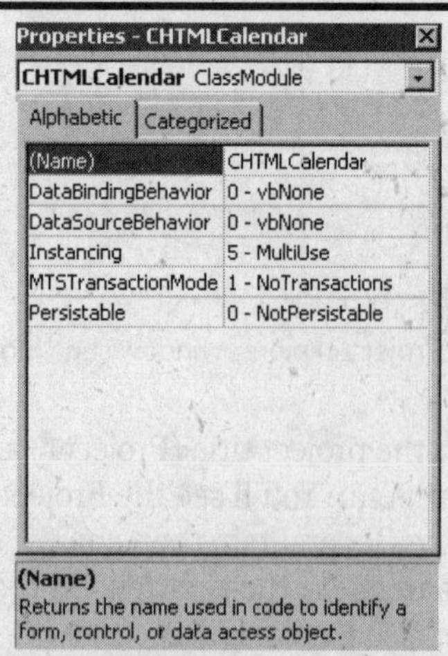

FIGURE 17.4: CHTMLCalendar Class Properties window

Because this object will run in MTS and needs to access the ASP intrinsic objects, you'll need to set some project references. Click the Project menu and select References. VB responds (eventually) by displaying the References dialog. The References dialog contains a list of all registered type libraries on your system, arranged so that selected items appear at the top of the list and other items appear in alphabetical order. If you're running Windows 2000, scroll through the list and select the COM+ Services Type Library entry. If you're running Windows NT 4, select the Microsoft Transaction Server Type Library entry. For both operating systems, select Microsoft Active Server Pages Object Library and Microsoft Active Server Pages ObjectContext Object Library. Click OK to save and close the dialog. If you reopen the dialog, your selections will appear at the top of the list (see Figure 17.5).

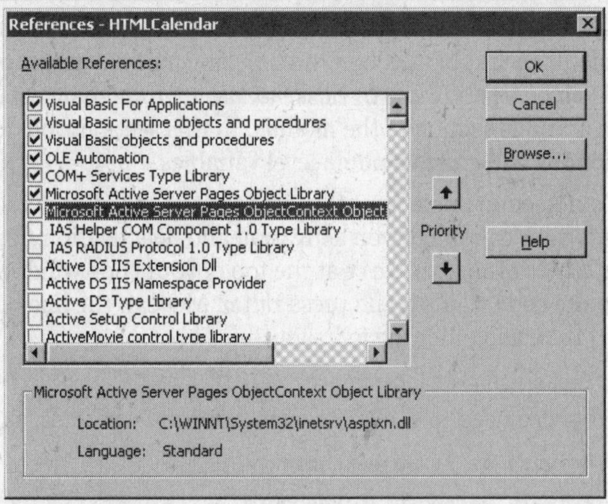

FIGURE 17.5: HTMLCalendar Project References dialog

Save your changes by clicking the File menu, then selecting Save Project1. You'll need to select a directory in which VB will save the project files. After saving the project the first time, the Save Project1 entry changes to the name of the current project followed by a Visual Basic Project (VBP) extension. For example, the filename will become `HTMLCalendar.vbp`.

Double-click on the `CHTMLCalendar` class to open a code window for the `CHTMLCalendar` class module. If you don't see the keywords `Option Explicit` in the first line, enter them at the top of the code window. At this point your code should look like Figure 17.6.

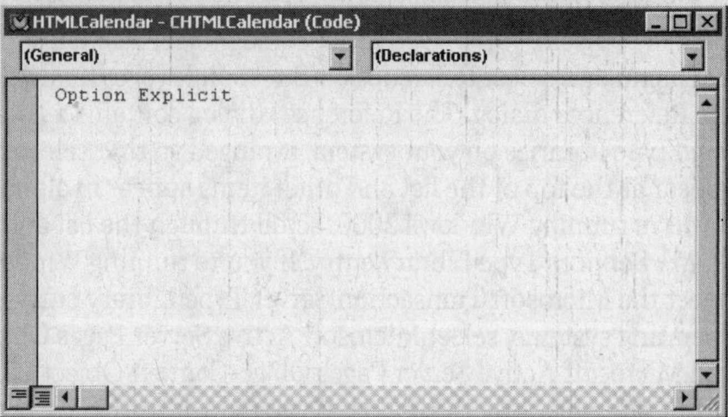

FIGURE 17.6: CHTMLCalendar code module

In VB, a class is a specific type of code module. There are other types of modules, but because there's only one module in this project, the terms *module* and *class* or *class module* are interchangeable. You're in the Declarations section of the module. In this section, you declare external functions and create module-level variables.

You need to implement the `ObjectControl` interface so that MTS will notify your component on activation and deactivation. If you don't see the line `Option Explicit` at the top of your code window, type the line into the code window and press Enter. Move to the line below `Option Explicit` and enter the following line:

```
Implements ObjectControl
```

You also need to declare two module-level variables, as follows:

```
Private oc As ObjectContext
Private Response As Response
```

Enter the preceding two lines immediately after the `Implements` statement, as shown in Figure 17.7.

It's usually a good idea to create a `Classname` property that you can use internally for error reporting. Begin on a new line and enter the following code:

```
Public Property Get Classname() As String
   Classname = "CHTMLCalendar"
End Property
```

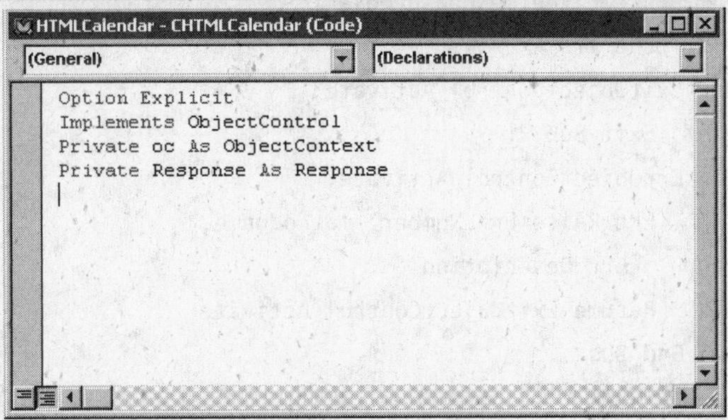

FIGURE 17.7: CHTMLCalendar Declarations section

In each method, create a `methodname` variable and concatenate the `Classname` property with the name of the method. For example:

```
Dim methodname As String
methodname = Classname & ".ShowCalendar"
```

If any error occurs within your method, you can set the `Err.Source` property to the value of the `methodname` variable to get the complete class and method name where the error occurred.

The `ObjectControl` interface exposes three events. These show up in the drop-down list at the top left of the code module. MTS raises an `ObjectControl_Activate` event whenever it activates your object. During the event, you can set the oc `ObjectContext` reference and obtain references to any intrinsic ASP objects your method needs. For example:

```
Private Sub ObjectControl_Activate()
  On Error GoTo ErrObjectControl_Activate
  Dim methodname As String
  methodname = Classname & _
    ".ObjectControl_Activate"
  Set oc = GetObjectContext()
  If Not oc Is Nothing Then
    Set Response = oc("Response")
  Else
    Err.Raise 50000, , _
      "Unable to set a reference to" & _
```

```
        " the Response object."
    End If
ExitObjectControl_Activate:
    Exit Sub
ErrObjectControl_Activate:
    Err.Raise Err.Number, methodname, _
        Err.Description
    Resume ExitObjectControl_Activate
End Sub
```

Similarly, MTS raises an `ObjectControl_Deactivate` event before deactivating your object. During this event, you should release any object references. For example:

```
Private Sub ObjectControl_Deactivate()
    On Error GoTo ErrObjectControl_Deactivate
    Dim methodname As String
    methodname = Classname & _
        ".ObjectControl_Deactivate"
    Set Response = Nothing
    Set oc = Nothing
ExitObjectControl_Deactivate:
    Exit Sub
ErrObjectControl_Deactivate:
    Err.Raise Err.Number, methodname, _
        Err.Description
    Resume ExitObjectControl_Deactivate
End Sub
```

MTS may also call a function asking if your object can be pooled. Visual Basic apartment-threaded objects may not be pooled, so you should respond with a `False` value. For example:

```
Private Function ObjectControl_CanBePooled() _
    As Boolean
    ObjectControl_CanBePooled = False
End Function
```

Paste or copy all three ObjectControl methods into the module. The order in which you enter the methods doesn't matter, but don't try to place them before the Declarations section.

The series of actions you've just gone through are (except for the Response references in the Activate and Deactivate events) completely generic—you can cut and paste the code into any class you plan to run in MTS/COM+.

The CHTMLCalendar component has only one public method—showCalendar. Listing 17.1 contains the entire method.

Listing 17.1: CHTMLCalendar Component—ShowCalendar Method (CHTMLCalendar.cls)

```
Sub ShowCalendar(aDate As Variant, _
  Optional align As Variant = "center", _
  Optional width As Variant = "300", _
  Optional height As Variant = "300", _
  Optional bgcolor As Variant = "lightcyan", _
  Optional cellcolor As Variant = _
    "lightcyan", _
  Optional cellhighlightColor As Variant = _
    "lightgreen", _
  Optional textcolor As Variant = "black", _
  Optional textHighlightColor As Variant = _
    "red")
  On Error Goto ErrShowCalendar
  Dim startDate As Date
  Dim endDate As Date
  Dim dt As Date
  Dim col As Integer
  Dim cellStyle As String
  Dim tableStyle As String
  Dim cellhighlightstyle As String
  Dim methodname As String
  methodname = Classname & ".ShowCalendar"
  If IsDate(aDate) Then
    aDate = CDate(aDate)
  Else
    Err.Raise 50000, , "Invalid Date argument"
  End If
  tableStyle = " style='background-color: " _
    & bgcolor & ";'
```

```
cellStyle = " style='background-color: " & _
  cellcolor & "; color: " & textcolor & ";' "
cellhighlightstyle = " style=" & _
  "'background-color: " & _
  cellhighlightColor & "; color: " & _
  textcolor & ";' "
startDate = CDate(CStr(Month(aDate)) & _
  "/1/" & CStr(Year(aDate)))
endDate = DateAdd("m", 1, startDate) - 1
With Response
  .Write "<form name='frmCalendar'" & _
    " method='post'>"
  .Write "<input type='hidden'" & _
    " name='calDate' " & _
    "value='" & FormatDateTime _
    (aDate, vbShortDate) & _
    "'></input>"
  .Write "<input type='hidden'" & _
    " name='selDate' " & _
    "value='" & FormatDateTime _
    (aDate, vbShortDate) & _
    "'></input>"
  .Write "<input type='hidden'" & _
    " name='startDate' " & _
    "value='" & FormatDateTime _
    (startDate, vbShortDate) & _
    "'></input>"
  .Write "<input type='hidden'" & _
    " name='Action' value=''>"
  .Write "<table align='" & align & _
    "' width='" & width & _
    "' height='" & height & _
    "' border='1' " & _
    "cols='7'" & tableStyle & ">"
  .Write "<tr style='height: 45px;'>" & _
    "<td id='cal_prevmonth'" & _
    " align='center'" & _
    " valign='center'>" & _
    "<img src='larr.gif'></td>" & _
    "<td colspan='5'" & _
    " align='center'><strong><em>" & _
    MonthName(Month(aDate)) & ", " & _
```

```
  Year(aDate) & "</em></strong></td>" & _
  "<td id='cal_nextmonth'" & _
  " align='center' valign='center'>" & _
  "<img src='rarr.gif'></td></tr>"
.Write "<tr>"
For col = 1 To 7
   .Write "<td" & cellStyle & _
   "align='center' " & _
   "valign='center' bgcolor='" & _
   cellcolor & "'><b>" & _
   Left(UCase(WeekdayName(col)), 1) & _
   "</b></tr>"
Next
.Write "</tr><tr>"
For col = 1 To Weekday(startDate) - 1
  .Write "<td" & cellStyle & "> </td>"
Next
For dt = startDate To endDate
  col = Weekday(dt)
  If Int(dt) = Int(aDate) Then
    .Write "<td id='cal_td'" & _
    cellhighlightstyle & _
    " align='center' valign='center'>" & _
    Day(dt) & "</td>"
  Else
  .Write "<td id='cal_td'" & cellStyle & _
    " align='center' valign='center'>" & _
    Day(dt) & "</td>"
  End If
  If col = 7 Then
   .Write "</tr><tr>"
  End If
Next
dt = endDate
Do While col < 7
  dt = DateAdd("d", 1, dt)
  col = Weekday(dt)
  .Write "<td" & cellStyle & "> </td>"
Loop
.Write "</tr></table>" & vbCrLf
.Write "</form>"
.Write vbCrLf
```

```
.Write "<scr" & _
  "ipt language='VBScript' " & _
  "for=cal_td event=onmouseover>" & vbCrLf
.Write Chr(9) & "window.event." & _
  "srcElement.style.color=" & Chr(34) & _
  textHighlightColor & Chr(34) & vbCrLf
.Write "</script>" & vbCrLf
.Write "<scr" & _
  "ipt language='VBScript' " & _
  "for=cal_td event=onmouseout>" & vbCrLf
.Write Chr(9) & "window.event." & _
  "srcElement.style.color=" & Chr(34) & _
  textcolor & Chr(34) & vbCrLf
.Write "</script>" & vbCrLf
.Write "<scr" & _
  "ipt language='VBScript' " & _
  "for=cal_td event=onclick>" & vbCrLf
.Write "dim el" & vbCrLf
.Write "dim daynum" & vbCrLf
.Write Chr(9) & "if " & _
  "window.event.srcElement." & _
  "style.backgroundcolor=" & _
  Chr(34) & cellcolor & Chr(34) & _
  " then " & vbCrLf
.Write Chr(9) & Chr(9) & "dayNum = " & _
  "window.event.srcElement." & _
  "innerText" & vbCrLf
.Write Chr(9) & Chr(9) & _
  "document.all(" & Chr(34) & _
  "selDate" & Chr(34) & ").value=" & _
  "dateAdd(" & Chr(34) & "d" & Chr(34) & _
  ", dayNum-1, cDate(document.all(" & _
  Chr(34) & "startDate" & _
  Chr(34) & ").value))" & vbCrLf
.Write Chr(9) & Chr(9) & "for each el " & _
  "in document.all(" & Chr(34) & _
  "cal_td" & Chr(34) & ")" & vbCrLf
.Write Chr(9) & Chr(9) & Chr(9) & "if " & _
  "el.style.backgroundColor=" & Chr(34) & _
  cellhighlightColor & Chr(34) & _
  " then " & vbCrLf
.Write Chr(9) & Chr(9) & Chr(9) & _
```

```
    Chr(9) & "el.style.backgroundColor=" & _
    Chr(34) & cellcolor & Chr(34) & vbCrLf
  .Write Chr(9) & Chr(9) & Chr(9) & _
    "end if" & vbCrLf
  .Write Chr(9) & Chr(9) & "next" & vbCrLf
  .Write Chr(9) & Chr(9) & _
    "window.event.srcElement." & _
    "style.backgroundcolor=" & _
    Chr(34) & cellhighlightColor & _
    Chr(34) & vbCrLf
  .Write Chr(9) & "end if" & vbCrLf
  .Write "</script>" & vbCrLf

  .Write "<scr" & _
    "ipt language='VBScript' " & _
    "for=cal_td event=ondblclick>" & vbCrLf
  .Write "dim el" & vbCrLf
  .Write "dim daynum" & vbCrLf
  .Write Chr(9) & "if " & _
    "window.event.srcElement." & _
    "style.backgroundcolor=" & _
    Chr(34) & cellcolor & Chr(34) & _
    " then " & vbCrLf
  .Write Chr(9) & Chr(9) & "dayNum = " & _
    "window.event.srcElement." & _
    "innerText" & vbCrLf
  .Write Chr(9) & Chr(9) & _
    "document.all(" & Chr(34) & _
    "selDate" & Chr(34) & ").value=" & _
    "dateAdd(" & Chr(34) & "d" & Chr(34) & _
    ", dayNum-1, & cDate(document.all(" & _
    Chr(34) & "startDate" & _
    Chr(34) & ").value))" & vbCrLf
  .Write Chr(9) & Chr(9) & _
    "document.all(" & Chr(34) & _
    "Action" & Chr(34) & ").value=" & _
    Chr(34) & "SelectDate" & Chr(34) & vbCrLf
  .Write Chr(9) & Chr(9) & "for each el " & _
    "in document.all(" & Chr(34) & _
    "cal_td" & Chr(34) & ")" & vbCrLf
  .Write Chr(9) & Chr(9) & Chr(9) & "if " & _
    "el.style.backgroundColor=" & Chr(34) & _
```

```
      cellhighlightColor _
      & Chr(34) & " then " & vbCrLf
    .Write Chr(9) & Chr(9) & Chr(9) & _
      Chr(9) & "el.style.backgroundColor=" & _
      Chr(34) & cellcolor & Chr(34) & vbCrLf
    .Write Chr(9) & Chr(9) & Chr(9) & _
      "end if" & vbCrLf
    .Write Chr(9) & Chr(9) & "next" & vbCrLf
    .Write Chr(9) & Chr(9) & _
      "window.event.srcElement." & _
      "style.backgroundcolor=" & _
      Chr(34) & cellhighlightColor & _
      Chr(34) & vbCrLf
    .Write Chr(9) & "end if" & vbCrLf
    .Write Chr(9) & "document.frmCalendar." & _
      "submit" & vbCrLf
    .Write "</script>" & vbCrLf
    .Write "<scr" & _
      "ipt language='VBScript' " & _
      "for=cal_prevmonth event=onclick>" & _
      vbCrLf
    .Write Chr(9) & "document.all(" & _
       Chr(34) & "selDate" & Chr(34) & _
       ").value=dateAdd(" & Chr(34) & _
      "m" & Chr(34) & ", -1," & _
      " document.all(" & Chr(34) & _
      "selDate" & Chr(34) & ").value)" & vbCrLf
    .Write Chr(9) & Chr(9) & _
      "document.all(" & Chr(34) & _
      "Action" & Chr(34) & ").value=" & _
      Chr(34) & "PrevMonth" & Chr(34) & vbCrLf
    .Write Chr(9) & _
      "document.frmCalendar.submit" & vbCrLf
    .Write "</script>" & vbCrLf
    .Write "<scr" & _
      "ipt language='VBScript' " & _
      "for=cal_nextmonth event=onclick>" & _
      vbCrLf
    .Write Chr(9) & "document.all(" & _
      Chr(34) & "selDate" & Chr(34) & _
      ").value=dateAdd(" & Chr(34) & _
      "m" & Chr(34) & ", 1," & _
```

```
          " document.all(" & Chr(34) & _
          "selDate" & Chr(34) & ").value)" & vbCrLf
        .Write Chr(9) & Chr(9) & _
          "document.all(" & Chr(34) & _
          "Action" & Chr(34) & ").value=" & _
          Chr(34) & "NextMonth" & Chr(34) & vbCrLf
        .Write Chr(9) & "document.frmCalendar." & _
          submit" & vbCrLf
        .Write "</script>" & vbCrLf
    End With
  ExitShowCalendar:
    Exit Sub
  ErrShowCalendar:
    Err.Raise Err.Number, methodname, _
      Err.Description
    Resume ExitShowCalendar
  End Sub
```

Basically, the `showCalendar` routine consists of a few variables, a form, and a single loop to write a table containing the calendar. The entire bottom half of the routine writes client-side script to control the actions a user can make with the calendar.

Note that all the arguments are defined as variants and most of them are optional. VB has the ability to define optional arguments that function exactly like the optional arguments you use with ADO methods—you can supply a value for the argument or not. If you don't supply a value, the code assigns a default value.

The method first sets up error-handling. Again, this is slightly different than VBScript. The `On Error Goto ErrShowCalendar` statement tells VB to resume processing at the `ErrShowCalendar:` label at the end of the method in the event of an error. VBScript, as you may remember, does not have an `On Error Goto` statement, just the `On Error Resume Next` statement.

The method defines variables, then checks to see if the `date` argument is a valid date. If not, it raises an error, which forces VB to resume processing at the error-handler beginning after the `ErrShowCalendar:` label. The code in the error-handler again raises the error to the calling code—in this case, the ASP page that instantiated the component. Why didn't I define error-handlers for the rest of the arguments? I should have, but because the other arguments define attributes for the HTML tags, it isn't critical. An improper value won't normally cause an error; the calendar just won't display correctly.

The calendar code itself calculates the starting and ending date for the month specified in the aDate argument. For example:

```
startDate = CDate(CStr(Month(aDate)) & _
  "/1/" & CStr(Year(aDate)))
endDate = DateAdd("m", 1, startDate) - 1
```

The other variable assignments are style settings. I included them for convenience to make the Response.Write statements easier to read and write. The calendar code itself writes a header row containing arrows so the user can change months. Next it writes the empty cells (if any) before the first day of the month; a cell containing a day number for each day in the month; and finally, the empty cells (if any) at the end of the month to fill out the calendar page. For the month 02/2000, using a width of 500 pixels and a height of 400 pixels, but using the default values for all other arguments, the calendar looks like Figure 17.8.

The last third of the showCalendar method writes client script to the browser. The code binds to several events for each cell: click, mouseover, mouseout, and dblclick. When you move the mouse over a numbered cell, the number changes color. When you click a numbered cell, the event code sets a hidden input control value, then highlights the cell by changing its background color. Note that any previously highlighted cells must first revert to the original background color. When you double-click on a numbered cell, the code highlights the cell, sets a hidden Action input control, and then submits the form.

Clicking on the month arrows also submits the form. The calling ASP page can determine the user's action by the value of the Request.Form("Action") variable. When the value is empty (which it will be when the user first requests the page) the user hasn't taken any action. Otherwise, the variable will contain one of the following values:

SelectDate means that the user double-clicked on a cell containing a day number.

PrevMonth means that the user clicked on the left arrow.

NextMonth means that the user clicked on the right arrow.

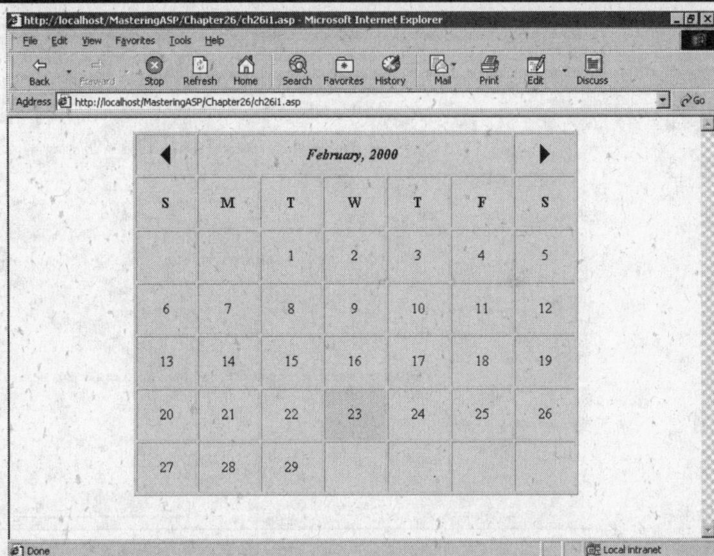

FIGURE 17.8: CHTMLCalendar for February 2000

You need to compile the `HTMLCalendar` component before you can run it in MTS. Click the File menu, then select `Make HTMLCalendar.DLL`. You'll see a file dialog. Select a location for your DLL. I suggest the Windows or WinNT system directory, but you may specify any local drive on your server. Click OK and VB will compile your component. If there are any syntax errors, the compiler will catch them. Fix the problem, and then repeat the compile process until the component compiles without errors.

Packaging the *HTMLCalendar* Component

For components you create with Visual Basic, you can create an installation program using the Visual Studio Package and Deployment Wizard (PDW). If your Web server is on the same computer you used to create the component in VB, you can skip the package and installation process; but if you plan to install the component on a different server, you need to create an installation program.

To launch the Wizard, click Start ➢ Programs ➢ Microsoft Visual Studio 6.0 ➢ Microsoft Visual Studio 6.0 Tools, and select the Package and Deployment Wizard. Enter the path to the project's VBP file in the project field, or select the VBP file from the browse dialog (see Figure 17.9).

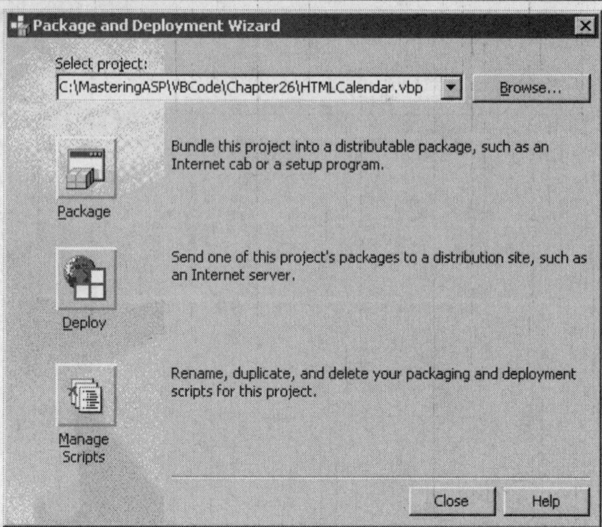

FIGURE 17.9: Visual Studio Package and Deployment Wizard

Click the Package button to create a new package. The Wizard will list several types of packages. Select the Standard Setup Package item, not the Internet Package item. Click the Next button and select the location for the setup files. Make sure you do not select the same directory as your project. Click the Next button to continue.

The Wizard will check the project files for dependencies. If it is unable to find the dependency information for one or more files, it will show you a list of those files. At that point, you can mark files that have no dependencies. Your DLLs may appear in this list, but other DLLs also appear. For example, you should see the `asptxn.dll` file. If you're using NT 4, you should see the `mtsax.dll` file because of the reference to the Microsoft Transaction Server Type Library. If you're using Windows 2000, you should see the `comsvcs.dll` file because the project references the COM+ Services Library. It's difficult to know exactly what to do with this information—I've never found it useful. If the Wizard can't find the dependency information, I can't either. I'm sure it's useful to someone and there's probably a wealth of PDW information available that may help you if you need it. You can probably ignore the dependency dialog without adverse consequences. An obvious exception is if you know that a component makes calls to an external DLL that *isn't* listed in the PDW process. Click the Next button to continue. The PDW shows you the list of files it will include with your component.

In this case, you have no special files to include with the installation, but you should check the list of files carefully. Make sure that all the required components and files appear. If your project requires external resource files, such as HTML files, image files, or text files, you must add them manually—the Wizard never includes any files of those types. If you need to add a file, click the Add button (see Figure 17.10).

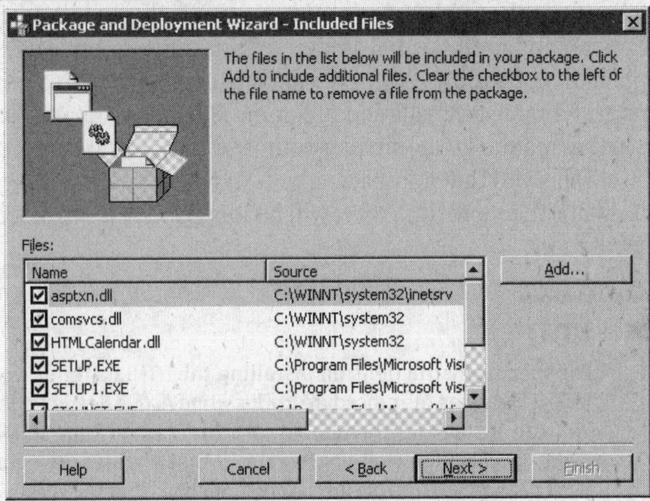

FIGURE 17.10: The PDW Included Files list

Click Next to continue. The Wizard typically marks DLLs for installation in the system folder. It also asks you which DLLs to mark as shared. Place shared DLLs in the system folder, and application-specific DLLs in the application folder. Click Next to continue. From the CAB options dialog, select Single Cab.

Follow the Wizard's instructions to complete the package process. Although they should not affect you for this project, be aware that there are many wizard and installation issues you may need to solve for other projects. The MSDN documentation includes information about many of these problems. Microsoft's Web site contains the most up-to-date version. The Microsoft newsgroups and information on the many VB Web sites can also help you solve installation problems. I urge you to take advantage of these resources by reading them before you undertake a complex installation.

The PDW is neither the most robust nor the most flexible installation program available. Third-party vendors supply much more powerful and configurable programs. The best of these can install essentially anything. As the programs gain in features, they also gain in difficulty. Each vendor has a set of Wizards. Some have customized scripting languages. The more involved your application installation is, the more difficult it will be to create the installation. Don't let the application installation languish while you tinker with background colors. You'll need a dedicated programmer and a substantial amount of time—two to three days for a simple application, possibly several weeks for a complex application—to create and test a robust installation program. The more you're willing and able to install manually, the simpler your installation will be. Unfortunately, the corollary to that approach is that the more you're willing to install manually, the more difficult it will be for anyone else to perform the installation.

NOTE

For specific instructions on installing the `HTMLCalendar` component into MTS/COM+, see the procedure in *Mastering Active Server Pages 3*, Chapter 20. You can install the component into the `MasteringASP` MTS package or COM+ application that you create in that chapter. Remember to set the `MasteringASPUser` role for the component so that IIS will have sufficient permission to launch it.

Using the *HTMLCalendar* Component

After installing the component into MTS/COM+, you can use the `HTMLCalendar` component just as you would any other component. Listing 17.2 shows an ASP script that displays the calendar.

Listing 17.2: ASP Script for `HTMLCalendar` Component (`ch17i1.asp`)

```
<%@ Language=VBScript %>
<%Response.Expires = -1%>
<html>
<head>
</head>
<body>
<%
Dim cal
```

```
Set cal = server.CreateObject _
  ("HTMLCalendar.CHTMLCalendar")
If Request.Form("selDate") = "" Then
  Call cal.showCalendar(Now, "center", _
    500, 400, "lightcyan", "lightcyan", _
    "lightgreen", "black", "red")
Else
  Select Case Request.Form("Action")
  Case "SelectDate"
    Response.write "You selected the date " & _
      Request.Form("selDate") & ".<br>"
  Case "PrevMonth", "NextMonth"
    ' OK, just show the calendar
  End Select
  Call cal.showCalendar _
    (Request.Form("seldate"), "center", _
    500, 400, "lightcyan", "lightcyan", _
    "lightgreen", "black", "red")
End If
%>
</body>
</html>
```

Using *CHTMLCalendar* with Frames

Because the calendar itself is pure HTML, it can adjust quite easily to differing sizes. For example, you can put the calendar in a small frame, then display information in another frame when the user clicks the calendar. To do this you need a `frameset` page—a page containing no <body> tag that defines the frame sizes, names, and initial page sources. Listing 17.3 shows the `frameset` definition.

Listing 17.3: `CHTMLCalendar frameset` **Definition** (`ch17i2.asp`)

```
<%@ Language=VBScript %>
<html>
<head>
<title>
Using the HTMLCalendar with Frames
</title>
</head>
<frameset cols="250,*">
  <frameset rows="250,*">
```

```
    <frame name="frameCalendar"
      src="ch17i3.asp">
    <frame name="frameBlank" src="blank.htm">
  </frameset>
  <frame name="frameMain" src="main.htm">
</frameset>
</html>
```

The `frameset` defines three frames: a 250 x 250–pixel frame in the top-left corner named `frameCalendar`, and a large frame on the right called `frameMain`. The portion of the screen under the calendar contains a frame named `frameBlank` that isn't used in this example. Listing 17.4 shows the ASP file for the `frameCalendar` frame.

Listing 17.4: ASP Source File for the `frameCalendar` Frame (`ch17i3.asp`)

```
<%@ Language=VBScript %>
<%Response.Expires = -1%>
<html>
<head>
</head>
<body>
<%
Dim cal
Dim calWidth
Dim calHeight
Dim calBackColor
Dim selDate
calWidth = 200
calHeight = 200
calBackColor = "#c0c0c0"
Set cal = server.CreateObject _
  ("HTMLCalendar.CHTMLCalendar")
If Request.Form("selDate") = "" Then
  Call cal.showCalendar(Now, "center", _
    calWidth, calHeight, _
    calBackColor, calBackColor, _
    "yellow", "blue", "red")
Else
```

```
    Select Case Request.Form("Action")
    Case "SelectDate"
      selDate = Request.Form("selDate")
    Case "PrevMonth", "NextMonth"
      ' OK, just show the calendar
    End Select
    Call cal.showCalendar _
      (Request.Form("seldate"), "center", _
      calWidth, calHeight, calBackColor, _
      calBackColor, "yellow", "blue", "red")
    %>
    <script language="VBScript">
      Dim doc
      Set doc = window.Parent.frames(2).document
      doc.All("calInfo").innerHTML = _
        "You selected the date <%=selDate%>."
      Set doc = Nothing
    </script>
    <%
  End If
  %>
  </body>
  </html>
```

The script in Listing 17.4 is almost identical to the script in Listing 17.2—both check the `form` variables `selDate` and `Action` to see if the user selected a date, and, if so, write the selected date. However, this script writes the selected date into the `mainFrame`. For example, if I double-click on the date 2/25/2000, the main frame contents changes to reflect the selected date (see Figure 17.11).

In this chapter, you've seen how to create a compiled component running in MTS/COM+ within a specified role, and then use it in conjunction with client-side scripts to create interactive browser frames that communicate with one another. That's quite an accomplishment! It's also the final component in the much larger picture known as a Web application.

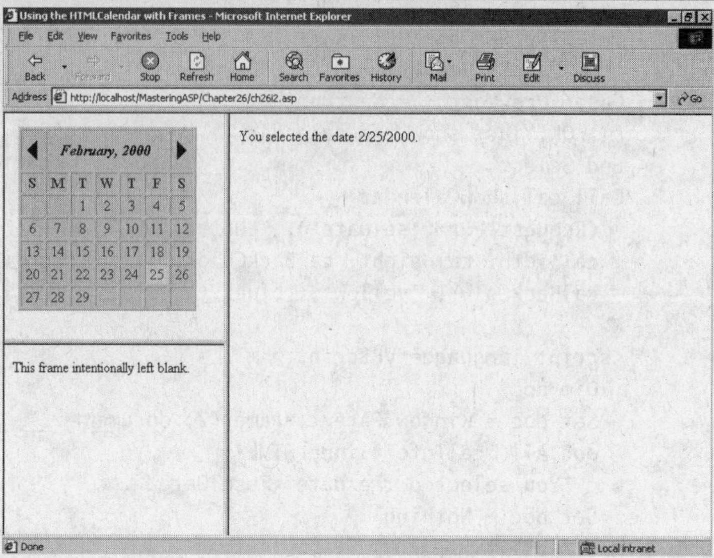

FIGURE 17.11: Using the HTMLCalendar component with frames

WHAT'S NEXT?

Now that you have intimate knowledge of the various pieces, it's time to take a step back and look at the big picture. In the next chapter, you'll go through the steps of planning your application, from defining an audience to creating a support plan. With this understanding of the overall process, you'll have all the tools you need to create a rich and robust Web experience.

Chapter 18

Planning Applications

Every application is different, so this chapter is not a procedure. At the same time, every application has common elements, so you should use this chapter as a way to jog your memory when planning a new application. You may not need all the features, but you are sure to need some of them. You should at least consider them in relation to your application. This chapter covers the requirements for a large application, but it applies equally well to smaller applications.

Adapted from *Mastering™ Active Server Pages 3*, by A. Russell Jones

ISBN 0-7821-2619-7 928 pages $49.99

Define the Audience

Before you begin any application you should consider the audience. You may or may not have a well-defined target audience. By well-defined, I mean that you may or may not know who the users are, what their average reading level is, how much experience they have with computers or with the subject of the application, and what equipment they have to run your application.

For example, if you're building a browser-based, front-end application to a mainframe application, you probably know, or can find out, exactly who the end-users are. You probably know which browser and which version they'll be using. You can find out the speed of the local machines. You can visit and talk with them to find out which features they would like, which features they absolutely have to have, and you can use them during development to try out your application, allowing you to make changes before deployment. However, if you're building an Internet application, you may have no control over the end-users. You'll need to plan for multiple browsers; unknown versions; slow computers; people who turn off graphics, change fonts, and have varying screen resolutions and color depth.

You may need to plan training into your application. While you may completely understand all the features, not everyone will. Find out how and when people want to use the application. A data-entry program that people use every day, all day, has different requirements than a data-entry application that people use once or twice a year. Consider colors carefully—a significant percentage of people are color-blind, so writing your informative messages in red over a yellow background is self-defeating.

What's the average age of the audience? You would probably write a different application for children than for adults—and you'd write a different application for teenagers than for senior citizens. Use language at an appropriate level and with appropriate content for the age of your audience.

Some people read extremely well while others are much better at absorbing information through spoken language and pictures. No one likes to use a computer to read page after page of text, regardless of how well the text is written. Consider the font size. After age 45, people generally have trouble reading small fonts. Take computer experience into account. People who are familiar with computers generally understand file systems, are unafraid to try new features, and can use a browser effectively; others refuse to take any action unless prompted when confronted with a new program.

Begin thinking about the help system at the beginning of the planning process. Do you need a help system? What should it contain? How will people access help? Consider language requirements. Does your application need to support multiple languages? If so, you'll want to write the application so it draws all text from resource files written in different languages.

No application, no matter how well written, can be successful unless it meets the needs of the people who use it. For that to happen, you must determine what those needs are before you write the application.

Determine Application Requirements

ASP applications require resources: network resources, server resources, browser resources, memory, database, security, and support and maintenance resources. All of these topics fall into the category of application requirements. For small test applications where you control the server, you can mostly ignore these requirements, but for larger applications, and those where you do not control the server, you'll need to do some advance planning.

How big is your application? How many programmer hours will it require? What about other support, such as subject-matter experts, system analysts, graphic artists, quality control personnel, technical writers, network and server support personnel, and database administrators? Human resources are the single greatest expense in building an application—and in most cases, people underestimate the costs involved in creating them. Coordinating human resources to deliver an application can be a difficult task, especially when rollout deadlines are imposed externally.

Human resources are only one aspect of application requirements. ASP applications also require machine resources. For example, you may be able to run your application on a single server, but which server? What are the disk space requirements? What are the memory requirements? Does the application require a database server? If so, which server? What's the size of the database initially? Eventually? Do you have a maintenance and backup plan in place? How will the application affect the network? Can the intended audience reach the server? Can they authenticate on that server? Does your application require resources on other servers?

Does the IUSR_MACHINENAME account on the server have access rights to those resources?

If any of these questions affect your application, you need to write a plan detailing which resources you will require, then follow the plan to ensure that everyone involved in the application rollout understands their role and tasks and can schedule for them appropriately. It won't do you any good to create an application that requires SQL Server if your company only has licenses for Oracle. The security requirements for applications that need authentication or need to access resources on other computers can be prohibitive. You need to ensure in advance that you have permission to set the server parameters and create the network accounts your application needs.

Create a Vision

You'll find that as you determine the audience and application requirements, you build a vision of the application that you can communicate to the various people involved. Use that vision to let others understand why you need the application and what it will do. The goal is to create a vision that others can share; if they can share your vision, they can help you make the application a reality. Without a shared vision, you'll be hard-pressed to co-opt others into working with you effectively.

Not everyone needs the same vision, and not everyone needs or wants to know about the application in its entirety. You probably want to communicate the vision differently to different individuals depending on their interests. For example, describing to a senior manager how the network architecture of your application will reduce resource contention doesn't constitute a shared vision, but the same language may be of great interest to a Network Administrator. Discussions of database relationships with a Database Administrator may win you friends, but the same vision, when shared with a data-entry clerk, may only tag you as a consummate bore.

With each group, you should share the portion of your application's vision that will gain a champion for the application. Unless you have total control of the human resources, the network, the server, and can tell the end-users what to do, you'll need some help. Champions are people in each area that can influence others. Pick the people who can help your application, then communicate your vision so they'll want the application. They will only want it if it solves a problem. Perhaps the application saves money or time. Perhaps it simplifies a task through automation. Perhaps it does none of these things, but provides integration with other applications they already have, or grafts an aesthetic face onto an unappealing application. The point is that each group has different interests and it's your task to create a vision that appeals to each group.

Plan the Interface

The interface is the public persona of your application. Some applications have no interface requirements—in fact, parts of your ASP applications, as you begin writing data-access and business components, won't need an interface. However, those portions that do require an interface are the ones that people see. You need to groom and plan them artistically and aesthetically, because if people don't like the interface, they're unlikely to use the application.

By the terms *artistically* and *aesthetically*, I don't mean you should add graphics or try to disguise the purpose of the application in favor of making it beautiful, I mean you should pay attention to the way you lay out controls, images, and text on the page. Take the time to align and size controls properly. Don't select a gray background color for text input fields—people think they're disabled or locked and won't try to type in them. Don't create a text field 200 characters wide if people are going to enter only 10 characters into the field. Similarly, leave enough room between controls. I've seen numerous applications—especially data-entry applications—where the designer has packed so many controls onto the screen that it's impossible to pick out the important features.

Think about how people will use the application. Try to make the application time-sensitive—by that I mean make the most common actions both easy to perform and as responsive as possible. Spend your efforts on the 30% of the application that people use every day. Minimize difficult input. Sure, it's hard to gather the information for pick lists and program intelligence into the application, but a program that responds rapidly and in consistent ways is much more pleasant to learn and use. Remember that many people don't like computers. Try to make the computer adjust to humans. If people want to see spreadsheet-like applications and reports, provide them. If you want to provide an alternate interface for those who would rather fill out forms, do that. Have the application remember its state from one session to another. There's little that's more irritating than having to reset your preferences because a program designer forgot to save them.

In addition to human interfaces, your application has programmatic interfaces. These are the points through which one module in your application communicates with the other modules. For example, passing information from page to page through `hidden form` variables is an interface. If, later on, you decide to modify the code or add functionality, you'll need to interact with your application at those points. Similarly, the names of functions, subroutines, methods, properties, and the arguments to those routines are an interface. Think about how the application will look to you or a maintenance programmer six months later.

As you move toward programming components, the programmatic interfaces gain importance. As you build more applications, you'll see that the programmatic interfaces often have lifetimes far beyond the front-end interfaces seen by the users.

Plan Database Requirements

ASP and Access have made it nearly painless to get a database application up and running, but for any substantive application, that's neither complete nor sufficient. When you build a database, you probably plan to gather information. Unless your application is so completely isolated that no one else wants to interact with the information you gather, it's highly likely that others will eventually need to interact with the database as well.

The database is the backbone of your application; therefore, it should be bulletproof. That means it should not accept information that doesn't meet requirements. It's easy to write code that tests for information validity, but you can't be sure everyone will write bulletproof code. While *you* would never allow an invalid value in a field, you can be sure that eventually one will slip through someone else's code.

Databases on the Web must service all the application's users, and because of the stateless nature of the Web, they are called upon to provide more information much more often than would normally be required in a standard client-server situation. Because database operations are inherently machine- and network-intensive, it's your job to minimize the volume of data that must traverse the network for any given request. That means your task is to learn to take advantage of the power of SQL to select only the required data. But that's only the beginning.

The relationships you build into your database during the planning stages will grow deep roots. For example, the way you plan to store something as simple as a phone number has major ramifications. Not all phone numbers are alike. Some phone numbers require area codes. Many people would prefer to dial numbers using their phone card PIN number to transfer charges. Some phone numbers have extensions. Foreign phone numbers are completely different than U.S. phone numbers. Consider the total phone numbers a person has. You might put the phone numbers in a Contacts table using fields like `HomePhone`, `WorkPhone`, `FaxPhone`, and `CellPhone`. But how many fields are sufficient? Those four may meet your application's needs today, but it's almost certain that however many fields you pre-define, someone will have a need for more.

You can circumvent this problem by normalizing the database. Put the telephone numbers in a separate table with the UserID as a foreign key and use `JOIN` operations. Add a field to that table called `TelephoneType`. Index the `UserID` field and the `TelephoneType` field, because those are the fields you'll use to look up values. After a database enters production, and especially after other programs begin using the database, it becomes much more difficult, if not impossible, to change the structure of the database.

Plan the interface to your database as carefully as you plan the names and arguments of your routines or the methods and properties of your objects. You can control access to the database through security, but your primary methods for controlling content are through stored procedures, triggers, and views. For example, you can (and often should) deny direct access to any database table. Instead, you provide `SELECT` access through views and stored procedures, and `INSERT` and `UPDATE` operations though stored procedures, defaults, and triggers. For example, if you have a `CreatedOn` field, you don't have to trust programmers to update the field. Write a default value or a trigger to insert the value. Create a rule or constraint that protects the field from invalid or out-of-range values. Don't expose the field for update.

You need to consider database administration. The rule of thumb is that you need to create at least four ASP pages for each top-level database table for administration purposes. These are: a page from which the administrator can select records to modify, a form for adding new records, a form for editing existing records, and a script to delete records. If you have password fields in your database, the administrator will need to be able to clear the passwords. You'll need a form where administrators can select an individual and a `clearPassword` script. If there are database processes that must be run on a schedule, such as archiving or deleting obsolete records, you need to create a mechanism that will launch the processes. You'll also need a way to let the appropriate people know if the process did or did not complete successfully.

Plan your data size requirements. Databases tend to grow over time. A SELECT query on an unindexed field may perform adequately when the database has a few hundred records. But when the database grows to hundreds of thousands of records, that same query will bog down the application. You need to plan for the future. Does the data expire or become obsolete? How will you remove obsolete data from the database? Manually? Automatically? What will you do with the records you remove? Discard them? Archive them?

The size of the data at any given time may also affect the application code. You should cringe whenever you see a query like `SELECT * FROM <Tablename>`. Unless you know the table contains a fixed number of rows, such queries are an invitation to disaster. The first few hundred rows won't matter, but when the code needs to display or winnow through thousands of records, it will make a huge difference in the responsiveness of your code.

How many servers will it take to service the total anticipated number of users? If it takes more than one, how will you split up or replicate the data? Test the queries using the database server's analysis tools. If the database doesn't have such tools built in, obtain them. These tools can help you find and anticipate problems. For example, the SQL Server Query Analyzer tool can show you the query plan for any query. You should particularly look for table-scan operations, because they mean the database was unable to find a suitable index to use, and therefore must read the entire column. For an enterprise application, spending a few hundred dollars to determine query efficiency can mean the difference between success and failure.

How do you plan to back up the database? What happens if the drive fails? If you don't have a backup plan, ask yourself how much data you can afford to lose. If the answer is none, then you must implement a fail-over plan and a backup plan. If you're willing to lose transactions in progress, you only need the backup plan. Sometimes, Server and Database Administrators have already solved the problem because your application shares space with a critical application—but don't be complacent—find out. If your application needs access to archived information, you'll need to build that into your plan. How do you obtain the archive? How do you load it? How long does that take?

You should be able to answer all these questions—or at least have asked them—before you begin building your application. If you think most of this doesn't apply to you as a program designer/developer, that such questions are the Database Administrators' (DBAs) job, then you should get ready for a long antagonistic relationship with the DBAs. Don't be surprised if some of these issues surface only after the application becomes successful, but try to anticipate your reaction. It's often difficult or impossible to spend time and money to implement all these features for applications that may not need them initially, and your application may not ever need them all. The point is, you need to understand and plan for database expansion, backup, data validity, security, and efficiency throughout the lifetime of the application.

Plan Object Responsibilities

If databases are the backbone of a modern Web application, objects are the legs. Objects in a Web application are often transient—created, used, and destroyed as quickly as possible. Consider the ASP intrinsic objects. Only the Application object is permanent; IIS creates and destroys all the others for each request. That's a lot of objects. Does the ASP engine really create all the intrinsic objects for each request or does it create them only when you write a reference in your code? Quite truthfully, I don't know, except for the `Request.ServerVariables` collection. The Microsoft documentation states that ASP creates the `Request.ServerVariables` collection only if you reference it, because the overhead involved in creating the collection is relatively high. In any case, the ASP object model has stood the test of time—it has remained relatively static ever since version 1. IIS 4 introduced transactional capabilities and added the ObjectContext object. IIS 5 introduced the `Server.Transfer` and `Server.Execute` methods, as well as the `Session` and `Application Contents` collections; but most methods and properties remain unchanged.

That's the type of stability you should strive for with your own objects. You'll want to plan an interface that will not need to change. Object modeling is beyond the scope of this book, but a little common sense can take you a long way. First, try to separate objects using the same type of logic you used to create normalized databases. That's not to say that an object's properties should always match the structure of a single table, but if your objects begin to span many tables, you might want to take a long hard look at the object's responsibilities. Try to create reusable objects. The more features you build into an object, the less generic it becomes. For example, you should never tie an object to a single database location by hard-coding a DSN or `ConnectionString` property into the object itself.

Try to capture the methods and properties that objects exhibit in the real world. For example, think of a Person object. Not all people are alike, but all have common elements. Build the common elements into a Person object, then create Child objects that both inherit and extend the capabilities of their common ancestor.

Create Data-Access Components

The most scalable Web applications use data-access objects to request data from and update database tables. That's not the most efficient way to develop your application—it's much easier and faster to write dynamic SQL queries directly into your ASP code than to plan and develop COM database components. Nevertheless, dynamic SQL queries can be used only by your application, whereas COM components may be used by many different applications. Data-access components become much more important when your application isn't the only application using the database.

The purpose of a data-access component is to mediate data transfer to and from the database. These components often run inside of Microsoft Transaction Server (MTS), which instantiates objects on demand, rather than on request. That means any given object may be shared between many different clients. Therefore, you should write (and use) the components with a strong bias toward efficiency over ease-of-use. For example, don't create large numbers of individual properties that must be set before calling a method that acts on those properties. Instead, pass the properties to the method. That way, MTS can provide a reference to the component, perform the work, and transfer ownership of the component to another process with only one call.

Similarly, try to write the components so they use database connections efficiently. If you know you need two forward-only record sets, retrieve them both in a single call using a stored procedure or chained SQL statements. By doing so, you minimize both the time and number of connections needed to retrieve the data.

Build the components so they meet the requirements of both program users and program administrators. Provide `select`, `update`, `insert`, and `delete` methods for every exposed column. It's often very difficult to gain permission to put data-access components on a production server, so try to anticipate future needs and build and test them during development.

Create Business Components

Business components contain the business rules that act on the data provided by data-access components. You often want to isolate these rules in a separate layer because they change more often than the front-end interface requirements. Consider an application that arranges route patterns for salespeople. The route data–the customer list and locations, resides in a database. Although the data changes constantly, the format of the data does not. You might build a data-access component to retrieve and update the data. On the other hand, the rules for calculating the route change constantly, depending on pricing, availability, the potential size of orders from different customers, and many other business factors.

The application must be able to adapt to the changing route rules. You do that by adding or changing business components. For example, one rule might be that salespeople must visit each customer a minimum of once each month unless the customer has been inactive for three or more months. Another might be that customers with total orders exceeding $1,000,000 per year receive a discount of 15% on all orders over $10,000, whereas customers with total orders between $500,000 and $999,999 receive a 10% discount. Customers with yearly orders totaling less than $500,000 get discounts that depend on the size of each individual order.

If (or rather, when) these rules change–perhaps the business focus changes to acquiring new customers, so discounts to smaller customers increase–the business logic must also change. Therefore, the main purpose of a business component is to isolate business rules so you can replace the logic inside the component without disturbing any other parts of the application.

Although this sounds simple, it's not. If the interface to the component changes, you must also change other parts of the application. The challenge is to design the components so you can change the logic inside the components without changing the external programmatic interface. Consider building an external interface that can adapt to changing needs. For example, a method that accepts an array of `Variant` parameters and returns a `Variant` data array is adaptable for many different purposes, albeit at the cost of efficiency. For example, you could pass it an ad hoc SQL statement and it would return the data. Don't design all of your data-access calls in this manner, but think about including one with each component.

TEST THE APPLICATION

Development is often a trade-off between efficiency and stability. While you may win praise for delivering an application on time, such praise will rapidly turn to censure if the application fails to work as anticipated. Therefore, don't forget to plan for testing. In my experience, there are, at minimum, three testing phases for an application. Each testing phase should answer one or more questions. The phases are:

Programmatic testing Does the application work according to specifications? This phase begins when code development begins and continues throughout the development of the application. As the program moves from development into maintenance, you must repeat this phase for every change to the application.

User testing Can the members of the target audience use the application to accomplish the task for which the application was designed? Do they use it? You can and should discover the answer to the first question before you deploy the application. You cannot answer the second question until after you deploy the application. Unfortunately, the answer to the second question is much more important than the first.

Goal testing Does the application meet the goals for which it was created? Depending on the application, the goals might involve an increase in productivity, or accuracy, or cost reduction. Such questions are rarely answered for several reasons. First, the application designers are usually satisfied when the application is complete—regardless of whether it is ever used. The end-users are usually more interested in completing tasks than in using your application—they're certainly not interested in measuring how well the application meets its goals; many of them may not be aware of the goals. Finally, measuring application success requires baseline measurements before application deployment. The people who envision, design, and create applications are rarely the ones who could accomplish the measurement; therefore, goal testing rarely occurs.

Think back to your targeted audience. What kinds of computers do they have? What network connection speeds? Which browsers and what operating systems? You must create a testing plan that takes these factors into account. Just because it works on your development system doesn't mean it will work on the target systems–it won't. I wish I had a quarter for each time a programmer has said "but it works on *my* system…." If you can't set up a laboratory environment that matches the target audience's hardware, set up a test server the users can reach, then schedule times where they can help you test the application. Don't just turn them loose with the application. Provide a script they can follow. Be sure they understand that it's a test. You can gain other benefits from testing in this manner. Interview the users afterward. Find out what they liked and didn't like. Find out which features are missing, which ones they didn't need, and which, if any, features they'd like to have added.

For solid development you need three servers: a development server, a staging server, and a production server.

NOTE

I've used the term server in the singular, but you should understand that applications requiring a server farm need to be tested in that environment.

You need these three servers even if you're the only developer. During the initial application development, programmers use the development server to write and test the code. For user and beta testing, place the entire application on the staging server. The staging server should be, as much as possible, an exact duplicate of the production server. Never make any changes to the staging server–make the changes on the development server, then migrate them to the staging server for testing. When you roll out the application, copy the application from staging to production. Changes must always flow in a single direction, from development, to staging, to production.

At this point, you might think you're done with the staging server, but you need to keep it. If the application needs any modification, you'll need to make the changes, test them, and then migrate the affected portions of the application to production. The development-staging-production cycle works only if you manage it carefully. There's a tremendous temptation to make changes on the staging and production servers, but you should resist that temptation, because if you make changes on the production server, they'll be overwritten if you ever move future changes into production from the staging server. Similarly, changes made on the staging server often disappear as programmers move code from development onto the staging server.

The development-staging-production cycle works for code, but doesn't work nearly as well for databases. After an application that collects user data is in production, you can't overwrite it with a staging copy of the database. Therefore, the cycle for databases works initially, before production, just like the code cycle; but after deployment to production, you must replicate the database from production to staging for testing. As you make changes and solve problems, you still can't copy the staging database into production unless you're absolutely certain the staging copy contains all of the data from the production copy—and it's difficult to be certain unless you can shut the production application down. Because many applications must run 24 x 7 in production, that may not be an option.

Fortunately, most database changes involve database objects—stored procedures, table definitions, view, indexes, etc.—not data. Therefore, your deployment task for databases is to build a process through which you can move a copy of the structure of a staging database into production without affecting the data. You'll need to be able to practice the operation on the staging database. Set up a process for changing the database in use from one copy on the staging database to another copy. I've found that the best way to do this is to have only one place in your application that defines database connection strings—for ASP applications, the `global.asa` file is a good place to put it. Remember that changing `global.asa` shuts down the application; if that's a problem for you, find another method to define the connection strings. Where you acquire the connection strings isn't nearly as important as acquiring them from only one place.

Create a Deployment Plan

Designing, building, testing, and debugging applications are the fun parts of program development. Deployment is rarely as satisfying because deployed machines are rarely completely under your control. You'll have the best chance of success, and deployment will be less painful if you follow these guidelines.

Prepare for Deployment

Deploying an ASP application isn't much different from deploying a standard Windows application, but there are three critical differences:

1. Anonymous Web applications run under different permissions than standard applications. Web applications using NT Challenge/Response run under the user's account on the server, but cannot authenticate across the network.
2. Web applications run on multiple threads. Resource contention that you may not see during development can become an issue after deployment.
3. The production server will not be your development server, won't have the same directory permissions that your server does, may not be the same service pack version, and will have different security settings. If you're lucky, you'll have administrator access to the production server. In both cases, you can help either yourself or the Server Administrators by following the guidelines in this chapter.

You need a minimum of two servers to test an installation—the staging server and a test server. They can't be the same server—in other words, you can't just publish the application to another virtual directory, because all paths, files, DSNs, graphics, virtual directories, permissions, DLLs, and other resources and settings presumably already exist and work on the development server. The point of testing the installation is that the target environment is usually unknown, and often uncontrollable. In other words, you may be delivering your application to a server that is radically different from your staging server.

Clean Up the Code

Now's a good time to go through the code and eliminate unneeded methods and variables. It's too early to remove any debugging code, although you should be able to easily turn the debug output on and off for testing.

- Check all component references and remove any unnecessary references. Installation programs often include external DLLs based on the project references list rather than the references the program actually uses.

- Delete unused files—you'll need a clean list to create your installation.
- Back up the project. As a developer, you're sure (or you should be) that the application runs perfectly right now. You should save that known state in case you make changes during the deployment process and want to undo them later, if you need the information to set path or file references.
- Make sure all file references within the project use relative URLs. Never include the server name or IP address in any code. The server name will always change. If your root directory name clashes with an existing name, or if, for whatever reason, the clients want to change the root to another name, your program will still work. You can obtain the server name and program root at runtime, with the `Server.MapPath` method.
- Search your program for references to external resources like log filenames, database DSNs, etc. As you find them, move them to the `global.asa` file and store them as Application-level variables. Change the code so it references the `Application` variables. That way you can change DSN names, sign-ons, passwords, and external file references easily, no matter where those resources are or what their names are. If security is an issue, put the references in an external file and encrypt the file. The point here is that those filenames, paths, machine resources, and database resources can and will change names and locations. In many cases, these changes are outside your control and will break your application. You want to get the references from a location that you can change easily, preferably without recompiling and reinstalling your application.
- Try to rename files specific to the application in a consistent manner. That makes it much easier to find and remember files later. It also decreases the risk that a file you're installing will conflict with the name of a file already on the system.
- Make a version number for your program and provide a method to retrieve it. For example, the About box found on the Help menu in most Windows programs provides that information. Although your browser-based application may not have an About box, you can provide a way to display it.

Generate Likely Errors

Generate errors for the things most likely to happen. By likely errors, I mean things your application depends on that tend to change over time. For example, if your application opens a connection to a database, shut the database down, then see how your application traps the error. Where do the errors appear? On the browser screen? In the NT Application Event log? In the Event Security Log? You need to know this so you can debug the application remotely on an unfamiliar server.

If your application needs write access to a directory, shut off that access. Delete log files and change Distributed Common Object Model (DCOM) permissions. All of these things are out of your control once the application leaves the development stage, but they all happen. Neither you nor anyone else on the development team will remember the information after a few weeks, so write down the exact error messages and the solutions.

If you follow this advice, you'll probably want to go through at least one more testing and revision cycle to beef up the error reporting. I can assure you this is time well spent if you're deploying to a remote server—one you can't physically reach or on which you don't have administrator permissions.

I often write hidden features into a program that can aid in debugging deployed applications. It's best to isolate these features as far as possible from other program requirements. ASP programs are excellent candidates for these programs because they're small, and they work as long as the server is working. Some examples are an ASP file that tests database connections; one that lists the contents of the `global.asa` file, one that checks resources; one that lets you run SQL code against a database, like the SQL Server Query Analyzer (iSQL) program. If you have FTP or FrontPage access to the target server, you can even write and deploy such applets after a problem occurs.

Put the error messages and solutions in an HTM file that accompanies your application and keep a copy for yourself. When you get a support call, you'll be able to tell the caller where to look and what to do to solve the problem.

Part iv

Deploy to a Test Server

If possible, install and test the application on a local server—one where you can physically access the machine, start, stop, and even reboot it.

While event logs can be helpful, other Server Administrators may not want to help you debug your application. Do not install any other code on the server unless you can also install the same code on all of the target servers.

Debugging an application in production is a skill that's different from debugging a program in development. Practice on your own server, not your production server; and practice on a test server, not the staging server.

Beta Test the Application

Many applications run perfectly when tested by the author, but fail miserably when tested by real users. By real users, I mean members of the target audience. Real users don't know what input the application expects, so they do unexpected things.

As early as possible, and on an ongoing basis during development, try to get several members of your target audience to use or at least critique the application. A decent sample is 5–10 people. You'll find that you can catch most of the bugs, misconceptions, and missing features if you let just a few people use the application.

A real beta test, though, occurs as a next-to-final step. Install the application on a server and let several people use it. They should treat the application as though it were the production version. Fix any problems that arise.

When the application has passed muster in beta form, you can remove the debugging code—it's ready for production. Be sure to test again without the debugging code—sometimes removing the code creates problems.

Determine the Production Server's Configuration

When you're delivering to a known production server, you may be able to call ahead to find out the configuration of that server. The earlier you can do this in the development process, the better. For example, it will do you no good to develop with the latest and greatest version of ADO if the target server is still running version 1.5. Similarly, taking advantage of the many convenient features of SQL Server version 7, such as 8000-character `varChar` fields, won't work if the production database server is still running version 6.5. Server Administrators are notoriously difficult when you tell them they must upgrade their equipment or software to accommodate your application.

If you're developing commercial applications, you will need to create more than one version of the application, design for the lowest common denominator, or be willing to give up possible sales to use the latest technology.

In all cases you'll want to design the application to isolate version-dependent issues, so you can change component versions and databases easily to meet the technical requirements of the customers. For example, if all of your database accesses happen via stored procedures, your application will work on any database where you can re-create the set of stored procedures. Moving the application from SQL Server to Oracle may be as simple as creating the tables and the stored procedures and copying the data. In contrast, the more database functionality you place in your code, the harder it will be to change the database.

I've sometimes found it useful to begin applications by having the program itself check resource availability and versions. While that may slow down application initialization, it's better than end-user error messages. Alternatively, you can write these checks so they are performed on demand—perhaps via Administrator options, or via an unreferenced back-door URL that runs a hidden page in your ASP application. Using these techniques, you can at least help determine problems after deployment.

Create an Installation Program

ASP programs, by themselves, don't need an installation package. If the target server already has ASP installed, you can simply copy the directory containing your application files and mark the directory as the source of a virtual directory on the target server. However, any components you have created or acquired that are not installed with ASP do need an installation program. That's because components require registration on the target server—you can't simply copy the DLL files to the target and expect them to work.

Configure the Target Server

Almost all ASP applications require a change to the server's configuration. At minimum you need to create a virtual directory. If your application requires write access to files, you will need to set NTFS file-access permissions as well. If you have a database, you must create and configure a DSN. For more complex applications, you may need to create special accounts or groups, set permissions, alter the registry, and install packages into MTS.

Capture the Server Configuration Settings

As soon as you create and test the installation package, capture the current settings for IIS and MTS from your test server. Screen captures work best, but you can write down all the settings as well. Be sure to capture them all.

If you're using an installer other than the Packaging and Deployment Wizard (PDW), one that can create virtual Web directories and perform MTS installations, you'll need to know the server settings to create your package. Otherwise, you or the Server Administrator will need to know them to configure the target server. There are too many settings to remember and you won't remember them long-term, so write them down. Put the settings, graphics and all, in the HTM file that accompanies the application, and keep a copy for yourself.

Dealing with Permissions Issues

It's been my experience that security issues arise for almost every ASP application deployment. Some of these problems you can solve in advance—the rest of them you'll need to solve during deployment. There's little chance that everything will run perfectly. If you trap the errors properly, practice the installation and document the settings from your staging server, you may only have a few problems. If you haven't done those things, I hope you're a lucky person.

Most security-related errors won't appear on the browser screen or in any log files generated by your application even if you trap them properly. The on-screen or in-log errors typically say something like Access Denied, which is not helpful. A better description of most security-related errors appears in the Event log. You need to check both the System log and the Application log if your application isn't running properly.

Most ASP application security errors occur when the IUSR_MACHINENAME account requests access or launch permission to a class, component, or file. In some cases these errors appear in the System or Application logs, in other cases they don't. When your own error-trapping and the system error-trapping don't provide enough information, you can use NT's auditing feature to help find the problem.

You need to be an Administrator to enable auditing for a computer. Document what you do–you'll want to turn it off later, and there's no easy way to turn off auditing without disabling all auditing. To enable auditing, start User Manager for Domains and click the Policies menu, then select the Audit entry. You can audit many things, but usually you need to audit only File and Object access to debug ASP applications. Work with your Server Administrator to enable auditing on the files, components, and other resources used by your application.

Despite all of these warnings and error-trapping resources, your application may still have problems. Microsoft's MSDN site and the newsgroups can sometimes provide expert advice.

Create an Application Support Plan

After deployment, you should be prepared to receive problem calls from end-users. Sometimes such calls are questions about how to activate or use the application, but sometimes they're problem reports. Unless you plan to take the calls yourself, you need to provide program documentation to the Help desk or to the people who work with the end-users to solve the problem. The work you did to document error messages and program requirements during the deployment phase should form the basis of your application support plan.

The people taking the calls will need to know the error messages that appear on the user's browsers and how those error messages relate to the application; otherwise they'll refer the errors to you. In many cases, errors that appear after deployment are infrastructure-related: the server's down, the network's down, the proxy or firewall won't allow access. Sometimes the errors are resource-related: a database server name changed, someone reset file permissions on the server, someone upgraded a DLL that's not backwardly compatible with your program code. Finally, some problems are code-related. Even with your best efforts, code-related bugs will occur. You need to plan how to resolve these problems, document them for the support personnel, and test any changes.

If all of this seems like overkill for your ASP application, it probably is. Not every application needs such an elaborate infrastructure, but at the same time, from a business standpoint, an application must not be dependent on a single individual. If you leave the company for another job, someone else will need to take over maintenance and support. Try to document the tasks you would want someone else to document for you if you were taking over the application.

WHAT'S NEXT?

Until now, you've been learning the various tools you need to know in order to build a robust Web application. Now that you've seen the basics, you're ready to venture into some new technologies. The next few chapters cover one of the more exciting new protocols to hit the scene in a while: XML. In the next chapter you'll learn what XML is and how it can help you and your site's visitors. You'll also learn how it relates to XSL and how to use XSL to add some style to your XML data.

PART V

XML

Chapter 19
Using XML/XSL with ASP

You have the database. You have the forms and the static pages. You have ASP scripts pulling it all together. Perhaps you even have Visual Basic components behind the scenes and client-side scripting in front of the curtain. What's next?

XML is becoming more important every day. In order to take advantage of the latest technologies, it would help you to understand more about XML and what it can do for your site.

XML is a flexible superset of HTML that:

- Is text-based
- Lets you define your own tags
- Is well-suited to complex hierarchical data
- Has the built-in technology to validate its own content
- Is a W3C standard

Adapted from *Mastering™ Active Server Pages 3*, by A. Russell Jones

ISBN 0-7821-2619-7 928 pages $49.99

Using an XML validating parser, you can ensure that an XML file contains the tags you expect, arranged in specified relationships, and the data within the tags meets specified expectations. XML is becoming increasingly important in business-to-business (B2B) Internet commerce.

In this chapter, I'll introduce you to ways you can use XML on the server, within the browser, and within your components to move your applications away from proprietary, program-specific code toward portable, standardized code.

NOTE

To run the examples in this chapter, you'll need IE 5 installed on both the client and server. You must also have the Microsoft XML parser version 2 or higher installed on both machines. You can obtain the latest XML parser from the MSDN site at `http://msdn.microsoft.com/xml/`.

BEYOND HTML

HTML provided millions of people with a way to put text and graphics on a computer screen without learning a complex programming language. As a display language, HTML has its limitations, but as the Web became ubiquitous, people began to try to force HTML to act as a data container. For example, programmers moved data to the browser in hidden form fields, hidden list boxes, and hidden frames both to increase interactivity and limit the number of server round trips. Developers often wrapped generic data in huge forms and submitted them to the server for processing, or resorted to automatic e-mail to move data from client to server.

On the server-to-server side, things weren't much better. There's never been a common way to transfer data from one program and one operating system to another. The closest we've ever come has been text files. Text files have been the lowest common denominator since the early DOS days—and text files can contain delimited fields, fixed-width fields, free-form text, and tokenized content. Each has its advantages. For example, to transfer the raw text of a novel from one computer to another, a free-form text file works perfectly well. Unfortunately, if you want to transfer formatted text from one computer to another, both computers must agree on the formatting symbols and what they mean.

In the earliest days of word processors, vendors created their own, proprietary file formats. These formats worked well enough within the application, but it was impossible to open a file generated in one word processor with a different word processing program. Entire companies grew up around the problems involved in translating one format into another, with mixed results. Nevertheless, for most people, the only way to move the files was to save them in plain text—thus losing all the formatting.

These proprietary file formats weren't limited to word processing. Databases, graphics programs, spreadsheets, project management software, page-layout applications, presentation software—each program had a proprietary format.

The Clipboard was the first easy method to move content from one program to another. The first efforts involved creating a memory buffer shared by all programs that could transfer plain text and bitmapped (BMP) graphics from one program to another. Through the Clipboard, for the first time, you could easily take numbers out of your spreadsheet and insert them into your word processor. Of course, they still lost all the formatting, but at least you could move the data.

With Dynamic Data Exchange (DDE), and later with Object Linking and Embedding (OLE), Microsoft made a huge leap. Suddenly, you could not only move data from one program to another, but you could preserve the format of that content, and even (by linking it) automatically update the inserted data when the source data changed. OLE was, and—as ActiveX—still is, a horrendously complex programming task. In addition, it was—and mostly, still is—Windows-specific. But it did provide a vision of multiple applications exchanging data seamlessly.

HTML, because of its ability to display word processor–like data, spreadsheet-like data, and graphics, all in a simple-to-learn and simple-to-understand package, took the major vendors by surprise. To their credit, almost all of the major application vendors embraced the new format eagerly. I guess they were as tired of file incompatibilities as the rest of us. HTML showed how a common file format could extend computing technology far beyond the workplace and make computing ubiquitous. You might say that HTML gave normal people a reason to buy a computer beyond bringing work home from the office.

Unfortunately, these vendors still had to deliver products, and as good as HTML is, a spreadsheet-like display isn't a replacement for a true spreadsheet. HTML is flexible enough to display data, but it has no concept of the content. The problem was, how could you build upon the simplicity and readability of HTML to create a common file format that could accommodate many different types of data and work across many different types of applications? The ideal file format would be text-based, let you define your own tags, be well suited for complex hierarchical data, have the built-in ability to validate its own content, and above all, be a worldwide standard. If these descriptions look familiar, re-read the introduction to this chapter. I've just described XML.

INTRODUCTION TO XML

Despite all the hype, XML is a very simple idea—the kind of idea that makes you wonder, "Why didn't I think of that?" The easiest way to understand XML is to look at some. Listing 19.1 shows an XML file that describes a person class.

Listing 19.1: XML Person Class File (ch19i1.xml)

```
<?xml version='1.0'?>
<class>
  <name>Person</name>
  <creator>Russell Jones</creator>
  <properties>
    <property type="text" name="lastname" readonly="false"
      maxlength="20" allownulls="false" value=""></property>
    <property type="text" name="firstname" readonly="false"
      maxlength="20" allownulls="false" value=""></property>
  </properties>
  <methods>
    <method type="function" public="true" name="getname"
      description=
      "Concatenates the FirstName and LastName properties
      into a single &quot;FirstName LastName&quot; string.">
    </method>
  </methods>
</class>
```

The code should look quite familiar to you. In fact, except for the tag names themselves, XML looks much like HTML. The file contains tags (markup) like `<class>`, `<name>`, and `<creator>`. Probably the strangest part of the file is the first line. In XML, the first line is required, and you must write it exactly as shown.

The rules for writing XML are simple:

- The first line must be `<?xml version='1.0'?>`.
- Tags are enclosed in angle brackets. Unlike HTML, tags are case sensitive and each tag must have a matching closing tag.
- Tags may contain *attributes* in the form `name="value"`. The quotes around attribute values are required. You may use either single or double quotes, but the quotes must match. In other words, you can't write an attribute like `somename="somevalue'` because the single quote at the end of the attribute value doesn't match the double quote at the start of the value.
- Tags may contain text, other tags, or both. Tag *content* lies between the starting and closing tag.

There is one exception to the rule that every tag must have a matching closing tag. You can write *empty* tags (those that contain no content) with the closing slash at the end of the tag, before the closing bracket. For example, the following two tags function identically, but the first has an explicit end tag, whereas the second uses the forward-slash shorthand:

```
<property type="text" name="lastname" readonly="false"
  maxlength="20" allownulls="false" value="">
</property>

<property type="text" name="lastname" readonly="false"
  maxlength="20" allownulls="false" value=""/>
```

The content of the file is essentially an outline. The tags delimit content of a particular type. Some tags contain other tags—these tags are called *parents*, and the contained tags are called *children*. As you look at the file, you can see that the designation of a tag as a parent or child depends on the context. If you look at the `<class>` tag, it is clearly a parent—it isn't contained within any other tags. However, the `<properties>` tag is both a child and a parent. It's a child of the `<class>` tag, but it contains two `<property>` tags; therefore, it's also a parent.

Internet Explorer 5 natively transforms XML files into outline format. If you look at Listing 19.1 in IE 5, it looks like Figure 19.1.

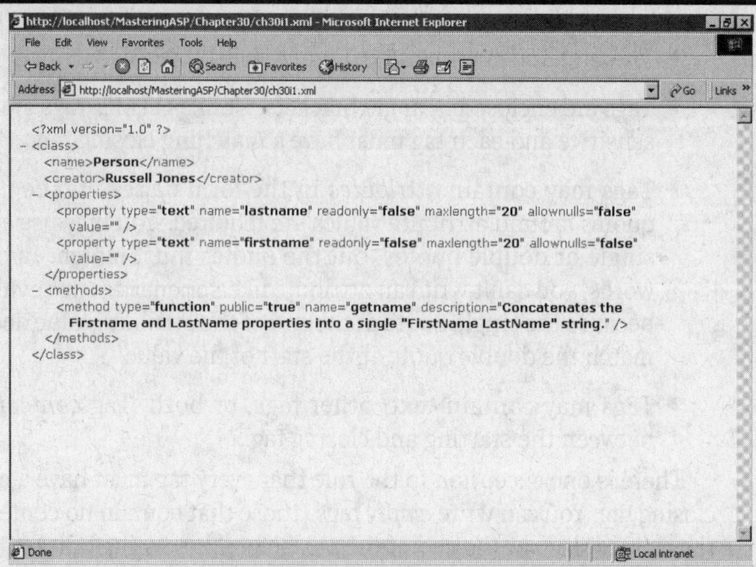

FIGURE 19.1: IE 5 native XML file view (`ch19i1.xml`)

The file initially appears as an expanded hierarchical outline. IE shows each tag that has children with a small minus sign next to the tag. You can't edit the file directly in IE, but you can open and close the parts of the document by clicking the minus sign (which then changes to a plus sign). Figure 19.2 shows the file with the `<properties>` tag closed.

The beauty of this file format is that if the tags are well named, you instantly know the purpose of the data the tag contains. If I were to write this same content into HTML, it might look like Listing 19.2. Figure 19.3 shows the file in a browser.

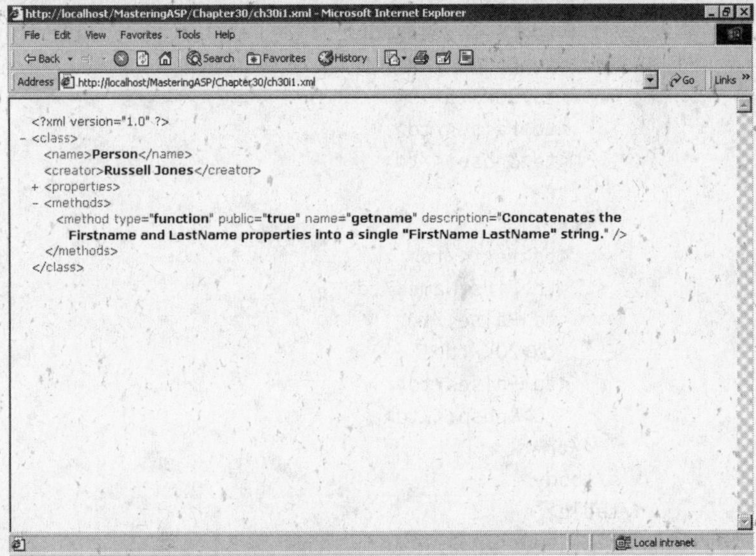

FIGURE 19.2: XML file with a closed tag (`ch19i1.xml`)

Listing 19.2: One Possible HTML View of the Content in Listing 19.1 (`ch19i2.htm`)

```
<html>
<head>
  <title>Person Class</title>
</head>
<body>
  <h2>Person Class</h2><br>
  <b>Creator</b>: John Bradford<br>
  <h3>Properties</h3>
  <table cols="6" border="1">
    <thead>
      <th>Type</th>
      <th>Name</th>
      <th>Read-only</th>
      <th>Max Length</th>
      <th>Allow Nulls</th>
      <th>Value</th>
    </thead>
    <tbody>
      <tr>
```

```
          <td>text</td>
          <td>LastName</td>
          <td>False</td>
          <td>20</td>
          <td>False</td>
          <td> </td>
        </tr>
        <tr>
          <td>text</td>
          <td>FirstName</td>
          <td>False</td>
          <td>20</td>
          <td>False</td>
          <td> </td>
        </tr>
      </tbody>
    </table>
    <h3>Methods</h3>
    <h4>getName</h4>
    <p>Concatenates the Firstname and LastName properties
    into a single "FirstName LastName" string.</p>
  </body>
  </html>
```

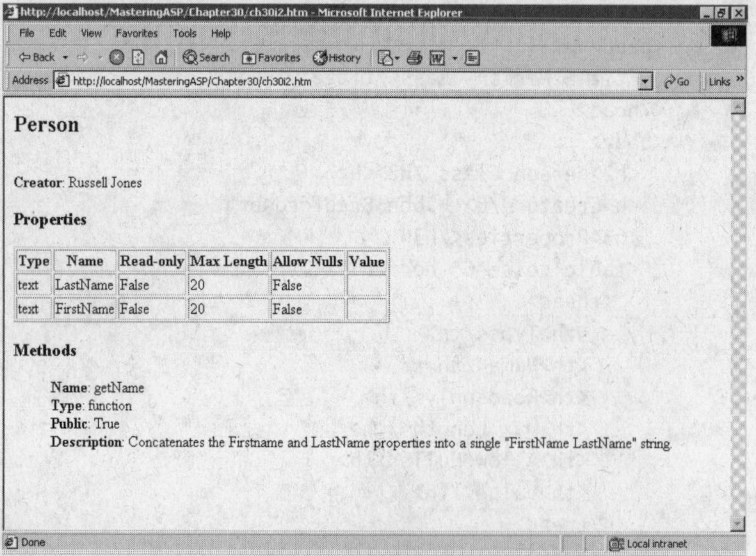

FIGURE 19.3: Listing 19.1 formatted as HTML (`ch19i2.htm`)

The two technologies are quite similar in content, but quite different in concept. The HTML version is much easier for a human to read, but the format makes it difficult for a computer to extract the content. For example, you might write some code to look for the word `Methods`, then read a list of methods contained between <h4> and </h4> tags. That code would then work as long as the page designer doesn't change the format of the page. In other words, the code to extract data from an HTML file is too closely tied to the display of the data.

In contrast, the XML file doesn't look as good on-screen and is more difficult for a human to read. However, it's much easier for a computer to extract data from the file.

Ideally, you would be able to place the data in XML, but display the data in HTML. That's the point of XML in a nutshell. XML is a generic data container that you can query and transform via code, applying formatting commands suitable for the display mechanism. The tool for querying and transforming the data in an XML document is called Extensible Stylesheet Language (XSL). In the remainder of this chapter, you'll see how to use XML as a data container and how to use XSL to transform that data into HTML.

Using the Microsoft XML Parser from ASP

You read XML files with a *parser*. There are several freeware and shareware parsers available, mostly written in Java. Microsoft provides a parser with IE 5 that you can use on the client or the server (assuming IE 5 is installed on the server). You can also download the parser as a redistributable file and install it on computers running IE 4 for use with your applications. The download URL is

```
msdn.microsoft.com/downloads/tools/xmlparser/xmldl.asp
```

The installed Microsoft parser file is `msxml.dll`. It's a COM component you can use with ASP, VB, C++, or any other development tool that understands COM. To use it in Visual InterDev, the easiest technique is to create a project reference to the Microsoft XML SDK Version X.X type library. The advantage of setting a reference in InterDev is that its built-in IntelliSense technology shows you the property and method calls available for each object. Of course, you don't have to set a reference—you can simply create the XML objects as with any other COM component. In this book, I'm using the XML SDK Version 2, but you can run all the code with the version installed with IE 5.

You can create an instance of the XML parser on either the server or the client, letting you perform data and transform operations on either side of the transaction. The advantage of this is that you can store and manipulate data on the server, using transforms to return HTML for non-IE browsers. Without changing much code, you can perform the same operations within IE—essentially offloading the process to the client and partitioning your application.

To create an instance of the XML parser on the server, use the following:

```
<%
   Dim domDoc
   set domDoc = Server.CreateObject("MSXML.DOMDocument")
%>
```

The previous statement creates an instance of an XML object called an XML DOMDocument object, which is the root object of the Microsoft XML object model. The DOMDocument object can read and write XML from files and streams. You use the `load` method to read a file. For example, to read the XML file in Listing 19.1 (which is in the file `ch19i1.xml`), you can write:

```
<%
   Dim domDoc
   Dim aFilename
   Set domDoc = server.CreateObject("MSXML.DOMDocument")
   aFilename = server.MapPath("ch19i1.xml")
   If Not domDoc.Load(aFilename) Then
     Response.Write "Could not load the file."
     Response.end
   End If
%>
```

As the DOMDocument object reads an XML file, it parses it into a collection of subobjects called nodes. The root node is a special node called the document element node. You can retrieve the document element by creating a node object and setting it to the node returned from the DOMDocument's `documentElement` method. For example:

```
<%
   Dim domDoc
```

```
   Dim aFilename
   Dim aNode
   Set domDoc = server.CreateObject("MSXML.DOMDocument")
   aFilename = server.MapPath("ch19i1.xml")
   If Not domDoc.Load(aFilename) Then
     Response.Write "Could not load the file " & _
       aFilename & "<br>"
     Response.end
   End If
   Set aNode = domDoc.documentElement
%>
```

Nodes can be one of several types, but the most important point is that all nodes share some common methods and properties. For example, all nodes expose an `xml` property. To view the XML loaded in the previous response, you can create an ASP page and send the XML to the browser as HTML (see Listing 19.3).

Listing 19.3: Reading/Viewing XML Code from ASP (`ch19i3.asp`)

```
<%@ Language=VBScript %>
<% option explicit %>
<%
   Dim domDoc
   Dim aFilename
   Set domDoc = server.CreateObject("MSXML.DOMDocument")
   aFilename = server.MapPath("ch19i1.xml")
   If Not domDoc.Load(aFilename) Then
     Response.Write "Could not load the file " & _
       aFilename & "<br>"
     Response.end
   End If
%>
<html>
   <head>
   </head>
   <body>
     <pre><code>
     <%
       Response.Write(server.HTMLEncode _
         ("<xml>" & domDoc.documentElement.xml & "</xml>"))
```

```
%>
</code></pre>
</body>
</html>
```

The code in Listing 19.3 loads the XML file `ch19i1.xml` and then displays the contents of the `xml` method for the document element node. You should notice that you must format the XML for viewing using the `Server.HTTPEncode` method; otherwise, the browser treats most of the XML data as markup and doesn't display anything. You should also notice that the XML doesn't look the same as when you simply loaded the same XML file directly into the browser. That's because the XML parser within IE applies special XSL formatting to XML files that you load directly. In this case, because the file is an ASP file, the MIME type is `text/html` by default. Therefore, IE has no idea that the file being loaded contains XML and it doesn't use the built-in XSL style sheet.

INTRODUCTION TO XSL

Reading a tokenized text file is no great feat; neither is reading it into an object hierarchy, but reading it in such a way that you can later query the resulting objects is. You can think of an XML file as a mini-database. The XML parser understands the database structure and can retrieve any set of data items or any specific data item for you. You retrieve data from XML using XSL.

When you use XSL in this way, you're *filtering* the XML. To filter XML, you use *XSL Patterns* to retrieve one or more nodes. There are two methods to retrieve nodes: `SelectNodes`, which returns a collection of nodes that match the specified pattern, and `SelectSingleNode`, which returns the first node that matches the specified pattern.

You can use XSL in another way to transform XML into another format. I'll show you how to use XSL to transform XML into HTML a little later in this chapter. For now, just remember that you can use XSL transforms for more than creating HTML—you could just as easily transform XML into a Word document, a spreadsheet, or a text file.

NOTE

For brevity, you can assume in the following examples that the code has already created a DOMDocument object called `domDoc` and loaded the `ch19i1.xml` file by executing the `DomDocument.load` method.

Querying XML with XSL

Using XSL queries, you can return one or more nodes from any location in an XML document. For example, to obtain the values of the `<class>` and `<creator>` nodes, you can query the `DOMDocument` element with an XSL query string. The value of a node is its `nodeValue` property. The `nodeValue` property tries to make intelligent decisions about the data type in the node. It returns a number if the node contains a numeric value and a date if it contains a date. If the parser can't determine the data type, it returns a string (the default). You can always obtain the node value as a string using the `text` property. Listing 19.4 shows the XSL query syntax to retrieve the nodes. In a browser, the result looks like Figure 19.4.

Listing 19.4: Retrieving Nodes with XSL Queries (`ch19i4.asp`)

```
<%
set aNode = domDoc.SelectSingleNode("class/name")
Response.Write "The class name is: " & _
  aNode.nodeValue & "<br>"

set aNode = domDoc.SelectSingleNode("class/creator")
Response.Write "The class creator is: " & _
  aNode.nodeValue & "<br>"
%>
```

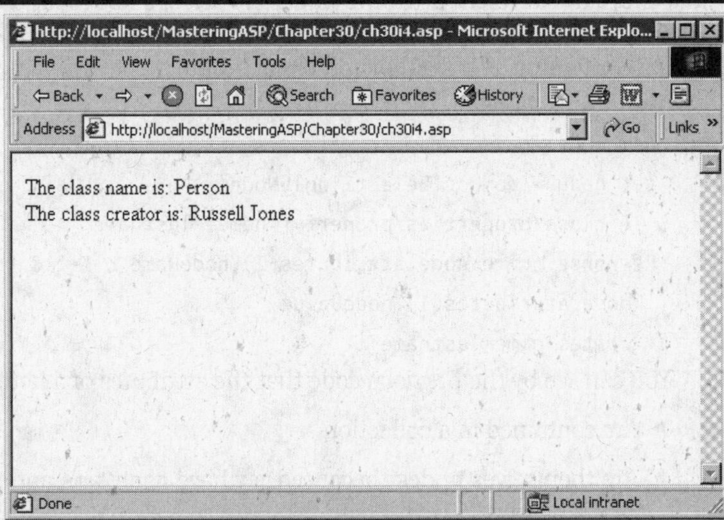

FIGURE 19.4: XSL query results (`ch19i4.asp`)

You can select several nodes at once with a query. When you do that, the query returns a collection of nodes in an IXMLDOMNodeList object. Don't be intimidated by the long name—the IXMLDOMNodeList object acts much like any other COM collection object. Because of its Java heritage, the XML parser uses a `length` rather than the more common `count` property to obtain the number of nodes in the collection. For example:

```
dim nodes
set nodes = domDoc.SelectNodes("class/properties/property")
Response.Write nodes.length ' writes 2
```

Using `For Each...Next`, you can easily iterate through all of the nodes in a collection. For example:

```
dim nodes
dim node
set nodes = domDoc.SelectNodes("class/properties/property")
For Each node in nodes
  Response.Write node.nodename & "=" & node.nodeValue _
    & "<br>"
Next
```

For nodes that have the same names, you differentiate between them by their attribute values. For example, there are two `<property>` tags, but they have different attribute values. To select a node based on an attribute value, you append a block in square brackets to the XSL query string containing an @ symbol and the attribute name and value you wish to find. For example:

```
dim node
set node = domDoc.SelectSingleNode _
  ("class/properties/property[@name='lastname']")
Response.Write node.attributes(1).nodeName & "=" & _
  node.attributes(1).nodeValue
' writes name=lastname
```

You can see by the previous code that the attributes of a node

- Are contained in a collection
- Are themselves nodes (because they have `nodeName` and `nodeValue` properties)

Iterating through XML

Internally, the XML parser treats attributes as nodes (for those who care, the `IXMLDOMAttribute` class inherits from `IXMLDOMNode`). Gaining access to node attribute names and values and iterating through them is almost exactly the same as iterating through nodes. Because you've seen so many collection iteration examples, I'm going to skip the short code example and jump directly to a more complex example containing the iteration code. Listing 19.5 shows you the rudiments of how generic code can become. The code iterates through the nodes of the XML file, displaying nodes without attributes as `<h2>` tags, and nodes with attributes as `<table>` tags, where the columns contain the attribute values. The listing introduces a few other useful properties, such as the `hasChildNodes` property, which returns `True` if the node has children.

Listing 19.5: Iterating through XML (`ch19i5.asp`)

```
<%@ Language=VBScript %>
<% option explicit %>
<%
  dim domDoc
  dim aFilename
  Dim node
  Dim nodes
  dim mainNodes
  dim mainNode
  dim attr
  dim root

  Set domDoc = Server.CreateObject("MSXML.DOMDocument")
  afilename =server.MapPath("ch19i1.xml")
  if not domDoc.load(afilename) then
    Response.Write "Could not load the file " & aFilename _
      & "<br>"
    Response.End
  end if
%>
<html>
<head>
</head>
<body>
<%
' display the root node
```

```
set root = domDoc.documentElement
Response.Write "<h1>" & root.nodename & ": " & _
  root.nodevalue & "</h1>"
Set mainNodes = root.childNodes
For Each mainNode In mainNodes
  If mainNode.hasChildNodes = False Then
    Response.Write "<h2>" & mainNode.nodeName & ": " & _
      mainNode.text & "</h2><br>"
  Else
    Response.Write "<h3>" & mainNode.nodeName & ": " & _
      mainNode.text & "</h3>"
    Set nodes = mainNode.childNodes
    If nodes.length > 0 Then
      Set node = nodes(0)
      If Not node.Attributes Is Nothing Then
        If node.Attributes.length > 0 Then
          Response.Write "<table border='1'>"
          Response.Write "<thead>"
          For Each attr In node.Attributes
            Response.Write "<th>" & attr.nodeName & "</th>"
          Next
          Response.Write "</tr>"
          For Each node In nodes
            Response.Write "<tr>"
            For Each attr In node.Attributes
              If attr.nodeValue = "" Then
                Response.Write "<td>" & " " & "</td>"
              Else
                Response.Write "<td>" & attr.nodeValue _
                  & "</td>"
              End If
            Next
            Response.Write "</tr>"
          Next
          Response.Write "</table>"
        End If
      End If
    End If
  End If
Next
%>
</body>
</html>
```

In Listing 19.5, I've used two collections—one for the collection of main nodes and those nodes that are direct children. The result is strikingly similar to the HTML example in Listing 19.2. Figure 19.5 shows how Listing 19.5 looks in a browser.

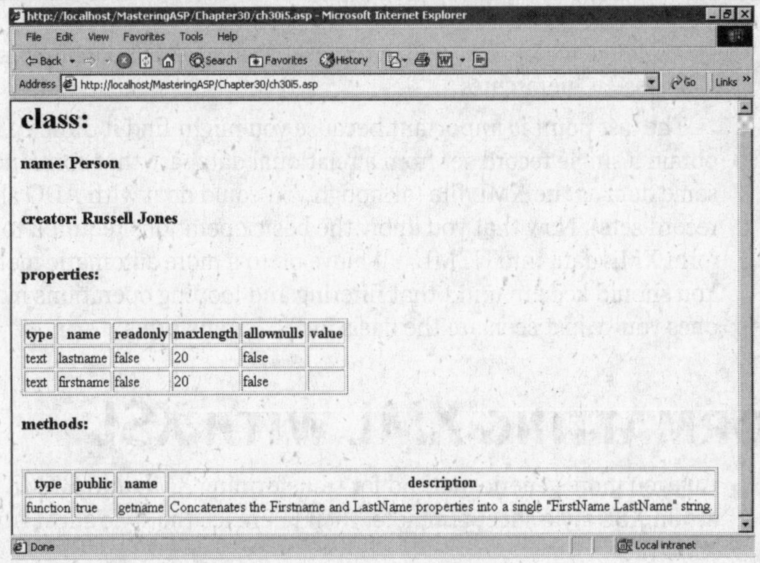

FIGURE 19.5: Iterating through XML (`ch19i5.asp`)

You're probably thinking this isn't any easier than creating the same type of display with record sets. Well, just wait—I'm not through yet. It's important to realize that the code is generic—it can display any XML file. So you can see that in action, I've saved most of the fields in the Employees table from the Microsoft Northwind sample database as an XML file. If you change the filename in the `ch19i5.asp` file from `ch19i1.xml` to `employees.xml`, you can see that the code works equally well with an entirely different record set.

The main points you should have by now are as follows:

- You can find any particular node via an XSL query.
- You can retrieve a collection of nodes with an XSL query.
- You can find one or more nodes that contain a specific attribute and value with an XSL query.

- You can iterate through node collections—whether the collection contains nodes or attributes—using identical syntax (because attributes *are* nodes).
- All nodes have the same properties and methods regardless of their position in the hierarchy.
- Unlike record sets, which represent tables, XML documents represent hierarchies.

The last point is important because you might find it difficult to obtain a single record set from a relational database that contained the same data as the XML file (although you could do it with ADO shaped record sets). Now that you know the basic operations required to transform XML data into HTML, I'll move on to a more automatic method. You should keep in mind that filtering and looping operations like the ones you've just seen are the basis for XSL transforms.

Formatting XML with XSL

An even more generic method for transforming XML into HTML is to create an XSL style sheet template, then reference the style sheet from the XML file.

XSL contains fewer than 20 element types (tags), each of which consists of XML! For example, the XSL element `<xsl:value-of/>` tells the parser to replace the tag with the value of an XML node.

NOTE

I've made use of the shorthand slash for an empty element. The slash is the equivalent of writing `<xsl:value-of></xsl:value-of>`. XSL is XML, so you *must* close all the tags.

If you don't select a specific XML node, the parser uses the current node. You can select a specific node using a `select` attribute containing an XSL query string. For example, the XSL element `<xsl:value-of select="class/name"/>` replaces the tag with the value `Person`, which is the value of the `<class><name>` tag in the XML file.

You can iterate through nodes using the `<xsl:for-each select="query">` element. For example, the following code iterates through each <property> tag in the XML file and selects the value of the name attribute:

```
<xsl:for-each select="class/properties/property">
   <xsl:value-of select="@name"/>
</xsl:for-each>
```

Listing 19.6 uses a new copy of the XML file introduced at the beginning of this chapter (ch19i6.xml). The XML content has not changed, but the file contains a reference to an XSL style sheet (ch19i6.xsl). To view the example, point your browser at the file ch19i6.xml.

Listing 19.6: XML File with XSL Style Sheet Reference

```
<?xml version='1.0'?>
<?xml-stylesheet type="text/xsl" href="ch19i6.xsl"?>
<class>
   <name>Person</name>
   <creator>Russell Jones</creator>
   <properties>
      <property type="text" name="lastname" readonly="false"
         maxlength="20" allownulls="false" value="">
      </property>
      <property type="text" name="firstname" readonly="false"
         maxlength="20" allownulls="false" value="">
      </property>
   </properties>
   <methods>
      <method type="function" public="true" name="getname"
         description=
         "Concatenates the Firstname and LastName properties
         into a single &quot;FirstName LastName&quot; string.">
      </method>
   </methods>
</class>
```

NOTE

Only IE 5 currently supports viewing XML files directly in the browser. I'll show you how to use the same techniques on the server and output HTML for non-IE browsers.

When IE loads the XML file in Listing 19.6, the XML parser recognizes the style sheet reference, queries the server for the XSL style sheet file, then applies the rules in the template to transform the XML data. The on-screen output is the result of the transformation. Figure 19.6 shows the result.

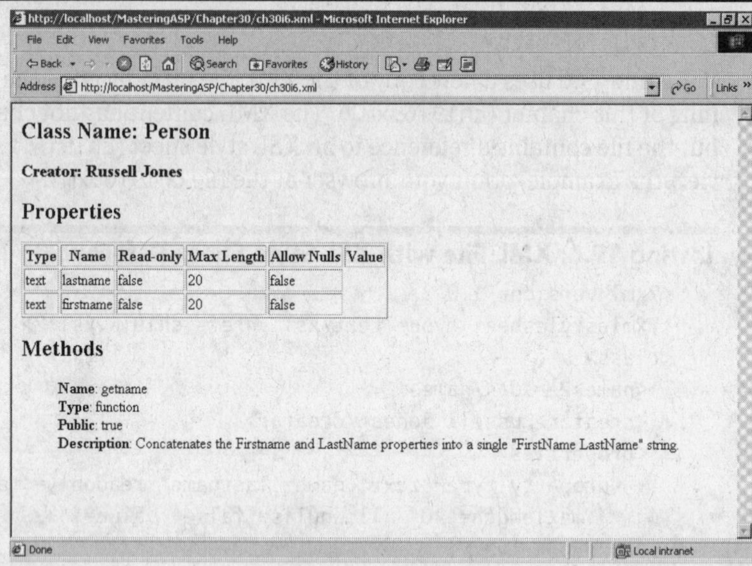

FIGURE 19.6: Transforming XML with an XSL style sheet

Interestingly, although the browser is obviously displaying HTML, if you right-click in the browser window and select View Source from the context menu, you won't see any HTML. The source is the XML file itself. The HTML lives only in your browser's memory space.

Transforming data on the browser with XSL is convenient and takes a big load off your server, but only works in IE. If you want to use this technology for down-level browsers, you must perform the XSL transform on the server. To do that, you call the `transformNode` method of the DOMDocument object. Listing 19.7 shows an example.

WHY SO MANY PROGIDS?

During this writing, I discovered that the ClassID for the `MSXML.DOMDocument` object is duplicated under another name—`Microsoft.XMLDom`. A little research turned up this information:

- There are six ProgIDs for creating XMLDOMDocument objects.
- `Microsoft.XMLDom` is version-independent.
- `Microsoft XMLDom 1.0` is version-dependent.
- `MSXML.DomDocument` is the class name of the object.

With version 2, all three ProgIDs create the same object—in other words, they all have the same ClassID {2933BF90-7B36-11D2-B20E-00C04F983E60}. The preceding ProgIDs all create Apartment-threaded DOMDocument objects.

There are three corresponding ProgIDs that create Free-threaded DOMDocument objects:

- `Microsoft.FreeThreadedXMLDom`
- `Microsoft FreeThreadedXMLDom 1.0`
- `MSXML.DOMFreeThreadedDocument`

Use one of the first set to create DOMDocument objects for use on a single page. If you absolutely must store a DOMDocument object at Session or Application scope, create a FreeThreadedDom Document object. It doesn't matter which ProgID you use as long as you're aware of the threading model. Personally, I'd advise you not to use any version-dependent code if you can avoid it.

Listing 19.7: Server-Side XSL Transform Example (`ch19i7.asp`)

```
<%@ LANGUAGE = VBScript %>
<%
  Dim XMLFile
  Dim XSLFile
  Dim domDoc
  Dim styleDoc
  XMLFile = Server.MapPath("ch19i6.xml")
  XSLFile = Server.MapPath("ch19i6.xsl")
  Set domDoc = Server.CreateObject("Microsoft.XMLDom")
  domDoc.async = False
```

Part v

```
    domDoc.Load (XMLFile)
    If domDoc.parseerror.reason <> "" Then
      Response.Write domDoc.parseerror.reason
      Response.end
    End If
    Set styleDoc = Server.CreateObject("Microsoft.XMLDom")
    styleDoc.async = False
    styleDoc.Load (XSLFile)
    If styleDoc.parseerror.reason <> "" Then
      Response.Write styleDoc.parseerror.reason
      Response.end
    End If
    Response.Write (domDoc.transformNode(styleDoc))
%>
```

The example loads an XML file and the XSL file. It makes no difference whether you load an XML file with a style sheet reference or without one. You can prove this by loading either `ch19i1.xml`, which has no XSL style sheet reference, or `ch19i6.xml`, as in the example, which does have a reference. Both versions work identically.

The final line in the listing performs the transform. The `transformNode` method accepts an XMLDOMNode object (remember that a DOMDocument object is a node) that must contain either a complete XSL style sheet or a style sheet fragment.

Caching Data with XML

You don't have to work with complete XML files to take advantage of XML. Using IE, you can load XML directly inline with HTML or use a URL reference to an XML file on a server, effectively caching the data on the client. To load inline XML into the browser, wrap the XML data with a `<XML ID="someID">` tag. You must provide the ID to be able to access the XML data from a script.

When you place XML inline into the browser it's called a *data island*, perhaps because it's an island of XML data in a sea of HTML.

TIP

You cannot use the processing instruction tag that begins stand-alone XML files (`<?xml version='1.0'?>`); use a plain `<XML ID="someID">` tag instead. You can place the processing instruction after the `<xml>` tag if you wish.

For example, Listing 19.8 is an HTML file that contains an XML data island.

Listing 19.8: XML Data Island Example (`ch19i8.htm`)

```
<html>
<head>
  <META NAME="GENERATOR"
    Content="Microsoft Visual Studio 6.0">
  <title></title>
</head>
<body>
  <xml id="xmlTest">
  <class>
    <name>Person</name>
    <creator>Russell Jones</creator>
    <properties>
      <property type="text" name="lastname" readonly="false"
        maxlength="20" allownulls="false" value="">
      </property>
      <property type="text" name="firstname"
        readonly="false" maxlength="20" allownulls="false"
        value="">
      </property>
    </properties>
    <methods>
      <method type="function" public="true" name="getname"
        description="Concatenates the Firstname and LastName
        properties into a single &quot;FirstName
        LastName&quot; string.">
      </method>
    </methods>
  </class>
  </xml>
</body>
</html>

<script for="window" event="onload" language="VBScript">
  Call readXML
</script>
<script language="VBScript">
  Sub readXML()
    Dim domDoc
```

```
      Dim s
      Dim N
      Set domDoc = xmlTest.XMLDocument
      On Error Resume Next
      s = "Class: " & domDoc.selectSingleNode _
        ("class/name").Text & vbCrLf
      s = s & "Creator: " & domDoc.selectSingleNode _
        ("class/creator").Text & vbCrLf
      s = s & "PROPERTIES" & vbCrLf
      For Each N In domDoc.SelectNodes _
        ("class/properties/property")
        s = s & "     " & N.Attributes(1).Text & vbCrLf
      Next
      s = s & "METHODS" & vbCrLf
      For Each N In domDoc.SelectNodes("class/methods/method")
        s = s & "     " & N.Attributes(2).Text & "(" & _
                          N.Attributes(3).Text & ")" & vbCrLf
      Next
      MsgBox s
    End Sub
  </script>
```

By caching data on the client in XML data islands, you have the complete power of the XML parser and XSL queries available to retrieve the data. But wait! It gets even better! You can create a very generic method to display a table in the browser from a record set. You write the data as an XML file, then load the file from the browser along with an XSL style sheet and perform the entire transformation within the browser.

For example, Listing 19.9 shows how to store Recordset data in the browser as XML and transform the XML on the client.

NOTE

You need to provide write and delete access for the test directory you're using for the `IUSR_MACHINENAME` account before the following script will run properly. It needs write access to persist the Recordset object in XML form and needs delete access to delete the file if it already exists.

Listing 19.9: Moving Recordset Data to the Browser (`ch19i9.asp`)

```
<%@ Language=VBScript %>
<% option explicit %>
<html>
```

```
<head><title>Transforming XML In the Browser</title></head>
<body>
<%
  Dim conn
  Dim R
  Dim F
  Dim fs
  Set conn = server.CreateObject("ADODB.Connection")
  conn.CursorLocation = adUseClient
  conn.Open "DSN=Northwind;UID=sa;PWD="
  Set R = server.CreateObject("ADODB.Recordset")
  R.CursorLocation = adUseClient
  R.Open "SELECT * FROM Products" & _
    " ORDER BY ProductName", conn, _
    adOpenStatic, adLockReadOnly, adcmdtext
  Set R.ActiveConnection = Nothing
  conn.Close
  Set fs = server.CreateObject("Scripting.FileSystemObject")
  If fs.FileExists(server.MapPath("products.xml")) Then
    fs.DeleteFile server.MapPath("products.xml")
  End If
  Call R.Save(server.MapPath("products.xml"), adPersistXML)
%>
<xml id="xmlData" src="products.xml"></xml>
<xml id="xslStyle" src="ch19i9.xsl"></xml>
<div id="xmlResult"></div>
</body>
</html>
<script for="window" event="onload" language="VBScript">
  Call showTable
</script>
<script language="vbScript">
  Sub showTable()
    Dim xml
    Dim xsl
    On Error Resume Next
    Set xml = xmlData.XMLDocument
    If Err.Number <> 0 Then
      MsgBox Err.Description
    End If
    Set xsl = xslStyle.XMLDocument
    If Err.Number <> 0 Then
      MsgBox Err.Description
```

```
      End If
      xmlResult.outerHTML = xml.transformNode(xsl)
      If Err.Number <> 0 Then
        MsgBox Err.Description
      End If
    End Sub
  </script>
```

I think what's most interesting about this script is how much it does with so little code.

At this point, you should be fairly comfortable with the rudiments of XML. Don't get complacent though, there's a lot more to learn. For example, you can sort and filter XML using XSL methods. You can update an XML data island, post it to the server, read the data into a Recordset object, then update a database. You can load an `ADO.DataControl` object with XML data in a data island, then bind controls on the page directly to the DataControl object.

If there's one technology (besides ASP, of course) that you concentrate on over the next few months, it should be XML. I urge you to continue exploring XML because it's going to be extremely important in your Web programming career. One excellent source is the MSDN Online XML Developer Center at `http://msdn.microsoft.com/xml/default.asp`. Microsoft has just released XML SDK Version 3.0, which extends XML even further throughout the application space.

Over the next few chapters, you'll learn more about using XML with ASP and databases. But first, here are a few notes about technologies I didn't cover in this chapter that you may find worthwhile:

- DHTML behaviors let you store code in a single location on the server that executes on the client. You can apply a behavior to any DOM object. For a good explanation of how to use DHTML behaviors, browse to

  `http://msdn.microsoft.com/workshop/Author/behaviors/howto/using.asp`

- XHTML redefines HTML in a transitional XML format. XHTML 1.0 became a W3C Recommendation in January 2000, and XHTML 1.1 was approved May 2001 to add a variety of tag modules. A good source of information is `www.w3.org/MarkUp`. You can find the W3C Recommendation for XHTML 1.1 at

  `www.w3.org/TR/2001/PR-xhtml11-20010406/`.

- XML-based scriptlets are the next version of server scriptlets. These text-based components register themselves as COM objects. You can call them from a browser without changing the page. For example, you might write a validation component as a scriptlet.
- The Simple Object Access Protocol (SOAP) is an XML-based, COM-like protocol that lets you make remote object calls over HTTP. Essentially, you can create an object on a remote server and then access its methods and properties. For more information, browse to

  `http://www.microsoft.com/mind/0100/soap/soap.asp`
- Java is a cross-platform language developed by Sun Microsystems. Despite the initial hype, Java has not developed into a super language; nevertheless, in addition to portability, it has three important features that VB does not have (yet). First, you cannot compile a method that calls another method that can raise an error without writing an error handler. This feature should be standard in every language. I think the greatest weakness of programmers is a lack of attention to error handling. This leads to weak applications, bad error messages, and frustrated users and support personnel. Second, Java lets you write multithreaded applications, so you can use it to write components that don't have the threading problems inherent in VB's Apartment-only threading model. Third, Java is rapidly becoming the non-Microsoft world's generic language, much as JavaScript/ ECMAScript is the preferred scripting language for all browsers except IE. You owe it to yourself to at least become familiar with Java.

WHAT'S NEXT?

Knowing XML helps you give your Web application broad new potential. The next chapter shows you how to combine this knowledge with your understanding of ASP. By integrating XML with IIS objects and building XHTML components, you can create new ways of transferring, manipulating, or displaying data. This, in turn, gives your application a high degree of flexibility not often found in today's Web site.

Chapter 20

XML AND ASP

XML started out as the ultimate client technology ("Build your own documents with your own structured language!"), but over time, most developers have come to realize that this original view of XML was both simplistic and naive. Most people have neither the time nor the resources to create an entire markup language. As the data-centric view of XML has begun to permeate the XML development community, the language has increasingly moved to the server or even farther back into the database stores.

Perhaps not surprisingly, XML has made significant inroads in two server-side technologies: Java and Active Server Pages. Entire books have been written about Java and XML, to the extent that many in the Java camp have proclaimed that XML and Java were made for one another. While I'd dispute this, the ability to leverage XML on the server in most languages makes it far more suited for its role there.

Adapted from *XML Developer's Handbook*™, by Kurt Cagle

ISBN 0-7821-2704-5 640 pages $49.99

In this chapter, I look at XML as a server technology as well as its relationship to Microsoft's Active Server Pages. The two form an uneasy alliance, although the most recent version of IIS provides somewhat better support for XML. I concentrate here on baseline solutions (because the adoption of Windows 2000 is still far from common in the marketplace as this chapter is being written).

Designing Server-Side XML

The term *Web application* is a relatively new one in the lexicon of developers. Applications that run on a single machine typically have very tightly coupled architectures, to such an extent that they seem largely seamless and monolithic. Programs such as Microsoft Word or Excel tend to best exemplify this principle: While Word, for example, actually consists of a fairly large number of discrete components, in practice most of the core functionality resides within a single application executable.

Client/server applications represent the next level of abstraction when dealing with programs. In this case, you're typically dealing with two primary programs: a server program that provides the data (and occasionally, but not often, the formatting of that data) and a client program that places a user interface on that data. The vast majority of accounting and inventory management systems fall into this category.

The Web application moves the level of abstraction up yet one more level. In this case, the client application is a browser that provides a rendering engine for some type of code (HTML, XML, or several others) while the server is a generalized program providing data based upon HTTP requests and posts. In other words, the client and server are both very generalized applications. Between client and server resides the application layer, where application calls are translated (usually through an interface such as Active Server Pages, Java Server Pages, CGI, or ultimately XML) into client-viewable code.

As a developer, you are undoubtedly familiar with most of this at the level of using the technology, but it's worth thinking about this architecture a bit in light of XML. If you assume that even the HTML that you are dealing with is, in fact, XML (that is, if you are working with XHTML), then some interesting possibilities begin to emerge for application design, either within an ASP script or as part of a component:

1. An HTTP request is made against the server, passing a number of parameters in the form of name/value pairs. *Suppose*

that the request information is then transformed into an XML document.

2. Specific parameters within the request are used to determine which specific action the ASP code will take. This action is expressed in the form of an XSL script.

3. The requested action, in turn, loads in other actions, perhaps through some kind of a "job" script written in XSL.

4. Data from external sources would, in turn, be output based upon the input from the job scripts and the initial request parameters.

5. Similarly, at various points along the path, resultant information (for example, the contents of a form) could be written out to external XML files or data sources.

6. Finally, the resultant information is formatted in a manner appropriate to the browser and sent back to it.

This is a very abstract view of the process of using XML on the server. In essence, this is the pipeline view; the XML flows along one or more pipes in this model, from the input based upon the `Request` object from the client to the output sent back to the client. This model works well when all of the elements are XML sources, although it can even be used with external data providers or consumers through the use of XML servers, which are primarily programs or DLLs that can communicate through either the XSL script interface or through XML parameters.

Building such an application can take more time to set up than one ASP page would (or even a couple of them), but the flexibility and strength that this model offers more than pays for itself in the long run. Some specific advantages to the pipeline view include:

Modularity You can use the same data stream and application interface to handle any number of different tasks.

Targetability You can target your output to any number of different sources simply by swapping one XSL transformation for another.

Portability By dealing with abstract operations, you can port your XML code to work with any W3C XSL server, regardless of operating system, browser, or platform.

Encapsulation The result of any such job is itself an XML stream that can, in turn, be incorporated into other XML clients.

One interesting upshot of all of this is that once you begin building a pipeline model your ASP or JSP code becomes much smaller and more manageable (and may, in time, disappear completely as specialized servers come into play) and that the development environment begins to look pretty exclusively like a single cohesive XML system.

INTEGRATING THE IIS OBJECTS AND XML

A significant amount of the processing in any ASP script goes to a simple process: retrieving and interpreting the parameters that come from forms or query strings in browsers. Some of this activity focuses on validation—is the data coming in well-formed or within bounds?—while much of it also deals with converting null values (unpassed parameters) to their default values.

The use of XML here can be a little problematic. In an ideal world, most of the processing should be able to take place within an XSL script, but even with the benefits of the `addParameter` method in the compiled XSL object, this still means a lot of procedural code needs to be written just to handle the simple act of setting up parameters. For example, Listing 20.1 shows a sample of code that is typically used for setting up an XSL script for processing, in this case for a page that shows the various messages available on a given message board.

Listing 20.1: Bad ASP Parameterization (`Listing20.1.txt`)

```
<%
' showListPageBad.asp
page=request.queryString("page")
if page="" then
  page=1
end if
recordSize=request.queryString("recordSize")
if recordSize="" then
  recordSize=20
end if
board=request.queryString("board")
set xslDoc=createObject("MSXML2.DOMDocument")
xslDoc.load server.mapPath("showListPageBad.xsl")
```

```
set param=xslDoc.selectSingleNode("xsl:param[@name='page']")
param.setAttribute "select",page
set param=xslDoc.selectSingleNode(_
  "xsl:param[@name='board']")
param.setAttribute "select",board
set xmlDoc=createObject("MSXML2.DOMDOcument")
xmlDoc.load server.mapPath(board+".xml")
response.write xmlDoc.transformNode(xslDoc)
```

So why is this kind of a page a problem? There are actually several problems here. The first and most pressing is a lack of modularity. The ASP page will work only for the situation where you want to show a list page, and only for the specific data contained therein. If you wanted to show the data in a different way, you would need a separate ASP page to handle this, which both degrades performance (since it increases the number of documents to cache) and makes management of the site more complex.

A second problem has to do with implementation of the `Request` object. Here, I have to know that the `Request` object has a specific set of interfaces and, moreover, that the information was specifically sent via either a GET or a POST command on the server. If I wanted to change the data source of this information (perhaps for testing purposes or maybe to cache commonly accessed pages automatically), I would have to provide an alternative `Request` object with identical interfaces.

Finally, the parameterization shown here is DOM-based: XSLT is supposed to minimize the interaction of DOM with the host environment, but if you have to spend all your time writing DOM parameter calls, then somewhere along the line you've lost sight of the advantages that XSLT offers. Since the DOM described here is very much a Microsoft implementation, the less reliance you have on the DOM in your XSLT code, the easier that it is to port to other systems (or vice versa).

Rethinking the *Request* Object

The `Request` object is a very useful (and surprisingly complex) component; although most people tend to use it to retrieve form or query-string information, in fact it controls four distinct collections:

Form The form collection contains information sent from HTML forms (and more generically contains information sent via the HTTP POST method). This is the most common way of sending large or complex data and can be used to send binary data as well as text data.

Query string The query string collection contains information sent from URL requests with query strings (the name/value pairs given after the ? character in URLs, and separated by an & character). More generically, `QueryString` contains information sent via the HTTP `GET` method. Query strings are the oldest HTTP command, but they are limited in length to 1,024 characters (give or take a few per implementation).

Cookies Cookies are bits of information that are kept by the client browser and are indexed by the same key mechanism that forms and query strings use.

Server variables These contain information that either the server itself retains or that is sent as part of the header information from the client. Unlike the other properties, these are typically a fixed set of tokens.

One useful characteristic of each of these collections is that you don't necessarily need to know the name of each key to invoke it; instead, you can enumerate through each of these collections and retrieve the keys directly, which, in turn, lets you retrieve the values associated with each key. This implies that it should be possible to make the `Request` object more generic, even conceivably turning it into an XML object.

If a mechanism exists to turn the `Request` object into XML, this means that the entire contents of the `Request` object can be passed directly into the XSL document without needing onerous ASP code to do the conversions. This simplifies the ASP code to such an extent as making it (almost) unnecessary. It also makes it easy to swap out this `Request` object with a different one (or an XML file that emulates such an object). The `passRequestObjectTo()` function and its two supporting functions, `getRequestXML()` and `setKeysCollection()` (Listing 20.2), do just this.

Listing 20.2: XML Response Creator Functions (`Listing20.2.asp`)

```
function getRequestXML(collectionsString)
  dim xmlDoc
  set xmlDoc = server.createObject("Microsoft.XMLDOM")
  xmlDoc.loadXML "        <keys/>"
  if collectionsString = "" then
    collectionsString = "all"
  end if
  collections=split(lcase(collectionsString),",")
  if collections(0) = "all" or collections(0) = "" then
    setKeysCollection xmlDoc,"querystring"
    setKeysCollection xmlDoc,"form"
```

```
    setKeysCollection xmlDoc,"cookies"
    setKeysCollection xmlDoc,"servervariables"
  else
    for each collection in collections
      setKeysCollection xmlDoc,collection
    next
  end if
  set getRequestXML = xmlDoc
end function

function setKeysCollection(xmlDoc,collectionName)
  set collectionNode=xmlDoc.createElement("collection")
  collectionNode.setAttribute "id",collectionName
  for each key in eval("request." + collectionName)
    set keyNode=xmlDoc.createElement("key")
    keyNode.setAttribute "id",key
    keyNode.text=request(key)
    collectionNode.appendChild keyNode
  next
  xmlDoc.documentElement.appendChild collectionNode
  set setKeysCollection=collectionNode
end function

function passRequestObjectTo(xslDoc)
  collectionsString="all"
  set requestDoc=getRequestXML(collectionString)
  set param=xslDoc.selectSingleNode _
    ("//xsl:param[@name='request']")
  if param is nothing then
    set param=xslDoc.documentElement.insertBefore _
      (xslDoc.createElement("xsl:param"), _
        xslDoc.selectSingleNode("//xsl:template"))
    param.setAttribute "name","request"
  end if
  while param.childNodes.length > 0
    param.removeChild param.childNodes(0)
  wend
  param.appendChild requestDoc.documentElement
end function
```

To use `passRequestObjectTo()`, you define and load your XSL document, then call it as an argument to `passRequestObjectTo`. This will, in turn, generate an XML `Request` object and place it into the `$request` parameter definition. At that point, the object is part of your XSL and can be referenced in the same manner that you reference other parametric information. (I use this extensively throughout the chapter, so there will be many useful examples shortly.)

The way the code is set up, the keys are automatically assigned to the `$request` parameter, replacing whatever previous code had been in place. To simplify placement, I also explicitly create a request parameter node as part of the `RequestUtils.xsl` file, which can then be imported into any XSL filter through the `<xsl:include mechanism>`. The whole script for `RequestUtils.xsl` is shown later in this chapter in Listings 20.4 and 20.5.

The core of the code, `setKeysCollection`, performs the actual XML creation: It enumerates through each collection in turn, retrieves the keys for that collection, and then uses the keys to get to the values associated with those keys. For a typical machine, this generates output that looks something like Listing 20.3. The query string that was sent to the server to generate this was given as the following:

```
http://localhost/xmlpro/getRequestKeys.asp?key1=This+is+
key+1&key2=Here+is+another+key.
```

TIP

Throughout this chapter (and other chapters), we've had to break some string, especially sample URLs, to fit the printed page. These examples are actually all on one line in "real life."

Listing 20.3: XML Request Format (`Listing20.3.xml`)

```
<keys>
  <collection id="querystring">
    <key id="key1">This is key 1</key>
    <key id="key2">Here is another key.</key>
  </collection>
  <collection id="form" />
  <collection id="cookies" />
  <collection id="servervariables">
  <key id="ALL_HTTP">
    HTTP_ACCEPT:image/gif, image/x-xbitmap, image/jpeg,
    image/pjpeg, application/ms-bpc, application/msword,
    application/vnd.ms-powerpoint, application/vnd.ms-excel,
    */*
```

```
    HTTP_ACCEPT_LANGUAGE:en-us,da; q=0.5
    HTTP_CONNECTION:Keep-Alive
    HTTP_HOST:localhost
    HTTP_USER_AGENT:Mozilla/4.0
    (compatible; MSIE 5.5; Windows 98)
    HTTP_COOKIE:ASPSESSIONIDFFFEMOBX=LMLNIAFBJJBEPLFBIIHCBD
    ME HTTP_ACCEPT_ENCODING:gzip, deflate</key>
  <key id="ALL_RAW">
    Accept: image/gif, image/x-xbitmap, image/jpeg,
    image/pjpeg, application/ms-bpc, application/msword,
    application/vnd.ms-powerpoint, application/vnd.ms-excel,
    */*
    Accept-Language: en-us,da; q=0.5
    Connection: Keep-Alive
    Host: localhost
    User-Agent: Mozilla/4.0
    (compatible; MSIE 5.5; Windows 98)
    Cookie: ASPSESSIONIDFFFEMOBX=LMLNIAFBJJBEPLFBIIHCBDME
    Accept-Encoding: gzip, deflate</key>
  <key id="APPL_MD_PATH">/LM/W3SVC/1/ROOT/xmlpro</key>
  <key id="APPL_PHYSICAL_PATH">d:\xmlPro\</key>
  <key id="AUTH_PASSWORD" />
  <key id="AUTH_TYPE" />
  <key id="AUTH_USER" />
  <key id="CERT_COOKIE" />
  <key id="CERT_FLAGS" />
  <key id="CERT_ISSUER" />
  <key id="CERT_KEYSIZE" />
  <key id="CERT_SECRETKEYSIZE" />
  <key id="CERT_SERIALNUMBER" />
  <key id="CERT_SERVER_ISSUER" />
  <key id="CERT_SERVER_SUBJECT" />
  <key id="CERT_SUBJECT" />
  <key id="CONTENT_LENGTH">0</key>
  <key id="CONTENT_TYPE" />
  <key id="GATEWAY_INTERFACE">CGI/1.1</key>
  <key id="HTTPS">off</key>
  <key id="HTTPS_KEYSIZE" />
  <key id="HTTPS_SECRETKEYSIZE" />
  <key id="HTTPS_SERVER_ISSUER" />
  <key id="HTTPS_SERVER_SUBJECT" />
  <key id="INSTANCE_ID">1</key>
```

```
      <key id="INSTANCE_META_PATH">/LM/W3SVC/1</key>
      <key id="LOCAL_ADDR">127.0.0.1</key>
      <key id="LOGON_USER" />
      <key id="PATH_INFO">/xmlpro/getRequestObject.asp</key>
      <key id="PATH_TRANSLATED">
        d:\xmlPro\getRequestObject.asp</key>
      <key id="QUERY_STRING">
        key1=This+is+key+1&key2=Here+is+another+key.</key>
      <key id="REMOTE_ADDR">127.0.0.1</key>
      <key id="REMOTE_HOST">127.0.0.1</key>
      <key id="REMOTE_USER" />
      <key id="REQUEST_METHOD">GET</key>
      <key id="SCRIPT_NAME">/xmlpro/getRequestObject.asp</key>
      <key id="SERVER_NAME">localhost</key>
      <key id="SERVER_PORT">80</key>
      <key id="SERVER_PORT_SECURE">0</key>
      <key id="SERVER_PROTOCOL">HTTP/1.1</key>
      <key id="SERVER_SOFTWARE">Microsoft-IIS/4.0</key>
      <key id="URL">/xmlpro/getRequestObject.asp</key>
      <key id="HTTP_ACCEPT">
        image/gif, image/x-xbitmap, image/jpeg, image/pjpeg,
        application/ms-bpc, application/vnd.ms-powerpoint,
        application/vnd.ms-excel, application/msword, */*</key>
      <key id="HTTP_ACCEPT_LANGUAGE">en-us,da;q=0.5</key>
      <key id="HTTP_CONNECTION">Keep-Alive</key>
      <key id="HTTP_HOST">localhost</key>
      <key id="HTTP_USER_AGENT">
        Mozilla/4.0 (compatible; MSIE 5.5; Windows 98)</key>
      <key id="HTTP_COOKIE">
        ASPSESSIONIDFFFEMOBX=LMLNIAFBJJBEPLFBIIHCBDME</key>
      <key id="HTTP_ACCEPT_ENCODING">gzip, deflate</key>
      </collection>
    </keys>
```

Note that the bulk of the XML code is actually dedicated to server variables and that these same server variables frequently contain highly useful information. For example, the HTTP_USER_AGENT key contains information about the browser client and can be used to customize output within your XSL transformations. Similarly, HTTP_ACCEPT_LANGUAGE can tell you what the standard written language is for the browser, making it easier to internationalize your content. You can retrieve path information, making it possible for XSL scripts to retrieve potential information about their file and directory environments. Finally, you can access information such as the IP address of the remote host, making it possible to identify machines that have been visited before without using cookies (but see the sidebar "The Onus of Privacy").

THE ONUS OF PRIVACY

If you ask people who use the Internet what their biggest concerns are about the medium, one topic that frequently comes up is invasion of privacy. People are rightly uncomfortable giving information over the Internet that may fall into the hands of unscrupulous people (not to mention direct marketing firms) and are much more uncomfortable when information is interpolated from the user without their permission or knowledge.

Ironically, though, being able to track machines is an integral part of the Internet, and the supposition that one user will typically use the same machine is true in almost every case. When combined with the ability to analyze structured data that XML provides, this means that it is possible to store and discern patterns of behavior for a given person without necessarily having detailed information about that person—when you go to a large, complex site, what you buy, how much you buy, where you visit, and more could be observed by keeping salient information keyed to an IP address, meaning that this information could form the basis for both good (providing a better user experience by customizing the interface to preferred settings, keeping contextual references handy) and not so good (targeted marketing, surveillance, and the like).

The genie, unfortunately, is out of the bottle, and only by using this information ethically can we, as developers, expect to continue to receive the support from our ultimate employers, the people who use our applications.

Working with Request Information

Once you have the `Request` object's information in XML and attached to the XSL document, retrieving the information internally does require a little legerdemain. Suppose, for instance, that you had an XSL script where you wanted to know whether the browser was IE 5 or above so you could use advanced features or deprecate the code accordingly.

If you've done any major server development at all, you know that answering this question (at least under IIS) is not anywhere near as straightforward as it should be. One solution that has evolved has been to keep a file with various browser capabilities associated with the HTTP_USER_AGENT string. The downside to this is that the file must be periodically updated to reflect more recent browsers coming into the market; otherwise, any code built upon this will revert to the default browser in the list, which generally reflects the state of the art as of 1994.

TIP

You can find more information about the Browser Capabilities DLL at `http://msdn.microsoft.com/workshop/server/Default.asp`**. Additionally, the file itself, shipped with both PWS and IIS, is called** `browscap.ini` **and should be located in your Windows** `System` **or** `System32` **folder.**

Short of incorporating this component, you can still attempt to parse the HTTP_USER_AGENT, and XPath now offers basic tools to let you do that. On my machine, running Microsoft's Personal Web Server, my IE 5.5 client returned the HTTP_USER_AGENT of `Mozilla/4.0 (compatible; MSIE 5.5; Windows 98)`, while Netscape returned `Mozilla/4.7 [en] (Win98; I)`. The key sequence for identifying Internet Explorer is the expression `MSIE 5.`, which serves to identify any 5.*x* versions (IE 4 is likewise designated with the `MSIE 4.` sequence). Thus, we can use these as markers.

Rather than incorporating the test directly into the working templates, it would be better to define the browser type and version ahead of time and place the resulting values into variables. Note that variables in XSL are not quite the same as for procedural variables: Once you define a given variable at a specific scope, you can't redefine that variable again at the same scope. Listing 20.4 demonstrates one technique for handling detection of the browser.

Listing 20.4: Defining Browser Types (`Listing20.4.txt`)

```
<xsl:variable name="userAgent">
  <xsl:value-of
    select="$request//key[@id='HTTP_USER_AGENT']"/>
</xsl:variable>
<xsl:variable name="browser">
  <xsl:choose>
```

```
        <xsl:when test="contains($userAgent,'MSIE')">IE
          </xsl:when>
        <xsl:otherwise>NS</xsl:otherwise>
      </xsl:choose>
    </xsl:variable>
    <xsl:variable name="version">
      <xsl:choose>
        <xsl:when test="contains($browser,"IE")">
          <xsl:value-of select="number(substring-before(
            substring-after($userAgent, 'MSIE '),';'))"/>
        </xsl:when>
        <xsl:otherwise>
          <xsl:value-of select="number(substring-before(
            substring-after($userAgent, 'Mozilla/'),' '))"/>
        </xsl:otherwise>
      </xsl:choose>
    </xsl:variable>
```

The expression

```
<xsl:value-of select="$request//key[@id='HTTP_USER_AGENT']"
```

demonstrates how to retrieve a specific defined value from the Request object; simply replace HTTP_USER_AGENT with the name of the query string property, the form property, or the server variable name that you want to request.

NOTE

The preceding code is obviously somewhat simplistic in that it recognizes only Netscape and Internet Explorer browsers. As there are something on the order of 135 different browsers currently on the market, you could, in fact, expand this considerably. The default, though, is that if there is no match with Internet Explorer, then the browser is assumed to be Netscape Navigator.

You can also see some of the power of the XPath functions through the combined use of `substring-before` and `substring-after`, which together can parse out the HTTP_USER_AGENT string to retrieve information on browser make and version. For Internet Explorer 5.5, the variable `$browser` will contain the string `IE`, and `$version` will have a numeric value of `5.5`. For Netscape Navigator 4.7, the same variables will hold the values NS and `4.7`, respectively.

Retrieving Documents Internally

When you write computer books, you get used to dealing with products before they actually see the shrink-wrapped stage, and the Microsoft XML parser is no exception. Certain core features of the XSL model were not implemented when this chapter was written, and there isn't necessarily a reason to anticipate that they will be before the product ships.

One of the more frustrating of these features is the `document()` function. This function retrieves the contents of an XML document and makes it available for processing with the XSL filter. However, it is possible to make both a script-based function that will emulate this and another (more powerful) one that will let you pull in an XML document and transform it with either an external XSL document or a local XSL template. This transform-within-a-transform mechanism can prove quite powerful because it essentially lets you create transformational scripts.

You can create a script in the newer XSLT format that lets you add functions into your XSLT XPath expressions. For example, you could create a JavaScript block, as shown in Listing 20.5, that includes a `document()` function, a `transformTree()` function, and a `transformDocument()` function. `document()` lets you pass a URL to retrieve the contents of an external document, while `transformTree()` lets you transform a node source from an XSL filter node, and `transformDocument()` loads the respective documents, converts them into XML trees, and then transforms them with `transformTree()`.

Listing 20.5: The `document()`, `transformTree()`, and `transformDocument()` Inline Definitions—Part of `RequestUtils.xsl` (`Listing20.5.xsl`)

```
<xsl:stylesheet version="1.0"
  xmlns:xsl="http://www.w3.org/1999/XSL/Transform"
  xmlns:utils="http://www.vbxml.com/utils"
  xmlns:msxsl="urn:schemas-microsoft-com:xslt">
<xsl:output method="xml" omit-xml-declaration="yes"/>
<msxsl:script implements-prefix="utils"
  language="Javascript"><![CDATA[
  function document(url){
    var xmlDoc = new ActiveXObject("MSXML2.DOMDocument")
    xmlDoc.async = false;
    xmlDoc.load(url);
    return xmlDoc;  }
```

```
    function transformTree(xmlDoc,xslDoc){
      var target = "" + xmlDoc.transformNode(xslDoc);
      return target;  }

    function transformDocument(sourceUrl,filterUrl){
      var xmlDoc = document(sourceUrl);
      var xslDoc = document(filterUrl);
      var target = transformTree(xmlDoc,xslDoc);
      return target;  }
  ]]>  </msxsl:script>
  <!- more inline code ->
  </xsl:stylesheet>
```

Once these are defined, you can then use them to load external XML files and store them in variables, where they, in turn, can be manipulated using similar techniques as you would use for the initial XML stream. For a simple example, suppose that you had an XML document that served as a table of contents to other XML documents, such as that shown in Listing 20.6.

Listing 20.6: A Simple Table of Contents (`Listing20.6.txt`)

```
<book title="XML Developer's Handbook">
  <chapter src="chapter1.xml" title="Why XML?"/>
  <chapter src="chapter2.xml" title="XML and DOM"/>
  <chapter src="chapter3.xml" title="XML and XPath/>
  <chapter src="chapter4.xml" title="XML Patterns"/>
  <chapter src="chapter5.xml" title="XPath"/>
</book>
```

You could combine all of the chapters into a single document through an XSL script that uses the preceding `utils:document()` definition, as shown in Listing 20.7.

Listing 20.7: Combining Chapters (`Listing20.7.xsl`)

```
<xsl:stylesheet version="1.0"
  xmlns:xsl="http://www.w3.org/1999/XSL/Transform"
  xmlns:utils="http://www.vbxml.com/utils"
  xmlns:msxsl="urn:schemas-microsoft-com:xslt">
<xsl:output method="xml" omit-xml-declaration="yes"/>
<msxsl:script implements-prefix="utils"
  language="Javascript"><![CDATA[
  function document(url){
    if (typeof(url) != "string"){
```

```
        url = url.text
      }
      var xmlDoc = new ActiveXObject("MSXML2.DOMDocument")
      xmlDoc.async = false;
      xmlDoc.load(url);
      return xmlDoc;  }
  ]]>  </msxsl:script>
  <xsl:template match="/">
    <book>
      <xsl:apply-templates select="//chapter"/>
    </book>
  </xsl:template>
  <xsl:template match="chapter">
    <xsl-copy-of select="utils:document(@src)"
      disable-output-escaping="yes"/>
    </xsl:template>
  </xsl:stylesheet>
```

TIP

While the code here is meant to showcase the use of scripting for acquiring documents, you should test your code to see whether `document()` has, in fact, been implemented before defining your own; the code will be faster and more robust.

This is a fairly easy application. For a more typical use of such code, let's return to the example that started out this chapter: the creation of a message board system. Each board is a separate file, with the messages contained in a hierarchical tree that shows primary messages and responses to those messages. The boards themselves have a table of contents file that lists all of the boards in the system, as shown in Listing 20.8.

Listing 20.8: Table of Contents for Boards (`Listing20.8.xml`)

```
<boards>
  <category id="site" public="yes">
    <board id="general">
      <title>General Site Board</title>
      <descr>This is essentially the "welcoming board" for
        the site.  Come here to introduce yourself, find out
        more about the site, or bring up important points to
        the general membership.</descr>
      <readAccess>0</readAccess>
```

```
      <writeAccess>1</writeAccess>
      <src>general.xml</src>
      <admin idref="cagle@olywa.net"/>
      <msgCount>3</msgCount>
      <baseMsgCount>2</baseMsgCount>
      <msgIndex>4</msgIndex>
    </board>
    <board id="announcements">
      <title>Announcements</title>
      <descr>This board contains notices from the site
        administrator concerning new features, technical
        problems, scheduled maintenance and the like.
      </descr>
      <src>announcements.xml</src>
      <readAccess>0</readAccess>
      <writeAccess>3</writeAccess>
      <admin idref="cagle@olywa.net"/>
      <msgCount>85</msgCount>
      <baseMsgCount>85</baseMsgCount>
      <msgIndex>86</msgIndex>
    </board>
    <board id="bugreport">
      <title>The Bug Report</title>
      <descr>This board is for use by members to report
        problems, bugs, and similar issues.</descr>
      <src>bugreport.xml</src>
      <readAccess>3</readAccess>
      <writeAccess>1</writeAccess>
      <admin idref="cagle@olywa.net"/>
      <msgCount>32</msgCount>
      <baseMsgCount>32</baseMsgCount>
      <msgIndex>33</msgIndex>
    </board>
  </category>
  <category id="xml" public="yes">
    <board id="xmlfaq">
      <title>XML Frequently Asked Questions</title>
      <descr>This site contains articles and information
        pertinent to XML, written by our selected group of
        gurus.</descr>
      <readAccess>0</readAccess>
      <writeAccess>2</writeAccess>
```

```
    <src>xmlfaq.xml</src>
    <admin idref="jean@halcyon.com"/>
    <msgCount>124</msgCount>
    <baseMsgCount>15</baseMsgCount>
    <msgIndex>129</msgIndex>
  </board>
  <board id="xmlstandards">
    <title>XML Standards</title>
    <descr>This board focuses on the latest actions of the
      W3C and relevant XML based standards.</descr>
    <readAccess>0</readAccess>
    <writeAccess>1</writeAccess>
    <src>xmlstandards.xml</src>
    <admin idref="jean@halcyon.com"/>
    <msgCount>252</msgCount>
    <baseMsgCount>76</baseMsgCount>
    <msgIndex>261</msgIndex>
  </board>
  <board id="xmldom">
    <title>XML Document Object Model</title>
    <descr>Learning the XML document object model? Got
      some cool tricks or effective programming
      techniques? This is the place to be.</descr>
    <readAccess>0</readAccess>
    <writeAccess>1</writeAccess>
    <src>xmldoc.xml</src>
    <admin idref="jean@halcyon.com"/>
    <msgCount>985</msgCount>
    <baseMsgCount>258</baseMsgCount>
    <msgIndex>1002</msgIndex>
  </board>
  <board id="xslt">
    <title>XSL Transformations</title>
    <descr>Discuss the use of XSL Transformations, show
      off your transforms or get help dealing with XSLT-
      related programming.</descr>
    <readAccess>0</readAccess>
    <writeAccess>1</writeAccess>
    <src>xslt.xml</src>
    <admin idref="jean@halcyon.com"/>
    <msgCount>392</msgCount>
    <baseMsgCount>125</baseMsgCount>
```

```
      <msgIndex>400</msgIndex>
    </board>
    <board id="xmlschemas">
      <title>XML Schemas</title>
      <descr>Learn how to leverage the XML schema or
        Microsoft's reduced dataset, DTDs, and more.</descr>
      <readAccess>0</readAccess>
      <writeAccess>1</writeAccess>
      <src>xmlschemas.xml</src>
      <admin idref="kc@halcyon.com"/>
      <msgCount>125</msgCount>
      <baseMsgCount>28</baseMsgCount>
      <msgIndex>129</msgIndex>
    </board>
  </category>
  <category id="services" public="yes">
    <board id="joboffers">
      <title>Offering Employment</title>
      <descr>Search this board for available XML and
        development-related positions.</descr>
      <readAccess>1</readAccess>
      <writeAccess>1</writeAccess>
      <src>joboffers.xml</src>
      <admin idref="cagle@olywa.net"/>
      <msgCount>65</msgCount>
      <baseMsgCount>56</baseMsgCount>
      <msgIndex>67</msgIndex>
    </board>
    <board id="componentoffers">
      <title>Component Needs</title>
      <descr>If you are a freelance developer and want to
        work on specific components, check out this site.
      </descr>
      <readAccess>1</readAccess>
      <writeAccess>1</writeAccess>
      <src>componentoffers.xml</src>
      <admin idref="cagle@olywa.net"/>
      <msgCount>64</msgCount>
      <baseMsgCount>62</baseMsgCount>
      <msgIndex>65</msgIndex>
    </board>
  </category>
```

```
    <!- more categories and boards as needed ->
  </boards>
```

Before you can enter a message board, you need to be able to see basic information about the board–its category and title, for example, as well as how many messages are currently on the board and, ideally, whether the message boards have changed since you last visited. The XML structure described here contains some of that information, but, as you may have noticed, it doesn't contain any information about dates or about the number of messages that the board contains. The filter that displays this information, then, will actually need to query the files that contain the actual message boards to retrieve this data.

The actual message board files have names that initially correspond to the ID of the board, but there's no strict requirement for this; it's an artifact of the way that the boards are set up in the first place. The `<src>` field could contain a fully qualified URL that points to a message board located on a different machine (or through a different interface, such as a SQL Server 2000 query filtered by a template).

ACCESS PERMISSIONS

Access permissions can be a fairly complicated problem to handle, especially when you are trying to build such systems across multiple platforms. While fairly primitive, the message boards contain a way of handling such permissions. A message board assumes that there are four classes of users on the system:

- Anonymous Users (0), who can often read messages on the site but can't post them.
- Registered Users (1), who can both read and write messages. Registered users are maintained in a user database.
- Authors (2), who have permission to read or write to specific message boards (the boards are contained in their user profiles). These may be content developers for something like a Frequently Asked Questions (or FAQ) board or may be members of a limited-access message board.
- Admin (3), who have the ability to read or write at all levels.

CONTINUED →

The attributes cascade: An Author can read any Registered User or Anonymous User message. A board can (and typically will) have different attributes for reading and writing. For example, even the most open board, one available to anonymous users, would only allow users to read the message board; they would have to register to write to it. In most cases, the Write permission is equal to or higher than the Read permission, but areas such as bug reports can actually serve as mailing services that are effectively write-only, since you're sending a message to an administrator. Finally, only the creator of a message (by definition a Registered User or above) can delete that message—the only exception to that being an administrator, who can delete any messages (or boards, for that matter).

Saving Documents Internally

I concentrate in this section on the mechanism in the `showBoards.xsl` script that determines both the number of messages and the ID of the most recent message within the board. Each message board retains an index generator that increments automatically when a new message is added. Although messages can be deleted, the generator won't be decremented again, so there is a guarantee that the index of any new messages will always be higher than that of existing messages. This is also a convenient way of bypassing the issue of date conversions, an issue that can prove awkward and error prone.

The message boards themselves are hierarchical in nature: A message can contain one or more messages that are responses to the initial message, which can, in turn, contain one or more messages, and so forth. A (small) part of one message board is shown in Listing 20.9.

Listing 20.9: A Message Board Fragment (`Listing20.9.xml`)

```
<board id="general" indexKey="4">
  <title>General Site Board</title>
  <descr>This is essentially the "welcoming board" for the
    site. Come here to introduce yourself, find out more
    about the site, or bring up important points to the
    general membership.</descr>
```

```
      <date>2/5/2000 2:25:15</date>
      <moderator>Kurt Cagle</moderator>
      <moderatorEmail>cagle@olywa.net</moderatorEmail>
      <messages>
        <message id="1">
          <title>
            <![CDATA[A starting message]]>
          </title>
          <date>2/6/2000 5:50:13 PM</date>
          <from>Kurt Cagle</from>
          <email>cagle@olywa.net</email>
          <isLive>yes</isLive>
          <body>
            <![CDATA[This is a basic message.]]>
          </body>
          <message id="2">
            <title>
              <![CDATA[Re:A starting message]]>
            </title>
            <date>2/6/2000 5:56:13 PM</date>
            <from>Kurt Cagle</from>
            <email>cagle@olywa.net</email>
            <isLive>yes</isLive>
            <body>
              <![CDATA[!This is a response to the previous
              message, and is actually contained in the
              message this is a response to.]]>
            </body>
          </message>
        </message>
        <message id="3">
          <title>
            <![CDATA[A second message]]>
          </title>
          <date>2/6/2000 6:15:13 PM</date>
          <from>Kurt Cagle</from>
          <email>cagle@olywa.net</email>
          <isLive>yes</isLive>
          <body>
            <![CDATA[This is another message at the same scope
            as the first message in the board.]]>
          </body>
```

```
    </message>
  </messages>
</board>
```

This example gives a basic idea about how the structure is set up, although it's worth remembering that a typical board may have hundreds or even thousands of messages associated with it. The XML does give rise to two distinct pieces of information worth knowing: the number of messages in total and the number of base messages, those that are not written in response to some other message, given in the table of contents XML as `<msgCount>` and `<baseMsgCount>`, respectively.

While the number of either message or base message can be calculated easily from the boards, you wouldn't want to retrieve this every time someone comes to the table of contents page. To see why, consider that a message board system may contain several dozen (or even several hundred) distinct boards. Opening up each of these large files, performing a count on their indices, then closing them again would be a significant hit even if you had only one person interacting with the message boards at any given time, and it is far more likely that dozens of people will be pulling from the boards simultaneously.

Instead, the most logical way of handling the problem is to update the table of contents whenever a change is made to any given board, changing only the information for the board that was modified. In that sense, the table of contents file begins to take on some of the capabilities of a registry, a comparison that I intend to exploit further. The XSLT filter `updateToC.xsl` (Listing 20.10) does this update by taking as a parameter the ID of the message board to be updated; opening the message board in question; retrieving the count of messages, base messages, and the index key; opening the TOC; recording the changes; and then saving the TOC from where it was loaded.

Listing 20.10: Updating the Table of Contents (Listing20.10.xsl)

```
<!- This assumes that toc.xml is the input stream ->
<xsl:stylesheet version="1.0"
  xmlns:xsl="http://www.w3.org/1999/XSL/Transform"
  xmlns:utils="http://www.vbxml.com/utils"
  xmlns:msxsl="urn:schemas-microsoft-com:xslt">
<xsl:output method="xml" omit-xml-declaration="yes"/>
<xsl:param name="boardID"/>
<msxsl:script implements-prefix="utils"
```

```
      language="Javascript"><![CDATA[
      function document(url){
        if (typeof(url) != "string"){
          url = url(0).text;
        }
        var xmlDoc = new ActiveXObject("MSXML2.DOMDocument");
        xmlDoc.async = false;
        xmlDoc.load(url);
        return xmlDoc;  }

      function persistDocumentTo(url,context){
        if (typeof(url) != "string"){
          url = url(0).text;
        }
        var xmlDoc = new ActiveXObject("MSXML2.DOMDocument");
        xmlDoc.documentElement = context(0).cloneNode.true;
        xmlDoc.save(url);
        return xmlDoc;  }
    ]]>  </msxsl:script>
    <xsl:template match="/">
      <xsl:variable name="boardRef"
        select="//board[@id=$boardID]"/>
      <xsl:variable name="board"
        select="utils:document($boardRef/src)"/>
      <xsl:variable name="newToc">
        <boards>
          <xsl:apply-templates select="//category"/>
        </boards>
      </xsl:variable>
      <xsl:copy-of disable-output-escaping="yes"
        select="utils:persistDocumentTo('toc.xml',$newToc)"/>
    </xsl:template>
    <xsl:template match="category">
      <xsl:choose>
        <xsl:when test=".[board[@id=$boardID]]">
          <category id="{@id}" public="{@public}">
            <xsl:apply-templates select="board"/>
          </category>
        </xsl:when>
        <xsl:otherwise><xsl:copy-of select="."/></xsl:otherwise>
      </xsl:choose>
    </xsl:template>
```

```
<xsl:template match="board">
  <xsl:choose>
    <xsl:when test=".[@id=$boardID]">
      <board id="{@id}">
        <xsl:variable name="msgCount"
          select="count($board//message)"/>
        <xsl:variable name="baseMsgCount"
          select="count($board//messages/message)"/>
        <xsl:variable name="msgIndex"
          select="count($board//messages/@indexKey)"/>
        <title><xsl:value-of select="$board/title"/></title>
        <descr><xsl:value-of select="$board/descr"/></descr>
        <readAccess>
          <xsl:value-of select="$board/readAccess"/>
        </readAccess>
        <writeAccess>
          <xsl:value-of select="$board/readAccess"/>
        </writeAccess>
        <src><xsl:value-of select="$board/src"/></src>
        <admin><xsl:copy-of select="$board/admin"/></admin>
        <msgCount>
          <xsl:value-of select="$msgCount"/>
        </msgCount>
        <baseMsgCount>
          <xsl:value-of select="$baseMsgCount"/>
        </baseMsgCount>
        <msgIndex>
          <xsl:value-of select="$msgIndex"/>
        </msgIndex>
      </board>
    </xsl:when>
    <xsl:otherwise><xsl:copy-of select="."/></xsl:otherwise>
  </xsl:choose>
</xsl:template>
</xsl:stylesheet>
```

To borrow a line from the movie *Ghostbusters*, the one thing you must avoid doing is crossing the streams; this is bad. To explain this, consider the difference between procedural and declarative languages. In a procedural language, you are dealing with objects with explicit properties that you can change. In a declarative language, you are dealing with streams; the XML coming in (from the `toc.xml` file) cannot be changed, but it can be duplicated (this is one of the reasons that an XSL variable cannot be changed once created).

This is essentially the technique that is used here: A stream is assigned to the variable `$newToc`, which duplicates the effects of the normal output stream. Thus, the template matches for category and board aren't, in fact, streaming to the default output stream but instead are being sent to the `$newToc` stream. This stream can then be persisted using the previously defined `utils:persistDocumentTo()` method. With a judicious bit of planning, the output of this object is the changed table of contents, which can, in turn, be passed back to the default output stream.

FROM PROPERTIES TO PLUMBING

The procedural programmers among you may be squirming a little bit about this last transformation. It seems like an incredible amount of work just to change a few properties, something that could be handled with JavaScript or VBScript in perhaps half the number of lines of code. It is a valid criticism, in this simple case in particular, but with the exception of the actual persistence code (an artifact of the current implementation, not of the language itself, and one that's not really all that necessary), the principles displayed here are handled completely within an XML context. You could swap out the category and message templates and replace them with any other matches you need without ever leaving an XML environment.

Moreover, it becomes possible to create handlers that are very generic. Since the structure involved here—an index file that contains references to other XML content files—is very common, this means that with some work you can essentially abstract out the whole process and create a mechanism for updating the index whenever any of its child files changes. As you read the other examples contained in this chapter (and in the book hereafter), start thinking about abstraction; it's one of XML's greatest strengths and an advantage that XML holds over the more objectified reality of OOP programming.

Persisting Session Data

The `Session` object is a staple of most ASP programming, but it runs into a number of limitations—specifically the following—that make it less than ideal in the XML/XSL world:

Cookies Sessions rely highly on client-side cookies. If such a cookie mechanism doesn't exist (or if the user turns cookies off), there is no clear-cut mechanism to retain state on the server.

Session Timeout A session keeps a connection "alive" so that the client and server know about one another. However, if a user leaves a connection inactive for too long, the session times out and relevant information gets lost.

Session Is an Object The `Session` object is just that: an object, which makes it awkward (though not impossible) to work within the context of XSL. It can, however, have its values retrieved through keys in a manner that is similar to the way that the `Request` object works.

Session Is External The `Session` object is a distinct part of the ASP environment and can't be queried through an internal XSL mechanism without passing it in from the outside.

Thus, a solution that either bypasses or enhances the capabilities of the `Session` object needs to be examined before any architecture is built onto it, since session maintenance is a key part of any server setup.

The first solution to this, and one that's already been alluded to in the previous section, is to design your architecture in such a way that you don't need to worry about state, by simply passing state information through query string or form. Unfortunately, this mechanism only really works for relatively simple state information; an anchor tag on an HTML form isn't going to have the depth to transmit large chunks of information, and it makes the code awkward to both write and debug.

The second solution is to convert the session state information into XML when the page instantiates and then convert it back into a `Session` object when the session terminates. This can actually work well for XML information when a session state is guaranteed, and this solution would use a mechanism similar to that of the `Request` object, as shown in Listing 20.11.

Listing 20.11: Session State Functions (`Listing20.11.vb`)

```
function getSessionXML()
  dim xmlDoc
  set xmlDoc = server.createObject("Microsoft.XMLDOM")
  xmlDoc.loadXML "<keys/>"
  set collectionNode = _
    xmlDoc.createElement("collection")
  collectionNode.setAttribute "id","session"
  collectionNode.setAttribute "sessionID",session.sessionID
  for each key in session.contents
    set keyNode = xmlDoc.createElement("key")
    keyNode.setAttribute "id",key
    keyNode.text = session(key)
    collectionNode.appendChild keyNode
  next
  set getSessionXML = xmlDoc
end function

function passSessionObjectTo(xslDoc)
  collectionsString = "all"
  set sessionDoc = getSessionXML()
  set param = xslDoc.selectSingleNode _
    ("//xsl:param[@name='session']")
  if param is nothing then
    set param = xslDoc.documentElement.insertBefore _
    (xslDoc.createElement("xsl:param"), _
    xslDoc.selectSingleNode("//xsl:template"))
    param.setAttribute "name","session"
  end if
  while param.childNodes.length > 0 then
    param.removeChild param.childNodes(0)
  wend
  param.appendChild sessionDoc.documentElement
end function
```

This function will end up passing a keys collection to the XSL filter under the parameter `<xsl:param name="session">`:

```
<keys>
  <collection id="session" sessionID="748945042">
    <key id="key1">This is the first session variable.</key>
    <key id="key2">Here's the second.</key>
```

```
    </collection>
  </keys>
```

This collection can be accessed in exactly the same way that the `Request` keys can: through the XPath expression `$session//key[@id='token']`, where *token* can take the name of any session key.

Setting new keys within an XSL document is a little more complex and lies at the heart of why session state is such a pain to maintain effectively. There is no easy way to pass any XML out of an XSL filter except through persisting and retrieving it or through passing it to the generic output stream. However, ASP sessions don't take place in a vacuum: typically, many users access the server simultaneously. If an XML stream is persisted to a standard file, there is no way to make sure that the file saved within the XSL filter has not been overwritten by another session before the current session has a chance to retrieve the file, short of uniquely identifying the file as belonging to this particular session.

Thus, a way of identifying the user uniquely is still required in this scenario. As it stands, in addition to the session tokens, the session XML stream also contains a unique `sessionID` attribute, attached to the `<collection>` node. This attribute is also used by the `Session` object itself and can be used to retrieve the XML file from its temporary storage place once the XSL script terminates.

With this information, you can create a local XML document in the XSL structure in script, then define four functions: `initializeSession()`, `setSessionVariable()`, `getSessionVariable()`, and `persistSession()`. `initializeSession()` takes the `Session` object as a parameter and creates a read/write version of the same object. `setSessionVariable()` passes the name of the variable and the given XML context into the session XML structure, either creating a new variable with the name or changing the contents of an existing variable. `getSessionVariable()` retrieves the named variable, and `persistSession()` saves the current state to a file called `_temp_sessionID.xml`, where `sessionID` is the current session ID (e.g., `_temp_748945042.xml`). The implementations of these four functions are shown in Listing 20.12.

Listing 20.12: XML Session Object Code (`Listing20.12.xsl`)

```
<!- This assumes that toc.xml is the input stream ->
<xsl:stylesheet version="1.0"
  xmlns:xsl="http://www.w3.org/1999/XSL/Transform"
  xmlns:session="http://www.vbxml.com/utils"
```

```
    xmlns:msxsl="urn:schemas-microsoft-com:xslt">
  <xsl:output method="xml" omit-xml-declaration="yes"/>
  <xsl:param name="session"/>
  <msxsl:script implements-prefix="session"
    language="Javascript"><![CDATA[
    Var session=new ActiveXObject("MSXML2.DOMDocument")
    function initializeSession(sessionContext){
      session.documentElement =
        sessionContext(0).selectSingleNode(
        "//keys").cloneNode(true);
      var keyNode = session.selectSingleNode(
         "//key[@id = '" + key + "']");
      return keyNode.getAttribute("sessionID")  }

    function setSessionVariable(key,context){
      var keyNode = session.selectSingleNode(
        "//key[@id = '" + key + "']");
      if (keyNode == null){
        var collectionNode = session.selectSingleNode(
          "//collection");
        keyNode = collectionNode.appendChild(
          collectionNode.createElement("key"))
          keyNode.setAttribute("id") = key
      }
      for (childNode in keyNode.childNodes){
        keyNode.removeChild(childNode);
      }
      for (childNode in context){
        keyNode.appendChild(childNode);
      } }

    function getSessionVariable(key){
      var keyNode = session.selectSingleNode(
        "//key[@id = '" + key + "']");
      if (keyNode != null){
        return keyNode;
      }
      else {
        return "#ERROR: No key named '" + key + "'#";
      } }
```

```
      function persistSession(){
        var sessionID = session.selectSingleNode(
          "//@sessionID").text
          persistDocumentTo("_temp_" + sessionID + ".xml",
            session);
      }

      function document(url){
        if (typeof(url) != "string"){
          url = url(0).text;
        }
        var xmlDoc = new ActiveXObject("MSXML2.DOMDocument");
        xmlDoc.async = false;
        xmlDoc.load(url);
        return xmlDoc;
      }

      function persistDocumentTo(url,context){
        if (typeof(url) != "string"){
          url = url(0).text;
        }
        var xmlDoc = new ActiveXObject("MSXML2.DOMDocument");
        xmlDoc.documentElement = context(0).cloneNode.true;
        xmlDoc.save(url);
        return xmlDoc;  }
    ]]>  </msxsl:script>
    <!- more code ->

    <xsl:param name="session">
      <keys><collection id="session" sessionID="0"/></keys>
    </xsl:param>
    <xsl:variable name="sessionID"
      select= "session:initializeSession($session)"/>
    </xsl:stylesheet>
```

Note the declaration of the <xsl:param> and <xsl:variable> tags at the end of the script. If the session isn't otherwise defined, then a dummy parameter value is set up that contains a collection but no keys. The `sessionID` isn't actually likely to be required in the XSL structure itself, but it serves as an excuse to invoke the `initializeSession()` method, which returns the session ID anyway and prepares the session XML object for use.

The getSessionVariable() takes a key name as a parameter and returns an XML context object, while setSessionVariable accepts both a key name and a context object:

```
<xsl:value-of
  select="session:getSessionVariable('formInfo')"/>
<xsl:value-of
  select="session:setSessionVariable('formInfo',.)"/>
```

SetSessionVariable(), by the way, returns a null string, so it has no impact on the output stream. Finally, persistSession() automatically saves as indicated earlier, likewise returning a null string to the output stream. persistSession() should be invoked prior to the XSL script terminating, as any changes made to the session state will not get reflected into the temporary file.

TIP

You can use these session variables to work with writeable variables in your XSL, although for both performance and portability reasons you should keep the use of such variables to a minimum.

Once the XSL filter terminates and you return to the ASP environment, you can use the function updateSession() to convert the XML file back into session variables, as in Listing 20.13. Note that if no initial session was supplied, then the session XML will be contained in the file named _temp_0.xml. Both the session ID file and the default file are automatically deleted.

Listing 20.13: Session State Functions (Listing20.13.txt)

```
function updateSession()
  dim xmlDoc
  set xmlDoc = server.createObject("Microsoft.XMLDOM")
  xmlDoc.async = false
  dim fso
  set fso=server.createObject("Scripting.FileSystemObject")
  filename = server.mapPath("_temp_"+server.serverID+".xml")
  if fso.fileExists(filename) then
    xmlDoc.load filename
    fso.deleteFile filename
  else
    filename = server.mapPath("_temp_0.xml")
```

```
      if fso.fileExists(filename) then
         xmlDoc.load filename
         fso.deleteFile filename
      end if
   end if
   if not (xmlDoc is nothing) then
      for each keyNode in xmlDoc.selectNodes("//key")
         session(keyNode.getAttribute("id")) = keyNode.xml
      next
   end if
end function
```

CAN YOU DO SESSIONS WITHOUT A *SESSION* OBJECT?

The Session object is a fairly heavily used part of most ASP development, but there is a hint here that you can get by without it.

The most difficult part of maintaining session state is retaining unique information about the user on the other end of the server. While server applications such as ASP maintain a unique ID that identifies a specific user profile, you can at least determine if the same machine is used in a transaction by looking at its REMOTE_ADDR (remote address) property in the Request object. Since that is passed in as part of the request XML structure, you can actually load a file with a reference to the IP address (such as _temp_127.0.0.1.xml), use the methods discussed in this section for referencing stored elements, and then persist the file back to the server's hard drive.

There are three minor problems with this technique. The first has to with the fact that a machine may have more than one user profile but only one IP address. This is not likely a major issue, by the way; the purpose of the Session object is to maintain state during a session, and a person disconnecting and another person reconnecting on the same machine during the same session is fairly unlikely.

A more serious issue comes from the fact that session timeouts exist for a reason: If your Web site takes a significant number of hits, your hard drive may quickly fill up with interim state files. If you do want to go this route, you should think about inserting a time stamp into an XML index file, then periodically removing all sessions older than a certain period.

CONTINUED ➞

Finally, file access is far slower than keeping `Session` objects in memory. If performance is an issue, you may be better off parameterizing the information you need from the session variables and passing that data in directly rather than building a `Session` object indirectly, at least at this point in the evolution of XML.

WORKING WITH OUTPUT STREAMS

Active Server Pages were originally designed for the purpose of "serving" Web pages, and they still perform that task admirably. However, as with most such Web servers, they do far more than just dish out HTML code. It is useful to switch contexts with ASP, moving it away from being a program that returns HTML upon request and focusing it instead on being a program that serves data streams upon request.

The `Response` object acts as the conduit that transmits formatted information to the client from the server, and as such it works well into the stream architecture that's been discussed in this chapter. `Response` has various properties and methods of interest to the XML developer, which are covered in Table 20.1.

TABLE 20.1: Response Properties and Methods

PROPERTY OR METHOD	WHAT IT DOES	IMPORTANCE FOR XML
`AddHeader(bstrHeaderName,bstrHeaderValue)`	Adds an HTTP header to the response stream.	Useful for sending document information to client.
`AppendToLog (bstrLogEntry)`	Adds a string to the IIS log session.	Useful for debugging.
`BinaryWrite(varInput)`	Writes out binary information to the client.	Principally useful with XML-HTTP.
`Buffer`	If true, then buffers output. Otherwise, page is sent at the termination of the ASP script.	Useful for controlling amount of XML sent to client for display. Used in conjunction with `Flush()`.

CONTINUED →

TABLE 20.1 continued: Response Properties and Methods

PROPERTY OR METHOD	WHAT IT DOES	IMPORTANCE FOR XML
`Clear`	Empties the buffer without transmitting any information.	Useful for controlling output on errors.
`ContentType`	Sets the MIME type of the document.	Usually needs to be set explicitly to `"text/xml"`.
`Cookies`	Lets you write cookies to the client.	Useful for storing general information; in theory, you could send an XML document into a cookie, though this is generally not recommended.
`End`	Terminates the ASP session and transmits the information to the client.	Usually only required with buffered output.
`Expires`	Gives the time in minutes until the page must refresh itself.	Setting expires to –1 will automatically force a refresh of the page, something that's essential to an ASP XML server.
`ExpiresAbsolute`	Gives an absolute time before the current page should no longer be cached.	Of minimal importance.
`Flush`	Clears the output buffer after sending the contents of the buffer.	Used heavily with buffered output, this can let you fine tune your output time.
`IsClientConnected`	Returns true if a client session is active.	Useful for determining if you need to refresh your state.
`Pics`	Collection for controlling content ratings for your page.	Minimally useful.
`Redirect(bstrURL)`	Redirects the source of the output stream to a new location.	This can prove handy with an XML server, as it allows techniques to perform conditional output based upon parameters rather than filenames.

CONTINUED ➡

TABLE 20.1 continued: Response Properties and Methods

Property or Method	What It Does	Importance for XML
`Status`	Sets the error status text of the page.	This can be useful for handling XML errors on the server, as you can modify this string to reflect errors in the object itself.
`Write(varText)`	Sends the specified text to either the output stream or to a text buffer.	The `Response` method that you will use for most XML output, unless you're working with XMLHTTP.

ASP code falls into two basic categories: code in which the page is relatively static and content that changes with each query, even given the same initial parameters. The `Response.Expires` property controls this, and understanding its use with XML is even more important than it is for HTML. `Expires` gives the number of minutes until the page expires (i.e., until a request to the server will force ASP to rerun the script instead of relying on a copy cached on the client).

If your content is relatively static—if you're serving up XML that doesn't have frequent updates; for example, you can get by without even setting the `expires` property—the client-side cache will maintain this information for the user's desired period. However, if the data changes frequently, you should set `response.expires = -1`. This will automatically force the page to refresh itself.

The `ContentType` property should also be set when outputting XML pages, although things get a little more complicated here. The `<xsl:output>` element can take as values either `xml`, `html`, or `text`, each of which sets the type of the XML stream to the appropriate MIME type (`text/xml`, `text/html`, and `text/plain`, respectively). However, the ASP content type (which is also set to the MIME type) will override this in all cases. With the current implementation of ASP, you should execute the line

```
Response.ContentType="text/xml"
```

prior to sending any data into the body of the output stream, if you want the output to be XML. If you're sending this to a browser, by the way, the `ContentType` header should control whether the browser displays the result as an HTML document or as an XML document.

Buffering output makes a great deal of sense when used in conjunction with XML. To turn buffering on, you should declare `Response.Buffer = true` before sending any information (header declarations or body content). This tells the ASP engine to save the building content into a text buffer rather than just sending it to the default output stream. You can fill a buffer partially (say, by writing a record in XML to the output stream via `Response.Write`) and then call `Response.Flush` to send the data to the client and clear the buffer. This works especially well when dealing with asynchronous XML structures on the client since you can catch updates via the `onreadystatechange` event to start processing your structure even before the whole document has been downloaded.

Buffering lets you do something else, too: handle errors effectively. Periodically, errors happen—the server for a critical piece of information has just busted a hard drive, a bad parameter was passed, and so forth. In this case, you can use buffering to halt the output production at the point where the error occurred, clear the buffer, then send an XML error message to indicate that a problem occurred, as shown in the following listing:

```
<%@LANGUAGE="VBSCRIPT%>
xmlDoc.buffer = true
xmlDoc.async = true
xmlDoc.load server.mapPath("myMisnamedFile.xml")
if xmlDoc.parseError.errorCode <> 0 then
  'create a quick object, then send it
  set errorDoc=createObject("Microsoft.XMLDOM")
  errorDoc.loadxml "<error/>"
  with xmlDoc.parseError
    errorDoc.setAttribute "errorcode",.errorcode
    errorDoc.setAttribute "charpos",.charpos
    errorDoc.setAttribute "linepos",.linepos
    errorDoc.setAttribute "line",.charpos
    errorDoc.setAttribute "srctext",.srctext
    errorDoc.setAttribute "url",.url
    errorDoc.text=.reason
  end with
  Response.Clear
  Response.Write errorDoc.xml
```

```
    Response.Flush
  else
    ' Handle the code
  end if
```

TIP

Establishing regular error-handling routines for your XML should be designed in from the start. While they don't improve the performance of the final Web application, they are crucial when developing.

Constructing XML Servers with ASP

Parametric XML is cool, but in many (if not most) cases, if you're trying to retrieve XML (or, for XHTML, see the "Building XHTML Components" section), loading several objects, setting up parameterization, and then dealing with the output can beg the question of why XML is so advantageous. However, you can take advantage of ASP to encapsulate this function not as a procedural function but as a URL with query-string or form parameters.

For example, consider that most of the XML operations that you are going to be dealing with will likely center around two areas: transforming an XML document with an XSL filter that has parameters, and querying an XML document for a specific XML node set. I faced this problem myself, and while the logical solution to the problem of transforming an XML document would be to use query-string name/value pairs as parameters, I couldn't think of a clean way of building an interface that differentiated parameters from filenames, for instance. Then it occurred to me that filtering out filenames to those that started with a unique token would do it.

Listing 20.14 is one of my workhorse functions: You pass the name of the XML resource in the `source` parameter, the name of the XSL resource in the `filter` parameter, and the `type` (content type) of the output as parameters in a form or a query string (where `type` defaults to `xml` but can also take the values of `html` or `text`).

Listing 20.14: XML Server Lets You Filter an XML Source with a Parameteric XSL Source. (Listing20.14.asp)

```
<%@LANGUAGE="VBSCRIPT"%>
<%
response.expires = -1
function processXML()
  src = request("source")
  xfilter = request("filter")
  mimetype = request("type")
  if mimetype = "" then
    mimetype = "xml"
  end if
  Response.ContentType = "text/" + mimetype
  set xmlDoc = createObject("Microsoft.XMLDOM")
  set xslDoc = createObject("Microsoft.XMLDOM")
  xmlDoc.async = false
  xslDoc.async = false
  xmlDoc.load server.mapPath(src)
  xslDoc.load server.mapPath(xfilter)
  for each key in request.queryString
    setParameter xslDoc,key,request(key)
  next
  for each key in request.form
    setParameter xslDoc,key,request(key)
  next
  response.write xmlDoc.transformNode(xslDoc)
end function

function setParameter(xslDoc,key,keyValue)
  if left(key,6) = "param_" then
    key = lcase(mid(key,7))
    set keynode = xslDoc.selectSingleNode _
     ("//xsl:param [@name = '" + key + "']")
    if not keynode is nothing then
      keynode.setAttribute "select","'"+cstr(keyValue)+"'"
    end if
  end if
  if left(key,6) = "param*" then
    key = lcase(mid(key,7))
    set keynode = xslDoc.selectSingleNode _
     ("//xsl:param[@name = '" + key + "']")
```

```
      if not keynode is nothing then
         keynode.setAttribute "select",".["+cstr(keyValue)+"]"
      end if
    end if

  end function

  processXML
  %>
```

Thus, for the message board example, I have a TreeView XSL control that displays the messages and their responses (the details of which are covered in the following "Building XHTML Components" section). To be able to apply to a message board a file that produces the list of messages in a tree-like structure (assuming both are in the same directory as the ASP file), you would need to use the following URL (this and other sample URLs should be on a single line):

```
http://www.myserver.com/xmlserver.asp?source=general.xml&
filter=simpleTreeView.xsl
```

The specific XSL transform, contained in the file `simpleTreeView.xsl`, employs a number of parameters that can determine the characteristics of the resulting tree. The parameters for the XSL function are passed using two prefixes: `param_` and `param*`. The distinction between the two is subtle but important. The expression `param_` points to a parameter that gets passed as a string into the XSL filter; `param_caption = body`, for example, translates into

```
<xsl:param name="caption" select="'body'"/>
```

On the other hand, `param*` actually passes an XPath expression, with `param*object=//message` translating as

```
<xsl:param name="object" select="//message"/>
```

For example, the `$caption` property determines what specific property in the message block is displayed (with the default being the `title` node). To change this to body, which would display the text of each message rather than the titles as the control's captions, you'd change the preceding URL to the following:

```
http://www.myserver.com/xmlserver.asp?source=general.xml&
filter=simpleTreeView.xsl&param_caption=body
```

Note that while this URL could be typed in at a browser window or generated from an anchor tag, it could just as easily be an argument passed to an XML load method (either on the client or, more importantly, on the server):

```
dim xmlDoc
set xmlDoc = createObject("Microsoft.XMLDOM")
xmlDoc.async = false
xmlDoc.load "http://www.myserver.com/xmlserver.asp?" & _
   "source=general.xml&filter=simpleTreeView.xsl&" & _
   "param_caption=body"
```

Additionally (at least in theory), as the following snippet demonstrates, the XPath `document()` method could also call the URL to retrieve such content into the XSL filter, although that feature wasn't implemented in the most recent MSXML component (though it should be in the final version).

```
<xsl:variable name="dynList"
   select="document(http://www.myserver.com/" & _
   "xmlserver.asp?source=general.xml&filter=" & _
   "simpleTreeView.xsl&param_caption=body)"/>
<xsl:copy-of select="$dynList"
   disable-output-escaping="yes"/>
```

As XSL becomes more mainstream, using ASP to serve it up in this fashion will likely become a common option. The same process can be used to retrieve a set of nodes, such as the set of all messages written by Kurt Cagle, sorted by date. Rather than placing this functionality in the ASP script, use the `xmlserver.asp` script, and call an XSL filter (`getFilteredRecords.xsl`) with the appropriate parameters, as shown in Listing 20.15.

Listing 20.15: `getFilteredRecords` **Can Be Used to Retrieve Nodes from an XML Document** (`Listing20.15.xsl`)

```
<xsl:stylesheet version="1.0"
   xmlns:xsl="http://www.w3.org/1999/XSL/Transform">
<xsl:output method="xml" omit-xml-declaration="yes"/>
<xsl:param name="collectionname" select="'messages'"/>
<xsl:param name="objectname" select="'message'"/>
<xsl:param name="sortby" select="'title'"/>
<xsl:param name="sorttype" select="'text'"/>
<xsl:param name="sortorder" select="'ascending'"/>
```

```
<xsl:template match="/">
  <xsl:element name="{$collectionname}">
    <xsl:apply-templates select="//*[name(.)=$objectname]">
      <xsl:sort select="$sortby" data-type="{$sorttype}"
        order="{$sortorder}"/>
    </xsl:apply-templates>
  </xsl:element>
</xsl:template>
<xsl:template match="*">
  <xsl:param name="criterion"
    select=".[from='Mark Wilson']"/>
  <xsl:for-each select="$criterion">
    <xsl:copy-of select="."/>
  </xsl:for-each>
</xsl:template>
</xsl:stylesheet>
```

To retrieve the aforementioned set of all messages written by Kurt Cagle, sorted by date, you could call the following URL (again, remember that we have to break these in print but this should actually be all on one line):

```
http://www.myserver.com/xmlserver.asp?source=messages.xml&
filter=getFilteredRecords&param_collectionname=messages&
param_objectname=message&param_sortorder=descending&
param*criterion=from='Kurt+Cagle'
```

Being able to combine the XML and XSL in a remote process, especially parameterized in this way, gives you a high degree of flexibility. Indeed, this best illustrates the concept of the remote server: By encapsulating the XML output of any operation behind a URL to an ASP or a related provider (such as a SQL Server computer or an Oracle database), you change these connections into anonymous sources—you know that they produce XML but, beyond that, you shouldn't know (or need to know) the specific implementation that generates that XML in the first place.

While the code discussed here has focused on the IIS objects and how they relate to XML, knowing how to be able to work with this information is as critical as knowing the API. In the next section, I look at a few sample applications for XML and ASP, returning first to the XML replacement for HTML: XHTML.

Building XHTML Components

One of the great ironies of XML development is that, three years after the XML standard first saw the light of day, the principal reason for creating it in the first place is still largely unfulfilled. The original intent of XML was to serve as a means to create output in browsers that was better suited to specific document requirements rather than relying on the context-poor HTML structure.

Unfortunately, only Internet Explorer 5.*x* supports the ability to view XML with a filter, although only with the browser, not when printed or displayed in source form (this will likely change with Internet Explorer 5.5). Netscape Navigator 4.*x* can't understand XML at all, although Navigator 6 looks as though it may be capable of displaying information in a few different, well-defined XML formats. For the vast majority of Internet users out there, client-side support of XML simply won't be a standard state of affairs for several years to come.

In a way, however, this state of affairs may actually have a silver lining. The wide diversity of different browsers that are currently in circulation, plus those yet undreamed, makes it difficult to create Web pages that can target more than the most dominant ones. If, however, a core HTML standard that were compliant with XML emerged from the W3C, it would be possible to use server-side code to customize the output for the appropriate browser.

Such a standard exists and is called XHTML. Approved in January 2000, the XHTML 1.0 Recommendation creates a version of HTML 4 that is fully compliant with the XML standard—quote-delimited attributes, properly terminated tags, the elimination of singleton tags, such as the `<option>` element's `selected` attribute, in favor of fully resolved attributes (i.e., `selected="yes"`). The changeover from HTML to XHTML is largely transparent.

Catching Namespace Tags

From the standpoint of the server developer, XHTML offers two primary benefits. First of all, since XHTML is, in fact, also XML, it is easy to create XHTML as part of a pipeline process: XHTML gets generated by one XSL transform, incorporates additional XHTML through a second XSL transform, and can then be tweaked to best fit the client browser.

A second advantage to XHTML is that you can actually create XHTML "behaviors": tags (with attributes or other interior content) that can be trapped by an XSL filter and replaced with other XHTML code. This is a mechanism that is becoming increasingly common with languages like Java Server Pages, where XML tags incorporated into the body of XHTML code trigger Java classes that modify the code, and is something that has been a staple of Macromedia's ColdFusion Server for years (albeit using proprietary tags rather than XML).

In essence, XML tag replacement involves a slight variation on the identity transformation. The simplest identity transformation is one in which the result stream is an exact duplicate of the source stream, as shown in Listing 20.16.

Listing 20.16: The Identity Transformation (Listing20.16.xsl)

```
<xsl:stylesheet version="1.0"
  xmlns:xsl="http://www.w3.org/1999/XSL/Transform">
<xsl:template match="/">
  <xsl:apply-templates select="*"/>
</xsl:template>
<xsl:template name="identity"
  match="*|@*|text()|comment()|processing-instruction()">
  <xsl:copy>
  <xsl:apply-templates select=
    "*|@*|text()|comment()|processing-instruction()"/>
  <xsl:copy>
</xsl:template>
</xsl:stylesheet>
```

In and of itself, the identity transformation is rather useless. However, by placing additional template matches after the identity template, you can catch exceptions to the general rule, so that when you run the script you will end up with the starting document but with the flagged tags converted into new XML (or XHTML) code. In short, you have the server-side analog of a client-side DHTML behavior.

As a simple example, consider an XHTML document that contains a tag for retrieving page hits, as shown in Listing 20.17. The tag is defined as part of the serv: namespace, a namespace that I specifically made up to contain some of the server-side tags of general utility to readers.

Listing 20.17: A Sample Page-Hits Page (Listing20.17.txt)

```
<html xmlns:serv="http://www.vbxml.com/serv">
  <head>
    <title>Page Visits</title>
  </head>
  <body>
    <h1>Page Visits</h1>
    <p>This page has been visited <serv:pagehits
      href="pagehittest.htm"/> times.</p>
  </body>
</html>
```

The page-hits data itself is contained in another XML file called pageHits.xml (Listing 20.18). This is indexed so that each page has its own page count.

Listing 20.18: The Page Hits XML Source File (Listing20.18.txt)

```
<pagehits>
  <pagehit href="pagehittest.htm" counter="415"/>
  <pagehit href="main.htm" counter="6215"/>
  <pagehit href="index.htm" counter="42814"/>
</pagehits>
```

The XSL script that then replaces the <serv:pagehits> tag is a modified identity transformation that also updates the appropriate counter information (Listing 20.19). Note that you do need to declare the serv: namespace in the filter, as otherwise the XSL parser will complain vociferously.

Listing 20.19: A Limited serv: Filter (Listing20.19.xsl)

```
<xsl:stylesheet version="1.0"
  xmlns:xsl="http://www.w3.org/1999/XSL/Transform"
  xmlns:serv="http://www.vbxml.com/serv"
  xmlns:service="http://www.vbxml.com/servimpl"
  xmlns:msxsl="urn:schemas-microsoft-com:xslt">
<xsl:output method="xml" omit-xml-declaration="yes"/>
<msxsl:script implements-prefix="service"
  language="Javascript"><![CDATA[
  function getPageHitCount(pageURL){
    var xmlDoc = new ActiveXObject("Microsoft.XMLDOM");
    xmlDoc.async = false;
    xmlDoc.load("pageHits.xml")
```

```
        var pageNode = xmlDoc.selectSingleNode(
          "//pagehit[@href = '" + pageURL + "']");
        if (pageNode == null){
          pageNode = xmlDoc.documentElement.appendChild(
            xmlDoc.createElement("pagehit"));
          pageNode.setAttribute("href",pageURL)
          pageNode.setAttribute("counter",0)
        }
        pageHitCount = pageNode.getAttribute("counter")
        pageNode.setAttribute("counter",
          parseInt(pageHitCount) + 1)
          xmlDoc.save("pageHits.xml")
        return pageHitCount  }
    ]]>  </msxsl:script>
    <xsl:template match="/">
      <xsl:apply-templates select="*"/>
    </xsl:template>
    <xsl:template name="identity"
      match="*|@*|text()|comment()|processing-instruction()">
      <xsl:copy>
        <xsl:apply-templates select=
          "*|@*|text()|comment()|processing-instruction()"/>
      </xsl:copy>
    </xsl:template>
    <xsl:template name="pagehits" match="serv:pagehits">
      <xsl:value-of select=
      "service:getPageHitCount(string(@href))"/>
    </xsl:template>
    </xsl:stylesheet>
```

You can the use the `xmlserver.asp` script discussed in the last section (Listing 20.14) to perform the server filtering, with the following URL:

```
http://localhost/messageboards/xmlserver.asp?source=
pagehitstest.xml&filter=servFilter1.xsl&mimetype=html
```

When this runs, it will return a sample page showing the number of times the page has been accessed. Additionally, if the page has never been referenced before, then the code actually creates a new `<pagehits>` node in the `pagehits.xml` document and initializes it.

TIP

Note that it would take relatively little effort to retrieve the page count number, convert the number to a string, then map each digit to a GIF filename (`coolNumber0.gif`, `coolNumber1.gif`, etc.). This gives you a quick-and-dirty, cool counter, which could be parameterized for any number of different image "fonts."

While such a script obviously works, the danger in creating such a server XSL script implementation is that you'll probably want the `serv:` namespace to represent several different services, and as the script for the page counter showed, such an XSL filter could get huge quickly. However, by taking advantage of the pipeline architecture, you could actually simplify the process immensely. The document containing the identity transform could also act as a switching station, where each service, in turn, used `xmlserver.asp` to perform the actual calls against the `document()` object, as shown in Listing 20.20.

Listing 20.20: A Switching `serv:` Filter (`Listing20.20.xsl`)

```
<xsl:stylesheet version="1.0"
  xmlns:xsl="http://www.w3.org/1999/XSL/Transform"
  xmlns:serv="http://www.vbxml.com/serv"
  xmlns:service="http://www.vbxml.com/servimpl"
  xmlns:msxsl="urn:schemas-microsoft-com:xslt">
<xsl:output method="xml" omit-xml-declaration="yes"/>
<xsl:template match="/">
  <xsl:apply-templates select="*"/>
</xsl:template>
<xsl:template name="identity"
  match="*|@*|text()|comment()|processing-instruction()">
  <xsl:copy>
    <xsl:apply-templates select=
    "*|@*|text()|comment()|processing-instruction()"/>
  </xsl:copy>
</xsl:template>
<xsl:template name="pagehits" match="serv:pagehits">
  <xsl:variable name="path">xmlserver.asp?
    source=stub.xml&filter=pagehits.xsl&param_href=
      <xsl:value-of select="string(@href)"/>
  </xsl:variable>
  <xsl:value-of select="document($path)"/>
```

```
</xsl:template>
</xsl:stylesheet>
```

In essence, this delegates the responsibility of generating the pagehits update to a separate filter (called pagehits.xsl) and parameterizes the @href attribute. Because the source XML at this point is unimportant—the pagehits.xsl file just works off the root node to generate its output—the path loads in a stub.xml file, which simply contains the single tag <stub/>. The new pagehits filter file (Listing 20.21) is also simpler, since it doesn't have to include the identity transformation.

Listing 20.21: The pageHits **Filter** (Listing20.21.xsl)

```
<xsl:stylesheet version="1.0"
  xmlns:xsl="http://www.w3.org/1999/XSL/Transform"
  xmlns:serv="http://www.vbxml.com/serv"
  xmlns:service="http://www.vbxml.com/servimpl"
  xmlns:msxsl="urn:schemas-microsoft-com:xslt">
<xsl:output method="xml" omit-xml-declaration="yes"/>
<msxsl:script implements-prefix="service"
  language="Javascript"><![CDATA[
  function getPageHitCount(pageURL){
    var xmlDoc = new ActiveXObject("Microsoft.XMLDOM");
    xmlDoc.async = false;
    xmlDoc.load("pageHits.xml")
    var pageNode = xmlDoc.selectSingleNode(
      "//pagehit[@href = '" + pageURL + "']");
    if (pageNode == null){
      pageNode = xmlDoc.documentElement.appendChild(
        xmlDoc.createElement("pagehit"));
      pageNode.setAttribute("href",pageURL)
      pageNode.setAttribute("counter",0)
    }
    pageHitCount = pageNode.getAttribute("counter")
    pageNode.setAttribute("counter",
      parseInt(pageHitCount) + 1)
    xmlDoc.save("pageHits.xml")
    return pageHitCount  }
]]>  </msxsl:script>
<xsl:parameter name="href"/>
<xsl:template name="pagehits" match="/">
  <xsl:value-of select="service:getPageHitCount($href)"/>
```

```
</xsl:template>
</xsl:stylesheet>
```

In this way, servFilter2.xsl could contain templates matching as many serv: tags as you choose to define, in turn delegating the actual implementation of the tags to different XSL filters. Of course, there is no requirement that you use the xmlserver.asp implementation; the URL could point to anything that generates a known XML stream, although parameterization methods will obviously be different.

Consider, for instance, a tag set that points to a URL that retrieves an XML block from a mobile server that returns the position of a laptop given by a global positioning satellite. The remote calls decouple the requirement that complex code exist on your server; indeed, the tags could call an XML-generating ASP script that, in turn, calls an XML-generating ASP script (or Java applet or related code) on another server that, in turn, calls the XML-generating code on the laptop. All you need to worry about is the immediate URL and the format of the XML code being received from the remote server.

Furthermore, your ASP code, in turn, may be used by another program to aggregate the locations of the laptops of the entire sales force and display them through a map drawn in SVG. This is one of the reasons that XSLT (and, consequently, XML) is so important. Everything becomes a stream, which is far more scalable in a distributed network than in an object-oriented environment.

A Configurable Outline Component

The code for setting up behaviors on the client can be immensely complicated. In addition to spending a great deal of time designing a component that can only be used on 20 percent of all browsers, development requires some intensely complex code for generating the output and really doesn't fit well into the XML paradigm. It would be far more satisfying to create something like a collapsible hierarchical view (for example) by placing the simpler tag

```
<serv:treeview source="generalMessages.xml"
   container="messages" object="message" caption="title"/>
```

into the XHTML code and preprocessing it on the server. Not only do you not have to worry about burdening your client with behaviors, but it's easier to make sure that the right code would be sent to the Netscape Navigator browser (or the Nokia XHTML component, or even the voice browser embedded into your client's car).

Creating a simple outline from XSLT is child's play; because XML is essentially hierarchical anyway, if you are outputting to XHTML, then you can use the HTML <LI> list element and either the <OL> or the <UL> tags for creating ordered (i.e., numbered) or unordered (i.e., bulleted) lists. What is not commonly appreciated, in part because HTML is very forgiving about not properly terminating a list element, is that the <LI> element is a container element: If you put another list element inside the first one, then that second list element will appear as a subordinate element.

Even better, if you put a list element inside of a <UL> or <OL> tag within another list element, then you have a transparent container that you can show or hide as a unit, which forms the basis for most collapsible tree implementations.

Thus, at its core, one of the more useful HTML structures looks something like Listing 20.22. The use of the <SPAN> element here is twofold: It makes it easy to apply styles just to the text without affecting any subordinate text, and it makes it easier to identify the children of a given node as elements (the <SPAN> is element 0, and the <UL> node is element 1).

Listing 20.22: A Sample HTML Outline (Listing20.22.txt)

```
<UL>
  <LI><SPAN>Chapter 1</SPAN>
    <UL>
      <LI><SPAN>Section 1</SPAN>
        <UL>
          <LI><SPAN>Topic 1</SPAN>
          <LI><SPAN>Topic 2</SPAN>
        </UL>
      </LI>
      <LI><SPAN>Section 2</SPAN>
        <UL>
          <LI><SPAN>Topic 3</SPAN>
          <LI><SPAN>Topic 4</SPAN>
        </UL>
      </LI>
    </UL>
  </LI>
  <LI><SPAN>Chapter 2</SPAN>
    <UL>
      <LI><SPAN>Section 3</SPAN>
        <UL>
          <LI><SPAN>Topic 5</SPAN>
```

```
        <LI><SPAN>Topic 6</SPAN>
      </UL>
    </LI>
    <LI><SPAN>Section 4</SPAN>
      <UL>
        <LI><SPAN>Topic 7</SPAN>
        <LI><SPAN>Topic 8</SPAN>
      </UL>
    </LI>
  </UL>
</LI>
</UL>
```

I wanted to be able to create a simple outline transform that would take a class of XML hierarchical structures and render them in the same way, regardless of the actual names of the elements being displayed. As an additional set of features, I wanted to have the ability to parameterize the output so that it could equally be able to render output both as bulleted points and as a classical outline (remember the I.A.i.a.1 format from your high school English classes?).

I also wanted to have the ability to display any field in the outline that I was dealing with in the original XML, not just the obvious title or caption field. By parameterizing this caption attribute, I could switch from seeing a message's title to a message's body, with the press of a button.

Finally, I wanted to be able to specify a JavaScript function that would get called any time a particular item in the outline was selected; I didn't yet want to add collapsible capability, but I did want the outline to be sufficiently intelligent that it could be interactive rather than static. The result that I came up with is shown in Listing 20.23.

Listing 20.23: A Parametric Outline Filter (`Listing20.23.xsl`)

```
<xsl:stylesheet version="1.0"
  xmlns:xsl="http://www.w3.org/1999/XSL/Transform">
<xsl:output type="html"/>
<xsl:param name="containername" select="'messages'"/>
<xsl:param name="objectname" select="'message'"/>
<xsl:param name="caption" select="'title'"/>
<xsl:param name="listtype" select="'ordered'"/>
<xsl:variable name="listContainer">
  <xsl:choose>
    <xsl:when test="$listtype='unordered'">UL</xsl:when>
    <xsl:otherwise>OL</xsl:otherwise>
```

```
      </xsl:choose>
    </xsl:variable>
    <xsl:param name="clickevent"><![CDATA[
      //alert(me.id);
      window.status=me.id;
    ]]></xsl:param>
    <xsl:param name="ordered1"
      select="'list-style-type:upper-roman'"/>
    <xsl:param name="ordered2"
      select="'list-style-type:upper-alpha'"/>
    <xsl:param name="ordered3"
      select="'list-style-type:lower-roman'"/>
    <xsl:param name="ordered4"
      select="'list-style-type:lower-alpha'"/>
    <xsl:param name="ordered5"
      select="'list-style-type:numeric'"/>
    <xsl:param name="unordered1"
      select="'list-style-type:disc'"/>
    <xsl:param name="unordered2"
      select="'list-style-type:circle'"/>
    <xsl:param name="unordered3"
      select="'list-style-type:square'"/>
    <xsl:param name="unordered4"
      select="'list-style-type:diamond'"/>
    <xsl:param name="unordered5"
      select="'list-style-type:disc'"/>

    <xsl:variable name="treelevelstylesheet">
      .ordered1 {<xsl:value-of select="$ordered1"/>;
                 cursor:hand;}
      .ordered2 {<xsl:value-of select="$ordered2"/>}
      .ordered3 {<xsl:value-of select="$ordered3"/>}
      .ordered4 {<xsl:value-of select="$ordered4"/>}
      .ordered5 {<xsl:value-of select="$ordered5"/>}
      .unordered1 {<xsl:value-of select="$unordered1"/>;
                   cursor:hand;}
      .unordered2 {<xsl:value-of select="$unordered2"/>}
      .unordered3 {<xsl:value-of select="$unordered3"/>}
      .unordered4 {<xsl:value-of select="$unordered4"/>}
      .unordered5 {<xsl:value-of select="$unordered5"/>}
    </xsl:variable>
```

```
<xsl:template match="/">
  <xsl:apply-templates
    select="//*[name(.)=$containername]"/>
</xsl:template>

<xsl:template match="*">
  <xsl:param name="treeLevel"/>
  <li>
    <xsl:attribute name="class">
      <xsl:value-of select="$listtype"/>
      <xsl:value-of select="$treeLevel"/>
    </xsl:attribute>
    <xsl:attribute name="id">
      <xsl:value-of select="@id"/>
    </xsl:attribute>
    <xsl:attribute name="onclick">
      handleTreeClick(this)
    </xsl:attribute>
    <span>
      <xsl:value-of select="*[name(.) = $caption]"/>
      (<xsl:value-of select="$treeLevel"/>)
    </span>
    <xsl:call-template name="drawNode">
      <xsl:with-param name="objectRef" select="*"/>
      <xsl:with-param name="treeLevel"
        select="number($treeLevel) + 1"/>
    </xsl:call-template>
  </li>
</xsl:template>

<xsl:template match="*[name(.)=$containername]">
  <script language="JavaScript">
    function handleTreeClick(me){
      <xsl:value-of select="$clickevent"/>
      event.cancelBubble=true;  }
  </script>
  <style>
    <xsl:value-of select="$treelevelstylesheet"/>
  </style>
  <xsl:call-template name="drawNode">
    <xsl:with-param name="objectRef" select="*"/>
    <xsl:with-param name="treeLevel" select="1"/>
```

```
      </xsl:call-template>
    </xsl:template>

    <xsl:template name="drawNode">
      <xsl:param name="objectRef"/>
      <xsl:param name="treeLevel"/>
      <xsl:element name="{$listContainer}">
        <xsl:apply-templates
          select="$objectRef[name(.) = $objectname]">
          <xsl:with-param name="treeLevel" select="$treeLevel"/>
        </xsl:apply-templates>
      </xsl:element>
    </xsl:template>
    </xsl:stylesheet>
```

To handle the requirements for customization rather than using the name of elements in the templates (say, `message`), I used a parameter (`$objectname`, for example) and then performed a match with the test `.[name(.)=$objectname]`. This is not efficient (in fact, it's hideously inefficient because it forces a match attempt on every node rather than using the optimized code for working with preexisting tokens), but it has the advantage of working for a fairly wide class of XML examples, essentially any code that has the following structure:

```
<category>
  <object @id="id1">
    <caption>A Caption</caption>
    <!- other elements ->
    <object @id="id2">
      <caption>A Caption</caption>
      <!- other elements ->
      <!- other objects ->
    </object>
  </object>
  <!- other objects ->
</category>
```

where `category`, `object`, and `caption` are all parametric in nature.

When dealing with XSLT scripts, parameters essentially take the role that public properties and methods do in procedural languages; because the results of XSLT transformations can be so much more extensive than is usually the case with functions, there tend to be more parameters than you would normally expect for just a function. The parameters for the outline filter are given in Table 20.2. Keep in mind that XSLT parameters, like those of Java but not of Visual Basic, are case sensitive.

TABLE 20.2: Parameters for the Parametric Outline Component

PARAMETER NAME	VALUES	WHAT IT DOES	REQUIRED
`Containername`	String	Determines the name of the element that contains the elements to be displayed (for example, `messages`).	Yes
`Objectname`	String	Comprises the name of the object itself (for example, `message`).	Yes
`Caption`	String	The name of the element that holds the caption or title for each item.	No (defaults to `title`)
`Listtype`	`'ordered'|'unordered'`	If ordered, the outline will display classical outline format (I.A.i.a.1. format). If unordered, the outline will be displayed using various bullet symbols.	No (defaults to `ordered`)
`Clickevent`	JavaScript code as String	Contains code that gets executed when a user clicks on an item. It can either be a block of JavaScript code or a function call to other code in the surrounding page. Use the me object to get access to the `list` element, or `me.id` to get access to the ID of the corresponding element in the source.	No (If no code is given, then clicking on an item performs no action.)

CONTINUED ➡

TABLE 20.2 continued: Parameters for the Parametric Outline Component

PARAMETER NAME	VALUES	WHAT IT DOES	REQUIRED
`Ordered1-5`	CSS rule as String	Provides the CSS rules that describe the nodes in ordered view. You can change the numbering character by setting the `list-style-type: CSS property`.	No (See code for assigned defaults.)
`Unordered1-5`	CSS rule as String	Provide the CSS rules that describe the nodes in unordered view. You can set the default bullets to one of the other standard bullet types using `list-style-type`, or assign the level a graphic as a bullet with `list-style-image:url (myImage.gif)`.	No (See code for assigned defaults.)

Thus, if you had a collection of <note> objects contained in a <folder> object, wanted to have the outline use bulleted points instead of numbers, and wanted to display the <body> node instead of the <title> node from your notes list, you could do this by calling the `xmlserver.asp` function as follows:

```
http://www.myserver.com/xmlserver.asp?source=notes.xml&
filter=drawoutline.xsl&mimetype=html&param_collectionname=
folder&param_objectname=note&param_listtype=unordered&
param_caption=body
```

One noteworthy point about the XSL script: The code includes a named template called `$drawNode`, which actually builds the `UL` or `OL` container for the `LI` elements. The advantage to using named templates is that they can be parameterized and can thus cut down on duplication in your code.

WARNING

Outline structures such as the one dealt with here are highly recursive in nature: They push information onto a stack every time the XSLT parser progresses from a parent level to a child level. While stock processing is an integral part of XSLT, system limitations can cause the stack to overflow, usually with fatal results. If you run into problems with large, deep data sets, you may want to limit the number of levels deep a message response can go (or work with an indexed hierarchical structure that points to a linear set of rich data).

A Dynamic TreeView Component

While outlines are useful, they can also be overwhelming. The collapsible TreeView structure has become a staple of most user interfaces. You can click a folder to open or close it, displaying or hiding the contents of that folder and revealing the files and subfolders contained within. In this way, you can hide detailed information about topics until the user specifically requests it, which is especially useful for complex, XML-related structures.

The most difficult part of working with TreeView controls isn't implementing them; they are not all that much more complex than creating an outline control. Rather, it's in understanding where they work best. A TreeView control should be considered a structure of nested objects. Thus, in the message-board view, a message board system holds multiple message boards, which in turn hold multiple messages, which in turn hold multiple responses. By selecting any of these items, you should see in a different display window some representation of that object–in essence, the properties associated with that object.

Too many people look at the hierarchical view of XML and automatically assume that such a structure maps easily to a TreeView structure. In practice, it usually doesn't, because even though an element referencing an object and an element referencing a property are identical in implementation, conceptually they are two very different things.

The TreeView component given here works on this assumption. This assumes a container/contained relationship along the lines of the previous outline control: a `<messages>`-type collection can contain multiple `<message>` objects, which can, in turn, contain `<message> Response` objects.

NOTE

A response is still considered a message, by the way—the only real difference between the two is whether the message is connected to the root object (`<messages>`) or is a child of other messages.

The Parametric Dynamic Tree (Listing 20.24) borrows considerably from the outline but is more suited for more formal applications. In the form as it exists right now, the Dynamic Tree only works in Internet Explorer 4 and above. (It requires the use of the CSS `display` property, which is not well supported in Netscape Navigator.) Unlike the outline, however, it can do such things as track the position of the cursor as it passes over items (the default is to underline them, but that is customizable) and select an item if clicked, and it can be set to both begin at a node other than the root and start with a given item visible.

Listing 20.24: A Parametric Dynamic Tree Filter (`Listing20.24.xsl`)

```
<xsl:stylesheet version="1.0"
  xmlns:xsl="http://www.w3.org/1999/XSL/Transform">
<xsl:output type="html"/>
<xsl:param name="containername" select="'messages'"/>
<xsl:param name="objectname" select="'message'"/>
<xsl:param name="caption" select="'title'"/>
<xsl:param name="childname" select="'message(s)'"/>
<xsl:param name="visibleid" select="''"/>
<xsl:param name="selectedid" select="''"/>
<xsl:param name="treeid" select="'tree'"/>
<xsl:param name="startfromid" select="''"/>
<xsl:param name="clickevent"><![CDATA[
  window.status=me.id;
]]></xsl:param>
<xsl:param name="folderstyle"
  select="'list-style-type:none;
    list-style-image:url(folder.gif);
    cursor:hand;'"/>
<xsl:param name="filestyle"
  select="'list-style-type:none;
    list-styleimage:url(file.gif);'"/>
<xsl:param name="selectedstyle"
  select="'background-color:navy;color:white;'"/>
```

```
<xsl:param name="highlightstyle"
  select="'text-decoration:underline;'"/>
<xsl:param name="defaultstyle"
  select="'font-size:11pt;font-family:Arial;'"/>
<xsl:variable name="treelevelstylesheet">
  .defaultstyle {<xsl:value-of select="$defaultstyle"/>}
  .folder {<xsl:value-of select="$folderstyle"/>}
  .file {<xsl:value-of select="$filestyle"/>}
  .selected {<xsl:value-of select="$selectedstyle"/>}
  .highlight {<xsl:value-of select="$highlightstyle"/>}
</xsl:variable>

<xsl:template match="/">
  <xsl:choose>
    <xsl:when test="$startfromid != ''">
      <xsl:apply-templates select=
        "//*[name(.) = $objectname][@id = $startfromid]"/>
    </xsl:when>
    <xsl:otherwise>
      <xsl:apply-templates select=
        "//*[name(.) = $containername]"/>
    </xsl:otherwise>
  </xsl:choose>
</xsl:template>

<xsl:template match="*">
  <xsl:param name="treeLevel"/>
  <li>
    <xsl:choose>
      <xsl:when test="*[name(.) = $objectname]">
        <xsl:attribute name="class">
          folder</xsl:attribute>
      </xsl:when>
      <xsl:otherwise>
        <xsl:attribute name="class">
          file</xsl:attribute>
      </xsl:otherwise>
    </xsl:choose>
    <xsl:attribute name="id">
      <xsl:value-of select="@id"/>
    </xsl:attribute>
    <xsl:if test="@id=$selectedid">
```

```
        <xsl:attribute name="onload">
          handleTreeClick(this,
            <xsl:value-of select="$treeid"/>)
        </xsl:attribute>
      </xsl:if>
      <xsl:attribute name="onclick">
        handleTreeClick(this,
          <xsl:value-of select="$treeid"/>)
      </xsl:attribute>
      <xsl:attribute name="onmouseover">
        handleTreeOver(this)
      </xsl:attribute>
      <xsl:attribute name="onmouseout">
        handleTreeOut(this)
      </xsl:attribute>
      <xsl:attribute name="onmousedown">
        handleTreeDown(this,
          <xsl:value-of select="$treeid"/>)
      </xsl:attribute>
      <xsl:variable name="childObjects"
        select="*[name(.) = $objectname]"/>
      <span>
        <xsl:value-of select="*[name(.) = $caption]"
          xml:preserve-space="yes"/>
        <xsl:if test="count($childObjects) &gt; 0">
          (<xsl:value-of select="count($childObjects)"/>
          <xsl:text> </xsl:text>
          <xsl:value-of select="$childname"/>)
        </xsl:if>
      </span>
      <xsl:call-template name="drawNode">
        <xsl:with-param name="objectRef" select="*"/>
        <xsl:with-param name="treeLevel"
          select="number($treeLevel)+1"/>
      </xsl:call-template>
    </li>
  </xsl:template>

  <xsl:template match="*[name(.)=$containername]">
    <xsl:call-template name="writeIEEventHandlers" />
    <style>
      <xsl:value-of select="$treelevelstylesheet"/>
```

```
      </style>
      <xsl:call-template name="drawNode">
        <xsl:with-param name="objectRef" select="*"/>
        <xsl:with-param name="treeLevel" select="1"/>
        <xsl:with-param name="treeID" select="$treeid"/>
      </xsl:call-template>
    </xsl:template>

    <xsl:template name="drawNode">
      <xsl:param name="objectRef"/>
      <xsl:param name="treeLevel"/>
      <xsl:param name="treeID" select="false()"/>
      <ul>
        <xsl:if test="$treeID">
          <xsl:attribute name="id">
            <xsl:value-of select="$treeID"/>
          </xsl:attribute>
        </xsl:if>
        <xsl:attribute name="style">
          display:
          <xsl:choose>
            <xsl:when test=
      "number($treeLevel)=1 or $objectRef//@id[.=$visibleid]">
              block</xsl:when>
            <xsl:otherwise>none</xsl:otherwise>
          </xsl:choose>
        </xsl:attribute>
        <xsl:apply-templates
          select= "$objectRef[name(.)=$objectname]">
          <xsl:with-param name="treeLevel" select="$treeLevel"/>
        </xsl:apply-templates>
      </ul>
    </xsl:template>

    <xsl:template name="writeIEEventHandlers">
    <script language="JavaScript">
      var oldNode=new Array();
      function handleTreeClick(me,treeID){
        if (me.className == "folder"){
          var container = me.children(1);
          if (container.style.display == "none"){
            container.style.display = "block";
```

```
          }
          else {
            container.style.display = "none";
          }
        }
        <xsl:value-of select="$clickevent"/>
        event.cancelBubble = true;  }

      function handleTreeDown(me,treeID){
        if (oldNode[treeID] != null){
          oldNode[treeID].className = "";
        }
        span = me.children(0)
        span.className = "selected"
        oldNode[treeID] = span;
        on handleTreeOver(me){
          span = me.children(0);
          if (span.className.charAt("highlight") != -1){
            span.className += " highlight";
          }
        }
        event.cancelBubble=true;  }

      function handleTreeOut(me){
        span = me.children(0);
        span.className = span.className.replace(" highlight","")
        event.cancelBubble = true;  }
    </script>
    </xsl:template>
    </xsl:stylesheet>
```

This example demonstrates both the advantage and the dangers of working with XSL—one of the principal problems is that JavaScript code is contained within the body of the script. The same rules apply to such code as apply to client code in ASP:

- You should refrain as much as possible from mixing the two blocks of code together.
- Client script code does not run in the same process as the XSL code output, unless encapsulated in an `<msxsl:script>` block.

- Because scripting code incompatibility is the largest area of difference between the major browsers, you should always make sure if you support multiple versions of code that you have them clearly delineated, preferably in different templates (or perhaps matching templates but with different modes).

Thus, I extracted the event-handling code that would be used by the nodes and placed them into a distinctly named template (`writeIEEventHandlers`). One modification that I could have made to the code would have been to retrieve the browser, then add the appropriate event-handling code for each distinct browser configuration; since the JavaScript is a separate template in each case, it makes the code much easier to handle (and one that becomes more amenable to `<xsl:include>` elements).

The results of processing the component again fall somewhere between the results generated by a function and the sophistication of an object. The parameters of the Dynamic Tree are given in Table 20.3; the list is similar to, but a little richer than, the list for the outline.

TABLE 20.3: Parameters for the Dynamic TreeView Component

PARAMETER NAME	VALUES	WHAT IT IS	REQUIRED
`Containername`	String	The name of the element t hat contains the elements to be displayed (for example, `messages`).	Yes
`Objectname`	String	The object itself (for example, `message`).	Yes
`Caption`	String	The name of the element that holds the caption or title for each item.	No (defaults to `title`)
`Childname`	String	The control indicates the number of child responses that the given message has.	No (If not included, the string showing this information is not displayed.)

CONTINUED ➡

TABLE 20.3 continued: Parameters for the Dynamic TreeView Component

Parameter Name	Values	What It Is	Required
`Clickevent`	JavaScript code as String	Contains code that gets executed when a user clicks on an item. It can either be a block of JavaScript code or a function call to other code in the surrounding page. Use the me object to get access to the `list` element, or `me.id` to get access to the ID of the corresponding element in the source.	No (If no code is given, then clicking on an item performs no action.)
`Visibleid`	String	If a value is given and an item has this ID, then the control will start with this item (and hence all of its parents) open.	No (If not included, then the tree only displays the topmost children and hides the rest.)
`Selectedid`	String	If a value is given and an item has this ID, then the item will automatically be selected. Note that such an item could still be invisible.	No (If not included, no item is initially selected.)
`Treeid`	String	If two or more such tree controls are included on the page, it is necessary to set `treeid` for each of them so that they are unique. This is required for maintaining state information.	No (Unless two or more controls are present, then yes.)
`Startfromid`	String	If this item is given and an item in the tree has this ID, then this will be displayed as the root node.	No (If this isn't given, then it is assumed that the container object is the root node of the tree.)

CONTINUED →

TABLE 20.3 continued: Parameters for the Dynamic TreeView Component

PARAMETER NAME	VALUES	WHAT IT IS	REQUIRED
`Folderstyle`	CSS String	Gives the CSS rule that describes the folder list item. Note that in the example it is assumed that the file `folder.gif` is in the same directory.	No (defaults to a folder icon view, if the GIF is available)
`Filestyle`	CSS String	Gives the CSS rule that describes the file list item. Note that in the example it is assumed that the file `file.gif` is in the same directory.	No (defaults to a file icon view, if the GIF is available)
`Selectedstyle`	CSS String	Gives the CSS rule that describes the appearance of the span when this item is selected.	No (defaults to white text on a navy rectangle)
`Highlightstyle`	CSS String	Gives the CSS rule that describes the appearance of the span when the mouse moves over the item.	No (defaults to underlined text)
`Defaultstyle`	CSS String	Gives the CSS rule that describes the default state of the text in all of the spans.	No

The principles behind this and the outline are similar, although this takes more advantage of DHTML to produce visual effects such as rollovers. That, however, brings up a good point about construction: In this case, the primary purpose of the XSLT is not to set up the eye candy but rather to create the underlying structure that supports the interactive elements. The XSLT script doesn't actually know about the behavior of the object, per se (with one minor exception); instead, it lets the browser take over this task while assigning the relevant CSS classes to each of the list elements.

The one exception to this rule comes from the use of the `visibleid` and `selectid` parameters. The `visibleid` property indicates that a given node should automatically be visible when the control starts, and the only way to do that is to make sure that its parent-container <UL> tags are also all visible. This is one of the reasons that the `display` property is kept distinct from the normal SPAN or LI style, since the CSS `display` property will be set or not set independent of any other class associations. Similarly, the `selectid` parameter determines what item should be selected, but rather than changing the visual appearance of that node it instead notifies the page (through the `onload` event) that when all of the elements for that section of the tree are completely rendered, the LI element with the `selectid` ID value should be handled as if it were clicked.

In other words, use the XSLT capabilities to set up the structural elements of the control, but turn over the interactive and rendering components of the control to a different language (such as CSS or JavaScript). Transform your data into structures with XSLT, decorate it with CSS, and enliven it with script (all of which can be delivered via the XSLT, of course).

ASP and XML exist in an uneasy alliance; clearly, ASP was never intended to serve as a host for XML, but it performs this task moderately well nonetheless. It has the necessary tools to provide XML streams from remote servers and to tie those streams together through XSLT or DOM. Also, ASP can provide a suitable environment for building distributed applications by making incoming, outgoing, and state-maintenance pipes available, although not necessarily in a clean fashion.

In this chapter, I deliberately stayed away from the most advanced features of IIS, both because the adoption of IIS 5 is still not widespread and because its capabilities really shine only when working in conjunction with XMLHTTP. Up until now, most of the concentration in working with code has been oriented towards scripting environments. However, XML offers significant advantages to the compiled environment of Visual Basic as well, and certain VB features, such as WebClasses, can significantly enhance XML's native flexibility and can radically simplify the pipeline architecture that will likely be the primary way of working with XML in the future.

WHAT'S NEXT?

XML and ASP make a powerful combination, but they're only the tip of the iceberg in presenting and manipulating XML data. In the next chapter, you'll learn more about Remote Data Services (RDS) as it relates to XML. You'll practice some useful data-binding techniques that will allow you to bind XML directly to your HTML controls. You'll also discover how to persist and update data in your database using XML recordsets, especially through the use of SQL Server 2000's new XML feature set.

Chapter 21

XML and MS Databases

XML is a language for representing structured information. As such, it's an ideal mechanism for exchanging information between different database management systems, or for building front ends for database applications that run on thin clients. Internet Explorer 5 supports XML, and Microsoft is adding XML support to its databases. ADO (ActiveX Data Objects), Microsoft's data access technology, supports XML already. SQL Server 2000 also supports XML natively.

In addition to adding XML features to the databases, Microsoft is enhancing XML support in Internet Explorer. As you probably know, any features added to Internet Explorer are also available to any language, like VBScript or Visual Basic. At this point, there are many XML tools, both on the database side and on the client side, but these tools are still rough around the edges. For one thing, you must write programs (or scripts, in

Adapted from *XML Developer's Handbook*™, by Kurt Cagle

ISBN 0-7821-2704-5 640 pages $49.99

the case of Internet Explorer) to parse XML documents. Eventually, XML must become transparent to developers so that we won't have to write code to manipulate the XML document itself. At this point, you must not only write code to process XML data, but you must use JavaScript to make sure your client applications will run in both browsers.

In this chapter, you'll learn how to retrieve XML-formatted data from a database, pass them to the client, and bind them to HTML controls. In the first part of the chapter, I review the Remote Data Services (RDS) and data-binding techniques that we touched on in Chapter 16. Once you learn how data binding works and you can bind a recordset to the HTML controls on a Web page, you'll be able to apply the same techniques to XML recordsets as well. You'll also learn how to use the XML Data Control and how to create data islands.

In the second half of the chapter, you'll learn how to use ADO's methods to persist recordsets in XML format and how to update the tables in the database through an XML recordset. You'll see the syntax used to mark changes in a recordset and how the modified recordset is submitted to the database and committed there. In the last section of the chapter, you'll learn about the new XML features of SQL Server 2000. You'll see how you can query SQL Server remotely through an HTTP connection and how to execute stored procedures against a SQL Server database remotely. As you will see, it is possible to directly access and manipulate SQL Server databases from within your browser.

NOTE

To retrieve the referenced files and programs from the Sybex Web site, go to `www.sybex.com` and search for this book using its title or ISBN (2971).

RDS AND DATA BINDING

Before examining the specifics of ADO's XML support, it is important to understand the basics of data binding. *Data binding* is the process of associating a control to a data field. When the underlying field changes value, the control is updated automatically. Likewise, when the viewer edits the control, the underlying field is updated automatically. The recordset whose fields are bound to the controls of a Form on a Web page is a disconnected recordset, and the changes are not immediately reflected to the database. The disconnected recordset is one of the most prominent features of ADO 2.1 and later versions; unlike the regular recordset we've been using for years, a disconnected recordset does not require an open connection to the database. It's populated through an open connection, but it maintains its data even after the connection to the database has been closed. Disconnected recordsets are updateable. You can edit their rows, and the changes can be committed to the database after the connection to the database has been established again. In this section, you'll see how to move a disconnected recordset to the client and display its fields on HTML controls.

HTML is nothing more than a language for formatting text to be displayed on a browser. Yet modern Web applications do not rely on static content that can be stored in HTML pages and transmitted to the client. For example, we want to be able to display field values on certain controls, but the exact fields that will be displayed on the controls are not known ahead of time. Thus we need a technique to bind the fields of a database to elements of a page, so that when we connect to the database, the elements will be populated automatically.

Visual Basic programmers have been doing this for years, but they can have a quick link to the database. However, Web applications can't assume that they have immediate access to a database. Despite this, it is possible for a Web page to "see" the fields of a database through the *Remote Data Services (RDS) Data Control*. As mentioned in Chapter 16, the RDS Data Control connects to a database server, such as SQL Server, and retrieves the data from tables. The viewer can then edit the data and update the database en masse.

If you're familiar with database programming, you already see the similarities between the usual Data Controls used in building database front ends with VB or other high-level languages (the DAO and ADO Data Controls) and the RDS Data Control. The main difference is that the RDS Data Control connects to the database over the HTTP protocol. Because dial-up connections are not fast enough for database operations, the RDS Data Control maintains the data in a disconnected recordset and updates the database only when requested. This happens at the end of a session. Now you'll see how to bind the fields of the recordset to HTML elements.

Binding Fields to HTML Elements

To review, the RDS Data Control can bind HTML elements to database fields, but it can also bind them to XML data. The following lines insert an RDS Data Control onto a page and specify the database it connects to, as well as a query to retrieve the desired data:

```
<OBJECT
   CLASSID=
   "clsid:BD96C556-65A3-11D0-983A-00C04FC29E33"
   ID="Products" WIDTH = 0 HEIGHT = 0>
   <PARAM NAME="Connect" VALUE="DSN=NWindDB">
   <PARAM NAME="Server" VALUE = "PROTO">
   <PARAM NAME="SQL"
   VALUE="SELECT * FROM Products">
</OBJECT>
```

This <OBJECT> tag tells the RDS Data Control to connect to a local database—the NorthWind database—and retrieve all the rows from the Products table. PROTO is the name of the machine on which SQL Server is running, and DSN is a Data Source Name that points to the NorthWind database.

NOTE

To set up a DSN, use the ODBC Data Source tool in the Control Panel (if you're using Windows 98) or in the Administrative Tools (if you're using Windows 2000).

Instead of connecting directly to a database, you can specify the name of a script with the URL attribute. The script will retrieve the data from the database server and return them to the client as a recordset. Here's the alternate <OBJECT> tag that uses the URL of a script to get the data:

```
<OBJECT
   CLASSID=
   "clsid:BD96C556-65A3-11D0-983A-00C04FC29E33"
   ID="Products" WIDTH = 0 HEIGHT = 0>
   <PARAM NAME="URL" VALUE="GetProducts.asp">
</OBJECT>
```

Both tags create a recordset—the Products recordset—on the client. By definition, this is a disconnected recordset, and you can bind its fields to HTML elements on the page (discussed in the next section). As you navigate through the rows of the recordset with its navigational methods, the values of the bound HTML controls are updated. If you edit a field (provided that the control allows editing), the new value is committed to the local recordset as soon as you move to another row. The changes are not sent to the server.

To update the underlying tables, you must call the disconnected recordset's `SubmitChanges` method. Another method, `Refresh`, discards the changes and reloads the recordset from the database.

Data Binding Properties

To bind an HTML element to the RDS Data Control, you must use the following two properties:

DATASRC This is the name of the RDS Data Control that contains the data. You must prefix the name of the data source with the pound sign (#) to indicate that the data source is local to the client.

DATAFLD This is the name of the field in the control to which the element is bound.

NOTE

For a review of the Data-Bound HTML Elements, see Chapter 16, Table 16.1.

To display a field on the page, use the SPAN tag as follows:

```
ProductID   <SPAN DATASRC="#Products"
             DATAFLD="ProductID">
            </SPAN>
ProductName <SPAN DATASRC="#Products"
             DATAFLD="ProductName">
            </SPAN>
Description <SPAN DATASRC="#Products"
             DATAFLD="Description">
            </SPAN>
```

The following statements display the entire recordset on a table:

```
<TABLE DATASRC="#Products">
<TR><TD>ProductID</TD>
  <TD><SPAN DATAFLD="ProductID"></SPAN>
  </TD>
  <TD>ProductName</TD>
  <TD><SPAN DATAFLD="ProductName"></SPAN>
```

```
    </TD>
    <TD>Description</TD>
    <TD><SPAN DATAFLD="Description"></SPAN>
    </TD>
  </TR>
  </TABLE>
```

As you can see, we don't have to specify more than a single row of the table. Since the data-bound element is a table, the browser knows that it must iterate through the entire recordset and create a new table row for each row in the recordset.

When we bind a table to a recordset, the DATASRC attribute is specified in the <TABLE> tag, so that we won't have to repeat it in every <TD> cell. The DATASRC attribute's value doesn't change from row to row.

The <TABLE> tag supports yet another attribute, DATAPAGESIZE, which specifies how many rows will be displayed on the table. The following tag will create a table with the first 20 products:

```
<TABLE ID="ProdTable"
   DATASRC="#Products" DATAPAGESIZE="20">
```

In this example, we've specified an ID for the table. This is because we want to be able to move to any group of 20 products. To do so, we must provide scripts for two buttons that take the viewer to the previous group and the next group, respectively. These buttons must call the control's PreviousPage and NextPage methods. The following statements insert two buttons after the table that implement the table's navigational methods:

```
<INPUT TYPE=Button VALUE="PREVIOUS"
   onClick="ProdTable.PreviousPage()"/>

<INPUT TYPE=Button VALUE="NEXT"
   onClick="ProdTable.NextPage()"/>
```

The ProductsTable.htm page on the Sybex Web site retrieves product information from the NorthWind database and displays it in tabular format on the browser. Before you open the document, change the following two lines in the definition of the RDS Data Control:

```
<PARAM NAME="Connect" VALUE="DSN=NWindDB">
<PARAM NAME="Server" VALUE = "PROTO">
```

The Connect attribute should be the name of a DSN on your computer, and the Server attribute should be the name of the computer on which SQL Server is running. Figure 21.1 shows a small section of the Products table with the product data.

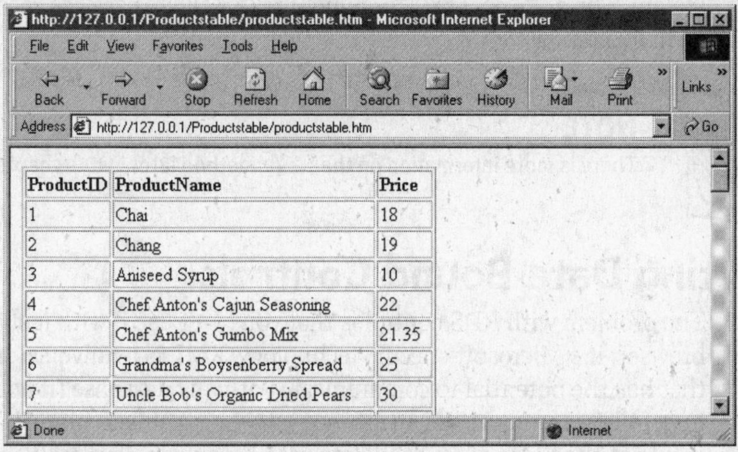

FIGURE 21.1: Binding a table to a disconnected recordset

NOTE

If you have only Access on your system, set up a DSN for the NorthWind database and omit the `Server` parameter.

Retrieving Data with ASP Files

If you want to use an ASP file on the server to retrieve the data, open the `ProductsTableScript.asp` file (on the Sybex Web site). You must copy the file to the root folder of the Web server, start your browser, and connect to the address `127.0.0.1/ProductsTableScript.asp`. The RDS Data Control will invoke the `GetProducts.asp` script (Listing 21.1), which will furnish the rows of the Products table.

Listing 21.1: The `GetProducts.asp` Script

```
<%
Set RS = Server.CreateObject("ADODB.Recordset")
RS.Open "Products", "DSN=NWINDDB"
```

```
RS.Save Response, adPersistXML
RS.Close
Set RS=Nothing
%>
```

The Save method places the recordset's rows directly in the Response stream. The adPersistXML argument tells ADO to save the recordset in XML format.

NOTE

There is more information on the Save method later in this chapter.

Editing Data-Bound Controls

The problem with RDS control is that you can't use it with just any browser; it's Microsoft-specific technology. XML is a universal language that has the potential to communicate with any database (if not now, hopefully someday in the near future). By being able to bind HTML elements to the fields of an XML data island, you can develop Web pages that allow viewers to edit the fields and update the database. The HTML elements that can be bound to fields (either database fields or XML fields) support the DATASRC and DATAFLD properties. DATASRC is the name of the database, or the name of an XML data island, in our case. DATAFLD is the name of the field we want to bind to the element.

If you want viewers to be able to edit the fields of the recordset, you must place a Text control in every cell of the table. Here are the statements of the previous table, only this time each cell is a Text control so that you can edit the fields. You'll see later how to commit the changes to the database.

```
<TABLE DATASRC="#Products">
<TR>
  <TD>ProductID</TD>
  <TD>
    <INPUT TYPE=Text DATAFLD="ProductID"/>
  </TD>
  <TD>ProductName</TD>
  <TD>
    <INPUT TYPE=Text DATAFLD="ProductName"/>
```

```
    </TD>
    <TD>Description</TD>
    <TD>
      <INPUT TYPE=Text DATAFLD="Description"/>
    </TD>
  </TR>
  </TABLE>
```

These revised pages have two drawbacks: There are too many rows to edit at once, and there's no mechanism to submit the changes to the database. We'll revise this page as we go along in the chapter. Also in upcoming sections, you will learn how to display a single row and allow the user to navigate through the recordset, as well as how to submit the changes to the database.

The XML Data Control

The previous section showed you how to connect an RDS Data Control to an XML recordset: You specify the URL of a script that returns a disconnected recordset. In this section, you'll learn how to do the same with the XML Data Control. In essence, the <XML> tag is the XML Data Control. The following statements will create an XML Data Control, name it Prod, and populate it with XML data:

```
<XML ID="Prod">
<Products>
  <Product>
    <ProductID>1</ProductID>
    <ProductName>ProductName1/ProductName>
    <UnitPrice>1.11</UnitPrice>
  </Product>
  <Product>
    <ProductID>2</ProductID>
    <ProductName>ProductName2/ProductName>
    <UnitPrice>2.22</UnitPrice>
  </Product>
{ XML statements for the remaining products }
```

```
</Products>
</XML>
```

The XML Data Control supports the same navigational methods as the RDS Data Control, and all the changes are maintained in a local XML recordset. After the viewer has edited the fields, your page should be able to transmit the modified rows to another script on the Web server that will update the database. This takes more than a call to the `SubmitChanges` method, and you'll see later in this chapter how to commit the changes to the database.

XML Data Islands

A recordset that's transmitted to the client as part of the HTML document is called a *data island*. The data island's fields can be bound to any of the HTML controls previously listed in Table 16.1. An advantage of the XML Data Control is that, technically, it's not an ActiveX control. This means you don't have to use the `<OBJECT>` tag to insert it on a page, and it can be used with any browser that supports XML.

The problem with XML data islands is in how they're created. Coding XML data islands by hand is obviously out of the question. Luckily, the major data access mechanism, ADO, supports XML, which means that the databases themselves don't have to support XML natively. In the following section, you'll see how to retrieve recordsets in XML format from Access and SQL Server. First, we'll look at ADO support for XML.

ADO Support for XML

ActiveX Data Objects is a key technology and one of the cornerstones of the Windows DNA (Distributed Network Architecture). Although ADO has limited support for XML right now, future versions will provide more elaborate XML support.

One of the most important features of ADO 2.5 is its ability to retrieve recordsets in XML format. ADO 2.5 can format recordsets as XML documents and save them in a file or in a `Stream` object. The Web server's response to the client is such a stream, and ADO can save a recordset in XML format directly to the `Response` object. The data are then sent to the client, where a client-side script can traverse the XML data and display, or otherwise manipulate, the rows.

The XML format contains information about the structure of the data, so the XML recordset carries with it a description of its structure as well as the data itself. Because XML is an open standard, you should be able to use XML recordsets to exchange structured data between any two machines. This is the promise of XML, but we aren't quite there yet. There are no tools that would allow you to store the structure of an Access database as an XML document and use it to create a DB2 database populated with the Access data. This situation may change in just a year, as Microsoft is pushing this technology and wants to incorporate it into flagship products like SQL Server.

NOTE

Since ADO is not database specific, the XML techniques discussed in this chapter apply to Access, SQL Server, and every other DBMS that has support for ADO.

Web developers who are not into database programming can also use an XML-formatted recordset. As long as they're familiar with XML and the DOM, they can work with this document without having to understand how the data is stored in the database, or even how to query the database.

In this section of the chapter, we'll explore how to use ADO to extract information from databases, format the recordset as an XML document, and display it on the client computer. You'll also see how to write a front end for the browser to edit the data and submit the changes back to the server in XML format.

Persisting Recordsets in XML Format

The ADO's recordset object supports the `Save` method, which stores the rows of the recordset to a file or a `Stream` object. In ADO jargon, saving the data to a file or `Stream` object is called *persisting the recordset*. The `Save` method can store the data in a proprietary binary format, in the ADTG (Advanced Data Table Gram) format, or in XML format. To store the recordset represented by the `RS` object variable to a file in XML format, use the following statement:

```
RS.Save fileName, adPersist
```

where *`fileName`* is the name of the file and *`adPersist`* is a constant that determines the structure of the file, and its value can be one of two constants: `adPersistADTG` or `adPersistXML`.

Assuming that you have Access installed on your system and you have created a Data Source Name for the NorthWind database, you can use the following VB statements to create a file with the rows of the Categories table in XML format. Just start a new VB project and enter the following lines in a button's Click event handler:

```
Dim RS As New ADODB.Recordset
FName = "C:\Temp\Categories.xml"
RS.Open "SELECT CategoryID, CategoryName, " & _
   "Description FROM Categories", "DSN=NWIND"
If Dir$(FName) <> "" Then Kill FName
RS.Save FName, adPersistXML
```

NOTE

If the file created by the code above exists already, the Save method won't overwrite it. Instead, it will cause a runtime error. That's why you must either delete the file or prompt the user for a different filename.

The first few rows of the RS recordset in XML format are shown in Figure 21.2.

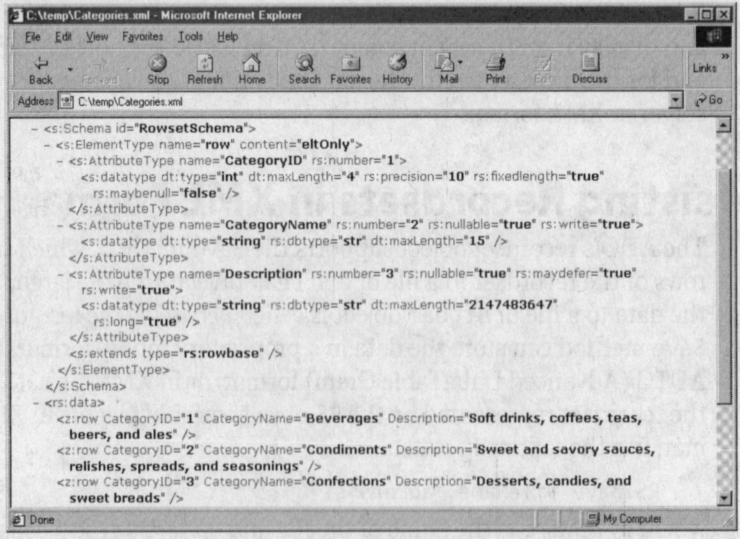

FIGURE 21.2: Persisting a table in XML format

If you want to access the database and produce XML output from within a server-side script, you can use the equivalent VBScript statements. With a server-side script, you need not save the XML-formatted recordset to a database. You can send it directly to the client by writing the output to the `Response` stream, as shown here:

```
Set RS = Server.CreateObject("ADODB.Recordset")
RS.Open "SELECT CategoryID, CategoryName, " & _
   "Description FROM Categories", "DSN=NWIND"
RS.Save Response, adPersistXML
```

TIP

You should probably insert a few HTML statements above and below the XML data island telling the client what to do with the XML data. Use the `Response.Write` method to send additional output to the client.

Though the XML document produced by the Save method (shown in Figure 21.2, displayed in Internet Explorer) looks quite elementary, let's take a close look at it. The appearance of the document, called `categories.xml`, may be of interest to developers, but it's not what typical viewers would like to see on their browsers. The simplest method to format the XML is to write an XSL file. I'm assuming that you'll find it easier to write scripts rather than XSL files. Thus, I will not discuss XSL files in this chapter.

Namespace Prefixes

The XML format used by ADO contains up to four sections, which—in XML jargon—are called *namespaces*. These sections are distinguished by a unique prefix, as shown in Table 21.1.

TABLE 21.1: XML Namespace Prefixes

Prefix	Description
s	Marks the beginning of the recordset's schema
dt	Marks the beginning of each row's data type
rs	Marks the beginning of the data section
z	Marks the beginning of each data row

The following rows in the `categories.xml` file in Figure 21.2, shown earlier, use three of the four available prefixes:

```
<s:AttributeType
  name="CategoryID" rs:number="1">
<s:datatype dt:type="int" dt:maxLength="4"
  rs:precision="10" rs:fixedlength="true"
  rs:maybenull="false" />
</s:AttributeType>
```

This section specifies the structure of a column. It's very unlikely that you will use this information on the client, but it's needed by ADO if you use the XML document to update a database.

The `dt` prefix appears in front of the row's data type attributes. Different data types have different attributes, of course. The *string* data type, for instance, doesn't have a precision attribute.

Later in the `categories.xml` file, you'll find the actual data. Each row in this section is identified with the z prefix:

```
<z:row CategoryID="2" CategoryName="Condiments"
Description="Sweet and savory sauces, relishes,
  spreads, and seasonings" >
```

(The `Description` line was broken to fit on the page.) If you select all the fields in the table, you'll see that the data section of the XML file contains a very long field, which is an image encoded as a sequence of characters. The image is not rendered on the client, because the content type of the file is text/HTML.

Although it is possible to include a textual representation of binary data in an XML-formatted recordset, it is not possible to directly bind the binary data to an `<IMG>` tag. To display a picture on a page with data-bound fields, use the `<IMG>` tag along with a URL, as shown here:

```
<IMG SRC="CategoryPicture.asp?CategoryID=XX">
```

The `CategoryPicture.asp` script reads the Picture column of the row in the Categories table that matched the specified Category ID. Most developers don't even store binary information in the database; they prefer to create image files in a specific folder and name them according to a key field in the database. This way they can easily match a row in the table to the corresponding file. For the Categories table, you should store each category's image to a file named *`xx.gif`*, where *`xx`* is the ID of the category.

The <s:datatype> attribute specifies the data type of each field, as well as other field attributes (whether the field can have a null value, for example). The data types that may appear in an XML file are shown in Table 21.2.

TABLE 21.2: XML Data Types

Type	Description
`bin.base64`	A binary object.
`bin.hex`	Binary values in hex format.
`Boolean`	A True/False value.
`Char`	A string that contains a single character.
`Date`	A date value in the format *yyyy-mm-dd*.
`DateTime`	A date and time value in the format *yyyy-mm-ddThh:mm:ss*. The time value is optional; if omitted, it's assumed to be 00:00:00.
`DateTime.tz`	A date and time value that includes time zone information in the format *yyyy-mm-ddThh:mm:ss-hh:mm*. The time zone information is expressed in hours and minutes ahead or behind GMT.
`fixed.14.4`	A fixed floating-point value with up to 14 integer digits and up to four fractional digits.
`Float`	A floating-point value.
`Int`	An integer value.
`Number`	A floating-point value.
`Time`	A time value in the format *hh:mm:ss*.
`Time.tz`	A time value that includes time zone information in the format *hh:mm:ss-hh:mm*. The time zone information is expressed in hours and minutes ahead or behind GMT.
`i1`	A single-byte integer value.
`i2`	A two-byte integer value.
`i4`	A four-byte integer value.
`r4`	A four-byte fractional value.
`r8`	An eight-byte fractional value.
`ui1`	A single-byte, unsigned integer value.
`ui2`	A two-byte, unsigned integer value.

CONTINUED →

TABLE 21.2 continued: XML Data Types

Type	Description
ui4	A four-byte, unsigned integer value.
Uri	A Universal Resource Indicator.
Uuid	A universally unique ID made up of hex digits.

The first thing to keep in mind when you work with XML recordsets generated by ADO (or SQL Server's native XML format, for that matter) is that the XML recordsets contain a description of the schema of the data. Not only that, but each row contains all the column values in a single tag, the <z:row> tag. As you will see later in the chapter, it takes some extra coding to get rid of the schema information. As far as the structure of the tags goes, Microsoft designers opted for a less verbose XML format: All the columns in a row are listed in the same <z:row> tag. For example, the line

```
<z:row CategoryID="2" CategoryName="Condiments"
Description="Sweet and savory sauces,
  relishes, spreads, and seasonings" >
```

corresponds to the following lines of straight XML code:

```
<Category>
<CategoryID>2</CategoryID>
<CategoryName>Condiments<CategoryName/>
<Description>Sweet and savory sauces, relishes,
  spreads, and seasonings<Description/>
</Category>
```

Updating XML Recordsets

The XML format used by ADO can also handle updates by storing edits, insertions, and deletions in the XML document itself. This is a very interesting feature, because it will eventually allow you to read data from any data source, edit it, and then post the changes to the original database. The software you use need not be aware of the capabilities of the database from where the data came. This is not the case right now, however. The various vendors are just beginning to add XML features to their databases, but it won't be long before XML becomes a standard feature for exchanging data between databases. But let's start by looking at the tags for updating recordsets.

Editing Rows

An edited row is specified with the `<rs:update>` and `<rs:original>` tags. The `<rs:update>` tag signifies the changes, and `<rs:original>` signifies the original row. Here's a typical example. The following lines correspond to the first row of the Customer table of the NorthWind database, after we have changed the CompanyName column from `BLAUER SEE DELIKATESSEN` to `BLAUER SEE DELIKATESSEN1` and set the `Region` field to `REGION`:

```
- <rs:update>
- <rs:original>
  <z:row CustomerID="ALFKI"
    CompanyName="BLAUER SEE DELIKATESSEN"
    ContactName="MARIA ANDERS"
    ContactTitle="Sales Representative"
    Address="Obere Str. 577" City="Berlin"
    Region="REGION" PostalCode="12209"
    Country="GERMANY"
    Phone="030-0074321" Fax="030-0076545" />
  </rs:original>
  <z:row
    CompanyName="BLAUER SEE DELIKATESSEN1" />
  </rs:update>
```

Notice that all the columns appear in the `<rs:update>` tag, even though only one of them was changed.

You may be wondering why ADO keeps track of the original values. ADO won't post any updates to the database if a row has been changed since it was read. If another user has already modified the same line after your application has read it, ADO will generate a runtime error and won't overwrite the edited columns. When the updates take place through a disconnected recordset, ADO needs to know what the values of the columns in the recordset were before it can commit any changes to the database.

Inserting Rows

Inserted rows appear at the end of the document in an <rs:insert> tag. The following lines add a new customer to the XML document:

```
<rs:insert>
  <z:row CustomerID="TEST" />
  <z:row CustomerID="TEST"
    CompanyName="TEST-CompanyName"
    ContactName="TEST-ContactName"
    ContactTitle="TEST-ContactTitle" />
  </rs:insert>
```

To summarize, you must follow these steps to persist a recordset to an XML document and to edit the persisted rows:

1. Create a disconnected recordset by setting its LockType property to adLockBatchOptimistic. You can persist all types of recordsets, but ADO won't reflect the changes in the recordset to the XML document representing the recordset. Other types of recordsets update the database as soon as a row is changed. Only disconnected recordsets maintain a list of changes and submit all the changes to the database at once.
2. Persist the recordset to an XML file. Do so by calling the recordset's Save method with the adPersistXML argument. ADO will convert the current recordset into an XML document and save it to disk. The disk file is a static image of the recordset the moment you saved it (in XML format, of course).
3. Edit the recordset and resave it as an XML file. ADO maintains internally all the changes made to the recordset. It's actually the Cursor service that maintains the changes, in addition to the original data. This is the information that will be stored to the database.
4. If you update the recordset by calling its UpdateBatch method, the changes will be committed to the database. An updated disconnected recordset doesn't contain any <rs:update> tags.

NOTE

If the Cursor engine can't commit the changes to the database, a runtime error will occur.

Deleting Rows

Deleted rows appear at the end of the document in an `<rs:delete>` tag. As an example, if you remove the customer with key ANTON from the Customers table of the NorthWind database, the following lines will be appended to the `<rs:data>` section of the XML file:

```
<rs:delete>
  <z:row CustomerID="ANTON"
    CompanyName="Antonio Moreno Taquer a"
    ContactName="Antonio Moreno"
    ContactTitle="Owner"
    Address="Mataderos 23129"
    City="M xico D.F." PostalCode="05023"
    Country="M xico" Phone="(5) 555-3932" />
</rs:delete>
```

As you can see, the entire row, not just the primary key of the row, appears in the XML document.

Editing Disconnected Recordsets: An Example

Let's look at an example written in Visual Basic of editing disconnected recordsets persisted in XML. The project is called `DisconnectedRS`, and it's also available on the Sybex Web site.

To begin, start a new project and add a reference to the Microsoft Active Data Object 2.5 Library to the project. Then place a Command button on the form and enter the following code in the button's Click event handler:

```
Private Sub Command1_Click()
Dim RS As New ADODB.Recordset
  RS.CursorLocation = adUseClient
  RS.LockType = adLockBatchOptimistic
  RS.Open "C:\Customers.xml"
```

```
    RS.Fields(1) = RS.Fields(1) & "1"
    RS.MoveNext
    RS.Delete
    Kill "C:\Customers.xml"
    RS.Save "C:\Customers.xml", adPersistXML
End Sub
```

The code is quite simple—a real recordset-editing application would be too complicated. But if you're familiar with ADO's basic features, you can easily develop a user interface for an application that allows users to edit any row.

When the Save method is called to persist the recordset to a local XML file, the updates are saved along with the original data. If you call the UpdateBatch method, however, the changes are committed to the XML representation of the recordset. The UpdateBatch method will make changes in the <rs:data> section of the XML document.

The code shown above edits the first row (by appending a single character to the CompanyName field value) and then deletes the next row. To add a new row, insert the following statements:

```
RS.AddNew
RS.Fields(0)="TEST"
RS.Fields(1)="TEST-CompanyName"
RS.Fields(2)="TEST-ContactName"
RS.Fields(3)="TEST-ContactTitle"
RS.Update
```

If you persist the recordset to an XML file, the following lines will be appended to the <rs:data> section:

```
<rs:insert>
  <z:row CustomerID="TEST"
    CompanyName="TEST-CompanyName"
    ContactName="TEST-ContactName"
    ContactTitle="TEST-ContactTitle" />
</rs:insert>
```

Multiple inserts appear together in as a single <rs:insert> section, but each row has its own <z:row> element.

This example uses the XML representation of a recordset, but there are no advantages to using XML with a desktop application. In the next section, you'll see how to pass the XML representation of a recordset to the client and how to get back the same recordset in XML format to update the database.

Passing XML Data to the Client

In addition to files, ADO recordsets can be persisted on `Stream` objects. A `Stream` object represents a stream of data, and the most common `Stream` object is the ASP `Response` object, which represents the stream of data from the Web server to the client. If you have ASP 3.0 installed on your server (ASP 3.0 comes with Windows 2000, and so does ADO 2.5), you can persist a recordset directly to the `Response` object. Use the following statement:

```
RS.Save Response, 1
```

where the second argument is the value of the constant `adPersistXML`. (ASP doesn't consult type libraries to resolve constant names.)

WARNING

If you use constant names in your code, as you should, make sure that you have declared them or have included the appropriate INC file. If not, VBScript will assume it's a variable and will initialize it to zero.

The statement shown above will create a recordset and send it to the client. The browser will see an XML document and will display the raw data. Normally, we don't want to display raw data to the client. Therefore, we add a client-side script, or an XLS file, to display the data in a more appropriate format. The XML data that are part of an HTML page form a so-called data island. The viewer sees what you display on the browser from within your script, not the raw XML data.

NOTE

If you're using VB to create the recordset, you don't have to declare the constants.

Now that you have seen how to create disconnected recordsets and how you can XML format the rows of a disconnected recordset, let's switch our attention to the client and see how to bind the XML-formatted data to HTML elements.

Creating and Using Data Islands

A section of XML data enclosed in a pair of XML tags forms a data island. You can create data islands by simply retrieving the desired data from the database and sending them directly to the client by persisting the recordset to the Response object.

First, create the Products.xml file by persisting the recordset with the rows of the Products table in the NorthWind database. Then create a file with the XML data going to the client with the following script:

```
<%
Const adPersistXML = 1
Set RS = Server.CreateObject("ADODB.Recordset")
RS.Open "Products", "DSN=NWINDDB"
RS.Save "C:\Products.xml", adPersistXML
%>
```

This short script generates a typical XML output. The XML output produced by the Save method is not really an XML island; it contains an <XML>, but this tag doesn't have an ID attribute. Thus we must surround the entire file by the following pair of <XML> tags:

```
<XML ID="Products">


</XML>
```

However, there is a problem with this solution: You can't have nested <XML> tags in an XML document. The correct solution is to rename the <XML> tags in the XML document generated by the Save method to something else and then embed the entire document in a new pair of <XML> tags. You can rename the existing <XML> tags into anything; I used the tag <ADOXML> in testing the scripts. Here are the first two and last two lines of the revised XML file:

```
<XML ID="XMLProducts">
<ADOXML    xmlns:s=


</ADOXML>
</XML>
```

Don't be concerned that if you open the edited file with Internet Explorer, you won't see anything. There's nothing wrong with the file; the XML document sent to the client has become a data island. The data are available to the client, but there's no script to tell the browser what to do with the data.

To turn the data island into an HTML page that can be displayed on the browser, let's add a few HTML statements to the XML file. To do so, we must add the following HTML elements and bind them to the fields of the recordset:

```
<HTML>
<TABLE DATASRC="#XMLProducts">
<TR><TD>
<TABLE DATASRC="#XMLProducts"
  DATAFLD="rs:data">
<TR><TD>
<TABLE DATASRC="#XMLProducts" DATAFLD="z:row" >
<TR>
<TD><SPAN DATAFLD="ProductID"></SPAN></TD>
<TD><SPAN DATAFLD="ProductName"></SPAN></TD>
<TD><SPAN DATAFLD="UnitPrice"></SPAN></TD>
</TR>
</TABLE>
</TD></TR>
</TABLE>
</TD></TR>
</TABLE>
</HTML>
```

If you want to be able to edit the table, replace the table's cells with Text controls. Figure 21.3 shows a section of the page with the NorthWind products displayed on a table. You will find the XML data island and the HTML code for binding the fields to a table's cells in the `ProductsXML.htm` file on the Sybex site. To create this file, I generated the recordset with the recordset's `Save` method and then edited it a little.

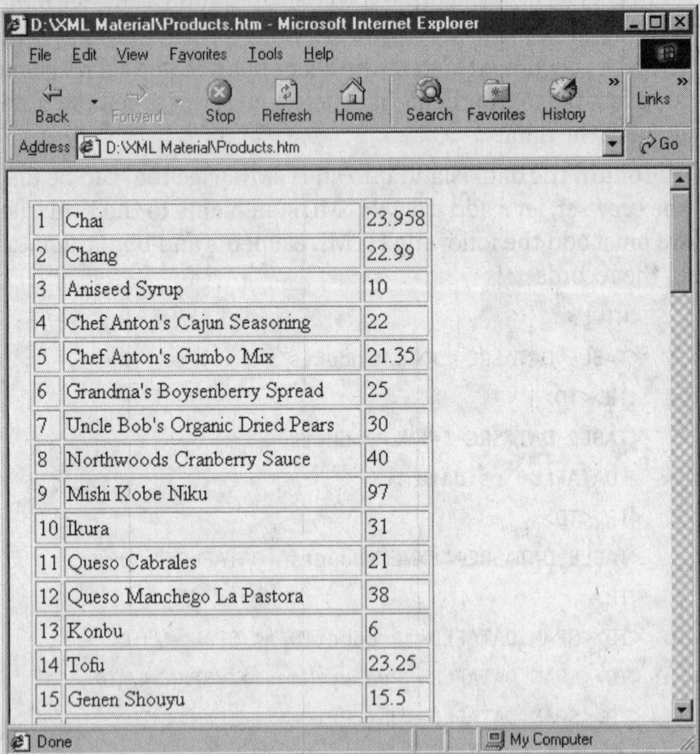

FIGURE 21.3: Displaying a data island on a table

I must explain the statements that bind the table to the data islands. They're quite different from the binding statements we've seen so far. The fields we want to bind to the table are the ones prefixed by the `<z:row>` tag. But these tags appear under the `<rs:data>` tag. So to skip the `<rs:data>` section, we bind the fields in the `<rs:data>` tag to a table that has no rows of its own. Then, within this table, we nest another table whose cells are bound to the fields in the `<z:row>` tag. You'll have to use this simple trick with all the data islands you create with ADO's `Recordset.Save` method. The alternative is to include an XSL file or a client-side script to exploit the XML document's DOM.

Creating Data Islands on the Fly

The example in the previous section demonstrates how to create XML data islands and process them on the client. As you have probably noticed, we had to edit the XML recordset. We persisted the recordset to an XML file, then edited it to convert the file into a form suitable for use as a data island on the client. Yet to make this technique more useful, we should be able to edit the XML data from within our server-side script. This would allow us to create XML data islands on the fly, without user intervention.

To do so, first we must insert an RDS Data Control that provides the data. The following <OBJECT> tag places an RDS Data Control on the page, which calls a script on the server to retrieve the data:

```
<OBJECT
  CLASSID=
  "clsid:bd96c556-65a3-11d0-983a-00c04fc29e33"
  ID="DSOCustomers" WIDTH="0" HEIGHT="0">
<PARAM NAME= "URL" VALUE="GetCustomersXML.asp">
</OBJECT>
```

The name of the script is `GetCustomersXML.asp`, and here's what it does. First, it creates a local recordset (on the Web server) with the desired data. Then, it saves the data on the `Response` stream:

```
<%
CN = "DSN=NWINDDB"
Set RSCustomers= _
  Server.CreateObject("ADODB.Recordset")
RSCustomers.Open "SELECT * FROM Customers", CN
RSCustomers.Save Response, 1
%>
```

When the page is loaded, the data island contains all the rows of the Customers table. The same script could accept a parameter to select customers from a specific country, customers who have placed an order in the last month, and so on. The script that provides the data doesn't change; the only thing that changes is the SQL statement that retrieves the data to populate the recordset. You can make this statement as complicated as you wish.

Once the data has been downloaded to the client, it's bound to the HTML elements of the HTML Form. If the data-bound elements allow editing of their content, the viewer can modify the recordset on the client. Of course, we should also be able to return the edited recordset to the server, where it will be used to update the database. You'll see how to post the data to the server shortly. But first, let's look at the code for editing the recordset on the client.

Navigational and Editing Operations

The code for binding the XML recordset's fields to Text controls on the Form is fairly simple, and you've seen it before. This time, we'll use the following statements to bind one row at a time to a few Text controls:

```
Company Name
<INPUT TYPE=TEXT DATASRC="#DSOCustomers"
  DATAFLD="CompanyName" SIZE="40">
</INPUT>
<BR>
Contact Name
<INPUT TYPE=TEXT DATASRC="#DSOCustomers"
  DATAFLD="ContactName" SIZE="30">
</INPUT>
Contact Title
<INPUT TYPE=TEXT DATASRC="#DSOCustomers"
  DATAFLD="ContactTitle" SIZE="25">
</INPUT>
```

This code binds the `CompanyName`, `ContactName`, and `ContactTitles` fields to three Text controls. You can add the statements to bind the remaining fields as well. When the page is loaded, you'll see the fields of the first row, as shown in Figure 21.4.

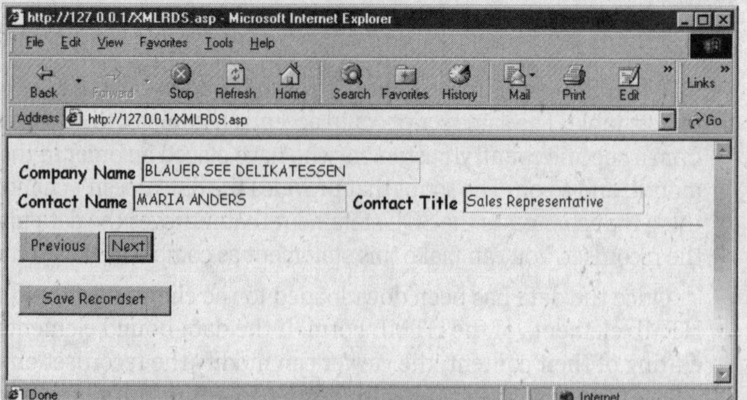

FIGURE 21.4: Editing an XML recordset on the client

We must also add a few buttons (shown in Figure 21.4) to allow the viewer to navigate through the recordset. Add the Previous and Next buttons with the following statements:

```
<INPUT TYPE=button
  VALUE="Previous" ONCLICK="PrevRec">
<INPUT TYPE=button
  VALUE="Next" ONCLICK="NextRec">
```

We must also provide the code for the PrevRec and NextRec buttons (seen as Previous and Next). This code must simply call the `MovePrevious` and `MoveNext` methods of the RDS Data Control:

```
Sub NextRec
  If Not DSOCustomers.Recordset.EOF Then
    DSOCustomers.Recordset.MoveNext
  End If
End Sub

Sub PrevRec
  If Not DSOCustomers.Recordset.BOF Then
    DSOCustomers.Recordset.MovePrevious
  End If
End Sub
```

Notice that the code examines the `BOF` and `EOF` properties to make sure that the script doesn't attempt to move before the first row or beyond the last row in the recordset.

Finally, we must add a button for submitting the changes to the server. The definition of this button, Save Recordset, is shown here:

```
<INPUT TYPE=button VALUE="Save Recordset"
  ONCLICK="PostData">
```

The `PostData` subroutine, which posts the modified recordset to the server, is the most interesting part of the page. The code uses the `XML-HTTP` object, which uses the HTTP protocol to pass XML-encoded data to the server. This script uses two of the `XMLHTTP` object's methods: the `Open` method to establish a connection to a script on the server, and the `Send` method to send the data to the server by reading the XML data from a `Stream` object. The last argument of the `Open` method indicates that the operation will not take place asynchronously. This object is an

ADO Stream object, which is populated with the Recordset.Save method. Here's the PostData subroutine:

```
Sub PostData()
   Set XMLHTTP = _
      CreateObject("Microsoft.XMLHTTP")
   Set StrData = CreateObject("ADODB.Stream")
   DSOCustomers.Recordset.Save StrData, 1
   XMLHTTP.Open "POST", "GetXMLData.asp", False
   XMLHTTP.Send STRDATA.ReadText()
End Sub
```

You may have noticed that this technique requires the presence of two objects on the client: the XMLHTTP and ADO objects. XMLHTTP comes with Internet Explorer, and ADO 2.5 (the ADO version that supports the Stream object) is also installed along with Windows 2000. The bottom line is that this technique works with Internet Explorer only. For the time being, Microsoft is ahead of Netscape in using XML as a universal data exchange protocol, but it's too early to say which methods will be adopted by the industry for exchanging XML data between servers and clients, especially for posting data to the server.

Listing 21.2 shows the entire document that allows editing of recordsets on the client.

Listing 21.2: Editing Recordsets on the Client (XMLRDS.asp)

```
<HTML>
<OBJECT CLASSID=
   "clsid:bd96c556-65a3-11d0-983a-00c04fc29e33"
   ID="DSOCustomers" WIDTH="0" HEIGHT="0">
<PARAM NAME= "URL" VALUE="Customers.xml">
</OBJECT>

<SCRIPT LANGUAGE=VBScript>
Sub PostData()
   Set XMLHTTP = _
      CreateObject("Microsoft.XMLHTTP")
   Set StrData = CreateObject("ADODB.Stream")
   DSOCustomers.Recordset.Save StrData, 1
   XMLHTTP.open "POST", "GetXMLData.asp", False
   XMLHTTP.Send STRDATA.ReadText()
End Sub
```

```
Sub NextRec
  If Not DSOCustomers.Recordset.EOF Then
    DSOCustomers.Recordset.MoveNext
  End If
End Sub

Sub PrevRec
  If Not DSOCustomers.Recordset.BOF Then
    DSOCustomers.Recordset.MovePrevious
  End If
End Sub

</SCRIPT>
<FONT FACE="Comic Sans MS" SIZE=3>
Company Name
<INPUT TYPE=TEXT DATASRC="#DSOCustomers"
  DATAFLD="CompanyName" SIZE="40"></INPUT>
<BR>
Contact Name
<INPUT TYPE=TEXT
  DATASRC="#DSOCustomers"
  DATAFLD="ContactName" SIZE="30">
</INPUT>
Contact Title
<INPUT TYPE=TEXT DATASRC="#DSOCustomers"
  DATAFLD="ContactTitle" SIZE="25"></INPUT>
<HR>
<INPUT TYPE=button
  VALUE="Previous" ONCLICK="PrevRec">
<INPUT TYPE=button
  VALUE="Next" ONCLICK="NextRec">
<P>
<INPUT TYPE=button VALUE="Save Recordset"
  ONCLICK="PostData">
</FONT>
</HTML>
```

Reading XML Data on the Server

Now we need a method to read the edited recordset on the server. The client-side script transmitted the data with the POST method, so we must use the Request object on the server to read the data. To read the data, use the recordset object's `Open` method, specifying that it should read from a file:

```
NewRS = Server.CreateObject("ADODB.Recordset")
NewRS.Open Request, , , , adCmdFile
```

Notice that no connection information is specified in the `Open` method. This technique will work only if:

- The recordset sent to the client is opened as a disconnected recordset. Only a disconnected recordset maintains the changes to the data, and not just the new values of the fields.
- The recordset is mapped to an RDS Data Control on the client, and not to an XML Data Control.
- The recordset that receives the XML data on the server is also opened as a disconnected recordset, so that you can call its `UpdateBatch` method to commit the changes.

Once the remote XML recordset is read into a local recordset on the server, you can call the `UpdateBatch` method to commit the changes to the database. The following script accepts the edited XML recordset on the server and posts the changes to the database.

```
<%
NewRS = Server.CreateObject("ADODB.Recordset")
NewRS.CursorLocation = adUseClient
NewRS.Open Request, ,adOpenKeyset , _
  adLockBatchOptimistic , adCmdFile
NewRS.ActiveConnection = "DSN=NWIND"
NewRS.UpdateBatch
NewRS.Close
Set NewRS = Nothing
%>
```

This script reads the data posted by the client. The `NewRS` recordset variable is opened with the `adLockBatchOptimistic` option, because it's a disconnected recordset. Then it connects the disconnected recordset to the database and calls the `UpdateBatch` method to update the database. This is the `GetXMLData.asp` script, which you will find on the Sybex site.

Hierarchical Recordsets

The recordsets we've used so far are uniform–each row contains the same number of columns. These recordsets are very similar to tables, although they may contain rows from multiple tables.

Another type of recordset contains not only rows from multiple tables, but the relationship between the tables they're based on. These are called *hierarchical*, or *shaped*, recordsets. They're made up of different sections, and each section has a different structure. Let's say you want a list of all customers in a city, their orders, and the items of each order. A hierarchical recordset with this information contains a row for each customer. Under each customer, there's another recordset with the customer's orders.

In this table, the customer rows have a different structure from the order rows, and the order rows have a different structure from the item rows. Thus the recordset carries with it information about the structure of the entities it includes, as shown in this example:

```
Customer 1
   Order 1
      Item 1
      Item 2
      Item 3
   Order 2
      Item1
      Item2
Customer 2
   Order 1
      Item 1
      Item 2
      Item 3
      Item 4
   Order 2
      Item 1
      Item 2
   Order 3
      Item 1
      Item 2
```

Each customer has one or more orders, and all the orders belonging to the same customer appear under the customer's name. Likewise, each order has one or more items, and all the items (detail lines) belonging to the same order appear under the order's ID.

Hierarchical recordsets are structured, and they lend themselves to XML descriptions. You can use ADO to produce hierarchical recordsets, but these recordsets are pretty useless outside ADO. You just can't process a hierarchical recordset on a computer that doesn't support ADO. However, if you translate a hierarchical recordset to an XML document, you can process it on every computer that supports XML.

The SHAPE Language

To create hierarchical recordsets, you use a special language, the *SHAPE language*. The SHAPE language supports all of the SQL statements, plus a few more keywords, to specify the relationships between the different recordsets. Following is the SHAPE statement that produces a hierarchical recordset with the customers, their orders, and the details of each order:

```
SHAPE {SELECT * FROM Customers} AS Command1
APPEND (( SHAPE {SELECT * FROM Orders}
  AS Command2
  APPEND ({SELECT * FROM [Order Details]}
    AS Command3
    RELATE 'OrderID' TO 'OrderID')
    AS Command3)
  AS Command2
  RELATE 'CustomerID' TO 'CustomerID')
AS Command2
```

Fortunately, you don't have to learn the SHAPE language to create hierarchical recordsets. The simplest method to define a hierarchical recordset is to use the visual database tools that come with Visual Studio. You can also write the statement yourself; conceptually, it's a little more complicated than straight SQL.

Building Hierarchical Recordsets with VB

Let's build a shaped recordset with VB. To do so, start a new VB project and enter the following statements in a button's Click event handler:

```
Private Sub Command1_Click()
Dim RS As New Recordset
ShapedCommand = _
   " SHAPE {SELECT * FROM Customers} AS" & _
   " Command1 APPEND (( SHAPE {SELECT *" & _
   " FROM Orders} AS Command2" & _
   " APPEND ({SELECT * FROM" & _
   " [Order Details]}  AS Command3 RELATE" & _
   " 'OrderID' TO 'OrderID') AS Command3)" & _
   " AS Command2 RELATE 'CustomerID' TO" & _
   " 'CustomerID') AS Command2"
RS.Open ShapedCommand, CN
RS.Save "C:\Temp\Sales.xml", adPersistXML
```

You must set the CN Connection object to point to the NorthWind database on your system. If you run the program and click the button, a recordset will be created and saved to a disk file as `Sales.xml`, which is shown in Listing 21.3.

Listing 21.3: The `Sales.xml` File

```
<xml xmlns:s=
"uuid:BDC6E3F0-6DA3-11d1-A2A3-00AA00C14882"
  xmlns:dt=
"uuid:C2F41010-65B3-11d1-A29F-00AA00C14882"
  xmlns:rs="urn:schemas-microsoft-com:rowset"
  xmlns:z="#RowsetSchema">
<s:Schema id="RowsetSchema">
  <s:ElementType name="row" content="eltOnly"
  rs:CommandTimeout="30"
  rs:ReshapeName="Command1">
    <s:AttributeType name="CustomerID"
    rs:number="1"
    rs:writeunknown="true">
      <s:datatype dt:type="string"
      dt:maxLength="5"
```

```
      rs:fixedlength="true"
      rs:maybenull="false" />
    </s:AttributeType>
    <s:AttributeType name="CompanyName"
    rs:number="2" rs:writeunknown="true">
      <s:datatype dt:type="string"
      dt:maxLength="40"
      rs:maybenull="false" />
    </s:AttributeType>
    <s:AttributeType name="ContactName"
    rs:number="3" rs:nullable="true"
    rs:writeunknown="true">
      <s:datatype dt:type="string"
      dt:maxLength="30" />
    </s:AttributeType>
  <s:ElementType name="Command2"
  content="eltOnly"
  rs:CommandTimeout="30"
  rs:ReshapeName="Command2"
  rs:relation="010000000200000000000000">
    <s:AttributeType name="OrderID"
    rs:number="1">
      <s:datatype dt:type="int"
      dt:maxLength="4"
      rs:precision="10"
      rs:fixedlength="true"
      rs:maybenull="false" />
    </s:AttributeType>
    <s:AttributeType name="CustomerID"
    rs:number="2"
    rs:nullable="true"
    rs:writeunknown="true">
      <s:datatype dt:type="string"
      dt:maxLength="5"
      rs:fixedlength="true" />
    </s:AttributeType>
    <s:AttributeType name="EmployeeID"
    rs:number="3"
    rs:nullable="true"
    rs:writeunknown="true">
      <s:datatype dt:type="int"
      dt:maxLength="4"
```

```
        rs:precision="10"
        rs:fixedlength="true" />
      </s:AttributeType>
      <s:AttributeType name="OrderDate"
      rs:number="4" rs:nullable="true"
      rs:writeunknown="true">
        <s:datatype dt:type="dateTime"
        rs:dbtype="timestamp"
        dt:maxLength="16" rs:scale="3"
        rs:precision="23"
        rs:fixedlength="true" />
      </s:AttributeType>
    <s:ElementType name="Command3"
    content="eltOnly"
    rs:CommandTimeout="30"
    rs:ReshapeName="Command3"
    rs:relation="010000000100000000000000">
      <s:AttributeType name="OrderID"
      rs:number="1" rs:writeunknown="true">
        <s:datatype dt:type="int"
        dt:maxLength="4"
        rs:precision="10"
        rs:fixedlength="true"
        rs:maybenull="false" />
      </s:AttributeType>
      <s:AttributeType name="ProductID"
      rs:number="2" rs:writeunknown="true">
        <s:datatype dt:type="int"
        dt:maxLength="4"
        rs:precision="10"
        rs:fixedlength="true"
        rs:maybenull="false" />
      </s:AttributeType>
      <s:AttributeType name="UnitPrice"
      rs:number="3" rs:writeunknown="true">
        <s:datatype dt:type="i8"
        rs:dbtype="currency"
        dt:maxLength="8" rs:precision="19"
        rs:fixedlength="true"
        rs:maybenull="false" />
      </s:AttributeType>
    </s:ElementType>
  </s:Schema>
```

To explore the structure of this script, I'll use one of the sample pages at the Microsoft XML site. If you connect to `msdn.microsoft.com/xml/general`, you will find a list of interesting samples. Connect to this URL, click the Sync TOC button, and when the frames with the TOC appear, click the Samples and Downloads link. Select the XML Data Source Object, and download it to your computer. After you have saved all the necessary files in a folder on your system, double-click the icon for the `dsoMap.htm` file, and you will see the page shown in Figure 21.5.

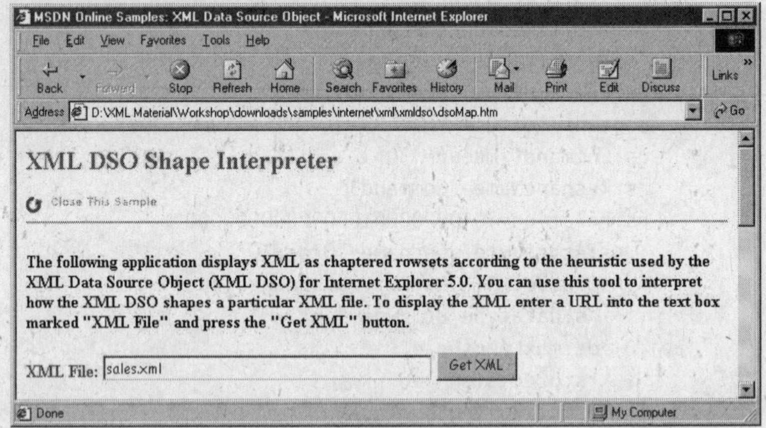

FIGURE 21.5: On this page, select the XML file to map

Enter **`Sales.xml`** in the XML File textbox, and click the Get XML button. Scroll to the bottom of the XML DSO Shape Interpreter page, and you'll see the two sections in the file: the schema section and the data section. Both items are hyperlinks, and you can click the `<rs:data>` hyperlink to see the data of the hierarchical recordset. This section is made up of `<z:row>` tags.

When you click the `<rs:data>` hyperlink, you'll see another table that contains the `<z:row>` hyperlink. Click this hyperlink and you will see the nodes of the parent recordset, which contains all the customers in the database, as shown in Figure 21.6. For each customer, you see the number of orders placed by the customer (in the TotInvoices column) as well as the total revenue for the specific customer (in the CustomerTotal column).

In each customer's Orders column is another hyperlink, leading to the child recordset that corresponds to each customer and contains all of their orders. For example, if you click the Orders hyperlink for the customer ANTON, you'll see all of Anton's orders, as shown in Figure 21.7.

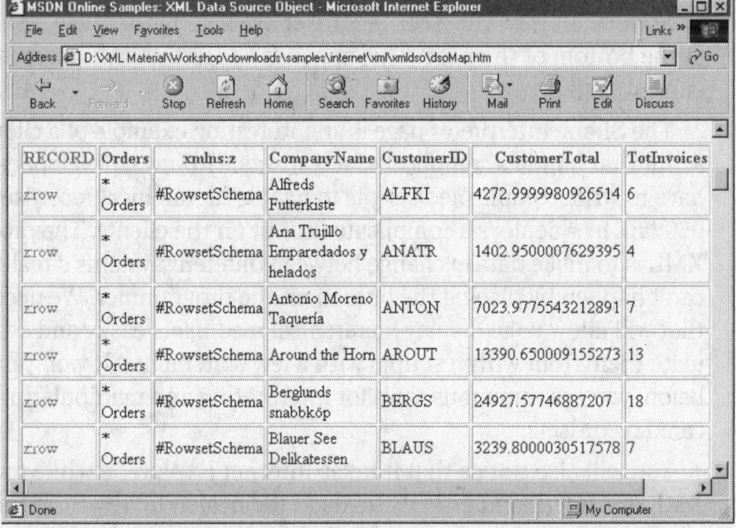

FIGURE 21.6: Viewing the customers in the `Sales.xml` recordset

This recordset contains each order's ID (in the OrderID column), as well as its total (in the OrderTotal column). The order's total is not stored along with each order; it's a calculated field. Each row in the Orders recordset has its own child recordset, which contains the order's detail lines. Click an order's `Details` hyperlink to see the order's details.

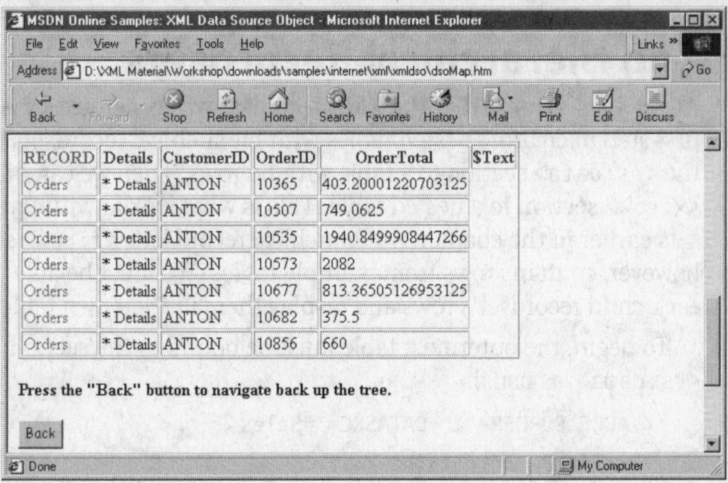

MSDN Online Samples: XML Data Source Object - Microsoft Internet Explorer
File Edit View Favorites Tools Help
Links
Address D:\XML Material\Workshop\downloads\samples\internet\xml\xmldso\dsoMap.htm
Go
Back Forward Stop Refresh Home Search Favorites History Mail Print Edit Discuss
RECORD Details CustomerID OrderID OrderTotal $Text
Orders * Details ANTON 10365 403.20001220703125
Orders * Details ANTON 10507 749.0625
Orders * Details ANTON 10535 1940.8499908447266
Orders * Details ANTON 10573 2082
Orders * Details ANTON 10677 813.36505126953125
Orders * Details ANTON 10682 375.5
Orders * Details ANTON 10856 660
Press the "Back" button to navigate back up the tree.
Back
Done
My Computer

FIGURE 21.7: Viewing a customer's orders

While you're exploring hierarchical recordsets with the DSOMap.htm page, you can view the XML recordset by clicking the View XML button at the bottom of the page. This appends the entire XML recordset to the current page.

The Shape Interpreter page is an interesting example of a client-side script that handles complicated recordsets. However, developers shouldn't have to write complicated scripts to handle hierarchical recordsets (and DSOMap.htm deploys a complicated script on the client). The promise of XML is to make data exchange between different systems a reality. This can't happen by placing the burden on the programmer. We need tools that will allow us to display hierarchical recordsets easily and even manipulate them from within scripts with a few statements. It won't be long before you see numerous tools for interpreting and manipulating complicated recordsets.

You will also notice that it takes Internet Explorer a while to load the XML document and bind its fields to the nested tables. Scripting languages are interpreted, not compiled, and they're not as fast as a compiled VB application.

DSOMap.htm is a helpful tool, in that it allows you to visualize both the structure of a hierarchical recordset as well as the data. However, this is not how you would display a hierarchical recordset on a page. A page made up of nested tables, like the one shown in Figure 21.8 in the next section, is more appropriate. Let's see how to create nested tables by binding a hierarchical recordset to a table.

Binding Hierarchical Recordsets

Again, let's assume that the XML recordset was generated by ADO. The first step in creating nested tables with hierarchical recordsets is to bind the <rs:data> section to a table with no rows. Then we can bind the <x:row> section to a nested table. This is what we did with flat recordsets earlier in the chapter. A hierarchical recordset's <z:row> section, however, contains rows from multiple tables. We must be able to separate each child recordset's rows and display them in their own table.

To begin, the outermost table must be bound to the section <rs:data>, as usual:

```
<TABLE BORDER="1" DATASRC="#Sales"
  DATAFLD="rs:data">
```

The first nested table corresponds to the customers, and it must be bound to the section `<z:row>`:

```
<TABLE BORDER="1" DATASRC="#Sales"
  DATAFLD="z:row">
```

Then, the cells of this table must be bound to the columns of the Customers child recordset:

```
<TD VALIGN=top><B>
  <SPAN DATAFLD="CompanyName"></SPAN></B>
</TD>
<TD>
```

To bind the next nested section in the recordset to an HTML table, use the following value of the DATAFLD attribute:

```
<TABLE BORDER="1" DATASRC="#Sales"
  DATAFLD="rs:data.z:row.Orders">
```

This table's cells must be bound to the fields of the Orders child recordset:

```
<TD VALIGN=top>
  <SPAN DATAFLD="OrderID"></SPAN></TD>
<TD VALIGN=top>
  <SPAN DATAFLD="OrderTotal"></SPAN></TD>
```

The details are a child recordset of the Orders recordset. Their table must be bound to the following field:

```
<TABLE BORDER="1" DATASRC="#Sales"
  DATAFLD="rs:data.z:row.Orders.Details">
```

The Details recordset, which is a child of the Orders recordset, is in turn a child of the Customers recordset.

Now let's look at Listing 21.4, the complete `Sales.htm` file. The file is fairly lengthy, but not difficult to understand.

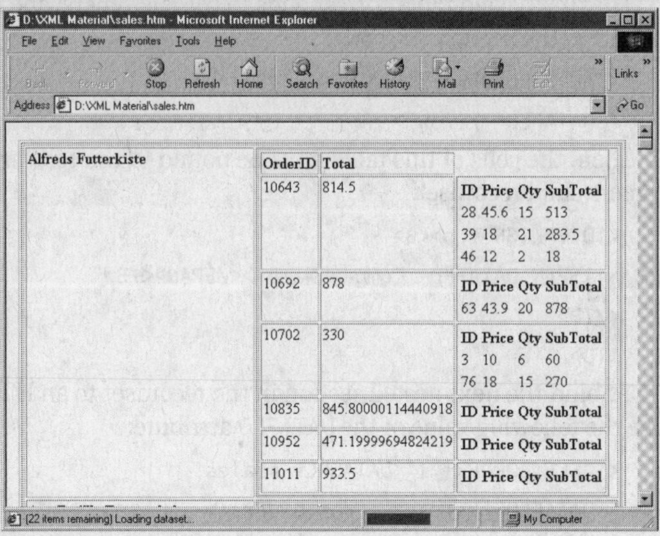

FIGURE 21.8: Binding a hierarchical recordset to nested tables on an HTML page

Listing 21.4: Binding Hierarchies to an HTML Table (`Sales.htm`)

```
<TABLE DATASRC="#Sales">
<TR>
  <TD>
    <TABLE BORDER="1" DATASRC="#Sales"
      DATAFLD="rs:data">
    <TR>
      <TD>
        <TABLE BORDER="1" DATASRC="#Sales"
          DATAFLD="z:row">
        <TR>
          <TD VALIGN=top><B>
            <SPAN DATAFLD="CompanyName"></B>
            </SPAN></TD>
          <TD>
          <TABLE BORDER="1" DATASRC="#Sales"
            DATAFLD="rs:data.z:row.Orders">
          <THEAD>
          <TR>
            <TD><B>OrderID</B></TD>
            <TD><B>Total</B></TD>
          </TR>
```

```
        </THEAD>
        <TBODY>
        <TR>
          <TD VALIGN=top>
            <SPAN DATAFLD="OrderID">
            </SPAN></TD>
          <TD VALIGN=top>
            <SPAN DATAFLD="OrderTotal">
            </SPAN></TD>
          <TD>
          <TABLE DATASRC="#Sales"
            DATAFLD=
            "rs:data.z:row.Orders.Details">
          <THEAD>
          <TR>
            <TD><B>ID</B></TD>
            <TD><B>Price</B></TD>
            <TD><B>Qty</B></TD>
            <TD><B>SubTotal</TD>
          </TR>
          </THEAD>
          <TBODY>
          <TR>
            <TD><SPAN DATAFLD="ProductID">
              </SPAN></TD>
            <TD><SPAN DATAFLD="UnitPrice">
              </SPAN></TD>
            <TD><SPAN DATAFLD="Quantity">
              </SPAN></TD>
            <TD><SPAN DATAFLD="LineTotal">
              </SPAN></TD>
          </TR>
          </TBODY>
          </TD>
        </TR>
        </TBODY>
        </TABLE>
        </TD>
      </TR>
      </TABLE>
    </TD>
  </TR>
```

```
      </TABLE>
    </TD>
  </TR>
</TABLE>
```

Viewing Reduced Recordsets

One of the most common and most useful applications of XML recordsets is to reduce the information displayed on the client. Let's say you want to display a hierarchical recordset with sales information. If you download a data island with the orders of a few customers, you are defeating the purpose of the data island. Clearly, you must download all the information in a single data island.

If you download all the information at once and display all the rows of the recordset on the same page, this page will be too long to be practical. The solution is to hide the child recordsets and let the user expand (and collapse) them as needed. This way, the viewer can quickly locate and view the desired information. When they're done with a child recordset (a customer's orders, or an orders' lines), they can simply hide it and move to another one.

To collapse and expand sections of the table, you must insert a script that reacts to the click of the mouse over a customer's name or an order ID. Assuming that the cells with the customers are named Orders and the nested tables with the orders are named OrdersTable, Listing 21.5 (`SalesTree.htm`) can be used to display and hide each customer's orders.

Listing 21.5: The Mouse Event Handlers for the Bound Recordset (`SalesTree.htm`)

```
<SCRIPT LANGUAGE=JavaScript
  FOR=Orders EVENT=onclick>
  rowID = this.recordNumber - 1;
  if (OrdersTable[rowID].style.display
    == "none")
  {
    OrdersTable[rowID].style.display
      = "inline";
  }
  else
  {
    OrdersTable[rowID].style.display = "none";
  }
```

```
    window.event.cancelBubble = true;
  </SCRIPT>


  <SCRIPT LANGUAGE=JavaScript
    FOR=Details EVENT=onclick>
    rowID = this.recordNumber - 1;
    if (DetailsTable[rowID].style.display
      == "none")
    {
      DetailsTable[rowID].style.display
        = "inline";
    }
    else
    {
      DetailsTable[rowID].style.display = "none";
    }
    window.event.cancelBubble = true;
  </SCRIPT>
```

This file is identical to the `Sales.htm` page we saw earlier, except that some of the HTML elements have different names and styles. Also, there is some added script that expands/collapses the orders and details for each customer.

The SalesTree page is shown in Figure 21.9. As you can see, the page lets you select a customer and view their orders and their order details.

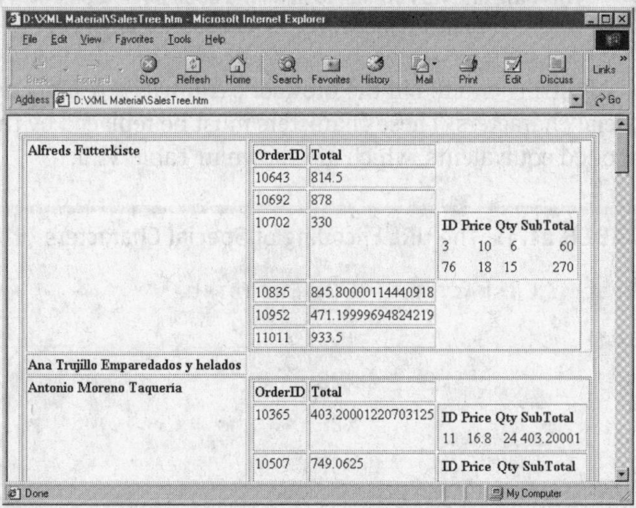

FIGURE 21.9: The SalesTree page

XML and SQL Server 2000

Everything we discussed in the earlier section titled "ADO Support for XML" applies to SQL Server as well, but SQL Server 2000 will have native support for XML. What this means is that SQL Server can produce XML-formatted cursors and transmit them directly to the client. The XML support for SQL Server is provided in the form of DLLs that sit between the DBMS and the Web server. These DLLs convert the cursors, returned by SQL Server in response to a query to XML data.

Let me start by showing you how easy it is to execute a SQL statement against a SQL Server database and retrieve a cursor in XML format. As you recall, a data island need not be included as is in an ASP file. You can use the SRC attribute of the <XML> tag to specify the URL of the XML file, or the URL of an ASP script that will return the desired data. The following lines can be entered in the browser's Address box to contact the SQL Server running on the same machine and execute a SQL statement against the NorthWind database:

```
http://127.0.0.1/NorthWind?sql=SELECT+
CategoryName,+Description+FROM+Categories
FOR+XML+RAW
```

NOTE

This long line was broken to fit on the book page. Don't worry about this—you can't break lines in the browser's Address box anyway.

Any string entered in the browser's Address box must not contain any special characters. These characters must be replaced by their URL-encoded equivalents, which are shown in Table 21.3.

TABLE 21.3: The URL Encoding of Special Characters

Special Character	URL Encoding
Space	+
+	%2B
/	%2F
?	%3F

CONTINUED ➡

TABLE 21.3 continued: The URL Encoding of Special Characters

SPECIAL CHARACTER	URL ENCODING
%	%25
#	%23
&	%26

Once you enter the appropriate information into the browser's Address box, SQL Server 2000 will execute the query and return the names and descriptions of the categories in the NorthWind database, as shown here:

```
<?xml version="1.0" encoding="UTF-8" ?>
<root>
<row CategoryName="Beverages"
    Description="Soft drinks  "/>
<row CategoryName="Condiments"
    Description="Sweet and Savory "/>
<row CategoryName="Confections"
    Description="Desserts, "/>
<row CategoryName="Dairy Products"
    Description="Cheeses"/>
<row CategoryName="Grains/Cereals"
    Description="Breads, crackers "/>
<row CategoryName="Meat/Poultry"
    Description="Prepared meats "/>
<row CategoryName="Produce"
    Description="Dried fruit  "/>
<row CategoryName="Seafood"
    Description="Seaweed and fish"/>
</root>
</xml>
```

Figure 21.10 shows how this file is rendered on your browser's window. This is an XML data island, and it contains row data but no information about the structure of the data in the cursor.

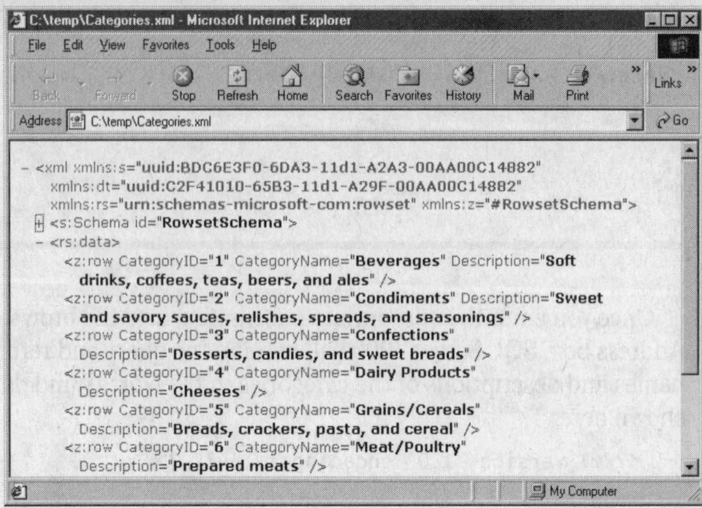

FIGURE 21.10: The XML-formatted cursor produced by SQL Server in response to a simple query

Being able to extract XML-formatted data directly from SQL Server is a very powerful feature, but we must still format the data as an HTML document. As you know very well by now, the simplest method to convert XML data to HTML documents is to use an XSL file. The XSL file should reside on the server, and you can include it in the response by simply adding its name to the previous URL:

```
http://127.0.0.1/NorthWind?sql=SELECT+
CategoryName,+Description+FROM+Categories
FOR+XML+RAW
&xsl=http://127.0.0.1/categories.xsl
```

The `categories.xsl` file must reside in the server's virtual folder.

Before you can contact SQL Server through the HTTP protocol, you must configure it accordingly with the `regxmlss` utility, which is described in the next section.

The *regxmlss* Utility

The `regxmlss` utility defines a virtual folder, which is the root folder of the SQL server. SQL Server will service requests made to this folder only, and this is where SQL Server expects to find all auxiliary files (like XSL or template files). Of course, this virtual root folder can have subfolders, just like the Web server's root folder.

The SQL server's virtual root folder is different from the Web server's home page so that the functionality of the two components is separated. I'm sure you don't want to place all the template files for accessing a database in the Web's root folder. Their place is the virtual folder of SQL Server. You can define an alias for the virtual root of SQL Server and map it to the Web server's physical root folder.

To specify the SQL server's virtual root folder, follow these steps:

1. Open the SQL server's menu and select the Configure IIS option to see the Register XML SQL Server Extensions dialog box (see Figure 21.11).
2. In the Internet Information Server section of the dialog box, specify the names of the IIS server (in the Site text box), the virtual root, and the physical folder (in the Directory text box) that will be mapped to the virtual root folder.
3. In the SQL Server section of the dialog box, set the name of the server and the name of the database. Note that all requests apply to this database, and you can't specify that a query be applied to a different database via the URL.
4. In the Connection Settings section of the dialog box, specify the type of authorization to be used.
5. To enable viewers to execute queries against a database through the HTTP protocol, select the Allow URL Queries check box at the bottom of the dialog box. To enable viewers to use templates for their queries, select the Allow Template Queries check box. (A *template* is a query that can be called by name, and it accepts parameters, just like stored procedures. Using templates and stored procedures is discussed later in this chapter.)

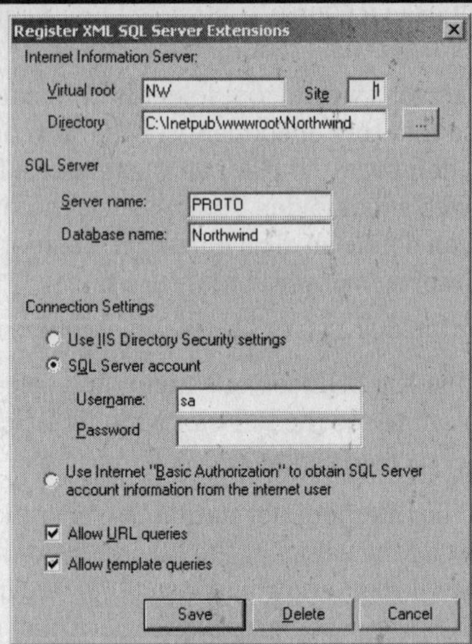

FIGURE 21.11: The Register XML SQL Server Extensions dialog box

SQL Server's XML Modes

The XML returned by SQL Server in response to a query over the Web can be in one of three different flavors. These flavors are called *XML modes*, and they are RAW, AUTO, and EXPLICIT.

RAW Mode

RAW mode converts each row into a single XML element, using the generic tag <row>. For example, the statement

```
SELECT ProductName, CategoryName
FROM Products, Categories
WHERE Products.CategoryID=Categories.CategoryID
FOR XML ROW
```

produces the following output (only the first few lines are shown):

```
<row ProductName="Chai"
  CategoryName="Beverages"/>
<row ProductName="Chang"
```

```
   CategoryName="Beverages"/>
<row ProductName="Aniseed Syrup"
   CategoryName="Condiments"/>
<row ProductName=
   "Chef Anton&apos;s Cajun Seasoning"
   CategoryName="Condiments"/>
<row ProductName="Ikura"
   CategoryName="Seafood"/>
```

AUTO Mode

AUTO mode returns a nested XML tree. Each table in the FROM clause is represented by an XML element, and the names of the fields become attributes. The same statement we used in the example of RAW mode will return the following rows, if you replace RAW with AUTO:

```
<Categories CategoryName="Beverages">
   <Products ProductName="Chai"/>
   <Products ProductName="Chang"/>
</Categories>
<Categories CategoryName="Condiments">
   <Products ProductName="Aniseed Syrup"/>
   <Products ProductName=
      "Chef Anton&apos;s Cajun Seasoning"/>
   <Products ProductName=
      "Chef Anton&apos;s Gumbo Mix"/>
<Products ProductName=
      "Grandma&apos;s Boysenberry Spread"/>
</Categories>
<Categories CategoryName="Produce">
   <Products ProductName=
      "Uncle Bob&apos;s Dried Pears"/>
</Categories>
```

As you can see, SQL Server is intelligent enough to consider the structure of the data and put together a hierarchical recordset, because this is exactly what you get in the AUTO mode. Each category section contains all the products in the category.

EXPLICIT Mode

EXPLICIT mode allows you to define the exact shape of the XML tree. In effect, you must visualize the XML tree and write your query following specific rules. These rules are described in SQL Server's documentation, so I will not discuss them here. Since the RAW and AUTO modes are simpler, I'll use them in the following section's examples.

TIP

You can use the Query Analyzer to experiment with the various XML modes and see the output they produce. However, you can't direct the XML output produced by a query in the Results Pane of the Query Analyzer to a client.

The *FOR* Clause

Here is the complete syntax of the FOR option:

```
FOR [mode][, schema][, ELEMENTS]
```

Notice that all arguments are optional. As you learned in the previous sections, the *mode* argument can be RAW, AUTO, or EXPLICIT. The *schema* argument specifies whether the recordset will contain schema information, and it can have the value DTD (Document Type Definition) or XML-DATA. The statement

```
SELECT ProductName, CategoryName
FROM Products, Categories
WHERE Products.CategoryID=Categories.CategoryID
FOR XML AUTO, DTD
```

will insert the following schema information at the beginning of the document:

```
<!DOCTYPE root
[<!ELEMENT root (Categories)*>
<!ELEMENT Products EMPTY>
<!ATTLIST Products ProductName CDATA #IMPLIED>
<!ELEMENT Categories (Products)*>
<!ATTLIST Categories CategoryName
  CDATA #IMPLIED>]>
<root>
```

The DTD option inserts the <root> element, and all data rows follow this tag. If you executed the same statement with the XMLDATA option, the following schema information will be inserted at the beginning of the document (the last four lines correspond to the first category):

```
<Schema xmlns=
  "urn:schemas-microsoft-com:xml-data"
  xmlns:dt=
  "urn:schemas-microsoft-com:datatypes">
<ElementType name="Products"
  content="textOnly" model="closed">
  <AttributeType name="ProductName"
    dt:type="string"/>
  <attribute type="ProductName"
    required="no"/>
</ElementType>
<ElementType name="Categories"
  content="mixed" model="closed">
  <element type="Products"/>
  <AttributeType name="CategoryName"
    dt:type="string"/>
  <attribute type="CategoryName"
    required="no"/>
</ElementType>
</Schema>
<Categories CategoryName="Beverages">
<Products ProductName="Chai"/>
<Products ProductName="Chang"/>
</Categories>
```

NOTE

If you omit the schema option, no schema information will be prepended to the document.

The ELEMENTS argument specifies that the columns will be returned as subelements. ELEMENTS can be used with AUTO mode only, and it produces straight XML code, which can be used as is in a data island. Let's try our sample statement with the ELEMENTS option:

```
SELECT ProductName, CategoryName
FROM Products, Categories
WHERE Products.CategoryID=Categories.CategoryID
FOR XML AUTO, ELEMENTS
```

The first few lines of the output produced by the preceding statement are shown here:

```
<Categories>
<CategoryName>Beverages</CategoryName>
<Products>
<ProductName>Chai</ProductName>
</Products>
<Products>
<ProductName>Chang</ProductName>
</Products>
</Categories>
<Categories>
<CategoryName>Condiments</CategoryName>
<Products>
<ProductName>Aniseed Syrup</ProductName>
</Products>
<Products>
<ProductName>Chef Anton&apos;s Cajun
             Seasoning</ProductName>
</Products>
```

OK, there's a catch here. The output produced by SQL Server doesn't contain an <XML> or <ROOT> tag, and it doesn't encode the text for transmission over the HTTP protocol.

Executing Stored Procedures

Stored procedures can be executed via a URL as easily as SQL statements. Actually, it's simpler to execute stored procedures, because the URL is simpler—it contains only the stored procedure's name and, optionally, one or more parameters. To call the Ten Most Expensive Products stored procedure of the NorthWind database, use the following URL:

```
http://127.0.0.1/NW?sql=execute+
[Ten+Most+Expensive+Products]
```

The square brackets are needed because the procedure's name contains spaces. This syntax uses the execute reserved keyword, followed by the name of the stored procedure.

If the stored procedure accepts parameters, you must supply their values either by ordinal position or by name. The Sales by Year stored procedure, also of the NorthWind database, expects two arguments: the beginning and ending dates, in this order. The names of the parameters are @BeginningDate and @EndingDate, respectively. Here's the definition of the Sales by Year stored procedure:

```
create procedure "Sales by Year"
  @Beginning_Date DateTime,
  @Ending_Date DateTime AS
SELECT Orders.ShippedDate, Orders.OrderID,
  "Order Subtotals".Subtotal,
  DATENAME(yy,ShippedDate) AS Year
FROM Orders
INNER JOIN "Order Subtotals"
ON Orders.OrderID = "Order Subtotals".OrderID
WHERE Orders.ShippedDate Between
  @Beginning_Date And @Ending_Date
```

To execute this stored procedure with the arguments 1/1/1998 and 12/31/1998, you can use either of the following two URLs:

```
http://127.0.0.1/NW?sql=execute+
[Sales by Year]+1/1/1998+12/31/1998
```

or

```
http://127.0.0.1/NW?sql=execute+
[Sales by Year]+@EndingDate=1/1/1998+
@BeginningDate=12/31/1998
```

Using the first form, you can specify the values of the parameters, as expected by the stored procedure. You don't have to know the names of the parameters, but you must know their order. With the second form, you use named parameters. You must know the names of the parameters, but you can specify them in any order, as you can see in the example.

Using Templates

In addition to XSL files, you can use templates to automate the process. Although it's possible to pass any statement as a URL, this requires a lot of typing, not to mention that you won't get the statement right the first time. As mentioned earlier in the chapter, it is possible to create template files with queries you want to execute against the database and call these template files by names, instead of supplying the actual SQL statement. The scripts need not be aware of the structure of the database. The database can prompt viewers for the values of some parameters and pass them as arguments to the template.

Another good reason for using template files is security. By placing a template file in the virtual root directory, you can enforce security by removing the URL query processing service on the virtual root. SQL Server will invoke the XML ISAPI to process the template file.

Finally, templates may contain other statements you want to include in your output. For example, you can insert the <XML> tags around the output, which are not produced automatically when you use the ELEMENTS argument in the FOR clause.

So, what exactly is a template file? A template is an XML file that contains SQL statements and parameters definitions like this:

```
<ROOT xmlns:sql=
  "urn:schemas-microsoft-com:xml-sql">
<SQL:query">
enter your SQL statements here
</SQL:query>
</ROOT>
```

The first and last lines are always the same; only the SQL statements change from template to template.

Let's create a template for retrieving product categories. To begin, enter the following code in a text file and store it in the SQL Server's XML-enabled root folder:

```
<ROOT xmlns:sql=
  "urn:schemas-microsoft-com:xml-sql">
```

```
<SQL:query">
SELECT CategoryID, CategoryName, Description
FROM Categories
FOR XML AUTO
</SQL:query>
</ROOT>
```

Assuming that the name of the template file is `AllCategories.xml`, you can execute this query against SQL Server by entering the following URL in your browser's Address Box:

```
http://127.0.0.1/NW/AllCategories.xml
```

If the template accepts parameters (and most templates do), use the following syntax:

```
<ROOT xmlns:sql=
  "urn:schemas-microsoft-com:xml-sql">
<SQL:query
  name1='value1' name2='value2'>
  { enter your SQL statement(s) here }
</SQL:query>
</ROOT>
```

Replace the strings *name1* and *name2* with the names of the parameters. *value1* and *value2* are the default values of the parameters, and they'll be used only if no values are specified in the URL.

The following template file will select the products of a specific category. Its name is `ProdByCategory.xml`, and it must be stored in SQL Server's root folder:

```
<ROOT xmlns:sql=
  "urn:schemas-microsoft-com:xml-sql">
<SQL:query
 SelCategory='3'>
 SELECT * FROM Products
 WHERE CategoryID = ?
</SQL:query>
</ROOT>
```

This template will select all the files in the category specified by the request. If no Category ID is specified, it will return the products belonging to the category with an ID of 3. To call this template passing the Category ID 4 as the parameter, connect to the following URL:

```
http://127.0.0.1/NW/ProdsByCategory.xml?
SelCategory=4
```

Using Update Grams

In the section "Updating XML Recordsets" earlier in this chapter, you saw how to post updates to a database using XML. SQL Server supports XML-based insert, update, and delete operations with a similar syntax. The statements for updating the database are called *grams*, and they can be used to post new rows and to edit or delete existing ones.

The syntax of an update gram is

```
<sql:sync xmlns:sql=
  "urn:schemas-microsoft-com:xml-sql">
  <sql:before>
    <TABLENAME [sql:id="value"]
               col1="value1"
               col2="value2"/>
  </sql:before>
  <sql:after>
    <TABLENAME [sql:id="value"]
               [sql:at-identity="value"]
               col1="value1"
               col2="value2"/>
  </sql:after>
</sql:sync>
```

`before` and `after` are keywords that specify field values before and after the update. The `sync` keyword delimits the operation, and everything between a pair of `<sync>` and `</sync>` tags is treated as a transaction. In other words, SQL Server will not update only a few of the fields if an error occurs. If one of the specified values is incompatible with the definition of the column, then the entire operation will be aborted.

In the `<before>` section, you specify the field values of an existing row. In the `<after>` section, you specify the new values for one or more fields. You must provide as many `column="value"` pairs as there are fields to be changed.

The <before> and <after> sections are optional. If the <before> section is missing, then it's assumed that you're inserting a new row to the database. The new row's fields must be specified in an <after> section. If the <after> section is missing, then the row identified by the field values in the <before> section is removed from the table.

It is possible to specify multiple updates in a single gram. If the <after> section contains rows with no matching entry in the <before> section, then these are new rows. The rows in the <after> section with a matching row in the <before> section are updated. Rows that appear only in the <before> section are deleted.

Inserting Rows

Following is an update gram that inserts a new row to the Customers table:

```
<ROOT xmlns:sql=
  "urn:schemas-microsoft-com:xml-sql">
  <sql:sync>
    <sql:after>
       <Customers CustomerID="NEW"
                  CompanyName="New Company"
                  ContactName="New Contact"
                  ContactTitle="New Owner/>
    </sql:after>
  </sql:sync>
</ROOT>
```

This is quite a URL, if you're thinking about submitting it to the server.

The information you retrieve from SQL Server via a URL is not a disconnected recordset. As a result, any changes you make are not going to be embedded in the recordset. The easiest approach is to create the update grams from within a client-side script and submit them to the server, just as you would submit a normal query via URL. Alternatively, you can call a template file and pass the values of the fields as arguments.

Most applications don't add rows to unrelated tables. A practical example is the insertion of a new order to the NorthWind database. To add an order, you must add a new row to the Orders table. SQL Server will automatically assign a new ID to the order. Then, you must use this ID to insert one or more rows to the Order Details table. Each item has its own row in the Order Details table, and all the rows that belong to the same order must have the same OrderID. The following statement will add a new row to the Orders table:

```
<sql:sync>
  <sql:after>
    <Orders sql:at-identity='newID'
    CustomerID='ALFKI'/>
  </sql:after>
</sql:sync>
```

newID is a variable name that will be assigned the ID of the new order. The OrderID field in the Order table is an AutoNumber field, so SQL Server knows which value to assign to the *newID* variable.

Now you can use this variable to add the order's details. For each detail, add a new row to the Order Details table and set the OrderID field to the value of the *newID* variable. The following statements add a single detail for the new order:

```
<sql:sync>
  <sql:after>
  <OrderDetails OrderID='newID'
                ProductID='11'
                Quantity='10'/>
  </sql:after>
</sql:sync>
```

Listing 21.6 is a page that adds a new order for the customer ALFKI. The order contains three items, for the products with IDs of 11, 12, and 13. To add the new order, the HTML page uses the `AddOrder()` function, which builds a template file. The contents of the template file are transmitted to the server by redirecting the script to the new URL.

Listing 21.6: The `AddOrder` **Script**

```
<HTML>
<SCRIPT>
  function AddOrder()
  {
    newOrderXML =
    "http://127.0.0.1/NW/?template=" +
    "<ROOT xmlns:sql='urn:schemas-" +
    "microsoft-com:xml-sql'>" +
```

```
            "<sql:sync>" +
               "<sql:after>" +
               "<Orders sql:at-identity='newID'" +
                           "CustomerID='ALFKI'/>" +
               "<OrderDetails OrderID='newID'" +
                              "ProductID='11'" +
                              "Quantity='10'/>" +
               "<OrderDetails OrderID='newID'" +
                              "ProductID='12'" +
                              "Quantity='20'/>" +
               "<OrderDetails OrderID='newID'" +
                              "ProductID='13'" +
                              "Quantity='30'/>" +
               "</sql:after>" +
            "</sql:sync>" +
         "</ROOT>"
         document.location.href = newOrderXML;
      }
   </SCRIPT>
   <BODY>
   Click here to
   <INPUT type="button" value="ADD ORDER"
          OnClick="AddOrder();">
   </BODY>
   </HTML>
```

You can modify this script so that it reads the values of the various fields from controls and builds the appropriate template file. This file isn't stored on the server. SQL Server simply executes it, and nothing is saved on the root folder.

An even better method to update the database is to write a stored procedure that accepts the same information we pass to the template file with the `AddOrder()` function and updates the database by adding new rows to the appropriate tables. The stored procedure should also be able to handle errors and return a True/False value indicating whether or not the operation was successful. It should also perform all the updates in the context of a transaction. The template file is also executed as a transaction, so that if a single insertion fails, the entire transaction is aborted.

Deleting Rows

To delete one or more rows in a table, specify the <before> section of the update gram and omit the <after> section. The sure method to delete the desired row is to supply its primary key. For example, the following statements remove the customers with ID TEST1 and TEST2 from the Customers table in the NorthWind database:

```
<ROOT xmlns:sql=
  "urn:schemas-microsoft-com:xml-sql">
  <sql:sync>
    <sql:before>
      <Customers  CustomerID="TEST1"/>
      <Customers  CustomerID="TEST2"/>
    </sql:before>
  </sql:sync>
</ROOT>
```

If the primary key of the row to be deleted is not known, supply as much information as possible to uniquely identify the row that you want to remove. The following statements attempt to locate a row in the Customers table with `ContactName="Joe Doe"` and `City="NY"`:

```
<ROOT xmlns:sql=
  "urn:schemas-microsoft-com:xml-sql">
  <sql:sync>
    <sql:before>
      <Customers ContactName="Joe Doe"
        City="NY"/>
    </sql:before>
  </sql:sync>
</ROOT>
```

If such a customer exists, it will be removed from the database. If two or more rows meet the specified criteria, then only the first row will be removed from the table. As you can understand, deleting rows with criteria other than the primary key is tricky, and you can't be sure that the deleted row was the one you intended.

Deleting Multiple Rows with One Statement

There are situations where you'll want to delete multiple rows with a single statement. For instance, to remove an order, you must first delete the details from the Order Details table. These are the lines whose OrderID field matches the ID of the order you want to remove. For example, the following statement will not remove all the rows whose OrderID field is 9840. Instead, it will remove only the first row that matches the criteria:

```
<ROOT xmlns:sql=
  "urn:schemas-microsoft-com:xml-sql">
  <sql:sync>
    <sql:before>
      <[Order Details] OrderID="9840"/>
    </sql:before>
  </sql:sync>
</ROOT>
```

To remove multiple rows from a table with a single statement, you must repeat the statement as many times as there are rows to be removed, or execute an action query against the database. The following statements will remove all the detail lines of the order with ID=9840:

```
<ROOT xmlns:sql=
  "urn:schemas-microsoft-com:xml-sql">
<SQL:query
  DELETE FROM [Order Details]
  WHERE OrderID = 9840
</SQL:query>
</ROOT>
```

As you may have guessed, the best method to remove an order is to write a stored procedure that accepts the ID of the order to be removed as an argument and that performs all the deletions as a single transaction. For example, you can define the following stored procedure that deletes the detail lines of an order:

```
USE NORTHWIND
CREATE PROCEDURE DeleteDetails
@OrderID int
AS
```

```
DELETE FROM [Order Details]
WHERE [Order Details].OrderID = @OrderID
```

You can call the `DeleteDetails` stored procedure to delete the detail lines of an order and pass the ID of the order whose details you want to delete as an argument:

```
http://127.0.0.1/NW?sql=execute+
DeleteDetails+19088
```

Templates vs. Stored Procedures

It seems that templates are nearly identical to stored procedures, and you can write a stored procedure instead of a template. Although this is true in most situations, template files can be used to execute multiple SQL statements. In fact, you can use template files that call stored procedures themselves.

Another good use of templates is to define update and delete grams. As you recall from our earlier discussion, the syntax of grams is a bit peculiar, and it takes a bit of effort to implement the gram from within a client script. You can insert all the tags of the gram in a template file and pass the necessary values as parameters.

NOTE

XML is an emerging standard, and ADO 2.5/2.6 provides rather limited support for XML-formatted data. Recently, Microsoft announced ADO+, which will provide better XML support, so you should check the Microsoft MSDN site for more information on this technology. According to recent announcements by Microsoft, XML will be one of the cornerstones of products ranging from databases to future versions of the Windows operating system.

What's Next?

Now that you have a good understanding of XML and databases, you have one more tool to explore before creating some sample sites. Building on your knowledge of XML and Windows DNA, the next chapter will introduce BizTalk, an invaluable technology for creating business applications for the Web.

Chapter 22

E-Commerce with Microsoft BizTalk

One of the most obvious arenas for the use of XML is business-to-business communication, sometimes known by the acronym *B2B*. However, the very flexibility of XML can be its downfall. If every organization defines its own schema for carrying business information, it's impossible for any two organizations to talk. So in this area, at least, standards for schema design are very important.

In this chapter, I review one such standard, *BizTalk*. Originally designed by Microsoft, BizTalk has become a multi-organizational specification of increasing importance in the crowded B2B market.

Adapted from *XML Developer's Handbook*™,
by Kurt Cagle
ISBN 0-7821-2704-5 640 pages $49.99

What Is BizTalk?

Microsoft announced the BizTalk Framework for e-commerce in March, 1999, with the stated goal of letting "software speak the language of business." The description of BizTalk has changed and become clearer in the intervening months. At first, it seemed as though Microsoft was promoting BizTalk as a refinement to Windows DNA, their process for creating distributed applications. But over time, the XML features of BizTalk have gradually assumed center stage. So far, there are three main parts to the BizTalk initiative:

- The *BizTalk Framework* provides a methodology and set of rules for creating XML schemas and tags to enable integration of business applications. These schemas are meant to be completely independent of software implementation details such as operating system or programming language.
- *BizTalk.org* is a quasi-independent industry group that supports collaboration among business organizations with an interest in BizTalk-compliant schemas. One of their most important activities is the maintenance of a library of BizTalk schemas.
- *Microsoft BizTalk Server 2000* is being promoted as "the industrial-strength, reliable operating environment for document transformation and routing to automate electronic procurement, business-to-business portals, and extranets, as well as automating value chain processes." Microsoft has also announced that BizTalk Server 2000 will include a graphical process-modeling environment.

In this chapter, I cover each of these parts of the BizTalk initiative in detail. You'll see what Microsoft is currently offering in this area, and I'll try to give you a sense of what you can implement today.

NOTE

This chapter is based on the BizTalk Server Technology Preview and may not reflect all of the features included in the final release of BizTalk Server 2000. You can download the BizTalk Server Technology Preview to get a look at parts of the BizTalk Server technology.

THE BIZTALK FRAMEWORK

Microsoft released version 1.0a of the BizTalk Framework Independent Document Specification in January, 2000. This document defines a set of XML tags that are designed to allow BizTalk-enabled applications to exchange information with one another. The specification defines an overall logical architecture for message passing between applications, defines key terms, and includes a set of XML tags that are used to encapsulate information in BizTalk messages.

In this section, I'll walk you through the details of the BizTalk Framework Independent Document Specification. At the end of the section, I'll show you a sample document that conforms to the specification.

NOTE

The BizTalk Framework Independent Document Specification is still evolving as Microsoft and its partners collaborate on refining the ideas in BizTalk. You should always be able to download the current version of the specification from `www.microsoft.com/biztalk/`. This chapter is based on version 1.0a of the specification.

The BizTalk Architecture

The overall architecture for BizTalk is a layered design vaguely reminiscent of the ISO/OSI seven-tiered architecture for networking, although considerably simpler. Figure 22.1 shows the components in this architecture.

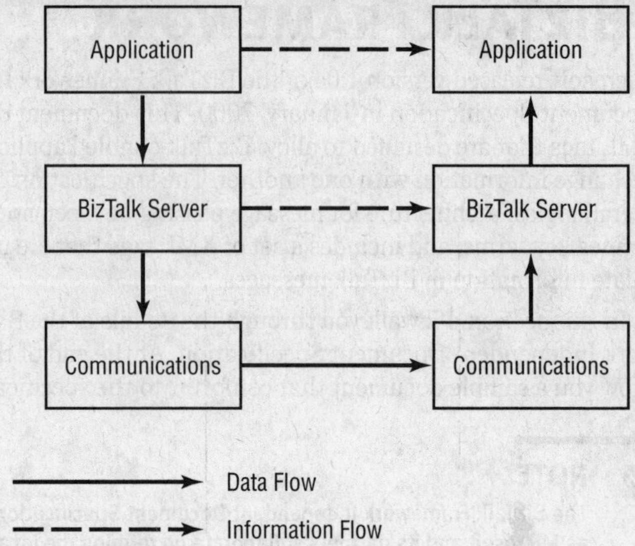

FIGURE 22.1: The BizTalk architecture

The BizTalk architecture includes three components:

The Application This is the business process that's sending or receiving data. This might be a purchasing program, a health care processing application, or any other business-specific application.

The BizTalk Server This is the server that knows how to interpret and route BizTalk messages. This might be Microsoft BizTalk Server 2000, but there's nothing to prevent other vendors from also shipping applications that function as BizTalk servers.

The Communications Layer This represents the network and communications infrastructure that moves messages from one BizTalk server to another. It might use a direct LAN connection, a dedicated dial-up line, an Internet protocol such as HTTP, or a message passing system such as Microsoft Message Queue (MSMQ). BizTalk is designed to be independent of the communications protocol used, and it doesn't care about the implementation details so long as messages actually get delivered.

In the BizTalk architecture, the logical flow of information differs from the physical flow of data. Physically, an application sends a message to the local BizTalk server, which sends it to the communications layer. This layer forwards the message to the communications layer on another computer, which passes the message up to the BizTalk server on the receiving end, which passes it to the receiving application. Logically, though, from the application's point of view, it is simply using BizTalk services to talk to another application. Similarly, the BizTalk server acts as if it's talking directly to another BizTalk server. Each layer in the architecture has its own distinct information that it processes.

BizTalk Definitions

To understand the BizTalk Framework, you need to understand the vocabulary that it uses. The key terms in the BizTalk Framework include:

Business Document This is the information that's being transferred from one application to another, formatted as an XML stream. The BizTalk Framework does not prescribe the schema for this stream. Rather, it's left to the implementers of the applications to agree on the business document schemas to use. One way to do this is by using schemas from BizTalk.org, discussed later in this chapter.

BizTags BizTags are a set of XML tags defined by the BizTalk Framework. These tags hold the information that passes from one BizTalk server to another. You can think of the BizTags as forming an envelope or wrapper around a business document.

BizTalk Document This is a business document together with the surrounding BizTags.

BizTalk Message A BizTalk document is encoded into a BizTalk message by the communications layer when it's sent. The details of this encoding can vary depending on the particular communications layer. I won't discuss BizTalk message formats in this chapter, because you're not likely to need to deal with BizTalk on this level.

Referring back to Figure 22.1, the business document passes between the two applications, the BizTalk document passes between the two servers, and the BizTalk message passes between the two communications layers.

BizTags

The BizTalk Framework defines a set of XML tags, called *BizTags*, to handle the delivery and addressing information that one BizTalk server requires in order to send a message to another BizTalk server. In this section, I'll review these tags one by one. In the next section, you'll see an example of a complete BizTalk document.

A BizTalk document must be enclosed in the <biztalk_1> tag and include a reference to the BizTalk namespace. This is what identifies the document as a BizTalk document. This tag and the namespace reference can take one of two forms:

```
<biztalk_1 xmlns=
  "urn:biztalk-org:biztalk:biztalk_1">
    document_contents
</biztalk_1>
```

or

```
<biztalk_1 xmlns="http://schemas.biztalk.org/
BizTalk/gr677h7w.xml">
   document_contents
</biztalk_1>
```

NOTE

In the tag examples in this section, italicized text such as *document_contents* indicates variables, information that is not part of the tag itself. Also, in formatting text for this book, URLs may be broken into multiple lines. These URLs should not be broken in actual use.

The first form of the <biztalk_1> tag uses a Uniform Resource Name (URN) to specify the location of the namespace definition on the Internet. Someday, this will be the preferred method of pointing to this definition. But at the moment, the Internet Engineering Task Force (IETF) hasn't finalized a URN definition for vendors to implement.

The second form of the tag uses a standard Web address to locate the namespace definition. This format allows today's tools to validate BizTalk documents against the schema.

The <header> tag is used within the <biztalk_1> tag to identify the header of the BizTalk document (the addressing and message processing information used by the BizTalk servers). The <body> tag is used within the <biztalk_1> tag to hold the business document being transmitted as part of this BizTalk document. These three tags fit together like this:

```
<biztalk_1 xmlns=
  "urn:biztalk-org:biztalk:biztalk_1">
```

```
    <header>
      processing_information
    </header>
    <body>
      business_document
    </body>
  </biztalk_1>
```

The other BizTags occur within the <header> tag. This makes sense, because the header section is where all of the information needed by the BizTalk server occurs. This information is precisely what BizTags are meant to contain.

The direct children of the <header> tag are the <delivery> tag and the <manifest> tag. The <delivery> tag contains delivery and addressing information for the BizTalk document. The <manifest> tag contains message content information.

The <delivery> tag is the parent of the <message>, <to>, and <from> tags. The <message> tag contains information about the message itself, while the <to> and <from> tags contain address information for the sender and recipient.

The <message> tag contains three child tags:

<messageID> This is an arbitrary message ID. It can be a sequential unique number generated by the sending BizTalk server, or a globally unique identifier (GUID). The BizTalk Framework does not specify a required format for this tag.

<sent> This tag is the time that the message was sent, according to the originating BizTalk server.

<subject> This is the subject of the message. Note that this is a subject determined by the BizTalk server, not by the originating application (which knows nothing about the content of BizTags).

The <from> and <to> tags have the same internal structure. Each of these tags can contain up to five other tags:

<address> This is a Uniform Resource Identifier (URI) describing the address of the sending or receiving system. The BizTalk server is responsible for resolving the URI address into a transport-specific address that can be understood by the communications layer in the BizTalk architecture.

<state> This tag is used by the BizTalk server to hold information used within the individual BizTalk server.

<referenceID> This is a unique identifier for the instance of the particular business process sending the message. This can be used when a reply to the message comes back to locate the destination process.

<handle> A refinement to the `referenceID`, this tag can be used to hold state information. For example, it might represent the step within a particular business process that transmitted the original business document.

<process> A refinement to the `handle`, this tag can be used to hold the account, process, or security information for the originating message.

The `<manifest>` tag contains information for the BizTalk server about the contents of the BizTalk message. Applications are free to send attachments along with business documents, and these attachments must be included with the message. Thus, the `<manifest>` tag contains the `<document>` tag and the `<attachment>` tag. The `<document>` tag must come before any instances of the `<attachment>` tag.

The `<document>` tag doesn't contain the document (that's in the <body> tag). Rather, it contains information about the document. The `<name>` tag is required and contains the name of the document. The `<description>` tag is optional and contains a description of the document. If there are multiple business documents within a single BizTalk document, then the `<document>` tag must be repeated multiple times, in the same order as the documents themselves.

The `<attachment>` tag can contain four child tags:

<index> This is a unique (within the context of the current BizTalk document) identifier for the attachment.

<filename> This is the filename of the attachment.

<description> This tag offers additional description of the attachment.

<type> This is a keyword identifying the type of attachment. If the attachment is itself a BizTalk document, then the type should be set to `biztalk`. Applications can define additional keywords to use here.

Putting the last several tags together, a full `<manifest>` section from a BizTalk document might look like this:

```
<manifest>
  <document>
    <name>PO 142787</name>
```

```
      <description>Purchase Order</description>
    </document>
    <attachment>
      <index>1</index>
      <filename>sig.jpg</filename>
      <description>
        Signature graphic
      </description>
      <type>jpg</type>
    </attachment>
  <manifest>
```

Finally, the <body> tag contains the actual business document. This document will itself be an XML stream, but the tags and schema used by this stream are not dictated by the BizTalk Framework. It's important, though, that the opening tag for the business document contains namespace information for the tags within the business document. If this namespace information is omitted, then the business document tags will be interpreted as part of the BizTag namespace, which will most likely cause an error. For example, BizTalk.org defines a sample Purchase Order schema with a schema definition located at `schemas.biztalk.org/BizTalk/cfwau8qx.xml`. You could use this within a <body> tag as follows:

```
  <body>
    <PO xmlns="http://schemas.biztalk.org/
    BizTalk/cfwau8qx.xml">
      purchase_order_information
    </PO>
  </body>
```

Table 22.1 lists the complete set of BizTags, and shows which ones are optional and which are required.

TABLE 22.1: BizTags

Tag	Parent	Required	Occurs
Address	to or from	Yes	Once
Attachment	Manifest	No	Zero or more
Biztalk_1	None	Yes	Once
Body	Biztalk_1	Yes	Once
Description	document or attachment	No	Zero or once
Delivery	header	No	Once
Document	manifest	Yes	One or more
Filename	attachment	Yes	Once
From	delivery	Yes	Once
Handle	to or from	No	Zero or once
Header	biztalk_1	No	Once
Index	attachment	Yes	Once
Manifest	header	No	Zero or once
Message	delivery	Yes	Once
MessageID	message	Yes	Once
Name	document	Yes	Once
Process	to or from	No	Zero or once
ReferenceID	to or from	Yes	Once
Sent	message	Yes	Once
State	to or from	No	Zero or once
Subject	message	No	Zero or once
To	delivery	Yes	Once
Type	attachment	No	Zero or once

A BizTalk Document

At this point, you've seen all of the components of a BizTalk document. Now it's time to see how they fit together. Listing 22.1 shows a sample

BizTalk document (`PurchaseOrder.xml`) encapsulating a business message that's written using the sample purchase order schema from BizTalk.org. In this listing, the BizTags are shown in boldface type. The normal type indicates the business document contained within the BizTalk document.

Listing 22.1: A BizTalk Document (`PurchaseOrder.xml`)

```
<biztalk_1 xmlns=
  "urn:biztalk-org:biztalk:biztalk_1">
  <header>
    <delivery>
      <message>
        <messageID>134576</messageID>
        <sent>2000-07-02T22:45:30+06:00</sent>
        <subject>Purchase Order</subject>
      </message>
      <to>
        <address>
          http://schmoop.com/po.asp
        </address>
        <state>
          <referenceID/>
        </state>
      </to>
      <from>
        <address>
          mailto:purchasing@schmoop.com
        </address>
        <state>
          <referenceID>241AA6</referenceID>
        </state>
      </from>
    </delivery>
    <manifest>
      <document>
        <name>PO 142787</name>
        <description>
          Purchase Order
        </description>
      </document>
    <manifest>
```

```
    </header>
    <body>
      <PO xmlns=
        "http://schemas.biztalk.org/
        BizTalk/cfwau8qx.xml">
        <POHeader>
          <poNumber>142787</poNumber>
          <custID>4718</custID>
          <description>
            Order for styrofoam cups
          </description>
          <paymentType>Invoice</paymentType>
          <shipType>Ground</shipType>
          <Contact>
            <contactName>
              Mel Schmoop
            </contactName>
            <contactEmail>
              Mel@schmoop.com
            </contactEmail>
          </Contact>
          <POShipTo>
            <attn>Schmoop</attn>
            <street>123 Willow Way</street>
            <city>Brook City</city>
            <stateProvince>WA</stateProvince>
            <postalCode>99999</postalCode>
            <country>USA</country>
          </POShipTo>
          <POBillTo>
            <attn>Schmoop</attn>
            <street>123 Willow Way</street>
            <city>Brook City</city>
            <stateProvince>WA</stateProvince>
            <postalCode>99999</postalCode>
            <country>USA</country>
          </POBillTo>
        </POHeader>
        <POLines>
          <count>1</count>
          <totalAmount>650.00</totalAmount>
          <Item>
```

```
            <line>1</line>
            <partno>S100</partno>
            <qty>325</qty>
            <uom>pkg</uom>
            <unitPrice>2.00</unitPrice>
            <discount>0</discount>
            <totalAmount>650.00</totalAmount>
          </Item>
        </POLines>
      </PO>
    </body>
  </biztalk_1>
```

BizTalk.org

Now you've seen how a BizTalk document is formed, but we haven't discussed the content of the business document that it contains. Developing and promoting standardized XML schemas to support business-to-business interchange is the mission of BizTalk.org.

BizTalk.org is an organization administered by the BizTalk Steering Committee. This is a group formed by Microsoft in conjunction with a number of partners. The charter members of the BizTalk Steering Committee are:

- American Petroleum Institute
- Ariba
- Baan
- Boeing
- Commerce One
- Concur Technologies
- Data Interchange Standards Association
- J.D. Edwards
- Merrill Lynch
- Microsoft
- Open Applications Group
- PeopleSoft

- Pivotal Software
- SAP

The main activity of BizTalk.org is to act as a repository for BizTalk schemas. The group also hosts a set of online discussion areas and provides news related to BizTalk on its Web site.

The BizTalk Web Site

The BizTalk Web site (`www.biztalk.org`) is divided into six major areas:

Home The home page includes breaking news about the BizTalk initiative, as well as quick links to important BizTalk information. From this page, you can also register with BizTalk. Registration is free, but it's required for access to some parts of the Web site.

Library The library page provides access to the BizTalk library of schemas. I'll discuss this more in the next section. From this page, you can also register to become a BizTalk contributor. You'll need to do this if your company wants to place a schema into the BizTalk library.

Community The community page provides a set of discussion groups for BizTalk-related topics. These range from a Newbies corner to several expert areas. The discussion groups are moderately active, and there are knowledgeable people available to answer your questions.

News The news page highlights news about BizTalk and related areas such as XML messaging and other industry XML initiatives. You can also sign up to receive e-mail notification of news items.

Resources The resources page provides a small selection of XML tools, white papers, and links.

Help The help page provides a list of frequently asked questions (FAQ) and general help with using the BizTalk Web site.

BizTalk Schemas

The BizTalk schemas are accessible through the library page on BizTalk.org. To find a particular schema, you'll need to search for it. There are two ways to search for schemas:

- You can enter a keyword or a comma-separated list of keywords to find schemas containing those keywords (such as "purchase" or "invoice").

- You can drill down through a list of industrial classifications to see all schemas that have been classed with a particular industry (the organization that submits the schema determines the classification).

TIP

To see a list of all schemas in the BizTalk library, enter a single space in the Keyword Search text box and click Search.

As of April 2000, the BizTalk library contained just over 400 schemas, submitted by a wide variety of organizations. Figure 22.2 shows one of these schemas in BizTalk.org's SchemaView application.

Schema View

Schema Name: CorporateEvents

Industry Group: On-Line Information Services

Organization: StreetFusion

Hosted by BizTalk.org: http://schemas.biztalk.org/c_call_com/mceil

Publish Date: 9/23/99 5:54:06 PM

Contributor: Peter Drayton

Summary: describes corporate events such as quarterly earnings releases, analyst conference calls, webcasts, and telephone replays.

Schema Interest

My organization uses the schema - please send me a notification email when it changes ☐

Register Interest

More Info on Schema Registration

View Schema	View Schema Source	Right Click to Download Schema*
View Doc		Right Click to Download Doc*
View Sample	View Sample Source	Right Click to Download Sample*

**To download these files, right click on these links and choose "Save Target As" or "Save Link As"*

FIGURE 22.2: BizTalk.org schema

BizTalk.org lets you perform any of these operations with a schema from the library:

View Schema Displays the details of the schema in an instance of Internet Explorer, formatted with a style sheet that displays everything for easy browsing.

View Schema Source Displays the schema as raw text within an instance of Internet Explorer. This lets you see what the schema looks like as a text file rather than as formatted XML.

Download Schema Downloads the schema from the library to your local computer.

View Doc Displays a description of the schema, contact information for the submitting organization, and other information about the schema.

Download Doc Downloads a copy of the schema documentation to your local computer.

View Sample Displays a sample document conforming to the schema in Internet Explorer, formatted with Internet Explorer's default XML style sheet.

View Sample Source Displays the sample as raw text within an instance of Internet Explorer. This lets you see what the sample looks like as a text file rather than as formatted XML.

Download Sample Downloads a copy of the sample document to your local computer.

BizTalk Server 2000

BizTalk Server 2000 is a server product designed to provide the "glue" between diverse business organizations. It provides a set of services that can help translate and transmit data, as well as tools to help you manage BizTalk documents.

The services provided by BizTalk Server 2000 include:

- Receiving documents via FTP, file drop-off, or message queuing
- Transmitting documents via HTTP, HTTPS, SMTP, STP, file drop-off, fax, or message queuing
- Parsing data from XML files and other industry-standard formats, such as ANSI X12

- Validating data against a specification and raising warnings to human operators when the data fails validation
- Document security

The components of BizTalk Server 2000 include:

- BizTalk Editor for creating document specifications
- BizTalk Mapper for specifying the rules to convert documents from one specification to another
- BizTalk Management Desk for overall management of data exchange with other organizations
- BizTalk Server Administration Console for managing BizTalk server services
- BizTalk Server Tracking for following documents through the organization and beyond

In the remainder of this chapter, I'll examine the services and components provided by BizTalk Server 2000. You'll see how you can use this product to automate B2B communications that use XML as their basic vocabulary. To see how the pieces fit together, I'll follow the major steps of setting up a BizTalk application to transform data from one format to another:

- Using BizTalk Editor to create specifications
- Using BizTalk Mapper to create a mapping
- Creating organizations
- Creating document definitions
- Creating agreements
- Creating pipelines
- Submitting documents
- Tracking documents

WARNING

This section of the chapter is based on the BizTalk Server Technology Preview, released in April 2000. For up-to-date information on the release of BizTalk Server, check the BizTalk Server Web site at `www.microsoft.com/biztalkserver`.

Creating Specifications with BizTalk Editor

The first step in using BizTalk Server is to define the format of the documents that I'll be using in this example. The tool for this is Microsoft BizTalk Editor. Figure 22.3 shows the process of editing a specification in BizTalk Editor. In this particular case, the Editor is showing the structure of a specification named `ProductionOrder1.xml`. The left pane shows the overall structure of the specification, while the right pane shows the properties of the selected node in the structure.

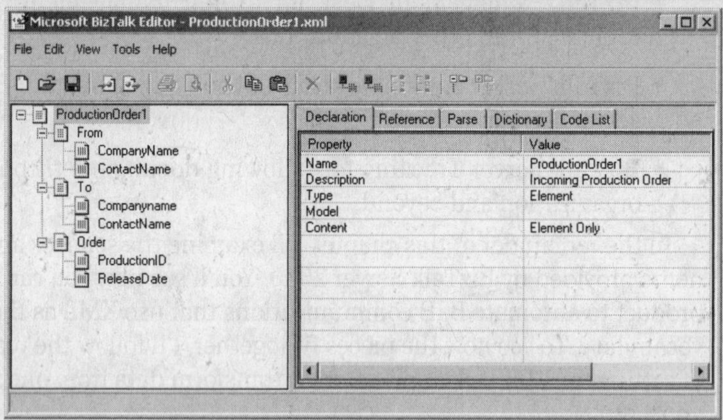

FIGURE 22.3: First schema in Microsoft BizTalk Editor

BizTalk Editor can design document specifications in a variety of formats, including XML, Edifact, and X12. If you're supporting legacy applications, you might need to define formats for Edifact or X12 standards. For new applications, it makes sense to use XML right from the start. To create a new XML specification, open BizTalk Editor, select File ➢ New, select Blank Specification as the specification type, and click OK.

The BizTalk Editor will help you build an XML schema for your document by letting you insert element and attribute nodes. You can do this from the Edit menu with the Insert Record and Insert Field menu items, or from toolbar buttons. As you insert each item, you can define the properties for that item.

TIP

The BizTalk Editor uses *record* to refer to an XML element and *field* to refer to an XML attribute. *Record* and *field* are general terms that are more familiar to people working with specifications based on legacy standards.

The right pane of the BizTalk Editor is divided into five sections by tabs:

Declaration The Declaration tab contains the basic information defining the element or attribute that's currently selected in the TreeView. For an element, this includes the Name, Description, Type (always Element), Model (should be left set to Closed), and Content (will be Element Only if the element has any attributes). For an attribute, this includes Name, Description, Type (always Attribute), Data Type, Data Type Values (only available if the Data Type is set to Enumeration), Min Length, and Max Length. Generally, you should supply at least a name for every node in the tree and data types for all attributes to help BizTalk verify document contents.

Reference For an element, the Reference tab lets you specify the minimum (0 or 1) and maximum (1 or many) occurrences of the element in the document. For an attribute, the Reference tab lets you specify whether or not the attribute is required.

Parse The Parse tab contains information used to extract information from non-XML files such as delimited, flat files, X12, or Edifact. This tab isn't used for XML documents.

Dictionary The Dictionary tab contains information that helps Edifact or X12 specifications validate data. This tab isn't used for XML documents.

Code List The Code List tab allows you to assign standard codes to fields in an X12 or Edifact specification. The X12 and Edifact standards specify lists of field codes. These codes are not used in XML documents.

NOTE

Some of these tabs will contain other information for non-XML document types.

In general, you should be able to build an XML specification fairly quickly with BizTalk Editor. To build a new specification, follow these steps:

1. Create the new specification.
2. Add the elements (records) to the root node or to their parent nodes.
3. Add the attributes (fields) to their parent nodes.
4. Set the minimum and maximum occurrence for each element on the Reference tab.
5. Set the data type and field size information for each attribute on the Declaration tab.
6. Set the required information for each attribute on the Reference tab.
7. Optionally, add element and attribute descriptions to the Declaration tab.

Saving a Schema with XML-DR

Once you've finished defining a schema in the BizTalk Editor, you can select File ➢ Save to save the schema in XML-Data Reduced (XML-DR) format. This format adds data type information to the XML schema information, and makes it possible for BizTalk Server to validate the data in incoming documents. For example, Listing 22.2 shows the saved XML-DR file (`ProductionOrder1.xml`) for the schema shown earlier in Figure 22.3.

Listing 22.2: An XML-DR File (`ProductionOrder1.xml`)

```
<?xml version="1.0"?>
<Schema name="ProductionOrder1"
b:root_reference="ProductionOrder1"
b:standard="XML" xmlns=
"urn:schemas-microsoft-com:xml-data"
xmlns:d="urn:schemas-microsoft-com:datatypes"
xmlns:b=
"urn:schemas-microsoft-com:BizTalkServer">
<b:SelectionFields/>

<ElementType name="To" content="empty"
model="closed">
```

```
<b:RecordInfo/>
<AttributeType name="ContactName"
d:type="string">
<b:FieldInfo/></AttributeType>
<AttributeType name="Companyname"
d:type="string">
<b:FieldInfo/></AttributeType>
<attribute type="Companyname" required="yes"/>
<attribute type="ContactName" required="yes"/>
</ElementType><ElementType
name="ProductionOrder1" content="eltOnly">
<description>
Incoming Production Order</description>
<b:RecordInfo/>
<element type="From" maxOccurs="1"
minOccurs="1"/>
<element type="To" maxOccurs="1"
minOccurs="1"/>
<element type="Order" maxOccurs="1"
minOccurs="1"/>
</ElementType><ElementType name="Order"
content="empty" model="closed">

<b:RecordInfo/>
<AttributeType name="ReleaseDate"
d:type="dateTime">
<b:FieldInfo/></AttributeType>
<AttributeType name="ProductionID"
d:type="string">
<b:FieldInfo/></AttributeType>
<attribute type="ProductionID" required="yes"/>
<attribute type="ReleaseDate" required="yes"/>
</ElementType><ElementType name="From"
content="empty" model="closed">

<b:RecordInfo/>
<AttributeType name="ContactName"
d:type="string">
<b:FieldInfo/></AttributeType>
<AttributeType name="CompanyName"
d:type="string">
<b:FieldInfo/></AttributeType>
```

```
<attribute type="CompanyName" required="yes"/>
<attribute type="ContactName" required="yes"/>
</ElementType></Schema>
```

Saving a Schema with WebDAV

While it can be useful to dump a schema to XML-DR so that you can see the XML that BizTalk Editor is creating, this is not how you should save a schema for use by BizTalk Server. Instead, you need to save your specification to a Web Distributed Authoring and Versioning (WebDAV) repository. To do this, select File ➢ Store to WebDAV in BizTalk Editor. This will open up a browse dialog showing you the folders on the WebDAV repository that your BizTalk server is currently using. You can work with this browse dialog just as you would with any other file-saving dialog box. Select or create a folder to hold your specification, assign a name, and click Save to save the specification to the repository.

WARNING

In the current implementation, a WebDAV repository is simply a folder on your hard drive, at `C:\Program Files\Microsoft BizTalk Server\BizTalk-ServerRepository`. However, you should always use the editor interfaces designed to store and retrieve documents to the repository, rather than treating it as a file folder, because there's no guarantee that the server will always use this implementation. BizTalk Server adds this folder as an IIS virtual directory and uses the HTTP protocol to communicate with the repository.

Translating Documents

One of the primary uses of BizTalk Server is to translate documents between the formats used by two business partners. For the examples in the rest of this chapter, I'll use two different schemas for a production order. The first is the one that you already saw in Figure 22.3; the second is shown in Figure 22.4. As you can see, although the two schemas contain much of the same information, there are some differences between them. In particular, the first schema treats the originating company, the receiving company, and the production order as three separate entities. The second schema sees both companies as attributes of an element named `TradingPartners`. There's also a piece of information (the date the production order was received) that's included in the second schema rather than in the first. In the following sections, you'll see how to use

BizTalk Server to seamlessly integrate documents based on these schemas despite these differences.

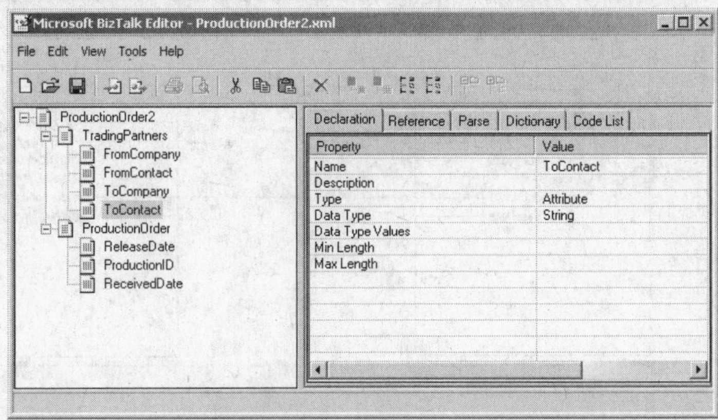

FIGURE 22.4: Second schema in BizTalk Editor

Creating a Mapping with BizTalk Mapper

To tell BizTalk Server how to convert a document from one format to another, you must create a *mapping*. A mapping is a set of instructions that tells BizTalk Server how two schemas are related. The tool for doing this is named, not surprisingly, BizTalk Mapper. Figure 22.5 shows BizTalk Mapper in action.

After launching BizTalk Mapper, the first thing you'll want to do is create a new mapping. This is a multiple-step process:

1. Select File ➢ New. This will launch a series of dialog boxes to guide you through the remaining steps.
2. Select a type for the source specification. This can be a file on your computer, a template for a general class of files (Edifact, X12, or XML), or a WebDAV file.
3. Select the actual source specification.
4. Select a type for the destination specification.
5. Select the actual destination specification.

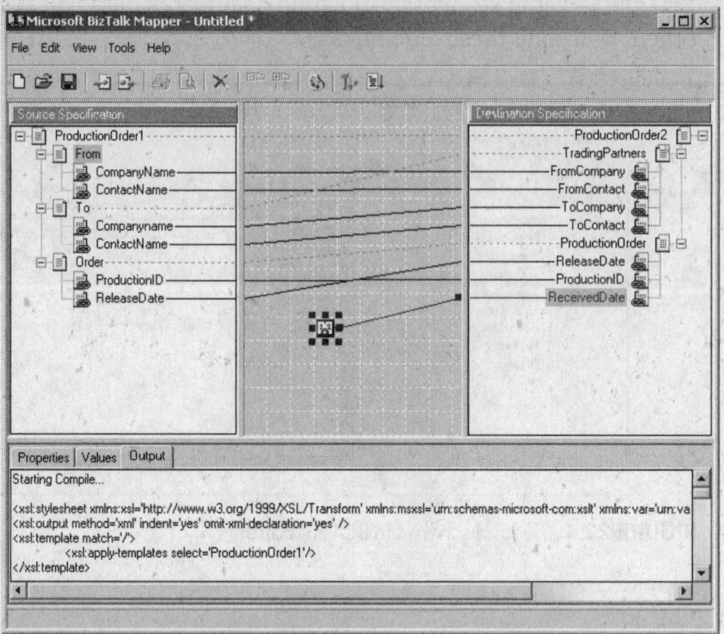

FIGURE 22.5: Microsoft BizTalk Mapper

After you've selected the source and destination specifications, BizTalk Mapper will populate the Source Specification and Destination Specification panes of its interface with the node information from your chosen specifications.

Once you've loaded the source and destination specifications, the next step is to indicate the corresponding fields between the two specifications. To do this, expand the source specification tree and the destination specification tree, locate a source field, and drag and drop it to the corresponding destination field. Repeat this step for each field that exactly matches between the source and destination.

Modifying Fields with Functoids

Sometimes field mapping will be enough to indicate the correspondence between a source specification and a destination specification. This will be the case if there are the same fields in both specifications but they're named differently or stored in a different order. However, specifications are much more powerful than this thanks to the use of functoids.

Functoids are bits of custom programming written in VBScript that can be used to modify fields as they're being copied from the source to the destination, or even to create entirely new fields. To use functoids in BizTalk Mapper, select View ➢ Functoid Palette, choose a category of functoid, and then drag the individual functoid that you require to the mapping area between the source and destination specification trees. You can drag inputs from the source specification tree to the functoid, and outputs from the functoid to the destination specification tree. Table 22.2 lists the functoids available with BizTalk Mapper.

TABLE 22.2: BizTalk Mapper Functoids

CATEGORY	FUNCTOIDS
String	Position of a substring, left characters, convert to lowercase, right characters, string length, extract substring, concatenate strings, remove leading spaces, remove trailing spaces, convert to uppercase
Mathematical	Absolute value, integer, maximum value, minimum value, modulus, rounding, square root, sum, difference, product, quotient
Logical	Greater than, greater than or equal, less than, less than or equal, equal, not equal, is a string, is a date, is a number, logical OR, logical AND
Date and Time	Add days, current date, current time, current date and time
Conversion	Character to ASCII, ASCII to character, decimal to hexadecimal, decimal to octal
Scientific	Arc tangent, cosine, sine, tangent, exponential, natural logarithm, power of 10, base 10 logarithm, power, arbitrary base logarithm
Advanced	Custom VBScript function

Functoids can also be chained to perform multiple operations. For example, you can remove leading and trailing space from a string field by following these steps:

1. Drag the remove leading spaces functoid to the mapping area.
2. Drag the remove trailing spaces functoid to the mapping area.
3. Drag from the source field to the remove leading spaces functoid.
4. Drag from the remove leading spaces functoid to the remove trailing spaces functoid.

5. Drag from the remove trailing spaces functoid to the destination field.

Saving a Mapping

Once you've created all the mappings that you need between the source and destination specifications, it's time to save the mapping. Before saving, you must select Tools ➢ Compile Map. This creates an XSL document describing the mapping. You can save the compiled map as an XSL file if you'd like to see the results of running BizTalk Mapper. Again, though, to be useful to BizTalk Server, the mapping must be saved into the WebDAV repository. Select File ➢ Store to WebDAV to save the mapping to the repository.

Creating Organizations with BizTalk Management Desk

After creating specifications for the source and destination documents and producing a map to transform the source into the destination, it's time to start working in Microsoft BizTalk Management Desk. BizTalk Management Desk is an integrated development environment that handles the details of BizTalk Server's operations. Figure 22.6 shows the BizTalk Management Desk. To the left are controls for selecting organizations and agreements; at the top are the current agreements and their status; below is an editor section that changes according to context.

The first task you need to accomplish is creating an organization to represent your own business unit. To do this, follow these steps:

1. Select File ➢ New ➢ Organization.
2. On the General tab of the Organization Editor dialog box, enter a name for the organization.
3. On the Identifiers tab of the Organization Editor dialog box, enter your Dun & Bradstreet or other identifier. You can skip this tab if you'd like.
4. On the Applications tab of the Organization Editor dialog box, enter the names of all the applications that are either document sources or document destinations for this organization. These are arbitrary names that will identify the applications with which BizTalk Server will communicate.
5. Click OK to save the organization definition.

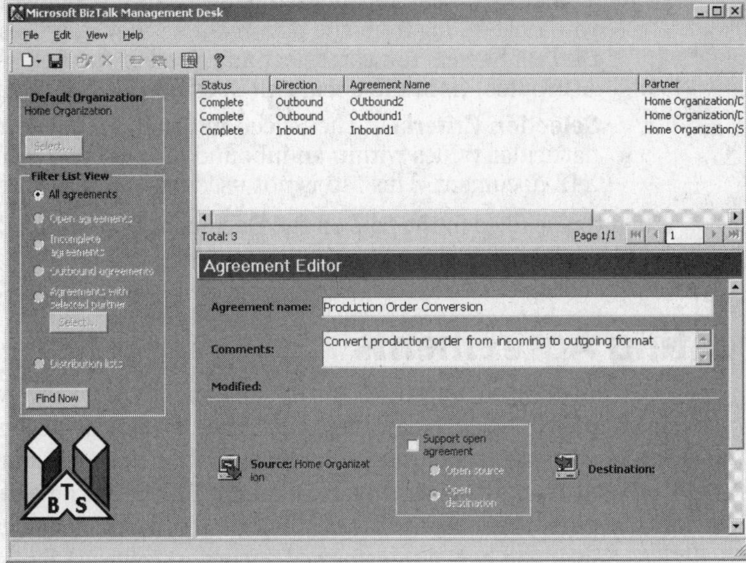

FIGURE 22.6: BizTalk Management Desk

You can create as many organizations as you'd like with BizTalk Management Desk. For this chapter's example, I created an organization named Home Organization with a number of applications including Production Order Source and Production Order Destination.

TIP

BizTalk Server can be used to transform documents within a single organization as well as to convert information sent from one trading partner to another.

Creating Document Definitions

After you've created the organizations that will interchange information via BizTalk Server, the next step is to create document definitions for the documents that will be interchanged. To do this, select File ➢ New ➢ Document Definition. This will open the Document Definition Editor, which has three tabs:

General On the General tab, you assign a name to the document definition and browse within a WebDAV repository to locate the specification for the document.

Tracking The Tracking tab lets you specify fields that you'd like to log from the document as they're processed by BizTalk Server. You can select any or all of the fields (XML Attributes) from the document specification for logging.

Selection Criteria The Selection Criteria tab lets you flag particular values within an inbound or outbound Edifact or X12 document. This tab is not used with XML documents.

When you've filled in the tabs on the Document Definition Editor, click OK to save the document definition.

Creating Agreements

After defining the organizations and document definitions involved in a business interchange, the next step is to create an agreement. An *agreement* represents the set of rules involved in moving data either into or out of BizTalk Server. All agreements have the BizTalk Server default organization as either the source or the destination. To move a document into BizTalk Server and have a transformed document come out elsewhere, you'll need to create two agreements and a pipeline. (Pipelines are discussed in the next section.)

To create a new agreement, select File ➢ New ➢ Agreement. Figure 22.7 shows an agreement being edited in the Agreement Editor, which is hosted exclusively within BizTalk Management Desk.

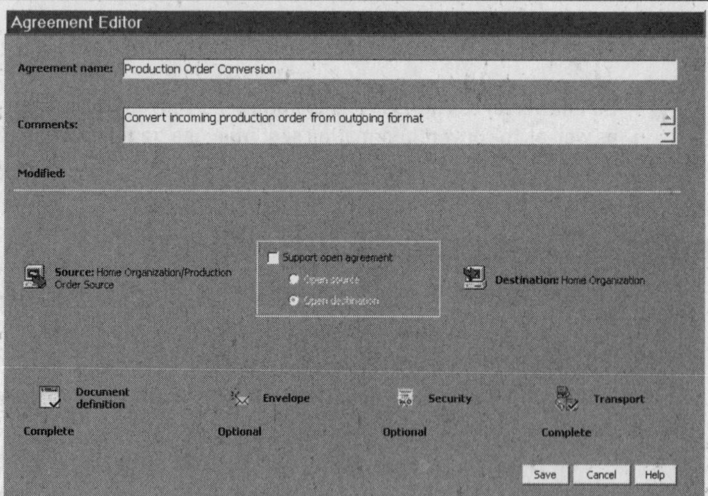

FIGURE 22.7: Creating an agreement

An agreement must have a source and a destination, a document definition, and a transport. Optionally, it can also have an envelope and security settings.

NOTE

Envelopes are used to provide routing information for documents in older formats such as Edifact and X12. They're not necessary for XML documents, and I don't cover them in this chapter.

To set the properties of a newly created agreement, follow these steps:

1. In the Agreement Editor, type in a name and description of the agreement.
2. Click the Source icon. This will open the Select an Organization dialog box. Select the organization that's the source of the document and the application that supplies the document.
3. Back in the Agreement Editor, click the Destination icon. This will open the Select an Organization dialog box. Select the organization that's the destination of the document and the application that supplies the document.
4. Again in the Agreement Editor, click the Document Definition icon. Select the document definition for the document that this agreement will process.
5. Optionally, click the Agreement Editor's Security icon and set the security properties for the agreement. You can choose whether to use MIME or custom encoding, whether to encrypt, and whether to digitally sign the document as it's being moved.
6. Click the Transport icon and select a Transport type and originating or destination location. You can choose from HTTP, HTTPS, SMTP, FTP, File, Fax, and Message Queuing transports.
7. Click Save to save the agreement after defining it. When you save an agreement, you can choose whether to save it as complete or as incomplete. Once you save an agreement as complete, it can no longer be edited. Before you can actually use an agreement, you must save it as complete.

NOTE

The transport type and address are used only on outbound agreements. The BizTalk Server Technology Preview requires assigning a transport to inbound agreements, but this transport is ignored by the server.

You can also use the Support Open Agreement check box to create an open-source or open-destination agreement. An *open-source agreement* can accept documents from many different sources; an *open-destination agreement* can send documents to many different sources. The source or destination that's left open must be specified when the document is submitted to BizTalk Server.

Creating Pipelines

To convert one document format to another with BizTalk Server, you need three things:

- An inbound agreement
- An outbound agreement
- A pipeline connecting the two agreements

A *pipeline* is simply the way that BizTalk stores the connection between a pair of agreements. Any given pipeline might include a map, or it might just move data from an inbound agreement to an outbound agreement with no changes. To create a pipeline, first click an outbound agreement in the upper pane of BizTalk Management Desk and then select File ➢ New ➢ Pipeline. This will open the Pipeline Editor, shown in Figure 22.8.

Once you've created a pipeline, follow these steps to set its properties:

1. Fill in a name and optional comments describing the pipeline.
2. Within Pipeline Editor, click the Source icon. Select the source organization and application in the Select an Organization dialog box and click OK.
3. Back in Pipeline Editor, click the Inbound Agreement icon to open the Select an Inbound Agreement dialog box. This dialog box shows the inbound agreements that are associated with the organization and application that you chose in step 2. Select the appropriate inbound agreement and click OK.

4. Again in Pipeline Editor, click the Inbound Document Definition icon and choose the document definition for the incoming document. The Select an Inbound Document Definition dialog box will show only the document definitions that match the inbound agreement that you chose in step 3.

5. The Pipeline Filtering icon allows you to look for specific values to be monitored in the inbound document. This is optional.

6. The Storage and Logging icon allows you to set storage formats and logging levels for the pipeline. This is optional.

7. In Pipeline Editor, click the Outbound Document Definition icon and select the document definition into which the document should be converted.

8. Optionally, click the Override Transport Defaults icon to modify the transport used for the outgoing document.

9. If you have a map to convert from the inbound document definition to the outbound document definition, uncheck the No Map check box, click the Map icon within Pipeline Editor, and select the appropriate map.

10. Click Save to save the pipeline.

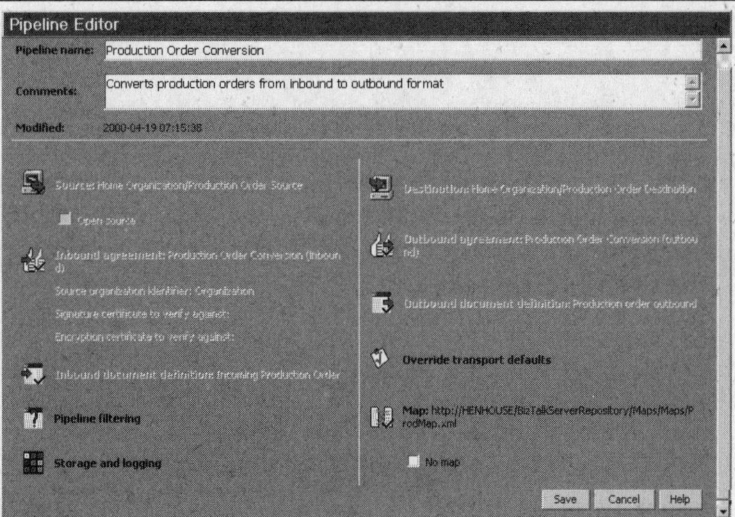

FIGURE 22.8: Adding a pipeline

Creating and Submitting Documents

To recap, here are the steps for using BizTalk Server 2000 discussed so far:

1. Create incoming and outgoing document specifications.
2. Create a mapping.
3. Create an organization.
4. Create inbound and outbound document definitions.
5. Create inbound and outbound agreements.
6. Create a pipeline.

At this point, BizTalk Server is ready to go to work. Referring back to the architectural diagram of BizTalk in Figure 22.1, you'll see that the "plumbing" is in place. What remains is to create and submit a document.

You can use any XML editor to create the document to be submitted. The format of the document must match that defined by the incoming document specification. For example, this document matches the sample production order specification I showed you earlier in the chapter:

```
<ProductionOrder1>
  <From CompanyName = "Integrated Industries"
    ContactName = "John Banbino" />
  <To CompanyName = "Owl Group Ltd"
    Contactname = "Ella Manfredi" />
  <Order ProductionID = "1425"
    ReleaseDate = "2000-03-14 11:30 AM" />
</ProductionOrder1>
```

BizTalk provides a set of COM interfaces that allow you to submit documents directly from an application such as a Visual Basic program or an ASP page. In order to submit a document that will use a map, you should reference these libraries:

- Microsoft BizTalk Server Core Type Library
- Microsoft BizTalk Server Interchange 1.0 Type Library
- Microsoft BizTalk Server StateEngine Type Library

The code for submitting a document is relatively simple. Listing 22.3 shows `SubmitDoc.frm`, a Visual Basic program that opens a document and submits it to BizTalk Server for processing.

Listing 22.3: Submitting a Document (SubmitDoc.frm)

```
Option Explicit
'Openness flag for not open agreements
Const MODELDB_OPENNESS_TYPE_NOTOPEN = 1

Private Sub cmdSubmit_Click()
  Dim objInterchange As New Interchange
  Dim txtStream As Object
  Dim fileSysObj As Scripting.FileSystemObject
  Dim strDocument As String
  Dim strHandle As String
  Dim strPipeline As String

  ' Retrieve the contents of the file that
  ' we want to submit
  Set fileSysObj = New _
    Scripting.FileSystemObject
  If fileSysObj.FileExists _
    (txtFileSource.Text) Then
    Set txtStream = fileSysObj.OpenTextFile _
      (txtFileSource.Text, 1, True)
    strDocument = txtStream.ReadAll
    txtStream.Close
    Set txtStream = Nothing
  Else
    strDocument = "Empty document"
  End If
  txtSend.Text = strDocument

  ' Specify the pipeline for BizTalk to use
  strPipeline = "Production Order Conversion"

  ' And actually submit the document
  strHandle = objInterchange.Submit _
    (MODELDB_OPENNESS_TYPE_NOTOPEN, _
  strDocument, , , , , , strPipeline, "", "")

  MsgBox "Document has been submitted"

End Sub
```

As you can see, the code to submit a document is straightforward. All of the work is done by calling the `Submit` method of the `Interchange` object. This method has the following arguments:

`lOpenness` A constant indicating whether the agreement is open-source or open-destination, or closed

`Document` The actual text of the document to submit

`DocName` The name of the document to submit

`SourceQualifier` Routing information to be submitted with the document

`SourceID` Routing information to be submitted with the document

`DestQualifier` Routing information to be submitted with the document

`DestID` Routing information to be submitted with the document

`PipelineName` Name of the BizTalk Server pipeline to use to convert this document

`FilePath` Override for the storage path of the converted file

`EnvelopeName` Envelope format to use for the pipeline (if any)

For most documents, you should be able to manage with just the arguments (`lOpenness`, `Document`, and `PipelineName`) that are used in this example.

Once you call the `Submit` method, BizTalk Server takes over. Assuming that you've properly defined all of the objects that it requires, the converted document will show up in the file, FTP, or other location that you've specified as part of the transport information for the outbound agreement. If anything goes seriously wrong, BizTalk Server will post a message to the Windows event log with the details.

Tracking Documents

BizTalk Server includes a Web-based tracking application that will help you see the activity on your server. This application is automatically installed at `http://servername/BizTalkDTA/` when you install BizTalk. This application uses ActiveX controls to allow you to query and display information from the BizTalk server's internal database. This information includes details of documents that have been sent or received by BizTalk Server and of interchanges between applications using BizTalk Server.

The tracking application allows you to perform these tasks:

- Search for interchanges and documents by agreement.
- Search for interchanges and documents by organization.
- Search for interchanges and documents by date.
- Search for data in fields captured by BizTalk Server.
- View the details and data of an interchange.
- View an activity log for an interchange.
- View document details.
- View document data in its native format or XML.

BizTalk Server Administrator

BizTalk Server Administrator is a Microsoft Management Console (MMC)–based application that gives you administrative access to the operations of a BizTalk server. Figure 22.9 shows the BizTalk Server Administrator.

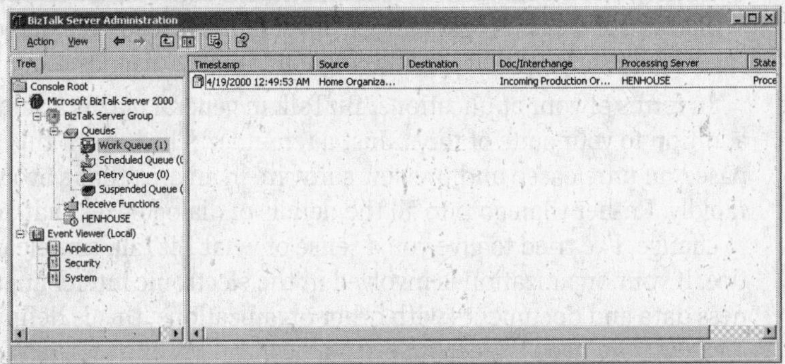

FIGURE 22.9: BizTalk Server Administrator

Just like any other MMC-based application, BizTalk Server Administrator arranges its functionality in a hierarchy. As you select nodes in the TreeView on the left side of the MMC window, details on those nodes appear in the list view on the right side of the window.

The topmost node is the Microsoft BizTalk Server 2000 node. This node allows you to create new BizTalk Server Groups.

The next level down is the BizTalk Server Group. A BizTalk Server Group is an arbitrary group of servers containing one or more computers. If you click a group node, the list view will show the status of all the servers in that group. A group also lets you add a new server.

The next level below the BizTalk Server Group includes three node types. These are the queues, the receive functions, and the servers themselves.

The queues node includes work, scheduled, retry, and suspended queues. Each of these shows the documents that are currently contained in the queue when the queue node is selected. Information displayed includes a time stamp, the current state of the work item, a description of any error, the source and destination organizations, the name of the document or interchange, and the interchange ID.

The receive functions node shows all of the receive functions on this server. A receive function is a BizTalk Server polling job. For example, to receive documents that are dropped off on an FTP server you need to set up a receive function that polls that server looking for new documents. From this node you can create new file, FTP, or MSMQ receive functions.

The server node shows the status of the selected server. You can start or stop the BizTalk Server from this node.

Finally, the BizTalk Server Administration console also shows the Windows 2000 event logs. This is convenient because BizTalk posts errors to the application log, making it a valuable diagnostic tool.

In terms of your applications, BizTalk in general makes a valuable addition to your suite of tools. Just a reminder: The bulk of this chapter is based on unreleased and preview software in an area that's evolving rapidly. Rather than go into all the details of dialog boxes that are certain to change, I've tried to give you a sense of what BizTalk can mean in practice. If your organization is involved in the electronic interchange of business data and documents with other organizations, this is definitely an area that you need to keep an eye on.

WHAT'S NEXT?

Now that you've experienced the different elements of a Web application, as well as a few technologies that enhance your projects, it's time to actually get your hands dirty with some specific examples. The rest of this book is dedicated to building typical Web projects. Using the tools you've learned, you'll create sample code and try new techniques that can be used in just about any type of Web project.

PART VI
Building Real-World Web Applications

Chapter 23

Building the User Interface

The first sample you'll design is an e-commerce store, or at least the key aspects of one. In the next chapter, you'll focus on the main ingredient of any store: the shopping basket. For now, we will work on building the core foundation of the store including navigation, site structure, and product data.

Adapted from *Visual Basic® Developer's Guide to E-Commerce with ASP and SQL Server™*, by Noel Jerke

ISBN 0-7821-2621-9 752 pages $49.99

Designing the Store Foundation

Our store is going to be made up of multiple ASP pages combined with a Visual Basic application for business rule management. These pages will be working against the database structure available on the Sybex Web site. Table 23.1 defines the pages in our store and the function of each. Most of the pages will not be reviewed here, but you can find a complete analysis of each part of this application in the *Visual Basic Developer's Guide to E-Commerce* cited on the first page of this chapter.

TABLE 23.1: ECStore Web Pages

Page	Description
`Footer.asp`	Included at the bottom of every display page on the site. It provides the closing structure for the navigation and primary content area.
`Header.asp`	Included at the top of every display page on the site. It provides the navigation structure.
`AddItem.asp`	Adds items to the shopping basket when the user selects a product.
`Basket.asp`	Displays all of the items in the user's shopping basket.
`Confirmed.asp`	Provides a confirmation message and thank-you when the shopper has completed an order.
`Default.asp`	Home page for the store.
`DeleteItem.asp`	Deletes an item from the shopping basket.
`Dept.asp`	Lists all of the departments in the store.
`EmailPassword.asp`	E-mails the profile password related to the specified profile e-mail address.
`EmptyBasket.asp`	Empties all items from the shopping basket.
`Global.asa`	Application level file that is executed each time a new application or session is started.
`OrderHistoryDisplay.asp`	Displays the order history of the shopper.
`OrderReceipt.asp`	Displays an on-screen order receipt.
`OrderStatus.asp`	Login page for the shopper's order history.

CONTINUED ➞

TABLE 23.1 continued: ECStore Web Pages

Page	Description
Payment.asp	Provides data input for the shopper's billing information.
Product.asp	Displays information on the specified product.
Products.asp	Displays all of the products in the specified department.
Profile.asp	Login page for the shopper to retrieve and edit their profile.
ProfileDisplay.asp	Displays the profile data for the specified shopper.
Search.asp	Provides search capabilities for finding products in the database.
Shipping.asp	Provides data input for the shipping information of the order.
UpdateBasket.asp	Updates the shopper basket items with the specified new quantities.
UpdateProfile.asp	Updates the shopper's profile.
ValidatePayment.asp	Validates the payment data entered by the shopper.
ValidateShipping.asp	Validates the shipping data entered by the shopper.

It is these core pages that will provide the environment for facilitating the shopping experience. There is an expected shopping process that we are trying to facilitate through the navigation and the various pages.

NOTE

To retrieve the referenced files and programs from the Sybex Web site, go to `www.sybex.com` and search for this book using its title or ISBN (2971).

Site Architecture

When the shoppers enters the store, they will typically follow one of several steps for beginning their shopping process. Ideally they will look at department and product data through browsing the store, or they may search for something specific.

We hope this browsing phase culminates in items added to the shopping basket and ready for purchase. The shoppers then have the opportunity to manage their shopping baskets and then check out. The checkout process will collect all of their key data, such as shipping and billing information. Once processed, they then can check their order history through a profile they set up online. Figure 23.1 diagrams the shopping process.

The navigation we design into the system certainly needs to provide a way to jump between any state that is appropriate. But, for example, we cannot allow shoppers to go to the payment page if there are no items in their shopping baskets. Likewise, if we go to the shopping basket before adding any items to it, we need to provide appropriate feedback to the users.

Finally, it is going to be critical that we maintain *state* throughout the entire process. We will need to be able to track the current shopper's ID so we can maintain their basket. Also, we will need to be able to maintain state on data entered into the various forms. For example, if the shopper gets to the payment page and decides they want one more item, we don't want them to have to enter their shipping information all over again.

To make this happen, we will be using session variables throughout the site to track data.

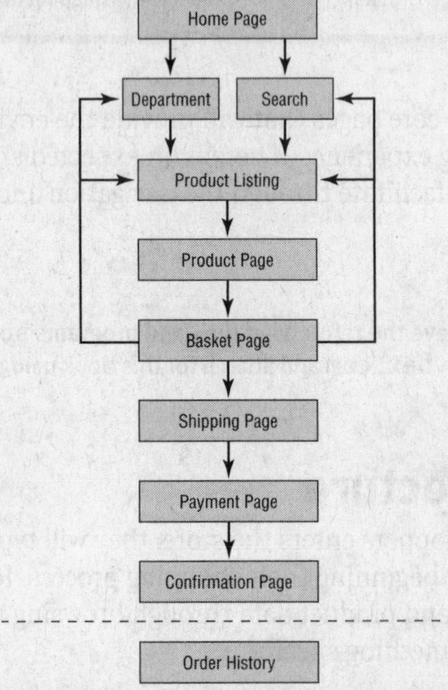

FIGURE 23.1: Shopping process

Project Setup

As shown in Chapter 10, we will need to set up a new development project on our Web server. Our sample store for this demonstration is called Wild Willie's CD Store. The store is going to sell some very unusual CD titles, some that even the biggest of Internet retailers would probably not carry (or want to carry).

The Sybex Web site contains SQL scripts for populating department and product data into the database structure and will be reviewed below. The Web site also contains all of the graphics for our store.

From the coding side of the store, we are going to keep things fairly simple in our ASP code. And, as you will see, good solid page-level development and breakout of code will more than meet our needs for the store development. The naming conventions in the code are straightforward and easy to understand.

One of the first pages we need to develop is the `global.asa` file, as shown in Listing 23.1. Functions from within this file are called every time a new application is started (when the Web site is started/restarted) or a new user session is started. It contains specific functions that are fired off depending on the request. For example, the `Application_OnStart` function will be executed when the Web site application is started. This is useful for initializing any parameters or settings upon startup. There is also a corresponding `Application_OnEnd` function. While we don't use these two in our sample store, they might be useful for storing global data such as statistical counts across the store, variable data related to the specific server, etc.

We do use the `Session_OnStart` function. Remember that we will need to track the ID of the shopper throughout the store. Of course, when the shopper first visits, there is no shopper ID, and we will eventually need to see if they have their profile set as a cookie on their machine. To ensure that this key variable is initialized properly, the `IDShopper` variable is initially set to 0. It will later get set to either a new shopper ID or an existing one from a stored profile on the user's machine. There is also a corresponding `Session_OnEnd` function, which is not used.

Listing 23.1: `Global.asa` **Page**

```
<SCRIPT LANGUAGE=VBScript RUNAT=Server>

'   ****************************************
'   Global.ASA - Fired off when each new
```

Part vi

```
    '  session is started for a new shopper.
    '  ***************************************

    '  Subroutine is fired off when the
    '  session starts.
    Sub Session_OnStart

    '  Start the shopper ID at 0.
    session("idShopper") = 0

    End Sub

    </SCRIPT>
```

The last little item we are going to need is an ODBC Data Source Name (DSN) to connect to the database. In this case we are using a File DSN, WildWillieCDs. Next we will be ready to prep the store with some sample data so the coding can begin.

NOTE

You may also consider using OLE DB as a connection. For building and testing purposes, using the SA username and the corresponding password makes the development process simpler. But be sure to lock down the security in production.

Loading Data

Since we haven't built the management side of the store yet, we need to go ahead and populate the store with some sample data. The Sybex site provides SQL scripts for inserting the data. But let's go ahead and review the data inserts to ensure it is clear how the tables are being populated.

First we will need to load the department table with department data. This will include the department name, the description, and the corresponding image. Listing 23.2 shows a sample insert.

Listing 23.2: Loading Departments

```
insert into department
  (chrDeptName, txtDeptDesc,
  chrDeptImage)
values('Funky Wacky Music',
  'The craziest music you have ever seen.' +
  ' Is it even music?','funk.gif')
```

Next we will need to load product data and then designate which department the products are assigned to. The first SQL insert shown below builds the product information. One sample CD, *Joe Bob's Thimble Sounds*, is added into the products table.

TIP

Be sure to check for single quotes and double them for proper insert into the database. Chapter 10 demonstrated this technique.

The next sample SQL code, in Listing 23.3, ties our new product with one of the departments. In this case, we are tying together the first product inserted with the first department inserted by building the relationship in the DepartmentProducts table.

NOTE

Be sure to run the `LoadDepts.sql` script first and then the `LoadProducts.sql` script. The second depends on the departments being in place and in the specified order.

Listing 23.3: Loading Products

```
insert into products
  (chrProductName, txtDescription,
  chrProductImage, intPrice,
  intActive)
values('Joe Bob''s Thimble Sounds',
   'Great thimble music that you will love!',
   'thimble.gif', 1000, 1)
insert departmentproducts
   (idDepartment, idProduct) values(1,1)
```

Some of our products will have attributes that we need to load. For example, in Listing 23.4, we will have T-shirts that the shopper selects from among different colors and sizes. The following two SQL statements insert our two attribute types, Size and Color, for our sample store.

Listing 23.4: Adding Product Attributes

```
insert into attributecategory
  (chrCategoryName) values('Size')
insert into attributecategory
  (chrCategoryName) values('Color')
```

Next we need to load in the names of the attributes in these categories. For example, in the Size category we will have Small, Medium, Large, and X-Large. The following SQL insert statements in Listing 23.5 create the attributes for the different categories.

Listing 23.5: Creating Attribute Categories

```
insert into attribute
  (chrAttributeName, idAttributeCategory)
  values('Small', 1)
insert into attribute
  (chrAttributeName, idAttributeCategory)
  values('Medium', 1)
insert into attribute
  (chrAttributeName, idAttributeCategory)
  values('Large', 1)
insert into attribute
  (chrAttributeName, idAttributeCategory)
  values('X-Large', 1)

insert into attribute
  (chrAttributeName, idAttributeCategory)
  values('Red', 2)
insert into attribute
  (chrAttributeName, idAttributeCategory)
  values('Blue', 2)
insert into attribute
  (chrAttributeName, idAttributeCategory)
  values('Green', 2)
insert into attribute
  (chrAttributeName, idAttributeCategory)
  values('White', 2)
```

Finally, we have to hook up our products to the different attributes. In this case, it will be the two T-shirts in Wild Willie's store. The following SQL statements in Listing 23.6 build the combination.

Listing 23.6: Assigning Attributes

```
insert into productattribute
  (idAttribute, idProduct)
  values(1, 9)
insert into productattribute
  (idAttribute, idProduct)
```

```
    values(2, 9)
  insert into productattribute
    (idAttribute, idProduct)
    values(3, 9)
  insert into productattribute
    (idAttribute, idProduct)
    values(4, 9)
```

This initial load of data will take care of the data requirements in this chapter. We will be loading additional data throughout this section.

BUILDING THE PAGE STRUCTURE

A good store design should provide consistent navigation throughout the shopping experience. Key navigational elements include a link to the department page, the shopping basket, the checkout process, and product searching.

In addition, we will provide a link to retrieve order status and to manage the shopper's profile, which will be retrievable between visits. Figure 23.2 shows the page layout.

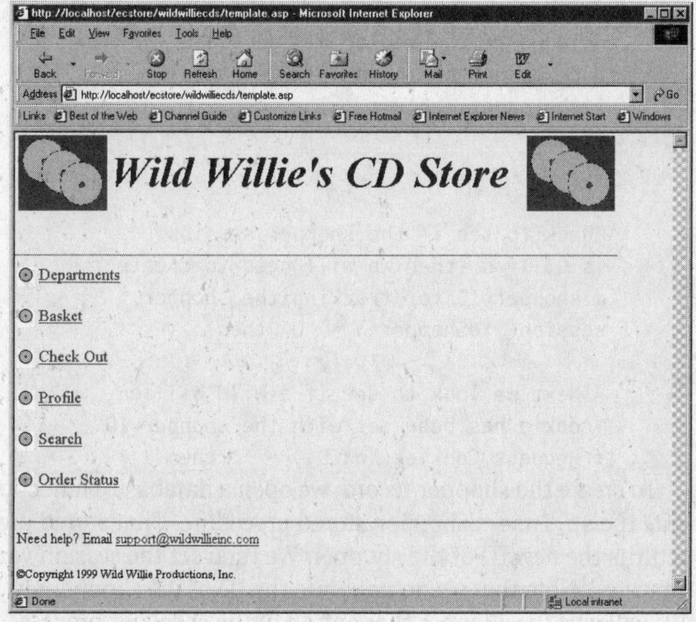

FIGURE 23.2: The store's navigation interface

Also note the elements at the bottom of the page. We will want to wrap our pages in a navigational structure that will be easy to manage. For example, perhaps down the road we want to add in a link to the specials offered on the site. We do not want to have to change all of the pages in the store to have this new link. Instead, we want to encapsulate the header and footer into include files that will build the page structure.

Header and Footer Pages

The `Header.asp` page, beginning in Listing 23.7, will build the structure of the site. It will also handle some key logic for setting up the shopper. The first section of the page handles checking to see if the ID of the shopper is set to 0 in the session (`idShopper`) variable.

If so, then we have to do a couple of tasks. The first is to see if there is a cookie set on the user's machine that contains a previous shopper ID. To check this, the WWCD cookie value is checked. If it is blank, then we know we need to create a new shopper tracking record. If not, then we will read the ID from the cookie.

Listing 23.7: `Header.asp` **Page**

```
<!-   Header.asp - This page should be
  included at the top of all pages in the
  store to define the navigation and layout
  of the pages. ->

<%

'  Check to see if the shopper session
'  is 0. If so then we will need to create
'  a shopper ID for tracking the shopper.
if session("idShopper") = "0" then

   '  Next we look to see if a Wild Willie
   ' cookie has been set with the shopper ID.
  if Request.Cookies("WWCD") = "" then
```

To create the shopper record, we open a database connection and execute the `sp_InsertShopper` stored procedure. That stored procedure returns the new ID of the shopper. We then set the session variable and continue. Note that we do not write the ID of the shopper out to a cookie. We will give the shopper that option in the checkout process.

Listing 23.8: `Header.asp` Page Continued

```
    '  Create an ADO database connection
    set dbShopper = server.createobject _
      ("adodb.connection")

    '  Create a record set
    set rsShopper = server.CreateObject _
      ("adodb.recordset")

    '  Open the connection using our ODBC
    '  file DSN
    dbShopper.open("filedsn=WildWillieCDs")

    '  Call the stored procedure to insert a new
    '  shopper since there is no cookie.
    sql = "execute sp_InsertShopper"

    '  Execute the SQL statement
    set rsShopper = dbShopper.Execute(sql)
    '  Set the shopper ID in the session
    '  variable.
    session("idShopper") = rsShopper("idShopper")
    else
```

If there is a cookie, then we will retrieve the shopper ID from the cookie. But that is not all we need to do. We also want to ensure that we retrieve the last open basket if there is one so the shopper can continue where they left off. The shopper ID is stored in the session variable. We then execute the `sp_RetrieveLastBasket` stored procedure to return the last basket. If a basket is returned, then the ID is stored in the session variable.

Listing 23.9: `Header.asp` Page Continued

```
    '  Retrieve the shopper ID from the cookie
    session("idShopper") = _
      Request.Cookies("WWCD")

    '  Create an ADO database connection
    set dbShopperBasket = server.createobject _
      ("adodb.connection")

    '  Create a record set
```

```
        set rsShopperBasket = server.CreateObject _
          ("adodb.recordset")

        '  Open the connection using our ODBC
        '  file DSN
        dbShopperBasket.open _
          ("filedsn=WildWillieCDs")

        '  Retrieve the last basket that the
        '  shopper used. Note that only baskets
        '  that are not completed will be returned.
        sql = "execute sp_RetrieveLastBasket " & _
          session("idShopper")

        '  Execute the SQL statement
        set rsShopperBasket = _
          dbShopperBasket.Execute(sql)
        '  Check to see if a basket has
        '  been returned.
        if rsShopperBasket.EOF <> true then

          '  Set the session ID of the basket
          session("idBasket") = _
            rsShopperBasket("idBasket")

        end if

        '  Indicate that a profile has NOT
        '  been retrieved.
        session("ProfileRetrieve") = "0"

        end if

      end if

      %>
```

Now that we have taken care of the business of setting up the shopper and the basket, we are ready to format the header of the page. Several tables are created that will hold the key sections of the page.

The first section of the page is the top row where the CD logo and the title of the page are shown. Following that table is the table that structures the navigation section of the page. The first column in the first row builds out the navigation links for each of the key sections. The second column is where the core content of the page will be displayed. Note that the `footer.asp` will contain the appropriate closing tags for the column, row, and table.

Listing 23.10: `Header.asp` **Page Continued**

```
<!- Set the default body tag for all
  of the pages ->
<body bgcolor="lightgoldenrodyellow"
  topmargin="0" leftmargin="0">

<!- This table defines the header
  for the page ->
<table width="680" border="0">
<tr>
  <td align="right" valign="center">
    <img src="images/cdlogo.gif"></td>
  <td><font size="7" color="blue">
    <b><i>Wild Willie's CD Store
    </i></b></font>
  </td>
  <td align="right" valign="center">
    <img src="images/cdlogo.gif">
  </td>
</tr>
</table>

<br><br>
<!- Dividing line ->
<hr width="680" align="left">

<!- This table defines the navigation
  for the page and the structure for
  placing the page content.->
<table width="680" border="0">
<tr>
  <!- Navigation column ->
  <td width="130" valign="top">
    <img src="images/cdbullet.gif"
      border="0" align="center">
    <font color="blue" size="4">
    <a href="dept.asp">Departments</a>
```

Part vi

```
    </font><br><br>
    <img src="images/cdbullet.gif"
      border="0" align="center">
    <font color="blue" size="4">
    <a href="basket.asp">Basket</a>
    </font>
    <br><br>
    <img src="images/cdbullet.gif"
      border="0" align="center">
    <font color="blue" size="4">
    <a href="shipping.asp">Check Out</a>
    </font>
    <br><br>
    <img src="images/cdbullet.gif"
      border="0" align="center">
    <font color="blue" size="4">
    <a href="profile.asp">Profile</a>
    </font>
    <br><br>
    <img src="images/cdbullet.gif"
      border="0" align="center">
    <font color="blue" size="4">
    <a href="search.asp">Search</a>
    </font>
    <br><br>
    <img src="images/cdbullet.gif"
      border="0" align="center">
    <font color="blue" size="4">
    <a href="OrderStatus.asp">
    Order Status</a></font>
    <br><br>
  </td>

<!- Spacing column between navigation
  and core content area    ->
  <td width="10"> </td>

<!- Start the column for the main
  page content ->
  <td valign="top" width="540">

<!- Note that the footer.asp include must
```

```
close out any page that has the header
include.The table will be closed out  ->
```

We used two stored procedures in this page. The first, sp_InsertShopper, creates a new row in the shopper table (see Listing 23.11). A new value is set in the identity column. We return that by referencing the @@identity system variable, which contains the last value.

Listing 23.11: sp_InsertShopper **Stored Procedure**

```
/*  Used to insert a new shopper
    into the database.
*/
CREATE PROCEDURE sp_InsertShopper AS

/*  Insert the shopper into the database and
    set the first and last name to blank */
insert into shopper
  (chrusername, chrpassword)
  values('', '')

/*  Return the identity column ID
    of the shopper */
select idShopper = @@identity
```

The second stored procedure, sp_RetrieveLastBasket, will return the last active basket the shopper was using (see Listing 23.12). It checks to ensure that only baskets that are not part of a completed order are returned. And, to return the last basket at the top of the record set, the DESC syntax returns them in reverse order.

Listing 23.12: sp_RetrieveLastBasket **Stored Procedure**

```
/*  Stored Procedure to retrieve the last
    basket for the shopper. */
CREATE PROCEDURE sp_RetrieveLastBasket

/*  Pass in the ID of the shopper */
@idShopper int

AS

/*  Select the basket data for all baskets
    assigned to the shopper and where the
    order was never finished. We sort the
```

```
      data in descending order so that the
      last basket is returned first. */
select * from basket
where idShopper = @idShopper and
   intOrderPlaced =0 and intTotal = 0
order by dtCreated DESC
```

Following the header, we will need to include the `footer.asp` in the bottom of the page. This page closes out the tags started in the header. And in this case, it gives us an opportunity to show a copyright notice, support e-mail, etc. Listing 23.13 shows the `footer.asp` page.

Listing 23.13: `Footer.asp` **Page**

```
<!-
   Footer.asp - This page should be included
   at the bottom of all pages in the store to
   close out the structure of the page.
->
<!-  Close out the content column
   started in the header ->
   </td>

<!-  Close out the row ->
</tr>

<!-  Start a new row to display the
      footer information ->
<tr>
<!-  Start a column, note the display
   across the four columns ->
   <td colspan="4" width="680">
      <HR>
      <!- Display the help email ->
      Need help?  Email
      <a href="mailto:support@wildwillieinc.com">
      support@wildwillieinc.com</a>
      <BR><BR>
      <!- Show the copy right ->
      <font size="2">&copy;Copyright 1999
      Wild Willie Productions, Inc.</font>
   </td>
</tr>
</table>
```

It is important that on all pages that display content to the user, these two pages are included at the top and bottom of the page. If only one or the other is included, then the page will not build properly because they contain opening and closing tags that relate to one another.

Building the Home Page

The home page for the store puts our header and footer into place and gives an entry point for the shopper. Right after the opening tags for the page, we include the `header.asp` page by using the ASP include syntax.

Then we put in the core information on the page, which in this case is just a welcome message. Following that, we close out the page with the `footer.asp` include. The home page code is shown in Listing 23.14.

Listing 23.14: `Default.asp` **Code**

```
<%@ Language=VBScript %>
<HTML>
<!-
  Default.asp - Home page for the store
  and provides a welcome message.
->

<!- #include file="include/header.asp" ->

<!- Opening screen text ->
Welcome to <font color="blue">
<B>Wild Willie's CRAZY CD</b></font>
store!  We have some of the wildest CDs
that not even the biggest of the CD stores
have.<br><br>

Select departments on the left to start
your shopping experience!

<!- #include file="include/footer.asp" ->

</BODY>
</HTML>
```

Figure 23.3 shows the store home page in all of its glory. The sample code on the Sybex Web site has all of the images appropriately linked, etc., to make everything pop up in the right place. Next we will move on to exploring the interactive functionality of the store.

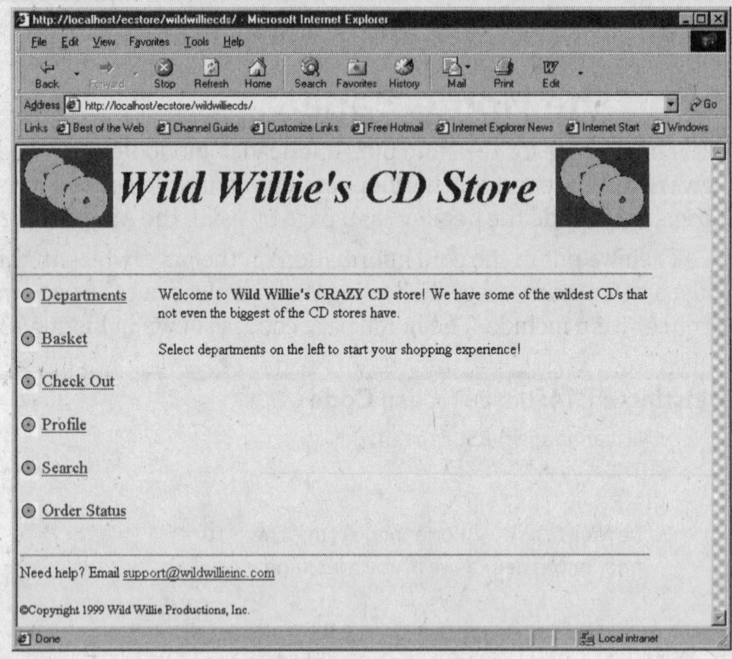

FIGURE 23.3: Default page for the store

Browsing Departments and Products

This section will focus on setting up a way for consumers to browse our store's departments and products. Now that we have the core page structure and the database loaded, we are ready to get started.

From a marketing standpoint, this can be the most critical aspect of enticing the consumer to spend some time window-shopping and maybe coming in. What is represented here is the underlying core functionality of the store. Yes, that may mean one even better than Wild Willie's.

Departments

The department page is built to display a list of departments in the store. In this case, we are going to show the department name and a corresponding image that represents the department. Listing 23.15 is the code for our department page. (It continues in listings 23.16 and 23.17.)

The page starts out with our standard structure that will have the header included.

Listing 23.15: `Dept.asp` **Page**

```
<%@ Language=VBScript %>
<HTML>
<!-
  Dept.asp - Displays the departments in the
  stores.
->

<!- #include file="include/header.asp" ->

<b>Select from a department below:</b><BR><BR>
```

Next we create a database connection and retrieve all of the departments in the database with the `sp_retrieveDepts` stored procedure. Then we are ready to begin looping through the departments and displaying the data.

Listing 23.16: `Dept.asp` **Page Continued**

```
<%

'  Create an ADO database connection
set dbDepts = server.createobject _
  ("adodb.connection")

'  Create a record set
set rsDepts = server.CreateObject _
  ("adodb.recordset")

'  Open the connection using our ODBC file DSN
dbDepts.open("filedsn=WildWillieCDs")

'  Call the stored procedure to retrieve
'  the departments in the store.
```

```
sql = "execute sp_RetrieveDepts"

'  Execute the SQL statement
set rsDepts = dbdepts.Execute(sql)

'  We will use a flag to rotate images
'  from left to right
Flag = 0
```

To make the listing visually interesting, we will rotate the department image display from left to right in relation to the text. With each pass, we retrieve the department name, the department image, and the ID of the department.

In each case, we are linking the image and name to the `products.asp` page where the products for the department will be listed. With each loop we check a flag and build the link appropriately.

Finally the page is closed out with the `footer.asp` link and the closing end tags.

Listing 23.17: `Dept.asp` Page Continued

```
'  Loop through the departments
do until rsDepts.EOF

'  Retrieve the field values to display the
'  name, image and link to the ID of the
'  department
chrDeptName = rsDepts("chrDeptName")
chrDeptImage = rsDepts("chrDeptImage")
idDepartment = rsDepts("idDepartment")

'  Check the flag
If Flag = 0 then

  '  Flip the flag
  Flag = 1

%>

  <!-  Display the image and the name
  of the department. In this case the image
  is on the left and the name on the right.
  ->
```

```
    <a href=
    "products.asp?idDept=<%=idDepartment%>">
    <img src="images/<%=chrDeptImage%>"
      align="middle" border=0>
    <%=chrDeptName%></a><BR><BR>
  <% else %>

    <!- Display the image and the name of
    the department. In this case the image is on
    the right and the name on the left.
    ->
    <a href=
    "products.asp?idDept=<%=idDepartment%>">
    <%=chrDeptName%>
    <img src="images/<%=chrDeptImage%>"
      align="middle" border=0>
    </a><BR><BR>

  <%

    '  Reset the flag
    Flag = 0

  end if

  '  Move to the next row.
  rsDepts.MoveNext

  loop

  %>

  <!- #include file="include/footer.asp" ->

  </BODY>
  </HTML>
```

In this page, we use one stored procedure, sp_RetrieveDepts, to return the products in the department (see Listing 23.18). In this case, we have a simple select statement that returns the data.

Listing 23.18: `sp_RetrieveDepts` **Stored Procedure**

```
/*  Stored procedure to retrieve all of
    the departments in the database */
CREATE PROCEDURE sp_RetrieveDepts AS

/*  Select all of the departments data */
select * from department
```

With that, we have our first interactive display page built for the store. Figure 23.4 shows the page with the sample data populated. Note that the images rotate from left to right around the product name. And each department is linked to display the products in the department.

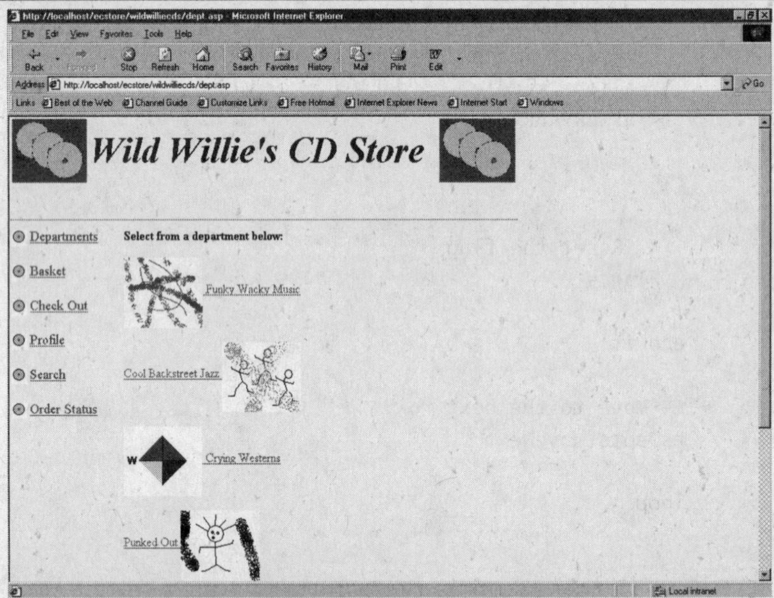

FIGURE 23.4: Department page

TIP

A couple of tips on designing the department page: If you have a large number of departments, you may want to list them in multiple columns instead of in a direct top-to-bottom list. This would simply require a bit of logic to rotate back and forth between columns in a table.

Next we move to the page that will display the products in the department that was selected from the `dept.asp` page. The ID of the department is passed on the URL to the `products.asp` page, as shown in Listing 23.19 (and continuing in listings 23.20, 23.21, and 23.22).

The first thing we do in the page is to create a record set, by which we can query the database. The `sp_RetrieveDept` stored procedure is used to return the department data for the specified department. The ID passed on the URL is passed into the stored procedure.

Listing 23.19: `Products.asp` **Page**

```
<%@ Language=VBScript %>
<HTML>
<!-
Products.asp - This page displays the
products in a department.
->

<!- #include file="include/header.asp" ->

<%

'  Create an ADO database connection
set dbDepartment = server.createobject _
  ("adodb.connection")

'  Create the record set
set rsDepartment = server.CreateObject _
  ("adodb.recordset")

'  Open the connection using our ODBC file DSN
dbDepartment.open("filedsn=WildWillieCDs")

'  Build the SQL statement. We are calling the
'  stored procedure to retrieve the department
'  information and passing in the ID of the
'  department
sql = "execute sp_RetrieveDept " & _
  request("idDept")
```

Once we have the SQL statement built, we are ready to retrieve the department data and display it as the header of the page. We will show the department image, name, and description. This will help to serve as a visual placeholder to indicate where the shopper has navigated.

For future use, we store the ID of the department requested in a session variable. That way when the shopper goes to the basket page, a link can be built back to the department they were shopping in. Thus, if the shopper is really interested in jazz music, they can quickly jump back to the Jazz department and keep shopping.

Listing 23.20: `Products.asp` **Page Continued**

```
'  Retrieve the departments
set rsDepartment = dbDepartment.Execute(sql)

'  Retrieve the product information
txtDescription = rsDepartment("txtDeptDesc")
chrDeptImage = rsDepartment("chrDeptImage")
chrDeptName = rsDepartment("chrDeptName")

'  Store the ID of the department being
'  referenced in the LastIDDept session
'  variable. This will allow us
'  to build a link on the basket back
'  to the department for further shopping.
session("LastIDDept") = request("idDept")

%>

<!-  Display the department image and name ->
<CENTER>
  <img src="images/<%=chrDeptImage%>"
  align="middle">
  <FONT size="4">
  <B><%=chrDeptName%></b></font><BR><BR>
</CENTER>

<!-  Display the description ->
<%=txtDescription%>  Select a product:<BR><BR>
```

Next we are ready to retrieve the products in the department. We once again create a new database connection and prepare a stored procedure to return all of the products. The ID of the department is passed to the stored procedure.

Listing 23.21: `Products.asp` **Page Continued**

```
<%

'  Create an ADO database connection
set dbProducts = server.createobject _
   ("adodb.connection")

'  Create the record set
set rsProducts = server.CreateObject _
   ("adodb.recordset")

'  Open the connection using our ODBC file DSN
dbProducts.open("filedsn=WildWillieCDs")

'  Build the sql statement to retrieve
'  the products in the department. The ID
'  of the department is passed in.
sql = "execute sp_RetrieveDeptProducts " & _
   request("idDept")

'  Execute the SQL statement and retrieve
'  the record set
set rsProducts = dbProducts.Execute(sql)
```

As with the department page, we are ready to display the images of the products rotating from left to right. As we loop through the products, a flag keeps track of the position of the last image.

With each product we are displaying the product name and the product image. As with the department, we link the image and name. In this case, we are linking to the product page and passing on the URL the ID of the product. Following that, we close out the page with the standard include and tags.

Listing 23.22: `Products.asp` **Page Continued**

```
'  We are going to rotate the images from left
'  to right.
Flag = 0

'  Loop through the products record set
do until rsProducts.EOF
```

```
' Retrieve the product information to
' be displayed.
chrProductName = rsProducts("chrProductName")
chrProductImage = rsProducts("chrProductImage")
idProduct = rsProducts("idProduct")

' Check the display flag. We will rotate the
' product images from left to right.
If flag = 0 then

  ' Set the flag
  flag = 1

%>

  <!- Build the link to the product
  information. ->
  <a href=
  "product.asp?idProduct=<%=idProduct%>">
  <img src=
  "images/products/sm_<%=chrProductImage%>"
  align="middle" border="0">
  <%=chrProductName%></a><BR><BR>

<% else %>

  <!- Build the link to the product
  information. ->
  <a href=
  "product.asp?idProduct=<%=idProduct%>">
  <%=chrProductName%>
  <img src=
  "images/products/sm_<%=chrProductImage%>"
  align="middle" border="0"></a><BR><BR>
<%

  ' Reset the flag
  Flag = 0

end if

' Move to the next row
```

```
rsproducts.movenext

loop

%>

<!- #include file="include/footer.asp" ->

</BODY>
</HTML>
```

We are using two stored procedures in this page. The first stored procedure retrieves the department by the ID passed into it (see Listing 23.23).

Listing 23.23: `sp_RetrieveDept` **Stored Procedure**

```
/*  Retrieve the department data */
CREATE PROCEDURE sp_RetrieveDept

/*  Pass in the ID of the department */
@idDepartment int

AS

/*  Select all of the data on the
    department */
select * from department
where idDepartment = @idDepartment
```

The second stored procedure returns the products assigned to the department (see Listing 23.24). In this case, we have to join together the Department table, the DepartmentProducts table, and the Products table. We are going to return all products where there is a matching department ID in the DepartmentProducts table.

Listing 23.24: `sp_RetrieveDeptProducts` **Stored Procedure**

```
/*  Stored Procedure to retrieve the products
    assigned to the specified department */
CREATE PROCEDURE sp_RetrieveDeptProducts


/*  Pass in the ID of the department */
@idDept int

AS
```

```
/*  Select the product data from the
    related products */
select * from products, departmentproducts

where products.idproduct =
  departmentproducts.idproduct and
  departmentproducts.iddepartment = @idDept
```

Now we can click any department listed on `dept.asp` and go to a listing of the products on the `products.asp` page. We can surf through each of the departments quickly by clicking the departments link on the navigation bar. Figure 23.5 shows the Funky Wacky Music department in our store.

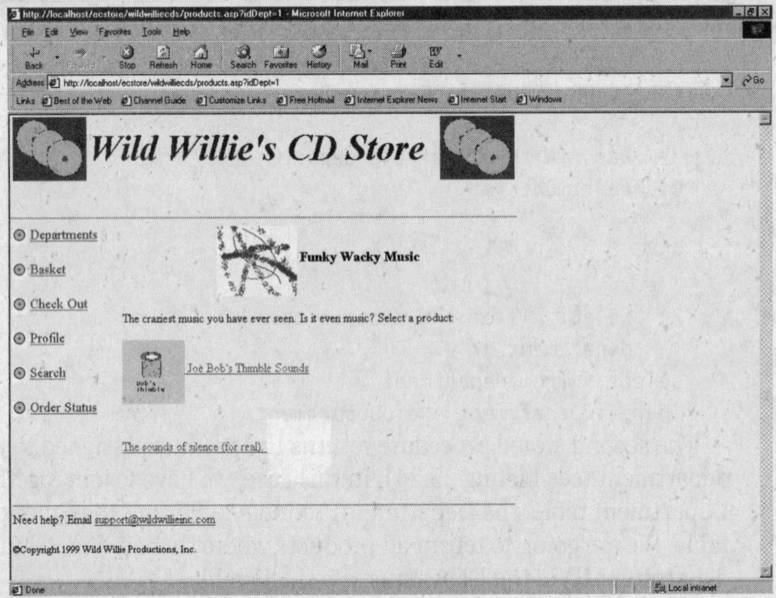

FIGURE 23.5: Department page

In this case we have two products tied to that department, *Joe Bob's Thimble Sounds* and *The Sounds of Silence* (for real). Note the department information display right below the header for the page.

If we click back to the department listing, we can select a new department, such as the Crying Westerns. Again, in Figure 23.6 we see the left-to-right positioning of the product images.

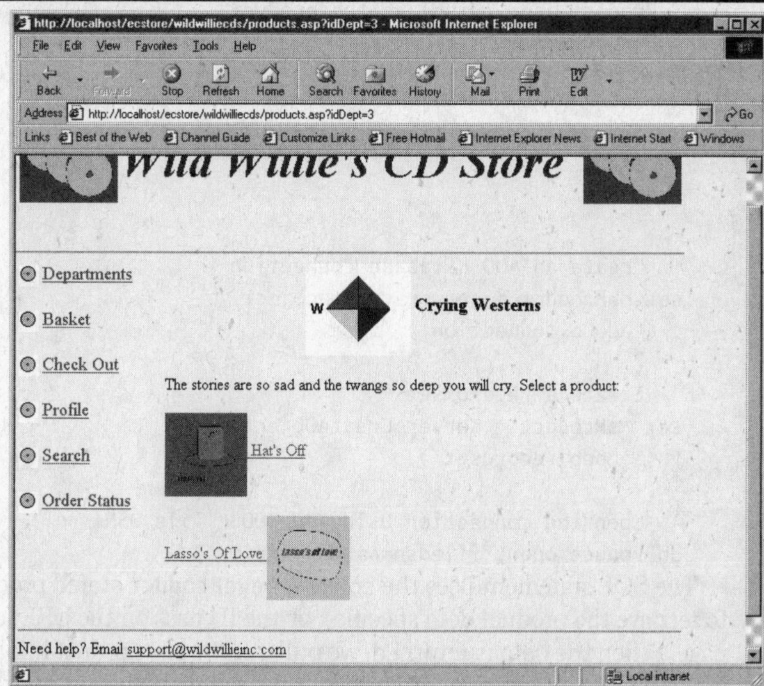

FIGURE 23.6: Crying Westerns Department

Now we are ready to actually look at some product data, the ultimate goal of the shopper.

Products

The product page, as shown in Listing 23.25 (and continuing in listings 23.26, 23.27, 23.28, 23.29, and 23.30), displays the product data selected from the `products.asp` page. This is where the shopper will be able to peruse the data in more detail and make a purchasing decision.

The page starts out in the usual fashion with the header include, and creates a database connection so we can retrieve the product data.

Listing 23.25: `Product.asp` **Page**

```
<%@ Language=VBScript %>
<HTML>
<!–
```

```
    Product.asp - Displays the product
    information.
->

<!- #include file="include/header.asp" ->

<%

'  Create an ADO database connection
set dbProduct = server.createobject _
  ("adodb.connection")

'  Create a record set
set rsProduct = server.CreateObject _
  ("adodb.recordset")

'  Open the connection using our ODBC file DSN
dbProduct.open("filedsn=WildWillieCDs")
```

The SQL statement uses the `sp_RetrieveProduct` stored procedure to retrieve the product data specified by the ID pass on the URL to the page. When the data is returned, we pull out the key product information including the description, product image, product name, product price, and the ID of the product.

Listing 23.26: `Product.asp` **Page Continued**

```
'  Execute the stored procedure to retrieve
'  the product and pass in the id of the product.
sql = "execute sp_RetrieveProduct " & _
  request("idProduct")

' Execute the SQL statement
set rsProduct = dbProduct.Execute(sql)

'  Retrieve the product data
txtDescription = rsProduct("txtDescription")
chrProductImage = rsProduct("chrProductImage")
chrProductName = rsProduct("chrProductName")
intPrice = rsProduct("intPrice")
idProduct = rsProduct("idProduct")
%>
```

We create a form that will post to the `additem.asp` page. When the form is posted, it will pass the key data to add the item to the shopping basket and track it until order completion.

We then start the table to display the product data. The image is on the left, and the name, description, and price are in the right column. We also provide input for the shoppers to specify the quantities they wish to purchase.

You will also notice that a series of hidden fields have been built. These fields are used to make basic basket data quickly available in the `additem.asp` page.

Listing 23.27: `Product.asp` **Page Continued**

```
<!- The additem.asp page will be called to
     add the product to the basket ->
<form method="post" action="additem.asp">

<!-  The table will provide the layout
      structure for the product. ->
<table border="0" cellpadding="3"
  cellspacing="3">

<!-  Row to display the product image,
  name and description.  ->
<TR>
  <!-  Display the image ->
  <td><img src=
     "images/products/<%=chrProductImage%>">
  </td>

  <!-  Show the product name and
  description ->
  <td valign="top">
    <CENTER><b><font size="5">
    <%=chrProductName%></font></b></center>
    <BR><BR>
    <%=txtDescription%><BR><BR>
  </td>
</TR>

<!-  Show the product price. An input
  quantity box is created. Also, several
```

```
    hidden variables will hold
    key data for adding the product to the
    database. ->
  <TR>
    <TD align="center">
      <B>Price:
      <%=formatcurrency(intPrice/100, 2)%></b>
    </td>

    <TD align="center">
      <B>Quantity:
      <input type="text" value="1"
        name="quantity" size="2"></b>
      <input type="hidden"
        value="<%=idProduct%>"
        name="idProduct">
      <input type="hidden"
        value="<%=chrProductName%>"
        name="ProductName">
      <input type="hidden"
        value="<%=intPrice%>"
        name="ProductPrice">
    </td>
  </TR>
```

Next we have to check to see if there are attributes for the product. Remember that for the T-shirts we loaded color and size attributes. The code below makes an assumption that we have two attributes of color and size. The database certainly will support many different variations of attributes.

We use the sp_Attributes stored procedure to retrieve the attributes. The ID of the product is passed into the query. We then check to see whether any attributes are returned.

Listing 23.28: Product.asp **Page Continued**

```
<%

'  Create an ADO database connection
set dbAttributes = server.createobject _
  ("adodb.connection")

'  Create a record set
```

```
set rsAttributes = server.CreateObject _
  ("adodb.recordset")

'  Open the connection using our ODBC file DSN
dbAttributes.open("filedsn=WildWillieCDs")

'  Execute the stored procedure to retrieve
'  the attributes for the products.
sql = "execute sp_Attributes " & _
  request("idProduct")

'  Execute the SQL statement
set rsAttributes = dbProduct.Execute(sql)

'  Loop through and display the attributes
'  for the product.
if not rsAttributes.EOF then

%>
<TR>
  <!-  Color column ->
  <TD>
```

We first process the color attribute. An option box is built that will list all of the different options. The value of each option will be the actual name of the attribute. Long term, we want to simply store the attribute names.

HANDLING PRODUCT SKUS

Different businesses handle product SKUs differently. Some will have the core product ID as the primary SKU, with attributes as just part of the order data. That is how we are handling attributes in this store. But many store SKUs will be combinations of the product ID, any attributes, etc. There are a couple of considerations to keep in mind when storing attribute data and product data in general. First, if the product mix changes frequently, then storing prices, attributes, etc., in the order may be critical. We would not want a price change to happen (or a color change, etc.) right after a shopper orders and then have them charged the new price. In general, the

CONTINUED ⟶

tack taken in this store is to take a *snapshot* of the product information at purchase. In the context of a much larger inventory management system, this may not be necessary.

As we are looping through all of the attributes for the product, we watch for a change from the color attribute to the size attribute. When that happens, we are ready to move on to building the next select box of size attributes.

Building the size attributes follows the same pattern as building the color attributes. That pretty much ends the display of our product data. Now the shoppers can make their selections.

Listing 23.29: `Product.asp` **Page Continued**

```
Color:
<!-  Select box for display the color
options ->
<SELECT name="color">

  <%

  ' Loop through the attributes.
  do until rsAttributes.EOF

    '  Check to see if we have moved
    '  beyond the color attribute in
    '  the list.
    if rsAttributes("chrCategoryName") <> _
       "Color" then

       ' Exit the do loop
       exit do

    end if

    %>

    <!- Build the option value for the
    color. The value will be the ID of the
```

```
    color ->
    <option value="
    <%=rsAttributes("chrAttributeName")%>">
    <%=rsAttributes("chrAttributeName")%>

    <%

    '  Move to the next row
    rsAttributes.MoveNext

  loop

  %>

</select>
</TD>

<!-  Site column ->
<TD>
Size:

<!-  Start the size select box ->
<SELECT name="size">

  <%

  '  Loop through the size attributes
  do until rsAttributes.EOF

    %>

    <!-  Display the options ->
    <option value="
    <%=rsAttributes("chrAttributeName")%>">
    <%=rsAttributes("chrAttributeName")%>

    <%

    '  Move to the next row
    rsAttributes.MoveNext

  loop
```

```
    %>

  </select>

  </TD>

</TR>

<%

end if

%>
```

Finally, the page closes out with a Submit button, the closing form tag, the footer include, and the end of the page.

Listing 23.30: `Product.asp` **Page Continued**

```
<!-  Show the submit button ->
<TR>
  <td colspan="2" align="center">
    <input type="submit" value="Order"
    name="Submit">
  </td>
</tr>

</table>

</form>

<!- #include file="include/footer.asp" ->

</BODY>
</HTML>
```

The first stored procedure used is `sp_RetrieveProduct`. This simply returns the product data based on the ID of the product passed to it.

Listing 23.31: `sp_RetrieveProduct` **Stored Procedure**

```
/*  Retrieve the product data */
CREATE PROCEDURE sp_RetrieveProduct

/*  Pass in the ID of the product */
```

```
@idProduct int

AS

/*  Select the product data */
select * from products
where idProduct = @idProduct
```

The sp_Attributes stored procedure returns all of the attributes for the specified product. To do this, we have to join four tables, including Products, Product-Attribute, Attribute, and AttributeCategory. The AttributeCategory table stores the Size and Color categories. The AttributeName table defines the color and size names in the categories. And the ProductAttribute table is a lookup of which attributes apply to the specific product.

The data returned from the stored procedure is ordered by the category name. That way in our loops above we can go down the list of all attributes and build select boxes with each break in category.

Listing 23.32: `sp_Attributes` **Stored Procedure**

```
/*  Returns the attributes in the database
    for the specific product.
*/
CREATE PROCEDURE sp_Attributes

/*  Pass in the ID of the product */
@idProduct int

AS

/*  select statement to return attributes
    for the product. */
select products.idproduct,
  attribute.idattribute,
  attribute.chrattributename,
  attributecategory.chrcategoryname

from products, productattribute,
  attribute, attributecategory

where
```

```
    products.idproduct = @idProduct and
      productattribute.idproduct =
      @idProduct and
      productattribute.idattribute =
      attribute.idattribute and
      attribute.idattributecategory =
      attributecategory.idattributecategory
    order by chrcategoryname
```

That does it for the development of the product page. Primarily, the page is created for the display of the product data. The real magic begins to happen when the user decides to add the item to their basket.

Figure 23.7 shows one of our sample product pages. The product image is placed on the left with the product data on the right. The price shows directly below the image. To order the product, the shopper would click the Order button, which would then fire off the `additem.asp` page.

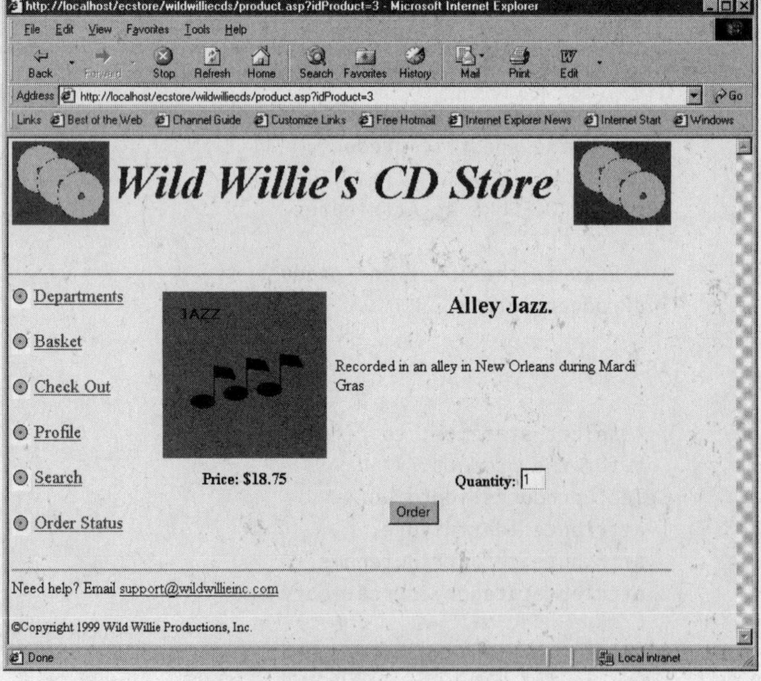

FIGURE 23.7: Product page for *Alley Jazz*

Figure 23.8 shows a product that has attributes. In this case it is the lovely and unique undershirt that costs $20. And, much to every shopper's delight, it comes in four different colors and four different sizes. The user will select a size and color combination and then add it to the basket.

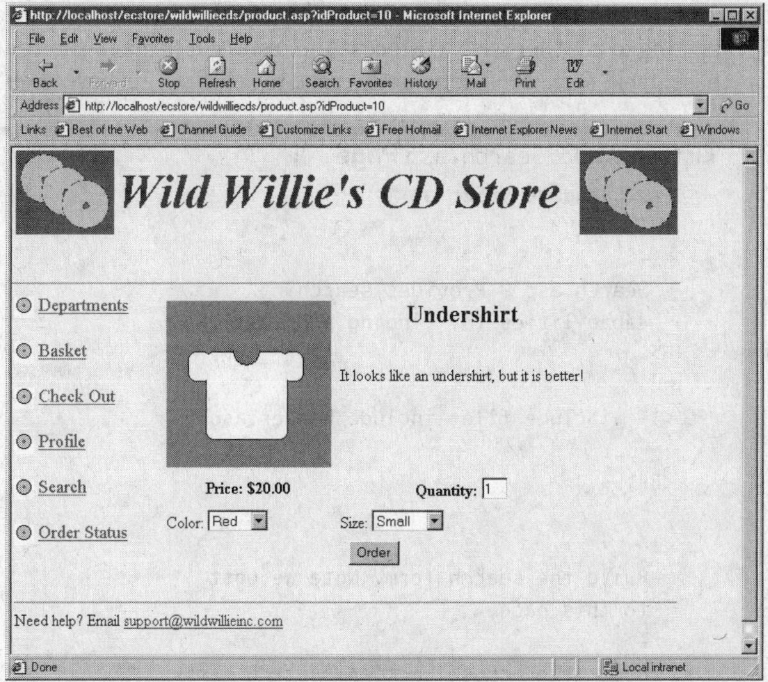

FIGURE 23.8: Product page for the undershirt

The shopper can now accomplish basic navigation through departments and products. Next we will take a look at how the shopper can find products through the search feature.

Searching

The search feature on the Web site is critical for allowing users to find products that meet their specific needs. In our store, we are going to provide two basic kinds of searches. The first is the standard keyword search. This search will be executed against the name and description fields using SQL syntax.

The second search option will be a search for products that fall into a certain price range. For example, I could search for products in the $10 to $20 price range that have "jazz" in the title or description.

The page begins in the standard fashion, as shown in Listing 23.33 (it continues in listings 23.34, 23.35, 23.36, 23.37, 23.38, and 23.39). The form for submitting the search has a bit of a different twist. Instead of posting to another page to process the results, it posts to the `search.asp` page itself. A check is done in the page to see if results have been posted.

Listing 23.33: `Search.asp` **Page**

```
<%@ Language=VBScript %>
<HTML>
<!-
  Search.asp - Provides searching
  capabilities for finding products.
->

<!- #include file="include/header.asp" ->

<BR>

<!-
  Build the search form. Note we post
  to this page.
  ->
<form method="post" action="search.asp">
```

The first thing we display is the search table. This will be shown even if a search has been executed so that the shopper can easily begin a new search after reviewing the results of the recent search. Note that we default the values to any previously input data.

Listing 23.34: `Search.asp` **Page Continued**

```
<!-  Table to display the search options ->
<table border="0">

<!-  Display the text search option ->
<tr>
  <td align="right">
    <b>Enter your search text:</b></td>
  <!-  Input text box ->
  <td align="right"><input type="text"
```

```
        value="<%=request("search")%>"
        name="Search"></td>
    </tr>

    <!- Provide a product price range search ->
    <tr>
      <td><b>Price Range:</b></td>
      <td align="right">
        Low:
        <input type="text"
        value="<%=request("low")%>"
        name="Low"></td>
    </tr>

    <!- High price search option ->
    <tr>
      <td></td>
      <td align="right">High:
      <input type="text"
      value="<%=request("high")%>"
      name="High"></td>
    </tr>

    <!- Break column ->
    <tr><td colspan="2"> </td></tr>

    <!- Submit button ->
    <tr>
      <td colspan="2" align="center">
        <input type="submit"
        value="Submit"
        name="Submit">
      </td>
    </tr>

    </table>

    </form>
```

Our next set of code on the page checks to see if a search request was posted to the page. We check out three post variables—search, low, and high. Following that, we go ahead and open our database connection in preparation for the search.

Listing 23.35: `Search.asp` **Page Continued**

```
<%

'  Check to see if a search request was
'  posted to page.
if request("search") <> ""  or _
  request("low") <> "" or _
  request("high") <> "" then

  '  Create an ADO database connection
  set dbSearch = server.createobject _
    ("adodb.connection")

  '  Create a result set
  set rsSearch = server.CreateObject _
    ("adodb.recordset")

  '  Open the connection using our
  '  ODBC file DSN
  dbSearch.open("filedsn=WildWillieCDs")
```

First the *low* value is checked to see if anything has been entered and, if so, to ensure that it was entered as a number. If nothing was entered, we default the lower value to 0. If something was entered, the value is retrieved and multiplied by 100.

The value has to be multiplied to provide a search against the prices in the database, which are stored in whole number values.

Listing 23.36: `Search.asp` **Page Continued**

```
  '  Check to see if the low search was
  '  set and is a number.
  If request("Low") = "" or _
    isnumeric(request("low")) = false then
    '  Default to 0
    Low = 0
  else
    '  Set value to the data entered. Note
    '  that prices are stored in whole
    '  number so we must multiply the value
    '  times 100.
    Low = request("Low") * 100
  end if
```

A similar check is done against the *high* value entered. If nothing was entered, then the value is defaulted to a very large dollar amount. If it was entered, as with the low price, the value is multiplied by 100.

Listing 23.37: `Search.asp` **Page Continued**

```
'  Check to see if the high search was
'  set and is a number.
if request("High") = "" or _
  isnumeric(request("High")) = false then

  '  Default to a very high number
  High = 99999999

else

  '  Get the value and multiply times 100
  High = Request("High") * 100

end if
```

The SQL query that searches for the results is based on the `sp_SearchProducts` stored procedure. The search key works as low and high prices are passed into the query. The query is then executed against the database and a result set is returned.

Listing 23.38: `Search.asp` **Page Continued**

```
'  Build a SQL query that will return
'  the requested products. The search text
'  and price range is passed in.
sql = "execute sp_SearchProducts '" & _
  request("search") & "', " & Low & _
  ", " & High

'  Execute the SQL statement
set rsSearch = dbSearch.Execute(sql)

%>

<!-  Start the list ->
<UL>
```

The results are returned from the query. We simply loop through the results and list the products in a bulleted list. If there are no products returned, then nothing is listed. Finally, the page is ended in the usual fashion.

Listing 23.39: `Search.asp` **Page Continued**

```
<%

  '  Loop through the record set
  do until rsSearch.eof

    '  Display the List
    response.write("<li><a href=" & _
    "'product.asp?idProduct=" & _
    rsSearch("idProduct") & "'>")
    response.write(rsSearch("chrProductName"))
    response.write("</a></li>")

    '  Move to the next record set
    rsSearch.MoveNext

  '  Loop back
  Loop

'  End the check
End If

%>

</UL>

<!- #include file="include/footer.asp" ->

</BODY>
</HTML>
```

The `search products` stored procedure (see Listing 23.40) takes in three parameters including the search text, the low price, and the high price. The SQL query uses the like capability to check the product name and the description to see if the keywords are found in the text. And finally, the price is checked against the low and high price.

SITE SEARCHING

Searching is an interesting topic when it comes to Web sites. There are two types of searches typically found on a Web site. The first is the unstructured type of search that a typical site search accomplishes. Tools such as Index Server crawl content files and index keywords in the content into a specialized database. Then a special query language can be used to query the database. The second is the database search, which typically can be done through languages such as SQL. The database search is like the database product search in the electronic commerce store.

In an e-commerce Web site, especially with a lot of products, the search may be one of the most popular pages on the site. Special focus can be given to features such as tracking keywords that shoppers are using to search, and building special keyword fields into the database to enhance the possibility of search hits. You can even get as sophisticated as to use recommendation engines like some of the major Web retailers (such as Amazon, CDNOW, and others).

Special focus should be given to the search features of an e-commerce store. While the traditional method of shopping through departments, department products, etc., is critical, don't overlook the important nature of the search. A good product database search can help site visitors find exactly what they are looking for, especially while the urge to buy is hot.

Listing 23.40: `sp_SearchProducts` **Stored Procedure**

```
/*  Stored procedure to search for
  products based on passed in parameters. */
CREATE PROCEDURE sp_SearchProducts

/*  Pass in the search text, low price and
  high price */
@SearchText varchar(255),
@Low int,
@High int

AS

/*  Select products from the data base
```

```
    where the product name or description
    contain the search text. And where the
    price falls in the given parameters.
    The products are ordered by the product
    name. */
  select * from products
  where (chrProductName like '%' +
    @SearchText+ '%' or
    txtDescription like '%' +
    @SearchText + '%') and
    (intPrice >= @low and intPrice <= @High)
  order by chrProductName
```

Figure 23.9 shows the site's search screen. Note the three input fields. To build a sample search, enter **jazz** into the search text box, **10** into the low price box, and **20** into the high price box.

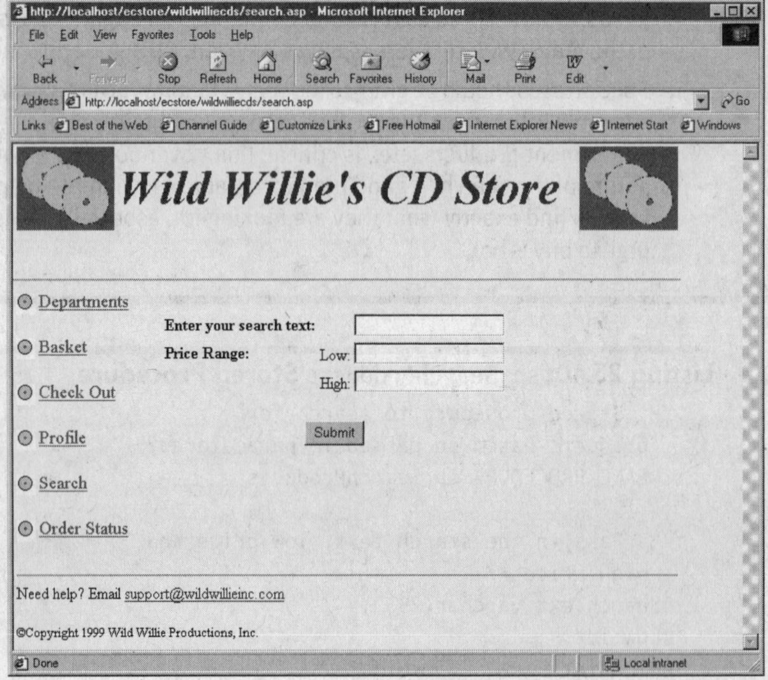

FIGURE 23.9: Search screen

Figure 23.10 shows the search results. In this case, our search returned one product, *Alley Jazz*. The shopper can then just click the link and be ready to buy.

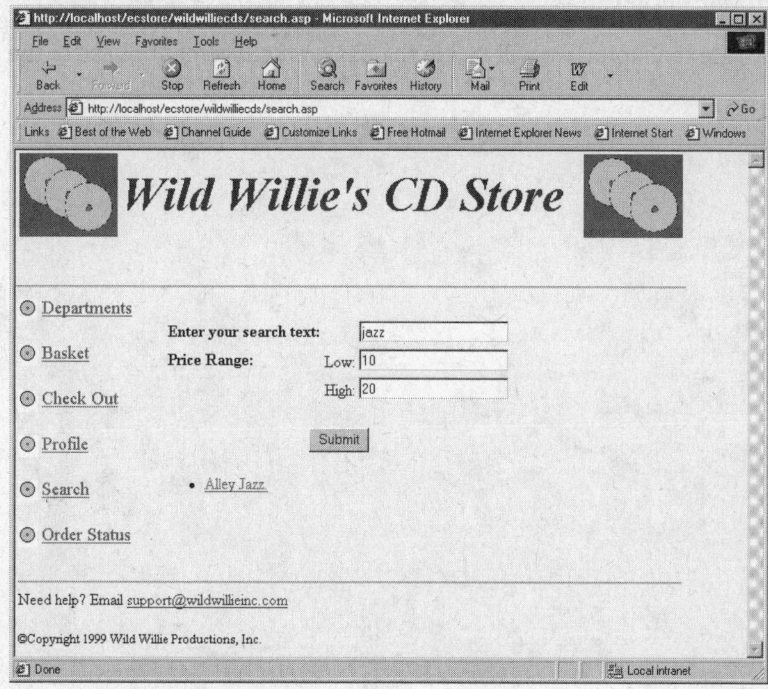

FIGURE 23.10: Search results

WHAT'S NEXT?

With the default, departments, products, and search pages, we have built the core infrastructure for presenting the store to the shopper.

There are a few key concepts to note about the build of these pages. The first is the use of the include files to provide the overall framework of the pages. By using the include files, we build a very encapsulated approach to the user interface that is changeable and easily scalable down the road.

Second is the implementation of the database structure. Through the use of the stored procedures, we have implemented the core department and product structure, including the product attributes, etc.

Finally, we have a platform for which we are ready to build the other half of the store, which supports the basket and checkout process. In the next chapter, we will tackle the basket management phase of the store.

Chapter 24

Making a Basket Case

In the last chapter, we made it possible for shoppers to browse and search for products at their leisure. Now we are ready to begin the basket management process.

The shopping basket is the foundational element of making the e-commerce store functional. This is where we want the shoppers to *park* products they are interested in, allowing them to continue and decide later what they ultimately want to purchase.

Adapted from *Visual Basic® Developer's Guide to E-Commerce with ASP and SQL Server™*, by Noel Jerke

ISBN 0-7821-2621-9 752 pages $49.99

Designing the Basket

The shopping basket is made up of several key functions that make it a very dynamic aspect of the Web site. Table 24.1 shows the core functions we will be adding into the shopping basket section of the Web site.

TABLE 24.1: Basket Functionality

Core Function	Description
Add item to basket	When the shopper is on the product page and hits the Order button, some magic needs to happen to add the product to the basket.
Display basket	When the shopper actually hits the basket page, we need to be able to list all of the items they've added to their basket and display the quantities.
Update basket items	If the shopper wishes to change the quantity ordered of any item in the basket, we need to provide the capability of changing the item quantities.
Remove item	If the shopper decides not to keep a certain item in their shopping basket, we need to provide a method for removing a selected item.
Empty basket	If, for some reason, the shopper decides to dump the whole thing, we can provide a function to empty the basket completely.

Figure 24.1 shows how the functions of the basket interact dynamically. On the top of the diagram, items are added into the basket. The shopper can empty the basket, adjust quantities, and remove items. So, without further ado, let's jump into the programming that makes all of this work.

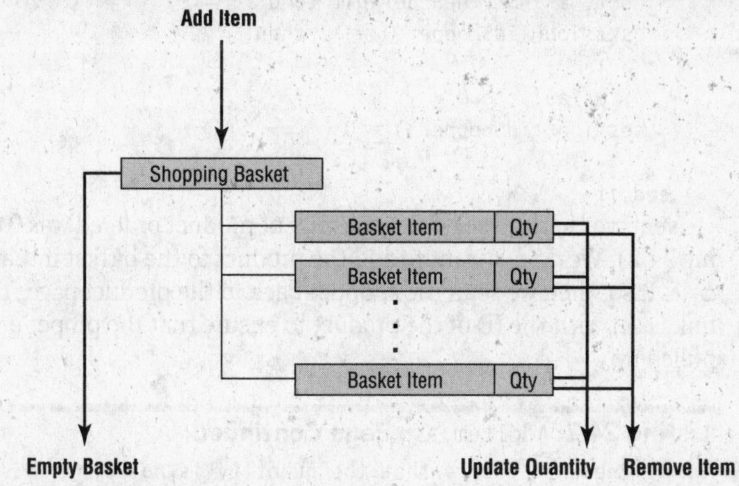

FIGURE 24.1: Dynamic interaction of basket functions

ADDING ITEMS

The first step in the process is adding items to the basket. This page is called when the user selects the Order button on the product page. Note that this page performs processing only. There is no information displayed directly to the user and it immediately redirects to a view of the basket produced by `basket.asp`.

The first step in the page is to check if there is a shopper ID assigned yet. If not, then we default the shopper ID to 0 so we can continue processing. Listing 24.1 begins the `AddItem.asp` code.

Listing 24.1: `AddItem.asp` **Page**

```
<%@ Language=VBScript %>
<%
'  ******************************************
'  AddItem.asp - This page is used to
'  add a selected product into the shopping
'  basket.
'  ******************************************

'  Check to see if a shopper variable has been
```

```
'  set. If not then default to 0.
if session("idShopper") = "" then

  '  Default to 0
  session("idShopper") = 0

end if
```

Next we check to see if the quantity of product ordered was 0 (see Listing 24.2). We do not want to add the product to the basket if that is the case. If so, then we send the shopper back to the product page. There the link is set with the ID of the product to ensure that the proper one is pulled up.

Listing 24.2: `AddItem.asp` **Page Continued**

```
'  Check to ensure that the quantity is not 0.
if request("quantity") = "0" then

  '  Send the user back to the product page.
  Response.Redirect _
    ("product.asp?idProduct=" & _
    request("idProduct"))

End If
```

Next we retrieve the values from the product page. Remember that the key product values are stored in hidden values on that page. Now we are able to retrieve them for our use here. On the product name, we are going to ensure that single quotes are doubled so we can insert the name into the database (see Listing 24.3).

Listing 24.3: `AddItem.asp` **Page Continued**

```
'  Retrieve the quantity
intQuantity = request("quantity")

'  Retrieve the id of the product
idProduct = request("idProduct")

'  Retrieve the product name
chrName = _
  replace(request("productname"), "'", "''")

'  Retrieve the product price
```

```
intPrice = request("productprice")

'  Retrieve the size
chrSize = request("size")

'  Retrieve the color
chrColor = request("color")
```

Next we have to ensure that there is a basket for this order session. We can't insert a basket item without a basket. The `idBasket` session variable is checked to see if it has been initialized (see Listing 24.4).

If it hasn't, then we open up a database connection to create the new basket. The `sp_CreateBasket` stored procedure is executed. In order to create a new basket, we have to assign a shopper ID so that it can be passed into the stored procedure.

Once the basket is inserted, we retrieve the new basket ID returned from the database (through an identity column). That value is then stored in our session variable.

Listing 24.4: `AddItem.asp` **Page Continued**

```
'  Check to see if a basket has been created
if session("idBasket") = "" then

   '  Create an ADO database connection
   set dbBasket = server.createobject _
     ("adodb.connection")

   '  Create a record set
   set rsBasket = server.CreateObject _
     ("adodb.recordset")

   '  Open the connection using our
   '  ODBC file DSN
   dbBasket.open("filedsn=WildWillieCDs")

   '  Execute the create basket stored
   '  procedure to create a new basket
   '  for the shopper
   sql = "execute sp_CreateBasket " & _
     session("idShopper")

   '  Execute the SQL statement
```

```
    set rsBasket = dbBasket.Execute(sql)

    '  Retrieve the id of the basket
    '  returned from the insert
    idBasket = rsBasket("idBasket")

    '  Set the basket id in the session variable
    session("idBasket") = idBasket

  else
```

If a basket already existed, then we would need to first see if this item is already in the basket. We don't want duplicate entries in the basket. What we really want is to simply increment the quantity based on whatever is in the basket.

We open a connection to the database and execute the `sp_CheckBasket-Item-Quantity` stored procedure, passing in the ID of the product and the ID of the basket to ensure we check the right item (see Listing 24.5).

Listing 24.5: `AddItem.asp` Page Continued

```
    '  Create an ADO database connection
    set dbBasket = server.createobject _
      ("adodb.connection")

    '  Create a record set
    set rsBasket = server.CreateObject _
      ("adodb.recordset")

    '  Open the connection using our ODBC
    '  file DSN
    dbBasket.open("filedsn=WildWillieCDs")

    '  Call the stored procedure to check
    '  the basket item quantity. The id
    '  of the product to check and the ID
    '  of the basket is sent in.
    sql = "execute" & _
      " sp_CheckBasketItemQuantity " & _
      idProduct & ", " & _
      session("idBasket")
```

```
    '  Execute the SQL statement
    set rsBasket = dbBasket.Execute(sql)
```

If nothing is returned, then we know that the item does not exist in the basket. If something is returned, then we need to update the basket item quantity for the existing item.

To do the update, the `sp_UpdateBasketItemsQuantity` stored procedure is called. We pass in the ID of the basket and the ID of the product. Also, we pass in the new quantity. This is done by accessing the current quantity returned from our previous query combined with the quantity the shopper just selected for the product. Then the user is redirected to the basket page (see Listing 24.6).

Listing 24.6: `AddItem.asp` **Page Continued**

```
    '  Check to see if the item is in the
    '  basket. If it is then we are going
    '  to update the quantity instead of
    '  updating it.
    if rsbasket.eof = false then

      '  If so, then we are going to update
      '  the basket quantity instead of
      '  adding a new item.
      sql = "execute" & _
        " sp_UpdateBasketItemsQuantity " & _
        session("idBasket") & ", " & _
        rsBasket("intQuantity") & ", " & _
        idProduct

      '  Execute the SQL statement
      set rsBasket = dbBasket.Execute(sql)

      '  Go to the basket
      Response.Redirect "basket.asp"

    end if

  end if
```

If we get to this point on the page, we are ready to actually add a new item into the BasketItems table. We call the `sp_InsertBasketItem` stored procedure to add the item to the basket.

Part vi

All of the key values are passed into the stored procedure including the ID of the basket, quantity, price, product name, ID of the product, size, and color. When the insert is finished, the shopper is sent to the basket page (see Listing 24.7).

NOTE

Many of our sample products do not include the size and color attributes. If these attributes do not exist, then nothing is returned from the request and the fields are blank in the database.

Listing 24.7: `AddItem.asp` **Page Continued**

```
' Create an ADO database connection
set dbBasketItem = server.createobject _
  ("adodb.connection")

' Create a record set
set rsBasketItem = server.CreateObject _
  ("adodb.recordset")

' Open the connection using our ODBC file DSN
dbBasketItem.open("filedsn=WildWillieCDs")

' Call the stored procedure to insert the new
' item into the basket.
sql = "execute sp_InsertBasketItem " & _
  session("idBasket") & ", " & _
  intQuantity & ", " & _
  intPrice & ", '" & _
  chrName & "', " & _
  idProduct & ", '"& _
  chrSize & "', '" & _
  chrColor & "'"

' Execute the SQL statement
set rsBasketItem = dbBasketItem.Execute(sql)

' Send the user to the basket page
Response.Redirect "basket.asp"

%>
```

The sp_InsertBasketItem stored procedure (Listing 24.8) handles the insert of the new item in the basket. The appropriate fields are passed in and then the SQL insert is executed.

Listing 24.8: `sp_InsertBasketItem` **Stored Procedure**

```
/*  Stored procedure to insert a new basket
    item */
CREATE PROCEDURE sp_InsertBasketItem

/*  Pass in the id of the basket, quantity,
    price product name, product price, ID of
    the product, size of the product and the
    color.
*/
@idBasket int,
@intQuantity int,
@intPrice int,
@chrName varchar(255),
@idProduct int,
@chrSize varchar(50),
@chrColor varchar(50)

AS

/*  Insert the item into the table */
insert into basketitem(idBasket, intQuantity,
  intPrice, chrName, idProduct, chrSize,
  chrColor)

values(@idBasket, @intQuantity, @intPrice,
  @chrName, @idProduct, @chrSize, @chrColor)
```

The sp_CreateBasket stored procedure creates a new basket for the shopper (Listing 24.9). This happens when a shopper visits the store and is a new shopper in the database, or an existing shopper who has completed orders for all existing shopping baskets.

The ID of the shopper is passed into the stored procedure. The insert is then executed to add the basket. The ID of the basket is returned from the stored procedure by using the @@Identity variable, which is set to the last value returned from the Insert.

Listing 24.9: `sp_CreateBasket` **Stored Procedure**

```
/*  Creates a new basket and returns the ID */
CREATE PROCEDURE sp_CreateBasket

/*  Pass in the ID of the shopper
    the basket will belong to.
*/
@idShopper int

AS

/*  Insert a new role into the basket and
    set the shopper ID
*/
insert into basket(idShopper)
  values(@idShopper)

/*  Retrieve the ID of the basket which
    will be in the @@identity variable value
*/
select idbasket = @@identity
```

The `sp_CheckBasketItemQuantity` stored procedure (see Listing 24.10) will return the basket item quantity for the specified product in the specified basket.

Listing 24.10: `sp_CheckBasketItemQuantity` **Stored Procedure**

```
/*  Checks the quantity of items in the
    basket for the specified product.
*/
CREATE PROCEDURE sp_CheckBasketItemQuantity

/*  Pass in the ID of the product and
    the ID of the basket
*/
@idProduct int,
@idBasket int

AS
```

```
/* Retrieve the quantity value */
select intQuantity from basketitem
where idProduct = @idProduct and
  idBasket = @idBasket
```

The sp_UpdateBasketItemsQuantity stored procedure (see Listing 24.11) handles updating the basket item quantity to the new value passed into the stored procedure. The item is identified by the ID of the basket and the ID of the product.

Listing 24.11: sp_UpdateBasketItemsQuantity **Stored Procedure**

```
/* Stored procedure to update the
   basket item quantity. */
CREATE PROCEDURE sp_UpdateBasketItemsQuantity

/* Pass in the ID of the basket, the quantity
   and the ID of the product (basket item). */
@idBasket int,
@intQuantity int,
@idProduct int

as

/* Update the basketitem table wit the new
   quantity for the product. */
update basketitem set intQuantity =
  @intQuantity
where idBasket = @idbasket and
  idProduct = @idProduct
```

Figure 24.2 shows a product page for *Joe Bob's Thimble Sounds*.

When you click Order, the item will be added into the basket and displayed. Figure 24.3 shows the basket when the product is added (we will review the basket display in the next section). Note that the quantity shown is 1 because that is what the shopper selected when the product was added.

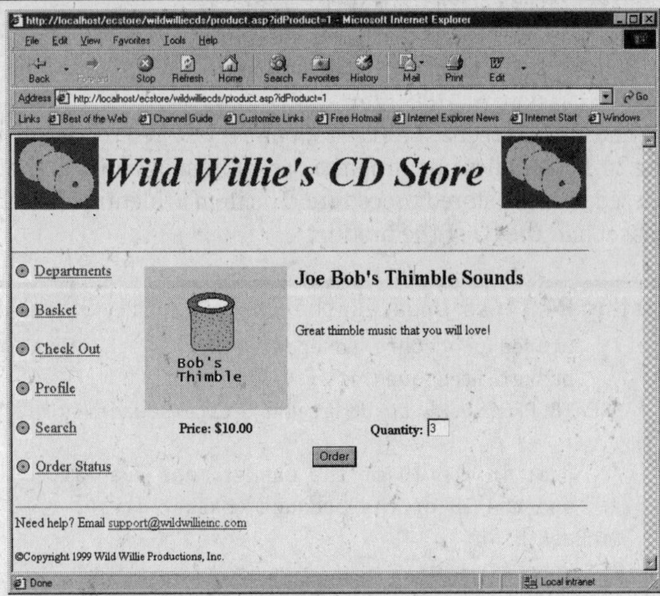

FIGURE 24.2: Product page to add to basket

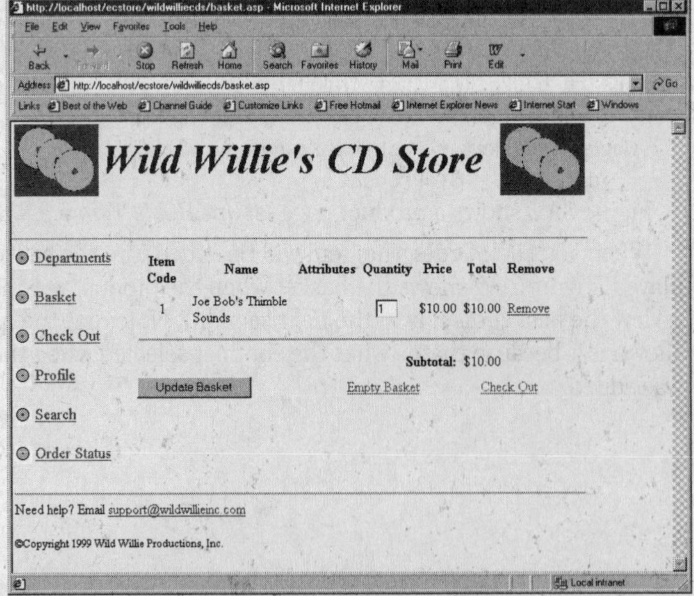

FIGURE 24.3: Basket with the product

Figure 24.4 shows the effect when three more copies of *Joe Bob's Thimbles* are added. Because that product is already loaded, a new item is not added to the basket. Instead, the quantity of the existing order is simply updated to reflect the total quantity of 4.

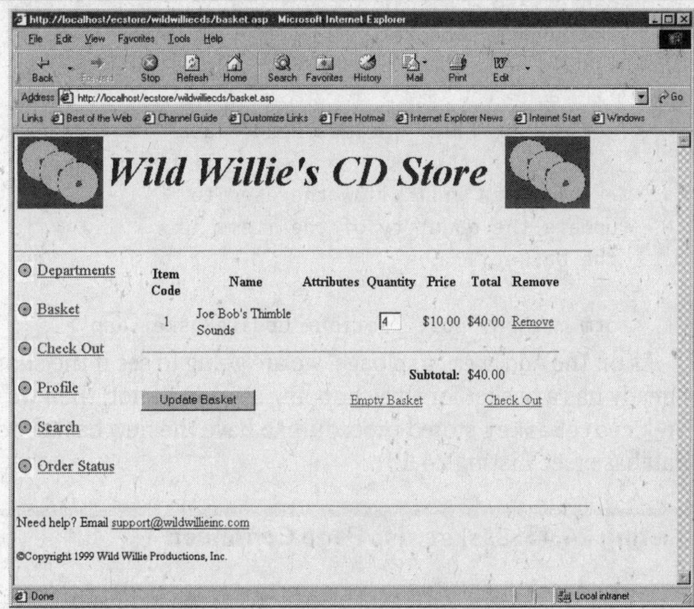

FIGURE 24.4: The basket page with the quantity updated

Now that you have seen that the basket works, let's dive into the code behind the basket.

DISPLAYING THE BASKET

The shopping basket is a list of items that need to be displayed on the page. The page starts in the standard fashion with the appropriate header file included. The page begins with a form that will be used for updating the quantities on the page. Listing 24.12 shows the `basket.asp` page and its corresponding stored procedures.

Listing 24.12: `Basket.asp` **Page**

```
<%@ Language=VBScript %>
<HTML>
<!-
  Basket.asp - Displays the items in
  the shoppers basket.
->

<!- #include file="include/header.asp" ->

<!- This form will allow the user to
  update the quantity of the items in
  the basket
->
<form method="post" action="UpdateBasket.asp">
```

As on the `AddItem.asp` page, we are going to see if the shopper already has a basket for this shopping session. If not, then we use the `sp_CreateBasket` stored procedure to have the new basket added to the database (see Listing 24.13).

Listing 24.13: `Basket.asp` **Page Continued**

```
<%

'  Check to see if the ID of the
'  basket is blank
if session("idBasket") = "" then

  '  Create an ADO database connection
  set dbBasket = server.createobject _
    ("adodb.connection")

  '  Create a record set
  set rsBasket = server.CreateObject _
    ("adodb.recordset")

  '  Open the connection using our ODBC
  '  file DSN
  dbBasket.open("filedsn=WildWillieCDs")

  '  Create a new shopping basket
  sql = "execute sp_CreateBasket " & _
```

```
      session("idShopper")

    '  Execute the SQL statement
    set rsBasket = dbBasket.Execute(sql)

    '  Retrieve the id of the basket
    '  returned from the insert
    idBasket = rsBasket("idBasket")

    '  Set the basket id in the session
    '  variable
    session("idBasket") = idBasket

  end if
```

Next we are ready to retrieve the basket items for the current basket. The `sp_RetrieveBasketItem` stored procedure is used to pull out all of the basket items for the current basket for the current shopper (see Listing 24.14).

Listing 24.14: `Basket.asp` **Page Continued**

```
  '  Create an ADO database connection
  set dbBasketItem = server.createobject _
    ("adodb.connection")

  '  Create a record set
  set rsBasketItem = server.CreateObject _
    ("adodb.recordset")

  '  Open the connection using our ODBC file DSN
  dbBasketItem.open("filedsn=WildWillieCDs")

  '  Execute the stored procedure to retrieve
  '  the basket items for the shopper.
  sql = "execute" & _
    " sp_RetrieveBasketItem " & _
    session("idBasket")

  '  Execute the SQL statement
  set rsBasketItem = dbBasketItem.Execute(sql)
```

If the basket is empty, then we will display an appropriate message to the shopper (see Listing 24.15). If not, then we are ready to loop through the items and display them.

Listing 24.15: `Basket.asp` **Page Continued**

```
    '  Check to ensure a basket has been
    '  created and that there are items in
    '  the basket
    if session("idBasket") = "" or _
      rsBasketItem.EOF = true then

    %>

      <!- Show the empty basket message ->
      <center>
      <BR><BR>
      <font size="4">Your basket is empty.</font>
      </center>

    <%

    else
```

E-COMMERCE STORE NAVIGATION

Into the core of our e-commerce store, we have built a navigational structure that allows shoppers to navigate to the shopping basket, departments, searching, and checking out.

Building in the link back to the department on the basket page helps facilitate the shopping process they were following. In a real physical store, we would not make the shopper go to a basket somewhere else and then have to walk all the way back to the department they were in. This link helps to facilitate the continuation of their shopping process.

There are some other elements of the shopping navigation process that we might want to consider. Many stores implement a forward/back feature on the product page to allow the shopper to move back and forth between products without navigating back to the department page.

Other considerations would include selling products in groups. For example, if we are selling a selection of bedding, in many cases the shopper would buy a complete set (including pillowcases, sheets,

CONTINUED ➡

etc.). In that case we might have other product templates that would allow multiple products to be displayed on one page and purchased in one group.

Considering these navigational issues is key to ensuring that your shoppers have the best experience in navigating the store. The type of navigational requirements is somewhat dependent upon the type of product being sold, but many of the principles outlined here are universal in utilization.

Before we begin the loop, we will display a link back to the department of the product from which a selection was just made. Remember on the `products.asp` page that we stored a session variable that indicated the last department viewed. We now check that session variable to see if it is set. If it is, then we build a link to that department for easy navigation back to the department in which the shopper was browsing (see Listing 24.16).

Listing 24.16 `Basket.asp` **Page Continued**

```
    '  Check to see if the last department
    '  is set based on where she ordered from.
    if session("LastIDDept") <> "" then

%>

<!-
    Show the link to go back to the department
    to make navigation easier.
->
<BR>
Click <a href="products.asp?idDept=
<%=session("LastIDDept")%>">
here</a> to continue shopping.
<BR><BR>

<%end if%>
```

Next on the page, we will create a table structure for displaying the products in the basket. The header is displayed first that shows the columns of data we will display in the basket (Listing 24.17).

Listing 24.17: `Basket.asp` Page Continued

```
<!- Build the basket table ->
<table border="0" cellpadding="3"
  cellspacing="2" width="500">

<!- Build the header row ->
<tr>
  <th>Item Code</th>
  <th>Name</th>
  <th>Attributes</th>
  <th>Quantity</th>
  <th>Price</th>
  <th>Total</th>
  <th>Remove</th>
</tr>
```

Next we will loop through the items in the basket. With each iteration, the product ID, product name, and any attributes are displayed. Following that, we display the product quantity currently selected to be purchased.

When the product quantity is displayed, the value of the text box is set to the product ID so that we can determine on the update page which product's quantity is changing.

Following the quantity, we display the product price and the purchase price. Remember that the prices are stored in the database in an integer format. To display the proper price, we have to divide the stored value by 100 to show the decimals properly. To display the price formatted properly, the `FormatCurrency` function is used to add the dollar signs, etc. The purchase price is calculated by multiplying the quantity by the product price.

Finally, the Remove option is built into the form. In our store, we are linking to the `deleteitem.asp` page. The ID of the product is passed on the URL to the page to indicate which item should be removed from the basket.

With each iteration, the subtotal is calculated and displayed after all of the basket items are displayed. At the end, the record set is moved to the next row and we loop back to show the next item (see Listing 24.18).

Listing 24.18: `Basket.asp` **Page Continued**

```
<%

'  Loop through the basket items.
do until rsBasketItem.EOF

%>

<!-  Show the row ->
<tr>
  <!-  Show the product id ->
  <td align="center">
    <%=rsBasketItem("idProduct")%></td>
  <!-  Show the product name ->
  <td><%=rsBasketItem("chrName")%></td>
  <!-  Show the product attributes ->
  <td>
    <% if rsBasketItem("chrColor") <> _
        " " then %>
    <%=rsBasketItem("chrSize")%>,
    <%=rsBasketItem("chrColor")%>
    <% end if %>
  </td>
  <!-  Show the product quantity ->
  <td align="center">
    <input type="text"
    value="<%=rsBasketItem("intQuantity")%>"
    name="<%=rsBasketItem("idProduct")%>"
    size="2">
  </td>
  <!-  Show the product price ->
  <td>
    <%=formatcurrency(rsBasketItem
("intPrice")/100, 2)%>
  </td>

  <!-  Show the product total cost ->
  <td>
    <%=formatcurrency(rsBasketItem
("intPrice")/100 * rsBasketitem
("intQuantity"), 2)%>
  </td>
```

```
    <!- Show the remove option. ->
    <td>
      <a href="deleteitem.asp? ↵
      idBasketItem=
      <%=rsBasketItem("idBasketItem")%>">
      Remove</a>
    </td>
    <!- Continue to calculate the subtotal ->
    <% subtotal = subtotal + _
      (rsBasketItem("intPrice") * _
      rsBasketitem("intQuantity")) %>

  </tr>

  <%

  ' Move to the next row
  rsBasketItem.MoveNext

  ' Loop back
  loop

  %>
```

After the products in the basket are displayed, we will show the current subtotal of the basket. Note that in the table, a break row is put in, and then in the next row, the subtotal is lined up under the purchase price column (Listing 24.19).

Listing 24.19: `Basket.asp` **Page Continued**

```
  <!- Build a break ->
  <tr>
    <td colspan="7"><HR></td>
  </tr>

  <!- Show the sub total of the basket ->
  <tr>
    <td colspan="5" align="right">
      <b>Subtotal:</b></td>
    <td>
      <%= formatcurrency(subtotal/100, 2) %>
    </td>
    <td> </td>
```

```
</tr>

</table>
```

TIP

To make the look of the basket more consistent, you might want to display images instead of a Submit button and text links. A form can be submitted with a graphic image as the button. And, of course, the images can be linked as well. That will provide more consistency in the interface.

The Submit button is displayed for submitting any quantity changes in the basket. Following that, we have links to the `emptybasket.asp` page and the `shipping.asp` page. Finally, the page is ended with the proper include and tags (see Listing 24.20).

Listing 24.20: `Basket.asp` **Page Continued**

```
<!- Show the submit button for the
      quantity update action ->
<table width="100%">


<td>
  <input type="submit"
  value="Update Basket" name="Submit"></td>


</form>


<!- Show the empty basket and check out
      links ->
<td>
  <a href="emptybasket.asp">
  Empty Basket</a></td>
<td><a href="shipping.asp">Check Out</a></td>


</tr>


</table>
```

```
<% end if %>

<!- #include file="include/footer.asp" ->

</BODY>
</HTML>
```

Now our basket is functional. Figure 24.5 shows the basket with several items displayed on the basket. Note the different quantities for each item and the total column showing the multiplied price. And at the bottom, the entire basket is subtotaled. Also, note the link in the line reading "Click here to continue shopping," which will take the shopper back to the department in which they were shopping.

NOTE

We are showing only the subtotal in the basket. The shipping and tax will be done in the checkout process. If your store has large shipping costs or unusual tax requirements, it may be prudent to show these charges at the basket level. But in many cases, this will require the shopper to enter at least a shipping and/or billing zip code.

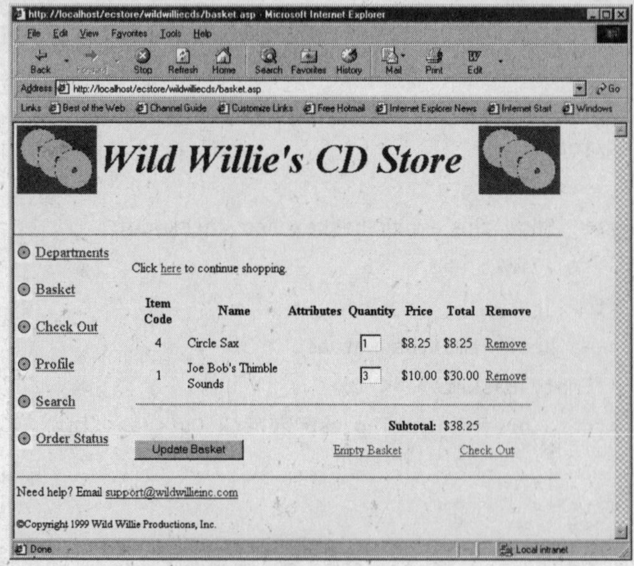

FIGURE 24.5: Basket page

That takes care of displaying the basket and setting all of the proper links to provide the shopper with the tools to manage the basket.

MANAGING THE BASKET

Now our shoppers have been able to add items in the basket and see their choices displayed. Next we will look at the tools to manage the basket. These will include the `UpdateBasket.asp` page, `DeleteItem.asp` page, and the `EmptyBasket.asp` page.

Updating the Basket

With our first page, `updatebasket.asp`, we will be building a non-display page that will process the update request. The first thing we'll do when the page is started is to open a database connection.

With the database connection, we will retrieve the shopper's basket items. The basket will be looped through with an update done on each product. A second record set is created to provide us with a connection to update each basket item as we loop through the basket items. Listing 24.21 is the code for the `UpdateBasket.asp` page we will review next.

Listing 24.21: `UpdateBasket.asp` **Page**

```
<%@ Language=VBScript %>
<%
  ' *******************************************
  '  UpdateBasket.asp - This page will read in
  '  new quantity for items in the basket and
  '  set them appropriately.
  ' *******************************************

  '  Create an ADO database connection
set dbBasketItem = server.createobject _
  ("adodb.connection")

  '  Create a record set
set rsBasketItem = server.CreateObject _
  ("adodb.recordset")

  '  Open the connection using our ODBC
  '  file DSN
```

```
dbBasketItem.open("filedsn=WildWillieCDs")

'  Retrieve the basket items
sql = "execute sp_RetrieveBasketItem " & _
  session("idBasket")

' Execute the SQL statement
set rsBasketItem = dbBasketItem.Execute(sql)

'  Create an ADO database connection
set dbUpdateItem = server.createobject _
  ("adodb.connection")

'  Create a record set
set rsUpdateItem = server.CreateObject _
  ("adodb.recordset")

'  Open the connection using our ODBC
'  file DSN
dbUpdateItem.open("filedsn=WildWillieCDs")

'  Loop through the basket items
do until rsBasketItem.EOF
```

In each loop, we retrieve the quantity value by accessing the ID of the product from our open record set. Remember that each quantity text field on the basket page has as its name the ID of the product. Thus, when we do the request call, we have to pass in the ID of the product we are currently looping through.

Next, the stored procedure, `sp_UpdateBasketItemQuantity`, is called to update the item with the new quantity (Listing 24.22). Note that the ID of the basket and the ID of the product are passed as well into the stored procedure.

Once the loop is completed, the shopper is sent back to the basket page. On the basket page, the quantities will be updated and the new line-item totals and subtotal will be displayed.

Listing 24.22: `UpdateBasket.asp` **Page Continued**

```
  '  Retrieve the quantity. We use the ID
  '  of the basket item from the database
  '  to retrieve the data from the correct
  '  input box.
```

```
        intQuantity = request(cstr _
          (rsBasketItem("idProduct")))

        '  Call the stored procedure to update
        '  the quantity
        sql = "execute" & _
          " sp_UpdateBasketItemsQuantity " & _
          session("idBasket") & ", " & _
          intQuantity & ", " & _
          rsBasketItem("idProduct")

        '  Execute the SQL statement
        set rsUpdateItem = _
          dbUpdateItem.Execute(sql)

        '  Move to the next item
        rsBasketItem.MoveNext

      loop

      '  Send the user to the basket page
      Response.Redirect "basket.asp"

      %>
```

The sp_RetrieveBasketItem stored procedure is used to get the basket items from the database for the specified shopping basket (see Listing 24.23). The ID of the basket is passed into the stored procedure.

Listing 24.23: sp_RetrieveBasketItem **Stored Procedure**

```
/*  Stored Procedure to retrieve the
    basket item from the database */
CREATE PROCEDURE sp_RetrieveBasketItem

/*  Pass in the ID of the basket */
@idBasket int

AS

/*  Retrieve the items for the specified
    basket */
select * from basketitem
where idBasket = @idBasket
```

Part vi

Figure 24.6 shows our basket page. We have two items, *Circle Sax* and *Joe Bob's Thimble Sounds*. The first has a quantity of 6 items purchased and the second has 9 items purchased.

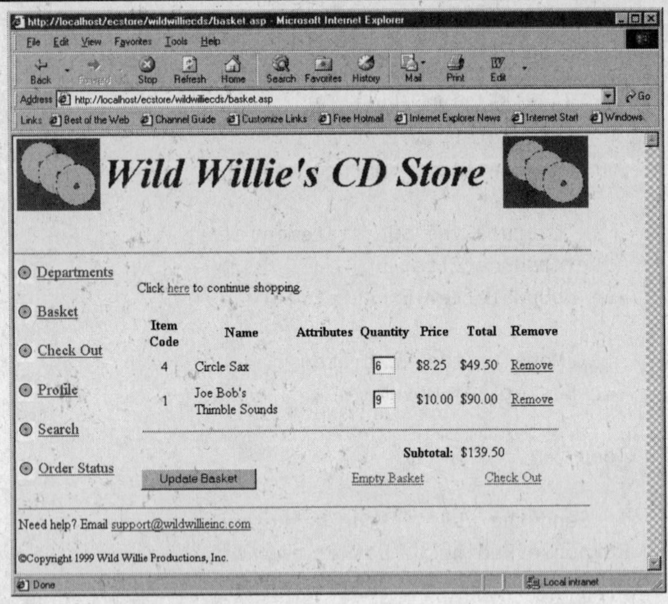

FIGURE 24.6: Preliminary basket

Now let's change the quantities to 3 each. Figure 24.7 shows the updated basket. Note that the quantities are updated, the line-item totals are updated, and the overall basket subtotal is updated.

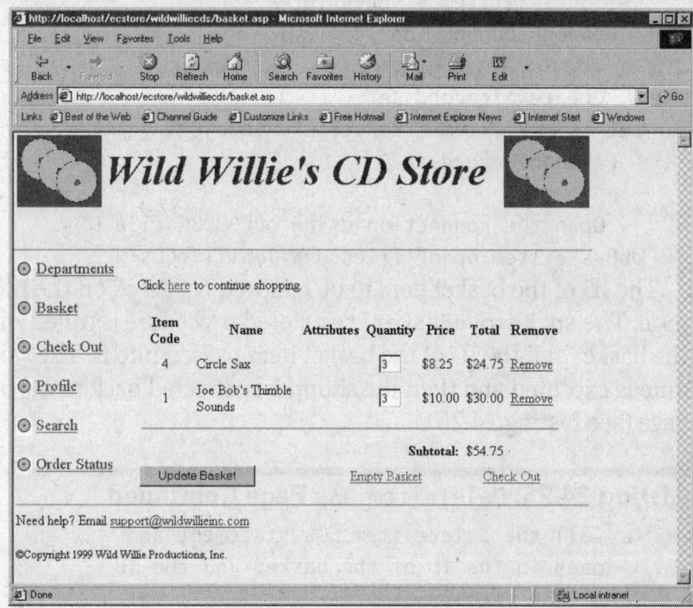

FIGURE 24.7: Updated basket

Deleting from the Basket

Our next page is also a non-display page. It is going to handle the processing of basket-item removal requests. The first step in the page is to open a database connection that will allow us to execute the remove request. The Active Server Page shown in Listing 24.24 accomplishes this task for us.

Listing 24.24: `DeleteItem.asp` **Page**

```
<%@ Language=VBScript %>
<%

   ' ******************************************
   ' DeleteItem.asp - Deletes the specified
   ' item from the shopping basket.
   ' ******************************************

   ' Create an ADO database connection
```

```
set dbBasketItem = server.createobject _
  ("adodb.connection")

' Create a record set
set rsBasketItem = server.CreateObject _
  ("adodb.recordset")

' Open the connection using our ODBC file DSN
dbBasketItem.open("filedsn=WildWillieCDs")
```

The ID of the basket item to be removed is passed on the URL to this page. The `sp_RemoveBasketItem` stored procedure is called with the ID of the basket and the ID of the basket item passed into it. The stored procedure is executed and then the shopper is directed back to the `basket.asp` page (see Listing 24.25).

Listing 24.25: `Deleteitem.asp` **Page Continued**

```
' Call the delete item SQL statement and
' pass in the ID of the basket and the id
' of the item.
sql = "execute sp_RemoveBasketItem " & _
  session("idBasket") & _
  ", " & request("idBasketItem")

' Execute the SQL statement
set rsBasketItem = dbBasketItem.Execute(sql)

' Send the user back to the basket page
Response.Redirect "Basket.asp"

%>
```

The `sp_RemoveBasketItem` stored procedure handles removing the basket item from the table. The ID of the basket and the ID of the basket item is passed into the stored procedure. Then the delete statement is executed to remove the row (see Listing 24.26).

Listing 24.26: `sp_RemoveBasketItem` **Stored Procedure**

```
/*  Stored Procedure to remove an item from
    the basket */
CREATE PROCEDURE sp_RemoveBasketItem

/*  Pass in the ID of the basket and
```

```
    the ID of the basket item to be
    removed.
*/
@idBasket int,
@idBasketItem int

AS

/*  Delete the item from the database */
delete from basketitem
where idBasket = @idBasket and
  idBasketItem = @idBasketItem
```

To test our functionality, Figure 24.8 shows a preliminary shopping basket with 5 items in it. Click the Remove option next to the T-Shirt Rip product.

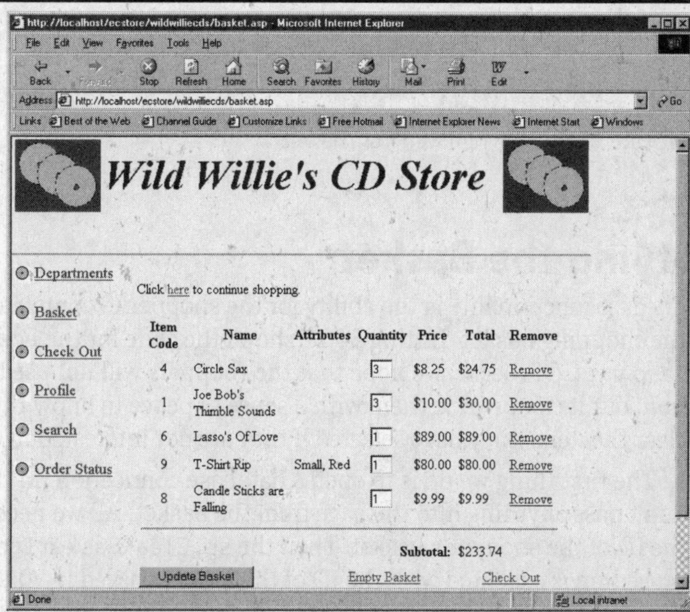

FIGURE 24.8: Preliminary basket

Figure 24.9 shows the item removed from the basket. Note that the subtotal is updated and the rest of the basket is still intact.

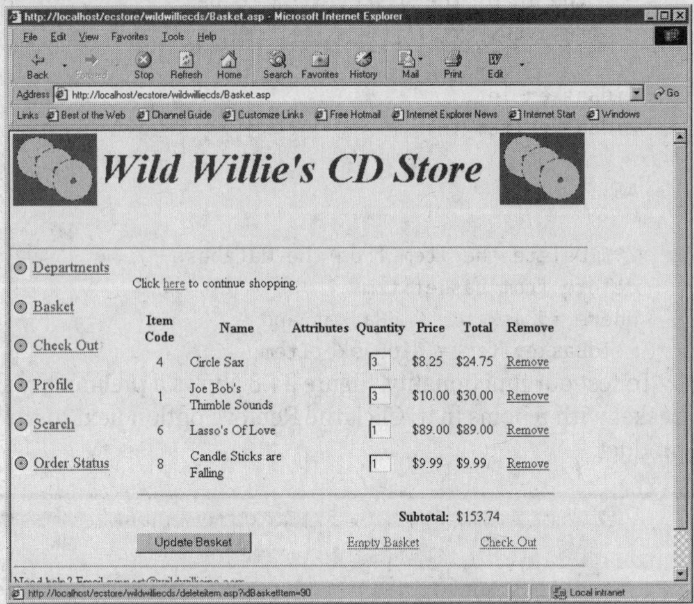

FIGURE 24.9: Item removed from basket

Emptying the Basket

The last functionality is the ability for the shopper to completely empty the shopping basket. Listing 24.27 shows the code for the `emptybasket.asp` page. Of course, we hope that the shoppers will not use this function, but it can provide them with a sense of peace to know that they can clear the items they have selected if they are not interested in ordering.

The first thing we do is to open a database connection. In this case, we don't pass anything into the page from the basket. All we need to know is the ID of the shopper's basket. Then the `sp_ClearBasketItems` stored procedure is executed with the ID of the basket passed in. Once that is done, the shopper is sent back to the `basket.asp` page.

Listing 24.27: `EmptyBasket.asp` Stored Procedure

```
<%@ Language=VBScript %>
<%
  ' *******************************************
  ' EmptyBasket.asp - This empties the items
```

```
'  in the basket.
'  ******************************************

'  Create an ADO database connection
set dbBasketItem = server.createobject _
  ("adodb.connection")

'  Create a record set
set rsBasketItem = server.CreateObject _
  ("adodb.recordset")

'  Open the connection using our ODBC file DSN
dbBasketItem.open("filedsn=WildWillieCDs")

'  Call the clear basket items stored procedure
sql = "execute sp_ClearBasketItems " & _
  session("idBasket")

'  Execute the SQL statement to empty
'  the basket
set rsBasketItem = dbBasketItem.Execute(sql)

'  Send the user to the basket page
Response.Redirect "basket.asp"

%>
```

The `sp_ClearBasketItems` stored procedure takes in the ID of the basket and then executes a delete statement to remove all basket items related to that basket (see Listing 24.28).

Listing 24.28: `sp_ClearBasketItems` **Stored Procedure**

```
/*  Clear the items in the basket */
CREATE PROCEDURE sp_ClearBasketItems

/*  Pass in the ID of the basket */
@idBasket int

AS

/*  Delete all items in the specified
    basket */
```

```
delete from basketitem
where idBasket = @idBasket
```

Figure 24.10 shows a standard shopping basket with multiple items.

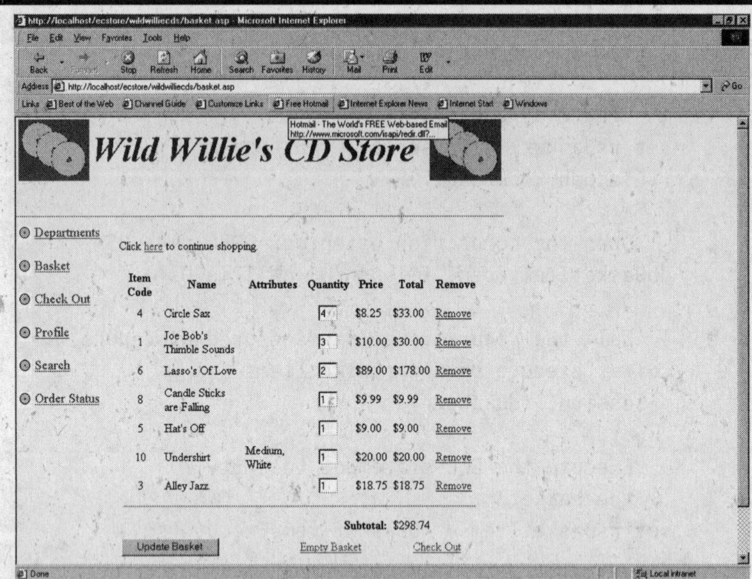

FIGURE 24.10: Preliminary basket

Click the Empty Basket option to remove all items from the basket. Figure 24.11 shows the standard error message indicating the basket is empty.

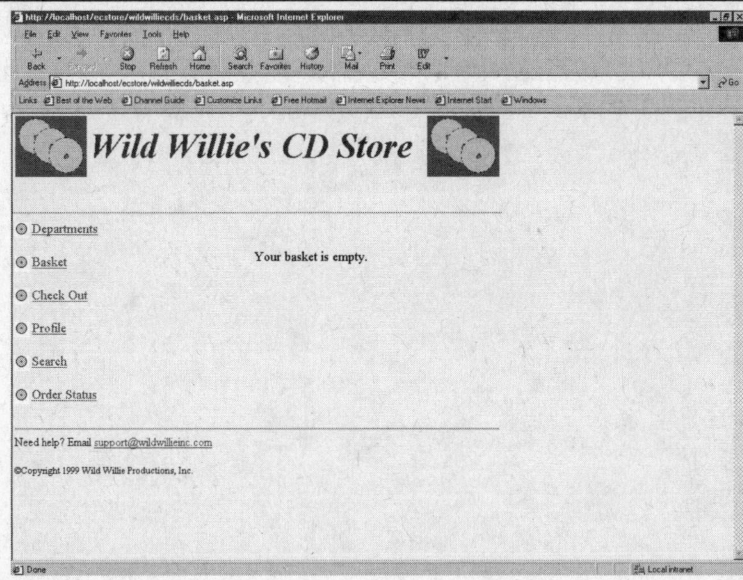

FIGURE 24.11: Basket cleared of all items

WHAT'S NEXT?

This covers the shopping basket and its role in the e-commerce process. The shopping basket is the key tool in the online shopping experience. It is the tool that shoppers will use to keep track of their interests and allow them to manage what they will ultimately purchase. It is also the stepping-off point to making the final purchase. In the next chapter, we will explore another aspect of an e-commerce site: promotional sales.

Chapter 25

On Sale

It's a sale! In this chapter we explore how to provide sale prices for our products, and how to promote those sale products. But sales are not limited to reduced prices. They can also include promotional offers like free shipping, which is another option we will explore.

Adapted from *Visual Basic® Developer's Guide to E-Commerce with ASP and SQL Server™*, by Noel Jerke

ISBN 0-7821-2621-9 752 pages $49.99

Designing the Sale Features

We already have fields in our Products table that will support setting sale prices and their effective date ranges. Listing 25.1 shows SQL code for setting up three initial items to be on sale in our store.

Listing 25.1: Setting Sale Prices

```
update products
set intSalePrice = 400,
  dtSaleStart = getdate(),
  dtSaleEnd = "1/1/2000"
where idproduct = 1

update products
set intSalePrice = 500,
  dtSaleStart = getdate(),
  dtSaleEnd = "1/1/2000"
where idproduct = 2

update products
set intSalePrice = 600,
  dtSaleStart = getdate(),
  dtSaleEnd = "1/1/2000"
where idproduct = 3
```

We will have many opportunities to query which products are on sale in our store. And, in the store manager, we will be able to manage the sale price settings for our products.

To handle the tracking of free shipping, we are going to need to add one field, `intFreeShipping (integer)`, into our basket table. This will be used to track whether or not free shipping was applied to the order.

We are also going to add a new table to indicate whether or not we are currently running a free shipping campaign. Table 25.1 shows the table structure.

TABLE 25.1: FreeShip Table

FIELD	DESCRIPTION
IdFreeShip	Primary key for the table
dtStartDate	Start date of the shipping campaign
dtEndDate	End date of the shipping campaign

The SQL code in Listing 25.2 will update the database tables appropriately.

Listing 25.2: Update Database Tables

```
ALTER TABLE dbo.Basket
ADD intFreeShipping int NULL DEFAULT (0)

CREATE TABLE dbo.FreeShip (
  intFreeShip int IDENTITY (1, 1) NOT NULL ,
  dtStartDate datetime NULL
  CONSTRAINT DF_FreeShip_dtStartDate
  DEFAULT (getdate()),
  dtEndDate datetime NULL
  CONSTRAINT DF_FreeShip_dtEndDate
  DEFAULT (getdate()),
  CONSTRAINT PK_FreeShip PRIMARY KEY CLUSTERED
  (
    intFreeShip
  )
)
```

To get the user side of the free shipping working, we will need to insert some sample data. Listing 25.3 shows the SQL statement to insert values into the FreeShip table.

Listing 25.3: Setting Free Shipping

```
insert into FreeShip(dtStartDate, dtEndDate)
  values(getdate(), '2/1/2000')
```

Now we are ready to begin building the user interface.

Building the Shopping Sale Features

Our code will be changed in two steps. The first step is for displaying sale items throughout the shopping process. The second step will be modifying the checkout process to support free shipping.

Implementing Sale Items

To get started, we will want to show a sale item along with the featured products on the home page of the store. But we'll have to be careful. We may have multiple sale products and we may not want to show all of them on the home page.

We will take the approach of selecting a sale product randomly and displaying it right before the featured products on the page. Listing 25.4 shows the code that should be inserted right before the featured product display code.

A database connection is opened and the `sp_RetrieveSaleProducts` stored procedure is called to return the sale products currently in the store.

Listing 25.4: `Default.asp` **Page**

```
<!-  Show the sale products.  ->
<b>On sale Today!</b><BR><BR>

<%

'  Create an ADO database connection
set dbSaleProd = server.createobject _
  ("adodb.connection")

'  Create a recordset
set rsSaleProd = server.CreateObject _
  ("adodb.recordset")

'  Open the connection using our ODBC file DSN
dbSaleProd.open("filedsn=WildWillieCDs")

'  Retrieve all of the current sale products
sql = "execute sp_RetrieveSaleProducts"
```

```
' Execute the SQL statement
set rsSaleProd = dbSaleProd.Execute(sql)
```

If products are returned, we will want to randomly select one to be displayed (see Listing 25.5). The stored procedure returns a column that is the total number of sale products. We can then use the `VBScript RND` function to randomly pick one of the items to be displayed.

Once the product is displayed, we then loop to the product in the record set returned. Once the product is found, then the product data is retrieved and displayed.

Listing 25.5: `Default.asp` **Continued**

```
' Ensure something is returned so it can
' be displayed
if not rsSaleProd.EOF then

  ' Seed the random number generator
  randomize

  ' Pick a random sale product to display.
  ' Note that the first column returned is
  ' the count of rows.
  Row = Int((rsSaleProd(0) - 1 + 1) * Rnd + 1)

  ' Loop to the row selected.
  for N = 1 to row - 1

    ' Move to the next row.
    rsSaleProd.MoveNext

  next

  ' Retrieve the product information
  ' to be displayed.
  chrProductName = _
    rsSaleProd("chrProductName")
  chrProductImage = _
    rsSaleProd("chrProductImage")
  dblSalePrice = rsSaleProd("intSalePrice")
  idProduct = rsSaleProd("idProduct")

%>
```

```
<!- Build the link to the product
    information. ->
<a href=
  "product.asp?idProduct=<%=idProduct%>">
<img src=
  "images/products/sm_<%=chrProductImage%>"
  align="middle" border="0">
<%=chrProductName%></a>
<font color="red"><b>
- Only
<%=formatcurrency(dblSalePrice/100, 2)%>
</b></font><BR><BR>

<%
  '  Set the flag to that the next
  '  featured product shows the image
  '  on the right.
  Flag = 1

end if

%>
```

We'll use a key stored procedure to retrieve our list of sale products (see Listing 25.6). The first thing done in the stored procedure is to get a count of the products currently on sale. That is needed for our random selection for the home page. The count is stored in a variable for return in our next select statement.

Next a query to retrieve the data for those sale products is done. The first column will return the count with each row.

Listing 25.6: `sp_RetrieveSaleProducts` **Page**

```
CREATE PROCEDURE sp_RetrieveSaleProducts AS

declare @cnt int

select @cnt = count(*) from products
where getdate() >= dtSaleStart and
  getdate() <= dtSaleEnd

select @cnt, *  from products
```

```
where getdate() >= dtSaleStart and
  getdate() <= dtSaleEnd
```

Next we will want to show a sale product on the navigation bar, along with our featured products. We will need to modify `header.asp` to include code to display a sale product.

Once again we will need to follow the same guideline to randomly select a sale item to be displayed on the navigation bar. Listing 25.7 shows the code changes for `header.asp`. This code goes right before the featured product listing.

As on the default page, we open our database connection and retrieve the list of sale products. We then randomly select one of the items and list it on the navigation bar. Note that the sale price will show on any page that is not the default or basket page, just like the featured products.

Listing 25.7: `Header.asp` **Page**

```
<hr>
<font size="2" color="red">
  Sale Products:</font>
<br><br>

<%

'  Create an ADO database connection
set dbSaleProd = server.createobject _
  ("adodb.connection")

'  Create a record set
set rsSaleProd = server.CreateObject _
  ("adodb.recordset")

'  Open the connection using our ODBC file DSN
dbSaleProd.open("filedsn=WildWillieCDs")

'  Retrieve all of the current sale products
sql = "execute sp_RetrieveSaleProducts"

'  Execute the SQL statement
set rsSaleProd = dbSaleProd.Execute(sql)

'  Check to ensure a product was returned.
if not rsSaleProd.EOF then
```

```
    '  Seed the random number generator.
    randomize

    '  Randomly get the product to be displayed
    Row = Int((rsSaleProd(0) - 1 + 1) * Rnd + 1)

    '  Loop to that product.
    for N = 1 to row - 1

      '  Move to the next row.
      rsSaleProd.MoveNext

    next

    '  Retrieve the product information
    '  to be displayed.
    chrProductName = _
      rsSaleProd("chrProductName")
    chrProductImage = _
      rsSaleProd("chrProductImage")
    dblSalePrice = rsSaleProd("intSalePrice")
    idProduct = rsSaleProd("idProduct")

    %>

    <!- Build the link to the
         product information.  ->
    <a href=
    "product.asp?idProduct=<%=idProduct%>">
    <%=chrProductName%></a>
    <font color="red">
    - <%=formatcurrency(dblSalePrice/100, 2)%>
    </font><br><br>

    <%

  end if

  %>
```

Now that we have our sale products showing up on the default page and the navigation page, we are ready to move to the product page. On the product page, we need to show the sale price for the shopper. We also need to modify the logic so that the sale price is added to the basket.

We need to add one section of code at the top of the product page that will check to see if the product is on sale. If so, then we will retrieve the sale price or default it to 0. Listing 25.8 shows the code to be added.

Listing 25.8: `Product.asp` **Page**

```
'  Check to see if the product is currently
'  on sale
if now >= cdate(rsProduct("dtSaleStart")) and _
  date <= cdate(rsProduct("dtSaleEnd")) then

  '  Set the sale price
  intSalePrice = rsProduct("intSalePrice")

else

  '  Default the sale price to 0.
  intSalePrice = 0

end if
```

Next we have to handle the display of the product price. In this case, we want to show the original price as well as the sale price. In Listing 25.9, we modify the price listing under the image to include a check to see if it is on sale. If so, then we show the text in red to indicate the sale price.

Listing 25.9: `Product.asp` **Continued**

```
<!-  Show the product price. An input
      quantity box is created. Also, several
      hidden variables will hold key data for
      adding the product to the database.  ->
<TR>
  <TD align="center"><B>Price:
    <%=formatcurrency(intPrice/100, 2)%></b>

    <!-  Check to see if the product is on
          sale.  ->
    <% if intSalePrice <> 0 then %>

      <!-  Show the sale price ->
      <font color="red"><b>
```

Part vi

```
        <BR><BR> On Sale Now for
        <%=formatcurrency(intSalePrice/100, 2)%>!
        </font></b>

      <% end if %>

    </td>
```

The code shown in Listing 25.10 continues to build the quantity and our hidden variables. Then we check to see if it is a sale product. If so, then the price we set in our hidden elements will be set to the sale price. When the item is added to the basket, it will have the sale price.

Listing 25.10: `Product.asp` **Continued**

```
    <TD align="center">
      <B>Quantity:
      <input type="text" value="1"
      name="quantity" size="2"></b>

      <input type="hidden"
      value="<%=idProduct%>"
      name="idProduct">

      <input type="hidden"
      value="<%=chrProductName%>"
      name="ProductName">

      <%
      '  Check to see if the product is on sale.
      if intSalePrice = 0 then
        %>
        <!-  Set the hidden price to
             the standard price.  ->
        <input type="hidden"
        value="<%=intPrice%>"
        name="ProductPrice">

      <%
      else
      %>
        <!-  Set the hidden price to the sale
             price.  ->
        <input type="hidden"
```

```
      value="<%=intSalePrice%>"
      name="ProductPrice">
    <%
    end if
    %>

  </td>
</TR>
```

TIP

If you have limited inventory of sale products, you might want to develop product limits in your store. For example, we might allow a shopper to purchase only four items within a certain time period for any sale products. This could be tracked by the shopper profile.

That's it for the sale product management on the store interface. Now let's take a look at it in action. Figure 25.1 shows the default page with our sale product listed before the featured products. Note how the images still flip-flop from left to right.

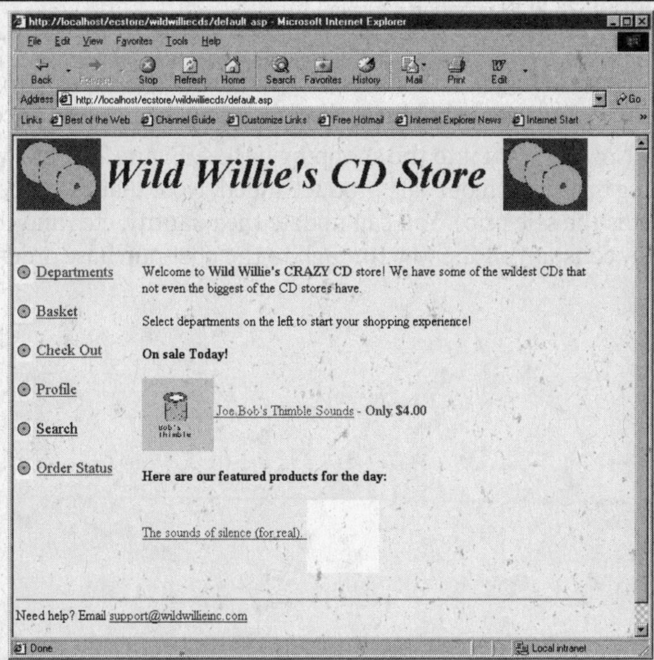

FIGURE 25.1: `Default.asp` sale product

Figure 25.2 shows the navigation bar on the department page. The sale product is listed directly above the featured products.

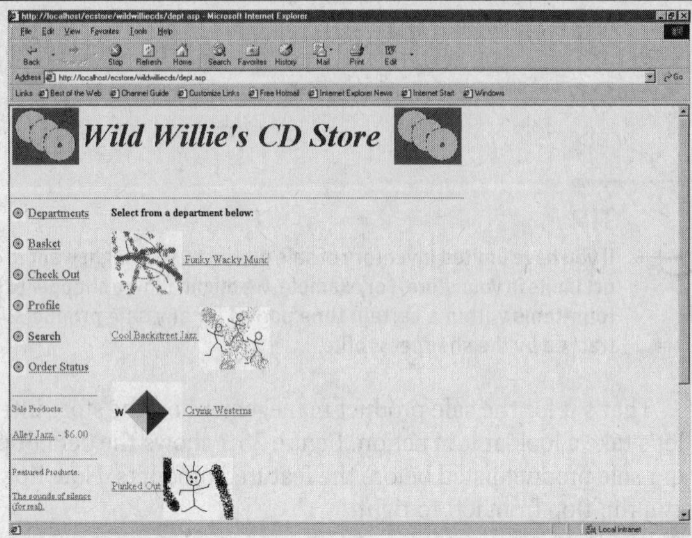

FIGURE 25.2: Navigation bar sale

Next, in Figure 25.3, we have a product that is on sale. Note the sale price (it appears in bold red) directly below the product price.

Now let's add it to the shopping basket. Figure 25.4 shows the shopping basket with our sale product added. Note that the price in the basket is the sale price. You can update the quantity, etc., and the price will stay constant all the way through to the post-purchase order detail.

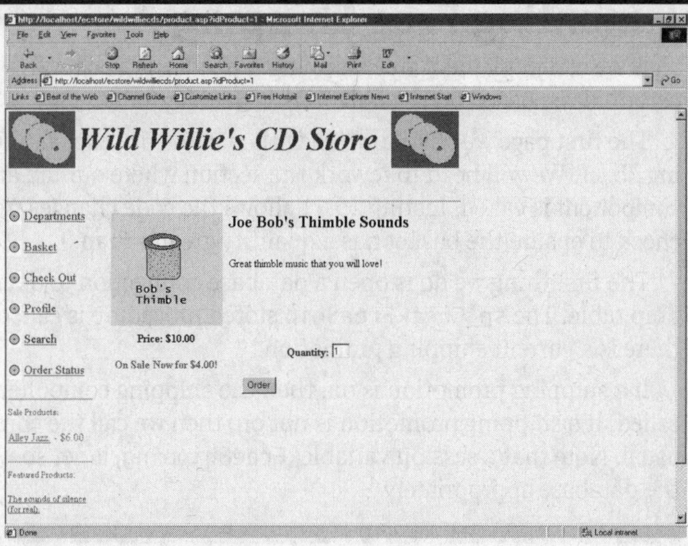

FIGURE 25.3: Product sale price

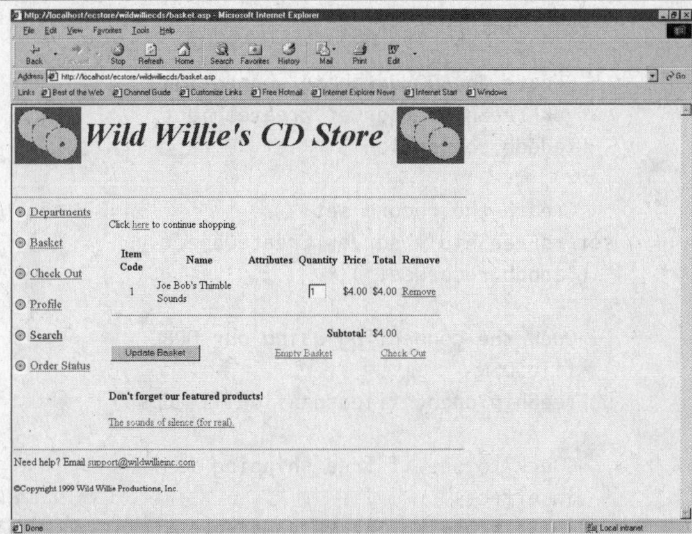

FIGURE 25.4: Basket sale prices

Implementing Free Shipping

Now we can implement free shipping. The idea is to have free shipping on certain days, based on the data in the FreeShip table.

The first page we need to work with is `Payment.asp`, as shown in Listing 25.11. We will need to rework the section where our tax and shipping component is called. Listing 25.11 shows the code changes from when we check to ensure the basket has a quantity greater than 0.

The first thing we do is open a database connection to query the FreeShip table. The `sp_CheckFreeShip` stored procedure is called to see if there is a current shipping promotion.

If a shipping promotion is on, then the shipping component is not called. If a shipping promotion is not on, then we call the component as usual. Note that a session variable, `FreeShipping`, is set so we can flag the database appropriately.

Listing 25.11: `Payment.asp` **Page**

```
    '  Check the quantity returned from
    '  the database
    if rsBasket("quantity") > 0 then

      '  Create an ADO database connection
      set dbFreeShip = server.createobject _
        ("adodb.connection")

      '  Create the record set
      set rsFreeShip = server.CreateObject _
        ("adodb.recordset")

      '  Open the connection using our ODBC
      '  file DSN
      dbFreeShip.open("filedsn=WildWillieCDs")

      '  Check to see if free shipping is
      '  in effect.
      sql = "execute sp_CheckFreeShip"

      '  Execute the statement
      set rsFreeShip = dbBasket.Execute(sql)

      '  Check to see if a row was returned
```

```
    ' which indicates free shipping is
    ' currently in effect.
  if rsFreeShip.EOF then

    ' Call the shipping function of
    ' our component. The quantity is
    ' passed in and must be in a long
    ' data type format. The Shipping fee
    ' is returned.
    Shipping = BizLogic.Shipping _
      (clng(rsBasket("quantity")))

    ' Indicate free shipping is not in effect
    session("FreeShipping") = 0

  else

    ' Default the shipping to 0.
    Shipping = 0

    ' Indicate free shipping is in effect.
    session("FreeShipping") = 1

  end if

else

  ' Redirect to the basket page since
  ' the quantity is 0
  Response.Redirect("Basket.asp")

end if
```

The next set of the code continues with our tax and total amount calculations (see Listing 25.12). Next we'll move into the display of the order totals. We will want to display to the shopper a message indicating that free shipping is currently in promotion. The message displayed next to the shipping total is changed to red and bold to indicate free shipping. (Otherwise it would be displayed in the usual fashion.)

Listing 25.12: `Payment.asp` **Continued**

```
' Store the shipping value in a
' session variable
```

```
session("Shipping") = Shipping

'  Store the quantity in a session variable
session("Quantity") = rsBasket("quantity")

'  Calculate the tax by calling the
'  Tax function of our component. We pass
'  in the shipping state and the order
'  subtotal. The value is also stored in a
'  session variable.
Tax = BizLogic.tax(session("chrShipState"), _
  clng(subtotal))
session("Tax") = Tax

'  Calculate the total and store in a
'  session variable.
Total = SubTotal + Shipping + Tax
session("Total") = Total

%>

<HTML>

<!- #include file="include/header.asp" ->

<BR>

<center>
<font size="5">
<b>Billing Information</b></font>
</center>

<BR>
<b>Order Recap:</b>
<BR><BR>

<!- Build a table to display the order
     total ->
<table>

<!-  Display the Subtotal ->
<tr>
```

```
    <td align="right">Subtotal:</td>
    <td>
      <%=formatcurrency(Subtotal/100, 2)%>
    </td>
  </tr>

  <!- Display the Shipping Value ->
  <tr>
    <td align="right">

      <!- Check to see if Free Shipping is in
           effect. ->
      <% if session("FreeShipping") = 0 then %>
        <!- Indicate standard shipping ->
        Shipping:
      <% else %>
        <!- Indicate free shipping ->
        <font color="red"><b>
        Free Shipping Today!
        </b></font>
      <% end if %>

    </td>
    <td>
      <%=formatcurrency(Shipping/100, 2)%>
    </td>
  </tr>
```

The stored procedure that we use checks to see if a free promotion is currently in place. The start and end dates are checked against the current system date using the `GetDate` function (see Listing 25.13).

Listing 25.13: `sp_CheckFreeShip` **Page**

```
CREATE PROCEDURE sp_CheckFreeShip

AS

select * from FreeShip
where getdate() >= dtStartDate and
  getdate() <= dtEndDate
```

That takes care of the display and calculation of the free shipping. Now our session variables are all set and will be stored in the database. We are ready to ensure that free shipping is stored in our order.

Listing 25.14 show the code for the ValidatePayment.asp page. We are going to update the code to set the calculated amounts in the basket. The sp_UpdateBasket stored procedure is modified to accept the FreeShipping settings. Note that the Shipping session variable will be set to 0 when there is free shipping.

Listing 25.14: ValidatePayment.asp **Page**

```
'*****************************************
' 6.  Update the basket with the final
'     order data.
'*****************************************

'  Finally we need to update the basket
'  with the final amounts for quantity,
'  subtotal, shipping, tax and total
   sql = "execute sp_UpdateBasket " & _
     session("idBasket") & ", " & _
     session("Quantity") & ", " & _
     session("Subtotal") & ", " & _
     session("Shipping") & ", " & _
     session("FreeShipping") & ", " & _
     session("Tax") & ", " & _
     session("Total") & ", 1"
```

As mentioned, we have to update the sp_UpdateBasket stored procedure to accept the free shipping settings (see Listing 25.15). A parameter is added to set the value of the free shipping, and then the update statement sets the field value.

Listing 25.15: sp_UpdateBasket **Page**

```
/*  Stored procedure to update the basket
  - values */
ALTER PROCEDURE sp_UpdateBasket

/*  Pass in the ID of the basket, the total
    quantity, the order subtotal, the shipping
    value, the tax value, the order total and a
    flag indicating the order was placed. */
```

```
@idBasket int,
@intQuantity int,
@intSubTotal int,
@intShipping int,
@intFreeShipping int,
@intTax int,
@intTotal int,
@intOrderPlaced int

AS

/*  Update the basket */
update basket set
   intQuantity = @intQuantity,
   intSubtotal = @intSubtotal,
   intShipping = @intShipping,
   intFreeShipping = @intFreeShipping,
   intTax = @intTax,
   intTotal = @intTotal,
   intOrderPlaced = @intOrderPlaced
where idBasket = @idBasket
```

SHIPPING CHARGES

There is more than one way to approach shipping charge reductions. We could provide logic that will give free shipping for orders over a certain amount, or we could provide free shipping on every third order. Each of these could be a key feature in providing incentive for the shopper to make that purchase.

Now let's test our free shipping logic. Be sure that the campaign data set in the FreeShip table is set to ensure the current date is within the campaign range.

Figure 25.5 shows the payment page indicating that the user will not be charged for shipping.

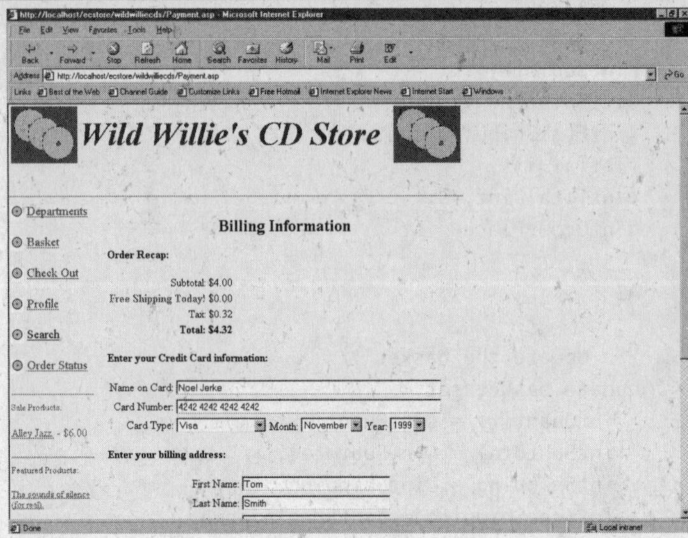

FIGURE 25.5: Free shipping

Go ahead and place the order. Check the order in the order status or order manager to ensure that the shipping values have been stored properly. Figure 25.6 shows our sample order detail.

http://localhost/ecstore/manager/OrderDetail.asp?idOrder=26&idShopper=1 - Microsoft Internet Explorer

Bill To:
Tom Smith
100 Main St.
Condo, VA 22609
555-555-5555
tsmith@nowhere.com

Ship To:
Tom Smith
100 Main St.
Condo, VA 22609
555-555-5555
tsmith@nowhere.com

Payment Data:
Card Name: Noel Jerke Card Number: 4242 4242 4242 4242
Card Type: Visa Card Expiration Date: 11/1999

Item Code	Name	Attributes	Quantity	Price	Total
1	Joe Bob's Thimble Soun		1	$4.00	$4.00

Subtotal: $4.00
Free Shipping: $0.00
Tax: $0.32
Total: $4.32

Submit Changes

FIGURE 25.6: Order detail with sale price and free shipping figure

Building the Sale Management Features

Now that we have seen the user interface in action, we are ready to tackle the management tools necessary to set our sale prices and manage the free shipping settings.

Managing Product Sales

Let's first tackle managing our sale settings. This will require an update to the ManageProduct.asp page, as shown in Listing 25.16.

Directly below the featured product code that we added to the manager, we need to add similar code to manage the sale settings. We need to set the price and the start and end dates. A row with text input fields for the intSalePrice field, the dtSaleStart field, and the dtSaleEnd field is added to the page.

Listing 25.16: ManageProduct.asp Page

```
<!-  Show the sale price settings.  ->
<tr>
  <td align="right"><b>Sale Price:</b></td>
  <td>

    <!-  Display an input box for the product
          sale price.  ->
    <input type="text"
    value="<%=rsProduct("intSalePrice")/100%>"
    name="intSalePrice" size="10">

    <!-  Show the start and end date for the
          sale price campaign.  ->
    Start Date:  <input type="text"
    value="<%=rsProduct("dtSaleStart")%>"
    size="10" name="dtSaleStart">

    End Date:  <input type="text"
    value="<%=rsProduct("dtSaleEnd")%>"
    size="10" name="dtSaleEnd">
  </td>
</tr>
```

Next we have to update the UpdateProduct.asp page to accept the new values and update the database. Listing 25.17 shows the code updates for the page. The values are retrieved from the form variables.

The stored procedure sp_UpdateProduct needs to accept the sale values. The values retrieved from the form are passed in.

Listing 25.17: UpdateProduct.asp Page

```
' Retrieve the sale price and start and end
' date for the sale price campaign.
intSalePrice = request("intSalePrice") * 100
dtSaleStart = request("dtSaleStart")
dtSaleEnd = request("dtSaleEnd")

' Create an ADO database connection
set dbProduct = server.createobject _
  ("adodb.connection")

' Create the record set
set rsProduct = server.CreateObject _
  ("adodb.recordset")

' Open the connection using our ODBC file DSN
dbProduct.open("filedsn=WildWillieCDs")

' Execute the SQL stored procedure to
' update the product data
sql = "execute sp_UpdateProduct " & _
     request("idProduct") & ", '" & _
     chrProductName & "', '" & _
     txtDescription & "', '" & _
     chrProductImage & "', " & _
     intPrice & ", " & _
     intActive & ", " & _
     intFeatured & ", '" & _
     dtFeatureStart & "', '" & _
     dtFeatureEnd & "', " & _
     intSalePrice & ", '" & _
     dtSaleStart & "', '" & _
     dtSaleEnd & "'"

' Execute the statement
```

```
set rsProduct = dbProduct.Execute(sql)

'  Send the user back to the product
'  manager page and pass back the product ID.
Response.Redirect _
  "ManageProduct.asp?idProduct=" & _
  request("idProduct")
```

Listing 25.18 shows the updated sp_UpdateProduct stored procedure. The first change is adding the parameter values for each of the fields. Following that, the updated SQL statement is modified to set these values.

Listing 25.18: sp_UpdateProduct **Page**

```
ALTER PROCEDURE sp_UpdateProduct

@idProduct int,
@chrProductName varchar(255),
@txtDescription text,
@chrProductImage varchar(100),
@intPrice int,
@intActive int,
@intFeatured int,
@dtFeatureStart datetime,
@dtFeatureEnd datetime,
@intSalePrice int,
@dtSaleStart datetime,
@dtSaleEnd datetime

AS

update products set
   chrProductName = @chrProductName,
   txtDescription    = @txtDescription,
   chrProductImage = @chrProductImage,
   intPrice = @intPrice,
   intActive = @intActive,
   intFeatured = @intFeatured,
   dtFeatureStart = @dtFeatureStart,
   dtFeatureEnd = @dtFeatureEnd,
   intSalePrice = @intSalePrice,
   dtSaleStart = @dtSaleStart,
   dtSaleEnd = @dtSaleEnd
```

```
where
    idProduct = @idProduct
```

The code changes to manage the sale prices are pretty simple. Figure 25.7 shows the product manager page with the sales fields displayed. These can be modified and the product data submitted.

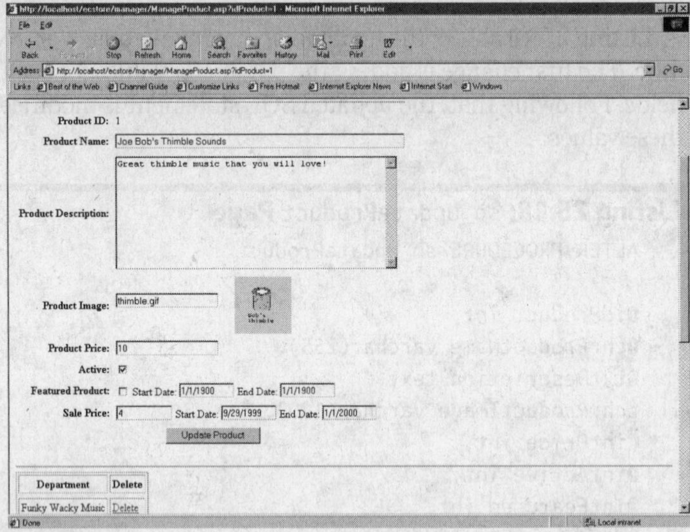

FIGURE 25.7: Product manager

After making appropriate changes, submit the product data. Figure 25.8 shows the product data with the sale data updated.

That's it for managing sales prices. Next we can move to managing the free shipping campaign.

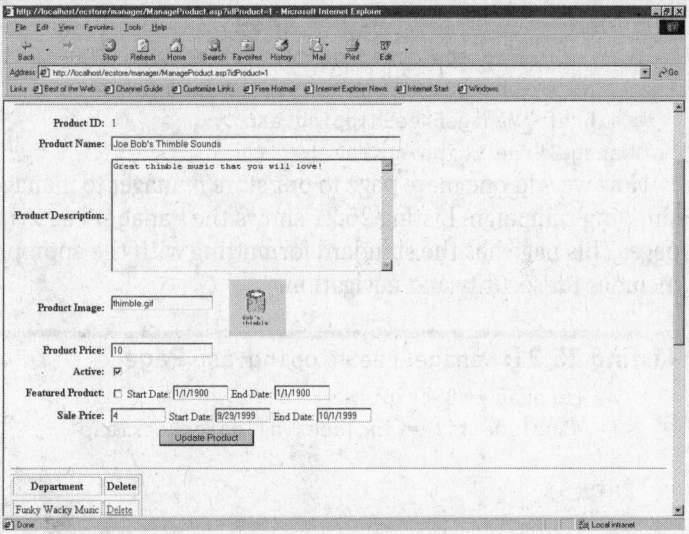

FIGURE 25.8: Updated sale price

Free Shipping Campaign Management

We currently do not have any facility for managing free shipping, so we will have to add one more item to our manager menu and `NavInclude` pages. Listings 25.19 and 25.20 show the updates to the appropriate pages that will add in the free shipping navigation.

In `ManagerMenu.asp` we add in one more row to the table that links to the `ManageFreeShipping.asp` page.

Listing 25.19: `ManagerMenu.asp` **Page**

```
<tr>
   <!- Manage free shipping ->
   <td><a href="ManageFreeShipping.asp">
        Manage Free Shipping</a></td>
</tr>
```

In Listing 25.20 the navigation bar has one more addition for linking to the Manage Free Shipping option.

Listing 25.20: `NavInclude.asp` **Page**

```
<!- Link to the management of free
      shipping. ->
<a href="ManageFreeShipping.asp">
Manage Free Shipping</a> |
```

Now we add one more page to our store manager to manage the free shipping campaign. Listing 25.21 shows the `ManageFreeShipping.asp` page. This page has the standard formatting with the appropriate includes for security and navigation.

Listing 25.21: `ManageFreeShipping.asp` **Page**

```
<%@ Language=VBScript %>
<!- #Include file="include/validatecheck.asp"
->
<HTML>
<!-
  ManageFreeShipping.asp - Provides options
  to set the next free shipping campaign date
  range.
->

<HEAD>
<META NAME="GENERATOR"
  Content="Microsoft Visual Studio 6.0">
</HEAD>
<BODY>

<!- #include file="include/navinclude.asp" ->


<BR><BR>
<B>Set free shipping campaign:
</b><BR><BR>
```

In Listing 25.22 we continue the page. The first thing we do is open a database connection to retrieve the current free shipping settings. The `sp_RetrieveFreeShip` stored procedure returns the data currently in the database.

Listing 25.22: `ManageFreeShipping.asp` **Continued**

```
<%
'  Create an ADO database connection
set dbFreeShipping = server.createobject _
  ("adodb.connection")

'  Create the record set
set rsFreeShipping = server.CreateObject _
  ("adodb.recordset")

'  Open the connection using our ODBC file DSN
dbFreeShipping.open("filedsn=WildWillieCDs")

'  The sp_RetrieveFreeShip stored procedure
'  returns the last settings in the database.
sql = "execute sp_RetrieveFreeShip"

'  Execute the statement
set rsFreeShipping = _
  dbFreeShipping.Execute(sql)
%>
```

Next a form is created for posting the start and end dates for the free shipping campaign. Then the form is completed with a submit form and the appropriate closing tags for the page (see Listing 25.23).

Listing 25.23: `ManageFreeShipping.asp` **Continued**

```
<!-  The changes will be posted to the
     UpdateFreeShipping.asp page.  ->
<form method="post" _
  action="UpdateFreeShipping.asp">

<!-  Start a table to show the start
     and end date.  ->
<table cellpadding="3" cellspacing"3">
<!-  Show the start date.  ->
<tr>
  <td align="right">Start Date:</td>
  <td>
    <input type="text" name="dtStartDate"
    value="<%=rsFreeShipping("dtStartDate")%>">
  </td>
```

```
</tr>
<!-  Show the end date.  ->
<tr>
  <td align="right">End Date:</td>
  <td>
    <input type="text" name="dtEndDate"
    value="<%=rsFreeShipping("dtEndDate")%>">
  </td>
</tr>

<!-  Show a submit button for the form ->
<tr><td align="center" colspan="2">
    <input type="submit" value="Submit"
    name="Submit">
</td></tr>
</table>

</form>

</BODY>
</HTML>
```

WARNING

The date functions here assume the use of a U.S. system locale, where dates are stored as mm/dd/yy. When filling out this form, be sure to enter your dates in this format; otherwise you may get an unexpected error.

The `sp_RetrieveFreeShip` stored procedure simply returns all of the data in the table. In reality, we are just working with the first row since we can have only one shipping campaign at a time. Note that we could provide management to set up multiple shipping campaigns and schedule them (see Listing 25.24).

Listing 25.24: `sp_RetrieveFreeShip` **Page**

```
CREATE PROCEDURE sp_RetrieveFreeShip AS

select * from FreeShip
```

The `UpdateFreeShipping.asp` page handles updating the data in the FreeShip table. The first thing we do is open a database connection. Then the `sp_UpdateFreeShip` stored procedure is called to make the changes to the database (see Listing 25.25).

Listing 25.25: `UpdateFreeShipping.asp` **Page**

```
<%@ Language=VBScript %>
<%

'  ******************************************
'  UpdateFreeShipping.asp - Handles updating
'  the free shipping campaign dates.
'  ******************************************

'  Retrieve the start date
dtStartDate = request("dtStartDate")

'  Retrieve the end date
dtEndDate = request("dtEndDate")

'  Create an ADO database connection
set dbFreeShip = server.createobject _
  ("adodb.connection")

'  Create the record set
set rsFreeShip = server.CreateObject _
  ("adodb.recordset")

'  Open the connection using our ODBC file DSN
dbFreeShip.open("filedsn=WildWillieCDs")

'  Execute the sp_UpdateFreeShip stored
'  procedure to change the dates.
sql = "execute sp_UpdateFreeShip '" & _
  dtStartDate & "', '" & dtEndDate & "'"

'  Execute the statement
set rsFreeShip = dbFreeShip.Execute(sql)

'  Send the user back to free shipping
'  manager page.
Response.Redirect "ManageFreeShipping.asp"

%>
```

Listing 25.26 shows the `update` stored procedure. The start date and end date are passed into it. In this case we are updating all rows that exist in the table.

Listing 25.26: `sp_UpdateFreeShip` **Page**

```
CREATE PROCEDURE sp_UpdateFreeShip

@dtStartDate datetime,
@dtEndDate datetime

AS

Update FreeShip set
  dtStartDate = @dtStartDate,
  dtEndDate = @dtEndDate
```

Order reporting must be updated also. We need to indicate that free shipping was in effect when the order was placed, and we cannot override that if the order is updated for some reason.

Listing 25.27 shows code for the `OrderDetail.asp` pages. To display whether free shipping is in effect, a check is done on the `intFreeShipping` field in the database. If the value is set, then we show text indicating free shipping; if not, then we show standard text. Also, we have to be sure to post the free shipping value to the `UpdateOrder.asp` page so that we can make the appropriate update. Thus, in each case we set a hidden input element with the shipping value so it will be passed to the next page.

Listing 25.27: `OrderDetail.asp` **Page**

```
<!- Show the shipping total of the basket ->
<tr>
  <td colspan="5" align="right">
    <!- Check to see if we have
          free shipping. ->
    <% if rsOrderReceiptHeader _
      ("intFreeShipping") = 1 then %>
      <!- Show that there is free
           shipping on this order. ->
      <b><font color="red">
      Free Shipping:</b></font>
      <input type="hidden" value="1"
        name="intFreeShipping">
    <% else %>
      <!- Show that there is
           standard shipping on this
           order. ->
```

```
          <b>Shipping:</b>
          <input type="hidden" value="0"
            name="intFreeShipping">
        <% end if %>
      </td>
      <td align="right">
        <%Response.Write formatcurrency_
          (rsOrderReceiptHeader_
          ("intShipping")/100,_
          2) %>
      </td>
    </tr>
```

The UpdateOrder.asp page handles updating the order data with any changes we have made. That may include changing quantities of items in the order, which in turn would affect the order total and calculated fields.

The first thing we do is update the section where all header values are retrieved from the form. We have to add one more option to retrieve the intFreeShipping value (see Listing 25.28).

Listing 25.28: UpdateOrder.asp **Page**

```
    '  Next we retrieve the core order data which
    '  includes the billing address and shipping
    '  address.  Note that the key fields are
    '  updated to ensure any single quotes are
    '  doubled.
    chrBillFirstName = replace(request_
      ("chrBillFirstName"), "'", "''")

    chrBillLastname = replace(request_
      ("chrBillLastName"), "'", "''")

    chrShipFirstName = replace(request_
      ("chrShipFirstName"), "'", "''")

    chrShipLastname = replace(request_
      ("chrShipLastName"), "'", "''")

    chrBillAddress = replace(request_
      ("chrBillAddress"), "'", "''")

    chrShipAddress = replace(request_
```

```
    ("chrShipAddress"), "'", "''")

  chrBillCity = replace(request_
    ("chrBillCity"), "'", "''")
  chrBillState = request("chrBillState")
  chrBillZipCode = request("chrBillZipCode")
  chrShipCity = replace(request_
    ("chrShipCity"), "'", "''")
  chrShipState = request("chrShipState")
  chrShipZipCode = request("chrShipZipCode")
  chrBillPhone = request("chrBillPhone")
  chrShipPhone = request("chrShipPhone")
  chrBillEmail = request("chrBillEmail")
  chrShipEmail = request("chrShipEmail")

  '  Get the free shipping setting for the order.
  intFreeShipping = request("intFreeShipping")
```

In Listing 25.29, the `UpdateOrder.asp` code changes are continued. As with the `payment.asp` page, we need to check to see if free shipping is in effect. If it is, then we cannot calculate shipping for the order.

Once the shipping value is set, then we can update the basket data with the new calculated values. If free shipping was in effect, then the shipping value will be set to 0. The `sp_UpdateBasket` stored procedure sets all of the values, including the `intFreeShipping` fields.

NOTE

Of course, there are a number of ways in which we could increase the sophistication of this procedure. For example, we could give an option in the manager to turn off free shipping for the order. Alternatively, we might allow multiple sets of dates to be used for free shipping promotions. The code has been written in such a way as to make such modifications easy.

Listing 25.29: `UpdateOrder.asp` **Continued**

```
  '  Check to see if there is free shipping
  '  on the order.
  if intFreeShipping = 0 then

    '  Create the Business Logic component to
    '  calculate the tax and shipping.
```

```
    set BizLogic = server.CreateObject_
      ("ECStoreBizLogic.TaxShip")

    '  Call the shipping function of
    '  our component. The quantity is passed
    '  in and must be in a long data type
    '  format. The Shipping fee is returned.
    Shipping = BizLogic.Shipping_
      (cLng(TotalQuantity))

  else

    '  Otherwise we default the shipping
    '  total to 0.
    Shipping = 0

  end if

  '  Calculate the tax by calling the Tax
  '  function of our component. We pass in
  '  the shipping state and the order subtotal.
  '  The value is also stored in a session
  '  variable.
  Tax = BizLogic.tax(cstr(chrShipState), _
    clng(subtotal))

  '  Calculate the new total.
  Total = subtotal + shipping + tax

  '  Build a SQL statement to update the
  '  basket data
  sql = "execute sp_UpdateBasket " & _
       idBasket & ", " & _
       TotalQuantity & ", " & _
       SubTotal & ", " & _
       Shipping & ", " & _
       intFreeShipping & ", " & _
       Tax & ", " & _
       Total & ", 1"

  '  Execute the SQL statement
  set rsOrderUpdate = dbOrderUpdate.execute(sql)
```

```
      '  Send the user back to the order detail
      '  page
      Response.Redirect _
        "OrderDetail.asp?idOrder=" & idOrder & _
        "&idShopper=" & idShopper

%>
```

Now let's take a look at our manager pages in action. Figure 25.9 shows the manager menu with the addition of the free shipping management option.

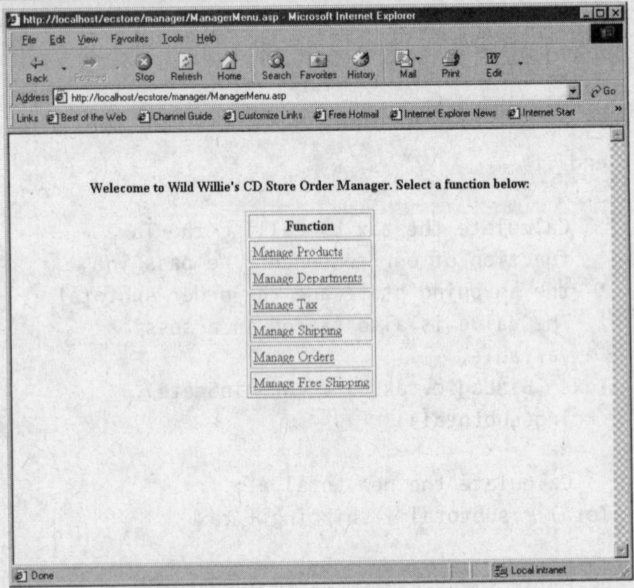

FIGURE 25.9: Manager menu

If we click that option, we'll see the free shipping management page, as shown in Figure 25.10.

There are only two fields for setting the next campaign dates. Figure 25.11 shows the campaign dates updated to reflect a new campaign period.

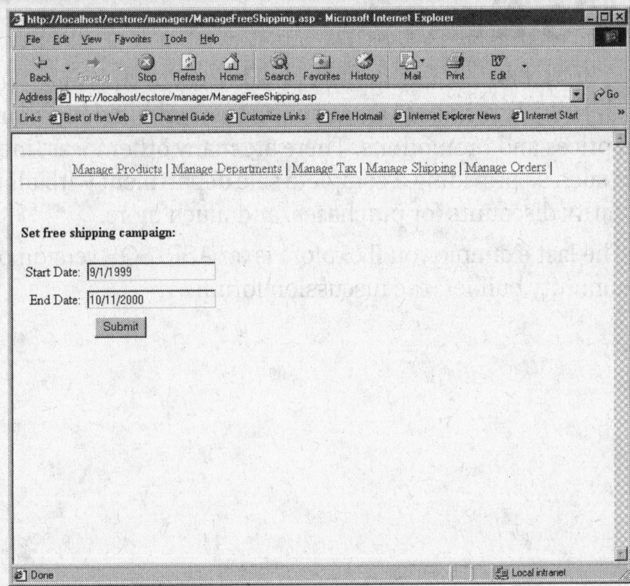

FIGURE 25.10: Free shipping management page

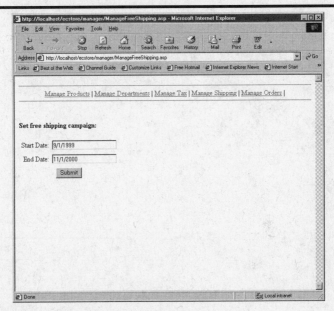

FIGURE 25.11: Free shipping campaign update

What's Next?

That does it for managing sales promotions in the store. We've just scratched the surface of what options we can build in for promoting special prices and promotions. There are many other ideas, including strategies such as providing a complete sale department with all items on sale, quantity discounts for purchases, and much more.

The last example you'll explore is an ASP/SQL version of the classic community builder: the discussion forum.

Chapter 26

Discussion Forums

This chapter tackles the kingpin of the community tools—discussion forums. Forums can be the lifeblood of a community Web site as they provide a central meeting place for site members to discuss the content of the site, issues, interests, news, and much more.

The basic principle of discussion topics and messages are at the core of any good forum solution, but there are any number of features and formats that the forums can include. In this chapter, we build the fundamental tools that make up a forum solution and that include the administrative tools as well.

Adapted from *E-Commerce Developer's Guide to Building Community and Using Promotional Tools*, by Noel Jerke

ISBN 0-7821-2865-3 544 pages $49.99

Designing the Application

The structure of the forums follows the "conversation" process. The forum administrator first starts out by setting up discussion sections. These can be thought of as buckets that the community administrator creates to lend focus to conversations.

Within those section buckets, the site visitor can create conversation threads. Ideally, the threads are topics related to the section topic set up by the administrator. Of course, the site visitors can title the thread anything they want.

Finally, within the thread, site visitors can post messages. These messages constitute the primary conversational tool of the forums with the sections and threads. Figure 26.1 depicts the structural flow of the forums we are designing.

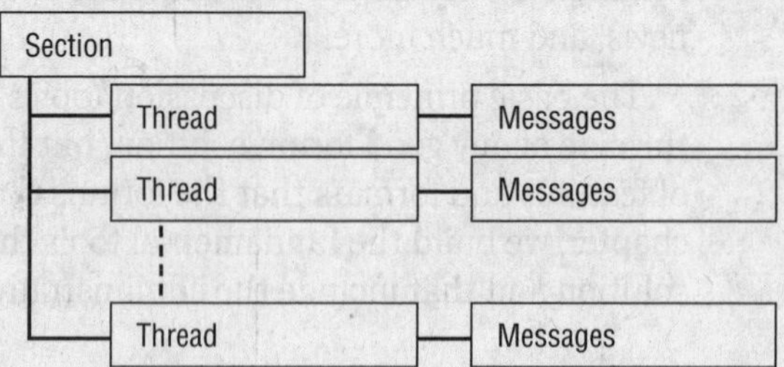

FIGURE 26.1: Discussion forums structure

With active forums, you need a solid administrative interface to keep up with your site visitors. The tool we build allows for the management of sections, threads, and messages. If you don't like what someone posts, you can edit or delete the message. If a visitor creates a thread that is not germane to the section, you can delete it.

Building the Database

Not surprisingly, our database structure is going to reflect the discussion structure outlined above. We have a slew of stored procedures that we'll use to manage the messaging database.

Tables

There are three tables as part of our forum data structure. Figure 26.2 shows the relationships between the Section, Thread, and Messages tables.

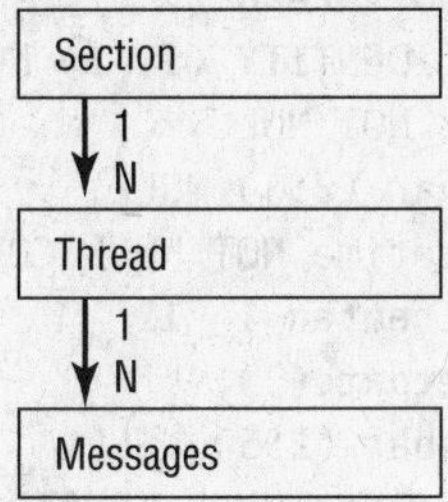

FIGURE 26.2: Forums database structure

We create a table to hold the section data. This table is related to the Thread table, which has a one-to-many relationship. Messages in the Message table will have a one-to-many relationship with the Thread table.

Listing 26.1 shows the SQL code to generate the Section table. Note that we store the date when the section was created. In addition, we store the last modification date to the section. Modification in this case means when any message is updated for that section. This enables the user to know when a new message has been posted for a quick look before browsing.

Listing 26.1: Section Table

```
CREATE TABLE dbo.Section (
  idSection int IDENTITY (1, 1) NOT NULL,
  chrName varchar (255) NULL,
  dtCreated datetime NOT NULL CONSTRAINT
  DF_Section_dtCreated_2__12
   DEFAULT (getdate()),
  dtLastMod datetime NULL CONSTRAINT
  DF_Section_dtLastMod_1__12
   DEFAULT (getdate())
)
GO
```

Listing 26.2 shows the SQL code to generate the Thread table. The ID of the section is stored in the table to identify to which section the thread is related. The name, date created, owner, and, of course, the date last modified are also stored. The owner is identified when logging in to the forums.

Listing 26.2: Thread Table

```
CREATE TABLE dbo.Thread (
  idThread int IDENTITY (1, 1) NOT NULL,
  idSection int NOT NULL,
  chrName varchar (255) NULL,
  dtCreated datetime NOT NULL CONSTRAINT
  DF_Thread_dtCreated_1__12
    DEFAULT (getdate()),
  chrOwner varchar (255) NULL,
  dtLastMod datetime NULL CONSTRAINT
  DF_Thread_dtLastMod_1__12
    DEFAULT (getdate())
)
GO
```

Our final table, Message, stores the messages of the forums. The ID of the thread is stored to make the relationship. The date the message was created, the text of the message, the owner, and the subject are also stored. Listing 26.3 shows the SQL script code to create the table.

Listing 26.3: Message Table

```
CREATE TABLE dbo.Message (
  idMessage int IDENTITY (1, 1) NOT NULL,
  dtCreated datetime NOT NULL CONSTRAINT
  DF_Message_dtCreated_3__12
    DEFAULT (getdate()),
  txtMessage text NULL,
  idThread int NOT NULL,
  chrOwner varchar (255) NULL,
  chrSubject varchar (255) NULL
)
GO
```

Stored Procedures

Next we create the stored procedures to manage all of the forum data. Let's first look at the stored procedures related to the section.

First for the section data we have the `sp_AddSection` stored procedure, as shown in Listing 26.4. This stored procedure handles inserting a new section into the database. The name of the section is passed in as a parameter.

Listing 26.4: `sp_AddSection` **Table**

```
CREATE PROCEDURE sp_AddSection

/* Pass in the section name */
@chrName varchar(255)

AS

/* Insert the section into the table */
insert into section(chrName) values(@chrName)
GO
```

If we add a section, we will of course want to be able to delete it. Listing 26.5 shows the code to create the sp_DeleteSection stored procedure. The ID of the section is passed in, and the SQL Delete function is used.

Listing 26.5: `sp_DeleteSection` **Table**

```
CREATE PROCEDURE sp_DeleteSection

/* Pass the ID of the section */
@idSection int

AS

/* Delete the section from the database */
delete from section
where idSection = @idSection
GO
```

The next stored procedure, sp_UpdateSectionName shown in Listing 26.6, manages updating the name of a section. The ID of the section and the new name is passed in as a parameter. The SQL Update function is used to update the data.

Listing 26.6: `sp_UpdateSectionName` **Table**

```
CREATE PROCEDURE sp_UpdateSectionName

/* Pass in the ID of the section and the
  name of the section */
```

```
@idSection int,
@chrName varchar(255)

AS

/* Update the name of the section for the
  specified section ID */
update section set chrName =
  @chrName where idSection = @idSection
GO
```

When we display the sections to the user, not only do we want to let them know when the last message update was done, but we also want to tell them how many messages are in the section. Listing 26.7 shows the `sp_RetrieveSectionPostCount` stored procedure that will retrieve the message count for the specified section.

To get the count for the section, we have to join the Message and Thread tables. Remember that the ID of the section is stored in the Thread table, thus we don't need to actually query the Section table directly.

Listing 26.7: `sp_RetrieveSectionPostCount` **Table**

```
CREATE PROCEDURE sp_RetrieveSectionPostCount

/* Pass in the ID of the section */
@idSection int

AS

/* Retrieve the number of messages posted
  for all threads in the section */
select count(*) from message, thread
where thread.idSection = @idSection and
  message.idThread = thread.idthread
GO
```

Our final stored procedure retrieves all the sections in the database. Listing 26.8 shows the code to create the `sp_RetrieveSections` stored procedure.

Listing 26.8: `sp_RetrieveSections` **Table**

```
CREATE PROCEDURE sp_RetrieveSections AS

/* Retrieve all the forum sections */
```

```
select * from section order by chrName
GO
```

Now we are ready to move on to the thread management stored procedures. These are similar to the section stored procedures.

Not unsurprisingly, our first stored procedure handles inserting a new thread into the database. The ID of the section related to the thread, the name of the thread, and the owner are passed in as parameters. The SQL script code used to create the stored procedure is shown in Listing 26.9.

Listing 26.9: `sp_InsertThread` **Table**

```
CREATE PROCEDURE sp_InsertThread

/* Pass in the ID of the section,
  the name of the thread and the
  owner of the thread */
@idSection int,
@chrName varchar(255),
@chrOwner varchar(255)

AS

/* Insert the new thread into the database */
insert into Thread
(idSection, chrName, chrOwner)
values(@idSection, @chrName, @chrOwner)
GO
```

Listing 26.10 shows the SQL code to create the `sp_DeleteThread` stored procedure. The ID of the thread is passed in, and the SQL Delete function is used to delete the thread.

Listing 26.10: `sp_DeleteThread` **Table**

```
CREATE PROCEDURE sp_DeleteThread

/* Pass in the ID of the thread */
@idThread int

AS

/* Delete the thread from the database */
delete from thread where idThread = @idThread
GO
```

Listing 26.11 shows the SQL code that handles updating a thread name and owner. The ID of the thread is passed in, and the name and the owner are updated.

Listing 26.11: `sp_UpdateThread` **Table**

```
CREATE PROCEDURE sp_UpdateThread

/* Pass in the ID of the thread,
  the name of the thread and
  the owner */
@idThread int,
@chrName varchar(255),
@chrOwner varchar(255)

AS

/* Update the thread name and owner for the
  specified thread */
update thread set chrName = @chrName,
  chrOwner = @chrOwner
where idThread = @idThread
GO
```

As with the sections, we want to indicate to the site visitor how many posts there are per thread. The `sp_RetrieveThreadPostCount` stored procedure, shown in Listing 26.12, takes in the ID of the thread and returns the count per thread. To get the count, we have to query the Message table by thread ID.

Listing 26.12: `sp_RetrieveThreadPostCount` **Table**

```
CREATE PROCEDURE sp_RetrieveThreadPostCount

/* Pass in the ID of the thread */
@idThread int

AS

/* Retrieve a count of all the messages
  posted for this thread */
select count(*) from message
where message.idThread = @idthread
GO
```

Finally, we have our stored procedure that returns all of the threads for a specified section. The ID of the section is passed into the stored procedure, and the related thread data is returned. `sp_RetrieveThreads` is shown in Listing 26.13.

Listing 26.13: `sp_RetrieveThreads` **Table**

```
CREATE PROCEDURE sp_RetrieveThreads

/* Pass in the ID of the section */
@idSection int

AS

/* Retrieve all of the thread for the
   specified section */
select * from thread where
   idSection = @idSection order by dtCreated
GO
```

Last but not least, we have our stored procedures to manage the message data. We have a similar set of functional stored procedures as we have seen for sections and threads, but we'll also need to add additional stored procedures for managing the paging through message data.

The first stored procedure that we'll build, `sp_InsertMessage`, inserts a new message into the table, as shown in Listing 26.14. We have a number of actions that have to take place aside from inserting the new message. We also have to update the corresponding thread and section data to indicate when the last update was completed.

Within this transaction, we'll update the section data to set the date last modified. And the thread data is updated to also indicate the last modification.

Listing 26.14: `sp_InsertMessage` **Table**

```
CREATE PROCEDURE sp_InsertMessage

/* Pass in the ID of the section,
   the ID of the thread, the subject
   of the message and the owner of
   the message */
@idSection int,
@idThread int,
```

```
@chrSubject varchar(255),
@txtMessage text,
@chrOwner varchar(255)

AS

/* Insert the message into the database */
insert into Message
(idThread, chrSubject, txtMessage, chrOwner)
values(@idThread, @chrSubject,
  @txtMessage, @chrOwner)

/* Update the date the section was last
  modified with a new message. */
update section set dtLastMod =
  getdate() where idSection = @idSection

/* Update the date the thread was last
  modified by adding the new message */
update thread set dtLastMod =
  getdate() where idThread = @idThread
GO
```

Next we have the sp_UpdateMessage stored procedure, shown in Listing 26.15, that updates the message data. The ID of the message, the subject, the owner, and the message are passed in as parameters.

Listing 26.15: sp_UpdateMessage **Table**

```
CREATE PROCEDURE sp_UpdateMessage

/* Pass in the ID of the message,
  the subject of the message,
  the owner of the message and
  the text of the message */
@idMessage int,
@chrSubject varchar(255),
@chrOwner varchar(255),
@txtMessage text

AS

/* Update the message data for the specified
  message */
```

```
update Message set chrSubject = @chrSubject,
  chrOwner = @chrOwner,
  txtMessage = @txtMessage
where idMessage = @idMessage
GO
```

We also have the obligatory stored procedure to delete a message from the database. Listing 26.16 shows the code for this stored procedure. The ID of the message is passed in and the SQL Delete function is used to remove the message from the database.

Listing 26.16: `sp_DeleteMessage` **Table**

```
CREATE PROCEDURE sp_DeleteMessage

/* Pass in the ID of the message */
@idMessage int

AS

/* Delete the message from the database */
Delete from message
where idMessage = @idMessage
GO
```

Listing 26.17 shows the SQL code to generate the `sp_GetMessage-CountByThread` stored procedure. The ID of the thread is passed in, and the number of messages related to that thread is returned.

Listing 26.17: `sp_GetMessageCountByThread` **Table**

```
CREATE PROCEDURE sp_GetMessageCountbyThread

/*  Pass in the ID of the thread */
@idThread int

AS

/*  Get the total number of messages posted
   for the specified thread */
select total=count(*) from Message
where idThread = @idThread
GO
```

Listing 26.18 shows the SQL code to generate the sp_RetrieveMessage stored procedure. The ID of the message is passed in, and the data is returned for the specific message.

Listing 26.18: sp_RetrieveMessage **Table**

```
CREATE PROCEDURE sp_RetrieveMessage

/* Pass in the ID of the message */
@idMessage int

AS

/* Retrieve the message data for
  the specified message */
select * from message
where idMessage = @idMessage
GO
```

The next stored procedure, sp_RetrieveMessages, retrieves all of the messages related to the specified thread. The SQL script code to generate the stored procedure is shown in Listing 26.19.

Listing 26.19: sp_RetrieveMessages **Table**

```
CREATE PROCEDURE sp_RetrieveMessages

/* Pass in the ID of the thread */
@idThread int

AS

/* Retrieve the messages for the thread */
select * from message
where idThread = @idThread
GO
```

Our last two stored procedures are related to retrieving messages looking forward or backward from a specific message. Because we have the potential for hundreds of messages per thread, we want to display those in reasonable increments for the user to view the data.

The first stored procedure, sp_RetrieveNextMessages, handles retrieving the set of messages after the specified message passed into the stored procedure for the specified thread. To execute the query, we want all messages with IDs greater than the ID passed in and ones where the thread ID matches the current thread being viewed. The SQL script code to generate the stored procedure is shown in Listing 26.20.

Listing 26.20: `sp_RetrieveNextMessages` **Table**

```
CREATE PROCEDURE sp_RetrieveNextMessages

/* The ID of the thread and the ID
  of the last message displayed */
@idThread int,
@idMessage int


AS

/* Retrieve the next set of messages in list
  for the specified thread */
select * from Message where
  idMessage >= @idMessage and
  idThread = @idThread
  order by dtCreated
GO
```

Our last stored procedure, shown in Listing 26.21, handles retrieving messages that were posted previous to the specified messages. Again we are retrieving messages that relate to the specified thread and, in this case, were posted prior to the current message.

Listing 26.21: `sp_RetrievePreviousMessages` **Table**

```
CREATE PROCEDURE sp_RetrievePreviousMessages

/* Pass in the ID of the thread and the
  last message displayed */
@idThread int,
@idMessage int

AS

/* Retrieve all messages for the thread
  in the list before the specified
  message */
select * from Message where
```

```
    idMessage < @idMessage and
    idThread = @idThread
    order by dtCreated
GO
```

That does it for our database programming for the forums. Now are we ready to put the database to work with our script code. First we need to take a look at the user interface code, and then examine the administrative interface.

Building the User Interface

The user interface follows a logical flow of leading the user through login, section selection, thread selection, and then message browsing.

The first page, `Default.asp`, handles having the forums users log in with a handle. They don't have to use the same login handle with each visit, nor do they have to remember a password. This is done as a way for users to identify each other and build conversations. Listings 26.22 and 26.23 show the code for the page.

Listing 26.22: `Default.asp` **Page**

```
<%@ Language=VBScript %>
<%
'*********************************************
'** Default.asp
'**
'** Provides a login form for the forum user
'*********************************************
%>
<HTML>
<HEAD>
</HEAD>
<BODY>

<center>
<font color="blue" size="4">
<B>Welcome to our Message Boards!</b>
</font>
```

A simple form to post the form data to `Section.asp` is created, and an input field that is used by the users to enter their handles is created.

Listing 26.23: `Default.asp` **Continued**

```
<BR><BR>
Please log in with a handle:

<!- Form to enter in a handle for being
  identified in the forums. ->
<form method="post" action="Section.asp">
<input type="text" value="" name="Handle">
<input type="submit" value="Submit"
  name="Submit">
</form>

</center>
<P> </P>

</BODY>
</HTML>
```

Next we have the `Section.asp` page, as shown in Listings 26.24 through 26.26. This page handles displaying the sections that are available in the forums. The page begins with our standard documentation header.

Listing 26.24: `Section.asp` **Page**

```
<%@ Language=VBScript %>
<% Option Explicit %>
<%
'*********************************************
'** Section.asp
'**
'** Displays the forums sections
'*********************************************
%>
<HTML>
<HEAD>
</HEAD>
<BODY>

<font color="blue" size="4">
Select a topic area below:
<BR><BR></font>
```

Now we create our database connection and execute the sp_RetrieveSections stored procedure. This returns all of the current sections in the database.

The first thing that the page does is to retrieve the handle entered by the user. We do not enforce any validation, so the users can remain anonymous if they so choose. The handle is stored in a session variable for easy access throughout the rest of the pages.

Listing 26.25: `Section.asp` **Continued**

```
<%

Dim dbForums      ' database connection
Dim rsForums      ' record set
Dim rsPostCount   ' record set
Dim SQL           ' string

' Get the handle of the message owner.
' We go ahead and double up an single quotes
' for on insertion into the database.
session("Handle") =
  replace(request("Handle"), "'", "''")

' Create an ADO database connection
set dbForums = _
  server.createobject("adodb.connection")

' Create record set
set rsForums = _
  server.CreateObject("adodb.recordset")

' Create record set
set rsPostCount = _
  server.CreateObject("adodb.recordset")

' Open the connection using our ODBC file DSN
dbForums.open("filedsn=Forums")

' Retrieve the sections for the forums
sql = "execute sp_RetrieveSections"

' Execute the statement and retrieve
```

```
' the record set
set rsForums = dbForums.Execute(sql)
%>

<!- Build a table to display the sections ->
<Table border=1 cellpadding="5"
  cellspacing="5">
<TR>
  <TH>Forum</TH>
  <TH># of Posts</TH>
  <TH>Last Post</TH>
</TR>
```

The section data is displayed in a table that includes the section name, the number of message posts, and the date of the last message posted. As we loop through the data returned from our first query, we execute the `sp_RetrieveSectionPostCount` stored procedure for each section. That returns the number of messages posted for that section. Note that the section name is linked to the `Thread.asp` page, and the ID of the section is passed on the URL.

Listing 26.26: `Section.asp` **Continued**

```
<%

' Loop through the forums
do until rsForums.EOF

' Get the a count of the number of
  messages posted
' for the current section.
sql = "execute" & _
  " sp_RetrieveSectionPostCount " & _
  rsForums("idSection")

' Get the count
set rsPostCount = dbForums.Execute(SQL)

%>

<TR>
  <td>
  <!- Build a link to the thread listing ->
```

```
        <a href="thread.asp?idSection= ↵
        <%=rsForums("idSection")%>">
        <%=rsForums("chrName")%></a>
        </td>
        <TD>
          <!- Display the number of messages ->
          <% = rsPostCount(0) %>
        </td>
        <td>
          <!- Show the date the message was
            last modified. ->
          <%=rsForums("dtLastMod")%>
        </td>
      </tr>

      <%

        ' Loop to the next row
        rsForums.MoveNext

      loop

      ' Close the database
      dbForums.Close

      %>

      </table>

      </BODY>
      </HTML>
```

The page is then closed out with the proper ending table tags, closed database connection, and end page tags. We next have the `Thread.asp` page, as shown in Listings 26.27 through 26.30. This page handles displaying the threads related to the section ID passed on the URL.

The first thing we do on the page is to check if the referring page was `Section.asp`. If so, then we store the current section in a session variable for each access throughout the thread and message pages. This is a bit easier than storing it on the URL throughout the entire process. The `Thread.asp` page can be accessed from other pages besides `Section.asp`, so we need to always know which section the user has currently selected so we can display the appropriate threads.

Listing 26.27: `Thread.asp` **Page**

```
<%@ Language=VBScript %>
<% Option Explicit %>
<%
'*********************************************
'** Thread.asp
'**
'** Displays all the threads for a section
'*********************************************
%>
<%

' Check to ensure we came from the
' section.asp page to display a list
' of threads.
if instr(1, lcase_
  (Request.ServerVariables("HTTP_REFERER")), _
  "section.asp") then

  ' Get the ID of the section.
  session("CurrentSection") = _
    request("idSection")

end if
```

We now need to ensure that the `CurrentSection` session variable is not empty. If it is, we need to send the user back to the section page so a section can be selected.

Next we build a simple navigation header for the thread page. This gives the user the option of returning to the section page or creating a new thread. Note that we are not using navigation includes, because each page has unique navigation options based on where the user is in the message drill-down process.

Listing 26.28: `Thread.asp` **Continued**

```
' Ensure we have a section ID so we can display
' threads
if session("CurrentSection") = "" then _
  Response.Redirect("section.asp")

%>
<HTML>
```

```
<HEAD>
</HEAD>
<BODY>

<!- Build the forums navigation ->
| <a href="section.asp">Forums List<a> |

<HR>
<BR>

<!- Build a link to create a new thread ->
| <a href="CreateThread.asp">
Create New Thread</a> |

<BR><BR>
```

We are ready to display the list of threads related to the selected section. The `sp_Retrieve-Threads` stored procedure is used to query the database for all threads related to the section.

Listing 26.29: `Thread.asp` **Continued**

```
<%

Dim dbForums     ' Database Connection
Dim rsForums     ' Record Set
Dim rsPosts      ' Record Set
Dim sql          ' String

' Create an ADO database connection
set dbForums = _
  server.createobject("adodb.connection")

' Create record set
set rsForums = _
  server.CreateObject("adodb.recordset")

' Create record set
set rsPosts = _
  server.CreateObject("adodb.recordset")

' Open the connection using our ODBC file DSN
dbForums.open("filedsn=Forums")
```

```
' Build a SQL statement to retrieve threads
' for the specified section
sql = "execute sp_RetrieveThreads " & _
   session("CurrentSection")

' Execute the statement and retrieve
' the record set
set rsForums = dbForums.Execute(sql)

%>

<!- Build a table to display the threads ->
<table border="1" cellpadding="5"
  cellspacing="5">

<TR>
  <TH>Topic</TH>
  <TH># of Posts</TH>
  <TH>Last Post</TH>
  <TH>Started By</TH>
</TR>
```

As with the section data, a table is set up to display the thread listing, including the topic name, the number of messages posts, the last message posted date, and the identity of the owner (handle). With each iteration of the recordset loop, the `sp_RetrieveThreadPostCount` stored procedure is called to return the number of message posts for each thread. Note that the thread topic is linked to the `Messages.asp` page with the ID of the thread passed on the URL.

Listing 26.30: `Thread.asp` **Continued**

```
<%

' Loop through the threads
do until rsForums.EOF

' Execute the SQL statement to retrieve the
' number of messages posted for the specified
' thread.
sql = "execute sp_RetrieveThreadPostCount " & _
  rsForums("idThread")
```

```
' Get the message count
set rsPosts = dbForums.execute(sql)

%>

<TR>
  <TD>
  <!- Link to display the messages
  for thread ->
  <a href="Messages.asp?idThread= ⤶
  <%=rsForums("idThread")%>">
  <%=rsForums("chrName")%></a>
  </td>
  <td>
    <!- Show the number of messages posted
      for the thread ->
    <%=rsPosts(0)%>
  </td>
  <td>
    <!- Show when the last messages was
      posted ->
    <%=rsForums("dtLastMod")%>
  </td>
  <td>
    <!- Show the thread owner ->
    <%=rsForums("chrOwner")%>
  </td>
</tr>

<%

' Move to the next row
rsForums.MoveNext

loop

' Close the databases
dbForums.Close

%>

</table>
```

```
<BR>

<HR>

<!- Show the forms navigation ->
| <a href="section.asp">Forums List<a> |

</BODY>
</HTML>
```

Finally, the page is closed out as appropriate. In addition to the navigation links on the top of the page, we include a navigation link at the bottom of the page to take the user back to the `Section.asp` page.

Next we have our page, `CreateThread.asp`, that is used by the user to create a new thread in the section. A check is done up front to ensure that the user has selected a section to post the thread to. If not, the user is sent back to the `Section.asp` page. The navigation to take the user back to the section page is included as well. The code for the page is shown in Listings 26.31 through 26.33.

Listing 26.31: `CreateThread.asp`

```
<%@ Language=VBScript %>
<% Option Explicit %>
<%
'*********************************************
'** CreateThread.asp
'**
'** Creates a new thread in the database
'*********************************************
%>
<%
' Check to ensure that we have a section ID to
' assign this new thread to.
if session("CurrentSection") = "" then _
  Response.Redirect("section.asp")
%>

<HTML>
<HEAD>
</HEAD>
<BODY>
```

```
<!- Build the forums navigation ->
| <a href="section.asp">Forums List<a> |

<HR>
<BR>
```

If the users do not enter their data correctly, there will be a parameter on the URL called `idError` with a value of 1. If it is set, we indicate to the user that there is an error.

Listing 26.32: `CreateThread.asp` **Continued**

```
<%

' See if there was an error in trying to insert
' a new thread.
if request("idError") = 1 then

%>

<font color="red">
You did not enter in a thread name.</font>
<BR><BR>

<%

end if

%>
```

A form is created to post to `InsertThread.asp`. The only field we ask the user to enter is for the Thread name. The page is then closed out with a closing navigation link.

Listing 26.33: `CreateThread.asp` **Continued**

```
<!- Form to insert a new thread. ->
<form method="post" action="InsertThread.asp">
<TABLE cellpadding="4">
<TR>
  <TD colspan=2>Enter in your Thread
  Information</td>
</tr>

<tr>
```

```
   <td align="right">Name:</td>
   <td>
   <!- Input field for the thread name ->
   <input type="text" value="" name="chrName">
   </td>
</tr>

<TR>
   <TD colspan=2 align="center">
   <input type="submit" value="Submit"
     name="submit">
   </td>
</tr>

</TABLE>

</form>

<HR>

<!- Show the forms navigation ->
| <a href="section.asp">Forums List<a> |

</BODY>
</HTML>
```

The InsertThread.asp page, as shown in Listing 26.34, handles inserting the new thread into the database. A check is done on this page to ensure that we have a section ID to associate with the new thread.

Listing 26.34: InsertThread.asp

```
<%@ Language=VBScript %>
<%Option Explicit%>
<%
'**********************************************
'** InsertThread.asp
'**
'** Inserts a new thread into the database
'**********************************************
%>
<%

Dim dbForums   ' Database Connection
```

Part vi

```
Dim rsForums    ' Record Set
Dim sql         ' String

' Check to ensure we have a current section ID
' to assign the thread to.
if session("CurrentSection") = "" then _
  Response.Redirect("section.asp")

' Ensure that a thread name was entered
if request("chrName") = "" then

  ' If not send the user back to the
  ' create thread page
  Response.Redirect _
    "CreateThread.asp?idError=1"

end if

' Create an ADO database connection
set dbForums = _
  server.createobject("adodb.connection")

' Create record set
set rsForums = _
  server.CreateObject("adodb.recordset")

' Open the connection using our ODBC file DSN
dbForums.open("filedsn=Forums")

' Execute the sp_InsertThread stored
' procedure to insert the new thread
sql = "execute sp_InsertThread " & _
  session("CurrentSection") & ", '" & _
  replace(request("chrName"), "'", "''") & _
  "', '" & session("Handle") & "'"

' Execute the statement and retrieve the
' record set
set rsForums = dbForums.Execute(sql)

' Close the database
dbForums.Close
```

```
' Send the user back to the thread page
Response.Redirect "thread.asp"

%>
```

Next we are ready to work on displaying messages. `Messages.asp`, shown in Listings 26.35 through 26.46, handles displaying a series of messages and providing page navigation through the messages. It is also the page that handles displaying a single message. When a single message is displayed, the list of messages is still displayed below it. This keeps the amount of back and forth navigation to a minimum.

A check is done to ensure that we have a thread ID set by linking to this page from `Thread.asp` or by checking the `CurrentThread` session variable.

Listing 26.35: `Messages.asp`

```
<%@ Language=VBScript %>
<% Option Explicit %>
<%
'*******************************************
'** Messages.asp
'**
'** Shows all messages for a thread
'*******************************************
%>
<%

' Ensure we arrived at this page after
' selecting a thread on the thread.asp page.
if instr(1, lcase_
  (Request.ServerVariables("HTTP_REFERER")), _
  "thread.asp") then

  ' Get the current thread ID
  session("CurrentThread") = _
    request("idThread")

end if

' If there is no thread ID then send the
' user back to the thread selection page
if session("CurrentThread") = "" then _
```

```
    Response.Redirect("Thread.asp")

Dim dbForums        ' Database Connection
Dim rsForums        ' Record Set
Dim connForums
Dim cmdForums
Dim sql             ' String
Dim MessageCount    ' Integer
Dim Count           ' Integer
Dim Direction       ' string
Dim NumDisplay      ' Integer
Dim dbMessage       ' Database Connection
Dim rsMessage       ' Record Set
Dim txtMessage      ' string
Dim chrOwner        ' string
Dim N               ' integer

' Static Variables
Dim adCmdText
Dim adCmdTable
Dim adCmdStoredProc
Dim adCmdUnknown
Dim adOpenForwardOnly
Dim adOpenKeyset
Dim adOpenDynamic
Dim adOpenStatic
Dim adLockReadOnly
Dim adLockPessimistic
Dim adLockOptimistic
Dim adLockBatchOptimistic

%>
<HTML>
<HEAD>
</HEAD>
<BODY>
```

We have two tiers of navigation on our message page. The first gives the user the option to link back to the section and thread pages, followed by our message navigation.

The message navigation puts a parameter on the URL that indicates if the user would like to move to the first, last, next, or previous messages. We display a maximum of 10 messages on-screen at one time.

Listing 26.36: `Messages.asp` **Continued**

```
<!- Top level navigation ->
| <a href="section.asp">Forums List<a>
| <a href="Thread.asp">Discussion
  Thread List<a> |

<HR>

<BR>

<!- Messages navigation ->
| <a href="Messages.asp?dir=First">First</a>
| <a href="Messages.asp?dir=Next">Next</a>
| <a href=
  "Messages.asp?dir=Previous">Previous</a>
| <a href="Messages.asp?dir=Last">Last</a>
| <a href="CreateMessage.asp">
  Create New Message</a> |

<BR><BR>
```

If there is a message ID on the URL, we know that we need to display the actual text of the message before we display the message list. A link is displayed to reply to the message that links to `CreateMessage.asp`.

Listing 26.37: `Messages.asp` **Continued**

```
<%

' Check to see if a request was made to display
' the contents of a message
if request("idMessage") <> "" then

%>

<!- Show the option to reply to the message ->
<a href="CreateMessage.asp">
Reply to Message</a>
<BR><BR>

<%

' Create an ADO database connection
```

```
set dbMessage = _
  server.createobject("adodb.connection")

' Create record set
set rsMessage = _
  server.CreateObject("adodb.recordset")

' Open the connection using our ODBC file DSN
dbMessage.open("filedsn=Forums")
```

The sp_RetrieveMessage stored procedure is called with the ID of the message passed as a parameter. The subject, owner, and date posted are all displayed in a table format.

Listing 26.38: Messages.asp **Continued**

```
' Retrieve the message based on the ID
sql = "execute sp_RetrieveMessage " & _
  Request("idMessage")

' Execute the statement and retrieve the
' record set
set rsMessage = dbMessage.Execute(sql)

txtMessage = rsMessage("txtMessage")
chrOwner = rsMessage("chrOwner")

%>

<!- Build a table to display the message ->
<table border="1" cellpadding="5"
  cellspacing="5">
<tr>
  <td align="right"><b>Subject:</b></td>
  <td><%=rsMessage("chrSubject")%></td>
</tr>

<tr>
  <td align="right"><b>Created By:</b></td>
  <td><%=chrOwner%></td>
</tr>

<tr>
  <td align="right"><b>Date Posted:</b></td>
```

```
    <td><%=rsMessage("dtCreated")%></td>
</tr>

<tr>
    <td align="right"><b>Message:</b></td>
    <td><%=txtMessage%></td>
</tr>

</table>

<%

' Close the subject
dbMessage.Close

end if
```

We are now ready to display the list of messages. We can change the number of messages displayed at one viewing by changing the NumDisplay variable. We also have a series of constants that are used in our database query.

Listing 26.39: Messages.asp **Continued**

```
' Set the number of messages to display
NumDisplay = 10

REM - ADO command types
adCmdText = 1
adCmdTable = 2
adCmdStoredProc = 4
adCmdUnknown = 8

REM - ADO cursor types
adOpenForwardOnly = 0 '# (Default)
adOpenKeyset = 1
adOpenDynamic = 2
adOpenStatic = 3

REM - ADO lock types
adLockReadOnly = 1
adLockPessimistic = 2
adLockOptimistic = 3
adLockBatchOptimistic = 4
```

```
' Create our database connection object
Set connForums = _
  Server.CreateObject("ADODB.Connection")

' Open the database connection
connForums.Open "FileDsn=Forums"

' Create a ADA command object
Set cmdForums = _
  Server.CreateObject("ADODB.Command")
```

We have a different twist in how we use ADO to query the database. Because we have to be able to move forward *and* backward to support the previous/next browsing functionality, we have to create an ADO command that supports moving to previous records. This is done with a recordset that is returned from our command object. When that command object is called, the `adOpenStatic` and `adLockReadOnly` parameters are used. These indicate that the data returned to the recordset is static, meaning it will not change, and is locked for read-only. That way, we can page through the recordset in either direction.

Listing 26.40: `Messages.asp` **Continued**

```
' Set the command type to 1 to evaluate
' the command as text. Also, the time out
' is set to 0.
cmdForums.CommandType = adCmdText
cmdForums.CommandTimeout = 0

' Set the command object connection
Set cmdForums.ActiveConnection = connForums

' Create a record set
Set rsForums = _
  Server.CreateObject("ADODB.Recordset")

' Execute the sp_GetMessageCountByThread
' message to get the number of messages
' in this thread
sql = "execute sp_GetMessageCountByThread " & _
  session("CurrentThread")
```

```
' Set the SQL Command
cmdForums.CommandText = sql

' Open the record set and use the adOpenStatic
' and adLockReadOnly parameters. adOpenStatic
' creates a static cursor in the record set.
' adLockReadOnly makes the record set read
' only.
rsForums.Open cmdForums, ,_
  adOpenStatic,adLockReadOnly
```

Next we check to see which direction the user wants to navigate in the messages. Based on the direction, we call sp_RetrieveNextMessages or sp_RetrievePreviousMessages stored procedures. In each case, the current thread ID and the last message ID are passed in to return the appropriate result set.

Listing 26.41: Messages.asp **Continued**

```
' Get the message count
MessageCount = rsForums("total")

' Set the direction
Direction = request("Dir")

' Check to see if we know the last message ID
' displayed. If not set it at 1.
if Session("idLastMessage") = "" then _
  Session("idLastMessage") = 1

' If there is no direction for the messages
' to be displayed then set it as "First"
if Direction = "" then Direction = "First"

' Build the SQL statement based on the
' navigational direction
select case Direction

  ' First of the list
  case "First":
    ' Execute the sp_RetrieveNextMessages
    ' stored procedure to get the next set
    ' of messages in the list, but we set
```

```
      ' flags to start at the first message.
      sql = "execute" & _
        " sp_RetrieveNextMessages " & _
        session("CurrentThread") & ", 1"
      session("idLastMessage") = 1

    ' Retrieve the next set in the list
    case "Next":
      ' Execute the sp_RetrieveNextMessages
      ' stored procedure to get the next set
      ' of messages in the list.
      sql = "execute" & _
        " sp_RetrieveNextMessages " & _
        session("CurrentThread") & ", " & _
        session("idLastMessage")

    ' Get the previous set of messages
    case "Previous":
      ' Execute the sp_RetrievePreviousMessages
      ' stored procedure to get the previous set
      ' of messages in the list.
      sql = "execute" & _
        " sp_RetrievePreviousMessages " & _
        session("CurrentThread") & ", " & _
        session("idLastMessage")

    ' Get the last set of messages in the list
    case "Last":
      ' Execute the sp_RetrievePreviousMessages
      ' stored procedure to get the last set of
      ' messages in the list. In this case we
      ' start at the very end of the list by
      ' passing a 1,000,000 message ID
      ' parameter
      sql = "execute" & _
        " sp_RetrievePreviousMessages " & _
        session("CurrentThread") & ", 1,000,000"

    ' Get the current list of messages
    ' being displayed
    case "Current":
      ' Execute the sp_RetrieveNextMessages
```

```
      ' stored procedure to get the next set
      ' of messages in the list. Note that the
      ' idLastMessage parameter will not have
      ' changed if the current set of messages
      ' is to be displayed.
     sql = "execute" & _
       " sp_RetrieveNextMessages " & _
       session("CurrentThread") & ", " & _
       session("idLastMessage")

 end select

 ' Close the record set
 rsForums.Close
```

Finally, the stored procedure is executed. Again, the appropriate parameters are used to return a result set that we can traverse forward and backward. We also check to see if any results are returned. If not, we simply start at the first message.

Listing 26.42: `Messages.asp` **Continued**

```
 ' Set the SQL command
 cmdForums.CommandText = sql

 ' Open the record set with the appropriate
 ' parameters
 rsForums.Open cmdForums, , _
   adOpenStatic,adLockReadOnly

 ' Check to see if we are at the end of the
 ' record set
 if rsForums.EOF then

   ' Retrieve the next set of message starting
   ' at the first message
   sql = "execute sp_RetrieveNextMessages " & _
     session("CurrentThread") & ", 1"
   session("idLastMessage") = 1

   ' Set the direction to next
   Direction = "Next"
```

Part vi

```
        ' Set the SQL statement
        cmdForums.CommandText = sql

        ' Close the record set
        rsForums.close

        ' Open the record set
        rsForums.Open cmdForums, ,_
          adOpenStatic,adLockReadOnly

    end if
```

Now we are ready to begin the display of the messages. We set a `Count` variable so we can track how many rows have been displayed; then the table is started. The message subject, date posted, and owner are displayed.

Listing 26.43: `Messages.asp` **Continued**

```
    ' Start our loop counter at 1
    Count = 1

    %>

    <BR>

    <!- Start the table to display the messages ->
    <table border=1 cellpadding="5"
      cellspacing="5">
    <tr>
      <th>Subject</th>
      <th>Date Posted</th>
      <th>Owner</th>
    </tr>
```

Next we have our logic to handle moving backward in the recordset. We have to do some fancy footwork to ensure that we don't hit the beginning of the recordset. If so, we have to end the loop. With each iteration, we store the last ID of the message so we can execute the next query when the user is ready to navigate to the next set of messages. In the end, we will have looped back to the first of the 10 messages we are going to display.

Listing 26.44: `Messages.asp` **Continued**

```
<%

' Check to see if the direction is
' moving backward
if Direction = "Last" or _
  Direction = "Previous" then

  ' Move to the last message in the record set
  rsForums.MoveLast

  ' Loop back
  for N = 1 to NumDisplay - 2

    ' Move back a row
    rsForums.MovePrevious

    ' See if we are at the beginning of the
    ' record set
    if rsForums.bOF then

      ' Exit the for loop
      exit for

    end if

    ' Set the last message displayed
    session("idLastMessage") = _
      rsForums("idMessage")

  next

end if
```

We do a quick check to ensure that we are not at the end or beginning of the recordset. If so, we need to reset to the first record. Then we begin looping through the messages, and the data is displayed. The message subject is linked back to the `messages.asp` page with the ID of the message on the URL.

Listing 26.45: `Messages.asp` **Continued**

```
' Check to see if we are at the beginning
' or the end of the file.
if rsForums.BOF and not rsForums.eof then

  ' Move to the first row
  rsForums.movefirst

end if

' Loop through the messages
do until rsForums.EOF

%>

<tr>
  <td>
    <!- Build a link to display the
       message ->
    <a href=
    "Messages.asp?dir=Current&idMessage= ↵
    <%=rsForums("idMessage")%>">
    <%=rsForums("chrSubject")%></a>
  </td>
  <td>
    <!- Show the data created ->
    <%=rsForums("dtCreated")%>
  </td>
  <td>
    <!- Show the message owner ->
    <%=rsForums("chrOwner")%>
  </td>
</tr>
```

We then have the recordset advanced to the next record, followed by a check to see if we are at the end of the recordset. If the direction was originally set to move forward, we store the ID of the last message for handling the next message direction move by the user. Our counter is then incremented, and if we have reached the number to display, the Do Loop is exited.

Listing 26.46: Messages.asp **Continued**

```
<%

   ' Move to the next row
   rsForums.MoveNext

   ' Check to see if we are not at the end of
   ' the record set and if the direction is
   ' moving forward.
   if not rsForums.eof and _
     (Direction = "Next" or _
     Direction = "First") then

       ' Get the ID of the message to store as the
       ' last message displayed
     session("idLastMessage") = _
       rsForums("idMessage")

   end if

   ' Increase the counter
   Count = Count + 1

   ' See if our counter meets the number
   ' displayed
   if Count = NumDisplay then exit do

loop

' Close the database connection
connForums.Close

%>

</table>

<font size="2" color="blue">
  <!- Display the message count ->
  There are <%=MessageCount%> messages
  in this thread.
</font>
```

```
<BR><BR>

<HR>

<!- Show the navigation for the forums ->
| <a href="section.asp">Forums List<a>
| <a href="Thread.asp">Discussion Thread
List<a> |

</BODY>
</HTML>
```

Finally, the page is closed out with a display of the number of messages in the thread and navigation links to the section and thread page.

This ends a very complex page that manages to provide forward and backward paging through the messages, displaying a message, and all the tracking it takes to manage the state of the user.

Next we have the `CreateMessage.asp` page, as shown in Listings 26.47 through 26.49. We first check to see if we have a thread ID to associate with the new message; then we have our navigation header.

Listing 26.47: `CreateMessage.asp`

```
<%@ Language=VBScript %>
<% Option Explicit %>
<%
'**********************************************
'** CreateMessage.asp
'**
'** Creates a new message in the database
'**********************************************
%>
<%

' Check to ensure a thread selection has been
' made
if session("CurrentThread") = "" then _
  Response.Redirect("Thread.asp")
%>

<HTML>
<HEAD>
```

```
</HEAD>
<BODY>

| <a href="section.asp">Forums List<a>
| <a href="Thread.asp">Discussion Thread
List<a> |

<HR>

<BR>
```

As when adding a new thread, we check the URL to see if an error parameter is set. If so, we indicate to the user that they didn't fill out the new message form properly.

Listing 26.48: `CreateMessage.asp` **Continued**

```
<%

' Check to see if there is an error.
if request("idError") = 1 then

%>

<!- Display the error message ->
<font color="red">You did not enter in
a message.
</font><BR><BR>

<%

end if

%>
```

The form is set up to post to the `InsertMessage.asp` page. We have two fields on the form. The first field is an input box for the message subject. The second field is a text box for the body of the message.

TIP

You might want to consider defaulting the Subject field to the subject of the message that is being replied to. This will require some additional tracking to pull the subject onto this page.

Listing 26.49: `CreateMessage.asp` **Continued**

```
<!- Form to pass the data so the message can be
  inserted. ->
<form method="post" action="InsertMessage.asp">

<TABLE cellpadding="4">

<TR><TD colspan="2">
  Enter in your Message</td></tr>
<tr>
  <td align="right">Subject:</td>
  <td>
  <!- Field to enter in the message subject. ->
  <input type="text"
    value="" name="chrSubject">
  </td>
</tr>
<tr>
  <td align="right">Message:</td>
  <td>
  <!- Text area to enter in the text of
     the message ->
  <textarea name="txtMessage"
    cols="60" rows="10"></textarea>
  </td>
</tr>
<TR>
  <TD align="center">
  <input type="submit" value="Submit"
    name="submit">
  </td>
</tr>

</TABLE>

</form>


<HR>

<!- Navigation bar ->
```

```
| <a href="section.asp">Forums List<a>
| <a href="Thread.asp">
  Discussion Thread List<a> |


</BODY>
</HTML>
```

Finally the page is closed out and the navigation links provided. Next we have the page `InsertMessage.asp` that processes the new message request. The code is shown in Listing 26.50. We do a check to ensure that we have a thread ID; if not, we send the user to the `Thread.asp` page.

We also check to ensure that the user has entered a subject and a message. If they have not, then the user is sent back to the `CreateMessage.asp` page with the error value set.

TIP

When we send the user back because of an error on this page as well as on the `CreateThread.asp` page, consider defaulting the fields with what they did enter. This would require the use of session variables to store and read the data.

Listing 26.50: `InsertMessage.asp`

```
<%@ Language=VBScript %>
<%Option Explicit%>
<%
'*******************************************
'** InsertMessage.asp
'**
'** Inserts a new message into the database
'*******************************************
%>
<%

Dim dbForums    ' Database Connection
Dim rsForums    ' Record Set
Dim sql         ' String

' Make sure we have a thread ID so we know what
' thread to assign the message to.
if session("CurrentThread") = "" then _
```

```
  Response.Redirect("thread.asp")

' Ensure message text and a subject have been
' entered.
if request("txtMessage") = "" or _
  request("chrSubject") = "" then

  ' If not send back to the createmessage.asp
  ' page
  Response.Redirect _
    "CreateMessage.asp?idError=1"

end if

' Create an ADO database connection
set dbForums = _
  server.createobject("adodb.connection")

' Create record set
set rsForums = _
  server.CreateObject("adodb.recordset")

' Open the connection using our ODBC file DSN
dbForums.open("filedsn=Forums")

' SQL statement to insert the new message
' into the database. Note that the relationship
' of the message is set by identifying the ID
' of the section and the ID of the thread.
sql = "execute sp_InsertMessage " & _
  session("CurrentSection") & ", " & _
  session("CurrentThread") & ", '" & _
  replace(request("chrSubject"), "'", "''") & _
    "', '" & _
  replace(request("txtMessage"), "'", "''") & _
    "', '" & _
  session("Handle") & "'"

' Execute the statement and retrieve the
' record set
set rsForums = dbForums.Execute(sql)
```

```
' Close the database connection
dbForums.Close

' Send the user back to the message
' listing page
Response.Redirect "messages.asp"

%>
```

If all of the values are in good order, the `sp_InsertMessage` stored procedure is used to add the message to the database. Note that the ID of the section, the ID of the thread, the message subject, the message text, and the message owner are passed to the stored procedure. The user is then directed back to the `Messages.asp` page.

This concludes the user interface side of our forums application. As we have seen throughout the book, the "design" isn't that pretty, but it can be gussied up to look very professional. The basic code here can be tweaked and improved upon to work smoothly in your environment.

Building the Management Interface

Next we move to the management interface for our forums. It stands to reason that the administrator will browse through the forums much in the way that a site visitor would. Thus, the flow of our administrative interface is going to closely parallel the user interface, but we'll insert the proper tools to add, update, and delete sections, threads, and messages.

WARNING

Our management interface works in real time. If you are performing edits, additions, or deletions, visitors on the site will see this happen in real time.

Our first page is `AdminSections.asp`, shown in Listings 26.51 through 26.53. One change from the user interface is that we do not need to have a handle to log in. You should also implement a security interface, but that is beyond the scope of this example.

The first thing we do on this page is execute the `sp_RetrieveSections` to retrieve the current active sections. We then build a table to display the sections.

Listing 26.51: AdminSections.asp

```
<%@ Language=VBScript %>
<% Option Explicit %>
<%
'*********************************************
'** AdminSections.asp
'**
'** List sections
'*********************************************
%>
<HTML>
<HEAD>
</HEAD>
<BODY>

<%

Dim dbForums     ' database connection
Dim rsForums     ' record set
Dim SQL          ' string

' Create an ADO database connection
set dbForums = _
  server.createobject("adodb.connection")

' Create record set
set rsForums = _
  server.CreateObject("adodb.recordset")

' Open the connection using our ODBC file DSN
dbForums.open("filedsn=Forums")

' Execute the stored procedure to retrieve the
' sections
sql = "execute sp_RetrieveSections"

' Execute the statement and retrieve the
' record set
set rsForums = dbForums.Execute(sql)
%>

<!- Start the table to display the sections. ->
```

```
<table cellpadding="5" cellspacing="5"
  border="1">
<tr>
  <th>Edit Section</th>
  <th>New Name</th>
  <th>Delete</th>
</tr>
```

The first row in our table is built to add a new section to the list. The page posts to `AddSection.asp` for processing. We have only one field that the administrator uses to enter the section name.

The current sections are now displayed. The section name is linked to `AdminThread.asp` with the ID of the section passed on the URL.

Listing 26.52: `AdminSections.asp` **Continued**

```
<tr>
  <td>Add a New Section</td>
  <td>

    <!- A form is created to insert a new
      section. ->
    <form method="post"
      action="AddSection.asp">
    <input type="text" value="" name="chrName">
    <input type="Submit" value="Add New"
      name="Submit">
    </form>
  </td>
  <td> </td>
</tr>

<%

' Loop through the sections
do until rsForums.EOF

%>
<tr>
  <td>
  <!- Link to the threads for the section. ->
  <a href="adminthread.asp?idSection= ⤸
  <%=rsForums("idSection")%>"> ⤸
```

```
    <%=rsForums("chrName")%></a>
    </td>
```

With the display of each section, we also need to build in an option to edit the section name. Another form is created that, in this case, posts to `UpdateSectionName.asp`. The current name is defaulted in the name field. Also, a hidden field is created with the ID of the section to be updated.

Listing 26.53: `AdminSections.asp` **Continued**

```
    <td>
      <!- A form is created for each section
        to the name can be updated. ->
      <form method="post"
        action="UpdateSectionName.asp">

      <!- The current name value is displayed. ->
      <input type="text"
        value="<%=rsForums("chrName")%>"
        name="chrName">

      <!- A hidden field stored the form ID so we
        know what form to update. ->
      <input type="hidden"
        value="<%=rsForums("idSection")%>"
        name="idSection">

      <input type="Submit" value="Update"
        name="Submit">
      </form>
    </td>
    <td>
      <!- Link to delete the section. ->
      <a href="deletesection.asp?idSection= ⤶
      <%=rsForums("idSection")%>">Delete</a>
    </td>
  </tr>

  <%

    ' Move to the next row
    rsForums.MoveNext
```

```
loop

' Close the database connection.
dbForums.Close

%>

</table>

</BODY>
</HTML>
```

Following the section update form, we have a link to delete the section with the ID of the section to be deleted passed on the URL. Finally, the page closes out with the appropriate closing tags.

Next we have the AddSection.asp page, as shown in Listing 26.54, which processes the addition of a new section. The new section name is posted to this page from AdminSections.asp.

Listing 26.54: AddSection.asp

```
<%@ Language=VBScript %>
<%Option Explicit%>
<%
'*******************************************
'** AddSection.asp
'**
'** Adds a new section to the database
'*******************************************
%>
<%

Dim dbForums    ' Database Connection
Dim rsForums    ' Record Set
Dim sql         ' String

' Create an ADO database connection
set dbForums = _
  server.createobject("adodb.connection")

' Create record set
set rsForums = _
  server.CreateObject("adodb.recordset")
```

```
' Open the connection using our ODBC file DSN
dbForums.open("filedsn=Forums")

' Execute the sp_AddSection stored procedure to
' insert the new section into the database.
sql = "execute sp_AddSection '" & _
  replace(request("chrName"), "'", "''") & "'"

' Execute the statement and retrieve the
' record set
set rsForums = dbForums.Execute(sql)

' Close the database connection
dbForums.Close

' Redirect the user back to the section admin
Response.Redirect "adminsections.asp"

%>
```

The sp_AddSection stored procedure is used to insert the new section into the database. Once the insert is complete, the user is sent back to the section administration.

We next have the page that processes the updating of a section name. The code for UpdateSectionName.asp is shown in Listing 26.55. The AdminSections.asp page posts to this page with the new name.

Listing 26.55: UpdateSectionName.asp **Page**

```
<%@ Language=VBScript %>
<%Option Explicit%>
<%
'***********************************************
'** UpdateSectionName.asp
'**
'** Updates the section name
'***********************************************
%>
<%

Dim dbForums    ' Database Connection
Dim rsForums    ' Record Set
Dim sql         ' String
```

```
' Create an ADO database connection
set dbForums = _
  server.createobject("adodb.connection")

' Create record set
set rsForums = _
  server.CreateObject("adodb.recordset")

' Open the connection using our ODBC file DSN
dbForums.open("filedsn=Forums")

' Executes the sp_UpdateSectionName stored
' procedure to update the name of the specified
' Section
sql = "execute sp_UpdateSectionName " & _
  request("idSection") & ", '" & _
  replace(request("chrName"), "'", "''") & "'"

' Execute the statement and retrieve the
' record set
set rsForums = dbForums.Execute(sql)

' Close the database connection
dbForums.Close

' Send the user back to the sections
' administration
Response.Redirect "adminsections.asp"

%>
```

The sp_UpdateSectionName stored procedure is used to update the section name for the specified section ID that is read from the hidden variable. The user is then sent back to the section administration.

Our last section administration page allows us to delete the specified section. The ID of the section is passed to the page. The sp_DeleteSection stored procedure is used to remove the section from the database. The user is then sent back to the sections administration. The code for the DeleteSection.asp page is shown in Listing 26.56.

Listing 26.56: `DeleteSection.asp`

```
<%@ Language=VBScript %>
<%Option Explicit%>
<%
'*********************************************
'** DeleteSection.asp
'**
'** Deletes a section from the database
'*********************************************
%>
<%

Dim dbForums    ' Database Connection
Dim rsForums    ' Record Set
Dim sql         ' String

' Create an ADO database connection
set dbForums = _
  server.createobject("adodb.connection")

' Create record set
set rsForums = _
  server.CreateObject("adodb.recordset")

' Open the connection using our ODBC file DSN
dbForums.open("filedsn=Forums")

sql = "execute sp_DeleteSection " & _
  request("idSection")

' Execute the statement and retrieve the
' record set
set rsForums = dbForums.Execute(sql)

dbForums.close

Response.Redirect "adminsections.asp"

%>
```

We now move to the thread administration. The functionality is similar to the sections administration and supports adding, editing, and deleting threads. The AdminThread.asp page is shown in Listings 26.57 through 26.60.

The first part of the page checks to see if we came from the adminsections.asp page. If so, we store the ID of the section in a session variable for easy administrative access throughout the thread and message pages. This is similar to the technique used in the user interface. If there is no section ID, we send the user back to the section administration.

Listing 26.57: AdminThread.asp

```
<%@ Language=VBScript %>
<% Option Explicit %>
<%
'*******************************************
'** AdminThread.asp
'**
'** Lists threads
'*******************************************
%>
<%

' Check to ensure that the linking page is
' the admin sections page.
if instr(1, lcase_
  (Request.ServerVariables("HTTP_REFERER")), _
  "adminsections.asp") then

    ' Set the current section ID we are
    ' working on
    session("AdminCurrentSection") = _
      request("idSection")

end if

' If there is no section ID then we can't
' display threads.
if session("AdminCurrentSection") = "" then _
  Response.Redirect("adminsections.asp")

%>
<HTML>
<HEAD>
```

```
</HEAD>
<BODY>
```

We also include navigation on each page, as we did in the user interface. The sp_Retrieve-Threads stored procedure is used to retrieve the threads for the specified section.

Listing 26.58: AdminThread.asp **Continued**

```
<!- Navigation ->
| <a href="adminsections.asp">Forums List<a> |

<HR>
<BR>

<%

Dim dbForums     ' Database Connection
Dim rsForums     ' Record Set
Dim sql          ' String

' Create an ADO database connection
set dbForums = _
  server.createobject("adodb.connection")

' Create record set
set rsForums = _
  server.CreateObject("adodb.recordset")

' Open the connection using our ODBC file DSN
dbForums.open("filedsn=Forums")

' Retrieve the threads for the current section.
sql = "execute sp_RetrieveThreads " & _
  session("AdminCurrentSection")

' Execute the statement and retrieve the
' record set
set rsForums = dbForums.Execute(sql)

%>
```

The first thing we display in our table is a form to add a new thread to the section. The form posts to AddThread.asp, the new name is passed in the form, and then we list the thread name. The name is linked to the message display for the thread.

Listing 26.59: `AdminThread.asp` **Continued**

```
<!- Start the table to display the threads. ->
<table cellpadding="5" cellspacing="5"
  border="1">
<tr>
  <th>Edit Thread</th>
  <th>New Name/Owner</th>
  <th>Delete</th>
</tr>

<tr>
  <td>Add a New Thread</td>
  <td>
    <!- Form to create a new thread. ->
    <form method="post" action="AddThread.asp">
    <input type="text" value="" name="chrName">
    <input type="Submit" value="Add New"
      name="Submit">
    </form>
  </td>
  <td> </td>
</tr>


<%

' Loop through the threads
do until rsForums.EOF

%>

<TR>
  <td>
    <a href="AdminMessages.asp?idThread=
    <%=rsForums("idThread")%>">
    <%=rsForums("chrName")%></a>
  </td>
```

We also build a form for updating the thread name and the thread owner. The form posts to the `UpdateThread.asp` page. The ID of the thread is also passed in a hidden form variable.

Listing 26.60: `AdminThread.asp` **Continued**

```
    <td>
      <!- Form to update the thread data. ->
      <form method="post"
        action="UpdateThread.asp">
      <!- Input field for the name. Defaulted
        to the current name. ->
      <input type="text"
        value="<%=rsForums("chrName")%>"
        name="chrName">

      <!- Input field for the owner. Defaulted
        to the current owner. ->
      <input type="text"
        value="<%=rsForums("chrOwner")%>"
        name="chrOwner">

      <!- Hidden field for the thread ID
        so we can update the right thread. ->
      <input type="hidden"
        value="<%=rsForums("idThread")%>"
        name="idThread">

      <input type="Submit" value="Update"
        name="Submit">
      </form>

    </td>
    <td>
      <!- Link to delete the thread. ->
      <a href="deleteThread.asp?idThread= ⤶
      <%=rsForums("idThread")%>">Delete</a>
    </td>
  </tr>

  <%

  ' Move to the next row
```

```
rsForums.MoveNext

loop

' Close the database
dbForums.Close

%>

</table>

<BR>

<HR>

<!- Navigation bar ->
| <a href="adminsections.asp">Forums List<a> |

</BODY>
</HTML>
```

A link is also built to the DeleteThread.asp page with the ID of the thread on the URL. The page is then closed out with the appropriate tags and with a navigation link back to the section administration.

Next, we have our page that handles adding a new thread to the database. The code for AddThread.asp is shown in Listing 26.61. The name of the thread and the owner (which is defaulted to Admin) is posted to the page. The sp_InsertThread stored procedure is used to insert the thread. Note that the section the thread is related to is read from the AdminCurrentSection session variable. The user is then redirected back to the thread administration.

Listing 26.61: AddThread.asp

```
<%@ Language=VBScript %>
<%Option Explicit%>
<%
'*******************************************
'** AddThread.asp
'**
'** Adds a new thread to the database
'*******************************************
%>
```

```
<%

Dim dbForums    ' Database Connection
Dim rsForums    ' Record Set
Dim sql         ' String

' Create an ADO database connection
set dbForums = _
  server.createobject("adodb.connection")

' Create record set
set rsForums = _
  server.CreateObject("adodb.recordset")

' Open the connection using our ODBC file DSN
dbForums.open("filedsn=Forums")

' Execute the sp_InsertThread stored procedure
' to insert the new thread into the section.
sql = "execute sp_InsertThread " & _
  session("AdminCurrentSection") & ", '" & _
  replace(request("chrName"), "'", "''") & _
  "', 'Admin'"

' Execute the statement and retrieve the
' record set
set rsForums = dbForums.Execute(sql)

' Close the database connection
dbForums.Close

' Redirect the user to the thread admin
Response.Redirect "adminthread.asp"

%>
```

We now have the `UpdateThread.asp` page that handles updating the thread name and owner. The code is shown in Listing 26.62. The `sp_UpdateThread` stored procedure is used, which passes the thread ID that is read from a hidden variable, the thread name, and the owner. Once the update is done, the user is redirected to the thread administration page.

Listing 26.62: UpdateThread.asp

```
<%@ Language=VBScript %>
<%Option Explicit%>
<%
'*********************************************
'** UpdateThread.asp
'**
'** Updates the thread name
'*********************************************
%>
<%

Dim dbForums   ' Database Connection
Dim rsForums   ' Record Set
Dim sql        ' String

' Create an ADO database connection
set dbForums = _
  server.createobject("adodb.connection")

' Create record set
set rsForums = _
  server.CreateObject("adodb.recordset")

' Open the connection using our ODBC file DSN
dbForums.open("filedsn=Forums")

' Execute the sp_UpdateThread stored
' procedure that will update the thread
' name and owner
sql = "execute sp_UpdateThread " & _
  request("idThread") & ", '" & _
  replace(request("chrName"), "'", "''") & _
  "', '" & replace(request("chrOwner"), _
  "'", "''") & "'"

' Execute the statement and retrieve the
' record set
set rsForums = dbForums.Execute(sql)

' Close the database connection
dbForums.Close
```

Part vi

```
' Send back to the administration threads
Response.Redirect "adminthread.asp"

%>
```

Finally, for the thread administration, we have the `DeleteThread.asp` page as shown in Listing 26.63. The ID of the thread to delete is passed on the URL to the page. The `sp_DeleteThread` stored procedure is used to delete the thread. The user is sent back to the thread administration page once the SQL statement has been executed.

Listing 26.63: `DeleteThread.asp`

```
<%@ Language=VBScript %>
<%Option Explicit%>
<%
'********************************************
'** DeleteThread.asp
'**
'** Deletes a thread from the database
'********************************************
%>
<%

Dim dbForums   ' Database Connection
Dim rsForums   ' Record Set
Dim sql        ' String

' Create an ADO database connection
set dbForums = _
  server.createobject("adodb.connection")

' Create record set
set rsForums = _
  server.CreateObject("adodb.recordset")

' Open the connection using our ODBC file DSN
dbForums.open("filedsn=Forums")

sql = "execute sp_DeleteThread " & _
   request("idThread")

' Execute the statement and retrieve the
' record set
```

```
set rsForums = dbForums.Execute(sql)

dbForums.Close

Response.Redirect "adminThread.asp"

%>
```

The first thing we display in our table is a form to add a new thread to the section. The form posts to `AddThread.asp`, the new name is passed in the form, and then we list the thread name. The name is linked to the message display for the thread.

Next we are ready to move on to the message administration. The messages flow in the same fashion as they did in the user interface, but we have the option of deleting and updating the messages.

Listings 26.64 through 26.66 show the code for the `AdminMessages.asp` page. We will not explore all the intricacies of the code; instead, we'll highlight the changes to support the administration.

Listing 26.64: `AdminMessages.asp`

```
<%@ Language=VBScript %>
<% Option Explicit %>
<%
'***********************************************
'** AdminMessages.asp
'**
'** Lists messages for a thread
'***********************************************
%>
<%

' Declare the variables
Dim dbForums            ' Database Connection
Dim rsForums            ' Record Set
Dim connForums          ' Database Connection
Dim cmdForums           ' ADO Command Object
Dim sql                 ' String
Dim MessageCount        ' Integer
Dim Count               ' Integer
Dim Direction           ' string
Dim NumDisplay          ' Integer
Dim dbMessage           ' Database Connection
```

```
Dim rsMessage        ' Record Set
Dim txtMessage       ' character variable
Dim chrOwner         ' string
Dim N                ' Integer

' ADO Static Variables
Dim adCmdText
Dim adCmdTable
Dim adCmdStoredProc
Dim adCmdUnknown
Dim adOpenForwardOnly
Dim adOpenKeyset
Dim adOpenDynamic
Dim adOpenStatic
Dim adLockReadOnly
Dim adLockPessimistic
Dim adLockOptimistic
Dim adLockBatchOptimistic

' Check to ensure the referrer
' is adminthread.asp.
if instr(1, lcase_
  (Request.ServerVariables("HTTP_REFERRER")), _
  "adminthread.asp") then

  ' Set the ID of the thread
  session("AdminCurrentThread") = _
    request("idThread")

end if

' If the value for the thread blank then send
' them back.
if session("AdminCurrentThread") = "" then _
  Response.Redirect("AdminThread.asp")

%>
<HTML>
<HEAD>
</HEAD>
<BODY>
```

```
<!- Build the navigation ->
| <a href="adminsections.asp">Forums List<a>
| <a href="adminThread.asp">
Discussion Thread List<a> |

<HR><BR>

| <a href=
"adminMessages.asp?dir=First">First</a>
| <a href="adminMessages.asp?dir=Next">Next</a>
| <a href=
"adminMessages.asp?dir=Previous">Previous</a>
| <a href="adminMessages.asp?dir=Last">Last</a>
| <a href="NewMessage.asp">
Create New Message</a> |

<BR><BR>

<%

' Check to see if there is an ID of a
' message to display
if request("idMessage") <> "" then

%>

<!- Link to reply to the message ->
<a href="NewMessage.asp">Reply to Message</a>
<BR><BR>

<%

' Create an ADO database connection
set dbMessage = _
  server.createobject("adodb.connection")

' Create record set
set rsMessage = _
  server.CreateObject("adodb.recordset")

' Open the connection using our ODBC file DSN
dbMessage.open("filedsn=Forums")
```

```
' Execute the sp_RetrieveMessage stored
' procedure to get the data for the
' specific message
sql = "execute sp_RetrieveMessage " & _
  Request("idMessage")

' Execute the statement and retrieve the
' record set
set rsMessage = dbMessage.Execute(sql)

' Retrieve the text of the message and the
' owner
txtMessage = rsMessage("txtMessage")
chrOwner = rsMessage("chrOwner")

%>
```

The section of our page that handles displaying a selected message now provides the administrator with the ability to edit the message. A form that posts to the `UpdateMessage.asp` page is created. Each field of the form is defaulted to the current values. The ID of the message is also passed as a hidden variable.

Listing 26.65: `AdminMessages.asp` **Continued**

```
<!- The form will post to UpdateMessage.asp to
  update the message data. ->
<form method="post" action="UpdateMessage.asp">

<!- Start the table to display the message ->
<TABLE cellpadding="4">

<TR><TD colspan="2">Edit Message</td></tr>

<!- Show the owner. The ID of the message is
  stored in a hidden variable so the right
  message data can be updated. ->
<tr>
  <td align="right">Owner:</td>
  <td>
  <input type="hidden"
    value="<%=rsMessage("idMessage")%>"
    name="idMessage">
  <input type="text" value="<%=chrOwner%>"
```

```
      name="chrOwner">
    </td>
  </tr>

  <!- Show the subject of the message. ->
  <tr>
    <td align="right">Subject:</td>
    <td>
    <input type="text"
      value="<%=rsMessage("chrSubject")%>"
      name="chrSubject">
    </td>
  </tr>

  <!- Show the text of the message. ->
  <tr>
    <td align="right">Message:</td>
    <td>
    <textarea name="txtMessage" cols="60"
      rows="10"><%=txtMessage%></textarea>
    </td>
  </tr>

  <!- Submit button ->
  <TR>
    <TD align="center">
    <input type="submit" value="Submit"
      name="submit">
    </td>
  </tr>

  </TABLE>

  </form>

  <%

  ' Close the database connection
  dbMessage.Close

  end if
```

```
' Variable that sets how many messages
' are shown in the list.
NumDisplay = 10

REM - ADO command types
adCmdText = 1
adCmdTable = 2
adCmdStoredProc = 4
adCmdUnknown = 8

REM - ADO cursor types
adOpenForwardOnly = 0 '# (Default)
adOpenKeyset = 1
adOpenDynamic = 2
adOpenStatic = 3

REM - ADO lock types
adLockReadOnly = 1
adLockPessimistic = 2
adLockOptimistic = 3
adLockBatchOptimistic = 4

' Create the database connection
Set connForums = _
  Server.CreateObject("ADODB.Connection")

' Open the database connection
connForums.Open "FileDsn=Forums"

' Create an ADO command object
Set cmdForums = _
  Server.CreateObject("ADODB.Command")

' Set the command type to 1 to evaluate
' the command as text. Also, the time out
' is set to 0.
cmdForums.CommandType = adCmdText
cmdForums.CommandTimeout = 0

' Set the command object connection to the
' forums connection
Set cmdForums.ActiveConnection = connForums
```

```
' Create a record set
Set rsForums = _
  Server.CreateObject("ADODB.Recordset")

' SQL statement to retrieve message count
' for the thread.
sql = "execute sp_GetMessageCountByThread " & _
  session("AdminCurrentThread")

' Set the command text
cmdForums.CommandText = sql

' Open the record set and use the adOpenStatic
' and adLockReadOnly parameters. adOpenStatic
' creates a static cursor in the record set.
' adLockReadOnly makes the record set read
' only.
rsForums.Open cmdForums, ,_
  adOpenStatic,adLockReadOnly

' Get the message count for display.
MessageCount = rsForums("total")

' Retrieve the direction of the navigation
Direction = request("Dir")

' If there is no last message set, then start
' at 1.
if Session("idLastMessage") = "" then _
  Session("idLastMessage") = 1

' If there is no direction, then start at the
' beginning of the list.
if Direction = "" then Direction = "First"

' Build the SQL statement based on
' the navigational direction
select case Direction

  ' First of the list
  case "First"
    ' Execute the sp_RetrieveNextMessages
```

```
      ' stored procedure to get the next set
      ' of messages in the list, but we set
      ' flags to start at the first message.
      sql = "execute"  & _
        " sp_RetrieveNextMessages " & _
        session("AdminCurrentThread") & ", 1"
        session("idLastMessage") = 1

    ' Retrieve the next set in the list
    case "Next"
      ' Execute the sp_RetrieveNextMessages
      ' stored procedure to get the next set
      ' of messages in the list.
      sql = "execute" & _
        " sp_RetrieveNextMessages " & _
        session("AdminCurrentThread") & ", " & _
        session("idLastMessage")

    ' Get the previous set of messages
    case "Previous"
      ' Execute the sp_RetrievePreviousMessages
      ' stored procedure to get the previous set
      ' of messages in the list.
      sql = "execute" & _
        " sp_RetrievePreviousMessages " & _
        session("AdminCurrentThread") & ", " & _
        session("idLastMessage")

    ' Get the last set of messages in the list
    case "Last"
      ' Execute the sp_RetrievePreviousMessages
      ' stored procedure to get the last set of
      ' messages in the list. In this case we
      ' start at the very end of the list by
      ' passing a 1,000,000 message ID parameter
      sql = "execute" & _
        " sp_RetrievePreviousMessages " & _
        session("AdminCurrentThread") & _
        ", 1,000,000"

    ' Get the current list of messages being
    ' displayed
```

```
  case "Current"
    ' Execute the sp_RetrieveNextMessages
    ' stored procedure to get the next set
    ' of messages in the list. Note that the
    ' idLastMessage parameter will not have
    ' changed if the current set of messages
    ' is to be displayed.
    sql = "execute" & _
      " sp_RetrieveNextMessages " & _
      session("AdminCurrentThread") & ", " & _
      session("idLastMessage")

end select

' Close the record set connection
rsForums.Close

' Set the SQL command to be executed
cmdForums.CommandText = sql

' Open the record set with the appropriate
' parameters
rsForums.Open cmdForums, , _
  adOpenStatic,adLockReadOnly

' Check to see if we are at the end of the list
if rsForums.EOF then

  ' Move to the first of the list if there
  ' are no results returned
  sql = "execute sp_RetrieveNextMessages " &_
    session("AdminCurrentThread") & ", 1"
    session("idLastMessage") = 1

  ' Set the direction
  Direction = "Next"

  ' Set the SQL command
  cmdForums.CommandText = sql

  ' Close the forums connection
  rsForums.close
```

```
    ' Retrieve the new record set of messages
    rsForums.Open cmdForums, ,_
      adOpenStatic,adLockReadOnly

end if

' Start the loop count at 1
Count = 1

%>

<BR>

<!- Create the table to display the
  messages list ->
<table border=1 cellpadding="5"
  cellspacing="5">

<!- Build the table header ->
<tr>
  <th>Subject</th>
  <th>Date Posted</th>
  <th>Owner</th>
  <th>Delete</th>
</tr>

<%

' Check to see if the direct is either
' the last set or the previous set. In
' both cases we are moving back in a record
' set of lists.
if Direction = "Last" or _
  Direction = "Previous" then

    ' Move to the last row in the returned
    ' record set
    rsForums.MoveLast

    ' Loop through the messages in the list
    for N = 1 to NumDisplay - 2
```

```
      ' Move back a row
      rsForums.MovePrevious

      ' Check to see if we are at the beginning
      ' of the record set
      if rsForums.BOF then

        ' Exit the FOR loop
        exit for

      end if

      ' Set the last message
      session("idLastMessage") = _
        rsForums("idMessage")

    next

  end if

  ' Check to see if we are at the beginning
  ' or the end of the record set
  if rsForums.BOF and not rsForums.eof then

    ' Move to the first record
    rsForums.movefirst

  end if

  ' Loop through the record set
  do until rsForums.EOF

  %>

  <!- Build the row to show the message subject,
    date created and message owner. ->
  <tr>
    <td>
      <a href=
      "adminMessages.asp?dir=Current&idMessage=
      <%=rsForums("idMessage")%>">
      <%=rsForums("chrSubject")%></a>
```

```
    </td>
    <td>
      <%=rsForums("dtCreated")%>
    </td>
    <td>
      <%=rsForums("chrOwner")%>
    </td>
```

An additional column is built in our Messages table to provide a link to delete the message. The ID of the message is passed on the URL to the `DeleteMessage.asp` page.

Listing 26.66: `AdminMessages.asp` **Continued**

```
    <td>
      <a href="DeleteMessage.asp?idMessage= ⮠
      <%=rsForums("idMessage")%>">
      Delete</a></td>
  </tr>

  <%

    ' Move to the next row
    rsForums.MoveNext

    ' Check to see we are at the end of
    ' the record set and we are moving in
    ' a forward direction.
    if not rsForums.eof and _
      (Direction = "Next" or _
        Direction = "First") then

      ' Set the last message
      session("idLastMessage") = _
        rsForums("idMessage")

    end if

    ' Increment our counter
    Count = Count + 1

    ' See if we have reached the maximum
    ' number of messages to display
    if Count = NumDisplay then exit do
```

```
loop

' Close the database connection
connForums.Close

%>

</table>

<!- Show the message count ->
<font size="2" color="blue">
  There are <%=MessageCount%> messages in
  this thread.
</font>

<BR><BR>

<!- Close out the navigation ->
<HR>

| <a href="adminsections.asp">Forums List<a>
| <a href="adminThread.asp">
Discussion Thread List<a> |

</BODY>
</HTML>
```

As with the user interface, we also have a page to create a new message. This page uses a process similar to the one on the user interface. The code has been updated to reflect the administrative navigation. Listing 26.67 shows the code for NewMessage.asp.

Listing 26.67: NewMessage.asp

```
<%@ Language=VBScript %>
<% Option Explicit %>
<%
'*********************************************
'** NewMessage.asp
'**
'** Adds a new message to the database
'*********************************************
%>
<%
```

```
' Ensure we came from a thread page to
' ensure we have a thread selected
if session("AdminCurrentThread") = "" then _
  Response.Redirect("AdminThread.asp")
%>

<HTML>
<HEAD>
</HEAD>
<BODY>

<!- Build the navigation ->
| <a href="adminsections.asp">Forums List<a>
| <a href="adminThread.asp">
Discussion Thread List<a> |

<HR><BR>

<!- Form to add a message to the
  thread list. ->
<form method="post" action="AddMessage.asp">

<TABLE cellpadding="4">

<TR><TD colspan="2">
  Enter in your Message</td></tr>
<tr>
  <td align="right">Owner:</td>
  <td>
  <!- Field to set the owner ->
  <input type="text" value="" name="chrOwner">
  </td>
</tr>
<tr>
  <td align="right">Subject:</td>
  <td>
  <!- Field to create a subject ->
  <input type="text" value=""
    name="chrSubject">
  </td>
</tr>
<tr>
```

```
    <td align="right">Message:</td>
    <td>
    <!- Text area to input the message ->
    <textarea name="txtMessage" cols="60"
      rows="10"></textarea>
    </td>
  </tr>
  <TR>
    <TD align="center">
    <input type="submit" value="Submit"
      name="submit">
    </td>
  </tr>

  </TABLE>

  </form>


  <!- Close out the navigation ->
  <HR>

  | <a href="adminsections.asp">Forums List<a>
  | <a href="adminThread.asp">
  Discussion Thread List<a> |

  </BODY>
  </HTML>
```

The AddMessge.asp page, shown in Listing 26.68, handles adding the new message to the database. This page is similar to the page on the user interface, but has been updated to reflect the administrative navigation and page structure.

Listing 26.68: AddMessage.asp

```
<%@ Language=VBScript %>
<%Option Explicit%>
<%
'*********************************************
'** AddMessage.asp
'**
'** Adds a new message to the thread list
'*********************************************
```

```
%>
<%

Dim dbForums    ' Database Connection
Dim rsForums    ' Record Set
Dim sql         ' String

' Check to see if a thread has been selected
' If not send the user to the thread selection
' page
if session("AdminCurrentThread") = "" then _
  Response.Redirect("Adminthread.asp")

' Create an ADO database connection
set dbForums = _
  server.createobject("adodb.connection")

' Create record set
set rsForums = _
  server.CreateObject("adodb.recordset")

' Open the connection using our ODBC file DSN
dbForums.open("filedsn=Forums")

' Execute the sp_InsertMessage stored
' procedure to make the new message.
sql = "execute sp_InsertMessage " & _
session("AdminCurrentSection") & ", " & _
session("AdminCurrentThread") & ", '" & _
replace(request("chrSubject"), _
"'", "''") & "', '" & _
replace(request("txtMessage"), _
  "'", "''") & "', '" & _
replace(Request("chrOwner"), _
  "'", "''") & "'"

' Execute the statement and retrieve
' the record set
set rsForums = dbForums.Execute(sql)

' Close the connection
dbForums.Close
```

```
' Send the user to the message admin page
Response.Redirect "adminmessages.asp"

%>
```

Our next page, shown in Listing 26.69, handles updating the message with changes made by the administrator. The `sp_UpdateMessage` stored procedure is used to update the message. Once the update is done, the user is redirected back to the `AdminMessages.asp` page.

Listing 26.69: `UpdateMessage.asp`

```
<%@ Language=VBScript %>
<%Option Explicit%>
<%
'*******************************************
'** UpdateMessage.asp
'**
'** Updates the data in an existing message
'*******************************************
%>
<%

Dim dbForums   ' Database Connection
Dim rsForums   ' Record Set
Dim sql        ' String

' Create an ADO database connection
set dbForums = _
  server.createobject("adodb.connection")

' Create record set
set rsForums = _
  server.CreateObject("adodb.recordset")

' Open the connection using our ODBC file DSN
dbForums.open("filedsn=Forums")

' Executes the sp_UpdateMessage stored
' procedure to update from the data entered
sql = "execute sp_UpdateMessage " & _
  request("idMessage") & ", '" & _
  replace(request("chrSubject"), _
  "'", "''") & "', '" & _
```

```
replace(request("chrOwner"), _
 "'", "''") & "', '" & _
replace(request("txtMessage"), _
 "'", "''") & "'"

' Execute the statement and retrieve the
' record set
set rsForums = dbForums.Execute(sql)

' Close the database
dbForums.Close

' Return to the messages administration
Response.Redirect "adminmessages.asp"

%>
```

Our final forum page handles deleting messages, as shown in Listing 26.70. If you don't like the content of something posted by one of your site visitors, then ZAP! You can kill it. The ID of the message is passed on the URL. The `sp_DeleteMessage` stored procedure is used to delete the message. Once it is deleted, the user is redirected back to the messages page.

Listing 26.70: `DeleteMessage.asp`

```
<%@ Language=VBScript %>
<%Option Explicit%>
<%
'*********************************************
'** DeleteMessage.asp
'**
'** Deletes a message from the database
'*********************************************
%>
<%

Dim dbForums   ' Database Connection
Dim rsForums   ' Record Set
Dim sql        ' String

' Create an ADO database connection
set dbForums = _
```

```
   server.createobject("adodb.connection")

   ' Create record set
set rsForums = _
   server.CreateObject("adodb.recordset")

   ' Open the connection using our ODBC file DSN
dbForums.open("filedsn=Forums")

   ' SQL statement to delete a message
sql = "execute sp_DeleteMessage " &_
   request("idMessage")

   ' Execute the statement and retrieve the
   ' record set
set rsForums = dbForums.Execute(sql)

   ' Close the database
dbForums.Close

   ' Redirect to the messages administration
Response.Redirect "adminmessages.asp"

%>
```

That does it for our sample forums code. The foundation has been laid for building a robust forum solution. Careful consideration of how frequently your forums will be used and what administrative tools are needed, as well as how these tools will be used, can greatly affect the final implementation.

Some additional features to consider include profiling, user editing of their messages, message searching, user moderation, and much more. One site to look at for successful forum implementation is www.Delphi.com.

NOTE

Information on testing the user interface is available for download. Go to www.sybex.com and search for *ASP, ADO, and XML Complete* by title or ISBN.

Conclusion

This is just one last example of the rich applications you can create with ASP and SQL Server. With the addition of the crown jewel of community Web sites–discussion forums–your site visitors have both valuable content and a method for discussing it. Your forums provide a multitiered conversation thread that facilitates member-to-member communication, and our administrative interface allows the site administrator to maintain control over the content of the forums.

At this point, you've covered a lot of ground in a short period of time. You've gone from a summary of your Web development tools through descriptions of the various languages and technologies at your disposal. Then you ventured even further to look at new technologies that are not yet in widespread use, but which will be soon. Finally, you pulled it all together with some samples that highlighted popular features of any Web application.

Now you have only one task left: experiment! The Web offers endless resources for taking your craft to the next level. With some creativity, there's no end to the applications you can create.

INDEX

Note to the reader: Throughout this index **boldfaced** page numbers indicate primary discussions of a topic. *Italicized* page numbers indicate illustrations.

Symbols

A

C

D

E

F

H

I

J

K

L

N

O

P

Q

R

S